The D-Day Dodgers

By the same author

In Enemy Hands
Sir Arthur Currie
Legacy of Valour
Spearhead to Victory
Welcome to Flanders Fields
Gallant Canadians

THE D-DAY DODGERS

The Canadians in Italy, 1943 – 1945

Daniel G. Dancocks

M&S

Canadian Cataloguing in Publication Data

Dancocks, Daniel G. (Daniel George), date.
  The D-Day Dodgers

Includes bibliographical references and index.
ISBN 0–7710–2544–0

1. Canada.   Canadian Army – History – World War, 1939–1945.
2. World War, 1939–1945 – Campaigns – Italy.   3. World War, 1939–
1945 – Canada.   I. Title.

D768.15.D36 1991   940.54'215   C91–093193–3

Designed by David Shaw & Associates Ltd.

Printed and bound in Canada on acid-free paper.

McClelland & Stewart Inc.
The Canadian Publishers
481 University Avenue
Toronto, Ontario
M5G 2E9

To my best friend, Cindy,
for putting up with me

Contents

List of Maps

References for maps from G. W. L. Nicholson, *The Canadians in Italy*, Reginald Roy, *The Seaforth Highlanders of Canada*, C. P. Stacey, *The Canadian Army, 1939–1945*, and G. R. Stevens, *The Royal Canadian Regiment*.

Acknowledgements

This book was made possible by a generous grant from the Alberta Foundation for the Literary Arts. It is no exaggeration to say that I would not be able to pursue my writing career without AFLA's support, and the encouragement and assistance of its executive director, Ron Robertson, and his assistant, Shirlee Smith Matheson. As I have said previously, I consider myself fortunate to live in a province which makes possible this kind of support.

The D-Day Dodgers resulted from a luncheon discussion with my publisher, Doug Gibson, and neither of us, I am sure, realized that the project would be as complex and lengthy as it proved to be. And while Doug continues to support and encourage my writing career, it was left to my editor, Pat Kennedy, to pare down my massive manuscript to its present, more-manageable state. My copy editor, Cy Strom, also laboured valiantly on the manuscript. However, any errors or omissions that may remain are mine alone.

A vast number of people cooperated with me on this project and made invaluable contributions. Among those who have been particularly helpful is Bill McAndrew at the Directorate of History, National Defence Headquarters, Ottawa. Bill is one of the few Canadian historians with an active interest in the Italian campaign, and while he gave me as much assistance as possible, he made no effort to change my thinking or opinions, even when they contradicted his own conclusions and beliefs. Others I wish to single out for their unselfish assistance include Strome Galloway, whose own writings are among the best to emerge from the campaign; George Kitching and Pat Bogert, who were bombarded with questions and who answered with patience and eloquence; Cliff Evans, who organizes the annual D-Day Dodgers' reunion in Orillia, Ontario; a couple of former Cape Breton Highlanders, Bill Matheson and Duncan Fraser, who were very kind (many of the latter's comments have been previously published in the Halifax *Mail-Star* and *Herald-Chronicle*, and appear here courtesy of the Halifax Herald Limited).

I interviewed or corresponded with many others, each of whom was helpful in his or her own way, including (in alphabetical order):

Ned Amy, Jack Anderson, Earle Barr, Norman Bell, Reg Brousseau, George Brown, G. Allan Burton, Ernie Buss, Barney Byrnes, J. Allan Calder, Ken Cashman, Ray Cross, Danny Danbrough, Ernest Danby, Angus Duffy, Clem Dick, Stocky Edwards, Stu Egglestone, Dick Fuller, George Garbutt, Barbara Gibson, Graeme Gibson, Tom Gilday, Joe Glass, Dave Goldberg, Dave Gordon, Ralph Grossi, George Hall, Victor Hall, Skid Hanes, C. Malim Harding, Doug Harkness, John Hebb, Ian Hodson, Max Holbrook, Bert Hoskin, Bert Hoffmeister, Bert Houle, Bert Hovey, Doug How, Frank Johnson, Rupe Leblond, John Lovelace, Don McLarty, Nelson Maddeau, Dick Maltby, A. Bruce Matthews, G. D. Mitchell, Howard Mitchell, Julius Molinaro, Amedeo Montemaggi, Oviglio Monti, Basil Morgan, Farley Mowat, Don Munro, Ross Munro, Len Murphy, Enos Nauss, Murray O'Dell, Lloyd Oliver, Tony Planinshek, Jack Parfett, Ed Patrick, Jimmy Quayle, Herb Rolston, Gordon Romkey, Bill Ross, Bob Sharp, Ray Sherk, Dick Shunn, J. Desmond Smith, Jean Smith, C. P. Stacey, Bob Stirling, Jim Stone, Bill Story, Bill Swinden, Keirn Wallace, Geoff Walsh, Cam Ware, Stan Waters, Denis Whitaker, Dick Whittington, Vic Worley, Henry Worrell, Bill Ziegler.

I also wish to acknowledge the cooperation and assistance of the staff at the regimental museums of Lord Strathcona's Horse (Bert Reed and Jim Weber) and Princess Patricia's Canadian Light Infantry (Bob Zubkowski).

Finally, I must thank four special people. The several exhausting months I spent writing this book took an enormous toll, and Cindy, David, Mitchell, and Jeanette bore the strain much better than I deserved. A writer's life is far from glamorous, and no one knows this better than they do.

The D-Day Dodgers

Scenes from a Far-Away War

"Fix bayonets!" I shrilled.

And so we went into our first and last bayonet charge in a war in which the bayonet was an almost total anachronism.

We scrambled over the wire, ripping our shorts and shirts and flesh, and went galloping clumsily up the slope. As we reached the crest we discovered why we had not all been slaughtered during this suicidal attack. A group of commandos was just completing an assault from the rear of the hill; instead of waving bayonets, they were sensibly hosing streams of lead into the buildings.

"Cor!" a commando sergeant said to me after we had finished sorting ourselves out. "You chaps *did* look loverly! ... Never seen nothin' like it 'cept in a flick with Errol Flynn."

For a second I was taken in – until I noticed the sardonic grins on the faces of the men.

– Farley Mowat, *And No Birds Sang*, pp. 79–80

The stench here is dreadful. There are two dead Germans ... and nearby a dead Hastings & Prince Edward private, still clutching his Bren gun, has swollen up so much that he is bursting the seams of his bushshirt and shorts. The Germans, as usual, are a green colour, a hideous combination with shocks of yellow hair. The Canadian is purply-black like our dead normally turn. I can't understand why the Germans decay differently.

– Strome Galloway, *Some Died at Ortona*, pp. 77–8

The sounds of battle were varied, deadly and distinct. Learn them and your chances of survival increased dramatically....

There was the high-pitched "burrp! burrp!" of the German MG 42, my own special nemesis, the human meat cleaver in action.... The sharp zip

1

and immediate wham of an 88, flat firing at high velocity. Get behind something, anything, but very, very quickly. . . . The almost inaudible cat-like hiss of a plunging mortar bomb, the first warning usually a blast in our midst with men broken and bleeding. . . . The unbelievable shattering roar of an artillery barrage, centuries-old buildings pulverized and the whole landscape metamorphosing in front of your eyes. Almost always ours. . . . The sharp crack of a rifle bullet snapping by your head, called sniper fire but usually a solitary German rifleman firing his Mauser 98 in a desperate, inaccurate gesture. Stop standing in the open like a clueless twit. The sharp, high-pitched rattle of a 9-millimetre Schmeisser sub-machine-gun. No worries whatsoever unless the owner was standing right in front of you.

And then a very special sound, the *Nebelwerfer*, or "Moaning Minnies," as we called them. Giant 150-millimetre rockets launched in sequence from a six-barrelled mount. Screamers mounted in their tails. Supreme morale-shatterers as they came howling at you through the night skies. . . . But they were very, very inaccurate. . . . Usually lots of time for cover. . . . The clank, grind, rattle, squeak, and unbelievable roar of tanks approaching at night. Fortunately, in my experience, always ours and not theirs. . . . And the roar of fighter planes, either diving and bombing or spitting out bullets and cannon shells. Two out of three times, mistakenly bombing their own and strafing their own. Over so quickly there was nothing to do but drop, press into the dirt, and hope. . . .

The sounds of war, all lethal and all designed for one purpose: to kill you.

– Jimmy Quayle, "The Sounds of Battle"

I remember once, during the winter on the Ortona front, seeing a battalion commander studying an aerial photo of the enemy territory the other side of no man's land. Suddenly he called to the artillery rep. . . .

"Come here quick," he shouted.

The gunnery officer . . . bounded across the room to where the colonel had his eyes glued to the stereos.

"Yes, sir!" he answered excitedly. "What is it?"

"Get onto your gun positions right away. I want a shoot on these three vehicles on the road here."

The gunner stopped in his tracks. His mouth fell open. He couldn't believe his ears.

"But sir!" he said, "that aerial photo is dated December 5th. This is February!"

"I know, I know," replied the infantry colonel. "But they may well be back there. Now's our chance to clobber them. Don't argue. Shoot."

So a concentration of 25-pounder shells went whirring overhead, expertly plotted to hit the non-existent vehicles as they reached a point a thousand yards or so further on – and, as the gunner later remarked, "six weeks after they had left the road, if not the country."

"Good," said the colonel, as he leaned back from the big photo mosaic, so carefully laid out on the farmhouse table, "that will show those Jerries we're not asleep!"

– Strome Galloway, *The General Who Never Was*, p. 196

Wartime Italy was a depressingly sad sight. . . . What a wonderful country it must have been before the war, with its beautiful vineyards, prosperous farms, warm, sunny climate, healthy livestock, and pretty girls. . . .

Now we found them a sad, defeated, poverty-stricken race. There were still wine and liqueurs, but inferior types as the vineyards had been neglected. The girls would give their bodies for a tin of bully beef or a package of cigarettes – or a ride any distance in an Army truck. I saw a woman with a dead dog wrapped in paper under her arm; they were desperate for food, particularly meat. I saw hundreds of Italians from ten years old to sixty or seventy years old, mostly women or men unfit for military duty, walking the 250 miles across Italy to the West coast. They were going to get a bag of grain to make flour, and carry it back to the East coast where there was no flour to make bread.

– Bill Swinden, letter to author

We moved into an Italian farmhouse during our advance. The place had either been looted by someone preceding us or the occupant family had torn things apart to gather up what they wanted to take with them when they left. What remained was a great pile of clothing on top of which was a complete bride-and-groom ensemble. Two of our wits tried them on, and had just gotten fully dressed . . . when the Germans counter-attacked. They must have been somewhat shocked to see a "bride" coming at them with a submachine-gun, and the "bridegroom" not too far behind with Bren gun blazing. Too bad we didn't have a war artist handy for that one.

– Bill Matheson, letter to author

It was around the Hitler Line, and we were going across a field, and here's the body of a this young Canadian soldier, lying on the ground. And there's the gouge of a shell explosion right in front of him, and it had killed him.

He's lying there, and he has a sheet of paper in his hand. I picked it up and read it, and it was a letter to his mother.

Why did he have that letter in his hand? Had he lived long enough to write it? I don't think so; there was no sign of a pencil. Had he written it just before he went into battle? Had he not sent it and even perhaps at the last minute pulled it out of his pocket to make sure that it'd be the last touch he'd ever have with his family? I don't know.

I even remember his name. He was with the West Nova Scotia Regiment, his name was Edward Drillio. He was a kid, I'd say eighteen.

– Doug How, interview with author

We had reached that point with reinforcements where the lads coming in were not trained. We had boys there of eighteen, nineteen, twenty, just out of school, with maybe three months' training. They'd scarcely learned how to drill or to fire a rifle. They probably wouldn't know how to take the pin out of a grenade. And it was a terrible experience to [see] untrained troops who were slaughtered like animals by a well-trained German force.

– Tom Gilday, interview with author

Nearby a burial party was grimly going about their task of unloading a truck filled with blanket-wrapped bodies, casualties of the latest attack. Gunner L. I. Brady . . . had recently heard that his 19-year-old brother had arrived in Italy to join the 48th Highlanders as a reinforcement. As if drawn by a hidden fear, he inspected several of the new graves and found to his shock and sorrow, that his younger brother's "I" tag was nailed to a makeshift cross.

– Vic Bulger, quoted in G. Mitchell, RCHA – *Right of the Line*, p. 129

Just after first light, when our tank support arrived, my company commander started shooting at the tanks and telling them to remove themselves from our position because "this was an infantry battle." One of our lost platoon commanders came into view while this was going on and distracted my company commander [who] took after the platoon commander, shooting with a pistol in each hand and calling the fleeing officer all kinds of [names] for having got lost during the battle. Luckily this did not result in any casualties.

I have yet to find out where my company commander was during the battle [prior to this], but battalion headquarters must have known where he was, since he later was awarded the Military Cross. Rank and social position have their advantages even in the midst of war.

– Bill Matheson, letter to author

What's misery? Well, if you're moving up to battle and the rain's coming down in sheets and the chill wind cuts through you like a knife and then you bed down for the night in the muck off the side of the road, that's misery. You try to pull your groundsheet or your gas-cape over your body to shut out the blinkin' rain but you fight a losing battle. And sleep is impossible as you squirm and squish in the cold oozy mud. That's misery. And then some xx!!ccxx!!!xxx sergeant comes along and roots you back out onto the road where you slither and slide and stumble around in a groggy haze and you wonder how in bloody hell you got into this goddam mess. You do most of your sleeping as you plod through the rutted mud, a sort of a coma and you don't see the guy in front of you stop and you walk up his backside. And you don't hear the S.O.B. lance-jack barking behind you to close up but you do hear the whispering whoosh of an incoming shell. You throw yourself wildly into the slimy muck of a ditch and you taste the awful crap that enters your mouth. Man, that's misery!

– Stan Scislowski, *Return to Italy, 1975*, p. 51

Following the war, one of my sons went to (Grade IV) school just before Remembrance Day, and the teacher asked if anyone in the class had a family member that had been in the war. On my son's affirmative reply, the teacher asked with whom I had served, to get a reply from my son: "I don't know, but he was with Julius Caesar at the Rubicon."

– Bill Matheson, letter to author

When I went to Mount Allison University, in middle age, I came across these two young fellows in their early twenties, laughing about a notice on the bulletin board. There was going to be a seminar at the University of New Brunswick about the Italian campaign. I asked, "Why are you laughing?" They weren't being nasty about it, they just said they couldn't imagine taking this seminar, talking about this vague, distant military campaign. "Well, you know," I said, "there are five thousand Canadians buried over there."

That sobered them up immediately. They just didn't know this.

– Doug How, interview with author

"Things Are Getting Very Monotonous"

1

By early 1943, the war against Germany had turned in favour of the Allies. The Battle of the Atlantic was being won by the American, British, and Canadian navies over the enemy's submarine fleet, securing the lifeline between the United Kingdom and North America. The Allies had also achieved decisive victories on both fronts where their ground forces were engaged – North Africa, where a quarter-million Germans and Italians were trapped in Tunisia, and the Soviet Union, where two hundred thousand Germans had been lost at Stalingrad.

Everyone knew that, sooner or later, the western Allies must invade continental Europe. But the British and American leadership disagreed sharply on the question of timing. The Americans were anxious to mount an invasion via the English Channel into occupied France as soon as possible, while the British, haunted by memories of the terrible bloodbaths on the Western Front during the Great War, preferred to delay this inevitable confrontation for as long as they could. American and British philosophies of war were diametrically opposed: American military doctrine was based on direct confrontation with the foe, and the shortest route to Berlin, the heart of the Third Reich, lay across the Channel and through France; the British, wary of the high human cost of this approach, preferred to use their naval superiority to chip at the periphery of occupied Europe until a weak point appeared. While Allied troops and equipment were assembled in Britain for the cross-Channel invasion (initially code-named "Round-up," later changed to "Overlord"), which was expected to take place in 1943, alternative theatres were sought; it was impossible for British and American troops to sit idly while the Soviets waged a war to the death with the main German armies. It was this need for action that had convinced the American president, Franklin Roosevelt, to commit his country's forces to the November 1942 invasion of northwestern Africa, Operation "Torch." The African landing, combined with the late-October victory of the

British Eighth Army at El Alamein, had spelled doom for the German and Italian formations in North Africa.

Winston Churchill, the cigar-smoking British prime minister, was only too happy to cultivate the North African campaign as a major theatre of war. British and Commonwealth forces had been fighting for some time in North Africa where the main opponent, initially, was Italy, the weak link in the enemy chain mail. "Africa," Churchill would write, "was the only continent in which we could meet our foe on land." In addition to the obvious necessity of keeping open the vital Suez Canal and denying the enemy free use of the Mediterranean Sea, the North African campaign also offered the possibility of "the destruction of the Italian Empire."[1] Such an outcome was most attractive to the British, who felt a certain enmity towards Italy, an ally in the Great War and now viewed as a jackal for its belated entry into this war after the German *Blitzkrieg* had conquered most of western Europe.

While it would be unfair, and inaccurate, to say that Churchill had a hidden agenda, it is clear that he had far more in mind than merely defeating the Axis armies in North Africa. He had revealed his intentions to the Soviet dictator, Joseph Stalin, when he travelled to Moscow in August 1942. Drawing a picture of a crocodile, symbolizing the enemy alliance, Churchill explained that it was his wish "to attack the soft belly of the crocodile as [the Soviets] attacked its hard snout."[2] In a message to Roosevelt the following month, Churchill referred to the possibility "of attacking the under-belly of the Axis by Sardinia, Sicily or even possibly Italy."[3] Thus was born the myth of the rugged Italian peninsula as the soft underbelly of continental Europe. "This was great oratory," notes the American historian, J. Lee Ready, "but militarily it made no sense whatsoever. The great politician had a habit of letting symbolic description of a situation take more importance than the situation."[4]

Churchill's case was reinforced when it became apparent that Round-up, the cross-Channel invasion of Europe, would not be possible in 1943. The buildup of the invasion force in Britain was going more slowly than anticipated, and Churchill was quite prepared to postpone the operation. "But if so," he cabled Roosevelt on 24 November, "it becomes all the more important to make sure that we do not miss 1944."[5] If it became necessary to delay Round-up, he was ready to recommend an alternative mission for 1943: "drive Italy out of the war."[6]

But the gulf between British and American intentions remained as broad and seemingly unbridgeable as ever. Roosevelt's chief advisers were anxious to proceed with Round-up in 1943 or, failing that, to concentrate instead on the war against Japan. Viewing North Africa as an end in itself, they refused to give serious consideration to expanded operations in that theatre. General George Marshall, the U.S. army's chief of staff, pointed out that, in order to secure the Mediterranean, the Allies would have to occupy "Sicily, Sardinia and Crete," and he doubted "whether . . . the large forces required for such a project could be justified. . . ."[7]

To resolve the frustrating deadlock, Churchill and Roosevelt met in mid January 1943 at Casablanca, in recently liberated Morocco. Accompanied by the Combined Chiefs of Staff, a committee comprising the heads of the Anglo-American armed forces, the two leaders discussed future strategy, not just in the Mediterranean but in all aspects of the global conflict. The Casablanca Conference resulted in the joint declaration by Roosevelt and Churchill that they would settle for nothing less than "the unconditional surrender" of Germany, Italy, and Japan. For the most part, the British and Americans resolved their differences amicably, with one notable exception – the Mediterranean theatre.

The advantages of widening the war there, so obvious to the British, were obscure so far as the Americans were concerned. To the British, Italy was the enemy's weak point, and the chief of the Imperial General Staff (CIGS), Sir Alan Brooke, argued for an invasion of Sicily. "If Italy were out of the war," Brooke stated, "Germany would be forced to occupy that country to replace Italian divisions in other Axis occupied countries, such as Yugoslavia and Greece." Brooke's American counterpart, George Marshall, continued to be unimpressed. "Every diversion on a side issue from the main plot," he warned, "acts as a 'suction pump.'"[8]

In the end, Brooke's view prevailed: the invasion of Sicily, code-named "Husky," was given the green light. The target date, according to the Casablanca directive, was July 1943, and the invasion had three goals: "(i) Making the Mediterranean line of communications more secure; (ii) diverting German pressure from the Russian front; (iii) intensifying the pressure on Italy."[9] The commander-in-chief would be the future United States president, Dwight Eisenhower.

Unfortunately, the Casablanca directive concerning Operation Husky was flawed. Observes American historian Carlo D'Este: "It established Sicily as an end in itself rather than as the first step in an agreed joint strategy for the Mediterranean."[10] Further friction between the allies was certain because, although the Americans did not yet know it, Churchill had no intention of stopping there.

The post-Casablanca preparations for the invasion of Sicily amount to a textbook study of how *not* to plan a military operation.

It took until the beginning of May 1943 to finalize Husky's plans. The planning process was, as Carlo D'Este points out, "plagued by interminable problems of organization and indecision,"[11] all of which were directly attributable to the peculiar nature of coalition warfare: there were too many cooks stirring the broth. Dwight Eisenhower, the charming and amiable four-star general from Kansas, organized a British-American planning staff, which took its code name, Task Force 141, from the room number of the Algiers hotel where it first met. Force 141, which later became the headquarters of the Fifteenth Army Group, set to work on Operation Husky on 12 February.

Although the planners at Force 141, in Algiers, were technically in charge of Husky, everybody in authority seemed to have a hand in the proceedings. At a very early stage, it was decided that the actual invasion would involve two invasion forces: one British (code-named Force 545), which would assault eastern Sicily, the other American (Force 343), assigned to the western part of the island. The British force, which was essentially the British Eighth Army, established its headquarters in Cairo, while the American force, which was later designated the U.S. Seventh Army, was headquartered in Rabat, Morocco. Naturally, both of these task forces had a say in Force 141's work, as did planners in far-off London and Washington, because some of the assault forces would be transported directly from the United Kingdom and the United States. (Although there were more than enough troops and equipment already in North Africa, limited shipping facilities meant that only a small fraction could actually participate in the initial invasion.)

Further complicating matters was the command structure in the Mediterranean. A British general, Sir Henry Maitland Wilson, was the theatre's commander-in-chief, but Eisenhower was in charge of Husky. Eisenhower's British deputy, General Sir Harold Alexander, commanded Husky's ground forces. The naval and air forces were also commanded by British officers, Admiral Sir Andrew Cunningham and Air Marshal Sir Arthur Tedder, respectively. The arrangement, says D'Este, eventually "led to one crisis after another."[12]

The planners had to juggle many factors in coming up with a practicable blueprint for invasion. Not the least of these was Sicily's geography, which was later descibed by an American corps commander, Omar Bradley:

Sicily is a lopsided triangular island, roughly 170 miles on the side, located a mere two and a half miles from Calabria in the toe of Italy. It is rugged and mountainous, dominated by the famous 10,000-foot Mount Etna. In 1943, its road system was primitive – narrow lanes winding along the coastlines or through the mountains. Its principal ports – famous from antiquity – were Messina on the northeast corner, Palermo on the northwestern corner and Syracuse on the southeastern corner. One could not imagine a more difficult place to assault with the mobile road-bound Allied armies of 1943, or conversely, an easier place for the Axis ground troops to defend.[13]

Because ports were considered to be natural strongpoints, planning focussed on beaches from the very beginning. The requirements were mind-boggling, as a British official historian, C. J. C. Molony points out: "Deep water close in shore; good anchorages; prevailing winds which do not establish a lee-shore; absence of currents and heavy swell or surf; a recognizable coastline . . . wide to give broad fronts and deep to give room for men, vehicles, and stores, firm, moderate in slope, not boulder-strewn." The planners also had to take into account the range of Allied fighter aircraft, and the location of Luftwaffe airfields. And they had to ponder questions to which there were no conclusive answers: how well would the Italians fight in defence of their homeland, and how many German reinforcements would be sent to Sicily?[14]

Inter-service rivalries caused many changes to Husky. According to Carlo D'Este, "the Navy wanted ports, the Air Force wanted airfields, both wanted dispersion of their forces," while the soldiers desired "a concentration of land forces mutually supporting one another."[15] None of this bickering came as a surprise to a tough, profane, swashbuckling American general, George Patton, a rising star among Allied commanders. "As usual the Navy and Air are not lined up," wrote the fifty-eight-year-old Patton. "Of course being connected with the British is bad. So far, this war is being fought for the benefit of the British Empire and for post-war considerations. No one gives a damn about winning it for itself now."[16]

General Bernard Montgomery proved to be the biggest obstacle facing the planners. The cocky little commander of the Eighth Army, famed simply as "Monty," wished to duplicate in Sicily his well-publicized victories in the North African desert, and so rejected any and every proposal that did not give him the most important tasks and objectives. A fifty-five-year-old career soldier, Monty was short (five-feet-seven), slight (147 pounds), and beak-nosed, but no one who met him ever forgot his piercing, grey-blue eyes. His casual dress – typically, he could be seen wearing chukka boots, knee-length socks, corduroy trousers or baggy khaki shorts, khaki shirt with the sleeves rolled up, and a black beret with two badges – reflected his preference for informality and his intolerance of military bureaucracy. He loved to be seen by his men, gathering them around his car and giving them a short speech delivered "in a high-pitched tone and an impeccable accent."[17] His flair for command was equalled only by his conceit. "General Montgomery's belief in his infallibility seemed absolute," writes British historian R. W. Thompson. "He appeared to be totally incapable of self-criticism, or even of conceiving that his general-ship might be less than perfect."[18]

Disdain and outright hostility among the key players were painfully evident. Eisenhower, the man treading the tightrope between British and American interests and juggling rivalries among the services, came in for much abuse. Patton had no sympathy for his fellow American's seemingly insoluble problems, railing that "he is such a straw man that his future is secure. The British will never let him go."[19] Montgomery's opinion of Eisenhower was hardly more flattering: "good chap; no soldier!"[20] Sir Harold Alexander, always impeccably attired and manicured, was held in even lower esteem. Patton considered Alexander to be "a sorry figure,"[21] while Monty made no attempt to conceal his feelings. As he explained to Patton: "George, let me give you some advice. If you get an order from [Alexander] that you don't like, ignore it. That's what I do."[22]

Beset by rivalry and conflict, the planning for Husky quickly bogged down, and for some time there was a real possibility that there would be no invasion of Sicily. The crisis was not resolved until 3 May, when Eisenhower intervened decisively, bowing to Montgomery's objections and enabling the project to proceed.

The Sicilian invasion was to be the largest amphibious assault of the whole war. The Normandy invasion, in June 1944, was bigger in terms of ships and aircraft, but more troops participated in the landings in Sicily. Husky's statistics are staggering: in round numbers, there were 180,000 troops taking part,[23] along with nearly 15,000 vehicles (including 600 tanks), and 1,800 guns, transported in and escorted by more than 3,000 vessels of every size and description.[24] These forces would operate under an umbrella provided by 2,500 aircraft.[25]

Saturday, 10 July 1943, was selected as D-Day, the date of the attack, which fell into the period of July's favourable moon, "that phase of the moon which gives the right amount of light for an operation which, for any reason, it is impossible to conduct in total darkness or broad daylight." Last light on 9 July would be 2133 hours, with moonset on the tenth at 0031, first light at 0439, and sunrise at 0546.[26] Zero hour, the actual time of the attack, would be 0245.

Long before a single soldier set foot in Sicily, both the Allied navies and air forces were hard at work to make the invasion a success. The sailors had to deliver, support, and sustain two Allied armies in enemy territory. Convoys had to be organized, not only in the Mediterranean but as far away as the United Kingdom and the United States, an undertaking of administrative coordination that allowed little margin for error. These thousands of vessels had to arrive in specific locations off the coast of Sicily at precisely the same time. Meanwhile, the air forces had begun the systematic bombing of Sicily. Axis airfields, industrial centres, and ports were prime targets for the Allied bombers (which included three Canadian squadrons, transferred from England for this purpose), but the missions were spread among Sicily, Sardinia, and the Italian mainland to deceive the enemy.

By the beginning of July, the stage was set for the invasion of Sicily. The final plans called for landings to be made along a hundred-mile sector of Sicily's southern shores. On the Allied left, the U.S. Seventh Army was to land three infantry divisions between Cape Scaramia and Licata, assisted by paratroopers of the 82nd Airborne Division. On the right, in the south-eastern corner of Sicily, the Eighth Army would land four divisions and the 231st (Malta) Brigade between Syracuse and Pozzallo, supported by the 1st Airborne Division. Although the invading armies were roughly the same size, the British were given, as Monty desired, the most important assignments. Their immediate objectives were the ports of Syracuse, Augusta, and Catania, as well as enemy airfields in the vicinity, such as Pachino. The Americans, in strictly a supporting role, were to prevent "enemy reserves moving eastwards against the left flank of Eighth Army."[27]

The invasion plan placed Sir Harold Alexander, the ground-force commander, at the mercy of "two primadonnas,"[28] Monty and Patton. "Alex," who was destined to be the last British-born governor-general of Canada, was fifty-one years old, a professional soldier and a veteran of the Great War. Although in the present war he had made his reputation saving armies that were apparently beyond saving (first at Dunkirk in 1940 and then in Burma in 1942), the charming Alexander had his hands full in this situation. "I don't think he was a very clever man," writes his biographer, Nigel Nicolson. "I don't think he had great imagination. . . . He was a country gentleman, almost uneducated, who never read a book . . . he was very much affected by the drama of war. He did see it as very romantic."[29]

Nor was Husky blessed with the best plan. Eisenhower admitted that, when he later remarked that "we should have made simultaneous landings on both sides of the Messina Strait, thus cutting off all Sicily and obtaining wholesale surrender." Indeed, this was precisely the course of action that German generals feared most. With its long, indefensible coastline, Calabria, the province that occupies the "toe" of the Italian "boot," represented the real danger point. "A secondary landing in Calabria," declared Generalfeldmarschall Albert Kesselring, the German officer in charge, "would have turned the landing in Sicily into an annihilating victory" for the Allies.[30]

However, as the British historian, C. J. C. Molony, notes: "In the circumstances it was remarkable that an agreed plan was formulated at all."[31]

The German-Italian alliance had been strained, too – by defeat. Germany's Führer, Adolf Hitler, had mixed feelings about his Axis partner. Although he was enchanted by the country ("My dearest wish," he would tell dinner guests, "would be to be able to wander about in Italy as an unknown painter") and intensely loyal to its Fascist leader, Benito Mussolini ("one of the Caesars"), Hitler realized that the Italians had been nothing but a burden since the start of the war, staggering from misadventure to defeat to disaster. "What neither the campaigns of Poland nor Norway, France, Russia nor the desert have succeeded in doing," he fumed, "the Italians are on the point of accomplishing – they are ruining the nerves of our soldiers." Italy was "only half an ally," said Hitler. "The Paris police . . . by themselves" could defeat the Italian army.[32]

The Führer controlled the entire German war effort, with increasingly disastrous effect. No unit, however small, moved without Hitler's knowledge or permission. While the Germans remained on guard against the expected cross-Channel invasion from Britain, the final defeat in North Africa in May 1943 had exposed southern Europe to possible invasion, too, and Hitler, obsessed with "the supreme principle of German overall strategy to keep fighting as far as possible from our homeland,"[33] took steps to deal with that threat. Thanks to skilful Allied deception, he was unsure where the enemy would strike next, but at a May planning conference, Hitler directed that "the southern periphery of Europe, whose bastions were the Balkans and the larger Italian islands, must be held."[34]

The German forces in the central Mediterranean came under the nominal direction of the Commando Supremo, the Italian high command, but the real power was exercised by the German commander-in-chief in the theatre, Albert Kesselring, an air force officer who emerged as one of the foremost military commanders of the Second World War. A devout Roman Catholic, the forty-eight-year-old Kesselring was nicknamed "Smiling Albert" for his optimism, which enabled him to serve Hitler, and for his charm, which enabled him to cooperate with the Italians. Although Hitler was slow to recognize the threat to Sicily, Kesselring had concluded that it was the most likely target for the Allies, and the field-marshal put to good use the two-month interval between the defeat in Tunisia and the Allied invasion of Sicily. The Tunisian campaign had drastically weakened the German defences in the central Mediterranean, but by the first of July, Kesselring had managed to station approximately forty thousand German troops in Sicily.[35] Despite the island's vulnerability, the ever-optimistic Kesselring hoped to hold it. He knew the difficulties the Allies would face in mounting a major amphibious operation in the Mediterranean, and even spoke of turning the invasion into "another Dieppe,"[36] a reference to the ill-fated Canadian raid on the French coast in 1942.

Despite his high hopes, Kesselring recognized that the key to the defence of Sicily rested in Italian hands. There were 230,000 Italian soldiers there, in the Sixth Army under sixty-six-year-old Generale d'Armata Alfredo Guzzoni. A powerful force on paper, Guzzoni's army was organized into two corps consisting of ten divisions. However, six of these divisions were coastal-defence formations, accurately described by Allied intelligence as having "an unbelievably low standard of morale, training and discipline."[37]

One coastal division, the 206th, bears out this description. So lamentable was its state that its commander, Generale di Divisione Achille d'Havet, was despondent. "Wherever I go," he complained, "I see company commanders behaving like cinema actors and leaving their men to engage in some childish occupation."[38] D'Havet raged at his chief of staff, who seemed to be "glued to the telephone. . . . This afternoon alone, between 1600 and 1850 hours, he had 53 . . . telephone calls." Nor were low morale, inadequate equipment, and poor training the division's only problems. Its feeble defences, "short belts of barbed wire and scattered minefields covered by machine-gun posts and occasional concrete pillboxes," were scattered along a seventy-mile stretch of the Sicilian coast between Gela and Syracuse. This was the sector where the Eighth Army would come ashore on 10 July.[39]

2

Military necessity launched the Allied campaign in Italy, but military politics consigned nearly half of Canada's overseas army to a theatre that was destined eventually to assume secondary importance in the overall war effort.

Until early 1943, Canada's small but important part in the war had appeared to be unfolding just the way William Lyon Mackenzie King wished. He was an odd little man, "baffling, weird, mystical, dull, dour and boring,"[40] in one historian's words, but politically the sixty-eight-year-old prime minister had few rivals, federally or provincially, thanks to his electoral scheming in the first few months of the war.

King had even survived a brush with his *bête noir*, conscription. In June 1940, he had brought in the National Resources Mobilization Act, giving his Liberal government sweeping powers to control industry and manpower. The NRMA also provided for limited conscription – for home defence only. When the Conservatives threatened to make an issue out of overseas conscription, King held a national plebiscite to free him from his pledge not to conscript men for overseas service. He won nearly two-thirds of the votes cast on 27 April 1942, but the fact that three-quarters of Quebecers voted against him was ample evidence that conscription was still a sensitive, potentially explosive, issue. King cautiously interpreted the results the same way as the *Toronto Star*: "Not necessarily conscription, but conscription if necessary."[41]

King's political battles were made easier by a booming economy. The war proved to be the perfect antidote to economic depression. There were, at long last, seemingly endless export markets for Canada's vast agricultural production, and the country also engineered what an American magazine, *Fortune*, called "an industrial miracle," emerging as the world's fourth-largest weapons and munitions manufacturer.[42]

The transformation of Canada's armed forces was no less remarkable. The army, navy, and air force, after languishing during the two decades following the Great War, now enjoyed world-class status. The Royal Canadian Navy grew from a handful of small ships to 471 vessels, making it the third-largest in the world by the end of the war. The Royal Canadian Air Force went to war with only thirty-seven modern aircraft, but became the world's fourth-largest air force. Out of a regular army which numbered just 4,261 (all ranks) in 1939, and 51,418 militiamen, Canada now had a full-fledged field army, the First Canadian Army, based in England and commanded by Lieutenant-General Andrew McNaughton. Formed in April 1942, Andy McNaughton's army was a quarter-million strong, organized into two corps and subdivided into five divisions and two independent tank brigades. McNaughton proudly likened his army to "a dagger pointed at the heart of Berlin," a phrase which put his stern countenance on the cover of *Time*, but which was to come back to haunt him.[43]

But, in the view of many, there was something missing from Canada's war record. While Canadian airmen defended Britain during the dark days of 1940 and now carried the war into the enemy's heartland, and Canadian sailors were helping to win the crucial Battle of the Atlantic, Canadian soldiers seemed to be doing very little. Aside from a small but successful 1941 expedition to destroy coal supplies in Spitsbergen in northern Norway, Andy McNaughton's highly trained men had participated in only one large-scale action prior to 1943. That occurred on 19 August 1942, the Dieppe Raid. The Second Canadian Infantry Division provided 4,963 men, the bulk of the raiding force, but an outrageously inept plan of attack, combined with inadequate naval support and lack of surprise, produced a major defeat and 3,367 casualties.

Dieppe was deeply disturbing to Prime Minister King. "I still have a feeling," he confided in his diary soon afterwards, "that the part of wisdom would have been to conserve that especially trained life for the decisive moment."[44] Later, mere mention of Dieppe was enough to strike terror into King's heart. Heavy casualties of this sort, he believed, would lead to conscription and political disaster, both for himself and for Canada.

Conserving life was King's primary concern. The best way to do that was to avoid combat, and the prime minister was quite content to keep the First Canadian Army in England until "the decisive moment," the eventual invasion of continental Europe. In this, he and Andy McNaughton were in perfect agreement.

When the First Canadian Infantry Division sailed from Halifax in December 1939, it would have been impossible to predict that three and a half years would pass before it went into battle. At first, no one really minded. The troops survived the winter of 1939–1940, which was one of the worst in English history, mindful that their fathers had undergone much the same experience twenty-five years earlier. Their one brush with war came during the fall of France in the spring of 1940, when a brigade was rushed to Brittany, "rather like tourists,"[45] before making a hasty return to Britain. In the wake of Dunkirk, where the British Expeditionary Force had been rescued from France at the cost of most of its equipment, the Canadian division assumed unusual importance, because for some time it was the only fully equipped, mobile formation of its size in the entire United Kingdom. With a German invasion expected almost daily during the bleak summer of 1940, the First Division – proudly dubbing itself "McNaughton's Travelling Circus"[46] – was moved to and fro across southern England, to deceive the Germans about Britain's counter-attack capabilities.

As the threat of invasion faded, the Canadian forces in the United Kingdom grew. By the end of 1940, a two-division Canadian Corps was formed, inheriting the reputation of its formidable predecessor in the Great War. From there, it was a logical and relatively easy step to form the first field army in Canadian history. But it was not nearly as easy to decide what to do with it.

While the rest of the world warred, the Canadian army trained. And trained. And trained some more. "Some of the training in England," recalls Victor Hall, a member of the West Nova Scotia Regiment, "was a hell of a lot harder than some of the action."[47] But the grind took its toll. "Things are getting very monotonous over here just waiting for our war to start," an artillery lieutenant, Duff Mitchell, wrote home in March 1941. "The Air Forces are having all the fun. . . . The men are getting pretty well fed up with the war."[48] By the end of 1942, the question was becoming increasingly common: "When the hell are we going to see some fighting?"[49]

The soldiers were not alone in asking that question. Observers were wondering the same thing. "In its inaction," says former CBC reporter Peter Stursberg, "the Canadian Army had set some kind of a record. A friend of mine, who was on a London newspaper, said that he thought it was the first time in military history that a volunteer army had been used as garrison troops."[50] Similar sentiments were expressed by the Montreal *Gazette*'s Lionel Shapiro, who noted that the Canadian army was "the first formation in the history of war in which the birthrate is higher than the deathrate."[51]

Impatience was noticeable at home, too. Public opinion, at least in English-speaking Canada, was finally coming into play, demanding that the army do more to win the war. In the space of a few days in November 1942, Winnipeg's *Free Press* commented that it would be "sensible to send a full division to some theatre of war," the Montreal *Gazette* headlined an alarming story, "Mental Illness in Overseas Army Laid to Inactivity and Anxiety," and a Great War brigadier-general, John Clark, told a Vancouver audience that the army's idleness "constitutes the greatest disgrace of the present war."[52] It was becoming apparent to Prime Minister King that Canada's army could not be kept out of battle for much longer.

King was also under pressure from James Layton Ralston, his minister of national defence. Colonel Ralston, a decorated battalion commander in the 1914–1918 war, felt that Canadian honour required a major effort by the army, and the sooner the better. Since assuming the defence portfolio in the summer of 1940, Ralston had been trying to get Canadian soldiers into combat. Each attempt had been rejected by King's cabinet war committee, but Ralston remained on a collision course with the country's top soldier.

Andy McNaughton advocated keeping the army united for the invasion of mainland Europe. Although he stated a willingness to detach divisions under certain unspecified circumstances, McNaughton believed "that the Canadian force proceeding abroad would, from necessity, be allotted a less important role and probably be decentralized under British command." This would not only relegate to Canada "an inferior role in the total Allied war effort," in McNaughton's view, "such splitting up would result in a very marked decrease in the effect we could have on the enemy."[53]

He was dealing from a position of strength only so long as there was the possibility of a cross-Channel invasion in 1943. However, as that prospect faded early in the year, McNaughton became isolated within the army itself. No one worked harder to undermine him than one of his own corps commanders, Lieutenant-General Harry Crerar. On 10 February 1942, he dined with the chief of the Imperial General Staff, Sir Alan Brooke, who complained in his diary that Crerar had harangued him about "the necessity of getting some Canadians fighting soon for imperial and political reasons." Brooke pointed out "that the main factor that had up to date militated against their use in Africa was the stipulation made by the Canadian Government that the Canadian Army must not be split up and must only be used as a whole – a conception that McNaughton had always upheld with the greatest tenacity. Crerar realised this concept must be broken down."[54]

At home, the political and public pressure continued to grow. March 1943 was the crucial month, when King met several times with Ralston and the chief of the General Staff, Lieutenant-General Kenneth Stuart. Appointed CGS in December 1941, Stuart was a former classmate of McNaughton's who, like Ralston, was a Great War veteran and shared his boss's desire to get Canadian troops into action sooner than later. Ralston and Stuart pursued this objective now, but the prime minister was not very sympathetic to their views. This "whole mischievous situation," as King called it, had arisen because "we have far too many men overseas than we should be keeping there – many should be in employment here." King, who had viewed Ralston with a jaundiced eye since the 1942 conscription crisis (Ralston, a strong advocate of conscription, resigned at one point but was later talked out of such a politically damaging move by the prime minister), believed that it was "my duty . . . to back up McNaughton rather than Ralston. Back of all else, there is a feeling between them which I think warps Ralston's judgment a bit."[55]

However, Ralston and Stuart had a trump card – the casualty projections for the cross-Channel invasion. There was no doubt that it was going to be very bloody, and they took advantage of King's fear of heavy casualties. In his diary, the prime minister confessed that "I have been afraid of a second Dieppe." The entry for 17 March confirms his concern "that our armies would simply be landed on European soil and massacred between the devil [Germany] and the deep blue sea."[56]

The ploy worked. Facing the prospect of very heavy losses in the cross-Channel invasion, which raised the spectre of conscription and a political crisis in Canada, King's earlier resolve began to crumble. Perhaps, after all, it would be better to allow at least part of the Canadian army to fight somewhere else, where casualties might be lighter. At this time, that somewhere else was Tunisia, and the prime minister finally agreed to cable Winston Churchill in mid-March that "the strong considerations with which you are familiar in favour of employment of Canadian troops in North Africa appear to require earnest re-examination."[57]

More than a month passed before the Canadian appeals bore fruit. On 23 April, General McNaughton was summoned to the War Office in London for a meeting with General Brooke. The Canadian commander departed with a formal, written request to commit "one Canadian infantry division and one tank brigade together with the necessary ancillary troops" to "certain operations based on Tunisia." Without even knowing the details of the those operations, the King government quickly gave its tentative approval, which McNaughton delivered to Brooke on 25 April. The only catch was that Ottawa required McNaughton to view the detailed plans and determine whether they constituted "a practical operation of war."[58]

McNaughton spent three days reviewing Operation Husky, the invasion of Sicily. Studying maps, reading reports, perusing orders, and holding discussions with senior War Office planners, he concluded that the plan was practical. It was not an easy decision for him to make, because it would divide his beloved his army and leave him in England with only part of the troops he had assembled and trained. Although he admitted that he was conscious that "public opinion in Canada was being incited to demand action," he insisted that his approval to commit Canadian forces to Husky was based "on purely military grounds." He did attach one condition: that the agreement related to "this specific operation only, and that if other operations were contemplated we would have to consult again."[59] McNaughton approved of the Sicilian operation because it was clearly a limited undertaking that would provide valuable experience and enable the First Canadian Army to be reunited prior to the cross-Channel invasion.

When McNaughton's assessment reached Ottawa, government approval followed swiftly. The prime minister did not yet know it, but he had committed Canadian troops to the biggest amphibious assault of the war.

The news, for the handful of senior officers who were notified, was electrifying: the First Canadian Infantry Division, with the First Canadian Army Tank Brigade, would be heading for the Mediterranean. With less than two months until the first departures, a whirlwind of preparations ensued.

These units were Andy McNaughton's choices, and they were good ones. McNaughton had commanded the division when it first went overseas in 1939. The first Canadian army formation to leave Canada, it had worked hard and trained hard during the subsequent three and a half years. Every member of this division wore on his upper sleeve a rectangular red patch inherited from the division's Great War predecessor, which had won renown by standing firm in the face of poison gas at Ypres in 1915 and had then gone on to become what one British general called "the pride and wonder of the British Army." The new First Division thus carried with it great expectations, and there was no reason to doubt that it would live up to them. Its nine infantry battalions included all three of Canada's regular-army units: The Royal Canadian Regiment (RCR), Princess Patricia's Canadian Light Infantry (PPCLI), and the Royal 22nd Regiment (the "Van

Doos"). The divisional commander was Major-General Harry Salmon, a highly regarded career officer who might have become Canada's top soldier had not fate intervened. His chief staff officer, Lieutenant-Colonel George Kitching, describes the Camberley-trained Salmon as "very demanding" and "a stickler for detail."[60]

Salmon was surrounded by capable officers. Of his four brigadiers, two were former militia officers: the divisional artillery chief, Bruce Matthews, from Toronto, and Howard Graham, the former Trenton mayor who commanded the First Brigade, which consisted of three Ontario battalions: the RCR, Toronto's 48th Highlanders of Canada, and the Hastings and Prince Edward Regiment. The Second Brigade was commanded by blustery, volatile Chris Vokes, a regular, as was portly Howard Penhale, a Great War gunner who led the Third Brigade. Vokes's brigade was mainly from Western Canada, comprising the Princess Patricias, the Edmonton Regiment, and Vancouver's Seaforth Highlanders of Canada, while Penhale oversaw an eastern formation, consisting of the Van Doos, New Brunswick's Carleton and York Regiment, and the West Nova Scotia Regiment.

The First Canadian Tank Brigade had been in England for two years. Commanded by Brigadier Bob Wyman, it contained the only formation in Canada's Sicilian contingent with actual battle experience. The Calgary Regiment, which was better known simply as the "Calgary Tanks," had lost twenty-nine tanks on the blood-soaked beach at Dieppe, where it had become the first Canadian armoured unit to see combat in this war. The brigade's other formations were the Ontario Regiment and the Three Rivers Regiment, which would soon prove themselves as proficient as their western cousins.

There was much to be done to prepare the Canadians for their trip to the Mediterranean. General Salmon established his divisional planning staff at Norfolk House in St. James's Square in London. This became the scene of countless conferences concerning training, intelligence, security, and administration, which included transportation arrangements and the provision of equipment and supplies. British liaison officers from the Royal Navy, the Royal Air Force, and the War Office also participated in the discussions.

Meanwhile, the decision to include the Canadians had been transmitted by Sir Alan Brooke to the Allied commanders for Husky, Generals Eisenhower and Alexander. Brooke explained that the Canadians had been selected for "political and military" reasons. "I very much regret this last minute change. We have been very carefully into its implications and consider it quite practicable."[61]

When Force 545, the British planning group ensconced in Cairo, learned that it had acquired a formation about which it knew nothing, it requested that General Salmon fly in for consultations. A twin-engined Hudson aircraft was made available for this purpose, and the flight was scheduled for Thursday, 28 April. Salmon was accompanied by several senior Canadian and British officers.

One officer who was supposed to accompany him was Lieutenant-Colonel Geoff Walsh, the First Division's chief engineer. Tall, slender, blue-eyed, the thirty-three-year-old Walsh was a regular soldier who viewed the excitement at Norfolk House with detached professionalism. When Walsh arrived at the London-area Hendon airfield that fateful Thursday morning for the flight to Cairo, he discovered that he had lost his seat to a top-priority naval courier. Walsh returned to London, where, he remembers, "I had a bit to eat, and I went back to Norfolk House. I just happened to notice [Salmon's] office door open, so I looked in there, and they all turned white." Walsh soon learned the reason for the shocked expressions on the faces of his colleagues: Salmon's Hudson – on which they assumed Walsh had been a passenger – had crashed soon after take-off, killing everyone on board.[62]

This tragic turn of events, under other circumstances, might have been catastrophic for the Canadians. But the divisional headquarters staff remained largely intact, and Andy McNaughton made an inspired choice as a replacement for Harry Salmon. He selected Guy Granville Simonds, an intense, English-born professional soldier, who had just celebrated (on 23 April) his fortieth birthday, shortly after his promotion to major-general and command of the Second Canadian Infantry Division. A grad-uate of Kingston's Royal Military College, a gunner by trade, Simonds had been a major on the First Division's staff when it went overseas in 1939, soon rising to the rank of brigadier. He was one of the few Canadians to impress General Montgomery, who was to call him the "only [Canadian] general fit to hold high command in the Second World War."[63]

Simonds took charge immediately. Striding into Norfolk House that very afternoon, he plunged into the rather daunting task of familiarizing himself with the preparations made to date. One factor in his favour was that there was not yet a firm plan for the Allied invasion of Sicily. But Simonds still had to study the vast accumulation of orders, reports, and maps that had been prepared to cover all eventualities. Two days later, he flew to Cairo, accompanied by several senior staff officers, including the very lucky Geoff Walsh. As a safety precaution, Simonds split his party in two: one, aboard a Liberator bomber, left on 30 April, while his own departed on 1 May, aboard a Hudson.

Delayed by sandstorms *en route*, Simonds did not reach the Egyptian city until the evening of the fourth. By now, the Allied high command had at last reached general agreement on the Husky invasion plan, with D-Day definitely scheduled for 10 July, and Simonds spent the next few days conferring with his Eighth Army commanders. The First Canadian Division, as part of Lieutenant-General Sir Oliver Leese's XXX Corps, would land on the extreme left of the Eighth Army's allotted area, on the Pachino peninsula in southeastern Sicily. The American Seventh Army would be well to the left of the Canadians, further along the coast, while on their immediate right would be the British 50th Division. The youthful Simonds prepared a plan of attack which he "cabled to England within 24 hours of my arrival in Cairo."[64]

While Norfolk House continued its top-secret preparations, virtually everyone else in the First Division and the First Tank Brigade remained ignorant of the Sicilian operation. Both formations were shipped to Scotland, where they underwent what the Canadian official history calls "a final period of advanced training" near Inverary in Argyllshire,[65] where they also re-equipped. Although they did not realize it at the time, the new weapons and equipment were standard issue in the Mediterranean theatre. Weapons included the American-made Thompson submachine-gun, nicknamed the "Tommy gun" or "Chicago piano" from its pre-war gangster days, a .45-calibre weapon capable of firing up to 650 rounds per minute. There was also the odd-looking, brand-new portable gun officially known as the "Projector, Infantry, Anti-Tank," soon to be famed by its simple acronym, PIAT. While the PIAT was issued to selected riflemen to carry into battle, the anti-tank platoon of each battalion was equipped with the heavier 6-pounder gun, an improvement over the 2-pounders previously used, while the divisional anti-tank regiment was armed with the still-heavier 17-pounder.

Among the vehicles delivered to the Canadians was an American-made amphibious truck, the DUKW, which was equally effective at carrying either supplies or assault troops. Pronounced "duck," this unimaginative acronym was merely the vehicle's factory serial initials. The DUKW was a two-and-a-half-ton, six-wheeled truck with a boat built around it. Afloat, it had a maximum speed of six knots, while ashore its cross-country performance was similar to that of the British army's three-ton lorry. DUKWs were just now being produced in the United States in large numbers, and one hundred were sent directly to Britain for the First Canadian Division, although they arrived too late to be utilized in the unit's combined-operations training for Sicily.

The armoured brigade received new tanks, in the form of the American-built M4 medium Sherman, which replaced their Canadian-made Ram. Al Cawsey, a lieutenant in the Calgary Tanks, recalls that "the Sherman didn't have much of a reputation" at this time. Its armour-plating was not particularly thick, and while its 75-millimetre gun was an improvement over the 6-pounders to which the Canadian tankmen were accustomed, it would prove to be no match in one-on-one fights with the bigger German tanks such as the Panther and the Tiger, which was often equipped with the superlative 88-millimetre gun. Still, says Cawsey, they "grew to love" the thirty-ton Shermans. The Canadians, he remembers, adapted quickly. "A crew of British instructors arrived, intending to spend a month with us, teaching us how to use the tanks, but after ten days our men, who were farmers and ranchers from Southern Alberta, knew as much about the tanks as the instructors."[66]

The administrative planning could have been a nightmare if it had been handled with anything less than professional competence. The Canadian troop convoys that were to sail from England in June would have to take every conceivable item, in sufficient quantities to sustain the division and tank brigade – a total strength of 1,851 officers and 24,835 other ranks – for at least three weeks following the invasion, and no detail was overlooked. The 30,000 tons of supplies included everything from special camouflage paint to mosquito nets.[67]

However, there was still one matter that had to be resolved. Who controlled the Canadians who were being sent to the Mediterranean? Although nominally under British jurisdiction, they were on their own in some administrative respects, such as providing reinforcements and looking after casualties. To oversee Canadian interests two thousand miles away from the elaborate Canadian Military Headquarters in London, a small staff under a lieutenant-colonel was set up at General Alexander's Fifteenth Army Group headquarters. But this did not fully answer Andy McNaughton's preoccupation with the question of control, and he reminded Guy Simonds of his "right to refer to the Government of Canada with respect to any matter in which the forces under your command are or are likely to be involved or committed or on any question of their administration which may require correction."[68]

By 1 June, the Canadian plans had been finalized. According to the division's chief staff officer, Lieutenant-Colonel George Kitching, the orders filled more than two hundred typewritten pages. "It was the last document of that size that was produced by the Division," he writes, "but it was recognized that the circumstances warranted it."[69] Sealed copies were placed on board each troopship. Labelled TOP SECRET, they were not be opened until after the convoys had sailed.

The strain had started to show by now. Simonds and the First Brigade's Howard Graham had not hit it off, and they were beginning to get on each other's nerves. Simonds, Graham noted, routinely addressed the other infantry brigadiers as "Chris" or "Pen," but called him by his surname. Graham was even more annoyed by Simonds's "abrupt and harsh criticism," first at a planning session at Norfolk House and later during a landing exercise on the Scottish coast. "I had the definite feeling that he wanted to get rid of me, a rank amateur," Graham complained in his memoirs. "Imagine, a lawyer in command of one of his brigades!"[70]

Graham was not the only senior officer to suffer Simonds's wrath. The divisional commander was enraged when he learned that the officer commanding the Three Rivers Regiment, Lieutenant-Colonel Leslie Booth, had prematurely opened his sealed orders. The unfortunate colonel was summoned to appear before the seething Simonds. "I was standing behind Booth," says George Kitching of the five-minute tirade, "and at one time I thought I would have to support him physically as he wilted from the blast."[71] Simonds only grudgingly allowed Booth to retain his command.

These episodes were soon overshadowed by the excitement of imminent departure. The loading of supplies began in various ports in early June, and all vessels were assembled in Scotland's River Clyde, where they awaited the departure of their respective convoys. The troops boarded their ships between 13 and 16 June, only vaguely aware of the complex sailing plans. The Canadians would travel in four convoys, consisting of 125 transport and escort vessels, each departing on different dates. There was a "Fast Assault Convoy," a "Slow Assault Convoy," and two follow-up convoys. The Fast Assault Convoy, which carried the troops taking part in the actual landing, departed on 28 June. Prior to that, the Slow Assault Convoy, with the reserve combat units, sailed in two groups, on 19 and 24 June. The follow-up convoys, scheduled to sail on 25 June and 1 July, carried non-essential personnel and equipment not required for the actual assault on the Sicilian coast.[72]

The Canadians departed quietly. When the Fast Assault Convoy sailed down the Clyde on 28 June, a PPCLI officer aboard the transport *Llangibby Castle* observed: "Citizens and soldiers, sailors and airmen, members of the women's forces, could be seen walking along the riverside or bathing on the beaches. It was to be our last view of a peaceful setting for a long time."[73]

Also watching were some very high-level eyes. In a naval shore establishment at Largs, overlooking the firth, a group of senior Allied officers met secretly "to study the problems of combined operations in a cross-Channel assault on the continent." The chairman, Admiral Lord Louis Mountbatten, interrupted the discussion and called the participants outside, where they watched darkness falling over the Canadian convoy as it moved into the open sea. "To at least one of these observers, General McNaughton, it must have been a profoundly moving experience to see the 1st Canadian Division thus setting forth on its path of high adventure."[74]

The troops remained ignorant of their destination until after the convoys put to sea. They listened to messages from generals Montgomery,

McNaughton, and Simonds, outlining their role in the impending invasion of Sicily, and details of the operation soon followed.

The news was received with enthusiasm, according to Farley Mowat, then a twenty-two-year-old lieutenant in the Hastings and Prince Edward Regiment. Mowat remembers his own reaction: "Sicily! I knew next to nothing of the place. Vaguely I recalled something about it being the home of the Mafia, and images of Al Capone and the Saint Valentine's Day massacre came to mind." Mowat and all other officers in the division were soon studying "maps and air photographs of the Pachino Peninsula-. . . containing First Canadian Division's objective: the town of Pachino and its nearby airfield. We pored over these maps and photos with such avidity that images of them still remain imprinted in my mind."[75]

It was, on the whole, a grand voyage. "That trip to Sicily was one of the most luxurious trips that I have ever taken," writes Howard Mitchell, then a captain with the Saskatoon Light Infantry, the First Division's support battalion. "There was plenty of room for everyone. And the food was wonderful. The cook baked fresh rolls every day. I have never tasted such delicious rolls anywhere."[76]

A mystery resulted from the nighttime passage of the Strait of Gibraltar. A member of the Calgary Tanks disappeared, and no one ever discovered whether he fell or jumped overboard.[77]

The searing sunshine in the Mediterranean stressed an absurd situation aboard an LST (landing ship, tank) carrying the Ontario Regiment. Just before the convoy sailed from Scotland, Captain Ned Amy had been sent ashore to purchase phonograph records for the vessel's public-address system. Amy returned with the only record he recognized: a copy of Bing Crosby's "White Christmas," with "Adeste Fideles" on the flip side. Christmas songs were not really appropriate to the torrid Mediterranean in the summertime, and it was not long before an angry cry went up all over the ship: "Throw Amy overboard!"[78]

But danger lurked in these waters, as both the fast and slow convoys discovered. On the afternoon of 6 July, Rear-Admiral Sir Philip Vian, seeing that he was ahead of schedule, abruptly reversed the direction of the Fast Assault Convoy in order to use up some time – and encountered a German U-boat moving in for the kill. Two British destroyers immediately attacked the would-be attacker, and Geoff Walsh, the divisional engineer, remembers seeing the enemy submarine "being blown out of the water, practically vertical. It was just like a movie."*[79]

---

* Walsh's memory is remarkable. In his interview with the author, he estimated that the destroyers "dropped about a hundred and twenty-five depth charges." The actual number was 127.[80]

The Slow Assault Convoy was far less fortunate. Sunday, 4 July, found it steaming at a leisurely eight knots off the North African coast, ninety miles west of Algiers. Suddenly, a torpedo struck the merchantman *City of Venice*, which later sank. Half an hour later, the transport *St. Essylt* was hit by a torpedo. The convoy's crisis continued the next day, when another transport, *Devis*, was torpedoed during the afternoon and sank within twenty minutes. The officer commanding the Canadian troops on board *Devis* was a thirty-six-year-old Calgarian, Major Douglas Harkness, a future federal cabinet minister. "I was in my cabin at the time the explosion took place," he recalls. "I rushed out, and the first thing I saw was the two rear wheels of a truck and half the body of a man, which was on the deck just outside the door." Harkness organized rescue parties to help the men trapped below deck, but with limited success: "We were only able to get a few up." The worst part came when he finally jumped overboard and subsequently endured what he calls "one of the worst experiences that I remember in the war." Destroyers criss-crossed the area, dropping depth charges, which Harkness believes "killed quite a few of our people that were in the water." With each explosion, he says, "you felt your insides being squeezed out. It was a terrible feeling." His misery ended a couple of hours later, when a destroyer fished him out of the warm water.[81]

The losses in these three sinkings were heavy. Fifty-eight men perished, and five hundred vehicles and forty guns were missing.[82] Particularly hard-hit was the divisional headquarters, which lost twenty-two of its twenty-six vehicles.[83] As George Kitching points out, these three vessels had been loaded with vehicles and signals equipment in equal portions, so that if one ship were sunk, the headquarters could still function smoothly. "The chance of all three ships being sunk," he claims, "was a million to one."[84]

No other mishaps befell the Canadian convoys, and around noon on Friday, 9 July, they joined up south of Malta for the final approach to Sicily. It was only now that the sheer magnitude of this operation became apparent, for the Canadians found themselves in the midst of thousands of ships, all headed in the same direction. But there was no time to admire the thrilling sight. During the afternoon, a sudden and violent storm swept through the area, and for several hours there was doubt whether the invasion could take place. Farley Mowat recalls that his ship, *Derbyshire*, "was wallowing like a drunken sow. . . . Everything that was not lashed down had come adrift: kitbags, weapons boxes, steel crates of ammunition, mess tins, tin helmets and nameless flotsam surged back and forth among the upturned tables, banging into stanchions and fetching up at the end of each long roll in dishevelled heaps against the bulkheads."[85] Then, as quickly as it blew in, the storm died away.

The troops spent the final hours before the invasion writing letters home, checking their equipment, praying, playing cards and dice. Aboard *Llangibby Castle*, a PPCLI company commander, Captain Donald Brain, proudly wrote that his men "were confident and cheerful and I can honestly say that I did not meet one man who showed conscious signs of nerves."[86] Chris Vokes, the gruff commander of the Second Brigade, attempted to inspire his men by urging them to "seek out and destroy the enemy wherever he may be found" and reminding them that "only cowards surrender." He concluded by wishing his troops "good luck – and good scalping."[87]

The long years of boredom were about to end.

PART ONE

Sunny Sicily

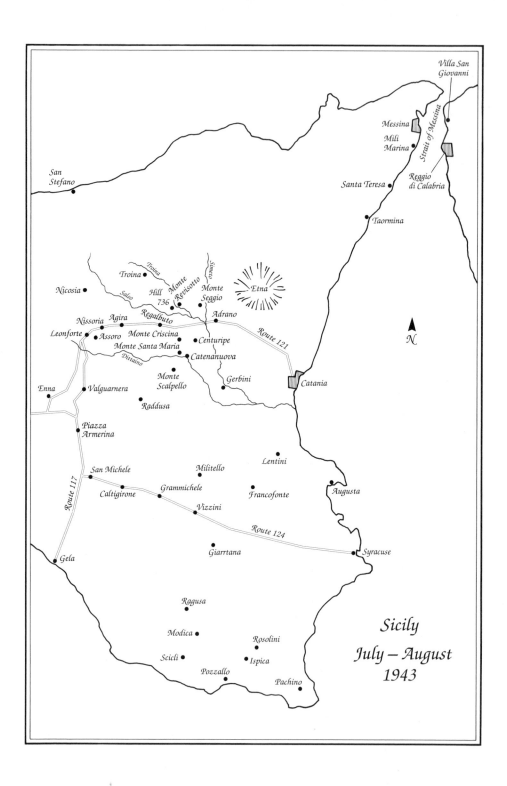

Villa San
Giovanni

Messina

Mili
Marina

Santa Teresa

Strait of Messina

Reggio
di Calabria

San
Stefano

Taormina

Troina
Troina

Nicosia

Monte
Revisotto

Hill
736

Monte
Seggio

Simeto

Etna

Salso

Nissoria

Agira

Regalbuto

Monte Criscina

Adrano

Route 121

Leonforte

Assoro

Centuripe

Monte Santa Maria

Dittaino

Catenanuova

Enna

Valguarnera

Monte
Scalpello

Gerbini

Catania

N

Raddusa

Piazza
Armerina

Lentini

San Michele

Militello

Route 117

Caltigirone

Grammichele

Francofonte

Augusta

Vizzini

Route 124

Gela

Giarrtana

Syracuse

Ragusa

Modica

Rosolini

Scicli

Ispica

Pozzallo

Pachino

Sicily

July – August
1943

CHAPTER ONE

"Fun and Games"

1

Canada's role in Husky was easier than anyone could have foreseen. Virtually unopposed, the Canadians suffered few casualties on 10 July 1943. Nevertheless, it was far from a textbook operation.

Code-named "Bark West," the Canadian landing sector was situated in a wide, curving bay known as Costa dell'Ambra (the Amber Coast). Bark West was divided into two sandy beaches, "Roger" on the right and "Sugar" on the left. The Hastings and Prince Edward Regiment and The Royal Canadian Regiment of Howard Graham's First Brigade, from Ontario, were assigned to Roger beach, while Sugar was given to Chris Vokes and the Second Brigade of western Canadians, led by the Seaforth Highlanders of Canada and Princess Patricia's Canadian Light Infantry. Three miles inland lay the main Canadian objective, the Pachino airfield, near the town of the same name. Defensive positions were few and far between in this sector. Aerial photographs revealed "about fifteen pillboxes and a score of machine-gun posts," but more worrisome were two coast-defence batteries. One, consisting of four 147-millimetre guns, was located a mile and a half from the Canadian beaches; the other, with four 6-inch howitzers, guarded the airfield.[1]

No one knew what to expect on Sicily's shores. Although the defences were sparse, they were capable of inflicting heavy casualties if the Italians chose to fight hard. A worst-case planning scenario included plans to be used "if a whole Brigade were destroyed before the beaches were reached." But the divisional commander, Guy Simonds, "had not the slightest doubt of the successful outcome of the operation." In a discussion with General McNaughton before leaving Britain, he had pointed out "the great superiority of force" being employed in Husky, as well as "the sound plans and the careful preparations."[2]

Events would show that Simonds's confidence was justified, but the youthful divisional commander would suffer some anxious moments. As they developed, the landings on the two Canadian beaches were to become dramatically different operations. While the Second Brigade, on the left, encountered only minor difficulties, the First Brigade's assault came dangerously close to complete collapse.

When the First Division's headquarters ship, HMS *Hilary*, anchored seven miles off the Costa dell'Ambra, D-Day was forty-eight minutes old. On shore, in the vicinity of Pachino, a spectacular fireworks display was under way, as Allied bombers pounded the airfield and the Italian defenders fired flak and flares in response. At the same time, the half-dozen transports carrying the assault formations slowed to a stop nearby, their landing craft loaded with troops and ready to be lowered into the sea. After the storm the previous evening, the weather was quite pleasant. Standing on the bridge of *Marnix van Sint Aldegonde*, CBC reporter Peter Stursberg noted that "the ship did not seem to be rolling so much . . . the wind had died to a gentle breeze. The sky was studded with stars and a small moon hung like a yellow lantern. There was a tense hush on the bridge, broken now and then by the jangle of the engine-room telegraph."[3]

In order to reach Sugar beach in time for zero hour, 0245, the Second Brigade's two assault battalions, PPCLI and the Seaforth Highlanders, set off at 0134. The brigade utilized LCAs (landing craft, assault); each lightly-armoured, flat-bottomed LCA carried about forty men, an infantry platoon plus a crew of four. Once in the water, the landing craft were marshalled in flotillas which were then led to the beaches by motor launches. The guide vessels were in turn aided by sonic buoys two miles offshore, but nighttime navigation was a hazardous undertaking in which guesswork was sometimes as important as the skills of the sailors.[4] The Canadians were riding in British landing craft, although Canadian craft were available; "Canadian soldiers and sailors, for this operation, were not to have the satisfaction of working together," lamented historian Joseph Schull. The four hundred men of the RCN's 55th and 61st flotillas, manning LCAs, and the 80th and 81st flotillas, equipped with LCMs (landing craft, mechanized), were assigned to British beaches during Husky. Another two hundred and fifty Canadian sailors were serving in Royal Navy landing craft and support ships.[5]

However, air cover for the Canadians was being provided by Canadian pilots, among others. From its base in Malta, Spitfires of the RCAF's 417 (City of Windsor) Squadron provided an umbrella for the ground and naval forces off Bark West. The only Canadian fighter squadron in the Mediterranean during World War II, 417 was commanded by Stan Turner, an English-born ace with twelve kills to his credit. The pilots were tired: since 6 July, 417 Squadron had escorted Canadian, American, and British bombers on their "shuttle-bombing of Sicily." The four days of intensive flying paid off on D-Day: over Bark West, at least, German aircraft were noticeable only by their absence.[6]

En route to the beaches, the naval bombardment exploded over the heads of the seasick Canadian infantrymen huddled in their little landing craft. The Saskatoon Light Infantry's Captain Howard Mitchell remembers it as "terrific. First there was a flash from the warships that seemed to light up everything. Then there were swishes overhead. Then the whole coastline seemed to literally rise up momentarily to be followed by clouds of smoke. Then came the report of the guns on the ship to be followed by the sound of the explosions on land."[7] The main support in Bark West was provided by the 15-inch guns of the Royal Navy monitor *Roberts*, supported by a cruiser and three destroyers, all directed by Admiral Vian on board HMS *Hilary*. *Roberts*'s firepower made a lasting impression. "We could feel the blast sweep over the ocean," recounted war correspondent Ross Munro, "although we were several miles away."[8]

Among the first Canadians in Sicily was Captain Don Brain of the PPCLI. So far as he was concerned, "everything functioned as smoothly as any drill parade." A final roll call on the transport *Llangibby Castle* was taken as each man reported to his landing craft and climbed aboard. Everyone sat quietly as the LCAs were lowered into the "slight swell" and started on their long journey to Sugar beach. "As we approached closer to shore," Brain later wrote, "flares could be seen being put up by an enemy even more uncertain than ourselves as to what to expect."[9]

Brain's B Company hit Sugar beach on schedule. Enemy small-arms fire, the captain recalled, "was almost negligible." More disconcerting was the deep water in which he and his men found themselves. "In a few instances men landed in water six feet deep and had to abandon their weapons and equipment and swim for it." His three platoons were not in exactly the right spot, but Brain swiftly organized them and rushed up the sandy shore. Enemy resistance came in the form of a few hand grenades and a machine-gun post whose two-man crew "we wiped out." In a nearby hut the Patricias found a sleepy Italian soldier "obviously just awakened by the noise as he had not yet had time to put on his uniform."[10]

Vancouver's Seaforth Highlanders were not quite so lucky. Instead of landing on the left of the PPCLI, they were put ashore on the right. The Seaforths splashed ashore to the skirl of bagpipes, which they had been ordered to leave behind in order to conserve weight in the first assault wave. It was an appalling thought for any Highland regiment to go into battle without its beloved bagpipes, but by a remarkable coincidence, these instruments were discovered to have been "accidentally" stored in the wrong boxes and brought ashore. According to the Second Brigade's Major Dick Malone, "they made a very happy sound that morning."[11]

Facing "practically negligible opposition," the two battalions of the Second Brigade quickly cleared Sugar beach. By 0400 hours, they had reported success to their brigadier, Chris Vokes, and started to move inland.[12]

Meanwhile, the First Brigade's landing on Roger beach was still getting under way. The delay resulted from a change of plan that was made when a shallow sandbar was discovered offshore. Since there did not appear to be sufficient clearance to enable LCAs to get across it, Brigadier Howard Graham was ordered to use larger LCTs (landing craft, tank); the LCTs were to transport the assault troops as far as the sandbar, where amphibious DUKWs would take them the rest of the way to the beach. Three LCTs, each carrying seven DUKWs, were assigned to the First Brigade, but they were more than two hours late. Graham's worst fears about the landing were being realized as he waited on the bridge of the transport *Glengyle*. "Words fail me," wrote the former Trenton mayor, "in trying to describe the frustration . . . during the two hours and more between the anchoring of the ships and the dispatch of my assault companies."[13]

On the headquarters vessel, HMS *Hilary*, General Simonds and Admiral Vian were growing impatient. "Will your assault ever start?" Vian signalled. Simonds sent Lieutenant-Colonel Pres Gilbride in the admiral's barge to deliver an urgent order: "You must get your assaults away in either LCTs or LCAs."[14]

Gilbride delivered his message at 0335, only to find that Graham's assault had at last begun. Deciding that it was better to do something than to do nothing, Graham had ordered the two assault companies of the Hastings and Prince Edward Regiment, on *Glengyle*, to embark in LCAs. Confusion ensued, according to Regimental Sergeant-Major Angus Duffy of the Hasty Ps, as the battalion was popularly known. "Despite all our training," he says, "things started to go haywire. The very high waves forced us to change our landing craft loads, and in the shuffle the mortars got lost, and then something else got lost, and then two of the craft in the process of being put into the water were destroyed by the high waves." The last straw came when the ship's captain turned on the lights. "We had been training for months to go in very quietly with absolutely no lights, and sitting below deck to accustom our eyes to darkness, but all of a sudden the lights were on and there was the greatest din you ever heard. Of course we were still about six miles out."[15] It was 0226 before the Hasty Ps were ready for the forty-foot descent to the water, but nearly an hour passed before they actually headed for shore.

Graham's other assault unit, The Royal Canadian Regiment, was delayed even longer. After a seemingly interminable wait, two LCTs finally showed up alongside the RCR's transport, *Marnix van Sint Aldegonde*, and the men began scrambling down nets to take their places in the bobbing landing craft. Captain Ian Hodson was dismayed to find that instead of six DUKWs, he was allotted only five into which to cram his company's 139 men, including ten engineers. "With such a crowd," he writes, "we overloaded these vehicles and presented a possible catastrophe."[16] It was a time-consuming process, and not even the curses of harried NCOs could speed it up.

Both battalions landed hours behind schedule. Two companies of the Hasty Ps touched down at 0445, but it was after dawn (the sun rose at 0546) when the RCR landed. The LCTs carrying the two RCR companies grounded on the sandbar, then the DUKWs waddled out and swam the rest of the way to Roger. The landing was unopposed, but as he led his company ashore, Captain Hodson was surprised to find, in a large hole on the beach, "two film crew surrounded by cases of film. How and when did they get there?"[17]

However, one company of the Hasty Ps did not reach Roger. The LCAs carrying Captain Alex Campbell's A Company, which was in the follow-up wave, ended up three miles west of their intended location. Lost but enthusiastic, the company invaded Sicily. Lieutenant Farley Mowat, the future author, was the first to leap from his landing craft, bravely shouting, "Follow me, men!" Stepping into eight feet of water, he was also the first to discover that the craft had grounded on an uncharted sandbar a hundred yards offshore. Carrying a Tommy gun, a revolver, small-arms ammunition, and grenades, Mowat sank "like a stone, striking the bottom feet-first. So astounded was I by this unexpected descent into the depths that I made no attempt to thrash my way back to the surface. I simply walked straight on until my head emerged." Over the din could be heard Campbell's roar: "Get on, you silly bastards! Get on with it!"[18]

Charging ashore, Mowat's platoon came under small-arms fire. His company sergeant-major, Chuck Nutley, a twenty-year militia veteran, died beside Mowat, a bullet through his neck. Nutley was the first Hasty P to die in battle in World War II. Mowat led his men on a wild bayonet charge, overrunning the flimsy defences on the beaches. Once they were established, Campbell guided his company eastward along the coast in search of the rest of the regiment. They were reunited that evening, "hot, hungry and desperately thirsty," in an olive grove northwest of Pachino.[19]

Aboard HMS *Hilary*, Simonds and Vian were breathing easier. At 0645, the divisional commander reported to XXX Corps headquarters that all of their initial objectives were in Canadian hands.[20]

"There was something fantastic about it all," recalls the CBC's Peter Stursberg, who came ashore on Roger beach. He admits that he was somewhat surprised by the peaceful scene, compared to the noisy landing exercises in the United Kingdom. "The early morning sun was shining now, and I could see the vineyards above the yellow-brown beach and the little white houses in the vineyards and a town spread out on the hills beyond. It was just like a coloured picture in a geographical magazine."[21] However, there was little time to admire the scanty scenery. The four Canadian assault battalions moving inland that hot July morning were finding that the green-clad Italians in this sector were only too happy to surrender. There were soon so many prisoners that they became, in Brigadier Graham's opinion, "something of a nuisance."[22]

The only real battle fought by Canadian troops on D-Day was fought by the Royal Canadians. By midmorning, all four companies in the battalion closed in on their prime objective, the Pachino airfield, deserted but extensively damaged. Then A Company, commanded by Captain R. G. "Slim" Liddell, moved towards the powerful battery a few hundred yards to the north. Heavily defended by machine-guns and manned by 130 soldiers, the battery put up a fight. Here, the RCR suffered its first combat fatality, Private G. C. Hefford, of St. Thomas, Ontario. But the Royal Canadians were not to be denied. Launching a savage attack, half a dozen privates turned the tide. Cutting their way through the barbed-wire entanglement protecting the position, they used rifles, Tommy guns, and grenades to knock out three enemy machine-guns. The Italians lost their ardour and surrendered *en masse*. This action resulted in the first two awards for gallantry to Canadian soldiers in Sicily: Private Joseph Grigas won the Distinguished Conduct Medal, while the Military Medal was given to Private Jack Gardner.

Reinforcements were joining the fray by now. The Second Brigade had landed the Loyal Edmonton Regiment,* while Toronto's 48th Highlanders were moving up to support the First Brigade. The Eddies patrolled vigorously, and one party found itself under small-arms fire from a nearby farmhouse. When they returned the fire, thirty-three Italians filed out with their hands in the air. "The only walking wounded from this first engagement with the enemy," wrote Captain Alan Macdonald, "were those who sampled the *vino*. It was a sour and belching vintage."[23]

The 48th's fighting was limited to fending off the young Sicilian panhandlers who flocked around the marching soldiers with appeals for "*Sigaretta! Cioccolato!*" The regiment was also greeted by "a squat, ancient Sicilian" who seemed rather pleased to see these men from Toronto. Waving his scarecrow arms, he screeched something like, "Forryet

---

* Formerly the Edmonton Regiment, it had been given royal permission to add "Loyal" to its title, reflecting its affiliation with the British army's Loyal Regiment. Oddly, while this approval had been given in July, the regiment did not receive notification until October. Although the battalion was unaware of the name change, it is technically correct to refer to it as the Loyal Edmonton Regiment at this time.

Eyelander! Forryet Eyelander!" It turned out that the elderly man had once owned a fruit store on Elizabeth Street, behind the University Avenue Armouries where the 48th drilled in peacetime.[24]

Everyone soon wilted in the heat. Tourist guides recommend against travelling in Sicily in July, and the Canadian invaders soon found out why. The temperature on 10 July rose to a sweltering 114 degrees Fahrenheit in the shade, of which there was precious little. The CBC's Peter Stursberg, finding that the "scorchingly hot" sun "was frying the skin on my face," sought shelter in a flimsy Italian pillbox, where he unpacked his typewriter and wrote his first invasion story. Even clad in shorts, everyone was soon soaked in sweat. As they marched, they choked on clouds of fine, white dust.[25]

By nightfall, the Canadians were digging in as much as three miles inland, and even further in some spots. The Pachino airfield had been secured by the RCR and, further west, the PPCLI had reached the road to Ispica, the first large town in the First Division's path. Most of the division was ashore, including the reserve Third Brigade. The West Nova Scotia Regiment had a leisurely landing in the afternoon, "when the beaches were wrapped in sunshine and silence and some of the beach maintenance crew were actually enjoying a swim!"[26] General Simonds had established his tactical headquarters "in a civilian hovel, 12 by 16, inhabited by an old woman, 11 guinea pigs, 4 dogs, a goat and 4 gallons of wine, all of which were quickly cleared out."[27] These quarters were far from luxurious, but most of the Canadians had to content themselves with the doubtful comfort of a slit trench, hastily scratched out of the hard, dry soil.

Darkness brought danger, though few were aware of it. Captain Howard Mitchell, commanding a Saskatoon Light Infantry mortar battery, was given a tempting target by the PPCLI: campfires glowing in a neighbouring grove of trees. However, Mitchell, who three times during the day had been ordered to fire on targets that turned out to be Canadians, carefully investigated before shooting. His caution was rewarded. Farley Mowat should thank him, because Mitchell discovered that the campfires belonged to the Hasty Ps, and held his fire.[28] At about the same time, The Royal Canadian Regiment proved to be its own worst enemy, when two companies opened fire on each other. In the dark they fought "a pitched small arms battle," with the regimental headquarters caught in the middle. Fortunately, the mistake was realized within a matter of minutes and the shooting stopped before anyone was hurt.[29]

It had been an exhilarating and memorable day. At a cost of thirty-two casualties, including seven dead, the Canadians had taken all of their objectives. They estimated that they had killed or wounded a hundred Italians, as well as capturing 650 – with a lot more to come. "Thus comes to a close the first day of continued fighting by Canadians in this war," one of Simonds's staff officers remarked in the divisional war diary. "Although thus far the enemy has been conspicuous by his absence and our advance had been far more rapid than was expected, this day will go down as an important one in Canadian military history."[30]

Perhaps it had been too easy. One Hasty P, resting in his slit trench in the olive grove near Pachino, spoke for many when he muttered, "Call this a war? Why, this is only fun and games. I wonder if it's all like this."[31]

2

Five thousand miles away, in Ottawa, a battle of another sort was taking place. Canada's capital city was in the scorching grip of a heat wave. While it was not as hot as Sicily, Friday, 9 July, had been "excessively warm, the hottest day, I think, thus far this year," according to a perspiring Prime Minister Mackenzie King.[32]

King was facing a roller-coaster of a day. Much of it was spent putting the finishing touches to his speech announcing Canada's part in the invasion of Sicily. Its theme, "Canada will not fail her fighting men," pleased him. "This, I thought, should attract the headlines and be the pledge of the nation at this time."[33]

But right up until the last moment, it appeared that he would not be able to deliver the speech. Two days earlier, Defence Minister Layton Ralston had delivered bad news: for security reasons, General Eisenhower's communiqué announcing the invasion would refer only to United States and United Kingdom forces. That was not acceptable to King, who insisted that the Canadian contribution to Husky be recognized, and he soon had his staff sending out telegrams and holding meetings, which made little headway. Eisenhower, unwilling to prematurely reveal to the enemy the make-up of his invasion forces, felt that it was important to delay for as long as possible confirmation of the commitment of Canadian troops; his only concession would be to allow King a brief statement, twenty-four hours after the invasion, revealing the presence of the Canadians. King was not impressed, knowing that it left him open to possible embarrassment in the meantime. He feared, with good reason, that press reports might refer to the Canadians, "and I would be left in the position of having, as Prime Minister, said nothing about our forces."[34]

As a last resort, King decided to take advantage of his friendship with the American president, Franklin Roosevelt. Telephoning the White House, King arranged for a Friday night meeting between Roosevelt and the Canadian *chargé d'affaires* in Washington, Lester Pearson. The future prime minister spent twenty minutes with FDR, who proved to be "most friendly and sympathetic." After considering a number of alternatives, the president, as Pearson later announced in a cable to Ottawa, "ended by accepting the view that a specific mention of Canada was preferable and said he would take steps to see that this was done and that the Canadian position generally was safeguarded in any proclamations or official announcements to be made on the launching of this operation."[35]

The prime minister could only wait and see. Shortly after midnight, Ottawa time, Allied Force Headquarters in Algiers issued the anticipated communiqué: "This morning Allied Forces under command of General Eisenhower began landing operations in Sicily." Ten minutes later, however, came a startling annoucement from the United States War Department in Washington, that "British, American and Canadian troops" were involved in the invasion.[36]

King, who was still up at that late hour, promptly issued to the press his own statement: "Armed forces of Britain, the United States and Canada are now in the forefront of an attack which has as its ultimate objective the unconditional surrender of Italy and Germany. All Canada will be justifiably proud to know that units of the Canadian Army are a part of the Allied force engaged in this attack."[37] After "a sandwich and some ginger ale and a bite with little Pat," his beloved terrier, King went to bed at one o'clock in the morning. He awoke in time to deliver his announcement on national radio seven hours later. But, the more he thought about this little episode, the more serious he realized the potential ramifications could have been. "I would have been wholly discredited today and the Cabinet as well. . . . I pointed out that had no announcement come about Canadians participating from their own government, my political career would have ended so far as this country is concerned."[38]

Canada was languishing in the summer doldrums. Despite the inconvenience of rationing, life went on with surprising normalcy. Baseball fans watched the major-league races develop: the New York Yankees were two games ahead of the hard-charging Detroit Tigers in the American League, while St. Louis led the National League. People were buzzing over the mysterious death of Sir Harry Oakes, an American-born entrepreneur who had made his millions mining gold in Ontario. Oakes, "one of the British Empire's wealthiest baronets,"[39] was found dead in his home in the Bahamas on 8 July, but the murder was never solved. Closer to home, Ontario was gearing up for a provincial election. Across the river from Ottawa, a judicial inquiry was under way into the administration of the Hull, Quebec, police over political interference in gambling and prostitution crackdowns between 1936 and 1940.[40]

Sicily shook Canada out of its complacency. As prime ministerial aide

Jack Pickersgill later wrote, "Despite the very large part Canadian sailors and airmen were taking in actual combat in 1943, the sense of remoteness of the war from Canada remained strong until the landing in Sicily."[41] From coast to coast, the Sicilian invasion received front-page headlines, and the editorial response indicated that Prime Minister King had correctly assessed its national importance. "There will be deep pride all over Canada today that, when the invasion of Europe began, our army stood in the forefront of the battle," commented the militant *Winnipeg Free Press* on 10 July. Most newspapers echoed those sentiments, but Fredericton's *Daily Gleaner* warned against "undue optimism and that a hard road lies ahead. This in brief means we must be ready for lists of casualties. Not since Dieppe have Canadian troops taken part in an assault but they will give as good an account of themselves as before."

Nothing captured the nation's imagination more than Ross Munro's first exclusive report from the invasion beaches for the Canadian Press. The Ottawa-born Munro, who went on to be a major figure in Canadian newspaper publishing, was later described by fellow reporter Wes Gallagher (himself the future general manager of the Associated Press) as "not only the top Canadian correspondent but one of the best five or six correspondents of the war. He combined great personal courage with extremely lucid writing and reporting."[42] His gripping accounts of the Dieppe raid had already brought him to national attention, but his first story from Sicily would make Munro's name a household word across Canada.

Allied Force Headquarters (AFHQ) had made elaborate arrangements to look after the needs of the fifty Canadian, British, and American accredited correspondents who were covering Husky for the world's major papers and news agencies. However, Munro slipped through the cracks; unlike the other reporters, he and the CBC's Peter Stursberg had sailed with the Canadian invasion force directly from Scotland and right through AFHQ's censorship plans. Stursberg, who was unable to bring ashore the bulky broadcast equipment required in those days, posed no threat to security. But Munro was something else again.

After a harrowing trip to the beach ("I don't know how I ever got ashore because of the five- and six-foot waves"), Munro accompanied the RCR inland and, after watching the capture of the Pachino airfield, trudged back to the beach to write his story. "It wasn't the best story I wrote, by any means, because I only wrote about seven hundred words." What made the story special was that it was Canadian, and it was the first one to come out of Sicily.[43]

It was late afternoon by the time he was finished writing. At 2100, after typing it up, he delivered the story to HMS *Hilary*, lying offshore. There was no press censor on board the destroyer, but an intelligence captain named Alan Chambers, a member of Parliament and a friend of Munro's, had a look at it, gave his approval, and handed it to the signals office. The army and navy wireless sets were tied up at the time, but Major Bill Gilchrist, a former newspaper editor from Saint John, New Brunswick, handed it to air-force wireless operators. Munro had fortuitously typed the word "Urgent" across the top of his copy, and these "operators considered it highest priority. It really had none at all."[44] The story was immediately relayed to Canada via a Royal Air Force wireless station in Malta and the British Air Ministry in London, which handed it over to Canadian Press. "Sure, I was blind lucky," he later said of this incredible turn of events, "but what the hell, everything in life is lucky, anyway."[45]

Munro's story caused "a major sensation," in Canada and elsewhere, not just because it contained the first detailed report of the Canadian invasion. "Because no other forces were mentioned in that first cable," explains fellow journalist Doug How, "it seemed for a while that the Canadians were winning Sicily all by themselves."[46]

If Canada was thrilled by the exploits of its soldiers, Dwight Eisenhower was, in Munro's words, "mad as hell." The Allied commander wanted to have the Canadian reporter arrested for violating AFHQ security, but, naturally, nothing happened. Munro had, overnight, become Canada's most famous war correspondent; he was untouchable, and so continued to cover the Canadian advance through sizzling Sicily. But his first day on enemy soil had given him what he fondly calls "the best beat I ever had. I [was] seven hours ahead of everybody else."[47]

It was the scoop of a lifetime. When the story under Munro's by-line appeared in newspapers across Canada, only the prime minister and a few of his closest associates appreciated how close to disaster Mackenzie King had come. Had "security" interests prevailed, King would have looked extremely foolish, being quoted in Saturday's newspapers referring merely to "Allied" troops, when the next day's editions carried the Munro story about the Canadians. It might not have ended his political career, but it would have undermined his credibility, among the public at large and within his own party. He had good reason to thank, as he did, "the Providence that saved the whole situation."[48]

3

Husky had been a triumph.

The Canadian success on the Sicilian coast was duplicated in the British and American sectors. The British to the right of the Canadians were securely ashore, despite numerous delays and navigational problems that deposited many units far from their intended landing locations. "The scene was less exciting," commented the Montreal *Gazette*'s Lionel Shapiro, who came ashore on a British beach, "than many landing exercises I had witnessed in England."[49] Forty miles west of the Canadians, the Americans had overcome considerable difficulties, including heavy surf, counter-attacks by German and Italian forces, and air raids. Husky's sole disappointment was the airborne phase, in which British gliders and American paratroopers were victimized by a deadly combination of faulty navigation by inexperienced pilots, strong winds, and enemy anti-aircraft fire.

Success was due not only to the superlative work of the Allied naval and air forces but to tactical surprise. The Germans had noted the increased shipping activity in the Mediterranean as early as 1 July, but despite the pounding of airfields in Sicily, Sardinia was considered to be the primary Allied objective. Not until the late afternoon of 9 July had aerial reconnaissance revealed that Sicily was the target, when the various convoys came together, "converging as if along the supporting strands of some huge spider's web upon Malta," in Admiral Sir Andrew Cunningham's words.[50] During the evening, the Italian forces on the island had been alerted to the threat, although the 206th Coastal Division was not notified until 2220, barely four hours before the invasion was scheduled to begin. The alarm failed to galvanize the Italians into action, because many senior officers had been lulled into a false sense of security by the storm earlier that evening. "The enemy were certain no possible disembarkation could be attempted on such a night," wrote Harold Macmillan, the British minister resident in the Mediterranean. "One of the captured Italian generals described it as a 'pyjama night,' i.e. they thought this was a perfectly safe night for a good sleep."[51]

The Germans were appalled by the performance of their Italian ally. Although there were exceptions, most Italian troops surrendered in droves, prompting Albert Kesselring, the German commander in the Mediterranean, to cable Berlin: "The Italian troops in the area under attack are almost a total loss. The German forces at the moment are not sufficiently large to carry out a decisive attack against any one of the enemy bridgeheads."[52]

Kesselring was quickly able to obtain for Sicily high-quality reinforcements, in the form of the 1st Parachute and 29th Panzer Grenadier divisions, along with General der Panzertruppen Hans-Valentin Hube and his XIV Panzer Corps headquarters. Hube, a one-armed veteran of the Great War, was "considered one of the ablest German armoured commanders."[53] But Kesselring had already resigned himself to the inevitable loss of the island. On 16 July, he met privately with Hube, telling him "that I was reckoning with the evacuation of Sicily, which it was his job to postpone as long as possible."[54]

In the face of minimal opposition, the Allies swept across southern Sicily. By Sunday night, 11 July, the Allies "were pushing ahead impetuously," as General Alexander later wrote, "and it seemed as though nothing could stop them."[55] On the right of the Eighth Army's front, Lieutenant-General Miles Dempsey and XIII Corps captured Augusta without a fight on the morning of 13 July and pushed up the coast towards Catania, while Sir Oliver Leese's XXX Corps, which included the Canadian division, drove inland for Caltagirone, Enna, and Leonforte. Further west, the U.S. Seventh Army was also gobbling up large chunks of arid Sicilian territory. Only an Allied mistake could deprive them of a swift and impressive victory – and a mistake is exactly what happened.

At Fifteenth Army Group headquarters, Alexander's intention was "to split the island in half," aiming for the strategic heart of Sicily, "the irregular triangle of roads in the centre around Caltanisetta and Enna,"[56] a sensible enough plan, but one that was doomed. As historians Dominick Graham and Shelford Bidwell note, it was Alexander's job to come up with "a good plan agreed by both army commanders" and to see "that his two fractious subordinates acted in a spirit of cooperation and obeyed their orders; and that every step was taken to destroy or capture the defeated Axis forces" in Sicily. "In all these Alexander conspicuously failed."[57]

Bernard Montgomery had his own ideas about conquering Sicily. There are few quality roads on the island, and Monty was quick to note the importance of Route 117, the highway to Enna, in the very heart of Sicily. This road was in the Seventh Army's area, but Monty proposed to Alexander that it should be given to the Eighth Army, warning that there was not room enough for both to operate beyond Vizzini. Alex agreed, and on the night of 13 July issued orders giving Route 117 to Monty.[58]

The Americans were outraged. The Seventh Army's General Patton saw immediately that the revised plan put "the Americans in a secondary role, which is a continuation of such roles for the whole campaign and may find the war ending with us being overlooked." The flamboyant Patton decided to get even rather than get mad. "Alex has no idea of either the power or speed of American armies," he wrote in his diary. "We can go twice as fast as the British and hit harder." He met Alexander and proposed that the Seventh Army make what he termed "a reconnaissance in force" into western Sicily. Alexander, agreeable as ever, gave his approval but proved once more his inability to control his lieutenants when Patton's reconnaissance blossomed into a full-scale drive on Palermo.[59]

The results were spectacular, if rather meaningless. The Americans rolled into Palermo on 22 July, having raced across Sicily like heavily armed tourists. Brigadier-General Maxwell Taylor of the 82nd Airborne observed that he and his fellow Americans undertook "a pleasant march, shaking hands with Italians asking, 'How's my brother Joe in Brooklyn?' Nicest war I've ever been in! Monty – he had a different problem – he was up against Germans."[60] The Germans were baffled by this headline-grabbing venture. Patton's army, Kesselring later pointed out, "just marched and captured unimportant terrain, instead of fighting at the [eastern] wing where a major decision had to be reached."[61]

But the important fact is that when the Eighth Army's drive stalled in the face of the stubborn and skilful German defence, Montgomery had to turn to the Seventh Army for help – only to discover that most of the Americans had gone off in the opposite direction! This forced his Eighth Army into a gruelling campaign in adverse conditions against a deter-mined and resourceful enemy in easily defended terrain. His only chance to salvage success lay with the one formation of his army that had not fought in the desert, the First Canadian Division. "The Canadian Division," Monty explained in his diary, "was really doing a big left hook moving on the outer circle on the left flank via Enna-Leonforte against Adrano. This was hilly country, and enemy demolitions made progress difficult. The net result was a strong left wheel done by the Canadians. The enemy is very stretched and I do not see how he can hold us off so long as we keep up the pressure."[62]

Monty's "big left hook" was a movement taken from the experience of his North African campaign. It had worked well in the desert, where vast, empty expanses were fertile ground for such manoeuvres, but the rough terrain of central Sicily was not nearly as accommodating. Moreover, he was pinning the Eighth Army's hopes on the efforts of a single untried division of Canadians. It was, notes American historian Carlo D'Este, "a tall order for a division in its first combat and largely bereft of transport in mountainous country which favoured the defender."[63]

CHAPTER TWO

"Too Fat"

1

On Sunday morning, 11 July, the Canadians prepared to resume their advance into Sicily. It was still dark when the troops were awakened – after sleeping on soil for the first night in twenty-seven, Toronto's 48th Highlanders awoke at 0245 – but the sun had risen high in the sky before they set off in long columns of infantry, tanks, and guns. Nearly a week would pass before the Canadians saw any real action. Their only opposition, initially, was provided by "the heat, the sun's glare and Sicily's choking white dust."[1]

Ispica, six miles up the road, became the first important town to fall to the Canadians. Perched on a 150-foot cliff, it might have posed a problem had it been defended. But the Loyal Edmonton Regiment marched in unopposed during the afternoon, to be met by "the frantic endeavours of the military population to surrender."[2]

This became the rule rather than the exception. By hundreds, thousands, the Italians laid down their arms, usually after firing a few token, face-saving shots. The biggest haul came on 12 July, when a thirty-man platoon of the Eddies captured 1,100 prisoners in Scicli, halfway between Modica and the coast. As a consquence, the roads were soon filled with Italian prisoners, most of whom were pleased that, for them, the war was over. "Columns of Italians without any guards were frequently seen," recalled war correspondent Ross Munro, "and as we passed them going to the front they would grin foolishly and give us the V-sign."[3] During the first two days, the Second Brigade alone collected 1,200 prisoners, who were marched back to the beaches "escorted by eight bored privates," according to the First Division's war diarist. "They seemed to be extremely happy captives and no trouble is expected from them."[4]

One of these Italians was prominent. The city of Modica, further along the road from Ispica, served as the headquarters for the 206th Italian Coastal Division, commanded by Achille d'Havet. D'Havet, who had been most distressed by the low morale of his division before the invasion, seems to have decided to surrender as soon as possible, but that proved to be surprisingly difficult. The problem was that d'Havet insisted on surrendering to an officer of appropriate rank. This meant that the PPCLI sergeant who discovered him hiding in a building in Modica was entirely unsuitable. He even refused to surrender to Lieutenant-Colonel Leslie Booth of the armoured Three Rivers Regiment.[5]

Eventually, d'Havet managed to surrender to the divisional commander, General Simonds. When Major Dick Malone, the future *Globe and Mail* publisher, arrived from Second Brigade headquarters to escort the reluctant Italian general to Simonds, Malone accepted the general's offer of the use of his Fiat staff car, and everyone "jammed in." Another problem arose on the way to Simonds's headquarters, when Malone realized that these Italian officers were still armed! "Clearly I couldn't march them up to Simonds carrying loaded pistols, so I stopped the car." A compromise ensued: they could keep their pistols, but Malone took the ammunition.[6]

The surrender, in the shade of an olive tree, was a brief formality. The two generals were a study in contrasts. Simonds, nattily attired in beret, bush shirt, and shorts, was young, lean, and self-confident. The portly d'Havet, according to the CBC's Peter Stursberg, was "a tired old man." Simonds took d'Havet's small automatic pistol, then returned it when the Italian asked to keep it.[7] After they exchanged a few words privately, d'Havet departed for interrogation at XXX Corps headquarters. For a souvenir, Simonds removed the little staff flag from the radiator cap of d'Havet's Fiat, but allowed Major Malone to keep the car, "a far more luxurious bus than our jeeps."[8]

The d'Havet surrender typified the comic-opera atmosphere of those first few days in Sicily. A sense of unreality prevailed in this very strange war in which there seemed to be no enemy, as The Royal Canadian Regiment found when it moved cross-country against Ragusa. The regiment's route took it past a hill on which sat a farmhouse, "a very ancient building with a flagged courtyard and iron gates." Captain Strome Galloway, whose magnificent upturned moustache was the envy of the entire army, was ordered to take two platoons and attack the place. Sixty heavily armed Canadians stormed into the yard, where they were greeted by a sleepy-eyed Sicilian couple who, to Galloway's amazement, dished out cheese, bread, and eggs to the dusty invaders on their door-step. "One would have thought," Galloway later remarked, "that in this remote country it was an everyday occurrence to be attacked by Canadians at dawn."[9]

Ragusa's capture was anti-climactic. Sent ahead in a carrier under a white flag, Captain Dick Dillon led an RCR patrol into the town of forty thousand, to find that the only military personnel were American. The U.S. 45th Division had occupied Ragusa the night before! This first encounter with their highly mobile fellow North Americans was a revelation to the footsore Canadians, who got the impression that "every American soldier had his own jeep."[10]

By Monday night, the First Brigade had reached the village of Giarratana, thirty air-miles from the invasion beaches, but fifty miles by twisting, turning mountain roads. The Canadians had yet to engage in any serious fighting, which was just as well, because the strenuous conditions of their march were more than enough.

The heat. The dust. No man who was there will forget Sicily's twin miseries.

The fine, white dust was reminiscent of flour. According to Cliff Evans, a Saskatoon Light Infantry veteran who turned twenty-one on 13 July, "you'd see the infantry marching along with handkerchiefs over their faces and you wouldn't see them from the waist down – you'd think they were walking in flour, the dust was just coming up on them."[11]

The heat compounded their misery. Recalls Farley Mowat, the Hasty P subaltern: "The heat was brutal – and there was no water. The sun became an implacable enemy and our steel helmets became brain furnaces. The weight of our personal equipment, together with weapons and extra ammunition, became almost intolerable."[12] The padre of the 48th Highlanders, Stewart East, endeared himself to the regiment during its killing march on 12 July by loading himself with water bottles borrowed from the quartermaster. His tall, dusty figure was a welcome sight as he hurried up and down the column dispensing drinks of water to the parched troops.[13]

These conditions took a heavy toll. Sunstroke, sweat, blisters: no one was immune. As usual it was the "poor bloody infantry" who had it the worst. Due to the sinkings en route to Sicily, the division was short of trucks, and while as many men as possible hitched rides on tanks or crowded onto every available vehicle of Canadian or Italian make, a lot of infantrymen were forced to walk. The long, dust-clouded columns of Canadians soon moved zombie-like. Only a few fell out to rest by the roadside; most walked in their sleep, "a trick learned on English training schemes."[14]

No one was more alarmed at their condition than Montgomery himself. His veteran divisions were having an "exhausting" time, and the conditions were having an even more serious effect on the newcomers from Canada. "The Canadian Div had definitely to be rested," he wrote on 13 July, "the men were not fit and they suffered severely from the heat and many got badly burnt; generally, officers and men are too fat and they want to get some flesh off and to harden themselves."[15]

So Montgomery prescribed a day and a half's rest for the Canadians.

Farley Mowat of the Hasty Ps chuckles at Monty's idea of rest. "Ah," he writes, "the unconscious humour of the military mind."[16] Instead of resting, the Canadians marched for miles under the same hot sun, across the same parched, dusty terrain, to listen to a pep talk by the Eighth Army's commander. Monty addressed each brigade in turn, inspecting each battalion before summoning the men to break ranks and surround him while he stood on his car. "So far you have met only the Italians, and they don't want to fight, but the Germans are tough, very tough, opponents. But I am confident that you can master them. I will make good plans. I wouldn't be here today if I didn't make good plans. But good plans need good soldiers to carry them out. I have confidence in you. You have confidence in me, and all will be well."[17]

By the end of the day, Montgomery was pleased with what he had seen and heard in the Canadian camp. "I spent this day visiting every unit in the Canadian Division and talking to the men," he wrote in his diary. "They are a grand Division and when we get them tough and hard and some of the fat off them, they will be absolutely first class."[18] It was well that Monty had confidence in these "fat" Canadians, because their division, utilizing the highway he had wrested from the Americans, would have to execute the left hook designed to outflank the growing German opposition across the Eighth Army's front.

The Canadians were the subject of much interest. Besides Montgomery, Admiral Lord Louis Mountbatten looked over their sector on 11 July, and the next day, General Eisenhower insisted on greeting them personally. However, when the American general came ashore on Bark West, Guy Simonds's divisional headquarters had already moved inland; the only Canadian officer he could find was an engineer captain, J. E. Moore of Vancouver. After a brief chat, Eisenhower shook hands with Moore, asked him "to convey his message of good wishes to the Canadians," and returned to his ship.[19]

One visitor who did not arrive was Andy McNaughton. The First Canadian Army commander had planned a trip to the Mediterranean at the end of May, more than a month before Husky, to survey the administrative arrangements for the First Division. He learned via the War Office that Montgomery had suggested instead that McNaughton visit "during operation Husky rather than before." In any case, McNaughton's involvement in high-level planning sessions delayed his departure until July.[20] He was accompanied by a small party of officers, including the Canadian chief of the General Staff, Ken Stuart, a brigadier named Charles Foulkes, and an aide, Lieutenant-Colonel Dan Spry.

McNaughton got no closer to Sicily than Malta. Arriving on the smaller island on 14 July, the Canadian general was informed by Sir Harold Alexander at Fifteenth Army Group headquarters that he could not travel to Sicily. Alexander hemmed and hawed about a "shortage of transport," and shrugged that he had received no instructions from the War Office about McNaughton's tour.[21] Brigadier Foulkes, like his fellow Canadians, was disgusted. "It was obvious from the start that we were not wanted," he later complained. "The only time any enthusiasm was shown by the British was when McNaughton asked for transportation to go back to England."[22]

Montgomery indeed did not want McNaughton in Sicily at this time. "The 1st Canadian Division had not been in action before," Monty explained in his memoirs, "and officers and men were just beginning to find their feet. Guy Simonds . . . was young and inexperienced. . . . I wasn't going to have Simonds bothered with visitors when he was heavily engaged with his division in all-out operations against first-rate German troops." Monty also contended that Simonds wanted no part of McNaughton either, quoting the divisional commander as saying: "For God's sake keep him away."[23] (According to British historian Nigel Hamilton, "Monty had in fact asked . . . Simonds if he wanted to be visited by McNaughton, but in such a way that Simonds was encouraged to say no.")[24] As a result, Montgomery had made it clear to Alexander that McNaughton was not to come to Sicily.

Montgomery's position was later defended by his chief of staff. Major-General Sir Francis de Guingand explained that Monty "was particularly insistent that during a battle nothing must be allowed to happen which might take a Commander's eye off the ball. This included visitors and lookers-on who had no real contribution to make." Added de Guingand: "Montgomery undoubtedly made an enemy, but he protected Simonds from possible embarrassment during a delicate phase of operations."[25]

McNaughton was thunderstruck. This was clearly a violation of his right, as the senior Canadian army officer overseas, to keep tabs on Canadian troops in the field. But there was nothing he could do, and after stewing in Malta for a couple of days, he travelled to Algiers, where he spent 17 July with General Eisenhower at Allied Force Headquarters. Eisenhower could hardly believe his ears when the Canadian described his difficulties with Montgomery. The American dismissed the British excuse, a lack of transport, as "silly." According to a memo drawn up by Colonel Spry, "General Eisenhower said that he was very sorry that the Canadian Army had not been associated with the U.S. Army so that he could have intervened and made General McNaughton's visit possible." However, he was understandably reluctant to get involved in what he considered to be a British internal matter.[26]

Angry and humilitiated, McNaughton flew back to the United Kingdom. He told Eisenhower that he was cutting short his Mediterranean visit "in order . . . to forestall any ill-considered action."[27] But he never forgave Montgomery.* On 20 July, when he returned to London, he had what Colonel Charles Stacey delicately called "a somewhat unpleasant interview"[29] with the chief of the Imperial General Staff, Sir Alan Brooke. McNaughton contended that, as "a matter of principle," it was imperative "that representatives of the Canadian Army would have access to our troops at all times. . . ." The CIGS argued vehemently, but finally (according to McNaughton) "apologized for any lack of courtesy and consideration which might have been shown to me."[30] The two men shook hands at the conclusion of their meeting, but Brooke revealed his intense annoyance in a letter to Montgomery: "You fairly infuriated him for forbidding him access to his troops in Sicily!! He wasted an hour of my time on his return explaining to me how strained imperial relations must in future be owing to such treatment, the serious outlook of his Government, etc. etc."[31]

The CIGS also knew something that McNaughton did not realize. Brooke and other authorities, noted Stacey, had "already launched, behind McNaughton's back, a campaign to procure his removal from command" of the First Canadian Army.[32] This incident was merely one more nail in McNaughton's coffin.

2

In Sicily, the Canadian advance resumed around midnight on 14–15 July. Two brigades hit the road, the First, led by the Royal Canadians, departing the area of Giarratana, while the Second set out from the vicinity of Ragusa. Passing through Ragusa, the Loyal Eddies suffered their first combat casualties: roof-top snipers killed three privates and wounded four others.[33] Those responsible were probably civilians, Fascist fanatics like the trio captured near Modica by the PPCLI on 12 July. Outraged, the Second Brigade's Chris Vokes had intended to shoot them; only Guy Simonds's intervention had prevented him from doing so. (He contented himself with having one of the Patricias administer a sound "thrashing" to the three unfortunate Italians.)[34] Following the Ragusa shootings, XXX Corps headquarters issued orders that hostages be taken in each town after its surrender.[35]

Outside Vizzini, the Hasty Ps passed through the RCR as the First Brigade led the way to the paved Route 124, the infantry riding in lorries or

---

* In September 1946, Montgomery sought a "private talk" with McNaughton during a visit to Canada, but the Canadian flatly refused to meet him. "I felt that I had received grievous injury from him," McNaughton scrawled in his near-illegible handwriting, "that he had stabbed me in the back. . . . I really did not wish to see him again."[28]

on tanks of the Three Rivers Regiment. This appeared to be a more prosperous region, with wide fields and increasingly lush vegetation.

Aside from isolated incidents of enthusiasm, the Canadians received a lukewarm reception from the Sicilian civilians. They had been warned to expect "that the civil population will greet the invading forces with sullen indifference, whether they are British, Canadian or American,"[36] and this generally proved to be the case. One reason for their apparent disinterest was perhaps historical: these khaki-clad invaders were merely the latest in a long line of conquering armies which included Byzantine Greeks, Carthaginians, Romans, Saracens, Normans, Spaniards, and Moors. (The Sicilians may have shown more emotion had they realized that the Allied invasion would bring with it Mafia leaders who had left the country years before – and were released from American prisons to help the Allies set up a provisional government.) The Canadians gained a poor impression of the Sicilians, which, according to Farley Mowat, "somehow seemed to sanction making these people's meagre possessions fair game. In any event, many of their pitiful little orchards (a handful of fig trees, pears or pomegranates) and garden plots (mostly melons and gourds) were casually looted."[37] It was a disturbingly commonplace practice, made easier by the fact that this land was not being liberated but conquered.

This island, about the size of Kluane National Park in the Yukon, was not a happy place. Sicily had been acquired by Italy in 1860, but its inhabitants had never considered themselves to be Italians. The brutality of Mussolini's Fascist regime had merely reinforced that sense of separateness. "The Sicilians were bewildered, poverty-burdened folk who had been ground into the barren earth they tried to farm," Ross Munro later wrote. This was, he believed, "the fraud of Italian Fascism; its victims were these crowds of starving, beaten people in every town." Fascism really meant "grand villas in the country and towns for the Fascist chiefs and squalor for the people."[38]

The next major town was Grammichele, ten miles from Vizzini. This community of thirteen thousand was relatively new by Italian standards, having been founded in 1683, after an earthquake. Grammichele, sited on a long 250-foot-high ridge that commanded Route 124, was an ideal spot to set up an ambush, and parts of two battalions from the Hermann Göring Division were preparing to do precisely that as the Canadians approached from the east.

The Hastings and Prince Edward Regiment and Three Rivers tanks ran right into the German ambush. It was 0900 when the leading troops and tanks of the mile-long column reached the outskirts of Grammichele, where they were greeted by a sudden storm of shells and machine-gun bullets. One Sherman and three carriers were knocked out in swift succession. It was here that a Hasty P who bore a famous Canadian surname lived up to his proud family's reputation. Huron Brant, a Mohawk Indian from Deseronto, Ontario, proved to be a one-man wrecking crew, single-handedly attacking a group of thirty Germans. Every one of the enemy was either killed or wounded, and Brant won the Military Medal for his brave efforts.[39]

The battle for Grammichele was brief but furious. British self-propelled guns put in a timely appearance and gave valuable supporting fire while the Canadian infantry and tanks attacked. When two companies of Hasty Ps outflanked the town, the Germans began withdrawing. By noon on 15 July, Grammichele had been cleared of enemy troops, and the Canadians were counting the cost of this first encounter with a real enemy. The skirmish had resulted in twenty-five Canadian casualties; German losses were unknown, but the Hermann Görings left behind the smouldering hulks of three Mark IV medium tanks and several flak guns. That afternoon, Lieutenant Farley Mowat wrote a friend in Canada: "It was exciting as hell."[40]

Brigadier Graham now put in a fresh regiment, the 48th Highlanders from Toronto, to lead the way to the next big town, Caltagirone. The 48th discovered along the highway another sordid side of modern warfare.

At the head of the Toronto regiment's advance was a carrier-reconnaissance party commanded by a young lieutenant named Eddie MacLachlan. Nicknamed "Punchy" because he had been a boxer in college, MacLachlan had a philosophy of war that was simple: "to get this ugly job done and then go home." His little force drove up Route 124 towards Caltagirone on the afternoon of 15 July. Crossing a ridge, the road made a hairpin turn which brought the Canadians to a cement and stone barricade. It was undefended, and Punchy MacLachlan signalled his troop to follow him. It was the last thing he ever did: there was a bone-jarring explosion and the carrier flipped into the air. When the smoke and dust cleared, MacLachlan and his driver lay dead, victims of a land-mine. They were buried side by side inside the front gate of a nearby estate, and the Highlanders pulled over to the side of the road and waited for the engineers to come up and clear a path.[41]

The First Division's chief engineer, Geoff Walsh, believes that mines were the single biggest problem encountered by the Canadians in Sicily. "You really didn't go anywhere or do anything," he says, "without checking for mines." Walsh, who was a lieutenant-colonel at the time, takes pride in the fact that the Canadian engineers were well prepared to meet this challenge. When he had accompanied Guy Simonds to North Africa prior to Husky, Walsh "was able to persuade Eighth Army to get me a collection of mines, both German and Italian, and get them back to the U.K. I got five instructors – a major, a lieutenant, and three sergeants – and I ran a mine school and put all the sappers through on the various types of [enemy] mines. And then we put all the pioneer platoons in each of the infantry battalions through, and we briefed the whole division on the mines. So we were really prepared and it was one of the best things we ever did." Indeed, Cec Rae, the South African who served as the Eighth Army's chief engineer, considered the Canadian engineers to be "the best trained" in the army.[42]

Italian mines could be "very tricky," says Walsh. The slightest jar could trigger them, and there was a joke among Eighth Army engineers that "you could always find an Italian minefield because there were always a couple of dead Italians around, because they were so sensitive that they used to blow themselves up." The Germans, he remembers, were "very clever" about installing their mines; they were often booby-trapped, so the engineers had to be very careful about removing them. Sometimes the enemy placed two or three mines on top of each other, and the engineers had to ensure that all were removed before vehicles passed by. Of course, it was not practical to remove all mines, just those in key locations. The rest were simply marked off with wire and a warning sign.[43]

However, mines were not allowed to interfere with the Canadian division's advance on Caltagirone that sweltering July day. General Simonds arrived before the engineers and ordered the 48th Highlanders to abandon their vehicles and proceed cross-country. There was good reason for Simonds's sense of urgency. The Eighth Army advance had stalled on the edge of the Catania plain, and General Montgomery had instructed General Leese of XXX Corps to "Drive the Canadians on hard."[44]

The Highlanders were in Caltagirone by midnight. As they approached the city of thirty thousand, the sound of explosions could be heard. This indicated that the Germans were abandoning the place, and they were gone by the time the 48th arrived. Booty from the battalion's bloodless victory included a pair of petrol dumps that the Germans had failed to destroy, as well as a large hospital, and 140 Italian soldiers. The Canadians also freed a group of American paratroopers who had been captured when blown off course during their D-Day landing.[45]

The advance resumed the following morning, 16 July, with the Second Brigade in the lead. Lieutenant-Colonel Jim Jefferson's Loyal Edmonton Regiment and a squadron of tanks from the Three Rivers Regiment formed the vanguard, headed for the next large town, Piazza Armerina. Just beyond San Michele di Ganzeria, Route 124 joined the Gela–Enna highway, Route 117, the highway that had been hijacked from the Americans. It was uphill much of the way, for Piazza Armerina, at 2,366 feet above sea level, was the highest community the Canadians had so far encountered.

The Loyal Eddies had smooth sailing until noon when, three miles south of Piazza Armerina, they ran into elements of the 15th Panzer Grenadier Division. In the face of German artillery, mortar, and machine-gun fire, the Edmontonians calmly deployed on either side of the highway and hunted the enemy on the nearby heights. So steep were these hills that the Three Rivers tanks were unable to raise their guns sufficiently to support the infantry, who had to rely on their own 3-inch mortars to pin down the defenders, until the arrival of British self-propelled guns. The fighting lasted all afternoon as, hill by hill, the Canadians drove the defenders from the commanding ground south of Piazza Armerina. These Germans were good: they waited for the cover of darkness before they finally withdrew from the town, and it was not until dawn of 17 July that the First Division could report Piazza Armerina as secure. This bitter little scrap had cost the Edmontons twenty-seven casualties, including six dead.[46]

The skirmishes at Grammichele and Piazza Armerina masked Guy Simonds's first command crisis. He would eventually emerge as Canada's outstanding general in World War II, but Sicily was for Simonds, as for the rest of his First Division, a learning experience.

There had been friction between Simonds and the First Brigade's Howard Graham right from the beginning. A veteran militiaman, who had the habit of chewing his fingernails, Graham was convinced that Simonds, a career officer, was prejudiced against him. Things had come to a head on Thursday, 15 July.

It was Graham's forty-fifth birthday, and shortly after daybreak he was ushering his brigade along the road to Vizzini when Simonds drove up. Without a greeting, he barked at Graham, "Why hasn't your brigade moved forward before this?" The brigadier replied that the Royal Canadians had already gone through Vizzini and the Hasty Ps were on their way through it, but Simonds was not satisfied with his explanation. Graham refused to discuss it further. "I assure you we haven't wasted any time," he icily told Simonds, "but I want to get forward now and we can continue this discussion at your 'O' Group this evening."[47]

But they met again later that morning outside Grammichele, when the Hasty Ps were ambushed. Soon after the fighting started and the Canadians had deployed, Simonds arrived at the headquarters of the Hasty Ps, where Graham had already agreed to Lieutenant-Colonel Bruce Sutcliffe's plan of attack. "I want this battle stopped," Simonds announced. "I don't like the plan."[48] Graham backed Sutcliffe, and Simonds finally agreed to let the Hasty Ps proceed with their attack. Success at Grammichele vindicated Graham and Sutcliffe, but the brigadier had been incensed by Simonds's interference, and he fumed about it for the rest of the day.

That evening, when Simonds held his orders group in a field west of Grammichele, Graham announced his decision. "I feel the time has come for us to part company," he informed the divisional commander, "and therefore I request release from my command at once." Simonds's brief reply – "You'll get a bad report for this" – merely reinforced Graham's determination to quit, and he stormed back to his brigade headquarters to write his letter of resignation.[49]

Word of the dispute soon reached Montgomery and, although he was under the impression that Simonds had fired Graham, the Eighth Army's commander was most distressed. "This is a great pity," he wrote XXX Corps's Sir Oliver Leese. "Graham is an excellent fellow and much beloved in his Bde; I expect Simonds lost his temper." Monty added: "Simonds is a young and very inexperienced Divisional general and has much to learn about command. He will upset his Division if he starts sacking Brigadiers like this."[50]

On Saturday, 17 July, a week after the invasion of Sicily, Graham met Montgomery at Oliver Leese's headquarters. Asked for his side of the story, the brigadier spent several minutes outlining his difficulties with Simonds. Monty listened patiently; he clearly had no intention of letting Graham quit. He ordered the brigadier to return to his command and assured him that he would have no further difficulties with Simonds. "Both of you are to blame," said Montgomery. "Just get on with the battle."[51]

The army commander was as good as his word. Simonds, evidently wishing to resolve the dispute, readily agreed to restore Graham to the First Brigade. "Howard," he said, calling him by his Christian name for the first time since taking command of the division, "let's just forget about this whole business; you go back to your brigade and I'll tear up this [resignation] note."[52]

Graham returned to First Brigade headquarters. In doing so, he deprived Lieutenant-Colonel George Kitching of a promotion, for Simonds had designated Kitching, his chief staff officer, as Graham's successor. Kitching's batman had even improvised a brigadier's red tabs and epaulettes for his uniform, but Kitching bore no hard feelings when informed by Simonds that he would remain a colonel for the time being. "I was glad," says Kitching, "because Howard Graham was a good friend."[53] Despite misgivings about going back to his command, Graham later wrote that this episode was never mentioned again and that his relations with Simonds were completely cordial from this time forward.[54] Indeed, Simonds soon recommended Graham for the Distinguished Service Order.

The Simonds–Graham flare-up would have been a great news story, but this was one time the censors prevailed over the war correspondents. "I didn't even get a chance to get a story out," Ross Munro later remarked. "The censors held the thing up."[55]

3

Under the blazing Sicilian sun, the First Division pushed ahead relentlessly. The Germans had bought twenty-four hours of precious time at Piazza Armerina, and General Simonds was anxious to press forward.

Fresh forces led the way. Howard Penhale's Third Brigade moved out of Piazza Armerina at noon on 17 July. Eight miles north of town stood an important junction. Its left fork was Route 117, swinging northwestward for Enna, fourteen miles away, while the right fork was a side road leading to Valguarnera, six miles further along. The hills and ridges guarding this intersection, a superb location for a defensive action, were manned by parts of two battalions of the tough 104th Panzer Grenadier Regiment, the same outfit that had so skilfully defended Piazza Armerina.

The Germans did their job well. It cost the Canadians another valuable twenty-four hours to force their way past the junction. The Third Brigade, led by New Brunswick's Carleton and York Regiment and Three Rivers tanks, experienced repeated delays, which were characteristic of the entire Italian campaign. Four miles north of Piazza Armerina, halfway to the junction, the invaders were stopped by a blown bridge. It was late afternoon before Canadian engineers constructed a detour and enabled the advance to resume.

Mortar and machine-gun fire slowed the Carletons' approach to the fork in the road. During the evening, the Royal 22nd Regiment passed through, only to be halted by a huge crater in a stretch of the road that could not be by-passed. Darkness had fallen by the time the sappers had repaired the route, but the French-speaking regiment resumed its forward movement by moonlight. The column was checked by a vicious little skirmish with Germans who attempted to cut off the Van Doos. The enemy troops suffered heavy losses in the attempt, but forced the Royal 22nd to dig in for the night.

The next day, 18 July, would see the biggest action to date involving the Canadians in Sicily. That night, studying his maps at divisional headquarters, Guy Simonds spotted an opportunity to cut off the German rearguard holding the intersection on Route 117. While Brigadier Penhale and his three battalions, supported by tanks and the full weight of the divisional artillery, pinned down the defenders, Simonds sent the reinstated Howard Graham and the First Brigade cross-country against Valguarnera. If all went according to plan, Sunday, 18 July would witness a sparkling Canadian success.

Both operations involved considerable difficulty. As always, the Germans made effective use of terrain that always seemed to favour them. Route 117 funnelled Penhale's brigade through a narrow pass, Portello Grottacalda, which led to a long ridge, Monte della Forma, which overlooked the junction. Penhale proposed to leave the Van Doos on the road to keep the enemy distracted at Grottacalda, while making two outflanking movements, on the right by the Carleton and Yorks and on the left by the West Nova Scotia Regiment.

It was a good plan, but it took most of 18 July to carry it out. The Carletons carried their objective, nicknamed "Beginners' Hill," in a spirited attack, backed by the fire of 120 guns. It was the first divisional barrage fired by Canadian gunners, who found Sicily's heat and dust wellnigh unbearable. Henry Worrell, a twenty-three-year-old member of the Royal Canadian Horse Artillery, recalls that the dust was often so thick that "you could hardly breathe. Everybody was just wearing shorts, and everybody was as black as your boots from the sun after a short span of time. The guns, you figured they'd fall to pieces, they shook so hard. They wouldn't recoil normally" in the excessive temperatures.[56]

The barrage was nearly deafening, reminding Ross Munro of "a long train going through a tunnel." Watching in rapt fascination, the war correspondent likened the shell bursts to "a grey forest of trees growing suddenly and magically before my eyes. As a shell hits the brown earth, the grey smoke billows up like a full-blown tree sprouting from the soil." Behind the barrage came the Carletons, "little clusters of men in dusty khaki moving cautiously forward and then running and falling flat as they took cover. Some men were hit and fell and didn't move. The others couldn't stop, and kept going, firing, dodging, creeping, sweating forward."[57]

Meanwhile, the West Novas executed their long left hook by making a gruelling march, stumbling and staggering through ravines choked with "tall reeds and jungle-like shrubbery," and wilting in the merciless heat as they crossed "steep bare slopes." Late in the afternoon, they arrived at the west end of Monte della Forma, "breathless but triumphant," only to discover that the Germans had pulled out, leaving behind thirty machine-guns and a self-propelled gun.[58]

By late Sunday afternoon, the intersection was securely in Canadian hands. However, Valguarnera – or Valcartier, as the Canadians called it – was still held by the Germans, despite the best efforts of the First Brigade. Howard Graham had dispatched two battalions to cut the road to this hilltop town, the Hasty Ps on the right and the RCR on the left. In single file, the Hasty Ps had set out from Piazza Armerina at 2130 the previous evening, each man lugging at least sixty pounds of equipment, including ammunition and rations. Their maps were so poor – "badly blurred copies of sketchy Italian originals," according to Farley Mowat – that they had to rely on compasses and their own wits to get them through ten miles of terrain in which "we could not go in any direction for more than twenty or thirty feet without being confronted either by an unscalable cliff or an impassable ravine."[59]

By dawn on the eighteenth, when the Carleton and Yorks were in action at Beginners' Hill, the rugged farm lads from Ontario were more or less in position along the road below Valguarnera. Almost immediately, the Hasty Ps were greeted by the sight of a German half-track towing a gun, evidently withdrawing from the road junction on Route 117. A PIAT interrupted its journey (marking the first time that Canadian troops had used this anti-tank weapon in battle), and it was soon joined by a dozen burning vehicles along the paved road. The biggest slaughter involved a convoy apparently carrying reinforcements for the disputed intersection on the Enna highway. Somehow oblivious to the danger, six trucks loaded with perhaps 150 soldiers drove past the Hasty Ps, who opened fire on this tempting target. Only eighteen Germans survived the ambush, and these were taken prisoner.

Captain Alex Campbell took this battle personally. Campbell, says Farley Mowat, "was possessed of a ferocious determination to kill as many Germans as he could, as they had killed his father in one war and his elder brother in another. The only *good* German, he liked to say, was a dead one – seven days dead under a hot sun." There were plenty of good Germans on the road to Valguarnera by the time Campbell was finished. "Alex concentrated his berserk fury on a single truck," recalls Mowat, "and when he had finished firing into it from a range of a dozen yards, his consuming hatred of the enemy must surely have been sated. Within that truck twenty or more Germans writhed and died."[60]

The Germans reacted to this intrusion with characteristic speed and force. During the morning, the Hasty Ps came under increasingly heavy mortar and artillery fire, and by early afternoon it was apparent that a full-scale attack was imminent. Running low on ammunition, and out of radio contact with brigade headquarters, Colonel Sutcliffe reluctantly withdrew his companies.

Had he known that The Royal Canadian Regiment was on the way, he might have held on a little longer. Led by Lieutenant-Colonel Ralph Crowe, a permanent-force officer from Guelph, Ontario, the RCR moved into position on the left of the Hasty Ps while the latter were pulling back. Crowe lost his second-in-command in the process. Major Billy Pope, a Tommy gun slung over his shoulder, came upon eight Hasty Ps who seemed lost, led them forward, and ran into three German tanks rumbling along the road from Valguarnera. Rather than retreat, Pope grabbed a PIAT and went after the tanks: he died in a hail of machine-gun bullets.

The Royal Canadians put up a spirited fight. Further along the contested road stood a three-hundred-foot knoll, terraced and cloaked in olive trees, and Colonel Crowe organized an attack. Crowe, "eager to keep the action rolling," led it himself.[61] Captain Strome Galloway's company was involved in the assault, which he calls "as mad a charge as any artist ever painted. I found the experience intensely exhilarating. Wearing my forage cap, and carrying my walking stick, I must have presented a rather amusing figure to my Company as they followed me down the slope of one hill and up over the crest of the next, firing while they went." The Germans were shooting back, and "a fusillade of small arms fire tore all sorts of gaps in our ranks." But the Canadian rush up the knoll was irresistible. "Leaping into tracked vehicles, the Germans drove off in speedy retreat," leaving the RCR in command of Valguarnera's southern approach, a mere half-mile from the town.[62]

While the RCR clung tenaciously to the roadside, Brigadier Graham had committed his remaining battalion. He sent the 48th Highlanders to take Valguarnera by making a long right hook. The Toronto regiment was to launch its final approach on Valguarnera from a ridge two miles south of the town, but when the Highlanders arrived they found the ridge to be strongly held by the Germans. Enemy snipers and machine-gunners pinned down the Toronto infantrymen for long minutes, until an English-born corporal took matters into his own hands. William Kay led his five-man section to dead ground, where they were immune to German fire, and followed it to the top of the ridge to a strongpoint defended by seventeen soldiers and three machine-guns. Although hit in the arm, Kay threw thirty-two hand grenades at the Germans, then led an attack. Three of his men were cut down but every German was killed or wounded. This strongpoint proved to be the key: the 48th Highlanders won the ridge and Kay won the Distinguished Conduct Medal.[63]

Valguarnera fell to the 48th that night. After dark, patrols slipped into the town to find the 10,000 inhabitants hiding behind locked doors and the Germans gone. It was a quiet conclusion to a difficult day. To clear the junction on Route 117 and the town of Valguarnera had cost 140 Canadian casualties, including 40 dead. Although the First Division had been slowed, the enemy was paying for it. As many as 240 Germans had been killed or wounded, and 250 more were prisoners, as a result of Sunday's actions. If nothing else, the enemy's high command was aware that it was dealing with a force to be reckoned with. "Near Valguarnera troops trained for fighting in the mountains have been mentioned," Generalfeldmarschall Kesselring reported to Berlin. "They are called 'Mountain Boys' and probably belong to the 1st Canadian Division."[64]

More would soon be heard from these "Mountain Boys."

CHAPTER THREE

The Red Patch Devils

1

The Canadians were learning on the job. Their first week or so in Sicily had made a visible impact on them. "Though this phase of their Sicilian fighting seemed later to have been a succession of minor clashes," writes Kim Beattie in his history of the 48th Highlanders, "it was all exciting. . . . It was only skirmishing war, but they were being welded, and they were gaining experience and confidence by the hour."[1]

This new-found confidence was about to be put to the test. On Monday morning, 19 July, the First Division continued its halting advance as the Second Brigade, led by Vancouver's Seaforth Highlanders, passed through Valguarnera, which was garrisoned by the Royal 22nd Regiment.

A few hours earlier, the brigadier, Chris Vokes, had had a brush with death. Vokes had hopped in his Jeep (dubbed by one wag a "Vokeswagen")[2] and sought out the headquarters of the Van Doos, to ensure that his units got past safely. In the early-morning darkness, Vokes drove up to a soldier standing in the middle of the road. Before the brigadier could say anything, the man pointed his weapon and shouted in what Vokes assumed was colloquial Quebec French. Vokes, furious, roared: "Stand to attention. And take that goddam gun out of my ribs." The soldier lurched to attention, while Vokes turned to his driver and said disgustedly, "Let's go on. This sonofabitch is drunk." Minutes later, a motorcycle dispatch-rider ran over the man, still standing in the middle of the road, and discovered that he was not a Van Doo but a German![3]

But the Second Brigade, once under way, found the going extremely slow. The Seaforths, and the PPCLI behind them, were soon forced by extensive enemy demolitions – craters in the road and blown bridges – to abandon their few vehicles. Rearguards of snipers, mortars, and machine-guns harrassed them on their march towards a crossroads five miles north of Valguarnera. The infantrymen were not able to secure this important site until late in the afternoon, after engineers had made the necessary repairs to enable the artillery's 25-pounders to move up in support. The countryside was growing more forbidding. Hills were now giving way to mountains; in the distance the troops could for the first time see Etna, the majestic, snow-capped volcano, forty miles to the northeast. None of these footsore Canadians could know that seventeen days of bitter fighting lay ahead.

On Monday afternoon, General Simonds held a planning conference at divisional headquarters. The First Division's immediate objectives were the twin towns of Leonforte and Assoro, perched two miles apart on a long, steep ridge. The heights of Assoro, standing tall "like a sharp, snaggly tooth,"[4] dominated the countryside for miles around, while Leonforte sat on Route 121, then the main east-west highway in Sicily, linking Palermo and Catania via Enna. Simonds decided to send the First Brigade against Assoro, while the Second Brigade took Leonforte. With these places secure, the division would execute General Montgomery's left hook and drive along 121 towards Adrano, via Nissoria, Agira, and Regalbuto.[5]

The division's two-pronged advance began around midnight. Both brigades had to cross the valley of the dry Dittaino while the Germans, in their observation posts hundreds of feet above them, were able to direct remarkably accurate artillery and mortar fire. The First Brigade soon encountered trouble which culminated in its biggest battle to date. When the 48th Highlanders secured a crossing over the Dittaino (although waterless, its bed was still an obstacle), the Royal Canadians passed through with Shermans of the Three Rivers Regiment. Nine tanks were knocked out by mines, and the Canadians were pinned down by accurate fire directed from Assoro's commanding heights, four miles away. In these circumstances, movement during daylight was impossible.

The pause gave Brigadier Graham a chance to plan his assault on Assoro, which he assigned to the Hastings and Prince Edward Regiment. At the headquarters of the Hasty Ps, in a farmhouse tucked in an olive grove, Graham huddled with the battalion commander, Bruce Sutcliffe, and his intelligence officer, Lieutenant Battle Cockin, a Cambridge-educated Englishman. The two senior officers were close friends: Graham had commanded the Hasty Ps in peacetime, while Sutcliffe had been his second-in-command. "Colonel Bruce" was a near-legendary figure in his late thirties, his hair prematurely grey after the tragic accidental deaths of his two children.

As soon as he saw the objective, Graham realized that its capture was going to be a difficult, if not impossible, task. "It was a formidable sight," he later wrote. "The ruins of an ancient castle stood high on a cliff, and to the left of this the road that should lead to Assoro (not in sight because it was beyond the crest of the cliff) rose in a series of hairpin turns up the side of this escarpment." Graham, using field-glasses to study the thousand-foot cliff, quickly ruled out the road as a feasible route: the Three Rivers tanks had proven that it was mined, and it was certain to be covered by machine-guns and mortars that would make the attempt suicidal. However, Graham noted an alternative approach. "The southeast face of the cliff was almost sheer, but there was a considerable amount of scrub, and we could discern what appeared to be goat tracks in places."[6] Sutcliffe studied the slope and agreed to make the attempt that night. He recognized that it was risky, but if surprise could be achieved, Assoro might be taken with light losses. Graham then departed for divisional headquarters to arrange for artillery support.

Within half an hour, Sutcliffe was dead. At midmorning, he and Cockin went out to get a closer look at the cliff they would soon be scaling. German observers spotted the two officers: a single shell screamed out of the sky and exploded with a cloud of yellow dust and black smoke. The colonel was killed instantly; Lieutenant Cockin later died of his wounds.

Howard Graham, summoned from divisional headquarters, hurried back to the Hasty Ps. There was no time for mourning over the death of his friend; the brigadier's concern at the moment was to consult with Sutcliffe's successor, Major Lord Tweedsmuir, the son of the former governor-general. The slender, intense, thirty-one-year-old major, who preferred to be called John Tweedsmuir (rather than the more correct John Buchan, Lord Tweedsmuir), but who was nicknamed "Long John" or "Tweedie," listened quietly as Graham outlined the plan of attack and agreed to implement it. If he had any misgivings, he kept them to himself.

By dusk, all was ready. At 2100, when the artillery began a four-hour diversionary bombardment between Leonforte and Assoro, the Hasty Ps set out for their date with destiny, under the concerned gaze of Howard Graham, just returned from the burial party for Sutcliffe. By now, however, the brigadier was having second thoughts. "The likelihood that Tweedsmuir would lose the whole battalion seemed almost a dead certainty . . . and I was about to tell him: nothing doing! But then I thought, my God, he just *might* pull it off. So I let him go . . . but I sweated blood for the next twelve hours."[7]

The Hasty Ps had been reorganized for the operation. In the lead was a special assault company, commanded by Captain Alex Campbell and comprising twenty picked men from each of the four rifle companies. Crossing the dry riverbed of the Dittaino in carriers, the Hasty Ps dismounted and, in single file, marched into the night. This was rough country; it took most of the night just to get to the foot of the cliff. The approach march took the battalion across "a maze of sheer-sided gullies, knife-edged ridges and boulder-strewn water courses."[8]

The potential for danger was underlined by the discovery of an unoccupied machine-gun post: crusts of dark bread on the ground indicated that it had been manned some time earlier. An even greater scare occurred soon afterwards. As the Hasty Ps descended yet another gully, they heard the clatter of stones in the darkness below. They froze, triggers on Bren guns and rifles, ready to open fire. "There was indistinct movement and then a herd of goats slowly emerged into the dim starlight and, behind them, a ragged Sicilian youth," Farley Mowat remembers. "He did not see us at first but the goats did and snorted as he drove them forward. Then he was face to face with me, gaping incredulously as he took in the motionless shapes of armed men on every side. He said not a word but passed slowly on as in a dream."[9] Breathing a collective sigh of relief, the Canadians pressed on.

It was close to dawn – 0400 – by the time they reached the bottom of the cliff. Here, Major Tweedsmuir made his final decision. Was it possible to climb the cliff? His reconnaissance that afternoon had left him uncertain, and even now he felt there was "no way to find out except to try it."[10]

They were in a race against time. Dawn was at hand, with the most difficult part of their operation still ahead of them. Fatigued by seven hours of hard marching, they nonetheless found the energy and determination to scale the heights. After negotiating a deep ravine running along the base of the cliff, Tweedsmuir split his battalion in two: Captain Campbell's assault company and a rifle company ascended on the left, while the young major led the remainder of the unit towards the right. Their climb lasted forty nerve-racking minutes, and in that brief interval, says Farley Mowat, "each of us performed his own private miracle. From ledge to ledge we oozed upward like some vast mould. Those who faltered clung with straining muscles until someone heaved from behind or hauled them from above. Weapons were passed up hand to hand; and no man dropped so much as a clip of ammunition . . . which was just as well, for any sound by one would have been fatal to us all."[11]

And then it happened. The sun was ready to peek over the eastern horizon, with the Hasty Ps nearing the top of the "wickedly steep" cliff,[12] when a sharp burst of machine-gun fire split the early-morning silence. It turned out that a reclusive private named A. K. Long had climbed into an observation post manned by four enemy soldiers. One of them, a sergeant, reached for a weapon, and Long riddled him with Tommy-gun bullets; the other three surrendered. A more important capture was a tripod-mounted telescope, which was almost certainly the instrument responsible for the death of Colonel Sutcliffe.[13] Some distance away, Major Tweedsmuir, who was almost at the crest, heard the burst of fire, but somehow the Germans in nearby Assoro did not. The Hasty Ps continued their climb, knowing they still had the advantage of surprise.

Minutes later, the first men reached the top of what came to be called Castle Hill. Fanning out, gripped by that surge of excitement that only a soldier knows, they quickly occupied the fragmentary ruins of the twelfth-century castle built by the Norman king, Roger II. Sicily had had many invaders, but these farm boys from southern Ontario were the first ever to capture this imposing position.

Standing on the hilltop, Tweedsmuir paused to admire the stunning view, but his thoughts were interrupted by a sniper's bullet clipping the ground beside him. After he scrambled for cover, Tweedsmuir received a stern lecture from the regimental sergeant-major, Angus Duffy. "We lost one commanding officer yesterday, we can't afford to lose another one today," Duffy growled. "Don't push your luck, sir."[14] (Duffy candidly admits that he had another reason for ensuring Tweedsmuir's safety: "the R.S.M. travelled with the C.O.")[15]

The Canadians had achieved complete surprise. From their vantage point around the Norman castle, they opened fire on the Germans in the village of Assoro immediately below. At that moment a convoy of a dozen trucks rolled into view, and within moments several had burst into flame. Lesser troops would have been routed, but these Germans, members of the 15th Panzer Grenadier Division, were good soldiers. They scrambled to return the Canadian fire. "I even saw," writes Farley Mowat, "two cooks abandon their pots and pans to seize rifles and open fire upon us."[16]

The enemy soon brought heavier weapons to bear, including the dreaded *Nebelwerfer*, better known as the "Moaning Minnie," a multi-barrelled mortar, which was not very accurate but which produced terrifying noises. The punishing bombardment soon shrouded the top of Castle Hill in a pall of smoke, dust, and death. "I lay flat on my belly behind a section of stone fence," Mowat recalls, "scrabbling at the rock-hard ground with my tin hat in a frenzied attempt to burrow into the heart of the mountain."[17]

Three miracles saved the Hasty Ps from destruction. "No two of these miracles would have been enough – it had to be all three," Tweedsmuir maintained. The first miracle related to his foresight in bringing along the biggest radio available. Distressed by the previous performance of the portable 18-set, the major had insisted on lugging an enormous wireless set normally found in a tank. This was carried to the foot of the cliff by a mule, which dropped dead at that point. Somehow, this huge radio was manhandled up Castle Hill, ensuring that the Hasty Ps would be able to summon the artillery's help if it was needed – and it was surely needed now. The second miracle was the captured telescope, which Tweedsmuir described as "fabulous . . . a major miracle in itself." The third miracle was personified by the new second-in-command, Major Bert Kennedy, a long-time militiaman who had trained in the artillery. Thus, the Hasty Ps had a powerful radio to communicate with the gunners, a range-finder to pinpoint targets for them, and Bert Kennedy, "an ex-gunner who was word-perfect in artillery communications."[18]

The Canadian artillery soon turned the tide. One by one, the German guns were put out of action or withdrawn to safer sites out of range of the Canadian 25-pounders. At least one attempted counter-attack suffered the same fate.

However, new troubles were in store for the Hasty Ps. They had brought with them only a limited amount of food, water, and ammunition, and supplies were running low. Now the Ontario farmers on Castle Hill "lay and suffered in that heat," as Tweedsmuir recounted. "The skin of our faces and arms and legs was scorched by the sun. Our heads were swimming with heat and exhaustion. . . . The rocks were too hot to touch, and so was the metal of our weapons. We had practically no water."[19]

It was clear that the Hasty Ps had to replenish their supplies if they hoped to hold on to the peak. A worried Tweedsmuir called an orders group, where it was decided to send someone to brigade headquarters to procure the necessary supplies. "There was a pause when the runner was mentioned," recalls the RSM, Angus Duffy, and "heads turned to me in expectation." This task seemed to be tailor-made for him, since he had pulled off a similar feat at Valguarnera, making four trips of seven miles each through rough terrain. When Duffy agreed to try it again, a company commander, Captain Bill Stockloser, was ordered to go with him.[20]

Duffy admits that he "was full of apprehension" as he set out on this long and dangerous journey. "I was still tired from Valguarnera and from the very tough and desperate climb up Assoro." If he had had more time to think about it, he might have believed that the whole thing was hopeless. "We had to descend from Assoro in broad daylight if we were to get a carrying party back up that night. It was almost certain that the enemy had closed the ring at the bottom of Assoro where we had come through the night before. Even if we did get through to Brigade HQ and get a carrying party, we had to return about 7 miles and climb the bloody hill again. No one could have that much luck!"[21]

Fortunately, Duffy did not have time to ponder his chances for success. With Captain Stockloser following, the RSM clambered down the cliff, expecting to be riddled with bullets at any moment. The Germans were not waiting at the bottom, and the two daring Canadians began working their way across the wasteland of the Dittaino valley. "We made short dashes from cover to cover, taking turns covering each other," Duffy remembers. "God, it is an awful feeling moving with your back to the enemy, expecting a blast any minute. Time is endless."[22]

Duffy's luck held. He and Stockloser arrived at First Brigade head-quarters at dusk. With Brigadier Graham at the time was the officer commanding the RCR, Ralph Crowe, who immediately volunteered two hundred of his men for the necessary carrying party, half to pack the supplies, the other half to act as guards. "Theirs was an outstanding example of one Regiment helping the other," says Duffy of the Royal Canadians, who loaded up with sixty pounds apiece. After the sergeant-major had a quick bite to eat, he led the carrying party into the night. By the time they negotiated the rough terrain and made their way to the foot of the cliff, Duffy estimated that there was only a half-hour of darkness left. He advised the RCRs to "stack the supplies and get clear of the hill;" to be caught here in daylight would have been "disastrous" for them. They took his advice and moved out, and the supplies completed their journey to the top of the hill on the backs of Hasty Ps.[23]

There was no question now: Castle Hill was theirs. Thanks to Angus Duffy's overnight exertions, the Hasty Ps had the ammunition and food and water to enable them to hold this crucial position. But the bulldog sergeant-major finally ran out of luck. That afternoon, he suffered a serious arm wound in a Moaning Minnie explosion, and was evacuated to hospital the following morning.[24]

Even before Duffy had set out on his mission to get supplies, efforts were under way to assist the Hasty Ps. During the afternoon of 21 July, Brigadier Graham had discussed the situation with Lieutenant-Colonel Ian Johnston of the 48th Highlanders of Canada. "My appreciation," Graham later wrote, "was that the Hastings, now certainly the main con-cern of the enemy, would draw his fire and his strength away from the axis of the road, and so permit the 48th Highlanders to be the left claw of a pincer that would either destroy the enemy or cause him to retire."[25]

The Highlanders started out at midnight. While Duffy was guiding the RCR carrying party with its precious supplies to Castle Hill, two 48th companies quietly worked their way up the hillside road, a series of flat loops, desperately hoping that the Germans were too busy with the Hasty Ps to send out patrols. In their final approach to the intersection outside of Assoro, the Torontonians left the road and worked their way up the steep – in some spots, nearly vertical – terraces on the west side of the mountain. They silently deployed just under the crest, and Major Don Banton reported to Colonel Johnston, "I have men so close under the rim we just heard Germans talking in front of the first house."[26]

At dawn, the 48th attacked. A red flare signalled a barrage by mortars and 25-pounder field guns, and the infantrymen swarmed across the road. Within minutes, it was all over. The T-junction secured, the Canadians now commanded the long, looping road, enabling engineers to repair the crater blocking the Three Rivers tanks. The Germans made half-hearted attempts to recapture the intersection, but when these failed the Canadians witnessed the unusual sight of the enemy in flight. Having lost the road, the only way out of Assoro was over the north cliff, which meant that the Germans had to abandon all of their equipment in the village, including four trucks and a multitude of mortars and machine-guns. Many even threw away their rifles in their haste to escape.[27]

By midday on 22 July, the 48th and the Hasty Ps had linked up, their friendly rivalry, for the time being, a thing of the past. The men of the 48th had condescendingly referred to the rural Hasty Ps as "Plough Jockeys," while the latter responded by calling the Highlanders "Glamour Boys." Now, amid the smoking ruins of Assoro, the two regiments formed a mutual admiration society. Nor had the Hasty Ps forgotten the help of the RCR – the permanent-force unit they had previously viewed with a jaundiced eye – or of the gunners who had saved them several times.

They had had lots of assistance, but the taking of Assoro had been a Hasty P show. It was a feat with few equals in military history, and the regimental history rightfully calls it "a spectacular triumph of endurance and initiative."[28] Ralph Allen, then a *Globe and Mail* reporter, wrote a fitting tribute in August 1943: "When the folks around Belleville, Trenton, Picton and Madoc are preparing their welcome for the Hasty Petes, they'll do well to note that the town hall steps are strictly out. The Hasty Petes have already done enough climbing to put a mountain goat on full retirement pension."[29]

Even the Germans were impressed. The commander of the 15th Panzer Grenadier Division, Generalmajor Eberhard Rodt, later wrote this assessment of the Canadians: "In fieldcraft [*Indianerkrieg*] superior to our own troops. Very mobile at night, surprise break-ins, clever infiltrations at night with small groups between our strongpoints."[30]

Oddly, not a single decoration was awarded for Assoro. But Colonel Bruce had been avenged.

2

While the Hasty Ps were fighting their epic battle at Assoro, a remarkably similar and equally desperate fight was taking place at nearby Leonforte.

During the morning of 20 July, after the Loyal Edmontons had secured a bridgehead over the Dittaino about five miles from Leonforte, Vancouver's Seaforth Highlanders took the lead, advancing up Route 121. With a population of twenty thousand, Leonforte was both larger and more modern than Assoro; and while it was not quite as high as Assoro, it was in an awkward location, according to historian George Stevens: "The town, oblong in shape and a kilometre in length, could be entered only along a twisty switchback road which crossed a deep ravine on the southern outskirts of the built-up area. The approach to this bridge (which had been destroyed) was on a reverse curve which gave the enemy on the high ground behind and to the east of Leonforte a clear field of fire."[31]

Unlike Assoro, there was no unguarded back-door: Leonforte had to be attacked frontally. And the town was held in strength by tanks and troops from two battalions of the 104th Panzer Grenadier Regiment.

The Seaforths attempted to outflank Leonforte. When that effort failed, a fighting patrol was sent directly into the town, where it was pinned down for much of 21 July. With difficulty, the patrol was extricated, and a full-scale assault was organized.

But the Seaforths were not able to launch it. The battalion commander, Lieutenant-Colonel Bert Hoffmeister, had called an orders group at 1530 in a farmyard to discuss the assault on Leonforte. As the officers were familiarizing themselves with the plan of attack, four Canadian shells intended for Leonforte fell among them. When the smoke and dust cleared, thirty officers and other ranks lay dead and wounded. Captain Howard Mitchell of the Saskatoon Light Infantry was among the first to reach the scene, and he was horrified by the sight of an injured officer. The memory haunts him today, he writes: "A fine young Canadian man, alive, lying on his side on the ground, shocked into immobility for the moment, his hands near his face, his legs and feet together, the only thing that was wrong was that his legs from below his knees to above his ankles were completely gone. Just as clean as could be. His clothes were not damaged and there was very little blood. His boots were even polished."[32]

Owing to the confusion caused by these casualties at Seaforth headquarters, the Second Brigade's Chris Vokes revised his plans. He designated the Loyal Edmonton Regiment to make the attack after nightfall on 21 July, supported by as much artillery as could be made available. (This was a busy time for the gunners, because they had to remain on call to aid the Hasty Ps at Assoro.)

The attack went in at 2130, half an hour after the shelling started. The barrage was a good one, and it forced the Germans to keep their heads down long enough for the Eddies to get into Leonforte. A savage street battle ensued, and all four Edmonton rifle companies were soon involved. Once in Leonforte, the infantrymen from northern Alberta were on their own. The artillery could not shell the place, because it was impossible to say precisely which buildings and streets were held by the Canadians; and until the engineers bridged the ravine, there was no way to get tanks and anti-tank guns into the town.

For a while, the situation appeared to be under control, with the

Edmontons holding a sizeable portion of Leonforte. But when the Germans counter-attacked with tanks and self-propelled guns shortly after midnight, a promising victory turned into a potential disaster. With neither artillery support nor anti-tank guns, the Eddies were faced with the choice of remaining in Leonforte and being wiped out, or withdrawing to safety.

The battalion commander, Jim Jefferson, made up his mind quickly, ordering his embattled companies to pull out of Leonforte under small-arms covering fire provided by the Seaforth Highlanders. However, Colonel Jefferson, with his headquarters and most of C Company, were cut off before they could get out of this death-trap. Jefferson, who was later awarded the Distinguished Service Order, deployed his hundred or so soldiers in a series of buildings in rough U shape and prepared to fight to the bitter end. Battalion headquarters were set up "in a wine cellar in the centre of Town." To make matters worse, his radio communication failed at this critical moment.[33]

At Second Brigade headquarters, Chris Vokes was beside himself with worry. "I felt the despair of failure," he later remarked. "I considered I had lost most of a fine battalion."[34]

This was a tough initiation for Vokes, a forty-year-old career officer. Bruce Matthews, the Torontonian who commanded the divisional artillery at this time, calls Vokes "an ideal Brigade Commander. His approach was simplicity as he knew the hazards of confusion in battle. . . . He was always close to the battle, large or small, and expressed himself in very strong terms about success or failure. At times he felt critical of his superiors but never wavered in his decisions to carry out operations as effectively as possible."[35]

It was impossible to have mixed feelings about Vokes, who would emerge as one of the dominant personalities in the coming campaign. Ross Munro described him as "a roughneck. I never knew a more profane man in my life."[36] For all his bluster, however, he was a likeable man. Barrel-chested, with a walrus moustache that he considered to be "a mark of distinction,"[37] he was rarely photographed without a hat to cover his balding head.

While Vokes despaired of losing the Eddies in Leonforte, Canadian engineers were attempting to build a bridge over the ravine south of town. A platoon of the 3rd Field Company had gone to work as soon as the attack went in. Despite mortar and machine-gun fire, the engineers attempted to assemble a portable Bailey bridge in the fifty-foot gap. This work was performed under the supervision of the divisional engineer chief, Geoff Walsh, who proudly points out that this was the first time on any battlefield that one of these bridges had been installed under fire, and his engineers did it in the dark. "Thank heavens I'd done a lot of training with my troops at night in Bailey bridging and so on, just in preparation for this sort of thing, and it paid off."[38]

The engineer chief was later awarded one of three Distinguished Service Orders that came out of this difficult project. The others went to Major Ken Southern, the officer commanding the 3rd Field Company, and to Major G. A. "Tiger" Welsh of the 90th Canadian Anti-Tank Battery. When two tanks and a small party of German infantry moved down the road from Leonforte, Southern collected a handful of Loyal Eddies and attacked. Although they were equipped only with small arms, their spirited showing discouraged the Germans from getting any closer to the construction site. Welsh applied the *coup de grâce* soon afterwards, manhandling two 6-pounder anti-tank guns across the ravine and knocking out a machine-gun post and one of the tanks. The major capped a good night's work, with the assistance of two engineers, by capturing twenty Germans on Leonforte's outskirts.[39]

With Colonel Walsh watching, the bridge was in place by 0430 hours on 22 July, and he delivered the good news to Second Brigade headquarters. But Brigadier Vokes remained despondent. "The poor Edmontons are decimated!" he moaned. "What's the use of a bridge?" Walsh shrugged and, having done his part, returned to divisional headquarters.[40]

While Colonel Jefferson and his Eddies continued to hold out, their situation was worsening by the minute. The Canadians were being systematically wiped out, being driven out of one house after another. Aside from the thirty men huddled with him in his wine-cellar headquarters in the middle of Leonforte, Jefferson had lost touch with the rest of his battalion.

The solution to his dilemma came in the form of a ten-year-old Italian boy. The youngster, identified only as Antonio Guiseppe, had been discovered in one of the houses held by the desperate Canadians, and Jefferson, running out of alternatives, placed his fate in the lad's tiny hands. Using an overturned apple barrel for a table, the colonel scratched out a note describing the situation and addressed it to "any British or Canadian officer."[41] Jefferson handed over the note and a handful of cash. "I gave young Tony whatever I had in my pockets at the time," the colonel recollected. "It must have been an adequate amount of money as I remember how his eyes bulged at the sight of it."[42]

Antonio Guiseppe saved the Loyal Eddies. Dodging bullets, shells, and German patrols, he made his way to the Canadian lines, where he was escorted to the despondent Chris Vokes at Second Brigade headquarters. When the brigadier read Jefferson's message, he was overjoyed. Convinced that the Edmontons had been all but destroyed, he now felt a "great ray of hope" that they could be rescued.[43] While the Italian youngster disappeared in the ensuing scramble to mount a rescue operation, Vokes never forgot him. Thirty years later, he was to return to Sicily and employ the assistance of local government and police authorities in an attempt to track down Antonio Guiseppe. Vokes's belated search effort failed, as he was told that these were probably the boy's Christian names, and very common ones, too.[44]

Vokes acted decisively, organizing a flying column of troops, tanks, and anti-tank guns. It was led by Captain Rowan Coleman, a PPCLI company commander, whose father, D. C. Coleman, was the president of the Canadian Pacific Railway. The captain, who would win the Military Cross this day, loaded his men on four Sherman tanks from the Three Rivers Regiment and on the trucks towing four 6-pounders from the 90th Anti-Tank Battery. The first attempt to cross the Bailey bridge, at 0645, failed in the face of heavy mortar and machine-gun fire. But a second attempt, at 0900, on the express orders of an anxious Vokes, succeeded in striking fashion. Roaring across the bridge at "breakneck speed," according to Coleman, the flying column suffered only a single casualty *en route* to Leonforte.[45]

The rescuers arrived in the nick of time. Indeed, it was almost a Hollywood finish, as a grateful Colonel Jefferson recounted: "Our leading tank was seen to be approaching. Simultaneously an enemy tank rounded a corner near Battalion Headquarters. The Canadian gunner was lightning on the trigger and the enemy tank exploded almost in our faces."[46] It was 0945 hours on 22 July; barely twelve hours had passed since the Eddies had entered Leonforte, but to the men trapped in the town it had seemed like an eternity.[47]

There was still heavy fighting to be done, both in town and in the surrounding hills, and it was not until nightfall that Leonforte could be considered secure.[48]

Unlike Assoro, for which no decorations were awarded, Leonforte garnered no less than twenty-one awards for bravery. One young member of the PPCLI particularly distinguished himself. Late in the afternoon, A Company launched an attack on a hill to the left of Leonforte, but the Patricias were soon pinned down by heavy machine-gun fire. Reinforcements arrived, in the form of a non-commissioned officer and two privates, with a Bren light machine-gun. This trio was ordered to knock out a German machine-gun post, but the NCO and one private were shot down within twenty-five feet of the objective. While the men of A Company watched in disbelief, the survivor, Private S. J. Cousins, picked up the Bren gun and, firing it from the hip, charged the enemy. Miraculously unscathed, he leaped among the Germans and killed all five of them. Reloading, he repeated the performance, charging another machine-gun post and wiping it out. In the face of Cousins's courageous attack, German resistance collapsed.[49]

Private Cousins should have won the Victoria Cross, the Empire's highest award for bravery in battle. He was recommended for it, but for some reason it did not go through. The Patricias themselves might be at fault, for not promoting it properly, and, as former staff officer George Kitching points out, "I don't think we thought of VCs in the Sicily days."[50]* Unfortunately, Cousins was killed a short time later (by an errant Canadian artillery shell); because the lesser medals for which he qualified as a private could not be awarded posthumously, his only recognition came in the form of a mention in dispatches.

At dusk on Thursday, 22 July, the First Canadian Division could be well pleased with its efforts. By brilliant manoeuvre and hard fighting, the Canadians had deprived the enemy of two key defensive positions, Assoro and Leonforte. The past three days had cost the division 275 casualties, the highest toll to date. Two-thirds of these had been incurred by the Second Brigade at Leonforte.[52]

The battles for Assoro and Leonforte were significant in ways that went beyond the justifiable pride felt by the participants. The make-believe war that had preceded these actions was over. Grammichele, Piazza Armerina, and even Valguarnera had been fought against rearguards who had no intention of holding their ground. But Assoro–Leonforte had involved a large, first-class German formation (all three battalions of the 104th Panzer Grenadier Regiment) which meant to maintain its strong positions for a long as possible.

---

* The Victoria Cross (VC) was the British Empire's highest award for heroism in the presence of the enemy. Lesser combat decorations were the Distinguished Service Order (DSO) and Military Cross (MC), which could be won by officers only. While the MC was a junior-officer's award, the DSO usually went to senior officers as a commendation for outstanding work by their units. When a junior officer won the DSO, it recognized an outstanding personal performance which could easily have merited a VC. Other ranks qualified for the Distinguished Conduct Medal (DCM) and the lesser Military Medal (MM), but these, unlike the VC, could not be awarded posthumously.

While the VC was open to all ranks, it was rarely awarded during World War II, in sharp contrast to the Great War. During 1914–1918, Canadians won sixty-four VCs; only sixteen were awarded during the latter conflict. There was no less heroism; standards were merely increased, for all decorations. "The correct allocation of honours and awards is of great importance, since it affects morale," the Canadian divisional commander, Guy Simonds, later commented. "If decorations are distributed too freely they lose their value in the eyes of the Army as a whole and to the recipients."[51]

3

The Canadian division carried with it the Eighth Army's hopes of smashing enemy resistance in Sicily's northeast corner. The remarkable successes at Assoro and Leonforte had been a striking demonstration of Canadian capabilities, and General Montgomery was counting on them to bail him out of his self-inflicted jam. With the Seventh Army gallivanting all over western Sicily, it would be several days before the Americans could get involved in the decisive area. Montgomery remained optimistic, however, that his army could overcome the Axis opposition arrayed against him. On 21 July, while the Hasty Ps were surprising the Germans at Assoro, Monty gave up any further attempts to take Catania by frontal assault; to continue would cost casualties he "could not afford." Accordingly, he issued orders for all formations except the First Canadian Division to go over to the defensive. In addition, the Canadians were excluded from the artillery-shell rationing imposed on the rest of the army (thirty rounds per day per 25-pounder). Canadian operations, Monty decreed, were "to continue without restraint directed on Adrano."[53] As if to spur them on, he showed up at Guy Simonds's headquarters on 22 July for a private talk with the youthful divisional commander.

Simonds issued his own orders on the evening of the twenty-second. The medieval town of Agira, eight miles from Leonforte, was the division's immediate objective. While the British 231st Brigade, temporarily attached to the Canadians, moved on Agira from the south, Simonds would mount his main effort eastwards down the main highway, Route 121. A mile from Leonforte was the intersection with the road (Route 117) running to Nicosia; three miles beyond lay the village of Nissoria, "an abject collection of stone hovels."[54] A series of low hills and ridges lay perpendicular to the highway, but it was assumed that no serious resistance would be encountered until the vicinity of Agira, an assumption soon to be proven terribly wrong.

The First Brigade, led by the 48th Highlanders from Toronto, moved out around midnight, but Simonds's hopes for a quick and easy advance on Agira were quickly dashed. Moving forward in the early-morning darkness, the 48th was ambushed near the junction, suffering a number of casualties from machine-gun and mortar fire. The Germans pulled back, and dawn found the Highlanders in possession of the intersection. But Friday, 23 July, had begun badly. The Second Brigade, which was to support the First, had difficulty moving into position around Assoro, and when patrols from the divisional reconnaissance unit, the 4th Princess Louise Dragoon Guards – an elegantly named regiment inelegantly nicknamed the "Plugs" or "Piddledy-Gees," from the acronym PLDG – encountered heavy fire on Route 117 near Nissoria, Simonds decided that his offensive needed a lot more weight behind it. At noon, he signalled a twenty-four-hour postponement in favour of a set-piece attack, supported by every available artillery piece.

It was one of Simonds's most controversial decisions. Until now, the Canadians had been successful by relying on what historian William McAndrew describes as "intelligent, imaginative and bold manoeuvre."[55] All that was to change with the plan of attack for Saturday, 24 July. With "priority call" on the Eighth Army's limited stockpiles of artillery ammunition, Simonds resorted to brute force. His former chief staff officer, George Kitching, notes that, until this point, circumstances had limited the artillery's role in the Sicilian fighting, and Kitching believes that Simonds, a gunner by training, wished to get the artillery more involved.[56] Nissoria was to be the first time that every available Canadian gun was backing an assault, but Kitching points out that Simonds was not alone in his faith in firepower. "I distinctly remember the feeling that permeated headquarters of 1 Canadian Division," he writes, "that nothing could stop troops that were going to be supported by 5 field regiments and 2 medium regiments. Over 150 guns in support of *one* battalion!"[57]

Under Simonds's plan, The Royal Canadian Regiment would attack at 1500 hours, advancing behind a barrage which would advance at the rate of a hundred yards every two minutes. Half a mile ahead, a smokescreen two thousand yards long would precede the attackers and guide Kittyhawk fighter-bombers assigned to bomb and strafe targets along the road, while six squadrons of medium bombers plastered Agira and environs. (In the event, the air support produced negligible results: the fighter-bombers raked the road with bullets and bombs without hitting much of anything, while a mix-up in communications scotched the bombing of Agira.)[58]

The response from those taking part was less than enthusiastic. Captain Ian Hodson, an RCR company commander, vividly recalls the orders group where the operation was outlined. "There was little flexibility in the plan," Hodson writes, "and no options for company commanders." The colonel, Ralph Crowe, indicated that the battalion would cross a number of report lines *en route* to the objective, and stressed that the attackers were "*not* to go beyond a given report line without authorisation." According to Hodson's recollection, Crowe saved the worst for last. "At the end of the 'O' Group, the CO looked at his watch, and ordered us out of the area we were occupying, saying that it was the first ground the gunners were going to fire on. We exchanged looks, as you can well imagine. Why was it necessary to fire on ground we held, why waste ammunition?"[59]

Despite the planning flaws, the RCR attack actually came close to succeeding. At zero hour on this hot, sunny afternoon, the barrage opened with a deafening roar. At first, the whole thing resembled a training exercise. The Royal Canadians threaded their way through several orchards and the khaki-clad Canadians "plucked apples, figs and plums from the trees as they passed along," according to Captain Strome Galloway, who munched on an apple.[60] Although pleasant enough, these surroundings slowed the soldiers, and the barrage moved onward, steadily, irrevocably, leaving the infantry further and further behind with each passing minute. The hills a half-mile east of Nissoria were saturated with high explosive between 1530 and 1600, but it was more than half an hour before the Royal Canadians were even close to the target area. The barrage that kept the enemy's heads down was long gone by then.

The RCR's Colonel Crowe reported at 1615 that Nissoria was secure. The only sign of opposition came in the form of a tank outside the village and a gun on the main street. Both of these were knocked out by Three Rivers Shermans accompanying the RCR. So far, the attack had been little more than a noisy afternoon stroll.

That changed as soon as the leading companies emerged from Nissoria's east end. Hiding in the hills ahead was part of the 104th Panzer Grenadier Regiment, so recently bested by the Canadians at Assoro and Leonforte. The Germans held their fire until the two forward companies were in the clear, and then let go with everything they had. The RCR's support companies were hit by a mortar barrage. Not even tanks could survive. As the infantry scattered, the Three Rivers Regiment rolled forward. Without infantry protection, the metal monsters were sitting ducks for enemy artillery, and the Three Rivers lost ten Shermans in a matter of minutes.[61]

For many, this was a revelation. Until now, the Shermans had been considered indestructible, and it was a distressing sight to see the tanks knocked out, some of them afire. A burning tank was said to have "brewed," and the infantry soon saw enough of them to give the Shermans the grim nickname, "Ronsons," after the cigarette lighter.

With no artillery available to help them (for the curtain of shells was falling far beyond the enemy-held positions and moving still farther away), the infantry responded with courage and initiative. Although D Company was nearly crippled by its heavy casualties in the maelstrom of fire in which it was engulfed, the other three companies managed to take refuge in dead ground nearby. Captain Galloway got on the radio to Colonel Crowe, who urged him to keep going. Consulting a fellow captain and company commander, Slim Liddell, Galloway "made a plan whereby we'd push on up a gully to the right of the Nissoria position and thus outflank the Germans."[62]

This plan worked. Leading their companies, Galloway and Liddell slipped through the gully without being seen by the enemy, and reached their objective. "We could see Agira plainly," says Galloway, "and were only a few hundred yards south of the highway leading in from Nissoria." At this point, wireless communications broke down. After posting his platoons in defensive positions and sending out patrols, Galloway tried without luck to contact battalion headquarters by radio to report success. However, he did get in touch with Captain Ian Hodson, who brought his company through the gully an hour later. The RCR now had three strong companies behind the Germans and overlooking their line of retreat.[63]

Fate intervened at this point. With radio communications breaking down, Colonel Crowe, in Nissoria, was anxious to restore control over his scattered battalion. Around 1800, hearing the sound of firing in the distance, he apparently concluded that his wayward companies had cleared the hills and reached their objectives. Setting out with a small party of signallers and engineers, he brazenly walked up the slope south of the road, calling, "RCR!" Not until he was wounded by a machine-gun bullet did Crowe realize that he had blundered into the heart of the enemy defences. Taking up a rifle, the colonel returned the fire, until a second enemy bullet killed him. (In the space of just a few days, the RCR had lost both its commanding officer and second-in-command; they were, ironically, the only officers of this regiment to die in Sicily.) The loss of both the colonel and his signallers meant that, for several crucial hours, there was no one to authorize the Royal Canadians to proceed past the report line they now occupied.[64]

The inflexibility of the battle plan was painfully apparent, and no one was more conscious of this than Ian Hodson, the senior officer among the trio of company commanders. Nearby, a sunken road appeared to lead into Agira, and if it had been up to Hodson, he would have continued the advance. "Agira was an important road junction for the enemy, and no doubt he would have hit us very hard, but I believe to this day, we could have, and should have, made a go of it."[65]

However, the decision was not that easy. Hodson had been told at least twice not to go further without orders, and he was wrestling not only with correct military procedure but with regimental politics. The RCR was one of the few battalions in which all the company commanders were captains; in other units, it was not unusual for one or two to be majors, but Hodson had been told "that there would be no promotion until we had proved ourselves in battle." Ignoring orders was hardly the way to win the approval of the commanding officer. So they waited, while a sergeant-major was sent back to report their position and return with instructions.[66]

The fog of battle had enshrouded divisional headquarters. By early evening, no one knew what had become of the RCR, except that one of its companies was decimated and the other three were missing. All that was apparent was that the RCR attack had not succeeded, and General Simonds ordered Brigadier Graham to commit another battalion and "keep up the pressure on the enemy through the night and to capture Agira as soon as possible."[67]

The Hasty Ps were now sent forward. Oozing confidence in the wake of Assoro, few seemed to mind that they were being sent into action, as Farley Mowat notes, "with no tank support, no artillery support, and no prior reconnaissance for a battle to be waged in darkness."[68] Lord Tweedsmuir, now a lieutenant-colonel, was certainly uncomfortable about it, but there was nothing he could do. "The only thing," he later wrote, "was to get as far as possible in the darkness and hope for the best."[69]

Tweedsmuir planned to outflank the enemy position by a wide move to the right, but Howard Graham was having second thoughts. The brigadier had ridden a tank into Nissoria to meet with the new RCR commander, Major Thomas Powers, fondly known to the regiment as "Pappy." Powers, like just about everybody else, had no idea what had happened to A, B, and C companies, but he was able to point out to Graham the enemy's positions on the hills to the east of the village. Graham returned to his headquarters to argue for a properly prepared set-piece attack by the whole brigade and every gun and tank that could be found. However, when he telephoned divisional headquarters with his proposal, he was informed that Simonds was asleep and his chief of staff, Colonel Kitching, refused to awaken him.

This was not as surprising as it might sound. The divisional commander had adopted, on Montgomery's advice, the practice of getting a sound night's sleep. "Simonds," explains Kitching, "expended a great deal of energy, both physical and mental, during the daylight hours of battle. To be at his best he needed seven or eight hours of sleep at night to recharge his batteries." He was not to be awakened "unless, in my opinion, a crisis had been reached which required his judgement. If it did not, I was to handle it in his name." Kitching had interrupted Simonds's sleep during Leonforte, to arrange a midnight meeting with a worried Chris Vokes, but he saw no need to do that in this instance. "I reminded [Graham] that Simonds had been very specific in telling him 'to keep up the pressure' by offensive operations and that if I woke Simonds he would, I was sure, be just as specific," Kitching comments. "The Hasty Ps had a good plan and had every chance of success. There had been no change in the situation generally and I could see no reason why Simonds should become involved. So my advice to Graham was to push on." Simonds endorsed Kitching's decision the next morning.[70]

The Hasty Ps jauntily marched off into a disaster. Sunday, 25 July, was just minutes old when they passed through Nissoria and deployed with help from an RCR patrol. But the darkness that Tweedsmuir hoped would cover his battalion instead betrayed it. The Hasty Ps ran into an unseen machine-gun post, and the jig was up. The alerted defenders fired flares that lit the night-time sky – "like it was Maple Leaf Gardens on a Saturday night," said one shaken survivor[71] – and raked the fields with machine-gun and mortar fire.

The Hasty Ps were trapped on the exposed hillside. Among the dozens of casualties was Tweedsmuir, who was bracketed by four mortar bombs and so badly injured that someone inquired whether he had been killed. "No," replied a private who crawled over to the colonel's side, "but he's so full of lead that he wouldn't float in molasses."[72] He was eventually pulled to safety by Pat Amoore, an Englishman attached to the regiment as an interpreter. "He grabbed me partly by the hair and partly by the collar," Tweedsmuir later wrote. "Anyhow, it was a great improvement on the conditions from which he retrieved me!"[73]

All too soon, dawn came, and the stubborn Plough Jockeys from Ontario realized that they had to pull out of this death-trap. The order was given, and the Hasty Ps, singly and in small groups, scurried back to Nissoria. This abortive attack cost them eighty officers and other ranks, the heaviest casualties suffered in a single day in Sicily by a Canadian unit.[74]

If one man symbolizes the tragic futility of that terrible morning, it was A. K. Long. This was the same Private Long who had captured the German observation post at Assoro. Quiet, introverted, Long was wounded in the stomach and legs by fragments from a mortar bomb, but refused to let his buddies drag him away. "He waved them off," writes Farley Mowat, "and when they saw him last he was sitting with his body braced against the shattered remnant of an olive tree, sucking on an empty pipe, and leafing through a pocket edition of *Macbeth*."[75] Long was never seen again.[76]

By morning, the situation was not hopeful. The Hasty Ps, whose operation had seemed to hold much promise, had failed dismally. And to make matters worse, the three RCR companies behind the enemy lines had been withdrawn.

No one was more mystified than the Royal Canadians themselves. After spending an uneventful night awaiting further instructions, the senior captain, Ian Hodson, "had come to the conclusion that as Battalion HQ did not know our circumstances as well as we did, that the order not to proceed should be ignored."[77] But before he could set out for Agira, Captain Dick Dillon arrived with orders to withdraw immediately.

Hodson and his fellow company commanders were stunned by this turn of events. They had had a quiet night; their only discomfort was the lack of rations. The Germans appeared to be ignorant of their presence. "I believe a golden opportunity – possibly a long-shot gamble – was lost," says Hodson, who accepts the responsibility for not moving towards Agira sooner. "I was the senior officer. . . . I've regretted it ever since and have often wondered how much time might have been saved, how many lives might have been saved, had I done what I should have done."[78]

However, the blame lies not with Ian Hodson, but with his superiors. The difficulties originated with Guy Simonds and his lavish artillery program, which restricted the infantry to a rigid plan. That was in turn adopted by Ralph Crowe, the personable battalion commander who kept a tight rein on his company commanders. A breakdown in communications was exacerbated by Crowe's death. And then either Howard Graham or Pappy Powers ordered the RCR to withdraw. The three companies came back over a route which "remained open and uncontested throughout" the action. "If they could be extricated, they could also have been reinforced," historian Bill McAndrew points out. "Why a battalion – or a brigade – was not sent round remains a mystery."[79]

It was a disillusioned group of RCRs who made their way back that day. Strome Galloway, whose company had suffered only twelve casualties so far, led his men on a long, roundabout route to the Canadian lines. At journey's end was a tin of cold stew, Galloway's first food in thirty-six hours. "Such is the sad account," he concluded with no little bitterness, "of what might have been a terrific success."[80] Forty-five Royal Canadians, including their commanding officer, had been sacrificed pointlessly.

When Simonds learned of the situation, Kitching writes, he "was not happy."[81] Two battalions had failed to break through, but Simonds "insisted" (Brigadier Graham's word) that the First Brigade commit its remaining battalion, the 48th Highlanders, to break through the Nissoria roadblock.[82]

The Glamour Boys of the 48th spent the day preparing for their assault. Zero hour on 25 July was 1800 hours. Major Don Banton's D Company led the Highlanders' attack behind an artillery and machine-gun barrage. Unlike the previous operations, which had demonstrated the enemy's vulnerability to the right, this one was aimed to the left. This surprised divisional headquarters; as George Kitching points out, the capture of the high ground north of Nissoria "would not necessarily force the enemy to withdraw. . . . In retrospect, I can't help feeling that Brigade HQ had not planned the battle correctly."[83]

The Highlanders soon ran into serious trouble. Although they encountered fierce resistance in the northern hills, their biggest problems were caused by the repeated breakdown in wireless communications, which prevented vital information from reaching battalion and brigade headquarters and denied the infantry artillery support at crucial times. Failures of this sort had dogged the Canadians from their arrival in Sicily, but their extent this night was unprecedented. Fingers were afterwards pointed at the Canadian-made 18-set, the portable radio used at battalion and company headquarters. Officers like the RCR's Ian Hodson "found it to be very frustrating. When a signaller heard something coming his way and hit the ground hard, very often the 18-set was jarred out of calibration. To reset it took time, especially if there was wireless silence."[84] When the radios did work, the mountainous terrain produced freakish conditions that restricted reception, especially at night. Faulty batteries were blamed; it was estimated that two-thirds were "duds or very weak."* Nor did it help that they were in constant use, thanks to the fact that signalling equipment was lost in the convoy sinkings on the way to Sicily. General Simonds contended at the conclusion of the campaign that the 18-set "did not meet the range demanded to control an infantry brigade when dispersed over a wide front and/or in great depth" and ordered that a half-dozen of the larger 22-sets, carried by mule, be allotted to each brigade. However, that solution came too late to help the 48th Highlanders at Nissoria.[87]

Despite the chaos, the 48th attack almost succeeded. The Germans, it seems, were just as confused as the Canadians, and at one point during the night the enemy fell back. Unfortunately, the Highlanders were unable to exploit the situation; instead of advancing in triumph, they were ordered to withdraw. The road to Agira, so tantalizingly open on the morning of 26 July, closed again when the Germans reoccupied the hills overlooking Nissoria. The 48th had suffered forty-four casualties, but they were rendered meaningless when the regiment was ordered to pull out.[88]

The First Division was right back where it started, two days earlier, with 171 fewer infantrymen, the combined losses of the three infantry battalions. While Nissoria was a minor action, it is noteworthy for the puzzling behaviour of the divisional commander, Guy Simonds, who later blamed his troops for failing to execute his plan. In a post-war interview, he cited "failure to follow the fire support closely enough . . . as the funda-

---

* Poor radio discipline was another factor which has never been addressed. Contends a former RCR signaller, Jack Anderson: "We were practically out of communication any time we went into action because on the approach march up, they would have us in communication for no reason, and then when we did get into action, then our batteries were dead." Anderson was so frustrated by his experiences that when the Sicilian campaign ended, he handed in his radio and served as a rifleman.[85] Unnecessary communications were another problem. The West Nova Scotia Regiment, making a night move through the mountains east of Valguarnera, received a coded message from Third Brigade headquarters. The intelligence officer decoded it: "Brown paint is now available at Brigade HQ."[86]

mental cause of the reverses suffered by units of the 1st Brigade in their attacks at Nissoria."[89] This was clearly a reference to the original assault by the RCR, and the brigadier, Howard Graham, was not impressed with Simonds's assessment. "I still resent," he wrote forty years after the war, "the effort to justify a bad plan by putting the blame for its failure on the backs of the troops."[90]

Of course, the trouble can be traced to the change in tactics, in which manoeuvre was sacrificed to firepower. "Instead of relying so much on the artillery barrage and fire planning, which takes time," says George Kitching, "I felt that 1st Brigade should have been told to take Agira in the quickest time. The enemy flanks were comparatively open and I had hoped that we would continue to defeat him by open warfare (*Indianerkrieg*) in which our junior officers were becoming adept.... For a strong force to operate on a narrow front, when faced by a weaker enemy, gives an advantage to the enemy."[91]

To make matters worse, Simonds committed the cardinal military sin of reinforcing failure, not once but twice. He might well have heeded the words of a young Canadian artillery captain who wrote in 1939: "Several independent company and battalion battles launched on a divisional front will meet with the repulses that lack of coordination and concentration always deserve." The author's name was Guy Simonds.[92]

It would be wise to remember also that in July 1943 Simonds had been a major-general for only four months. As Strome Galloway observes: "Often cited since the war as Canada's most brilliant field commander, which he probably was, Simonds had much to learn about his job while in Sicily."[93]

4

By the time the 48th Highlanders had been withdrawn, General Simonds and his staff were already preparing a new offensive along Route 121. Chris Vokes's Second Brigade was committed on Monday evening, 26 July, behind an even bigger barrage than the one arranged earlier for the First Brigade. Vokes himself was the biggest difference between the operations. Several years younger than Howard Graham, Vokes also had a much more forceful personality. And his preparations were characteristically sound. "He was meticulous and very careful as to detail," George Kitching recalls of Vokes, "but once he was satisfied and knew that we at Div HQ would give him all the support he needed, he gave his orders clearly and forcefully."[94] Three general objectives had been identified by divisional planners: the high ground immediately east of Nissoria (code-named "Lion"), where the First Brigade had been repulsed; another low ridge ("Tiger") a thousand yards closer to Agira; and the crest ("Grizzly") within a half-mile of Agira, linking Monte Crapuzza, north of the road, and Monte Fronte, south of Route 121. The PPCLI would take Lion and Tiger, allowing the Seaforth Highlanders to pass through and capture Grizzly.[95]

At 2000 hours on 26 July, the barrage burst over the heads of the PPCLI assault companies and crashed into the German defences blocking Route 121 east of Nissoria. Seventeen minutes later, the Patricias went forward. Captain Rowan Coleman, whose flying column had rescued the Loyal Eddies at Leonforte, led C Company south of the road towards Lion. Only one of Coleman's three platoons was intact by the time the objective was reached; parts of the others got lost in the dark. They found that the artillery had done its work with deadly effect: fifteen stunned survivors of the shelling surrendered immediately, the first of seventy prisoners taken by the PPCLI. One captured officer was so dazed by the barrage that he asked to see the "automatic field gun" he supposed the Canadians were using.[96] Others were not quite ready to quit and C Company faced what Coleman called "a spirited grenade and tommy-gun fight" before it could report Lion's capture.[97]

But that was the only thing that went right for the Patricias. With Lion more or less in PPCLI hands, A and B companies were to pass through and strike for Tiger, a thousand yards east. Both of them lost their way; as had happened to the RCR on the twenty-fourth, the barrage rolled onwards with no one following it.[98]

As the evening wore on, it became evident that the attack was not proceeding according to plan. At Second Brigade headquarters, Chris Vokes was fuming. It was bad enough that he was situated in a quarry which, he later complained, "was the home of all the fleas in Sicily."[99] Worse, he had little idea what was going on: Lion apparently had been taken, but Tiger remained a question mark. Although the lack of information was frustrating, it did not prevent him from making a critical decision: at midnight he committed Lieutenant-Colonel Bert Hoffmeister's Seaforth Highlanders.

The Seaforths set out for Tiger, but they had to fight their way through that part of Lion still held by enemy machine-gunners and tanks. At 0425, A Company's Major Henry "Budge" Bell-Irving, the future lieutenant-governor of British Columbia, reported: "Forward elements on 'Tiger.'"[100]

This brief report actually marked the start of a morning-long battle. When they were stopped by heavy fire, Bell-Irving led his company to the right along "a donkey trail." With dawn approaching, Bell-Irving's company clambered up a slope and dug in. The arrival of daylight brought a pleasant surprise: "Purely by good luck," he later commented, "'A' Company had arrived at the very centre of the 'Tiger' objective."[101] But it took several more hours to clear Tiger. Reinforcements reached Bell-Irving during the morning, and by 1100 the position had been secured.

From here, the Seaforths could plainly see their next goal. Two miles to the east stood Grizzly, the high ground flanked by Monte Fronte and Monte Crapuzza; beyond, shimmering in the midday heat, was Agira, "a pile of white, jagged masonry cluttering up the top of an otherwise noble mountain."[102] What the Canadians could not see was that they were facing fresh troops. Their objective was held by a battalion of the 15th Panzer Grenadier Regiment, which had relieved the worn-out 104th Panzer Grenadier Regiment.

Chris Vokes was at his hard-driving best this day. Not content to sit in his flea-infested headquarters, he ranged the battlefield to gauge the progress being made by his units. Realizing the need to maintain the momentum, he rushed up machine-guns, tanks, and anti-tank guns, and arranged a barrage to support the Seaforths in an assault on Grizzly. He also called in air support: at noon, medium bombers pounded Agira, while Kittyhawk fighter-bombers strafed and bombed the enemy's Grizzly positions.

The Seaforths, attacking at 1400 hours, pulled off a splendid manoeuvre. Monte Fronte, south of the highway, was the objective of Major Bell-Irving, his company now reduced to fifty, all ranks. The square-topped hill was defended by a full company of Germans, who were undaunted by Canadian shelling and produced such a volume of small-arms fire that Bell-Irving halted his attack and sought an alternative. He found it in an unlikely location: the south side of Monte Fronte, precipitous and probably undefended. Leaving a platoon to distract the defenders, Bell-Irving led the rest of his company to the right, cleverly utilizing the cover provided by the orchards and vineyards on the terraces. Scaling the three-hundred-foot cliff, the Seaforths took the enemy by surprise.

The Germans quickly recovered, and a fierce battle ensued. It lasted for the rest of 27 July and all night long. When his platoon was pinned down by fire from a machine-gun post, Private Frederick Webster, a Native Indian from Lytton, B.C., crawled forward with his Bren gun and opened fire at close range, forcing the enemy gunners to keep their heads down and enabling some Seaforths to wipe out the post. Webster won the Military Medal for his heroism.

"By fire, movement and plenty of guts"[103] – Colonel Hoffmeister's words – the outnumbered Seaforths prevailed. Their casualties were surprisingly low: two dead and five wounded, compared to at least seventy-five Germans killed, fifteen captured, and an unknown number wounded. Bell-Irving considered the light losses in his company to be "particularly remarkable in that there was a concerted attack against them just after midnight in the form of one of the only – if not the only – bayonet charges ever made against the Seaforths in this war."[104]

By dawn on 28 July, Monte Fronte was firmly in the hands of the weary Seaforths. They had fought and marched more than eight miles to get to this commanding position, an exploit later recognized with the award of the Distinguished Service Order to the commanding officer, Bert Hoffmeister, and to the hard-working Bell-Irving.

In the meantime, Brigadier Vokes had committed his reserves against Grizzly north of Route 121. When it became apparent that the Seaforths would have to concentrate their efforts against Monte Fronte, Vokes personally summoned the Loyal Eddies into action late in the afternoon of 27 July but, delayed by rough terrain and then by darkness, the Edmontons did not attack Grizzly until 0300 on the twenty-eighth. The barrage that was to accompany them had been fired long ago, but they were undaunted. While one company stormed Monte Crapuzza – which turned out to be undefended – two other companies attacked a nearby hill crowned by "a walled cemetery characteristically bordered by tall, sombre cypress trees."[105]

Dubbed Cemetery Hill, it proved a tough nut to crack. According to Lionel Shapiro of the Montreal *Gazette*, "the tombstones bristled with machine and anti-tank guns,"[106] and there were four times as many defenders as attackers. Major Bill Bury led D Company's bayonet charge. The popular Bury was one of those officers who preferred to wear a beret instead of a steel helmet; he was killed by a bullet in the head. (The northern Alberta community of Bury Ridge commemorates him.) But his men stormed the hill and took it. Grizzly's last bastion had fallen.

Agira fell later in the day. The PPCLI entered the town during the afternoon, receiving "quite an ovation" from the residents and a rude reception from an enemy rearguard of snipers and machine-gunners. At the cost of one dead and eleven wounded, the Patricias mopped up Agira by 1800 hours, capturing forty-three Germans and killing "about 15" others.[107] As if in celebration, a five-hour rainstorm swept the Sicilian hills that evening, the first rain the Canadians had seen since coming to this parched island.

So ended the First Division's biggest battle of the Sicilian campaign. Originally intended as a one-day undertaking, the struggle for Agira had lasted five full days and cost 438 Canadian casualties. The Germans had, by employing a skilful defence in favourable terrain and by taking advantage of questionable Canadian tactics, bought valuable time, but they had paid dearly for it. The 104th Panzer Grenadier Regiment lost an estimated 200 killed, and its successor, the 15th, suffered 125 dead. These units had lost another 430 men taken prisoner by the Canadians.[108]

One prisoner paid a tribute to the determination of the Canadian infantry. Allowed to interview some Germans captured in the fighting at

Nissoria, Ross Munro sought out an officer who could speak English. The German had high praise for the Canadians, whom he recognized by the distinctive red patch on their sleeves: "We see the Red Devils coming and we fire our mortars hard. But the Red Patches just keep coming through the fire. I can't understand it. Other troops we fought lay down and took shelter when the mortars fired right on top of them. The Red Patches are devils."[109]

CHAPTER FOUR

"A Proper Schemozzle"

1

There was good reason for the warm welcome given the Canadians by the citizens of Agira. Most Sicilians were in a celebratory mood, because Il Duce, Benito Mussolini, had been deposed on 25 July.

Mussolini had known for some time that he was in trouble. "It is defeat in war," he stoically wrote, "that brings about the fall of a régime," and 1943 had witnessed nothing but defeat so far as Italy was concerned, beginning with catastrophe in North Africa, followed by the invasion of Sicily, the first intrusion by the Allies on Italian territory. After an emergency meeting with Hitler in northern Italy, Mussolini returned to Rome on 20 July to discover that his capital had been subjected to its first major air raid, when 560 Allied bombers blasted Rome's railway marshalling yards and nearby Ciampino airfield. This, so far as sagging civilian morale was concerned, was the last straw. On 24 July, after a rancorous ten-hour session of his Grand Fascist Council, which had not met since 1939, Mussolini reluctantly resigned. The next morning, he was arrested, and Italy's aging King Vittorio Emanuele III announced the formation of a government under the seventy-one-year-old Marshal Pietro Badoglio.[1]

While Sicilians openly rejoiced at the fall of Mussolini, who had brought so much misery to their island, the reaction in Germany was considerably different. Adolf Hitler was infuriated, denouncing Vittorio Emanuele as "a weakling,"[2] and plotting his revenge. Within forty-eight hours of Mussolini's fall, the Germans were preparing plans to take over Italy in case their erstwhile ally collapsed or surrendered, a possibility which had been openly considered since May.

Most Germans, however, were far from dismayed at the prospect of losing their Axis partner. Hitler's propaganda chief, Joseph Goebbels, lamented in his diary the lack of fighting prowess of the Italians, pointing out that while "the Germans have stood their ground in Sicily . . . the Italians . . . capitulated, sometimes a whole division at a time, headed by the divisional commander." The Germans had a word for the Sicilian situation: *Riesenauri*, "one hell of a mess."[3]

The Allied high command might have used the same word to describe Sicily, for the campaign was bringing out the worst aspects of coalition warfare. George Patton's Seventh Army completed its private war by making a triumphant entry into the Sicilian capital, Palermo, on 22 July, and the next day Omar Bradley's II Corps reached the north coast of the island.

But Patton's manoeuvre had done more harm than good. Several crucial days would pass before the Americans could concentrate their strength for an eastward drive on Messina, the next step in the reduction of the island. The drive on Palermo had looked spectacular on maps, and although Patton's reputation in the newspapers was enhanced by it, his fellow American commanders were not impressed. Bradley considered Patton to be "a rather shallow commander. . . . He was primarily a showman. The show always seemed to come first."[4]

In the meantime, the Eighth Army's drive on Catania had stalled in the mountainous terrain south of volcanic Etna. A change in tactics was necessary; a troubled Bernard Montgomery began to realize that he could not beat Sicily's German defenders without American help. On 25 July, when he and Patton met for the first time since D-Day, Montgomery proposed that the Americans utilize both major highways north of Enna and drive towards Messina with four divisions. Patton was pleased, surprised, and suspicious. Within three days, however, he had decided that Monty really wanted an Anglo–American race to Messina. "This is a horse race, in which the prestige of the U.S. Army is at stake," he declared. "We must take Messina before the British."[5]

Why the sudden change of heart by Montgomery? The fact is that he was losing interest in the Sicilian campaign. Its outcome was a foregone conclusion; the only question was how long it would take to complete the conquest of the island. Monty had bigger things in mind, as he revealed on 23 July – even as the Canadian division was beginning its eastward push along Route 121 towards Agira – when he cabled Sir Harold Alexander: "Consider the whole operation of extension of war on to mainland must now be handled by Eighth Army as once SICILY is cleared of enemy a great deal of my resources can be put on to mainland." By giving Patton the lion's share of the remaining work on Sicily, Monty could rest his own army and prepare to cross the Straits of Messina, although Allied strategists had not even decided at this point whether to take that step.[6]

The final Allied offensive on Sicily would be under way by Sunday, 1 August. On that date, Patton, after gathering his forces, was to launch his army north of Etna, while the Eighth Army's operation, code-named "Hardgate," would be spearheaded by Sir Oliver Leese's XXX Corps. Leese planned to utilize two divisions, the First Canadian against Regalbuto on the night of 30–31 July, and the newly-arrived British 78th Division against Centuripe two nights later, followed by a joint drive against Adrano, the key to the main German defensive position at the foot of Etna.

2

It fell to Canadian troops to launch the beginning of the end of the Sicilian campaign. Temporarily attached to the British 78th Division for Hardgate, Brigadier Howard Penhale's Third Brigade was to mount a preliminary operation near the "unpretentious and dirty village" of Catenanuova.[7]

For the past week, while the rest of the First Division had battled its way along Route 121, the Third Brigade had been operating in a semi-independent role on a parallel axis following the arid Dittaino valley. Things had started badly on 23 July, when a twenty-eight-man patrol of the Carleton and York Regiment was wiped out: every member was either killed or captured.[8] That night, possibly emboldened by this episode, two corporals from the Hermann Göring Panzer Division approached the West Nova Scotia Regiment under a white flag. Taken to battalion headquarters, they stated that unless the West Novas surrendered "within the next hour," they would find themselves "attacked in overwhelming force." The adjutant, Captain Clary Higgins, told them to "go to Hell." Nothing untoward happened.[9]

The Nova Scotians played a key role in the capture of Catenanuova. After the Royal 22nd Regiment captured Monte Scalpello, a razor-back ridge towering three thousand feet over the valley of the dry Dittaino, the West Novas attacked Catenanuova at midnight on 29–30 July. Twenty-four minutes earlier, seven regiments of British artillery laid a curtain of shells twelve hundred yards wide across the Dittaino. The West Novas, supported by the Carleton and Yorks, followed the barrage into and through the battered village, which fell with surprising ease. Only later did the Canadians learn that the defenders, in "an unusual case of German cowardice,"[10] had fled. The village had been held by the 923rd Fortress Battalion; because of its "shameful" retreat, the unit was disbanded and its officers court-martialled.[11]

Counter-attacks were not long in coming. The rough terrain, "all hills and folds, slashed by gullies and studded with cactus and olive groves," according to regimental historian Thomas Raddall, "made it possible for their assault groups to approach and appear without warning," resulting in several hours of confused fighting.[12]

One highlight, among many that day, was the Military Cross won by A Company's acting commander, Lieutenant Ross Guy. At one point, German infantry backed by machine-guns and a self-propelled gun firing at point-blank range drove the West Novas back, and Guy reorganized his men in "the dubious cover of a cactus grove and the more substantial protection of a low stone wall." From these positions, they stopped the enemy attack. Guy, in radio contact with battalion headquarters, called for artillery fire from a troop of British self-propelled guns. Although he had had no training in giving artillery targets, Lieutenant-Colonel Pat Bogert gave him a crash course over the radio, and Guy started calling out coordinates for distant targets, correcting them as he observed the explosions. "By some good fortune," he later modestly reported, "fire was brought down on the enemy and forced them to retreat," leaving behind fifty-four dead.[13]

The Third Brigade had done its job, giving the 78th Division a springboard for its attack towards Centuripe. And while casualties had been reasonably light, tougher times were in store for the brigade, and particularly for the gallant West Novas. While the 78th Division struck out for Centuripe, northeast of Catenanuova, Penhale's brigade moved cross-country to fill the narrowing gap between the 78th and the First Canadian Division further north. It was slow going, as the Carleton and York Regiment discovered, negotiating goat tracks winding among steep, arid hills. The West Novas, meanwhile, moved further to the left, to Monte Peloso on 31 July, then advancing on Monte Criscina, midway between the hamlet of Rosamarina and the village of Centuripe. German prisoners warned that the hill was held by paratroopers, members of the recently arrived 3rd Parachute Regiment.[14]

On Monday morning, 2 August, the Nova Scotians were ordered to take Criscina, which the Germans were believed to have abandoned. Two companies sent to occupy the hill found out otherwise. As they moved across the flat, open ground, the German paratroopers opened fire on them, pinning down both companies. Casualties mounted rapidly; the slightest movement drew a hail of bullets and mortar bombs, which led to the nickname, "Whistling Hill." The West Novas were trapped there all afternoon. Not until nearly sundown, when some Vickers machine-guns arrived to provide covering fire, could the survivors of the two companies safely withdraw. It had been the regiment's worst day in Sicily: nineteen dead, twenty-seven wounded.[15]

The stretcher-bearers were overworked, looking after the casualties. Victor Hall, a twenty-two-year-old from Lunenburg, had no time to think about what he was doing. "You just sort of jumped in and did it, to the best of your ability. Whether we did it right or wrong, I don't know." A stretcher-bearer's job, says Hall, was to perform first aid:

All we had to work with was big shell dressings [and] sulphanilamide [anti-bacterial] powder. When a guy got wounded, you ripped open his clothes to get at the wound, and you soaked that in sulphanilamide powder – it was like putting flour on it – and you put big dressings on it, maybe one, two, three, or four. And if his leg was broken, you always used his other leg as a splint. We had morphine all the time, little individual Syrettes, quarter-grain Syrettes of morphine. If the guy was in pain we always gave him a shot of morphine. And we'd mark an M on his forehead, so they knew that he'd had morphine.

Having been made as comfortable as possible, the wounded were taken first to the regimental aid post, and then by Jeep or truck to a field ambulance farther back. But not everyone was lucky enough to get that far. "We had a good many that we pronounced dead right then and there. You'd cover his face with something, stick a rifle in [the ground] by him. I helped to bury dozens and dozens of boys. That was part of our job, too."[16]

Whistling Hill was the last fight by the West Novas in Sicily. Plans for a night assault on Monte Criscina were cancelled when the British took Centuripe and the Canadians captured Regalbuto. Outflanked, the para-troopers evacuated the hill in the darkness, but it was not the last time the Canadians would face these tough fighers on an Italian battlefield. Its task with the 78th Division completed, the Third Brigade reverted to Guy Simonds's command on 3 August.

The fall of Regalbuto capped a bitter, five-day battle by the balance of the Canadian division and the 231st Brigade. Regalbuto was regarded as an important outpost by the Germans, who moved up fresh troops to defend it. For the first time since Grammichele, the Canadians were to grapple with elements of the Hermann Göring Division, which held Regalbuto with its engineer battalion, reinforced with tanks and artillery. These combat engineers were superb soldiers; in Tunisia, forty of them had routed an entire battalion. And they had been given instructions to hold Regalbuto "at all costs."[17]

The 231st Brigade led the drive on Regalbuto. While the two Canadian brigades had battled for Agira, the British brigade, known as the Malta Brigade because of the long service on that island by its three battalions, had come out of the hills to the south and cut Route 121 behind Agira by capturing Monte Campanelli, where the Canadian war cemetery was later located. The 231st began its advance on Regalbuto, six miles east along the main highway, on the morning of 29 July. After a late-evening skirmish with Hermann Göring engineers dug in along a rocky ridge south of

Regalbuto and running parallel to the road, the British backed off and awaited daylight before making their next move.

Regalbuto was arguably a stronger position than either Nissoria or Agira. The terrain, dotted with almond and olive groves, was unusually rugged, even by Sicilian standards. Besides the heavily-defended ridge, Regalbuto was ringed by several hills, including Tower Hill to the east, so named for the old stone look-out on its summit, and Monte Tiglio to the south, where a deep gorge added to the difficult terrain.

The battle opened on Friday night, 30 July, and lasted into Saturday. At the cost of 109 casualties, which attested to the severity of the fighting, the Malta Brigade captured the high ground north and west of Regalbuto, enabling the Canadians to enter the fray.[18]

The Royal Canadian Regiment was the first unit to be committed. After a six-mile march during the evening of 31 July, the RCR was ordered to swing south of Regalbuto and take Tower Hill, whose capture would force the Germans to evacuate the town. However, these orders were not received until late in the day, and darkness had fallen before the battalion commander, Pappy Powers, was able to take his company commanders on a reconnaissance patrol. Captain Strome Galloway complained in his diary that "a recce by a blind man would be just as good." Based on the sketchy information provided by a British patrol, Powers hastily scratched out his plan of attack: three companies in succession, at half-hour intervals, would move out as soon as the officers returned to their companies.[19]

Major Powers confidently declared that his men would "show the Limeys how it's done," but it turned out to be "a proper schemozzle," according to Galloway. No one had seen the steep-sided gorge that lay in their path, and it did not appear on their maps. And there was a German tank parked on the leading company's forming-up place. After a short scrap, D Company worked its way around the tank, then blundered into the gully, where it was later joined by A and B companies. Confusion reigned supreme. Strome Galloway deployed his company "on the steep, terraced slope on the enemy side" of the gully, but every attempt to find a way out of this confined position was stopped by German machine-gun fire.[20] There was no lack of gallantry among the Royal Canadians. The Military Cross was later awarded to Lieutenant Buck Bowman for his audacious leadership, while Private Jim Bancroft won the Military Medal by rescuing two wounded men under a hail of machine-gun fire.

Sunday, 1 August, was a long, hot day for the RCR companies trapped in the gully. "The day passed slowly and the sun blistered down," Strome Galloway wrote in his diary. "Our thirst and hunger was maddening. Occasionally the enemy would let all hell loose and hit the opposite bank behind us." The RCRs spent fourteen hours here, with little water and food to ease their misery. With the blessed arrival of nightfall, they were withdrawn.[21]

Galloway is still disgusted by that experience. "The Regalbuto affair," he writes, "was typical of what happens when things are so rushed that a proper reconnaissance of the ground cannot be made before moving into the attack.... Night attacks are never easy, even when the planning and reconnaissance [are] carried out in daylight, but when [these are] done after dark anything can happen, and usually does – to the enemy's advantage." Had this been an isolated incident, it might have been forgotton, but Galloway would see it happen repeatedly in the coming months. It was, says Galloway, as if the time-honoured military adage, "Time spent in reconnaissance is seldom wasted," had been rewritten by the Canadian army: "No time for reconnaissance, get going!"[22]

The Hastings and Prince Edward Regiment was sent in next. The battalion was in a buoyant mood, due to the return from hospital of the regimental sergeant-major, Angus Duffy, who had been wounded at Assoro. His arm was still in a sling, but the increasing numbers of casualties arriving for medical treatment told him that the regiment, his "family," needed him. Duffy left the hospital without permission and hitch-hiked across Sicily, and later heard that "the Red Tape boys [were] setting in motion the mill to charge me with desertion!"[23]

Perhaps inspired by Duffy's presence, the Hasty Ps succeeded. In sharp contrast to the RCR operation, the Plough Jockeys from southern Ontario were given sufficient time to reconnoitre and plan an attack under their acting commander, Major Bert Kennedy, whose artillery training had come in so handy at Assoro. Now, Kennedy, ill and suffering from a minor leg wound, led his men into action after dark on 1 August. Working their way from hill to hill south of Regalbuto, the Hasty Ps stormed and captured Tower Hill the next morning.

However, Regalbuto had already been abandoned. During the morning, a patrol from the 48th Highlanders slipped into the town and discovered that the Germans were gone. The defenders on Tower Hill had been a rearguard to cover the withdrawal of the troops, tanks, and guns defending Regalbuto. There were few civilians in the town; because of the extensive artillery and aerial bombardment to which it had been subjected, most of the inhabitants had fled. The CBC reporter, Peter Stursberg, who arrived soon after its capture, was appalled at the damage inflicted on Regalbuto. "Houses were gaping open," he later wrote, "and beds and chairs hung crazily over the broken floors. Some of the buildings looked like doll's houses with their fronts off. Rubble filled the streets to such an extent that a bulldozer had to clear the way for our vehicles."[24]

With the fall of Regalbuto, the Canadian division had unknowingly entered the final phase of operations in the Sicilian campaign. While the First and Malta brigades had reduced Regalbuto, the Second Brigade had patrolled aggressively to the north, in the valley of the dry River Salso. For several miles, this terrain was, according to the official history, "unsurpassed in difficulty by any that had gone before." Three notable features had to be seized along the way to Adrano: Hill 736, Monte Revisotto, and Monte Seggio. Until these heights were taken, there could be no safe advance along the river flats.[25]

Into this forbidding zone plunged the Loyal Edmonton Regiment, after a patrol reported that Hill 736, six miles northeast of Regalbuto, was undefended. However, the patrol also warned that "the trails were dried-up stream beds filled with rocks, and going would be difficult even for personnel on mules," a mule train was organized to haul food and ammunition, as well as the battalion's 3-inch mortars and the medium machine-guns of the supporting unit, the Saskatoon Light Infantry.[26]

Pack animals had been used since the early days of the campaign. Plagued by the shortage of trucks, the West Nova Scotia Regiment had sent out a party to scour the countryside for mules and donkeys, paying the owners with "IOUs 'signed' by General Montgomery, Winston Churchill, Roosevelt, Mackenzie King and other worthies who came to mind."[27] They were as valuable as they were cantankerous. "As nobody spoke a language the mules understood," a Seaforth subaltern, Don Harley, later remarked, "and further, as no one understood the mules, we as a support platoon were inefficient and somewhat disorganized." Indeed, Lieutenant Harley was hospitalized when a terrified mule kicked him in the head.[28] The Royal Canadian Army Service Corps eventually organized a ninety-animal platoon for each infantry brigade.[29]

At midnight on 1–2 August, the Edmontons set out. Since they were out of touch much of the time with the rest of the division, war correspondents called them "the Lost Battalion."[30] This was a misnomer; the regiment knew where it was, even if no one else often did. The four rifle companies spent the next four days moving into position for the assault on Hill 736, clashing several times with enemy outposts cleverly concealed in the wilderness terrain.

His grey hair making him look much older than his thirty-six years, Major Archie Donald led the attack. Artillery support was provided by the 25-pounders of the 3rd Canadian Field Regiment, with communications being maintained by an improvised chain of 18-sets and shouted commands. The Eddies' determination was personified by Lieutenant John Dougan, who was wounded in both arms and hands. Gripping his revolver in both injured hands, and ignoring intense pain, he guided his little force across three hundred yards of open ground to the objective. Forty-five men made the final attack upon Hill 736's summit, which was defended by an estimated one hundred Germans. It was no contest: those enemy soldiers who survived the onslaught fled.[31] Donald won the Distinguished Service Order, Dougan got the Military Cross, and Ross Munro later called the Loyal Edmonton Regiment "the finest in the 1st Division during the Sicilian campaign."[32]

Events elsewhere, meanwhile, were having an impact on the Canadian drive through the central Sicilian wilds. The loss of Agira, Regalbuto, and Centuripe to XXX Corps had convinced the Germans to abandon their endangered defences in front of Catania and to withdraw into the main defensive position around the foot of Etna. The withdrawal was marked by extensive demolitions and destruction of ammunition dumps across the front of XIII Corps, and General Montgomery urged XXX Corps to step up its efforts to capture Adrano, the loss of which would disrupt the enemy defences. On the afternoon of 4 August, Sir Oliver Leese ordered the 78th Division to continue its northward push across the Salso and Simeto rivers via Route 121, while the Canadians were to capture Monte Revisotto and Monte Seggio, then force their way through the valley of the Salso.[33]

At this point, Guy Simonds hatched a plan worthy of his reputation as Canada's foremost tactician. Ascending the hill at Centuripe, which offered a panoramic view of the whole battlefield, he saw one of the rare opportunities to properly utilize tanks. The junction of the Salso and Troina rivers gave way to a flat-bottomed valley leading to the Simeto (a real river, unique in this part of Sicily at this time of year). Simonds hurried to Chris Vokes's Second Brigade headquarters to propose an improvised "striking force" to take advantage of the ground and of the situation. Under the command of Lieutenant-Colonel Leslie Booth, this force would consist of Booth's Three Rivers Regiment, the Seaforth Highlanders, and a reconnaissance squadron from the Princess Louise Dragoon Guards, supported by self-propelled and anti-tank guns. First thing the next morning, "Booth Force" would speed down the Salso valley and seize the high ground overlooking the Simeto. "I think that such a move will startle the enemy," Simonds wrote Vokes that evening, "and will probably result in a good mix up in the open country where the Tanks will really be able to manoeuvre. I think Booth will handle such a party well."[34] Clearly, Simonds had forgiven the Three Rivers colonel for his indiscretion in opening his secret instructions prior to departure from Scotland for Sicily.

Thursday, 5 August, would prove to be one of the most propitious days for Canadian soldiers in Sicily. Booth Force surged down the valley at 1000 hours. Within half an hour, after a pleasant drive past orange and lemon groves, the Canadians were practically on their objective, defended by fanatical machine-gunners belonging to the 3rd Parachute Regiment. C Company of the Seaforths dismounted and by rushes began ascending the hill, accompanied by Booth's Shermans. The paratroopers, although lacking anti-tank guns, were cleverly concealed, and Booth "found that the best way to deal with them was to have the tanks scout around the terrain and clean out all suspicious looking places with 75mm H.E. and with blasts of machine-gun fire."[35]

By early afternoon, it was all over. Canadian casualties were light. Forty-three Seaforths were killed or wounded, and two members of the Three Rivers Regiment died in an action historian Reginald Roy rightly describes as "a classic example of exploitation, speed and co-operation."[36] Leslie Booth was later awarded the Distinguished Service Order, a distinction which confirmed Guy Simonds's faith in him.

There was more fighting to be done, but it was anti-climactic. The Loyal Edmonton Regiment had to capture Monte Revisotto, while the PPCLI took Monte Seggio, both falling into Canadian hands on 6 August. The Patricias had their problems. Two companies managed to get lost in the darkness, and by the time they assaulted the hill, the Germans had pulled out.

The Patricias gained Monte Seggio and lost their commanding officer. Chris Vokes had been unhappy with Lieutenant-Colonel Bob Lindsay throughout the Sicilian campaign. The brigadier had been "furious" when two companies of the battalion lost their way during the attack at Nissoria, and Seggio was the last straw. "I felt they had missed an opportunity to deal the enemy a telling blow," Vokes explained,[37] and three days later, he fired Lindsay and replaced him with the second-in-command, Major Cameron Ware, who realized a boyhood dream by taking command of the PPCLI.[38]

(Lindsay was one of two Canadian battalion commanders to lose their jobs in Sicily. The other was Dodd Tweedie, the amiable commanding officer of the Carleton and York Regiment, who was the victim of an apparent personality clash with his brigadier, Howard Penhale.)[39]

When the Van Doos established a bridgehead over the Simeto during the morning of 6 August and sent patrols into Adrano, the Canadian division's operations in Sicily drew to a close. Its five-day drive along the Salso valley had cost the Second Brigade "more than 150 casualties," nearly two-thirds of them among the Loyal Eddies in their strenuous struggles for Hill 736 and Monte Revisotto.[40]

With the fall of Adrano at Etna's foot, the First Division was squeezed out of the line. The whole Allied front was surging forward. Catania had fallen to the British on 5 August, while the Americans had taken Troina, northwest of Adrano, on the morning of the sixth. The constricting front of the advancing armies meant that some formations could be rested, and Montgomery, with one eye still on an as-yet-unauthorized invasion of the Italian mainland, selected the Canadian division for this honour. "It was a well-earned rest," according to the official historian, Gerald Nicholson.[41]

"Apparently this campaign is almost sewed up in the bag," the RCR captain, Strome Galloway, wrote in his diary on 7 August. "For the next few days we remain in our present position" in the vicinity of the Simeto. "That means the RCR will stay in an orange grove and a pear orchard. Well, we've been in far worse places!"[42]

They were now veterans. In their first prolonged confrontation with the enemy, they had proven themselves worthy of the enormous reputation won by their fathers on the battlefields of France and Flanders in 1914–1918. In some respects, they were professionals. Most had enlisted in 1939, and for nearly four years they had done nothing but train for the task of killing Germans. The Canadian engineer chief, Geoff Walsh, considers that the First Division was "extremely well trained and, when I look back on it, far better trained than the divisions we put into Normandy [in the summer of 1944]."[43]

Senior British commanders were pleased with their performance. "The Canadians have made a successful debut," Alexander signalled Prime Minister Churchill on 2 August, "and are fighting well."[44] No less an authority than Montgomery himself gave a ringing endorsement of their capabilities. As he wrote on 27 July to the CIGS, Sir Alan Brooke, "The Canadians are going great guns; they are very willing to learn and they learn very fast; they will be one of the best Divisions I have in due course."[45]

His most adept student was the divisional commander, Guy Simonds. What Montgomery liked best about this young, handsome major-general was that he appeared to be a mirror-image of himself – intense, dedicated, ruthless. All he needed, Monty informed Andy McNaughton, was a bit of polishing to perfect his command skills: "Simmonds [sic] has got to learn the art of command just as his Division has got to learn the art of battle fighting. I shall teach him; and he is learning well. He will be a 1st Class Div. Comd. in due course, and he will have a 1st Class Division."[46]

Simonds was the best general officer Canada produced during World War II. Innovative, daring, ambitious, he had few rivals among Canadian battlefield commanders. But the short campaign in Sicily revealed all of his flaws, including strict adherence to occasionally unrealistic plans, even to the point of reinforcing failure. He had committed these errors at Nissoria, a minor action by any measure, but he went on to repeat them on a grander scale, with greater consequences, in Normandy in August 1944 and in the

Howard Graham showed that he had much to learn about dealing with subordinates. But mistakes are an inevitable part of war, and it must be said that Simonds was under an incredible amount of pressure throughout the Sicilian campaign. Not only was he aware that he was being vetted by Monty, he was being watched by an entire nation of armchair generals. He was commanding a division whose predecessor had achieved near-legendary status during the Great War. The unrelenting strain must have had some effect, personally and professionally. This, too, was part of his learning experience and something that could never be duplicated in training.

The Canadian general later attributed success in Sicily to teamwork. "What I want to emphasize," he said in a CBC interview, "is that all these operations have been successful because each arm and service has gone full out to do its share – and though the spectacular actions sometimes fall to individual units and the infantry bear the brunt of the fighting, the ultimate success has resulted because of the contributions made by all."[47]

Sicily had been a proving ground for the Canadians. The cost, while not as high as anticipated, was heavy enough. In four weeks of fighting on this arid island, Canadian casualties totalled 2,310: 562 dead, 1,664 wounded,* 84 taken prisoner. (Most authorities refer to the losses in Sicily as "light," but these figures rival Canadian combat casualties in the battles around Ortona that were to come during December.) All of the dead were eventually collected and reinterred in a cemetery on a lonely hilltop east of Agira. The Agira Canadian War Cemetery is the only exclusively Canadian military cemetery in Italy.

3

Sicily was an exciting, even exhilarating, experience for one small, dedicated group of individuals. Only a handful of Canadian war correspondents reached the battle zone, and they milked it for every story they could get out of it. They included Ross Munro of Canadian Press, the CBC's Peter Stursberg, and Lionel Shapiro of the Montreal *Gazette*. Munro, famous across Canada thanks to his report from the D-Day beaches, continued to keep close to the troops as they sliced into Sicily. "It was a breath-taking business keeping up with the speeding Division," he remembers, "and trying to write its day-to-day story as it happened. We could never bivouac

---

* These figures were far below those anticipated by the Canadian medical authorities. Their worst-case scenario forecast 3,200 wounded who would require evacuation during the first seven days of the invasion, 1,500 more during the second week, and a weekly average of 875 for the balance of the campaign.[48]

trying to write its day-to-day story as it happened. We could never bivouac in the same place for two nights and we bounced around in a jeep throughout the daylight hours, going to the forward units to check on some incident and then rushing back to headquarters to get more information."[49]

The newspapermen had it easy, compared to their CBC colleague, Peter Stursberg. Because there had been no room in the invasion fleet for the bulky recording equipment he required to do his job, Stursberg could do no more than write stories and cable them to his office in Tunis. Later, Stursberg flew to Allied Force Headquarters in Algiers, where the nearest shortwave station was located, and transmitted his stories to London, where they were re-recorded for transmission to Canada. They were recorded once again at CBC studios in either Montreal or Toronto before being aired.[50]

When Stursberg returned to Sicily, he took with him an engineer, Paul Johnson. Together, they scored a broadcast first by recording the pipe band of Vancouver's Seaforth Highlanders, who played "Retreat" before a huge crowd in the main square in battered Agira on 30 July. This was the first sound recording to come from conquered territory; while the CBC broadcast it across Canada, the BBC beamed it around the world.[51]

One of the most beloved newsmen was the Toronto *Telegram*'s Bert Wemp, a decorated Great War flyer and a former mayor of Toronto. Charged with covering Toronto's contributions to the war effort, he carried out his assignment with boundless enthusiasm. Wemp became famous for his query: "Anybody here from Toronto?" His stories, said fellow journalist Wallace Reyburn, "read like the Toronto telephone directories." His colleagues joked that if and when Rome was captured, his report would read: "Today Rome was liberated. Among those present from Toronto were . . ." Wemp was ribbed so often about his Toronto bias that one day he agreed to visit the Loyal Edmonton Regiment. "Do you know something," he said on his return a couple of hours later, "it was amazing. I hadn't been there five minutes before I met four guys from Toronto!"[52]

Censorship was a fact of life for the correspondents. A few veterans, like Ross Munro, "didn't find it that tough,"[53] but others, no less gifted, encountered difficulties. The *Globe and Mail*'s Ralph Allen, whose temper matched his red hair, had a much different opinion of the censors, contending that they often "reached depths of stupidity hitherto unplumbed by man." Allen once filed a story that ended with the sentence, "It was a capsule inferno." In his cable, however, the sentence was shortened to "IT WAS CAPSULE INFERNO." The censors deleted it with the explanation: "The name of the town of Capsule Inferno has not been released yet."[54]

These men were not the only ones recording Canada's war in Sicily. The First Division brought with it a historical officer, Captain Gus Sesia, and a war artist, Lieutenant Will Ogilvie. They could thank for their appointments Major Charles Stacey, who was in command of the tiny Historical Section at Canadian Military Headquarters in London. "The British scorned the idea of having historians in the field," but Stacey saw to it that the Canadians attached historical officers to divisions and corps, although it took some time to assemble a qualified staff. A staff officer, Sesia was given "a crash course in historical work" by Stacey and sent to Sicily with the First Division.[55]

Like everyone else in the division, Sesia had to learn his trade on the job. He later complained to Stacey that senior officers treated him, initially, "as a headquarters dogsbody instead of letting him get out to interview knowledgeable people and advise units and formations on how to keep their records, which was what he was there for."[56] Eventually, by trial and error, Sesia was able to work out a method of interviewing people about their combat experiences. In the beginning, most officers were frustratingly reticent, but once Sesia honed his skills, he found that most talked "a blue streak."[57]

Sesia's field reports, together with those of his successors, proved to be invaluable in the compilation of the excellent official history, *The Canadians in Italy*. But his work had more immediate value. As Major (soon to be Lieutenant-Colonel) Stacey, at CMHQ in London, sifted through the documents, it occurred to him that this was "material of great potential training value. Here was information hot off the griddle, about how the war was being fought by those in contact with the enemy, the problems they were encountering and the expedients they were using to overcome them. Should this material merely be filed away for the 'future use of the Official Historian'?" Stacey thought not, and he began circulating summaries to high-ranking authorities. He added with characteristic modesty: "I would like to think that the information we circulated this way made a tiny contribution to winning the war."[58]

Significant though Sesia's work was, it was overshadowed by the contributions of the divisional war artist. "The historical triumph in Sicily was Will Ogilvie's," Stacey maintained. "I know of no other pictorial record of a campaign anywhere to match the one Ogilvie made in Sicily."[59]

Forty-two years old, the South African-born Ogilvie was the first official war artist hired by Stacey, and his colleagues, such as Charles Comfort and Lawren Harris, considered him to be the best of the Canadian artists. "Ogilvie," writes historian Bill McAndrew, "combined a soldier's capacity to endure nonsense with an artist's imagination to identify essence." Wading ashore on D-Day with his sketch books and pencils waterproofed in a gas cape, Ogilvie drew his first sketches of activities on the beaches. Hitch-hiking from unit to unit, walking when a ride was not available, he compiled his "notes," as he called his drawings and sketches, which he completed later.[60]

The fruits of Ogilvie's labour of love comprised "35 magnificent water-colours," which Stacey believed constituted "a really amazing record of the Canadian operations in Sicily." These were the first of approximately three thousand sketches, drawings, watercolours, and oil paintings compiled by Canadian artists in the course of the Italian campaign. Sadly, the vast majority of these works have never been seen. Stacey found it "extraordinary . . . that the custodians of those pictures in Canada – the National Gallery and more recently the Canadian War Museum – have never given the public an opportunity of seeing them all together in one place."[61]

4

Ten days after the Canadians were pulled out of the line, the Sicilian campaign formally ended. On the morning of Tuesday, 17 August, Sir Harold Alexander cabled Prime Minister Churchill: "By 10 A.M. this morning, August 17, 1943, the last German soldier was flung out of Sicily and the whole island is now in our hands."[62] Thirty-eight days had passed since the invasion.

That morning, George Patton had won his race to Messina. Elements of the U.S. 3rd Division entered the city at 0600, four hours ahead of the British 4th Armoured Brigade and a commando unit. Amid great fanfare, the publicity-conscious Patton entered Messina in triumph.

Incredibly, the Germans escaped. Even as the Americans prepared to capture Messina, the one-armed German corps commander, Hans Hube, had crossed the Strait of Messina with the last of his rearguard. The Germans had engineered one of the most dramatic escapes from disaster in military annals: in the first fifteen days of August, the Germans moved 39,951 troops, 94 guns, 47 tanks, 9,605 vehicles, as well as 17,000 tons of ammunition, fuel, and miscellaneous equipment across the straits. In addition, the Germans ferried an estimated 62,000 Italians to the mainland.[63]

Comments American historian Carlo D'Este: "The Allies should have ended the campaign with a stunning victory; instead, by any objective assessment, they gathered a harvest of bitter fruit."[64] The balance sheet offered scant consolation. The Germans lost an estimated 5,000 killed, together with 6,663 men taken prisoner, 78 tanks and armoured cars, 287 guns of various calibres, and 3,500 vehicles. Estimates of Italian casualties totalled 2,000 dead, 5,000 wounded, and 137,000 captured (although the figure is probably closer to 160,000). Allied losses exceeded 19,000 killed, wounded, and taken prisoner: 11,843 by the Eighth Army, 7,402 by the Seventh.[65]

Neither Montgomery nor Patton (already in Eisenhower's doghouse for slapping shell-shocked soldiers) distinguished himself in Sicily, but they were not the only culprits. A list of Allied shortcomings would fill a book; perhaps the biggest was the failure to exploit the command of the sea. As British historian J. F. C. Fuller comments, "in coastal operations he who commands the sea can nearly always find an open flank leading to the enemy's rear – the decisive point in every battle."[66] But, aside from two minor landings by the Seventh Army and one by the Eighth in August, the soldiers made no effort to utilize this advantage.

There has been much criticism of the Allied conduct of the campaign. Many critics quote Germans like Albert Kesselring, who later wrote that "the Allied conception of operations offered many chances" for decisive victory, but these were lost through their "methodical procedure."[67]

Much of the criticism is valid, but most of it overlooks the campaign's obvious merits. Sicily had been a conservative, low-risk undertaking. At a time when the war's momentum was slowly swinging in favour of the Allies, it served as a morale-booster and confidence-builder, not only to the Allied soldiers in the field but – of equal importance – to the civilians supporting them at home.

CHAPTER FIVE

"Morale Is Excellent"

1

"Where do we go from 'Husky'?"[1] President Roosevelt had asked that question in mid-May, but two summit conferences were required before it was answered.

Prime Minister Churchill knew what he wanted to do. As early as 4 April, a month before the plans for Husky had been finalized, the British leader had written that the capture of Sicily was, by itself, "a modest and even petty objective." The real goal should be the Italian mainland, with Sicily serving as "a stepping-stone." Even if Mussolini could keep his country at war, "a footing both on the toe and heel of Italy" would offer advantages, including access to the Balkans, "so that we can foment the insurgents of Albania and Yugoslavia by weapons, supplies and possibly Commandos."[2]

With Husky's preparations under way, Churchill and his advisers had travelled to Washington to confer with Roosevelt. Their conference, code-named "Trident," had begun at the White House on 12 May and reopened the Anglo–American dispute over strategy. All agreed that it would be impossible to mount the cross-Channel invasion of Europe prior to the spring of 1944, which meant a period of several months of inactivity at the conclusion of Husky. The British chiefs of staff argued in their position paper that it was "unthinkable that we should be inactive during these critical months when Russia is engaging about 185 divisions,"[3] and advocated that Italy be knocked out of the war before the end of 1943.

The Americans were not impressed. Resurrecting the arguments presented at the Casablanca Conference in January, they remained reluctant to commit themselves to further effort in the Mediterranean, fearing that the drain on resources might further delay the cross-Channel invasion of Europe, now scheduled for the spring of 1944. Brooke, to his surprise, found that there was still bitterness among his American colleagues who, he wrote, "are taking the attitude that we led them down the garden path by taking them to North Africa. That at Casablanca we again misled them by inducing them to attack Sicily. And now they do not intend to be led astray again."[4]

With difficulty, a compromise was worked out. In exchange for a British commitment to a target date (1 May 1944) for the cross-Channel invasion, soon to be code-named "Overlord," the American chiefs of staff lifted their opposition to limited operations in the Mediterranean. The resolution signed by Churchill and Roosevelt authorized General Eisenhower, "as a matter of urgency, to plan such operations in exploitation of 'Husky' as are best calculated to eliminate Italy from the War and to contain the maximum number of German forces" – but the final decision on specific operations would be left to the Combined Chiefs of Staff. There was only one certainty, that no additional forces would be allocated to this theatre; four American and three British divisions were to be transferred to the United Kingdom after 1 November to participate in Overlord, and the air forces in the Mediterranean would also be substantially cut back.[5]

Preliminary planning for a possible invasion of mainland Italy had been under way since the end of May at Eisenhower's Allied Force Headquarters. The planners were governed by one cardinal principle, that any landing must be protected by Allied air power. This reduced the selection of invasion sites to a 180-mile radius from northeastern Sicily, for that was the maximum range of a Spitfire. But no decisions were made until Husky's outcome had been ascertained. Eisenhower's planners, anticipating that the campaign in Sicily would be over by 15 August, proposed several operations, but the most promising were code-named "Baytown" (a British crossing of the Strait of Messina at Reggio di Calabria), "Buttress" (a British amphibious operation thirty-five miles up the coast from Reggio), and "Avalanche" (an Anglo–American landing in Salerno Bay, south of Naples).

The choices were made on 16 August, when Eisenhower hosted a conference of commanders-in-chief at Carthage. At this meeting, the consensus was "to proceed at the earliest possible moment to a full-scale invasion on the lines of the boldest plan which had been considered." Given the limited numbers of landing craft available in the theatre, only two operations were possible: Baytown and Avalanche.[6] Baytown was assigned to Montgomery's Eighth Army, while Avalanche was handed to the newly-organized U.S. Fifth Army, under Lieutenant-General Mark Clark.

Monty, as usual, was unhappy with the arrangements. "In my view," he later wrote, "AVALANCHE was a good operation to carry out; everything should have been put into it from the very beginning, and all endeavours concentrated on making it a great success. This was not done."[7] His own operation, Baytown, did not seem to offer much potential. The Eighth Army, coming ashore at Reggio, would be separated from the Fifth Army at Salerno by three hundred miles of rugged mountainous terrain. If Monty's forces got into trouble, Clark's army would soon threaten the enemy rear; but if Clark got into trouble, it would be extremely difficult, if not impossible, for the British to bail him out.

Geography, it seems, did not play a significant role in planning the invasion of mainland Italy. There was woefully little grasp of the difficulties the invaders would face, according to British historian G. A. Shepperd, who points to the Apennine mountain range which runs the length of Italy and the rivers that plunge from the peaks. "These natural barriers inhibit large-scale military movement except on the established coastal roads, particularly in winter when rivers are often in spate," Shepperd writes. "In addition the extensive mountainous areas, themselves formidable barriers, favour the defence and operations launched against 'the grain of the country' invariably prove both slow and costly."[8] There was, in historian Sir William Jackson's view, plenty of evidence to indicate "that the soft underbelly of Europe might turn into a crocodile's tail."[9]

There were few precedents. Any student of military history could have informed the politicians and the planners that, while Italy has been invaded many times over the centuries, almost all of the invasions came from the north, through the Alps. Only once had an invader landed in the south of Italy and made it all the way to the north, the Byzantine general, Belasarius, in the sixth century.

But before anything could be launched, the Americans and British renewed their dispute over strategy. This time their arguments took place in an unlikely location: Canada. Amid great fanfare, President Roosevelt and Prime Minister Churchill travelled to Quebec City for a conference code-named "Quadrant."

Prime Minister King was only too happy to host the conference. As the leader of a medium-sized power, he had to tread warily, according to C. P. Stacey. "A country of 'medium' status, which makes a contribution to victory materially less than those of the great powers, but large enough to be valuable and to represent a heavy sacrifice on its own, is in an awkward position," Stacey noted. "In certain circumstances it may feel with some resentment that it is pouring out blood and treasure in accordance with plans which it had no share in making and over which it has little or no control."[10] And this is exactly what happened.

King was quite content to leave the war's direction to Churchill, despite the apparent drawbacks. For information about the conduct of the war, the Canadian prime minister relied almost exclusively on summaries prepared by Churchill, but these were rarely satisfactory. (It was not until September 1942, for example, that Canada had been notified of the impending invasion of North Africa, Operation Torch; and after Casablanca, Churchill's summary had made a vague reference to "further amphibious offensive operations on a large scale" in the Mediterranean, but had said nothing about invading Sicily.)[11] In return for subordinating Canada's interests to the Allied cause, King asked only for recognition of the part Canada was playing. A modest demand, it was sometimes forgotten amid the war's major crises, as the prime minister had discovered when he had wished to announce the participation of Canadian troops in Husky.

Therefore, King, who was always willing to sacrifice substance to appearance, was delighted when he was asked to host a summit conference at Quebec City in August. It had been Roosevelt's idea, and Churchill readily agreed. King could not participate, of course, since that would set a precedent and possibly encourage other secondary allies to have a say in strategy. But that hardly mattered to King, who readily saw the public-relations advantages of staging this important meeting on Canadian soil. "My own feeling," he told his diary, "is that Churchill and Roosevelt being at Quebec, and myself acting as host, will . . . really be very helpful for me personally," by silencing media and opposition jests that Churchill and Roosevelt were "our war leaders."[12]

The Château Frontenac provided a plush, picturesque setting for the Anglo–American talks, but the gulf between the allies remained as wide as the majestic St. Lawrence itself. From the very first meetings, on 14 August, it was evident that the American position remained unchanged. "We must not jeopardise our sound overall strategy," declared a U.S. chiefs of staff paper, "simply to exploit local successes in a generally accepted secondary theatre, the Mediterranean, where logistical and terrain difficulties preclude decisive and final operations designed to reach the heart of Germany."[13]

Sir Alan Brooke, the chief of the Imperial General Staff, grew increasingly frustrated. No one angered him more than his American counterpart, George Marshall, who continued to vigorously oppose continued fighting in the Mediterranean, despite Brooke's vehement arguments. Discussions on 15 August, he told his diary, "settled nothing. I entirely failed to get Marshall to realize the relation between cross-Channel and Italian operations." The CIGS was appalled when Marshall responded with "a threat . . . that if we pressed our point, the build-up in England would be reduced to that of a small corps and the whole war reoriented towards Japan."[14]

The British responded with a counter-proposal. Churchill suggested that the Allies might undertake a campaign in Italy with strictly limited objectives. "Although I have frequently spoken of the line of the Po or of the Alps as being desirable objectives for us this year in Italy, it is not possible to see so far at present. A very great advantage will have been gained if we stop at the Leghorn–Ancona line [north of Rome]."[15]

By the time the Quebec Conference concluded on 24 August, a number of crucial decisions had been made. The key points, for the purposes of the Italian campaign, included confirmation of the 1 May 1944 target date for Overlord, with that operation being guaranteed priority call on resources. A diversionary invasion of southern France would be undertaken in conjunction with Overlord. And, finally, General Eisenhower was given the green light to knock Italy out of the war and to apply "unrelenting pressure" on the German forces in Italy.[16]

This sudden decisiveness was caused by events elsewhere, which had influenced the conference in favour of continued operations in the Mediterranean. In the midst of their discussions came the secret but electrifying news of peace feelers from Italy's new leader, Marshal Badoglio. Churchill and Roosevelt promptly ordered Eisenhower to initiate discussions, which led to the signing of an armistice on the afternoon of 3 September, although it was not announced until the eighth. (Italy later joined the United Nations by declaring war on Germany on 13 October.) At almost the same time came word from Sir Harold Alexander, on the morning of 17 August, that the Sicilian campaign was officially over. The previous day, Eisenhower's planning conference in Carthage had agreed to mount Baytown and Avalanche against the Italian mainland. Since the commander-in-chief clearly considered these operations to be both practicable and desirable, the Combined Chiefs of Staff were not disposed to disagree and advised that Churchill and Roosevelt give their blessings. "We did so with alacrity," said Churchill, "indeed, it was exactly what I had hoped and striven for." The British prime minister now had what he would fondly call the "Third Front."[17]

Although Mackenzie King had no part in the Quebec Conference, he played the Quebec Conference for its maximum public-relations value. He greeted visitors, had his photograph taken with Churchill and Roosevelt, and hosted dinner parties and receptions. ("These continued lunches, dinners and cocktail parties," Sir Alan Brooke later complained, "were a serious interruption to our work.")[18] In return, Churchill kept him posted on the progress of his discussions with the American president.

Word of the imminent surrender of Italy led naturally to a discussion of the Allied plans to invade the mainland – and possible Canadian participation. Churchill explained to the prime minister that the Canadian formations in Sicily had been taken "out of the fight for a time in order to get ready to invade Italy." However, Churchill indicated that there was a problem with the Canadian army chief overseas, Andy McNaughton, who had raised the legal question "as to whether our men going to Italy was to be regarded as part of the one operation." Surprised, King told Churchill that "I had always understood that Sicily was simply a step to invading Italy, and to the invasion of Europe from the South."[19]

In the meantime, a cable arrived from McNaughton asking for clarification of this point. The First Army commander was under the impression that the First Division and the armoured brigade were to be returned to the United Kingdom at the conclusion of the Sicilian campaign; Sir Archibald Nye, Brooke's deputy, had earlier advised him that these forces would be "brought back at a not distant date," probably late autumn 1943, "before large-scale operations against North-West Europe."[20]

However, McNaughton's political and military masters in Ottawa had other ideas. They were quite anxious to invade the Italian mainland, for they seemed to share Britain's unspoken enmity towards Italy. After Italy's entry into the war, in June 1940, seventeen thousand Canadians of Italian descent had been declared "enemy aliens" by the federal government, and seven hundred were interned without explanation for up to three years. (It would not be until fifty years later that the Canadian government would apologize for this action.) Now, the army's chief of staff, Ken Stuart, sent a telegram to McNaughton, notifying him that the Allied high command would be authorized "to use Canadians in extension of operations to Italy."[21]

The Canadians were not only going to Italy, they would lead the invasion.

2

Paradise soon ended for the Canadians relaxing around the Simeto. Between 11 and 13 August, the division was transported to the southern edge of the Catania plain, north and east of Grammichele, where it had had its first clash with German troops. It was "a tiresome and dusty trip," according to the RCR captain, Strome Galloway. "In fact, everyone was covered from head to toe in white dust. It was about an eighth of an inch thick on the peak of my cap and my moustache was snow white."[22] The First Division was joined here by the First Army Tank Brigade, soon to be redesignated the First Armoured Brigade. The new camps around Militello and Francofonte would be their home for the rest of August.

Compared to the Simeto, this location left much to be desired. With little shade available, they were exposed to the blast-furnace of the sirocco, a dry, warm breeze which blows across the Mediterranean from North

Africa. "It's a most excellent thing for the laundry business," an artillery captain, David Mathieson, commented in a letter home, "as one can hang up a drippy pair of socks and take 'em down dry in a few minutes." However, it was also a decidedly unhealthy area, with malaria, jaundice, sand-fly fever, and dysentery prevalent.[23]

Medical problems soon arose, and malaria was the worst. Mepacrine tablets to combat the disease had been issued to the Canadians *en route* to Sicily, but the precaution was not taken seriously. The divisional medical officer, Colonel C. H. Playfair, defended his personnel on the grounds that information about malaria "trickled in slowly and seemed incomplete. Time for planning was brief, and there was no time for extensive training of special personnel." Whatever the reason, the inadequate arrangements had dire results. In the second half of August, 1,184 actual or suspected cases of malaria were diagnosed among the Canadians, which amounted to what the official medical history describes as "an epidemic of serious proportions."[24]

The food, for most, was less than palatable. Cliff Evans, at that time a twenty-one-year-old veteran of the Saskatoon Light Infantry, recalls that the heat ruined much of the food. Canned bully beef was particularly affected, he remembers: "the heat was so great that the can would expand and when you opened the can it would run out."[25] Food parcels known as "compo packs," a new innovation which met with a mixed response from the troops, contained a variety of food to sustain fourteen men for twenty-four hours. "Designed by some chairborne genius in England," their contents were less than mouth-watering, according to an obviously disgusted Farley Mowat: "hard-tack biscuits in lieu of bread; canned yellow wax, misleadingly labelled margarine; tins of M & V (unidentifiable scraps of fat and gristle mushed up with equally unidentifiable vegetables); canned processed cheese which tasted like, and may well have been, casein glue; powdered tea, milk and sugar, all ready mixed; turnip jam (laughingly labelled strawberry or raspberry); eight (count them) tiny hard candies for each man. . . ."[26] The unpalatable M & V was dubbed "munch and vomit."[27]

Fortunately, bartering with civilians improved things considerably. Although it was a forbidden activity, most men were soon enjoying an improved diet that included canteloupe, watermelon, pomegranate, grapes, eggplant, tomatoes, pasta, and goat cheese. Among the items the Canadians gladly offered for trade were their rations of Victory, or "V," cigarettes. These "hideous products of India," relates Strome Galloway, were rumoured to be "made out of dried camel dung; at least not tobacco, of that I am sure!"[28]

Despite these inconveniences, the Canadians loved being part of the

Eighth Army. The army had acquired "a great fighting reputation" since its creation in September 1941, General Simonds told the CBC's Peter Stursberg, and he was pleased to report that the Canadians "have been accepted both by its commander and by the formations in it as fully fledged members."[29]

What the Canadians, especially in the lower ranks, liked best was the Eighth Army's air of informality, and they took full advantage of it. Even Montgomery, who cared more about performance than appearance, was surprised by the liberties taken by the Canadians with their apparel. He loved to relate the story of the day his staff car passed a convoy of trucks that had been stopped at the side of the road. When Monty pulled over to have a look, he was greeted by one Canadian truck driver who, he related, "saluted by doffing a silk hat – *and he was stark naked*!"[30]

Guy Simonds was somewhat less tolerant. A vain man who was always immaculately dressed (his nickname at the Royal Military College was "The Count"), he usually expected his men to take the same kind of pride in their appearance. He did make exceptions, however. The divisional engineer, Geoff Walsh, recalls riding with Simonds soon after he issued an edict demanding the troops spruce up their uniforms. Walsh was aware that his bulldozer operators were free spirits, but even he was horrified when they came around a corner and there, sitting on a D-7 bulldozer, was the operator, shirtless and wearing a silk top hat. Walsh braced for a blast from the general, but Simonds surprised him by merely saying, "Well, he seems to be doing a good job!"[31]

With the Canadians in reserve, divisional headquarters made a determined effort to restore some dignity to the proceedings. At this point, recalls Farley Mowat, "a horde of tormentors," non-combatant staff officers, descended upon the hot, dusty plain "and subjected ... the men to ... a pointless persecution, beginning with detailed inspections of everything from carburettors to foreskins." Training resumed, too, much to the disgust of the troops. Mowat contends that "the training was often asinine. . . . It seemed to us that instead of being rewarded for our victories, we were being forced to do penance." Recreation and entertainment left a lot to be desired. The former was limited to a vigorous sports program ("ah, the joys of the hundred-yard dash!") and swims in the sea in closely-guarded convoys, the latter consisted of two-hour concerts by military bands. But all towns and villages were placed out of bounds to Canadian soldiers, who Mowat says "were treated like inmates of a reform school."[32]

Not all of the so-called "brass hats" were dedicated to making a misery of their men's lives. Chris Vokes, the Second Brigade's gruff commander, decided that it was in everyone's best interests to establish a brothel. Morality, he later explained, did not enter the picture: "the mentality of a soldier in the field is that he wants to get drunk and he wants to get laid, because these are pleasant things he may perhaps never experience again. There is no use being mealy-mouthed about it, or not recognizing the fact." However, the brothel was not permitted to open. In his memoirs, Vokes blamed Eighth Army headquarters for killing it, George Kitching, then the senior staff officer at the Canadian divisional headquarters, says the real reason is that "the padres of his brigade and the other senior padres of the division told him that they would not allow it."[33]

While the soldiers "relaxed," the war in the sky continued unabated. Indeed, the air war was one of the most satisfying aspects of the entire Sicilian campaign. For the loss of 375 aircraft, the Allies had destroyed or captured 564 German and 546 Italian planes; of these, 740 had been shot down.[34]

Canadian fighters and bombers had played an important part in this success story. Wellington bombers of the RCAF's 331 Wing had worked unceasingly to cripple the enemy's defensive capability in Sicily and on the southern mainland. Between 4 and 17 August, the three squadrons of Canadian bombers – 420 (City of London), 424 (City of Hamilton), and 425 (Alouette) – focussed their efforts on the Strait of Messina, where the Germans were staging their remarkable evacuation. Repeatedly defying the massive concentration of searchlights and anti-aircraft batteries, the Wellingtons returned night after night to disrupt the enemy movement. Not until Wednesday, 18 August, did 331 Wing receive a well-earned rest; that date marked the first night in August that the RCAF aircraft were not airborne. In the previous seventeen days, one squadron had staged sixteen raids and the others had each mounted fifteen.[35]

The three Wellington squadrons were soon transferred back to the United Kingdom. By the time their temporary duty in the Mediterranean theatre ended in early October, they had flown 2,127 sorties, dropped 3,746 tons of bombs, and dropped 10 million propaganda leaflets. Theirs had been, according to the British official history, "a distinguished spell of service."[36]

Canadian fighter pilots were busy, too. The only Canadian Spitfire squadron in this theatre, 417 (City of Windsor), was one of fifteen fighter formations based on the Catania plain around Lentini, midway between Catania and Augusta, "in the heart of a great valley of wheat."[37] In the two months it was based at Lentini West, 417's work was mainly routine. The Canadian Spitfires spent most of their time "patrolling over Catania and Gerbini, escorting Kittyhawks and medium bombers as they attacked Cape Milazzo and shipping in the Messina strait, and making fighter sweeps along the north coast of the island."[38]

The Luftwaffe was seldom in evidence in Sicily, aside from the periodic night-bombing raids, but the Allied fighter squadrons around Lentini discovered that the enemy still had teeth. The Germans had made a few half-hearted attempts to bomb the airfields, but these had not amounted to much – until the night of 11 August. An estimated fifty German bombers made a routine appearance over Augusta, then swung westwards. Flight Lieutenant Bill Olmsted, a Hamilton native who was a member of the RAF's 232 Squadron, was sitting outside his tent having a beer and swatting flies, under a moon bright enough to read by, when the first signs of trouble appeared: flares, anti-aircraft fire, and explosions at an aerodrome to the east. Within moments, the "loud and clear" drone of approaching aircraft engines told him to find cover, and Olmsted raced to the nearest slit trench.[39]

From this vantage point, the young Canadian pilot watched a disaster unfold. "The 'drome rapidly became a blazing inferno as ammunition dumps exploded and fuel supplies burned fiercely. The grass started to burn, aircraft caught on fire, and our few ack-ack gunners were obliterated. The fires, the moon, and the flares made the scene incredibly brilliant with every potential target clearly exposed."[40]

It was all over in less than an hour. As the Germans triumphantly winged into the darkness, they left behind raging fires and delayed-action bombs which continued to explode for the next two days. "Soon everyone was yelling for stretchers," Olmsted recounted. "There were many killed and wounded. . . . Other victims had been blown to bits and their bodies would never be found."[41]

The Allies paid dearly for overconfidence which hovered close to negligence. Out of more than three hundred Spitfires based on the Lentini airfields, Olmsted estimated that only twenty were flyable in the wake of the raid. Most of these were Canadian planes, for 417 Squadron emerged almost unscathed, with only seven Spitfires being damaged and no casualties among its personnel. But Lentini was now firmly lodged in the squadron's history. "For weeks and months thereafter, the old-timers delighted in indoctrinating newcomers with blood-curdling stories of a night in hell."[42]

There were plenty of signs that the army would soon be back in action. A steady stream of senior officers kept the Canadians on their spit-and-polished toes. The first to appear, on 18 August, was Lieutenant-General Miles Dempsey, who commanded XIII Corps, in which the Canadian division was now serving. A familiar face appeared two days later, when Montgomery, accompanied by Guy Simonds, visited the troops. As was his fashion, Monty summoned the men to gather around while he stood on his car. "I regard you now as one of the veteran divisions of my army," he told them, "just as good as any, if not better."[43]

The Canadians "lapped it up," according to the RCR's Strome Galloway. Most generals, says Galloway, were as remote "as Mackenzie King or Gracie Fields," but Monty was different. "Six distinct levels of command existed between the man with the rifle and 'Monty.' These levels were platoon, company, battalion, brigade, division and corps. Yet, to the private soldier the Army Commander seemed to be his own personal commander, with no one else really in between."[44]

Andy McNaughton showed up, too. At the invitation of General Alexander, he arrived in Sicily on 21 August for a six-day stay, during which McNaughton was kept continually busy, touring the Sicilian battlefields and visiting every Canadian unit. He was still smarting from his humiliation at Montgomery's hands in July. Although the Canadian commander never forgave him, Monty did attempt to make amends by writing a long personal letter during the campaign, describing the First Division's exploits, then inviting McNaughton to his villa in the east-coast resort of Taormina, overlooking the strait. It was a luxurious home, and McNaughton could not resist a gibe: "Not going soft, are you, Monty?" The remark, according to Lord Chalfont, reduced his host to "a condition of speechless rage."[45]

McNaughton was in high spirits by the time he flew back to London. "Everywhere morale is excellent – the troops are in fine condition and full of confidence," he reported to National Defence Headquarters in Ottawa.[46]

By the time McNaughton departed, preparations for the invasion of mainland Italy were well under way. Canadian planning for Operation Baytown began as soon as General Dempsey at XIII Corps issued his preliminary instructions on 14 August. Dempsey intended to cross the strait with two divisions, the British 5th on the left on a two-brigade front, and one brigade from the First Canadian Division on the right. Villa San Giovanni was the initial British objective, while the Canadians were to take Reggio di Calabria and its airfield. Dempsey directed that the Canadians would drive directly inland from Reggio, while the British followed the coastal highway northwards.

Three days later, General Simonds released his own plan, which named Howard Penhale's Third Brigade as his assault formation. Detailed planning followed, amid sweltering temperatures and clouds of flies, and the Canadian invasion plan was finalized by 24 August.

No one was sure what to expect from the enemy. Of course, the Italians could not be considered a serious opponent, after their performance in Sicily. The Canadian sector was thinly manned, but two forts near Reggio caused concern. One was known to be unoccupied, but the other boasted four huge 280-millimetre howitzers, with a range of five miles, protected by concrete walls twelve feet thick. The Germans were another matter. A Canadian intelligence summary on the last day of August placed two enemy battalions behind Reggio (the nearest Germans, in fact, turned out to be two battalions of the 29th Panzer Grenadier Division at Bagnara, fifteen miles up the coast). As D-Day, scheduled for 3 September, approached, the critical question remained unanswered: "Would the Germans offer any determined resistance to a landing in southern Calabria?"[47]

It promised to be a physically demanding campaign. The Calabrian peninsula is a mountainous region with few roads. Immediately beyond Reggio, the ground rises to a plateau, the Aspromonte, its granite face steep and terraced. Its highest point is Monte Montalto, 6,400 feet above sea-level. The state highway – Route 18 north of Reggio, Route 112 to the south – ringed the peninsula, "for the most part squeezed tightly against the railroad which hugged the entire shoreline." Inland, two lateral roads, Routes 111 and 112, linked the east and west coasts. "Masterpieces of engineering," these roads snaked their way up and over the Aspromonte, "their gradients stiffer and their turnings more frequent than in any part of Italy outside the Alps." But there were no other major roads, which meant that, as in Sicily, the Canadians would be operating in terrain which offered every advantage to the defenders, whether their intention was to hold the ground or merely to delay the invaders' advance.[48]

It was easy to select a landing site, because there were few suitable ones on the Calabrian coast. The only decent beaches on the strait lay between Villa San Giovanni, the eastern terminus of the Messina ferry, and Reggio, seven miles south, and XIII Corps selected a three-mile front in two gentle, sandy bays divided by the Torrente Torbido, a *fiumara*, a steep, deep watercourse that was dry for most of the year. The Canadian sector, code-named "Fox," was subdivided into two beaches, "Amber" and "Green." The Germans had landed here during their evacuation from Sicily, proving its suitability for landing craft; the enemy had also conveniently left vehicle tracks in the sand leading to the beach exits. The West Nova Scotia Regiment would land on the left, on Amber beach, and strike for Point 305, the site of the Italian coastal battery with its four howitzers, while another Maritime unit, New Brunswick's Carleton and York Regiment, stormed ashore on Green and pushed south through Reggio for the aerodrome. The Royal 22nd Regiment would land a short time later and push inland. Units of Howard Graham's First Brigade would follow through and take the long and winding road that led to San Stefano and Gambarie, atop the Aspromonte.

By 31 August, the Canadian division was ready for its part in Baytown.

The Third Brigade's two assault battalions moved by stages to Mili Marina, just south of Messina and directly across from Reggio, while the Van Doos were taken to Catania. The other two infantry brigades were transported to assembly points near their embarkation beaches at Santa Teresa, ten miles up the coast from Taormina. A mile offshore could be seen the huge rocks which, according to mythology, had been hurled by the enraged Cyclops after Ulysses and his men fled from Etna. Officers of all units were taken to Mili Marina to observe the opposite coast. The RCR's Strome Galloway, viewing the far shore through binoculars, found it "a strange, unreal experience peering at the enemy occupied mainland of Europe from our island springboard."[49]

After nightfall on 2 September, the assault troops were moved from their hiding places in the hills around Mili Marina down to the beaches to await the arrival of their landing craft. The noted war correspondent Ross Munro strolled among the West Novas and Carletons and was surprised to see how relaxed these Maritimers were, sitting on the sand, munching on hardtack, "yawning and joking." Shortly before midnight, LCAs and LCMs began touching down along the shore, and the troops crowded onto them. "There was the crunch, crunch, crunch of a thousand boots on the sand and hobnails on the metal ramps as the infantry went aboard."[50]

By 0230 hours, the little fleet was on its way. "The sea was dead calm, and the faint moonlight gave just enough visibility to disclose general outlines."[51] Seven miles ahead stood the Italian mainland. The Canadians were about to become the first Allied troops to return to continental Europe to stay.

PART TWO

The Spaghetti League

Southern Italy
1943 - 44

CHAPTER SIX

"A Most Curious War"

1

The Italian campaign came to be commonly called "the Spaghetti League," and the Canadians entered it when they splashed ashore at 0430 hours on Friday, 3 September. The date marked the fourth anniversary of Britain's declaration of war.

The two-hour crossing had been uneventful, save for the covering bombardment which exploded over the heads of the invaders crammed into their little assault crafts. At 0330, with the Canadian invasion fleet halfway to Reggio, 530 British artillery pieces, augmented by some American heavy guns and 120 naval guns of varying calibres, opened fire. Reporter Ross Munro, huddled in the landing craft carrying Brigadier Howard Penhale, was dazzled by it. To Munro, it seemed as if the Sicilian shoreline behind him "were exploding in one destructive and supernatural eruption."[1] But Munro, on his fourth amphibious operation, later came to consider it as a colossal waste. "I think they probably used more ammunition that night than they used anywhere before and maybe more ammunition than a division used on D-Day [in Normandy in June 1944]. It was ridiculous. Monty wanted a show."[2]

But there was a more significant aspect to this operation. "This was indeed a Canadian attack on Reggio," Munro observes.[3] Not only were Canadian fighter planes overhead, but "Canadian soldiers and Canadian sailors were operating together at last," wrote historian Joseph Schull. Twelve LCMs of the Royal Canadian Navy's 80th Flotilla took part in Baytown, ferrying Canadian men and supplies across the strait. For the sailors, this was their last hurrah in this theatre, because the Canadian naval presence in the Mediterranean, never large, was soon to dwindle. In October, the 80th Flotilla would return to the United Kingdom, joining the three landing-craft flotillas that had participated in Husky.[4]

The soldiers were ashore by dawn, but both Canadian assault battalions were widely dispersed. Navigation had been hindered by great clouds of dust and smoke caused by the bombardment, which obscured the shore, and by the sharp tidal currents in the strait. The West Novas, hoping to land on Fox Amber beach, put only one company, A, ashore at that point; half of the other assault company landed two miles to the north, in the British sector, while the rest of B was carried far to the south and landed right at Reggio.

Happily, it was an unopposed landing, even easier than at Pachino two months before. The beaches were deserted: no mines, no barbed wire, no defenders. The Canadians had landed in continental Europe – Hitler's celebrated *Festung Europa* – without being shot at or suffering a single casualty. At 0526, the Canadian sector was reported secure.[5]

The assault battalions speedily rounded up their missing sub-units and hurried inland to take their objectives. The Carletons, now commanded by Lieutenant-Colonel John Pangman, swiftly occupied Reggio, which was formally surrendered that morning by a few Italian officers, the first enemy seen by the Canadians on the mainland. "Italian coastal defence troops surrendered everywhere," recalls Munro. "They first came in by hundreds and then by battalions. Without guards they passed back to the beaches to be taken away."[6] After taking the airfield (which was in use by Allied fighters that night), the Carletons dispatched a patrol which raced down the coast as far as Melito. Along the way, this party rounded up a thousand prisoners.[7]

The West Novas, meanwhile, headed for Point 305 and its battery of coastal guns frowning high over the invasion site. The two enemy forts were deserted, save for a pair of sergeants who were only too happy to give up; later, members of the fifty-five-man garrison, which had fled during the bombardment, appeared from nearby hiding places. The forts boasted impressive armament: four 280-millimetre howitzers, along with four 75-millimetre and two 20-millimetre guns. This imposing array of weaponry was captured without a fight, "a comic anti-climax to the night's anticipations and the grim climb in the dawn."[8]

The Royal 22nd Regiment had a similar experience. Landing at 0700 hours, the Van Doos ascended from the beaches to the Reggio–San Stefano road, passing a fort *en route*. The defenders enthusiastically surrendered. According to a CBC correspondent, Marcel Ouimet, the Van Doos discovered "the [Italian] officers having breakfast in their well-pressed uniforms and freshly-polished boots while a few yards away navy guns lay idle, their caissons filled with shells."[9]

Senior officers were soon coming ashore, accompanied by the follow-up units. The brigadier, Howard Penhale, landed at 0630, followed later in the morning by Guy Simonds and Bernard Montgomery, who stepped onto Italy's mainland at 1030 hours. "It was," Monty wrote that evening, "a great thrill once more to set foot on the Continent from which we were pushed off three years ago, at Dunkirk!!"[10] Penhale experienced "the stiffest resistance of the day." The portly brigadier established his headquarters at the Reggio zoo, where "a loose wildcat," escaped from a shell-torn cage, took "a fancy to the Brigade Commander." The animal was driven off by small-arms fire.[11]

The absence of opposition forced the Canadians to improvise. The original plan had called for Howard Graham's First Brigade to pass through the Third, with Chris Vokes's Second driving inland. But, with no resistance in sight, Simonds ordered Penhale to take Graham's objectives; only then would the First Brigade move ahead. Toronto's 48th Highlanders, behind skirling pipes, led the Ontario brigade up the long, winding road towards San Stefano, with the Hasty Ps close at hand. In the opposite direction, hordes of Italians marched happily into captivity. "They refused to take their capture seriously," Farley Mowat complains, "and they showed a boundless desire to fraternize and to be amiable even to the extent of wishing to supply the addresses of their girl friends to the Canadians who would soon be going north."[12]

Not even darkness halted the Canadians. It was 0200 hours on 4 September before the 48th and Hasty Ps finally stopped for a welcome sleep on the steep, wooded slopes. They were only five miles inland, but they had travelled at least twice that distance along the tortuous road from Reggio. "The day had been a scorcher," says the 48th regimental history, "but now they experienced the great contrast between the palpitating, oppressive heat of the Sicilian plain [and] Italy's cool, mist-shrouded slopes."[13]

As they slept in meadows and along the roadside, the tired Canadians could take satisfaction in the day's work. The invasion of mainland Italy had cost nine Canadian casualties, all wounded, although none of these injuries had been incurred by the assault formations on the beaches of Calabria. There had been no shortage of prisoners: XIII Corps rounded up an estimated three thousand Italians (and three Germans) on D-Day. The British 5th Division, supported by Shermans of the Ontario Regiment, had pushed along the coast road to the outskirts of Scilla. "We never fired a shot, but we had a lot of fun," recalls Captain Ned Amy, who was serving with the Ontarios. "It was beautiful country on that side of the peninsula, just sheer drops into the water."[14]

For five more days, the Canadians drove into the heart of Calabria. It was rugged terrain, reminding Ross Munro of "the Laurentians or parts of the Rockies" in Canada.[15] The single, narrow road allocated to them was soon dubbed "Maple Leaf Highway," decorated with signs featuring a gold maple leaf on a red background and featuring the order, YOU ARE A CANADIAN – DRIVE LIKE ONE.[16] General Simonds was forced to deploy his brigades one at a time on the mountain road, which featured hair-raising hairpin turns overlooking sheer drops of more than a thousand feet.

It was ideal countryside for delaying tactics, executed with excellence by enemy demolition teams. The first of many man-made obstacles was located near the village of Straorini, where the Germans had blown the bridge. The seventy-foot gap was expertly filled by a Bailey bridge (described as "overgrown Meccano sets" by one regimental history)[17] installed by the 1st Field Company, Royal Canadian Engineers, but the episode set the pattern for what was to follow: "craters, blown bridges and more craters."[18] The engineers soon became the unsung heroes of the Canadian advance. Doug Harkness, the future cabinet minister who was serving as second-in-command of the 1st Anti-Tank Regiment, says the engineers "did a terrific job. If it hadn't been for the Bailey bridges, I don't know how long we'd've been stuck there in southern Italy."[19]

Steady if slow progress was made by the Canadian division. On 4 September, on the outskirts of the village of Gambarie, the 48th Highlanders became the first Canadians to clash with enemy troops in mainland Italy. Gambarie, a ski resort in a pine forest, was defended not by Germans but by Italians – Fascist militia known as "Black Shirts." In a brief, one-sided battle the Highlanders killed nine and captured thirty other Black Shirts, along with six field guns and four machine-guns. The prisoners revealed that Germans had been there, but had pulled out just two hours earlier. The booty also included two hundred folding bicycles, which were soon put to good use. B Company rode them fifteen miles north to Delianuova, only to discover that this place, too, had been abandoned by the Germans.[20]

The Second Brigade now moved into the lead, striving to reach Cittanova, a large town on Route 111, one of the lateral highways which crosses the Aspromonte from coast to coast. When the PPCLI were slowed by demolitions along Route 112, Brigadier Chris Vokes sent the Loyal Edmonton Regiment cross-country along a "doubtful track" which might lead to Cittanova.[21]

The Eddies also ran into Italian troops, a hundred German-trained paratroopers of the élite 184th (Nembo) Division, who surprised the Canadians by putting up a spirited fight. "They were exceptionally well turned out," wrote Lieutenant-Colonel Jim Jefferson, "and obviously knew what they were doing. While the action was relatively short, they made a determined stand." The terrain proved to be an even bigger obstacle, and it took the Edmontons most of 7 September to find the track which led overland to Cittanova, followed by a night march through uncharted mountain country. Somehow, they did it, trooping into the town at 0300 hours on the eighth, as the Patricias were approaching from the other side.[22]

Cittanova would always hold happy memories for the men from the Canadian prairies. During their brief stay, the Eddies informally adopted a little boy named Angelo, fitting out the youngster with a pair of boots and sharing rations with him. "I'll always remember Angelo's mother offering the 'widow's mite,' two eggs, to repay us in some way for being kind to her son," wrote Major Jim Stone, a company commander at that time. Twenty-five years later, Stone returned to Cittanova to look for Angelo, the child "who sang so beautifully and who cried his eyes out when he could not leave with us." Sadly, he and his mother had long since moved away, and no one knew their whereabouts.[23]

The West Novas, meanwhile, had a scrap with the same Italians who had hindered the Edmontons. The Nova Scotia battalion was leading the Third Brigade's advance from Delianuova, following in the footsteps of the prairie unit. At 0200 hours on 8 September, the battalion commander, Lieutenant-Colonel Pat Bogert, called a halt, unaware that the Italian paratroopers were camped nearby. An Italian patrol stumbled into the West Nova position, and shooting broke out in the darkness. Colonel Bogert quickly assessed the situation and sent a company to outflank the blue-and-grey-clad paratroopers. The Italians were driven back to a ravine, where Bogert demanded that the officer in command, a major, surrender. "He was reluctant at first, but finally agreed," Bogert recalls.[24]

The West Novas had killed six Italians and captured fifty-seven others, at a cost of two dead.[25] Unfortunately, as Bogert points out, the skirmish was unnecessary. "We were in fact no longer at war with Italy, but neither we nor the Italians knew it."[26]

Word of Italy's surrender came over the BBC news at 1830 hours. It arrived in time to enliven the dinner-table conversation at Guy Simonds's headquarters, where several hidden bottles of Scotch were retrieved to celebrate the occasion. While most Canadians greeted the surrender news with indifference, or at most guarded optimism, Italians – soldiers and civilians alike – went wild over the news. Those who had not already surrendered now hurried into the nearest Canadian lines, entertaining their captors "with a display of flares and the joyous discharge of rifles and machine-guns."[27] Buildings were soon graced with graffiti: "Finito Benito."[28]

By the morning of the ninth, there was another major news story: the Anglo–American landing at Salerno, near Naples. These events, important enough in themselves, directly affected the Canadians. Speed was essential if the Eighth Army were to have an impact on the operations developing in southern Italy at this time. While the British 5th Division, following the coast along the state highway, was enjoying relatively smooth sailing, the Canadian division was stalled in the Calabrian mountains.

There were no suitable interior roads, but Route 106, which ran from Reggio around the southern and eastern coasts of Calabria, seemed promising. The divisional axis was thus switched to the coast.

An improvised flying column had already demonstrated the value of the coastal highway. Lieutenant-Colonel Cy Neroutsos, a former Montreal chemist who commanded the Calgary Tanks, had not been pleased that his tanks were being left out of action, for no apparent reason. Anxious to contribute, Neroutsos obtained permission to form a Jock column, a collection of "all the odds and sods that I could get together," which was nicknamed "X Force."[29]

Neroutsos, ordered to "push up the road as far as I could," raced his Jock column along the coast. It was a pleasant journey, with the seashore on one side and a succession of summer homes and sleepy villages on the other. X Force had reached Locri, sixty-four miles from Reggio, by nightfall on 7 September, after an uneventful drive, highlighted by the sighting of a submarine. "We weren't sure whether to shoot at it or not; it might be a friend, it might be a foe, but it wasn't doing anything so we left it alone," remembers Bob Sharp, a sergeant who later commanded the King's Own Calgary Regiment in peacetime.[30]

The few Italians encountered by X Force readily surrendered, and by late afternoon on 10 September, the Canadians had travelled another sixty miles, reaching Catanzaro, a city of twenty thousand that lay five miles from the coast. The capture of Catanzaro was, as Neroutsos proudly points out, "entirely a bloodless affair." The brief history of X Force ends here, for the Jock column had served its purpose and was disbanded.[31]

Not far from Catanzaro lay a prize of sorts. The 104th (Mantova) Division, fully equipped and a potential threat if it chose to ignore the national surrender, was headquartered in the area, and both the Hasty Ps and the Royal Canadians later claimed to have captured it. However, it was a modest achievement, because the commander, Generale di Divisione Guido Bologna, a "fat and sweating gentleman," was quite happy to hand over his fifteen thousand men and all of their weapons, vehicles, and supplies.[32]

By now, the Canadians were self-conscious about their appearance. Compared to the nattily-attired Italians, they resembled ragamuffins. They were still clad in their tropical clothing, a necessity in summertime Sicily but utterly inadequate for the mountains of mainland Italy with autumn on its way. Until supplies of warmer battledress arrived, most Canadian soldiers dressed in whatever captured clothing appeared to offer a degree of warmth, with hilarious results. A PPCLI subaltern, Syd Frost, described himself in a letter to his mother back home in Toronto:

I would like to have a picture of myself now. Besides a good bit of mustache, I've got a good week's beard. My uniform consists of whatever I can get to keep warm, and it is a bit chilly this morning. I have an old pair of German pants, a summer drill shirt, home-knit sweater, German shirt, battle dress blouse, and a pair of Australian boots! Fine looking officer, eh wot! I've got maps, binoculars, compass, etc, hung about me, and . . . I usually carry a German pistol or my issue revolver. My head-dress is anything I happen to have at hand: a beret, skull cap, field service cap, or nothing at all. All in all, I am a peculiar looking specimen.[33]

After a four-day break at Catanzaro, the Canadians went back to work, putting on a dazzling display of mobile warfare.

Their drive into mainland Italy resumed on Wednesday, 15 September. It was a wild ride, and accidents were inevitable on the precarious coastal highway, portions of it "merely a modified form of goat track"[34]: one claimed the lives of three members of the 48th Highlanders when their truck overturned.[35] Then there was the more familiar danger, booby traps. Four engineers were killed and one wounded when they attempted to dismantle a roadblock.[36]

As usual, the engineers were never far from the front, and were often in the lead. The divisional engineer chief, Geoff Walsh, roved far ahead in his Jeep, "to assess what had to be done so we could prepare the troops properly to do the job. It was easier to go and take a look yourself." The Germans continued to try to slow the Canadians by demolishing many of the bridges that lay along their route, but the engineers had the answers. Instead of installing the portable Bailey bridges – which were in short supply, in any event – the Canadians constructed "Irish" bridges, filling the gaps with stones, which enabled water to trickle through while the convoys of vehicles continued on their hectic journey.[37]

By Friday night, 17 September, the leading elements of the division had reached the area of Spezzano, Cassano, and Villapiana, a hundred miles from Catanzaro. Along the way, the Canadians were given a new and urgent assignment. The large town of Potenza, 125 miles north, was a key road and rail centre, and General Alexander named it as the Eighth Army's prime objective during the next phase of operations. The corps commander, General Dempsey, ordered Guy Simonds and his division to take it.

Simonds created a Jock column, similar to X Force, which had been so spectacular a week earlier. Composed of Calgary Tanks, with artillery, machine-guns, and engineers, its primary element was the West Nova

Scotia Regiment. It was commanded by Lieutenant-Colonel Pat Bogert, after whom this improvised unit was named "Boforce."

In the early afternoon of the seventeenth, Boforce set off on a sixty-hour dash to Potenza. Colonel Bogert's column followed the coastal highway for twenty-five miles to Nova Siri, then swung inland along Route 92. "The countryside was mountainous," says the West Novas' history, "with dense forests of conifers and deep gorges like the hills of Cape Breton, with an admirable site for a German ambush at every turn of the dizzy road."[38]

By nightfall on 19 September, Boforce had reached Potenza. The column had been delayed by blown bridges, but the speed of the Canadian thrust had caught the Germans by surprise, for they had no time to conduct their usual thorough job of demolitions and mine-laying. Potenza, a town of thirty thousand, sat on a twenty-seven-hundred-foot hill overlooking the dry bed of the River Basento. Besides a number of fine churches, Potenza boasted many blocks of modern apartment buildings, which offered ideal defensive positions. Unsure whether the town was defended – he had had conflicting reports – Bogert waited until after dark before sending three companies into Potenza.[39]

The white buildings gleamed in the moonlight as the West Novas crossed the valley into the town. Potenza, they found, was defended by a hundred paratroopers, equipped with "an unusually large number of automatic weapons,"[40] and a fierce firefight soon broke out.

By daylight on 20 September, it was apparent that the West Novas would need help. "I had men in Potenza," Bogert remembers, "but exactly where in this big town it was impossible to say, which made artillery support virtually impossible." Brigadier Penhale – watching the battle with General Simonds from the West Novas' headquarters across the valley – sent the Van Doos to outflank Potenza to the east, while Boforce's engineers cleared the approach to the town. "When our tanks rather reluctantly moved forward," says Bogert, "we found the enemy gone."[41] They left behind sixteen prisoners, members of the 3rd Parachute Regiment, but the fighting had cost the West Novas six killed and twenty-one wounded.[42]

With Potenza as a base, the Canadians confined themselves to patrolwork for the rest of the month, and prepared for their next phase of operations. The First Division could look back with fondness on its work during September. Its 375-mile advance from Reggio had been highlighted by the absence of heavy fighting, as reflected by the relatively light casualties: 32 killed, 146 wounded, 3 prisoners of war.[43] But the sickness toll was alarming – 1,500 men were ill, most of them suffering from malaria and jaundice (infectious hepatitis).[44]

The most notable case of illness was that of the divisional commander, Guy Simonds. On 22 September he was confined to quarters with jaundice; a week later, he was evacuated to a British casualty clearing station at Bari. The Second Brigade's blustery Chris Vokes was named as acting divisional commander. "I was rather startled to find myself in command of the division," Vokes would write, pointing out that Howard Penhale was the senior brigadier at this time. "I had no expectation that it would happen."[45]

In Vokes's place at the head of the Second Brigade was the Seaforths' Bert Hoffmeister. A militia officer and business executive from Vancouver, Hoffmeister was emerging as a major figure in the Canadian army's contingent in Italy. "He was just so bloody efficient and so dynamic," war correspondent Doug How says of Hoffmeister. "He'd walk through shell fire as though it didn't exist. A tremendous soldier."[46]

Both appointments, originally intended to be temporary, were confirmed on 1 November, when Vokes was promoted to major-general and Hoffmeister became a brigadier.

2

As the Canadians and British had discovered, the Germans were not prepared to put up a fight in the extreme south of Italy's mainland. And it took the enemy until early November 1943 to formulate a firm policy.

Hitler, as always, was reluctant to give up ground. His generals had repeatedly urged retreat in Russia, and the Führer had just as adamantly rejected their advice. Italy was no different. "The Führer will not withdraw from the Italian mainland under any circumstances," Joseph Goebbels had recorded in his diary in February 1943. "He has no intention of retreating north to the river Po, even if Italy itself pulls right out of the war. It is the supreme principle of German overall strategy to keep fighting as far as possible from our homeland."[47]

Yet for several weeks it seemed as if Hitler would abandon southern Italy. This was the advice of his favourite field-marshal, Erwin Rommel, the famed and feared "Desert Fox," who had been appointed in August to command the newly created Army Group B in northern Italy. Rommel argued that it was not practical to defend Italy anywhere other than in the far north, where the threat of Allied amphibious operations would be minimized. His belief carried considerable weight, because Hitler had already resolved that "at a time yet to be decided" Rommel would assume responsibility for all German forces in Italy.[48]

But Rommel was almost alone in advocating the evacuation of most of mainland Italy. Albert Kesselring, the commander-in-chief in southern Italy, insisted that the Allied advance could be blocked below Rome, where the narrow peninsula required only half the troops necessary to man the mountains in the north. But Kesselring's optimism was not wholly appreciated by Hitler, who considered him to be "incredibly naive politically."[49]

The Allied invasion of mainland Italy on 3 September, followed five days later by Italy's surrender, had infuriated Hitler. "It is in fact quite obvious that our Italian alliance has been of much more service to our enemies than to ourselves," he raged. "If, in spite of all our efforts, we fail to win this war, the Italian alliance will have contributed to our defeat!"[50]

For several days, the picture had seemed quite bleak for Germany, but events in Italy combined to restore the Führer's confidence. The first was Operation "Achse," or Axis, which Hitler had prepared in case of Italy's betrayal. As soon as the surrender became known, German forces seized control of the country and disarmed the Italian armed services. By the time the operation was over, the Germans acquired 440 tanks, 2,000 guns, and 500,000 rifles, and had shipped to Germany 268,000 Italians (soldiers and civilians, who were utilized as forced labour), and 50,000 Allied prisoners of war.[51]

On 12 September, Mussolini had been rescued by German commandos from his prison in the ski resort Gran Sasso d'Italia, the highest peak in the Apennines, northeast of Rome. Mussolini was later returned to power as the leader of a puppet state in northern Italy. The Germans also defied Allied air and naval power by successfully evacuating Corsica and Sardinia. "It was completely incomprehensible to us," Kesselring later commented, "that the withdrawal of the German forces from Sardinia and Corsica could have been carried out with almost no interference by the Allied sea and air striking forces. This enabled over thirty thousand soldiers with full equipment to be transferred safely to the mainland." The garrison was reorganized into the 90th Panzer Grenadier Division, a welcome addition to Kesselring's weak forces.[52]

To top it all off, the Germans had come within an ace of defeating the Allied landing at Salerno. Only naval guns and air power saved the American and British ground forces from being crushed by the enemy armour; the situation became so serious that an evacuation plan was drawn up. But by the evening of the sixteenth, the Germans had to admit failure.

The cumulative effect of these events was to restore morale and confidence to the German leaders. The only difficulty, for Hitler, was that his advisers were convinced that the the real objective of Allied operations in the Mediterranean was not Italy, but the Balkans, and the Führer refused to commit substantial forces until the enemy's intentions had been made clear.

Until that happened, it was Kesselring's job to buy time. With no reinforcements available, Kesselring ordered Heinrich von Vietinghoff's Tenth Army to conduct a fighting withdrawal to the Bernhard Line between Gaeta and Ortona, eighty-five miles apart. According to Kesselring, the Bernhard Line (the Allies labelled it the Winter Line) was "one of a series of defensive lines to be occupied . . . in the retrograde movement toward Rome."[53] Although the line was only partly built at this time, Kesselring hoped "to create an impregnable system of positions in depth, and so save German blood."[54]

Meanwhile, Hitler vacillated. Unable to assess Allied intentions accurately, and torn between the conflicting views of Rommel and Kesselring, the German leader wrestled with the problem.

Finally, in early November, Hitler would make up his mind: he would fight for Italy. On the fifth, he would assign Rommel to northwestern Europe, where he was to oversee the strengthening of the coastal defences for the impending Allied invasion. The next day, appointing Kesselring his supreme commander in Italy, the Führer's instructions specified that "the Bernhard Line will mark the end of withdrawals." On the twenty-first, Kesselring was designated Commander-in-Chief Southwest, while his two field armies became Army Group C.[55]

A disappointed Rommel wrote his wife, "Maybe I aroused no great hopes that the position would be held."[56]

The German defence of Italy may have been hastily improvised, but the Allied plans for the conquest of the peninsula left even more to be desired. "If the planning and conduct of the campaign in Sicily were bad," General Montgomery later wrote, "the preparations for the invasion of Italy, and the subsequent conduct of the campaign in that country, were worse still."[57]

During August, Monty had tried repeatedly to get some direction from General Alexander. Not until the twentieth did the army-group commander give him an outline of the proposed invasion of the mainland. On 5 September, two days after his forces landed on Italy's toe, Monty was still pressing, unsuccessfully, for a definite plan of action. "We must have a master plan and know how we propose to develop these operations," he argued, to no avail.[58]

But the lack of direction could be seen even higher. Not even the campaign's primary proponent, Winston Churchill, could make up his mind. His first inclination was for a strictly limited advance that did not necessarily include either Naples or Rome. On 9 September, the day of the Salerno landing, he had advocated an advance to the main German defence line, whereupon the Allies would build "a strong fortified line of our own," and remain on the defensive until the spring of 1944, when a decision could be made regarding offensive operations. In the meantime, the Allies could "supply agents, arms, and good direction" to the partisans in the Balkans.[59]

He was soon singing a different tune. On 13 September, in a telegram to the Combined Chiefs of Staff, he argued that "our prime duty is to accelerate the build-up in Italy.... We must on no account be guilty of failing to nourish the battle.... This is the moment for intensification of effort and for running small-scale risks audaciously. If we fail to profit by our good fortune now, we shall lose in History the credit we have so painfully gained."[60]

As the Allies drove deeper into Italy, Montgomery's concern mounted. In his diary on 20 September, he scribbled a stinging indictment of Allied planning: "There was no object laid down. The whole affair was haphazard and untidy – in fact typically British."[61]

The campaign unfolded haphazardly and untidily. Although the Salerno landing had come within a hair's breadth of disaster, it had been saved at the cost of British-American relations in Italy. The American commander, Mark Clark, believed that Monty dragged his heels in coming to the aid of the hard-pressed Fifth Army, which had staved off defeat before British and American patrols linked up on 16 September. When Monty declared, "I ... saved their bacon,"[62] Clark never forgot the slap in the face.

Once the Fifth Army broke out of its beachhead, it drove towards Naples, while Monty's Eighth Army headed for the airfields around Foggia in southeastern Italy. These had been secured by the beginning of October. But by the end of October, the Allied position had improved only marginally. Monty continued to complain that Allied planning was still "haphazard and go-as-you-like," and he realized that there was trouble ahead unless the campaign was given some strategic direction, and quickly. To Monty, it was a simple matter. "The Allies," he wrote, "have not got the resources in [landing] craft and shipping to fight two major campaigns at the same time. If ITALY is to be the main theatre, then turn the tap on there and leave it on till you have got what you wanted. . . . If Western EUROPE is to be the main theatre, then turn the tap on there; in this case you must not expect spectacular results in ITALY."[63]

To make matters worse, the Allies were also working against the calendar. The Quebec Conference's deadline of 1 November, when divisions and landing craft would be removed from Italy and dispatched to the United Kingdom in preparation for Overlord, was fast approaching. Churchill pleaded with Roosevelt against prematurely shifting the landing craft. "This will cripple Mediterranean operations," he argued, "without the said craft influencing events elsewhere for many months."[64]

The Anglo–American strategy rift, so carefully patched at Quebec, was re-opening. Churchill sought desperately to keep the campaign going. "We must not let this great Italian battle degenerate into a deadlock," he cabled Roosevelt on 26 October, once again raising the stakes. "At all costs we must win Rome and the airfields to the north of it. The fact that the enemy have diverted such powerful forces to this theatre vindicates our strategy. No one can doubt that by knocking out Italy we have enormously helped the Russian advance in the only way in which it could have been helped at this time. I feel that Eisenhower and Alexander must have what they need to win the battle in Italy, no matter what effect is produced on subsequent operations."[65]

Lack of commitment continued to endanger the Italian campaign. There was no over-all plan, comments British historian Nigel Hamilton, "for no one knew why the Allies were in Italy, apart from the need to 'knock Italy out of the war' and to take possession of the Foggia airfields. Now that Italy *had* been knocked out and the Foggia airfields [captured by] Eighth Army, there was a vacuum in the councils of Allied power."[66]

Incredibly, Canada was preparing to pour more men and equipment into this strategic vacuum.

3

Five thousand miles from Italy, life in Canada continued to be almost embarrassingly normal in September 1943. As Labour Day approached, most people were looking forward to the last long weekend of summer. Two million children were getting ready to go back to school, as an opinion poll (one of the earliest conducted by George Gallup, through the Canadian Institute of Public Opinion) indicated that 76 per cent of Canadians approved sex-education classes in the schools.[67]

The nation had been thrilled by the news of the invasion of mainland Italy. From coast to coast, editorial opinion was unanimous. "Canada is proud to have her brave men in the vanguard of this new advance," remarked the *Toronto Star* on 3 September. "They will acquit themselves with honor to their native land; in some cases their adopted land." Declared the *Winnipeg Free Press*: "Germany, we profoundly believe, knows that the war is lost." In Ottawa, the *Evening Citizen* welcomed "the opening of the second front," but warned, perceptively, that "hard fighting" lay ahead; "the Italian mainland does lend itself to stubborn defence operations such as the three German divisions put up in Sicily."

Prime Minister Mackenzie King was pleased to see these sentiments. The country seemed to be fascinated by the Italian campaign, which made him even happier – because he had just approved a proposal to dispatch another division, complete with a corps headquarters, to the Mediterranean.

The proposal had first been made on 10 July, the date that Canadian troops took part in the invasion of Sicily. King had composed a long memo regarding his afternoon meeting with Defence Minister Ralston and Lieutenant-General J. C. Murchie, the vice-chief of the General Staff. Murchie was representing Ken Stuart, the CGS, who was on his way to the Mediterranean but who had sent a report proposing the dispatch of another division to that theatre.

The meeting had rehashed the familiar debate between keeping the Canadian army intact for the cross-Channel invasion, as Andy McNaughton preferred to do, or getting it into action as soon as possible, anywhere, in order to obtain combat experience, for the fighting men and their commanders. "R. clearly favours early action for most or all of our men," wrote King, who just as clearly – at this moment – favoured McNaughton's policy. The prime minister argued that it made more sense to conserve Canada's army for the final showdown, "to bring Hitler to his knees."[68]

It was evident, so far as Ralston and Stuart were concerned, that McNaughton was the stumbling block. If the stubborn general could be removed, or at least discredited, the prime minister might be more amenable to their arguments. As historian C. P. Stacey has noted, "both Ralston and Stuart were convinced that McNaughton had to go."[69]

In late July, Ralston had flown to England to join Stuart for a confrontation with McNaughton, who was still smarting from his humiliation at Montgomery's hands in Sicily. McNaughton, understandably, had nothing good to say about Allied strategy in the Mediterranean, and Ralston and Stuart were unable to convince him of the merits of transferring a corps headquarters and another division to that theatre. Stuart bluntly told him that this proposal would be pursued, with or without his approval. Stuart even went so far as to threaten to disband McNaughton's headquarters and place the remaining Canadian formations in the United Kingdom under British command – an "extraordinary" suggestion, according to Stacey, flying "in the face of military good sense as well as the Canadian tradition."[70]

McNaughton bowed to the inevitable. Although he angrily accused Ralston of not caring "anything about the Canadian Army,"[71] he reluctantly gave his approval to the plan to post a Canadian corps in the Mediterranean theatre, on the understanding that it "would return to the United Kingdom if the decisive attack on Germany was to be launched from here."[72]

But Ralston and Stuart were out to get McNaughton. Before returning to Canada to attend the Quebec Conference, they had compiled evidence that the army commander was unfit for his position, reporting to Prime Minister King that senior British commanders "had expressed surprise at the judgment McNaughton had shown in military exercises earlier in the year" and that they "no longer felt confidence in McNaughton's capacity to command troops in actual combat." Stuart even went so far as to suggest Harry Crerar as a successor, stating, with considerable exaggeration, that the British were "particularly enthusiastic" about him, that "he was an exceptionally good officer, and . . . very popular with the men."[73]

However, King wavered. His mistrust of Ralston and his respect for McNaughton notwithstanding, he was haunted by the spectre of conscription, knowing that if the army was heavily engaged, casualties would be commensurate; if conscription became necessary, he feared for national unity. As recently as 18 June, King's war committee had been given an estimate forecasting 115,000 Canadian casualties in the next sixteen months. "No word I have thus far heard caused me greater pain in my heart than the thought all of this implied in the lives of the men serving in the Army and to our young country."[74] It was, for King, a crucial consideration.

By the end of August, he had decided what to do: the First Canadian Army must be split. (And make no mistake, it was King's decision. "If King had sided against Italy, with any determination," historian Stacey wrote later, "I think there can be little doubt that he would have carried the day.")[75] As he commented in his diary, "The more of our men participate in the campaign in Italy, the fewer there are likely to be who will be involved in the crossing of the Channel which, as Churchill says, will be a very tough business." On the thirty-first, in a meeting with Churchill, he had outlined the Canadian desire to dispatch a division and a corps headquarters to the Mediterranean.[76]

Churchill agreed to consider King's request, but for a time it appeared that McNaughton had nothing to worry about. On 14 September, the Canadian general was told by Sir Alan Brooke that the ultimate factor was the availability of shipping, a conundrum which plagued Allied planning throughout the war. The CIGS warned that the situation was so serious that not only was it unlikely that more Canadians could be sent to the Mediterranean, but it was doubtful that the First Division could be brought back to England before the invasion of France.[77] Even Ken Stuart realized that the chances of building up Canadian forces in Italy were "remote."[78]

An intense lobbying campaign by the Canadian government paid off. Badgered by Vincent Massey, Canada's high commissioner in London, Churchill pressured the War Office to find a solution.

On 7 October, Brooke told McNaughton that he had come up with a plan to accommodate the Canadians. The CIGS wished to bring XXX Corps headquarters and the veteran 7th Armoured Division to England; if a Canadian armoured division went to the Mediterranean, the two units could simply swap equipment, which would minimize the transportation difficulties. Pending approval by both Churchill and King, preparations for the transfer were begun immediately under the code name "Timberwolf." Because of shipping schedules, the Canadians would be moved in three stages: 25,000 troops would move to Italy in November, followed by 10,000 in December and 4,000 in January.[79]

Prime Minister King was pleased with this development. "There will remain a Canadian Army Corps in Britain. Then, when the main assault comes, instead of our men bearing the brunt of this assault, it will be divided between the British, Americans, and ourselves. . . . This, I think, will mean a considerable saving of life of our own troops and it will also have the advantage of Canada sharing in such successes as there may be in the south as well as in the north."[80]

On 12 October, Churchill cabled to Ottawa a formal request to carry out the transfer, and Timberwolf was launched the next day, as soon as Prime Minister King's approval was received. McNaughton selected Harry Crerar's I Corps headquarters, as well as the newest of his formations, the Fifth Armoured Division, to go to Italy. Originally organized in March 1941 as the First Armoured Division, it had arrived in the United Kingdom in the autumn of that year. Later redesignated the Fifth Armoured Division, it underwent a number of organizational changes, but by the autumn of 1943 its primary components were the Fifth Armoured Brigade (Lord Strathcona's Horse, British Columbia Dragoons, and 8th New Brunswick Hussars) and the Eleventh Infantry Brigade (Cape Breton Highlanders, Perth Regiment, and Irish Regiment of Canada). The key support elements included a motorized infantry battalion, the Westminster Regiment, a reconnaissance unit, the Governor-General's Horse Guards, and an armoured-car unit, the Royal Canadian Dragoons. However, the division would need a new commander; Major-General C. R. S. Stein was about to be declared medically unfit for further overseas service.

The corps commander, General Crerar, and an advance party flew to Algiers on 24 October, to make administrative preparations for the move from Britain to Italy. The balance of his headquarters, with ancillary units and the armoured division, sailed from Scotland on 27 October.

These forces were unwanted. No one in the Mediterranean had been informed of the decision, and the key players reacted with astonishment. The Allied commander-in-chief, General Eisenhower, complained to the Combined Chiefs of Staff that "the arrival of these troops at this time is likely to cause us considerable embarrassment. . . . The aspect which causes me most concern is the pressure I anticipate will be put upon me to get these troops into action at an early date. I cannot guarantee to do this."[81] General Alexander, the army-group commander, was intensely annoyed. "The proposed move of the Canadian Armoured Division has come as a complete surprise to me," he telegraphed Brooke. "We already have as much armour in the Mediterranean as we can usefully employ in Italy. I should have preferred another Canadian Infantry Division. . . . I do not want another Corps Headquarters at this stage. I shall be grateful if I can be consulted in future before matters of such importance are agreed upon."[82]

McNaughton carried out his orders, but he was not happy about them. With the dispatch to Italy of a corps headquarters, two divisions, and an armoured brigade, First Canadian Army in England was left with a single corps and three divisions (one armoured and two infantry), plus an independent armoured brigade, but McNaughton could do nothing except rage privately about "the deliberate break-up of the Canadian Army."[83] (A British corps was later added to the army, which was now Canadian in name only.) McNaughton later complained that the decision to reinforce the Mediterranean "had been a political one; not a military one." He also warned Prime Minister King that "there is a real danger of the Army 'evaporating' unless we can hold the control that we should over our own men; that there is this danger of it being used in pieces."[84]

His resignation followed soon afterwards. Told by Ralston that he could remain in command of the army, but that he would not be permitted to lead it into battle, McNaughton resigned in early November. To avoid a political crisis, he agreed to the prime minister's request to step down at an unspecified later date. However, it all became academic when his health deteriorated dramatically in December, forcing him to request his immediate replacement. Late in the month Ken Stuart, pending Harry Crerar's return from Italy in early 1944, temporarily took over the army headquarters he was so willing to disband.

It was a sad end to McNaughton's military career. While no one could credibly contend that he was the right choice to lead the First Canadian Army into combat, it was nevertheless a shabby way to treat the man known as the "father of the Canadian Army." Although McNaughton would return to the national stage within a year, war correspondent Lionel Shapiro contended that "his illness was not of the body. He suffered from a broken heart." Recalling his famous statement comparing the Canadian army to a dagger pointed at the heart of Berlin, Shapiro noted that "McNaughton's dagger had become more handle than blade."[85]

The final chapter in this episode was to be written in May 1944, when the Canadian government began pleading with the British to reunite its overseas forces. Over the signature of General Murchie, who succeeded Stuart as CGS, a cable would be dispatched on 19 May to the First Army's General Crerar, declaring that "from a national point of view," it was now "highly desirable" that "such formations now serving in the

Mediterranean theatre . . . should be grouped under unified Canadian Command." Crerar was instructed to present this case to British authorities.[86]

Even before I Canadian Corps fought its first action in Italy, the Canadian government, which had lobbied long and hard to get it there in the first place, sought the return of the corps to northwest Europe, a corps which had been unwanted by the British commanders in the Mediterranean. The Canadian army in England had been split, over the vigorous protests of Andy McNaughton, who lost his job in the process. Now it had come full circle. "Canadian policy in this matter, doubtful at best, was made to look thoroughly silly," Stacey sagely noted. "A policy which is inimical to effective national control of the forces, and at the same time is open to criticism on military grounds, has little to recommend it."[87]

CHAPTER SEVEN

"Monty's Mountain Goats"

1

Campobasso, a picturesque city nestled in the eastern foothills of the Apennines, was the next Canadian objective. After resting in the vicinity of Potenza, the Canadians were moved northwards to Lucera, where they would operate on the left of a two-pronged thrust mounted by the Eighth Army. While the British 78th Division followed the main highway from Foggia along the east coast towards the small port of Termoli, the First Canadian Division was sent into the mountains from Lucera, due west of Foggia. Twelve miles from Lucera, Route 17 climbed rapidly, "following a sinuous course which doubled and sometimes trebled the airline distances between the hilltop towns along its route." The first town was Motta Montecorvino, the goal of another one of the those grand improvisations, a Jock column comprising Princess Louise Dragoon Guards armoured cars, the Calgary Tanks, and The Royal Canadian Regiment, with the usual array of anti-tank and field guns, commanded by Lieutenant-Colonel Cy Neroutsos of the Calgaries. The vanguard of the First Division moved out of Lucera during the morning of Friday, 1 October, past the great castle dating back to Frederick II.[1]

It soon became apparent that the Germans intended to fight for possession of Motta. The Plugs leading Colonel Neroutsos's flying column came under heavy machine-gun and shell fire shortly after 0800 hours, and the Canadians deployed for a tank-infantry assault. Because of a massive traffic jam between Foggia and Lucera, it took most of the day to arrange an assault by two squadrons of Calgary Shermans and two platoons of Major Strome Galloway's B Company of the RCR. The tanks broke into Motta – Lieutenant A. J. Charbonneau won the Military Cross when his Sherman attacked an enemy anti-tank gun head-on – but the infantry were soon pinned down by enemy artillery and machine-guns. "It only took a short time for me to realize," Galloway wrote in his diary afterwards, "that my two platoons were not going to be strong enough to carry the town. . . . Every time they tried to get forward they drew heavy fire from both flanks.

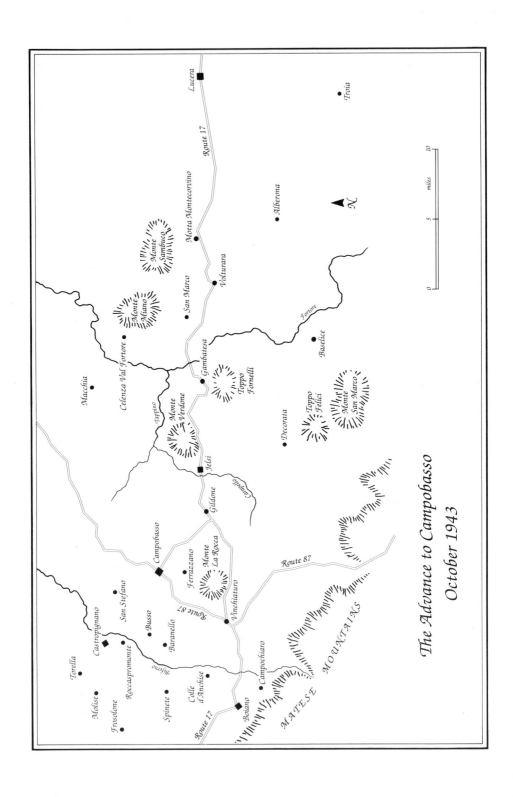

The Advance to Campobasso
October 1943

The ground was such that there was no other line of advance open for a daylight attack." A heavier attack, with artillery support and another company of the RCR, was laid on that night. This, too, ran into severe opposition, which was finally broken when Galloway's men outflanked the town. The Germans wasted no time pulling out, and Galloway watched them leave: "Ten enemy vehicles with full headlights could be seen tearing down the winding road on the other side of the town, in full flight, making for the high ground to the West."[2]

The rest of the Royal Canadians swarmed into Motta, and a happy Lieutenant-Colonel Dan Spry greeted Galloway: "The Mayor of Motta, I presume?" The major replied, "Sir, the town is yours!"[3] But this savage little battle had cost the RCR seven dead and a similar number of wounded.

More stiff fighting lay ahead. The German paratroopers – the same unit which had held Potenza – had merely retired to another ridge a little over a mile away, where the Calgaries ran into grief. A single anti-tank gun stopped the advance cold by knocking out six Shermans in swift succession. The German gunners were in "a beautiful position," according to Sergeant Bob Sharp, and they calmly "picked off the lead tank, and picked off the sixth tank, then picked off the four in between."[4]

These Canadians had experienced the enemy's new and effective delaying tactics. These called for, according to the official history, "determined and fierce resistance up to an unpredictable point, then rapid withdrawal to another dominant feature."[5] The terrain was ideal for such tactics, according to Pat Bogert, who commanded the West Nova Scotia Regiment at this time:

The [few] roads were intersected by water-courses, mountain torrents or dry river beds – serious obstacles and good defensive positions. Kesselring's men did not mind surrendering Italian ground provided that a good price was paid. At each obstacle we found the bridge blown, mines laid, and well-armed infantry seemed to be in some strength (in reality, probably a company or less) but every man with an automatic weapon and plenty of ammunition. We would launch an attack, perhaps in battalion strength, and suffer a few casualties. As we closed on the enemy position he would withdraw, leaving his unexpended ammunition and perhaps some weapons. There were few pieces of flat ground off the road where guns could be deployed or vehicles parked; these would be registered by enemy artillery and engaged when he thought we had occupied them.[6]

This is precisely what happened beyond Motta, at Monte Sambuco, Volturara, and San Marco, where the gallant Strome Galloway was wounded. By 6 October, a five-day advance had carried the Canadian division to the River Fortore, eighteen miles from its starting point at Lucera. The Third Brigade took over the lead, but the Canadians continued to find the going slow. (They might have felt better had they been able to read the war diary of the 26th Panzer Division, which noted that "the First Canadian Infantry Division had appeared again, which explains the rapid advance of the enemy.")[7]

The Germans continued to make skilful use of mines to further slow the Canadian advance along the few roads available to them. Among the forty types of anti-tank devices employed by the enemy was the Tellermine, "a flat, cylindrical metal body with a pressure cover to set off the main igniter," which packed a ten-to-twelve-pound charge.[8] Some were encased in wood or plastic, which made them difficult to detect, while others were detonated by a ratchet system, set to explode after a certain number of vehicles had depressed the mechanism. Captain Howard Mitchell, commanding his mortar battery in the divisional support unit, the Saskatoon Light Infantry, observed the disheartening effects of the delayed-action mines. "In one ten foot section of the road," he writes, "I saw three vehicles blown up the same day. A squadron of tanks had gone over the road. The second truck in the convoy was blown up. The engineers searched and found nothing. Fifty more trucks passed and then another explosion. More searching, twenty more vehicles passed, then another explosion."[9] One Tellermine detonated under a Jeepload of wounded men; four members of the 48th Highlanders died in the blast.[10]

The slow Canadian advance was causing concern at Eighth Army headquarters. "Canadian threat against Campobasso and Vinchiaturo meeting stiff opposition," General Montgomery had signalled General Alexander on 5 October, suggesting that an American division of the Fifth Army "operate energetically" to "force the enemy to give ground in front of the Canadians."[11] However, the Americans were too busy to offer meaningful assistance. By now the British, supported by tanks of the Three Rivers Regiment – in action for the first time since Sicily – had captured Termoli, and the Germans were free to concentrate their limited resources against the Canadians, who were still thirty miles from Vinchiaturo. It was obvious that things were not going to get easier.

After further skirmishes with the 29th Panzer Grenadier Division at Gambatesa and Toppo Fornelli, and at Jelsi and Gildone, the Canadians finally moved to within striking distance of Campobasso. The First Brigade's Howard Graham was given added incentive to capture Campobasso quickly, when he was paid a visit by the corps commander, General Dempsey. Graham assured the British general that his brigade would be in Campobasso by 14 October, barring a heavy counter-attack. "Good," replied Dempsey, "if you have cleared the place by the 15th, I'll bring you a bottle of Marsala."[12]

Led by Toronto's 48th Highlanders, the First Brigade set out at 0630 hours on Wednesday, 13 October. By midmorning, the 48th was within two miles of Campobasso, without having seen an enemy soldier. Then one company, inspecting the hilltop village of Ferrazzano, skirmished with a small group of Germans. This clash alerted the enemy to the impending threat to Campobasso, and heavy shell-fire was played along the road, forcing the 48th to take cover and delaying the arrival of The Royal Canadian and Hastings and Prince Edward regiments until after nightfall. As a result, the assault on Campobasso was postponed until morning: it would be mounted by the RCR, with a diversionary attack from Ferrazzano by the Hasty Ps.

Surprisingly, Campobasso fell without a fight. The Royal Canadians entered the city at 0530 hours on 14 October to find that the enemy had pulled out. (To save face, the 29th Panzer Grenadier Division later reported that it evacuated Campobasso "after a hard battle," possibly because the city had once served as the headquarters of Albert Kesselring, the enemy commander-in-chief in Italy.)[13] As promised, Brigadier Graham got his bottle of sweet Sicilian wine from General Dempsey. "But, sad to say, I did not taste a drop," he wrote, for the bottle fell off his table and smashed to pieces.[14]

When Bert Hoffmeister's Second Brigade, after a gruelling cross-country push parallel to Route 17, captured nearby Vinchiatura the next day and pursued the Germans to the River Biferno, the Canadians were given some time to rest and reorganize. While the infantry patrolled along the Biferno, and the Canadian artillery honed their counter-battery skills to discourage the enemy's long-range shelling, Campobasso became the centre of attention. This provincial capital consisted of an old town, at the foot of a 350-foot, thirteenth-century citadel, and "a modern section, whose wide streets were flanked by imposing municipal and provincial administrative buildings, banks and schools – all built during the Fascist era."[15]

The Canadians had big plans for Campobasso. "With typical North American hustle Campobasso in a matter of days had been converted into the best-remembered recreation centre of the war," wrote historian George Stevens. The amenities included canteens operated by the Salvation Army, the YMCA, the Canadian Legion, and the Knights of Columbus, clubs for officers and for other ranks, theatres, cinemas, reading rooms, and mobile baths. Campobasso, noted historian Stevens, "was christened 'Maple Leaf City' and the Italian civilians undoubtedly obtained a most favourable if not entirely accurate impression of how Canadians lived it up at home."[16]

Since the major recreational activities for Canadian soldiers were, as Chris Vokes pointed out earlier, "to get drunk" and "to get laid," it is difficult to see how the Italians could possibly have formed a "favourable" impression of Canadians.

Perched in the mountains around Campobasso, Canadian soldiers found a new nickname for themselves. "They seem to like sticking us right up in the hills," artillery Major Duff Mitchell noted in a letter home, "so we have nicknamed ourselves 'Monty's Mountain goats.'"[17]

During the second half of October, the division consolidated its hold on the east bank of the Biferno. It had been assumed that the opposing formations, the 26th Panzer and 29th Panzer Grenadier divisions, would withdraw to the far side following the capture of Campobasso, but it was soon apparent that the remaining enemy outposts would have to be attacked. However, these proved to be no match for battle-hardened units like The Royal Canadian Regiment, which attacked the village of Busso on 19 October. Captain Tommy Burdett, temporarily commanding Strome Galloway's B Company, "staged a perfect battle-drill movement" and captured the twenty-man garrison.[18]

The Canadians were soon attempting to pry the enemy out of their holdings on the far side of the Biferno. On the extreme left, the Carleton and Yorks pushed towards Boiano, the first town on Route 17 west of the Biferno, but they took a roundabout route to get there. For six days, the hardy New Brunswickers worked their way along the foot of the Matese Mountains, a sheer wall to their left, in terrain that was virtually impassable. Along the way, they occupied Campochiaro, where they became the subjects of a famous photograph showing them crouching and crawling along a narrow, stepped street in search of snipers. The fighting was sporadic, as the Germans obeyed their orders to delay the Canadian advance for a short time before withdrawing. The capture of Boiano, on 24 October, was anti-climactic: it had been heavily bombed and shelled during the past several days, and the enemy had vacated it. The Carletons had completed their task with only thirteen casualties, but forty other men were classified as ill, most of them suffering from exhaustion.

In the meantime, the Loyal Eddies and Princess Patricias had established a bridgehead at Colle d'Anchise and Spinete in a hard-fought battle, but the biggest operation on the Biferno involved all three battalions of the First Brigade. The far bank facing Howard Graham's formations was an "almost sheer rampart," upon which were perched two villages, Roccaspromonte and Castropignano (the latter soon dubbed "Castropigface" by the Canadians), a mile apart. Patrols confirmed that the only suitable crossing point for vehicles was at the site of the demolished bridge on the road to Campobasso. Graham decided to send the Royal Canadians across the river at two spots to capture Roccaspromonte and Castropignano. This would enable the engineers to build a bridge, while the 48th Highlanders and Hasty Ps attacked Molise and Torella.[19]

Some remarkable patrol work by the Hasty Ps had set the stage for this attack. In one foray, four scouts slipped across the river one night and established an outpost in a vineyard. When dawn arrived, they realized that they were in the midst of a panzer-grenadier battalion headquarters. Not the least deterred, they sneaked up to the stone building that was being used as an NCOs' mess, captured a German orderly, drank his coffee, and escaped with the prisoner in tow – all in broad daylight! Another scout, Private George Langstaff (described by Farley Mowat as "lean and soft spoken, with penetrating eyes and a flair for guerrilla operations") spent a full day studying a German company headquarters and the surrounding area. At dusk, his notes completed, he shot the company commander and slipped back to his own lines.[20]

The RCR, in the late afternoon of 24 October, found Roccaspromonte vacated, and Castropignano was captured that night after a brief skirmish. However, a stiff fight awaited them at a nearby hill, Point 761, where a machine-gun post held out until the next day. The 48th Highlanders then passed through and advanced towards Torella, but Brigadier Graham halted them to await armoured support, which arrived on the morning of the twenty-sixth, in the form of Ontario Shermans. Even with tanks, the Highlanders had difficulty crossing "the treeless, rolling uplands"; enemy fire sweeping the bare ridges in front of Torella cost the 48th more than twenty casualties, including Private Alf Kneen, who had his injured arm amputated by a stretcher-bearer and then asked, as he was being carried away, "Please give me the ring off that hand, eh?" That night, the Germans withdrew, and Torella fell to the Highlanders on the morning of 27 October.[21]

At the same time, the Hasty Ps crossed the Biferno and marched to Molise. It was an unopposed but arduous advance, across twelve miles of wooded ravines and ridges. In Molise, they were greeted by, in the words of Lieutenant-Colonel Lord Tweedsmuir, "a formidable array of Italian flags and a very shifty looking mayor." This area was a Fascist hotbed, and Tweedsmuir's suspicions were confirmed within a few days by uncannily accurate long-range shelling that inflicted twenty casualties – including six dead – in a short period. Convinced that their positions were being revealed to the enemy by local Fascists, Tweedsmuir called in the shifty-looking mayor and warned him that unless the shelling ceased, he might shoot some townspeople. "That," said the youthful colonel, "quieted them down."[22]

This action ended major operations by the Canadian division for the time being. By the end of the month, the Germans withdrew to the River Sangro, but by then the Canadians, relieved by British formations, had moved into reserve. "It had been manoeuvres with live ammunition rather than war," historian George Stevens later wrote of this period. "The adversary was terrain rather than Germans; timing and mobility counted far more than courage and weight of metal."[23] The division and armoured brigade had suffered 630 casualties in the advance from the Foggia plain. The heaviest losses were incurred by the 48th Highlanders, who lost 96 men without fighting a major action. This was, says the official history, "striking evidence of the exacting nature of the routine infantry task" in mountainous Italy.[24]

Illness remained a nagging problem. Non-battle casualties during October totalled 2,572, with another 1,859 in November, sixteen times the normal sick rate. "On the whole," says the official Canadian medical history, "sickness presented a more serious medical problem than battle casualties" in this period, and posed "a potential danger to Canadian fighting power."[25]

For the majority of the Canadians, November 1943 was an opportunity to rest and reorganize. On the first of the month, Chris Vokes's and Bert Hoffmeister's promotions (to major-general and brigadier, respectively) were confirmed. Guy Simonds's appointment to command of the soon-to-arrive Fifth Armoured Division was officially announced, and the youthful general bade farewell to the infantry, taking with him George Kitching, who was promoted to brigadier and given command of the armoured divison's infantry brigade.

Another change involved the Third Brigade's Howard Penhale, the gentlemanly Great War veteran, who was replaced by Brigadier Graeme Gibson, fresh from England. Penhale's days had been numbered, for Chris Vokes had considered the Third to have been "the worst brigade in the division in Sicily."[26] Some regimental officers complained he issued "confused" orders,[27] but Ross Munro, the war correspondent, believed that Penhale was simply "too fat" to be taken seriously.[28]

During the month, 1,500 reinforcements arrived to replace the dead, wounded, and ill, although the First Division remained 350 below its authorized strength. Forty-eight-hour leaves were granted for Maple Leaf City, and 4,000 men per week poured into Campobasso to enjoy its comforts.[29] Those in search of intellectual stimulation went to the Beaver Club, where a two-day exhibition of Canadian war art was held in early November. The fifty-four watercolours were viewed by 3,137 soldiers, a "gratifying" number, according to the recently-arrived war artist, forty-three-year-old Charles Comfort. Comfort was pleased "to see knots of men assembled about the paintings and carrying on animated discussions, recalling personal experiences at a particular location, and discussing the merit of the work."[30] Somewhat less aesthetic, and somewhat more anaesthetic, was the work of a PPCLI officer who devised an alcoholic concoction which became legendary at the Aldershot Officers' Club. The "Campobasso Stinger" consisted of "gin, cognac and Rooster Blood – the raw Abruzzi red wine"; it was, according to one survivor, "appalling."[31]

But Campobasso's delights were strictly limited, and winter was on the way. There were unmistakable signs all through November: peasants toiled in their fields, cutting back and tying up vines and collecting firewood, while the leaves changed colour and fell from the trees and bushes. It was soon raining nearly every day, and in the near distance, mountain-tops turned white with their first covering of snow. When it did not rain, a thick mist pervaded the countryside. Farley Mowat, the intrepid intelligence officer of the Hasty Ps, fumed in a letter to a friend that Italy's climate was "the worst in the whole bloody world. It either burns the balls off you in summer, or freezes them off in winter. In between, it *rots* them off with endless rains. . . . The first travel agent I see back home with a poster of Sunny Italy in his window is going to get a damn big rock right through the glass."[32]

Campobasso's delights might have been modest, but the Third Brigade and its new commander, Graeme Gibson, had little time to enjoy them. The Eighth Army was about to launch a major offensive across the Sangro, upon which the Germans based their formidable Bernhard, or Winter, Line, the main defensive position below Rome. The Third Brigade's task was two-fold: to stage diversionary operations along the upper Sangro, while at the same time interfering with the enemy's scorched-earth policy, which was denuding the countryside of billets and provisions required by Allied troops. Furthermore, the brigade had to pretend that it was the whole Canadian division, in the hope of deceiving the Germans about General Montgomery's actual intentions.

Gibson's brigade started out on its sixty-mile move from Campobasso to the Sangro on Sunday, 14 November. The move was an engineering triumph, for the Germans had destroyed every bridge and culvert along the way, in addition to cratering roads and dynamiting overhanging cliffs to cause landslides. They also had had time to paint signs. "Welcome to Canadian boys. Come and spend Christmas with us,"[33] read one, while another taunted, "Build your Bailey bridge so we can come back and blow it up."[34] Besides ploughing countless detours and making innumerable repairs, the engineers put up ten Bailey bridges during the second half of November, including a 180-foot span that was completed in less than eighteen hours. The steady rain often turned to snow, and the poor roads were soon reduced to tracks of churned-up mud, yet the Royal Canadian Army Service Corps somehow managed to maintain a steady supply of rations, gasoline, and ammunition, the latter requiring up to 12,000 rounds of 25-pounder ammunition for large-scale bombardments.[35]

The devastation along the Sangro had been conducted with typical Teutonic thoroughness. There were occasional skirmishes between Canadian patrols and parties of paratroopers; the West Novas ambushed one group on 17 November, killing four and forcing the rest to flee. But they were too late to prevent the enemy from scorching the earth. In a zone five miles wide and ten miles long, between Castel di Sangro and Sant' Angelo, "the Germans had seized all food stocks and cattle, evicted the unfortunate inhabitants and then demolished and burned their homes." When the Royal 22nd Regiment arrived in the village of San Pietro during the evening of the eighteenth, not a house had been left standing. The brigade war diary recounted a sad litany of destruction: "Castle del Guidice visibly burning. . . . S. Pietro flattened, also burning. Ateleta observed burning. Capracotta also burning." Thousands of refugees had to be fed, clothed, and sheltered by the Canadians, adding a further strain to the divisional transportation system.[36]

By the twenty-second, the Third Brigade had done its job well. Aggressive patrolling and skilful shooting by the artillery had cleared the Germans from the near side of the Sangro, with one exception. An estimated twenty to thirty paratroopers were holed up in a monastery atop Point 1009, the rocky pinnacle that towered over Castel di Sangro. The West Novas were assigned the task of clearing the Germans from this vantage point, and at 0100 hours on 23 September, Captain F. H. Burns and B Company set out to take it.

Burns and his men walked into a trap. In the rain and darkness, the Nova Scotians worked their way up the muddy, slippery slopes, and found that there was only one way to get at the monastery, along a narrow path. Burns deployed two platoons to give covering fire from below, while Lieutenant J. B. "Blackie" Blanchard's platoon, firing Bren guns and hurling grenades, rushed the building.

"All hell broke loose," recalls stretcher-bearer Victor Hall. The attackers were caught in a cross-fire by skilfully-sited machine-guns arrayed around the approach to the monastery. Blackie Blanchard fell mortally wounded, but he lived long enough to order his platoon to withdraw. Only a handful escaped, despite the desperate efforts of the rest of the company to come to their rescue. Lieutenant Gordon Romkey, who had recently rejoined the regiment after being wounded in Sicily, was ordered to take his platoon to the right, to try to outflank the Germans. "I ran across to have a look at it," he remembers, "and my batman followed me – he got killed." But the cliff was too steep, and the Germans were now showering them with hand grenades. With the approach of daylight, the West Novas were left with an unpalatable choice, retreat or die. According to Hall, "we all ran for our lives."[37] In a matter of minutes, the battalion had lost five killed, ten wounded, and sixteen taken prisoner.[38]

Two days later, the West Novas returned to Point 1009. Instead of stealth, they relied on overwhelming force. Two companies scaled the cliffs, while mules brought up mortars and machine-guns of the Saskatoon Light Infantry, and nine field regiments of Canadian and British guns blasted the peak with a prolonged bombardment. But it was unnecessary; the paratroopers had evacuated the place the previous night. "All we found," recalls Lieutenant Romkey, "was three wounded members of the company."[39] Hidden in the cellar, these men had survived the bombardment behind the monastery's four-foot-thick walls.

Point 1009 marked the last action, and the only major one, by the Third Brigade on the Sangro. On 26 November, units of the British 5th Division began moving into the sector, and Brigadier Gibson's battalions headed for the rear. But the rest of the Canadian division had left the Campobasso area for the coast, in preparation for one of the most famous of all Canadian battles, Ortona.

2

During the northward Canadian advance, a new element had entered the picture: escaped Allied prisoners of war (PWs). The first of these had been encountered as early as 26 September, when the Princess Louise Dragoon Guards had passed forty of them on the road to Campobasso, and these numbers increased steadily through October and November on the Biferno and Sangro rivers. Bedraggled and footsore, most staggered in with incredible tales of hardship, harrowing escapes, and the unfailing kindness and courage displayed by Italian peasants in the rugged mountains of the interior.

When the Allies invaded the mainland of Italy, there were an estimated seventy-four thousand Allied PWs in the country. Housed in prison camps in various locations, they were mainly British soldiers, sailors, and airmen who had been captured in the fighting in North Africa and elsewhere in the Mediterranean. But every nationality was represented in Italian prison camps, including Americans, Australians, New Zealanders, Indians, and South Africans, along with a handful of Canadians, mostly flyers.

They led "a peculiar type of life,"[40] as Flight Sergeant Arnold "Skid" Hanes had discovered early on. A member of the RAF's 274 Squadron, Hanes had been one of the first Canadians to be captured in this theatre when his Hurricane fighter was shot down on 7 December 1941 near

Tobruk, Libya. Hanes, who broke both legs, an arm, and a shoulder in the crash, was, as a Canadian, something of a novelty. He was interrogated extensively by the Italians who, more than anything, were puzzled as to why Canada was at war with them. On crude crutches, he ended up at a prison camp, Campo Concentramento Prigionieri di Guerra (CCPG) 59, near Sevigliano, not far from the Adriatic coast near Ascoli. Conditions here, Hanes discovered, were most primitive. "We had cockroaches, we had bedbugs, we had lice, we had fleas. We didn't live any differently than the average peasant in Italy!" he jokes today, although at the time it was not so amusing.[41]

The food was poor and the war news worse at that time, and discipline became the key to maintaining morale. "Everybody would try to look smarter than the Italian guards," Hanes remembers. "If it meant shaving with a broken beer bottle, if you didn't have a razor blade, do it. And if you had to sleep on your pants to put a press in 'em, do it. Everybody tried to keep himself clean, not only to impress the Italians, but to keep up morale." There was also a "fantastic" amount of talent in the camp, and there was little difficulty in finding actors and musicians to provide entertainment.[42] They also played cards (particularly poker and bridge) and attended informal classes run by fellow prisoners.

Easily the most popular pastime for PWs was escaping: dreaming about it, planning it, or actually doing it. Flight Lieutenant Don McLarty, an Ottawa pilot who served with 33 Squadron (RAF) in the desert (where he had been shot down in October 1942), recalls that an elaborate organization was in place by the time he arrived at CCPG 78, near Sulmona, sixty miles east of Rome. "We had an escape committee, of course, like most prison camps did. If you had an escape plan, you had to get the approval of the escape committee [which] was usually chaired by the senior British officer in the camp. Unless it was a very sound plan, they usually denied you authority to attempt it, because that would jeopardize any good plans that were in the making." A plan that was accepted was given full support, including Italian money, maps, and compasses, much of it obtained from guards who could be bribed. Any papers that could not be purchased were forged. "We had tremendous forgers," says McLarty. "They could produce any kind of document you needed."[43]

Tunnels were the favourite method of getting out of the camps, but it was very difficult to get rid of the soil. The prisoners dumped it in their gardens, McLarty recounts, "and they'd keep getting higher and higher, and the Italians'd get more and more suspicious. You'd flush it down the toilets, you'd put it up in the false ceilings. You'd try to hide soil in any possible way." Few were successful; when the Italians discovered a tunnel, they would fill it with cement.[44]

The prisoners' spirits had soared as the war turned in favour of the Allies. They were able to keep track of events via illicit radios constructed by electrical experts in the camps. Allied victories in late 1942, El Alamein in October and the Torch landing in November, had raised their hopes to new heights, but the crunch came with the sensational news of Italy's surrender. Senior British officers had received orders over their secret radios to "stand fast and await the arrival of the Allied army. Do not allow your men to escape and roam about running unnecessary risks."[45] Most heeded these orders, which they relayed to their men.

Typical of the camps was CCPG 21, near Chieti. The morning after the surrender announcement, the walls were unmanned: the Italian guards were gone. The senior British officer, a colonel, soon summoned the prisoners onto the parade square and declared that everyone must "remain in camp. Anyone disobeying these orders is subject to court martial at a later date! You will be kept informed of any changes in my directive." The camp, which housed more than two thousand PWs, most of them officers, meekly submitted to the German takeover several days later.[46] They were among the fifty thousand former prisoners who were transferred to prison camps in Germany.

But thousands of others took to the hills in a desperate bid for freedom. Many had simply walked out the unguarded front gates of some camps; others cut holes in the barbed-wire fences as the laconic Italians watched them. Most were soon recaptured, like the veteran from Sevigliano, Skid Hanes. After two weeks of freedom, Hanes and a number of other PWs were discovered hiding in a ravine. The grey-clad German soldiers fired their machine-guns over the heads of the escapees and, in Hanes's colourful phrase, "scared the living shit out of us." Without an alternative, they surrendered, and soon found themselves being transported to Germany by train across the Brenner Pass. "That was a hell of a trip," he remembers. Three nights and four days, and if you can imagine a boxcar packed so tight with men that no one could lie down – you couldn't even sit down, we had to take turns." There were no toilet facilities, little food, and "we were dying for water at times." His journey ended near Dresden, deep in Germany, at Stalag IVB, where he was to spend the rest of the war.[47]

Better luck was enjoyed by Don McLarty and Ray Sherk, a flying officer from Toronto, who escaped from CCPG 78. But they got away with little time to spare. "We didn't get very far before the Germans arrived," recalls McLarty. "They immediately encircled the camp, and they took it over." While McLarty and Sherk watched from a vantage point on the mountain overlooking CCPG 78, the Germans held a roll call, determined how many men were missing, and then they "came after us. So our mountain-climbing was aided by German bullets and shells going off all around us."[48]

Freedom was seemingly short-lived. After climbing the mountain for two days, McLarty and Sherk crawled up to a water-hole to fill their canteens. "I guess there was, in total, some sixteen Germans who just came at us from all directions and recaptured us." The Germans dragged the despondent PWs further up the mountain in search of other escapees. Tired, hungry, and thirsty, they had trouble keeping pace with the enemy soldiers, and the officer in charge finally sent the prisoners back to the water-hole, escorted by a single guard. It was near evening by now, and the Canadians had a ludicrously easy time escaping once more. "We told the German that we had to look after the call of nature," says McLarty, "and we went over a small ridge and we took off."[49]

They were free again, but for how long? The escaped airmen took refuge in a small cluster of trees nearby, then spent several anxious hours. "Ray Sherk and I hid under a pile of leaves, each of us with our head against a tree, and these Germans came marching through the trees looking for us, and they went on either side of us, and I could hear Ray's heart beating – I could hear the leaves rustling – and he could hear mine, no doubt! They tended to be very noisy. They fired off their machine-guns to try to frighten us. They tossed hand grenades around. They went through us twice and missed on both occasions."[50]

When they resumed their flight in the mountains of central Italy, McLarty and Sherk encountered an English-speaking Italian, who guided them to a village, where a woman, Maria Carbori, took them to a cave some distance away. They hid there for the next seventeen days. "This woman brought us food almost daily," recalls a thankful McLarty. "She'd walk up the two or three miles from the village to the cave and feed us."[51]

On the seventeenth day in the cave, they were nearly discovered by a German patrol; after that close call, they decided to resume moving southwards. "Ray had a tremendous sense of direction, he knew his stars, and we did most of our walking at night," McLarty explains.

We walked a long way over a period of forty-five days. We had to cross rivers, we had to cross valleys. The problems you encountered were dogs that smelled you out at night and would come barking at you, and you never knew when the Germans were going to come. You could never cross a bridge, because they were guarded by the Germans; we had to swim rivers.

The mountains were frightening. You'd think you were at the top, and there was always another ridge. You just had to keep going, until you eventually got to the top. We were going across the mountain ranges most of the time, so that meant going over a range and across a valley, a river, and a main highway, and up the mountains on the other side. We did a lot of mountain-climbing.

To make matters even more interesting, says McLarty, "Ray tended to be a little aggressive and wanted to sabotage German trucks all the time, and we had a number of pretty close calls."[52]

Some of these were frightening. At one point, they were hidden by peasants in a haystack for the night. Before sunrise, an Italian boy warned them that the Germans were coming. "We went up into some trees," says McLarty, "and at dawn we watched the Germans arrive in two trucks. They poured gasoline on the haystack and set a match to it. It just went up in flames." They had another narrow escape after they took refuge in a farmer's tool shed. Again, a child warned them to get out, McLarty recalls, "and sure enough, we got up into the trees and the Germans came and blew the door in and threw hand grenades into the tool shed."[53]

Everywhere they went, Italian peasants offered help. Among the many who provided food, shelter, and guidance, was an Italian doctor, Torinto Sciuba, who had provided medical treatment in the prison camp and had let it be known that he would assist anyone who tried to escape. Another "helper," as they came to be called, was a grizzled Italian shepherd known only as Bartolommeo. "A small sturdy middle-aged man with pointed features and serious dark-brown eyes," Bartolommeo was fifty-three years old, a Great War veteran who had spent fourteen months as a PW in Austria-Hungary. He guided the two Canadians, and a South African named Uys Krige, through some of the worst and most dangerous terrain.[54]

With plenty of help, in addition to their own wits and endurance, they worked their way through the German lines along the Sangro in early November. This was perhaps the most harrowing experience of all, according to McLarty. "At one point, there was artillery firing 360 degrees around us. In the course of that battle, we were able to get through and met up, funnily enough, with the Canadian Seaforth Highlanders, who didn't know whether to accept our story or not, but they did give us bacon and eggs and Canadian cigarettes. It was a great day for us."[55]

No PW could hope to escape without Italian aid. But not all Italians were friendly. "We were warned to stay in the mountains and keep away from any large areas," recalls a CCPG 78 escaper, Ed Patrick of Toronto, a bomber pilot who had been shot down in the desert in October 1942, "because there were still Fascisti in all these areas. Stay with the peasant people, because they were anti-Mussolini and anti-Tedeschi, or anti-German, and they would help."[56]

It was sound advice, as every PW discovered for himself. Patrick was eventually picked up by a patrol from the Van Doos, but it was a poverty-stricken family in the mountains of central Italy who provided him with the most enduring and cherished memory of this fateful period in his life. Soon after fleeing, with six others, from CCPG 78 on 12 September, he took refuge in the village of San Vittorino. There he was befriended by the Orsini family, Aquilino and his wife and their son and two daughters, who stoically accepted the terrible risk involved in offering aid to the Canadian. "It must be remembered," he writes, "that these courageous people were aware that they would be shot if they were caught sheltering us, and the rest of the villagers tortured." Patrick would never forget the ten days or so that he spent here. "Everyone in the village knew I was staying with the Orsinis. . . . The children were the alarm system, they would come running, yelling, 'Tedeschi' (Germans) as soon as they heard motorcycles leaving Caramonica across the valley. I would then be hidden in a wood pile until the 'all clear' was given." They shared what little food they had, and even provided him with spare clothing, at a time when many civilians, instead of shoes, were shod in "'Mussolini scarpe,' which consisted of of a piece of old rubber tire, roped or wired on."[57]

The inevitable time to move on came too soon. "It was not easy saying goodbye," Patrick recalls. "Aquilino walked with me for some distance. . . . We embraced and I'm not ashamed to say I had tears in my eyes, as did he. That was the last time I saw Aquilino and his family."[58]

These good Samaritans risked their lives, loved ones, and property for complete strangers. They had everything to lose and virtually nothing to gain by helping these desperate strangers from a foreign land. They certainly did not profit financially. The British paid the princely sum of £1 for each prisoner escorted through enemy lines, while the Germans offered a reward equivalent to £20 to any Italian who turned in a PW. And the risks were tragically real. It was later estimated that five hundred Italians were executed by the Germans for aiding or sheltering the escaped prisoners.[59]

The young Canadians who benefitted from the courage and generosity of Italian peasants, young and old, male and female, would never forget. Nearly half a century has passed, "but time will never erase my memory," says an ever-grateful Ed Patrick. "Needless to say I owe a debt of gratitude to the Orsinis, the villagers of San Vittorino and other Helpers, which I will never be able to repay."[60]

3

"I will hit the Boche a crack that will be heard all over Italy."[61] General Montgomery's brave words, uttered in mid-November, came back to haunt him.

By now, Montgomery was openly contemptuous of General Alexander, and never missed an opportunity to denigrate him. "He does not understand the business [of war]," Monty complained of Alexander, "and he is not clever; he cannot grasp the essentials." At a planning conference to discuss the forthcoming campaign, Alexander attempted to outline his ideas, but Monty interrupted his superior with characteristic rudeness. "Sit down," he told Alexander, "I'll show you how to do it."[62]

Such plans that had existed had been completely upset by the German decision to defend Italy south of Rome. Instead of a dash to Rome, the Allies now faced a strenuous winter campaign in rough terrain; its difficulty was ensured by the alarming numbers of enemy troops and tanks pouring into Italy. By the end of October, the thirteen Allied divisions found themselves facing nearly twice as many German divisions.* Rome remained an important goal of the Allied forces in Italy, but the enemy's decision to fight invited a new objective: to pin down German forces and keep them away from the decisive arena, in northwestern Europe. "If we can keep the enemy 'on his heels' until [the spring of 1944]," Alexander concluded in a 21 October paper, "we shall be certain of retaining in Italy the divisions already there; we might even draw still more into the theatre."[63]

The Italian campaign had been given its *raison d'être*. It meant that Allied forces would continue to fight in difficult terrain, often in adverse weather conditions, against an enemy who was well-equipped, skilful, determined, and numerically strong. Theirs would be a costly and frustrating war of attrition.

The immediate goal was to pierce the German *Winterstellung*, or Winter Position, which consisted of the Bernhard and Gustav lines. Mark Clark's Fifth Army, operating on the west coast of Italy, due south of Rome, had already launched its offensive in early October, but progress was slow and costly. The rain-swollen River Volturno proved to be a significant obstacle, and the Anglo–American attack soon bogged down in the mountains beyond it. Clark managed to break through the enemy defences on the Volturno, but twenty miles and four weeks later, he had to close down his operations because of bad weather, nightmarish terrain, and heavy

---

* The use of divisions is a convenient but not necessarily an accurate measurement. By the second half of the war, there was a vast discrepancy in the quality of German divisions, and few if any maintained their authorized strength in men or equipment. For instance, an infantry division in 1939 contained 16,000 men; by 1943, the establishment had been reduced to 12,000, but the actual strength of most was below that figure. While there is more consistency with Allied divisions, here, too, there were significant differences in the capabilities of infantry, armoured, and airborne divisions.

losses. The Fifth Army had shot its bolt, even before the Eighth Army launched its offensive on the Adriatic coast.

Plans for the capture of Rome were finalized on 8 November. The Eighth Army would launch its offensive across the Sangro on 20 November, while the Fifth resumed its drive on Rome from the south ten days later. In addition, Alexander hoped to make an amphibious landing on the west coast of Italy, just south of Rome, pending high-level deliberations to arrange the necessary landing craft.

Both army commanders were confident of success. The Fifth Army, in particular, faced a daunting task, to break through the Mignano Gap, cross a river, the Rapido, twelve miles beyond, breach the Gustav Line anchored by the Benedictine monastery at Cassino, and drive through the valley of the Liri and Sacco rivers to Frosinone, fifty miles southeast of Rome. At this point, the amphibious landing would be made, catching the Germans in a vise. "Don't worry," an optimistic Mark Clark told a friend, "I'll get through the Winter Line all right and push the Germans out."[64]

Montgomery knew this was nonsense. The Fifth Army, he was sure, would get hung up in the mountains, and Rome would fall to his Eighth Army. After driving across the Sangro, past the small port of Ortona, to Pescara, he planned to swing westwards and cross the Apennines on the lateral highway to capture the Italian capital with the 2nd New Zealand Division. "It is a very powerful Division," Monty wrote; "20,000 men and 170 tanks; it will take a bit of stopping." With the New Zealanders leading, the Eighth Army would "get in behind the German divisions facing 5 Army. These German divisions will either have to come out of it and retire hurriedly, or be cut off. In any case I hope to accompany the N.Z. Division into ROME!!"[65]

On the eve of his offensive, he issued a message to be read to all his troops. "The enemy has been outfought by better troops ever since we first landed in SICILY, and his men don't like what they are getting," said Montgomery. "The Germans are in fact in the very condition in which we want them. WE WILL NOW HIT THE GERMANS A COLOSSAL CRACK."[66]

Much of his talk was bravado. The offensive was being spearheaded by a new headquarters, V Corps, under Lieutenant-General Charles Allfrey. This was Monty's first look at Allfrey, and he did not like what he had seen since the corps had become operational in October. "He is not yet up to the standard of my other Corps Commanders; he is inclined to fiddle about with details, is very slow, and is inclined to bellyache." An even bigger concern was the weather. "I *must have* fine weather," Monty wrote. "If it rains continuously I am done." But his hopes dwindled, as heavy rain fell during the middle of November, swelling the Trigno and Sangro rivers.[67]

The Eighth Army's offensive was launched on the night of 19–20 November. The 78th Division got across the swollen Sangro, only to be thrown back by violent counter-attacks within two days. Montgomery was livid at the failure, and angrily summoned Charles Allfrey to his headquarters "and told him that his Corps was completely amateur according to Eighth Army standards; there was a lack of 'grip' and 'bite,' and things must change at once."[68]

Instead of a breakthrough battle, the Eighth Army soon found itself in a slogging match. The attackers were fighting not just Germans but the elements as well. The heavy rains turned the normally sedate Sangro into a raging torrent, and it took a week to establish a bridgehead a mile-and-a-half deep and seven miles wide. Once that was done, however, Montgomery was able to organize a more powerful attack, accompanied by the overwhelming artillery support which was his trademark. By 1 December, the Eighth Army had broken the Bernhard Line on the Adriatic and thrown the German defenders back to the River Moro. Inland, the 2nd New Zealand Division crossed the Moro and mounted a drive towards the ridgetop town of Orsogna, whence the Eighth Army could attack towards the little port of Ortona and the inland town of Chieti.

The rainfall intensified. On 4 December, the Sangro rose eight feet; by the next morning, Monty wrote, "all bridges over the river were under water and most washed away." The Eighth Army commander was facing failure, and he did not like it. "I don't think we can get any spectacular results," he wrote Sir Alan Brooke, "so long as it goes on raining; the whole country becomes a sea of mud and nothing on wheels or tracks can move off the roads."[69]

There would be two more weeks of hard fighting, but the New Zealanders would be unable to capture Orsogna, even with assistance from the 8th Indian Division. In the meantime, more fresh forces were brought into the battle. On the morning of 4 December, V Corps' Charles Allfrey signalled the Canadian divisional commander, Chris Vokes: "You must get over the River Moro as soon as possible."[70]

That terse order sent the Canadian division into its bloodiest month of the whole Italian campaign.

CHAPTER EIGHT

Bloody December

1

The Canadians were in high spirits as they moved into battle. "Who's for Reigate?" they laughed while boarding lorries, recalling happier days in England. "This tram for Twickenham!"[1] Other memories of their long years in Britain were revived when the First Division relieved the battle-weary 78th Division. "Blimey, it's the ruddy Canadians," muttered one mud-encrusted Tommy when he spotted the incoming Royal Canadian Regiment. Another called out, "'Ow did y'leave our wives back 'ome?" Replied a quick-witted Canadian: "Satisfied."[2]

Ahead lay Ortona. Two roads were available to the Canadian division, including the relatively modern Route 16, which hugged the coast. The other was an older highway which took a torturous route from the farming village of Sant' Apollinare, across the Moro River to San Leonardo, to link up with the Ortona–Orsogna road. From the Moro, Ortona "was four crow-flight miles away, but seven by road across the grain of four 500-foot ridges."[3] Dotted with hamlets and villages, the country was a "well-farmed area ... covered with olive groves and with vineyards which produced some of the finest table grapes in Italy."[4]

The valley of the Moro presented a somewhat imposing obstacle. From his vantage point on the high ground south of the river, the divisional war artist, Charles Comfort, surveyed the terrain with a trained eye. "The valley below was typical of the water courses that channel this coastal plain, two hundred feet perhaps to its floor, a thousand yards across. At the bottom, a muddy stream, high at this season, meandered through shrubs and vetches and occasional clumps of willow. . . . The reverse slope, with its burden of olive, rose in gentle folds to its crest, the highway snaking up its flank toward San Leonardo."[5]

The divisional commander, Chris Vokes, chose to cross the Moro at three points. After studying patrol reports, the general decided to establish bridgeheads on Route 16, near the mouth of the Moro; at San Leonardo; and at Villa Rogatti, a village two miles upstream from San Leonardo.

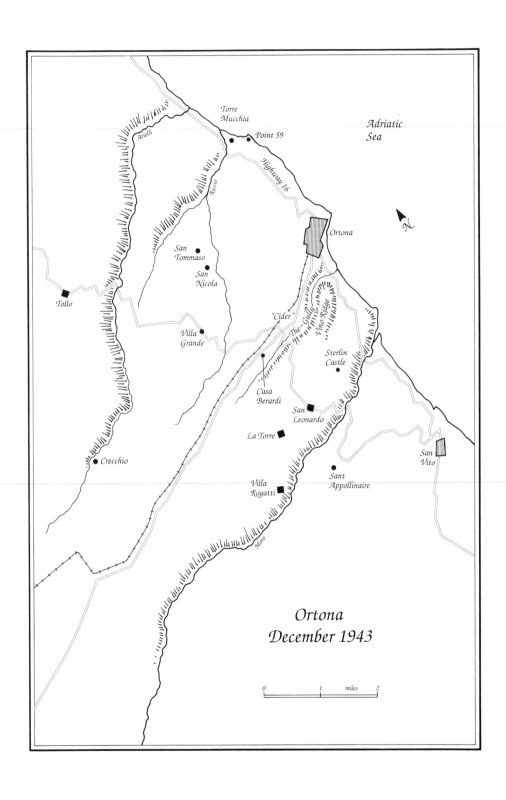

Torre
Mucchia

Point 59

Arielli

Adriatic
Sea

Highway 16

Riccio

Ortona

San
Tommaso

San
Nicola

Tollo

"Cider"

The "Gully"

Vino Ridge

Villa
Grande

Sterlin
Castle

Casa
Berardi

San
Leonardo

La Torre

San
Vito

Crecchio

Sant
Appollinaire

Villa
Rogatti

Moro

Ortona
December 1943

0   1   miles   2

From these positions, he could exploit towards his immediate objective, code-named "Cider," the junction of the old inland highway with the Ortona–Orsogna road. The trio of battalion-sized operations would be mounted at midnight on 5–6 December. The Hasty Ps were to cross the Moro on the right, while the Seaforth Highlanders of Canada took San Leonardo in the centre; the PPCLI, on the left, were ordered to capture the village of Villa Rogatti, two miles upstream from San Leonardo. All three crossings had one common feature: they would be silent attacks, without artillery support, in hopes of surprising the enemy.

Even as the division prepared these attacks, it was in danger of being cut off. When the Sangro flooded on the fourth, submerging or carrying away every bridge, British engineers redoubled their efforts to complete an all-weather bridge to maintain the precious supply line into the combat zone. The flooding was to prevent the Third Brigade from rejoining the division for two more days; even when it crossed the Sangro on 6 December, it had to leave behind two hundred of its heavier vehicles. In the meantime, the Royal Canadian Army Service Corps innovated by utilizing the amphibious DUKWs to ferry supplies around the mouth of the Sangro; on 7 December alone, they moved fifty thousand rounds of artillery ammunition, ten thousand gallons of gasoline, and forty thousand rations in aid of the offensive operations on the Moro.[6]

The first Canadian attacks along the Moro produced mixed results. On the right and in the centre, the Hasty Ps and Seaforths gained tentative toeholds on the far bank, which they were forced to relinquish in the face of furious counter-attacks. The only clear-cut success was gained by the PPCLI.

At midnight, three companies of Patricias slipped across the Moro at an unguarded ford. It was "a beautiful little exercise," recalls the battalion commander, Cam Ware, who was later awarded the Distinguished Service Order. "I'm all for silent attacks. It was a complete surprise to the Germans. There was food on the tables" in the hilltop village, as the Patricias converged on it from different directions. By dawn, after a short but savage street battle, they had captured Villa Rogatti. The village was still under mortar and sniper fire, and the Patricias braced for counter-attacks.[7]

Monday, 6 December, was an anxious day. On the left, the PPCLI repelled repeated attacks by the 200th Panzer Grenadier Regiment. Colonel Ware's British tanks were, as he had anticipated, "having a hell of a time" getting across the Moro, and his riflemen were left on their own that morning. Beginning at 0900 hours, the Germans charged through the olive groves, and Major W. D. "Bucko" Watson's company bore the brunt of the attacks. Watson won the Military Cross as his company stood firm, but only by the narrowest of margins. The tanks, eight Shermans of the 44th

Royal Tank Regiment, arrived in time to play a decisive role in the afternoon battles for the bridgehead.

At 1330, the Germans attacked again, led by nine Mark IV tanks. For
two hours the fighting raged in and around Villa Rogatti, but Ware's little
force was more than equal to the challenge. "Give the British tanks full
marks," he says, they "were terrific" in repelling the enemy.[8] Two Shermans
were knocked out, but five Mark IVs were left burning on the battlefield.
The enemy also left behind more than forty prisoners, and an estimated
hundred dead. The PPCLI casualties totalled eight killed, fifty-two
wounded, and eight captured.[9]

Meanwhile, the Hasty Ps had finally established their bridgehead near
the mouth of the Moro. The battalion was under the command of Major
Bert Kennedy, who had just spent twenty-five days as a prisoner of war.
Captured during the approach to Campobasso in mid-October, Kennedy
had escaped from his captors and made his way back to Allied lines,
rejoining the Hasty Ps in time to succeed Colonel Tweedsmuir when he fell
ill with jaundice.

The previous night's abortive operation had convinced Kennedy that he
could make a successful crossing, and when the First Brigade's Howard
Graham concurred, Vokes gave him permission to try again. After a
twenty-minute bombardment by field guns of the 2nd Field Regiment, and
supported by mortars of the Saskatoon Light Infantry, the Hasty Ps put
two companies across the river at 1400 hours on 6 December. But the
attackers were soon pinned down. When their radios failed, and smoke
from the heavy shelling by both sides obscured the situation, Kennedy
crossed the Moro to find out what was going on.

It was not a promising picture. Kennedy saw that his two companies
were being cut to pieces; they would have to withdraw. But a new crisis
arose. One company, trapped on the far side, could not get back, and
Kennedy agonized over the fate of his men before making his decision: he
would lead his remaining two companies across and try to salvage a lost
battle.

At 1430, Kennedy personally led the reinforcements across the Moro.
German shelling had intensified by now, but the Plough Jockeys from
Ontario were not to be denied. By early evening, the Hasty Ps had carved
out a small bridgehead six hundred yards wide and five hundred yards
deep. It was a perilous position, as the intelligence officer, Farley Mowat,
vividly remembers:

What followed was the kind of night men dream about in afteryears,
waking in a cold sweat to a surge of gratitude that it is but a dream. It
was a delirium of sustained violence. Small pockets of Germans that

had been cut off throughout our bridgehead fired their automatic weapons in hysterical dismay at every shadow. The grind of enemy tanks and self-propelled guns working their way along the crest was multiplied by echoes until it sounded like an entire Panzer army. Illuminating flares flamed in darkness with a sick radiance. The snap and scream of high-velocity tank shells pierced the brutal guttural of an endless cannonade from both German and Canadian artillery. Moaning Minnie projectiles whumped down like thunderbolts. . . . Soldiers of both sides, blundering through the vineyards, fired with panicky impartiality in all directions.[10]

It was a time for heroes. Bert Kennedy, who, like Cam Ware, was later awarded the Distinguished Service Order, seemed to be everywhere, offering encouragement, redeploying his men in the best positions available. British tanks tried and tried, but the thirty-ton Shermans were still unable to cross the boggy bottom of the Moro valley. When the rumble of enemy tanks in the distance foretold of trouble, Company Sergeant-Major George Ponsford organized parties to manhandle two of the battalion's one-ton anti-tank guns across the river. Then they ran out of ammunition. (Asked by his men what to do, Captain Lyall Carr had a ready answer: "Make military noises!")[11] At that point, the resourceful regimental sergeant-major, Angus Duffy, came through once more, as he had in Sicily, bringing over a mule train loaded with ammunition and food.[12]

By nightfall on 6 December, the Canadian division was across the Moro in two places. While the Seaforths had failed to establish a bridgehead at San Leonardo, the Patricias had a firm hold on the far bank at Villa Rogatti and the Hasty Ps were barely hanging on near the mouth of the Moro. At divisional headquarters, Chris Vokes later wrote that he "was now faced with a big decision – how to exploit the success of the PPCLI." Vokes elected to shift his main effort to the left. While the Loyal Edmontons prepared to pass through the Patricias, the Seaforths were ordered to shift from San Leonardo to support them.[13]

But Vokes's engineers had bad news. After studying the riverbanks, they informed him that it "was not possible" to build an assault crossing at either of his bridgeheads. The only practicable site, they said, was the demolished bridge on the road to San Leonardo.[14]

Vokes drew up a new plan. To reduce the divisional frontage, the Villa Rogatti bridgehead would be handed over to the 8th Indian Division, and the Canadians would exploit the slim hold being maintained by the Hasty Ps. "It was a significant decision," notes the official history, "for it meant that instead of outflanking San Leonardo from the left and then advancing along the grain of the country the Canadians were now to become involved in a series of costly frontal assaults in which advantages of topography lay with the defenders."[15]

The situation was doubly disappointing, for three days later, Indian engineers completed at Villa Rogatti a Bailey crossing which they aptly named "Impossible Bridge." Commented the explosive Vokes: "I can tell you I was in an evil temper when I learned about this, but by then it was too late."[16]

The battle for Cider crossroads was planned in two phases. It would open on the afternoon of 8 December with a two-pronged attack by Howard Graham's First Brigade, when The Royal Canadian Regiment moved into the Hasty Ps' bridgehead and mounted a right hook on San Leonardo. At the same time, Toronto's 48th Highlanders would cross the Moro and attack La Torre, midway between Villa Rogatti and San Leonardo. From this firm base, the Second Brigade, supported by the First Armoured Brigade, would push towards the junction on the Ortona–Orsogna road. But, like every Canadian plan prepared this month, this would fall short of expectations.

The attack went in at 1630 hours, after a sixty-minute bombardment by the full divisional artillery, assisted by British and Indian batteries, 350 guns in all. This massive display of firepower marked the beginning of a tough month for the dedicated gunners who worked so hard to make success by the infantry possible. One of these gunners was Sergeant Ben Malkin, of the 3rd Field Regiment, who later became a noted war correspondent. "Somebody said each 25-pounder round cost the Canadian taxpayer $12.50," writes Malkin. "We didn't care. We fired our guns when our infantry needed our support, and when they didn't need it during a pause in the action, we fired anyway."[17]

Across the Moro, war artist Charles Comfort watched the attack unfold. It began with the "cataclysmic shock" of the bombardment. "Instantly the pastoral valley became a valley of death. . . . The first impact was of sound, gigantic and preprosterous sound. . . . It battered and pounded the eardrums from all sides. . . ." Amid the destruction emerged a pattern which fascinated the artist: "neat rectangles were searched and scorched with fire, the finger pointing here and then there. Soon they all fitted together with diabolic accuracy, like the parts of a gigantic puzzle." Comfort was utterly astonished to hear the sound of small-arms fire, indicating that people had not only survived the shelling, but were now fighting in it.[18]

The shell fire certainly impressed the 48th Highlanders. "We didn't expect such a fearful uproar," a corporal said afterwards, "and we thought for an instant that we'd been trapped by the Germans. You couldn't see anything; it was like a raving madhouse." It was an overcast afternoon, with the promise of more rain, but two companies of the Toronto High-landers crossed the Moro with little difficulty – a sprained ankle was the only casualty in one company, but a single German shell killed seven men in the other assault unit – and captured La Torre by nightfall. Lieutenant-Colonel Ian Johnston brought up the rest of the battalion and ordered it to dig in. "I don't think the Germans know we're here," he told his officers that night. "But get ready for daylight!"[19]

It was a different story for the Royal Canadians, who were mounting what Strome Galloway calls an attack "in the best World War I tradition,"[20] with the four companies passing each other through a succession of objective lines into San Leonardo, a mile and a half away. Attacking southwestwards along a winding lane, soon to be dubbed "Royal Canadian Avenue," the RCR would attack across the front of the 361st Panzer Grenadier Regiment. When it works, this kind of operation is described as "bold"; when it fails, it is "foolish." This one did not work.

Within moments of moving forward, Captain Slim Liddell's A Company was hit by an enemy mortar barrage that wiped out an entire section. When B Company swung wide to avoid the fire, Major Strome Galloway and his men got lost in a tangled vineyard, with darkness descending. When the major finally risked a light, he "discovered that we were well behind enemy lines," and hurriedly led his company in the right direction. "We heard German shouting," he writes, "but in the dark managed to bypass them and get oriented. . . . How we got back without running into trouble I'll never know. I was in a complete rage by this time and would have almost welcomed a fight."[21]

The RCR was stopped halfway to San Leonardo. As the other two companies passed through Liddell and Galloway's, the Germans delivered a violent artillery and mortar barrage, followed by a counter-attack with tanks. This was checked by a desperate measure: Lieutenant-Colonel Dan Spry called down Canadian artillery fire practically on top of his own regiment. Lieutenant Jimmy Quayle, whose platoon endured the misery of being shelled by his own side, will never forget that experience. "The volume of fire was unbelievable," he writes. "Shell after shell after shell like an artillery conveyor belt with no cover except small shallow holes from previous shells."[22] Colonel Spry then took advantage of the bright moonlight to pull back to a modest height, forever known to the regiment as "Slaughterhouse Hill," where the four companies dug in.

On the Moro, Canadian engineers were labouring valiantly to clear the way for tanks. Waiting in vain for a success signal from San Leonardo, sappers of the 3rd Field Company went to work after dark on a diversion around the blown bridge on the road from Sant' Apollinare. Under the direction of Major F. B. Fraser, they toiled through the night, ignoring "continual machine-gun, mortar and shellfire." Sapper Milton McNaughton, operating a D-7 bulldozer which sounded "like a regiment of tanks," ploughed a rough road across the river bed and through the far bank. When the enemy fire grew unbearable, McNaughton was forced to take cover. But his impatience grew with each passing minute. "Aw, the hell with this," he finally said, and taking a rifle he scrambled across the river. He returned some time later with two prisoners in tow, then jumped back onto the bulldozer and finished his job. By 0600 hours on 9 December, the diversion had been completed, and within the hour Shermans of the Calgary Regiment were roaring through. The engineers were rewarded for their efforts: Fraser won the Distinguished Service Order, while McNaughton, who was recommended for the Victoria Cross, received the Military Medal.[23]

This development came in the nick of time. Just a few hours earlier, Brigadier Graham, who was suffering from a duodenal ulcer which would soon incapacitate him, had returned from the bridgehead (a heroic feat, which earned him a bar to the Distinguished Service Order he had won in Sicily) to notify General Vokes "that it is not possible for me to form the bridgehead as ordered by you."[24] Vokes's battle plan was already being revised; instead of jumping off from a firm base at San Leonardo, the Second Brigade would first have to take the village.

This task was given to Major Ned Amy, commanding A Squadron of the Calgaries. The twenty-five-year-old Maritimer had only recently joined the regiment, after serving since Sicily with the Ontario Regiment. Heading into his first action with the Calgaries, Amy vividly remembers receiving his instructions from the First Armoured Brigade's commander, Bob Wyman. "They haven't taken the bridgehead," Brigadier Wyman said. "You take it now."[25]

With those brief instructions, Amy set out. On his twelve tanks rode Captain Alan Mercer's D Company of the Seaforth Highlanders. They were mercilessly shelled the whole way. Careering along the road as it wound down to the Moro, two tanks failed to negotiate a sharp bend and rolled over a thirty-foot cliff. On the far side, a half-mile from the Moro, another tank was knocked out by a mine. The disabled tank blocked the road, but Amy managed to manoeuvre four Shermans past it and led them towards San Leonardo.[26]

A Seaforth subaltern stole the show at this point. Lieutenant John McLean led his platoon into San Leonardo and swiftly drove out the defenders in a door-to-door battle. In the process, he killed at least eight of the enemy and captured eighteen others, along with ten machine-guns. McLean was awarded the Distinguished Service Order, a rarity for junior officers and, in these circumstances, tantamount to a Victoria Cross.[27]

The Germans, characteristically, wasted no time counter-attacking. Twelve tanks, backed by a substantial infantry force, charged through the olive groves. But Major Amy, with only four Shermans and thirty-nine infantrymen, more than held his own. Amy's gunner knocked out a German tank, an older-model Mark III, at 150 yards, while Lieutenant A. J. Charbonneau destroyed a Mark IV at point-blank range. The latter episode gave Amy one of his fondest wartime memories: a Seaforth who had been lying helplessly in the path of the oncoming enemy tank ran over to Charbonneau's Sherman and exclaimed, "You big cast-iron son-of-a-bitch, I could kiss you!"[28]

The Germans retreated, and San Leonardo was at last secure. Ned Amy won the Military Cross for the "determined and gallant manner" in which he orchestrated its capture.[29]

Counter-attacks of this nature were the order of the day on Thursday, 9 December. Most were directed at the fragile bridgehead held by the hard-pressed Hasty Ps and Royal Canadians. The day's biggest counter-attack hit them early in the afternoon, at a time when the RCR was extremely vulnerable. One company, D, had virtually ceased to exist on account of heavy casualties, C Company had been sent back across the Moro to help with the wounded and prisoners, and B Company had moved up to reinforce the Seaforths at San Leonardo. A Company was about to depart from Slaughterhouse Hill when the action started, and only one of its platoons, Lieutenant Mitch Sterlin's, was in position to face the attacking Germans. This handful of Canadians made the most of it.

Mitch Sterlin did not look like a heroic leader. An honours student in chemistry at the University of Montreal, he was, in the words of his best friend and fellow subaltern Jimmy Quayle, "highly intelligent but stocky, overweight and poorly coordinated." But his "sheepish grin" endeared him to his men, and they stayed at his side in defence of a two-storey stone house on Royal Canadian Avenue, a building destined to go down in regimental annals as "Sterlin Castle."[31]

Again and again, the Germans swarmed around Sterlin Castle. Again and again, they were driven back by the pudgy lieutenant and his brave men. At least thirty German corpses were later found lying around the battered house. Among the enemy dead was a bespectacled and decorated Afrika Korps veteran who was wearing a Red Cross armband and carrying a Schmeisser submachine-gun. "Either he was a stretcher bearer who decided to get in on the scrap, or else he used the Red Cross to protect him while he charged across open ground," writes Strome Galloway. "Anyway, it didn't."[32]

But it was a dead Canadian who made the greatest impression on Galloway. The body of Lance-Corporal R. M. Stuart "was found slumped over his rifle, his eye right along the sights and his finger on the trigger. In front of his slit trench were several clips of ammunition laid out in a neat row so that he could reload quickly. A couple of dead Huns sprawled forward of his trench. Stuart, himself, had been drilled between the eyes."[33]

Sterlin's embattled platoon held out until the supply of ammunition was exhausted. Then the boyish-looking lieutenant abandoned Sterlin Castle and led his surviving men to safety. Surprisingly, Sterlin was not decorated for his sterling performance, nor was Sergeant R. W. Menzies, whose sharpshooting accounted for at least half a dozen of the enemy dead. But Sergeant A. J. Hocking and Lance-Corporal C. J. Davino, who manned a 2-inch mortar with devastating effect from a nearby shell hole, were both awarded the Military Medal.

While Mitch Sterlin made his amazing stand on Royal Canadian Avenue, the Hasty Ps repelled a counter-attack by the 200th Panzer Grenadier Regiment. By now, these farm lads from Ontario had prepared a killing ground that even a German professional soldier might appreciate. The entire defensive zone had been registered by artillery and mortars, with machine-guns set up to fire on fixed lines. The panzer grenadiers charged into the heart of this position, with results described by the war diary: "'A' Company on the left flank withheld their fire until the Germans had reached a vineyard some two hundred yards to their front, and then called for observed mortar fire and opened up with small arms, catching at least a company, and cutting them up completely. On 'B' Company's front another company was allowed into an enfiladed ravine and then annihilated by crossing machine-gun fire."[34] The enemy retreated, leaving "about 170 dead and 50 prisoners behind them."[35]

The Canadian division had taken its first step towards Ortona. San Leonardo had been captured, and the Hasty Ps were secure in their bridgehead. At divisional headquarters, the war diarist celebrated victory by writing on the night of 9 December: "This day will be remembered by the 1st Canadians for a long, long time. We had our first real battle on a divisional level with the Germans." The enemy had conceded San Leonardo and the River Moro to the Canadians, and were rushing reinforcements to the embattled sector. Fritz Wentzell, the Tenth Army's chief of staff, authorized the transfer of the élite 1st Parachute Division to Ortona, "so that [the Canadians] will be prevented from getting there at all costs." In the meantime, the battered 90th Panzer Grenadier Division pulled back to a new defensive line.[36]

The enemy selected a strong position. In front of the Ortona–Orsogna road, and running parallel to it, was a narrow and deep gully. Three miles in length, it served as a natural barrier, running from the coast until it petered out among the vine-tangled, mud-covered foothills. "It was too narrow to be vulnerable to anything except plunging fire," commented historian George Stevens, "but it was deep enough to house a garrison in burrows from which machine gun teams could emerge in a twinkling and man emplacements along its lip. In addition it provided sanctuary for outposts and infiltrators who shifted about almost at will under cover of the olive trees and the vine trellises."[37] Fellow historian Reginald Roy says this gully "was a trench, anti-tank ditch and a natural obstacle all rolled into one."[38]

It would take its place in Canadian military annals as, simply, "The Gully."

2

Cider crossroads was within their grasp, and the Canadians wasted no time reaching for it. Intelligence told them that the Germans had fallen back, that "the next defensive stand by the enemy would be made on the Arielli or the Foro Rivers several miles beyond."[39] On Friday morning, 10 December, the Second Brigade rolled out of San Leonardo. Brigadier Hoffmeister's intention was to strike quickly, capture the crossroads, then clear the enemy from the vine-covered near side of The Gully, known as "Vino Ridge." The first phase was an Alberta operation, featuring infantry from Edmonton backed by the Calgary Tanks. Once they had secured the road junction, the PPCLI would drive along Vino Ridge, the springboard for the final drive to Ortona, which was clearly visible in the distance.

It was wet and dreary as the Alberta troops and tanks charged out of San Leonardo at 0900 hours. They were accompanied by what is described in the Edmontons' history as "a monumental barrage."[40] Within an hour, they had secured the intermediate objective and at 1310 came word that the three leading companies and their supporting tanks had reached Cider. The battalion commmander, Lieutenant-Colonel Jim Jefferson, notified Hoffmeister, who subsequently ordered the Patricias into action.

Unfortunately, the Eddies were not on Cider, or even close to it. The only man who seems to have been aware of this was the PPCLI's commanding officer, Cam Ware. "Christ, you're not on the crossroads. Look at them!" he remembers telling Jefferson at the latter's headquarters near San Leonardo. From this vantage point, it should have been obvious that no Canadians were anywhere near Cider. Jefferson, for reasons he alone knew, insisted that his men were on the objective. Ware realized that if he sent his troops onto the ridge, they could be cut to ribbons by any enemy force still at the crossroads and the high ground around it.[41]

But Ware's protests were to no avail. The PPCLI attack "made no sense at all," according to Ware, and his fears were fully realized. His battalion, supported by Calgary Shermans, was decimated on Vino Ridge. Raked by machine-gun and mortar fire from the flank and rear, the Patricias were quickly pinned down, and then pummelled by a bombardment that presaged a German counter-attack from The Gully. Ware called off the attack, but his "entirely unnecessary" casualties included three company commanders.[42]

It was an inauspicious beginning. At divisional headquarters, staff officers scrambled for another look at their intelligence reports. Only now did they appreciate the tactical significance of The Gully which smiled sardonically from the maps. There were few alternatives. An approach to Ortona along the coast road was ruled out, because any advance would be under direct observation, and enfiladed from the high ground along the Ortona–Orsogna road. That left Chris Vokes with the choice of attempting to outflank The Gully by striking straight west to the road, then driving towards Ortona, or forcing a passage to Cider crossroads and then exploiting northwards. Vokes selected the latter, more direct route. His decision committed the Canadians to more than a week of hard and costly fighting.

The battle for The Gully opened in earnest on Saturday, 11 December. It was a day of futile fighting for the three battalions of Bert Hoffmeister's Second Brigade. On the right, the Patricias worked their way across Vino Ridge and its tangle of vineyards and olive groves, liberally laced with anti-tank mines and booby traps. When they reached the edge of The Gully, they dug in within easy grenade-throwing range of the enemy. In the centre, the Loyal Edmontons tried again to reach Cider crossroads, but repeated attempts to advance produced a maelstrom of small-arms and mortar fire in which no man could hope to live. Nor could the Seaforth Highlanders, backed by tanks of the Ontario Regiment, break through on the left. The day's action made it clear that there was no easy way to get through these defences.[43]

By noon, General Vokes had made up his mind to commit his reserves right away. Graeme Gibson's Third Brigade had finally arrived in the area, after being delayed by the bottleneck at the flooded Sangro. The brigade was far from fresh, having spent three strenuous weeks along the upper Sangro. The first of Gibson's battalions to be sent into the battle was the West Nova Scotia Regiment. The West Novas moved up during the afternoon of the eleventh, to pass through the Seaforths and attack across The Gully to Casa Berardi, a three-storey, square, stone farmhouse about a mile from Cider crossroads. The battalion commander, Pat Bogert, was quietly confident. "On the way," he recalls, "I spoke to Syd Thomson of the Seaforths, who told me that we would not reach our objective. I told him that we would. He was right and I was wrong."[44]

The Nova Scotians attacked at 1800 hours. Darkness was descending over the battlefield as they slogged across the forbidding terrain with two companies leading and one in support. "The landscape was bare, with an occasional battered stone farmhouse and its usual small orchard of gnarled naked olive trees, worthless for cover, and the usual straggle of vine poles and wires, a curse to men laden with arms and equipment and moving in the dark." While the defenders were shrouded in the shadows of night, the Canadians stood out clearly in the moonlight. They were finally stopped within a hundred yards of The Gully. "The true nature of the gully was now apparent," writes regimental historian Thomas Raddall, "for the Germans had popped up as if by magic out of the earth, and the volume of fire showed that the place was strongly held along its whole length."[45]

Digging in for the night, the West Novas prepared to resume the attack in the morning. However, they never got the opportunity to do so, for the Germans launched no less than four fierce counter-attacks in the cold rain. The Nova Scotians held their hard-won ground, but at the cost of more than sixty casualties, including Colonel Bogert, who was wounded by a bullet in the leg.

Three consecutive days' fighting had failed to breach the The Gully, but Chris Vokes ordered yet another attempt to be made the next day. This would be spearheaded by his other Maritime battalion, the Carleton and Yorks, supported by the Calgary Tanks and as much artillery as could be made available to the division. Zero hour was set for first light on the thirteenth, 0600 hours. At the same time, probing attacks were to be made on the flanks by the Patricias and West Novas.

The Carletons' attack started promisingly. The two leading companies, closely following the barrage, overran three machine-gun nests and captured twenty-one prisoners. It must have been disconcerting to discover that these were not panzer grenadiers, but rather paratroopers from the newly arrived 3rd Parachute Regiment, which had just taken over this vital sector. The tough paras lived up to their reputation; within an hour, the Carletons had been stopped cold.[46]

There was one exception. D Company actually got across The Gully, only to find itself cut off. For nine hours, this heroic band of Maritimers fought against overwhelming odds. Every rescue effort was driven back in a hail of bullets and mortar bombs, and their only hope was to hold out until nightfall, when they could try to split up and make their way back to the Canadian lines. But they ran out of ammunition, and the paratroopers moved in for the kill.

Captain Graeme Simms, known to just about everyone as "Buck," now faced one of those decisions that an officer hopes he never has to make. "Buck and I had sixteen months to relive that moment," recalled his artillery officer, Captain Robert MacNeil, "and I could never fault him for waving his map and calling us to get up slowly."[47] Three officers and thirty-two other ranks were now prisoners of war.[48]

Among them was Earle Barr, a twenty-six-year-old company sergeant-major, who soon learned that these paratroopers were not only tough but fair. Barr watched in amazement when, after a German struck a Canadian with a shovel, an enemy NCO hauled his man aside, chewed him out, and threatened to have him shot if he ever did anything like that again. Barr, heartened by this display, approached the German with an unusual request, explaining that one of his men, who had been killed by a bullet between the eyes, was carrying in his pack a large sum of money won at gambling. "His family is hard-up," Barr explained, "and can use the money." The paratrooper, who spoke good English, promised to do what he could. When Barr was freed from prison camp after the war, he returned to New Brunswick and found that the young man's family had, indeed, received his winnings. It was a remarkable display of battlefield compassion, and gave Barr "a lot of respect for the Germans."[49]

While the main Canadian assaults fared poorly, a series of probing attacks pointed out a weak spot in the German defences. Combat teams comprised of West Novas, Seaforths, and Ontario tanks had struck westwards, attaining remarkable results. In one sortie, a platoon of the West Novas and three tanks of the Ontario Regiment knocked out two Mark IV tanks and captured a third.[50] Later in the day, a Seaforth–Ontario combat team enjoyed similar success in the same area, capturing nearly a hundred Germans. After pausing to reorganize, Major H. A. "Snuffy" Smith led his tanks down the road to Ortona. They were stopped just short of Casa Berardi, and during the evening Smith fell back to guard the point where his little force had breached the enemy position.[51]

Here, it seemed, was the key to The Gully. The task of unlocking it was handed to the only Canadian battalion not yet committed to battle beyond the Moro, the Royal 22nd Regiment. "I had every confidence they would succeed with little difficulty," Vokes later explained, "because intercepted wireless messages indicated that the 90th Panzer Grenadier Division had been badly decimated and was not confident that it could withstand a further onslaught. Unfortunately, unknown to us, the 90th was relieved on the night of the 13–14th by the 1st Parachute Division. One company of the Royal 22nd and seven Ontario Regiment tanks would be opposed by a fresh battalion of the best German troops in Italy."[52]

The French-Canadians were to attack in the morning; before the day was out, one of them would win the Victoria Cross.

The Van Doos were scheduled to attack at 0700 hours on Tuesday, 14 December. The battle plan called for the infantry, supported by as many

Shermans as the Ontario Regiment could recover from the mud, to follow Snuffy Smith's tank tracks through The Gully, deploy on the high ground beyond, then attack along the road towards Cider crossroads. They would be preceded by an hour-long bombardment. A creeping barrage fifteen hundred yards wide, fired by corps and divisional artillery, would precede the Royal 22nd.

The Van Doo attack was to be spearheaded by two companies, commanded respectively by Captains Paul Triquet and Ovila Garceau. Triquet, a thirty-three-year-old native of Cabano, Quebec, was in a jovial mood as he led C Company towards The Gully that morning. "We're really going to get Jerry," he called to Major Jean Allard.[53] Major Smith's seven surviving Shermans were available to accompany the Van Doos.

Without waiting for the tanks to arrive, Triquet's company, eighty-one strong, moved out as soon as the bombardment ended. The shell fire had been "so terrifying," the captain later commented, "that some men were on the verge of panic."[54] The impact on the enemy was even greater. Emerging from the far side of The Gully, the Canadians rounded up "at least thirty men with an officer," according to Triquet.[55]

Attacking as planned along the road towards Cider crossroads, Triquet soon ran into problems. A German tank hidden behind a nearby house opened fire, threatening to disrupt the whole Canadian operation. Working forward by sections to distract both the tank and its infantry covering force, the French-Canadians brought up a PIAT. Sergeant J. P. Rousseau dashed into the open with his thirty-two-pound weapon, and fired at point-blank range. The bomb struck just under the turret and detonated the tank's ammunition. The Mark IV exploded with a resounding roar, and Rousseau was subsequently awarded the Military Medal. The PIAT, a cross between an anti-tank rifle and a bazooka, was not a popular weapon, and there had been many complaints about its performance, both in Sicily and on mainland Italy. But no one complained much after Rousseau's performance on the road to Ortona.[56]

Meanwhile, Major Smith's seven Shermans roared up out of The Gully. One was knocked out by a German Mark III, which was in turn destroyed by the Ontarios. Smith arrived to find Triquet's company under attack by three more enemy tanks, all of which were quickly destroyed. It was evident that the Germans were not going to be surprised on this road as they had been the day before. Nor was that the only difficulty. Captain Garceau and his men were nowhere in sight; D Company had taken a wrong turn in the darkness, and eventually ended up in the West Novas' lines. Triquet was undaunted: he had about fifty men and six tanks, and at 0830, he gave the signal to attack.[57]

The slow but steady advance was a superb display of cooperation by infantry, armour, and artillery, and of leadership by Major Smith and Captain Triquet. "It was one long Calvary," said Triquet, who was particularly inspiring. In the face of withering fire, with men dropping all about him, Triquet rallied his company. "They can't shoot!" he called. "Never mind them! Come on!"[58] There was no time to stop; the wounded were given first aid and then left where they had fallen. Smith's Shermans rolled ahead irresistibly. Two were knocked out, but not before accounting for three more German tanks.

A mile from Casa Berardi, Triquet's company was down to thirty men, now reorganized into two small platoons, each commanded by a sergeant; the captain, who seemed to be leading a charmed life, was the only officer still standing. But Triquet, who was only beginning to tap his storehouse of brave words, was undaunted. "There are enemy in front of us, behind us and on our flanks," he shouted over the din. "There is only one safe place – that is on the objective."[59]

On and on they went, the Van Doos and their Ontario tanks. "In this final rush," Triquet later wrote, "I was continually on the run between my two reduced platoons and Major Smith. I often had to jump on his tank and drop gravel on the turret to attract his attention and point out targets. My young French Canadians were superb. They showed great courage against vastly superior forces."[60]

They were finally pinned down two hundred yards from Casa Berardi. The whitewashed house stood on the edge of The Gully, in Thomas Raddall's words, "like a tall square ghost peering hollow-eyed over the battlefield."[61] But the distance might have been two hundred miles away, so heavy was the machine-gun and sniper fire raking the Canadians. It was now 1400: seven hours had passed since Triquet's company had begun its attack. Starting with eighty-one men, he now had just fourteen.

The Ontario tanks fired smoke shells to cover their advance and, with Triquet at their head, the Van Doos charged. The smoke screen gave them sufficient cover to reach the safety of the *casa*'s stout stone walls, now pocked by bullet and shell marks. While the French-Canadians routed the paratroopers inside, Major Smith spotted a German tank approaching. Using his own smoke screen to good advantage, he destroyed it with a single shot. But another of his Shermans had been knocked out, giving rise to one of those stories that make war such a fascinating study. All five crew members were wounded; their ammunition expended and no way to get out of the tank, they were to spend three days on the battlefield before being rescued.[62]

By 1530, Triquet had captured Casa Berardi. The grim-faced captain listened to his radio crackle with orders from battalion headquarters: "Hold your position at all costs and wait for reinforcements."[63] Triquet had only a handful of men, with five Bren guns and five Tommy guns, but very little ammunition, and the four gallant Shermans parked outside were also low on shells for their overheated 75-millimetre guns. Those resources, he decided, were sufficient to defend the place. As he posted his soldiers in shell holes and hastily dug slit trenches around the house, Triquet remembered a famous phrase uttered by a French general during the Great War. It seemed appropriate and he repeated it now: "Ils ne passeront pas!" ("They shall not pass!")[64]

Triquet was the picture of inspiration. He was round-faced and moustachioed and his eyes twinkled as he laughed in the face of danger. But his imperturbable features masked his real feelings. "You know, when you're caught in something like what we'd all been through, you're always scared," he said later. "Anyway, anyone who's *not* scared at a time like that is a fool!" Officers are not supposed to show fear, and he remembered with a chuckle the calming effect of his words as he scrambled from shell hole to shell hole, offering encouragement to his men. "The reaction you'd get was terrific! The bravest man in war is always the private, because he can only follow and it takes a brave man to do that."[65]

Reinforcements reached Casa Berardi after dark. Captain André Arnoldi and B Company arrived first, followed by the rest of the Royal 22nd during the night. Paul Triquet was later rewarded with a promotion to major and with a trip to Buckingham Palace, where King George presented him with the Victoria Cross, the first won by a Canadian in the Italian campaign. "I never expected the Victoria Cross for myself," he would comment. "All of my men were recommended for something. My only worry at the time was to organize a new company, because mine had been destroyed."[66] Snuffy Smith, the Ontario tank commander, won the Military Cross for his efforts.

The Canadians were here to stay, but the battle for Cider crossroads was far from over. The Van Doos and Ontario tanks at Casa Berardi were isolated on the far side of The Gully, and it was imperative that the rest of the division come to their assistance. It was also painfully clear that the paratroopers now facing the Canadians would have to be driven out or killed. Even as the battle for Casa Berardi raged, the Hasty Ps and Patricias had made repeated efforts to link up on the right, but without success in the face of heavy fire.

This led to renewed frontal attacks against The Gully, in a bid to reach the crucial crossroads. On Wednesday, 15 December, the Carleton and York Regiment made another brave attempt to break through, but the early-morning attack lasted barely an hour before the hardy New Brunswickers were forced to dig in two hundred yards closer to The Gully.

It was time to pause and prepare another major effort. The First Division had been fought to a standstill at The Gully. The rookie divisional commander, Chris Vokes, was undergoing a bloody initiation in the biggest battle so far experienced by the Canadians in Italy. "He got himself into a jam," remembers his engineer chief, Geoff Walsh. "He frittered away everything, and everything was committed, and he had no reserves, which is a terrible thing."[67]

To make matters worse, Vokes was under intense pressure to get the job done. At Eighth Army headquarters, General Montgomery was forming a poor opinion of Vokes as he watched his "colossal crack" reduced to something approximating a bad joke. Monty, suspecting that the Canadians were not pulling their weight, dispatched his current liaison officer, Colonel Dick Malone, to interview Vokes. "Old Monty wants to know what the problem is," Malone explained, "why you are getting along so slowly."[68]

"You tell Monty," raged Vokes, "if he would get to hell up here and see the bloody mud he has stuck us in, he'd know damn well why we can't move faster."[69]

Monty did come up to have a look, on 15 December, bringing with him the chief of the Imperial General Staff, Sir Alan Brooke. Under the gaze of these high-ranking and critical British generals, the pressure applied to the Canadian commander must have been almost unbearable.

Vokes responded with a plan to break the deadlock. He would rely on the artillery to blast a path through The Gully for Toronto's 48th Highlanders and the battered Royal Canadian Regiment, both belonging to the First Brigade. The brigade was now commanded by the RCR's Dan Spry, since Howard Graham had finally been evacuated as medically unfit because of his ulcers. And Vokes had decided to take the indirect approach to Cider. His three-phase plan called for the 48th Highlanders to push across The Gully west of Casa Berardi as far as the road to Villa Grande. This would be known as Operation "Morning Glory." The next phase ("Orange Blossom") would launch the Royal Canadians at a right angle, through Casa Berardi to the crossroads. The final phase would see the Second Brigade pass through and capture Ortona.

This plan was predicated on firepower. Morning Glory and Orange Blossom would be accompanied by a 250-gun barrage, which would move at the rate of a hundred yards every five minutes, with curtains of fire to seal off the flanks. The preparations for Morning Glory included a preliminary shelling, which enabled the gunners to register the target lines for their barrage (unfortunately, it was not possible to do this for Orange Blossom, because a number of factors, including the RCR start line, were not yet certain). To stockpile the enormous amounts of ammunition to be expended, the Army Service Corps toiled for three days, making thirty-five-mile round trips to haul shells from the Sangro. For the 25-pounders alone, this amounted to sixteen thousand rounds.[70]

The gunners were operating under great adversity. With their guns mired in mud up to the hubs of the wheels, it was a chore to do almost anything. On 18 December, one field regiment, the Royal Canadian Horse Artillery, would fire 8,800 rounds, totalling 111 tons of high explosive. It was an "extraordinary" achievement, according to the unit historian, "especially with so much ammunition man-handled from road to guns through wet muck." More than a few paid for their dedication to duty. "In those days before proper ear protectors, many of the gunners became deafened – some permanently impaired – from the blasts of their guns and the nearby explosions of enemy shells or bombs."[71]

Before this powerful assault was launched, the pitiful remnant of the West Nova Scotia Regiment was ordered to make another probing attack, to make sure that the Germans were still holding the crossroads in strength. Now commanded by Major Ron Waterman, the West Novas mustered only 160 riflemen for this operation. Supported by three tanks, they attacked The Gully at 1600 hours on 17 December.

The Germans were still there, and the West Novas were stopped in their tracks. Most of them could do little more than take cover in the face of the fusillade that greeted them, but a few actually got into The Gully, including Lieutenant Gordon Romkey. "I can guarantee you we got in close to them, because I got shot with a pistol bullet in the side of the head, and that ended my war." Romkey was brought back to his own lines, but he was unconscious for more than a week.[72]

This abortive effort virtually eliminated the Nova Scotia unit as an effective fighting force, if only temporarily. Its losses in The Gully now totalled 44 dead and 150 wounded.[73] But the regiment's sacrifice on the seventeenth cleared the way for Toronto's 48th Highlanders the next day.

Morning Glory was a sensational success. The barrage burst over the heads of the 48th Highlanders at 0800 hours on Saturday, 18 December. Twenty minutes later, Major John Clarke and Captain Lloyd Smith led their partially deafened companies forward, with tanks of the Three Rivers Regiment in close support. The barrage, Clarke said later, was "perfect," and he was pleased that his men were able to keep close behind it, despite the mud clutching at their feet and ankles. "The shell curtain carried us right to the objective." Only five of the twelve supporting Shermans made it through the mud, but they arrived in time to aid Clarke's company in wiping out the sole remaining strongpoint. Twenty-three paratroopers were captured after what the regimental history describes as "an insane flurry of killing."[74]

By 1030, Morning Glory was all over. The 48th had consolidated on its objective, for which the battalion commander, Ian Johnston, was awarded the Distinguished Service Order. The cost had been comparatively light: four dead and twenty wounded.[75]

The divisional artillery commander, Brigadier Bruce Matthews, takes understandable pride in this operation, whose code name came, appropriately, from a flower on his family crest. "Morning Glory," he writes, "was a good illustration of close artillery support on a one-battalion front. Registration of the co-ordinates of the barrage produced fall of shot in relatively even ground providing a high degree of confidence in the infantry. . . . These almost ideal conditions were rarely encountered in Southern Italy."[76]

But Orange Blossom was a near-disaster. Everything that went right in the initial attack went wrong in the follow-up program. Matthews had worried about this part of the plan. Unlike Morning Glory, the artillery had not had the opportunity to register targets beforehand, and it fired the Orange Blossom barrage strictly from inaccurate maps. It was later discovered that there was "a 500-metre error on about three sheets of the Italian map with British grids superimposed." There were other difficulties, including "an unsecured and, in fact, undefined start line," and the rough terrain made it "impossible for infantry to follow the barrage . . . fall of shot was very erratic." Matthews reflects: "I have always felt that I should have refused to undertake such a fire plan, but it is difficult to refuse in the face of an urgent request."[77]

Orange Blossom opened at 1145 hours. Within minutes, trouble became evident. Canadian shells were falling among both the Carleton and Yorks, on the near side of The Gully, and the 48th Highlanders, on the far side. Adjustments were made to the barrage; part of it was advanced four hundred yards, other portions were cancelled, giving enemy machine-gun posts a reprieve. The results were disastrous for the two RCR assault companies.

"Never before," Strome Galloway notes, "during either the Sicilian or Italian campaign, had the Regiment run into such a death trap." The RCR's C and D companies were virtually wiped out, suffering more than a hundred casualties. Losses among the officers and NCOs were appalling: Major Gerry Nelson, commanding D Company, died in the attack, and C Company's Captain Chuck Lithgow was severely wounded. All six platoon commanders were casualties, including the likeable young lieutenant, Mitch Sterlin, who was killed so soon after his platoon's brilliant battle at Sterlin Castle a few days earlier. C Company, or what little was left of it, ended up under the command of a corporal, G. C. "Red" Forrest, who conducted a twenty-four-hour running battle before bringing in the survivors. Forrest was later awarded a well-merited Distinguished Conduct Medal.[78]

Even the acting battalion commander, Major Bill Mathers, was wounded, but The Royal Canadian Regiment was far from finished. Mathers was replaced by the second-in-command, Major Ian Hodson, who was suffering from what Galloway calls "as bad a case of jaundice, plus malaria, as I have ever seen."[79] Within hours, Hodson was ordered to renew the attack on Cider. The acting brigade commander, Dan Spry, felt not only that the RCR could capture the crossroads but that it was necessary in order to maintain morale.

The Royal Canadians justified Spry's confidence. Backed by the same kind of superlative artillery support that had made Morning Glory a sparkling success, and assisted by tanks of the Three Rivers Regiment, the RCR overran the crossroads during the afternoon of 19 December. The two-company attack was commanded by Major Strome Galloway, who recalls that his men "went in with great dash."[80] In sharp contrast to the previous day's setback, this attack succeeded at the cost of only three casualties, including the regimental sergeant-major, Victor Lewington, who was wounded in the buttocks. (Lewington swore that he was shot by the Three Rivers tanks!) Despite the light losses, the RCR saw some stiff fighting, and Captain Tommy Burdett won the Military Cross taking out a machine-gun post in the basement of a house.[81]

By 1630 hours, Galloway's men had secured the battered crossroads, "one complete mass of smoking shell craters and blasted trees,"[82] but darkness had fallen before the Royal Canadians could consider the position secure. Even so, the tough German paratroopers stubbornly continued to man machine-guns in the area, and Galloway, who assumed temporary command of the battalion in relief of the desperately ill Ian Hodson, reports that two days afterwards "we were still clearing houses within five or six hundred yards of our position."[83]

The RCR had been reduced to an effective fighting strength of less than two hundred officers and other ranks, but the capture of Cider crossroads had moved the First Canadian Infantry Division another step towards its most famous battle – the struggle for Ortona itself.

3

No one anticipated a fight in Ortona. Experience had shown that the enemy, having been driven from The Gully, would withdraw to the next natural obstacle. The Arielli, a small stream three miles north of Ortona, seemed to offer the Germans everything they required for a defensive position. Eighth Army headquarters looked at Ortona only in terms of what it offered as a potential administrative and rest centre. Consequently, Ortona had been spared the aerial bombardment to which most towns and villages in the army's path had been subjected.[84]

Ortona was a picturesque community. Its old section, dating back to the fifteenth century, was huddled around a dilapidated castle on a precipitous cliff overlooking Ortona's artificial harbour, formed by a pair of stone breakwaters. Nearby was the great dome of the cathedral of San Tommaso, visible for miles around. While the older part of town consisted of "tall, narrow houses and dark, cramped streets," the newer section to the south and west was laid out in rectangular blocks, although most streets were very narrow. Because of a deep ravine west of town and the cliffs and sea on the other, there was only one way into Ortona, along Route 16, which turned into the Corso Vittorio Emanuele, the main street. This thoroughfare led to the town square, the Piazza Municipale.[85]

Very few of its ten thousand residents were still in Ortona in December 1943. The Germans had removed large numbers of able-bodied males to work as slave labour in northern Italy or in Germany, while a great many others had fled to the mountains. In a way, this was a good thing, for these people were spared the sight of the systematic and almost total destruction of their town. The enemy had already started the process. The harbour had been wrecked, blocked by sunken vessels and the moles breached. And the paratroopers defending Ortona had sealed off all side streets with rubble, in order to channel the attackers along the Corso Vittorio Emanuele. The central square, the Piazza Municipale, had been turned into a killing ground, the surrounding buildings filled with machine-guns, anti-tank guns, and mortars carefully sited to lay down a murderous cross-fire. The Canadians would complete Ortona's demolition during the week-long attempt to conquer it.[86]

"Everything before Ortona," General Vokes later commented, "was a nursery tale."[87]

The Canadians approached cautiously. At noon on Monday, 20 December, the Loyal Edmonton Regiment, supported by Shermans of the Three Rivers Regiment, followed a slow but steady barrage along the main road into Ortona. With their exposed left flank shrouded by a smoke screen, the Eddies reached the edge of town before encountering enemy fire, and the battalion commander, Jim Jefferson, decided against a night fight and ordered his men to dig in. Medium machine-guns of the Saskatoon Light Infantry moved up to assist, along with 17-pounders of the 90th Anti-Tank Battery.

Still not sure what to expect, the Edmontons continued to proceed cautiously the next day. Weakened by its previous losses and not having received reinforcements, the battalion was temporarily organized into three half-strength companies of sixty men apiece for the coming battle. Tuesday, 21 December, marked the beginning of what Colonel Jefferson later called "the town fighting proper." By nightfall, working their way from house to house, the prairie soldiers were within a quarter-mile of the heart of Ortona, the Piazza Municipale.[88]

When pre-dawn patrols on the twenty-second reported that the Corso Vittorio Emanuele was clear of roadblocks for three hundred yards, Major Jim Stone proposed a startling plan. He arranged for the supporting Three Rivers Shermans to drive along the Corso Vittorio Emanuele in low gear, with sirens wailing and guns blazing. This was designed to surprise and dazzle the Germans, and it almost worked.

"We started off," Stone recalls, "and the noise was absolutely deafening. We got a hundred yards without a shot being fired at us. I swear to God, if the tanks had kept going, they'd have gone straight through the first day. But the leading tank stopped, and I was so mad I got up and I beat on the tank and I asked, 'What the hell's the matter?' 'Well, you never know, there might be mines.' And, of course, the whole impetus was lost, the enemy started to shoot, and then we got stuck."[89]

Despite the enemy fire and the deadly mines, the Eddies made it to the Piazza Municipale by dark, but that was as far as they went on 22 December. While the tanks were stopped at a roadblock, Jim Stone led his company into the enemy's coldly calculated killing ground. They were promptly pinned down by five machine-guns at the entrance to the *piazza*, including three in a nearby building, but these tough Albertans went after their antagonists. Private C. G. Rattray and two buddies rushed the building and cleared the ground floor. Rattray stormed upstairs by himself, single-handedly capturing five paratroopers and the three machine-guns. Meanwhile, Stone directed the destruction of another machine-gun post (dispatched by a well-aimed grenade) and an anti-tank gun. Darkness ended the advance and the killing, for a few short hours.[90]

If 22 December demonstrated anything, it was that the Loyal Edmonton Regiment alone would not be sufficient to capture the town. A company of Seaforth Highlanders had been brought in during the day to cover the left flank, and the rest of the battalion entered the battle on the twenty-third, in addition to the PPCLI's scouts and snipers. Colonel Jefferson and the Seaforth's Major Syd Thomson divided Ortona between them, with the Corso Vittorio Emanuele the boundary. This gave each of the two western units, the Edmontons on the right and the Seaforths on the left, a more manageable front of only 250 yards. Even so, they had their hands full.

"In Ortona," writes American historian Robert Wallace, "the Canadians became, among the Allied soldiers, the acknowledged masters of house-to-house fighting."[91] But they had to learn the hard way. As the Eddies' after-action report notes, "street fighting is an acquired art and ... there are only two ways to acquire it – by careful planning and training and a high standard of discipline, or by bitter experience."[92]

Two battalions of German paratroopers defended Ortona, and they did it with the skill and determination for which they were justly famed. They welcomed the attacking Canadians to Ortona with a vast and perplexing array of defences. The sturdiest stone houses had been turned into strongpoints. In others, the front walls were demolished, exposing their interior to German fire. The rubble from this demolition work not only served as sometimes-defended roadblocks but as cover for parties of paratroopers changing positions. Other abandoned buildings were usually booby-trapped, sometimes with delayed explosive charges. Every street was covered by anti-tank weapons, and while the paratroopers never counter-attacked in Ortona, they often infiltrated into captured areas, unexpectedly popping up behind the Canadians. This tactic tied up "a larger number of [Canadian] troops than was necessary for the actual operation."[93]

The Canadians had a few tricks up their sleeve, too. They quickly learned that tight control and coordination were vital. Ortona was divided and subdivided into battalion, company, and platoon objectives, the latter sometimes consisting of two or three houses. A platoon would take its objective with one section, while the rest provided covering fire from neighbouring buildings. It could be suicidal to send men into the streets, so that most movements were done out of view, as troops moved from house to house via courtyards and balconies. When this was not possible, they employed a technique called "mouse-holing." Using an explosive charge, or pick and shovel, they would break through the walls on the upper floors of adjoining buildings.[94] Then, "stair by stair, room by room," they would clear the house and move on to the next one.[95] In some cases, they could clear entire blocks without setting foot in the street. Mouse-holing was an innovation of the Loyal Eddies' Captain Bill Longhurst, although some sources (such as the Canadian official history) say that it had been taught in battle drill schools in Britain since 1942. "I'd been to battle drill schools," says Jim Stone, "and I'd never heard of it."[96]

The Three Rivers Regiment lost three Shermans in the course of the fighting in Ortona, but the infantry later described the contribution of the tanks as "invaluable in spite of the cramped surroundings. They were used by the attackers both singly and in small numbers as assault guns or as pillboxes. They were also used to carry ammunition and mortars forward to the fighting troops and to evacuate wounded over bullet swept ground."[97] An appreciative Colonel Jefferson described their work as "wonderful."[98]

Tank losses could, and perhaps should, have been much heavier, for Ortona's narrow streets were a poor place for Shermans to fight. One dramatic episode illustrates their difficulties. A tank commanded by Sergeant J. W. Chapman was knocked out by an explosive charge, and Chapman was severely injured. A call for assistance was answered by another Sherman, commanded by Major Frank Johnson, and Trooper R. D. Gareau, driving a scout car. Johnson had a personal interest in this rescue mission, for Chapman was a boyhood friend from Trois Rivières. Gareau volunteered to hook a tow cable to the front of Johnson's tank and attach it to the rear of the disabled Sherman. The major covered him with his 38-calibre Smith and Wesson pistol, because the tank's Browning machine-guns could not be raised high enough to deal with the enemy lurking behind the second-storey windows of the buildings overlooking the street.[99]

The rescue went smoothly. Gareau hooked up the cable, and the disabled tank was hauled to a safe spot. Unfortunately, Sergeant Chapman died of his wounds two days later. Major Johnson recommended Gareau for the Military Medal, but it was turned down, says Johnson, "on the grounds that Gareau had merely done his duty."[100]

The close-quarter fighting virtually neutralized the Canadian and British advantage in artillery. Except where the infantry could pinpoint specific targets, the gunners generally had to confine themselves to harassing enemy movements along the coastal road north of town. But the Canadians could call on plenty of explosive firepower, from their hand grenade, the Type 36 which could be bowled down hallways, to the PIAT, "an ideal weapon for street fighting," according to Jefferson. They learned that their own 2-inch mortars could be most effective fired through windows. The Saskatoon Light Infantry's heavier 4.2-inch mortars worked so well that on a single day of the battle, 1,100 of these bombs were fired.[101]

A pleasant surprise, and devastatingly effective, were the anti-tank guns, both the infantry's own 6-pounders and the 17-pounders of the 90th Anti-Tank Battery. Major Tiger Welsh, who had won the Distinguished Service Order in Sicily for his superb work with anti-tank guns, had no qualms about putting these weapons to work. "There were no enemy tanks to shoot up in Ortona," he later commented, "but why remain idle when you can save lives?"[102] They could get into places where Shermans could not go, and fire at sharper angles than the tanks. George Brown, a lieutenant who commanded the Edmontons' anti-tank platoon, says his guns were in action without a break. "I can't remember how many bloody barrels we went through. Eventually, instead of us going back to pick up ammunition at the ammunition park, they sent up the big trucks loaded with ammunition. We were firing it as fast as we could. That's where I lost my hearing."[103]

And when all else failed, the Canadians resorted to the characteristics for which they are noted: initiative and courage. These attributes were reflected in the large number of decorations awarded to the participating units. Five officers won the Distinguished Service Order and three others were awarded the Military Cross; the Military Medal was given to seven other ranks.

Quarter was neither requested nor received. The savagery reached its peak on 26 December, when Eddies' Lieutenant E. D. Allen and his twenty-three-man platoon occupied a two-storey building that had been booby-trapped. The explosive charge killed all but Lance-Corporal Roy Boyd of Wembley, Alberta, who was trapped under heavy girders and cement blocks. While the dead were being removed, someone heard sounds coming from beneath the rubble, setting off a furious rescue effort. In the confined interior of the ruined house, there was room for only two men to work, and Corporal J. H. Johnman and Private R. J. Williams clawed their way into the wreckage, passing chunks of mortar and bricks to a chain of helpers behind them. By the time Boyd was pulled out, he had spent more than three days buried alive. Later, interviewed in hospital, a grateful Boyd commented, "It's like coming back from the dead." [104]

By then, the Eddies had more than evened the score, as the CBC's Matthew Halton recounted. After getting into a house by mouse-holing, "one officer, the Regimental Interpreter, crawled alone to a window of this building to hear the Germans talking. He heard an officer upbraiding his men for having let the Canadians get into the top floor. Then the Canadian crept away and found some of the engineers. In half an hour the engineers had placed charges of high explosive under the building. And after the Canadians on the top floor had been warned to get out, the building was blown up and 48 or 50 Germans in it were killed or crushed." [105]

It is one of the oddities of this "death frenzy" (Halton's words) that the Canadians came out of it with high regard for the paratroopers who fought so hard. "When it was all over," recalls the Eddies' Jim Stone, "somebody asked me, 'If you had to do this again, what would you like for troops?' I said, 'German paratroops.' They were first-class soldiers. And I remember one of them, wounded, an NCO shot in the head, and he was dying at the side of the street. I went out to him to see if I could do anything for him. He could speak a little English, and all he said was, 'We could beat you.'" [106]

One never really knew what to expect of these paratroopers. At the height of the fighting, a Seaforth stretcher-bearer found himself huddled for cover in the same room with a German. The paratrooper, who spoke some English, respected the first-aid man's non-combat status; they did, however, get into "a strong argument about the war in general" before going their separate ways. [107] On another occasion, the Germans shot a stretcher-bearer as he tried to carry a wounded man to safety. This was offset by the parachute sergeant who came out under fire to tend to a wounded Canadian. [108]

Major Doug Harkness remembers Ortona as the place where he had his closest brush with death in the whole war. The future cabinet minister, while bringing up rations to his embattled anti-tank gunners, "walked into a small square and I guess an 88 came down and exploded practically at my feet. It blew me head over heels backward – I was badly shaken and I crawled away." Staggering into the Eddies' headquarters a short distance away, he was given a drink by Colonel Jefferson to calm his nerves. Today, at age eighty-seven, he knows that he was lucky to survive that moment. "Any shell has one weak place and it splits away from that, so there's a small arc where there's no metal coming out," he explains. "I happened to be in that small arc, I guess."[109]

A day-by-day reconstruction of the battle is impossible. The inexorable but agonizing Canadian advance was measured, at times, in mere yards: doorway to doorway, courtyard to courtyard, rooftop to rooftop. Reality rudely mocked the early optimism. Captain Howard Mitchell, whose SLI machine-gun battery was supporting the grim street-fighters, recalls attending the daily orders groups at the Loyal Edmonton Regiment's head-quarters, where Colonel Jefferson outlined his plans. "At the first Orders Group he laid out plans to get to Pescara. The next day the objective was to take Ortona. The third day we had to reach a line midway through Ortona. After that . . . he would start off the Orders Group by saying, 'Well, we will see what we can do today.' It was marvellous how he bore up under strain."[110]

Everyone was soon feeling the strain. Jefferson's Seaforth counterpart, Major Syd Thomson, admits that after several days of street fighting in Ortona, "I was just about exhausted, practically living on rum, no sleep." However, Thomson's spirits were restored by a visit from his brigadier, Bert Hoffmeister. "On this particular day Bert came into Ortona and said, 'Great show, Syd, terrific show, you are doing great.' He patted me the back when all I wanted to say was 'For Christ's sake, Bert, can't I have a rest?' There was no way I could say that to him." Hoffmeister, says Thomson, "was a commander who would come to the front. . . . Bert never showed fear. During a sticky battle morale is as important, if not more important, than good tactics. On the scale of 1 to 10 morale will go from 4 to 9 just by the appearance of a senior commander in the line when and where the bullets are flying. Bert understood this." Thomson understood it, too; his personal direction of the battle, where the bullets flew thickest, afterwards brought him the Distinguished Service Order.[111]

Under the circumstances, it would have been easy to forget Christmas, but for many of these men, it was their fifth Christmas overseas, and the battalion quartermasters were determined that it not be overlooked. The Eddies were so heavily engaged that only small groups of officers and other

A comic-opera atmosphere prevailed during the first few days following the Allied invasion of Sicily on 10 July 1943, with the wholesale surrender of thousands of Italian soldiers. Among them was a divisional commander, Achille d'Havet, seen here being presented to Major-General Guy Simonds of the First Canadian Infantry Division. (National Archives of Canada/PA 138376)

The Canadians were introduced to real warfare when they finally came to grips with German troops, a week after landing. The casualties included Lieutenant-Colonel Ralph Crowe (right), commanding officer of The Royal Canadian Regiment, and his second-in-command, Major Billy Pope, killed within six days of each other in July 1943. (National Archives of Canada/ PA 132777)

Princess Patricia's Canadian Light Infantry in action north of Valguarnera on 20 July 1943. The dusty, parched terrain is typical of much of Sicily. (National Archives of Canada/PA 166750)

Mule trains were invaluable for moving weapons and supplies across the rugged Sicilian countryside, as shown by this party of The Royal Canadian Regiment. The temperamental mules proved to be equally useful when the campaign later moved into the mountainous Italian mainland. (National Archives of Canada/PA 168705)

One of the most stirring exploits of the entire war was the capture of Assoro by the Hastings and Prince Edward Regiment on 21 July 1943. Above is the view from Castle Hill, looking towards Leonforte, which was captured the next day by the Loyal Edmonton Regiment and Princess Patricia's Canadian Light Infantry. (Cindy Delisle)

The hilltop town of Agira, as it appears today. It was captured on 28 July by the First Canadian Infantry Division after five days of heavy fighting. (Cindy Delisle)

The Eighth Army's legendary commander, Sir Bernard Montgomery, loved to visit his troops and give them informal pep talks. Here Monty is seen addressing men of the Calgary Regiment in Sicily, August 1943. (National Archives of Canada/ PA 168548)

In the wake of the Allied invasion of mainland Italy, on 3 September 1943, the Canadians made extraordinary progress against minimal opposition. After a 375-mile advance, Shermans of the Calgary Regiment are shown carrying infantry of the West Nova Scotia Regiment into Potenza on 20 September. (National Archives of Canada/ PA 144113)

Campobasso, captured by the First Canadian Infantry Division on 14 October 1943, was quickly converted into a major leave centre known as "Maple Leaf City." (Cindy Delisle)

Members of the Carleton and York Regiment work their way up a steep street in the mountain village of Campochiaro, 21 October 1943. (National Archives of Canada / PA 114482)

When the Canadians went into action on the River Moro on 5-6 December 1943, it marked the start of their bloodiest month of fighting in the entire Italian campaign. Here, members of the Hastings and Prince Edward Regiment move forward through mud and tangled vineyards. (National Archives of Canada / PA 136215)

After establishing bridgeheads across the Moro, the Canadians pushed towards the small port of Ortona, only to find their line of advance blocked by The Gully. Attack and counter-attack raged back and forth for more than a week before the Canadians finally prevailed. (Cindy Delisle)

A crucial moment in the battle for The Gully came on 14 December, when Captain Paul Triquet's company of the Royal 22nd Regiment, supported by tanks of the Ontario Regiment, staged a stirring assault on Casa Berardi. This sturdy house is still occupied by a smiling *signora* and her family. A plaque on the near wall memorializes its capture by the Van Doos. (Cindy Delisle)

Paul Triquet proudly displays the Victoria Cross he won for his role at Casa Berardi. (National Archives of Canada/PA 157376)

The Loyal Edmonton Regiment moves cautiously into Ortona. This week-long battle, over Christmas 1943, established the Canadians as experts in the art of street-fighting. (National Archives of Canada / PA 116852)

Lance-Corporal Roy Boyd of the Loyal Eddies, being rescued after spending three days buried in the rubble of a booby-trapped building in Ortona. (National Archives of Canada / PA 152748)

ranks could be spared at a time to head to the rear for a bite to eat, but the Seaforth Highlanders were able to stage a more elaborate meal. The battalion headquarters had been established in the Chiesa di Santa Maria di Constantinopoli. The padre, Roy Durnford, greeted the dirty, unshaven, weary men as they trooped in, a company at a time: "Well, at last I've got you all in church!" In his diary, Durnford recounted that memorable meal:

> The floor had been cleared and tables set up, and it was heartwarming to see the tablecloths and chinaware some of the boys had scrounged, and the beer, cigarettes, chocolate, nuts, oranges and apples. There was soup, roast pork with applesauce, cauliflower, mashed potatoes, gravy, Christmas pudding and mince pies – all excellent and a credit to the cooks....
>
> What a concert of noise! As relief and relaxation took hold, the talk became louder and greetings and jokes were shouted.... Above the din one could sometimes hear machine-gun fire and shells. It was wonderful to hear so much laughter so close to so much death and suffering.... My heart grieved to see them, after their brief two-hour respite, turn their faces again to the battle.[112]

For many of these brave young men, it was their last meal.

4

Christmas 1943 was not a happy one for units of the First Brigade. While the Second Brigade slogged its way yard by heartbreaking yard through Ortona's streets and alleys, General Vokes had launched an outflanking attack two miles west of the battered town. The acting brigadier, Dan Spry, received instructions on 22 December – "only three more shooting days till Christmas," the soldiers joked blackly[113] – to commit his three infantry battalions, supported by tanks of the Ontario Regiment. Attacking in succession, in what was really an extension of the Morning Glory operation, they were to clear the Germans from the high ground due west and north of Ortona, thus cutting off the town's fanatical defenders.[114]

The attack would be led by the Hastings and Prince Edward Regiment, jumping off from the Tollo road and pushing north for a thousand yards, where the 48th Highlanders of Canada would pass through and capture the twin villages of San Nicola and San Tommaso. The woefully-weak Royal Canadian Regiment would complete the venture by driving cross-country northeastwards to the coast. Plenty of artillery was available (four field and three medium regiments), but an overnight rainfall made it unlikely that the tanks would be able to do much to help the infantry.

The Hasty Ps were not looking forward to their return to action. They had come out of the line on 19 December, following nearly two weeks of continual combat. After resting in an olive grove near San Leonardo, Farley Mowat notes that he and the rest of the battalion "would have been content to bivouac on the frozen tundra of Siberia, so long as we knew we would be left alone for a healing time."[115]

But there was no time for healing. They attacked at 0930 hours on 23 December. As he did so often, Bert Kennedy – now holding the rank of lieutenant-colonel and barely recovered from a bout of jaundice – played a crucial role. When the initial assault by two companies bogged down in the face of heavy fire, Kennedy went forward to see what could be done. After running a gauntlet of bullets and shells ("Not once did he dive for cover or even so much as hunch his shoulders," recalls Mowat, who accompanied him),[116] he quickly organized a new assault, moving up one of his reserve companies and putting out a call for the Ontario Shermans, churning through the mud somewhere to the rear. When the tanks failed to arrive, the Hasty Ps attacked on their own. Driven back by enemy fire, they tried again, this time with the tanks. By dusk, the Ontario infantry and tanks were on the objective. But it took them until the middle of the following day, Christmas Eve, to consolidate the position, as persistent paratroopers repeatedly infiltrated their exposed position. The tireless Kennedy, after moving up his remaining company, rallied his men: "Take it easy, lads! No matter what happens we will look after you."[117]

In the meantime, Toronto's 48th Highlanders had taken their turn. The battalion commander, Ian Johnston, opted for a surprise assault relying solely on the unit's small arms. As the 48th passed through the Hasty Ps, they appeared to be headed for disaster. Their attack, records the regimental history, "would have to be in the rain, at night instead of in daylight, without tanks instead of with their support, without artillery support except for general fire, with both flanks wide open and, perhaps most serious of all, without any kind of reconnaissance – just a blind advance in the rain and dark."[118]

A muddy footpath meandered into enemy-held territory, and Johnston decided to follow it to the hilltop objective a mile away. Johnston deployed the 48th in single file, then gave terse orders to Major John Clarke, whose company was at the head of the column. "Lead on – let's go!" said the colonel, and the Glamour Boys trudged into the chilly night.

No officer dared use a flashlight, or any other kind of light, to consult a map, so the troops blindly followed Clarke, hoping for the best. Along the way, they interrupted a Christmas party, capturing thirteen Germans who were opening parcels in an isolated farmhouse.

At last, they halted. No one seemed to know where they were, and Johnston hurried up to consult with Clarke. Risking a quick peek at their photos, they were pleasantly surprised to find that they were right on their objective! They had reached it without firing a shot.

That was the good news. The bad news was that they were cut off. After digging in, Johnston sent a pre-dawn patrol to link up with the Hasty Ps and bring up ammunition and rations, but it returned to report that the path behind them was blocked. Fortunately, the Germans did not seem to be aware that an entire Canadian battalion was in the midst of their defences – although they would find out soon enough.

The RCR now entered the fray. On 21 December, the regiment had marked its diamond anniversary (Canada's senior infantry unit, it had been created in 1883), but it was a mere shadow of the battalion that had crossed the Moro in such high spirits earlier in the month. To carry out its allotted task of cutting the coastal road, the RCR had to pass through the 48th, which was now isolated somewhere to the north. Small wonder that Dick Dillon, whose company was to lead the RCR assault, muttered "Are you serious?" when Major Strome Galloway, the acting battalion commander, pointed out the objective on that bleak Christmas Eve. Captain Dillon's concern was valid; he was wounded and the attack failed.[119]

The twenty-fifth of December found all three battalions of the First Brigade scattered about the "complete quagmire" west of Ortona, where they endured steady machine-gunning and shelling by the enemy. "It is hard to believe this is Christmas Day," Strome Galloway scribbled in his diary. "A year ago we did an assault landing exercise at Inverary. We had our Christmas celebration in Possingworth Park, Sussex, in January. I wonder when we'll have it this year." Christmas dinner at RCR headquarters' *casa* consisted of bully beef, bread, and wine. By now, there was no hope of getting to the road along the coast; the RCR's job was to fill the gap between the Hasty Ps and the 48th. This was done but at the cost of forty-five killed and wounded.[120]

The Hasty Ps lost a cherished veteran on Christmas Day. Major Alex Campbell, the big company commander whose hatred for Germans was matched only by his courage, had returned on the twenty-fourth from a stay in hospital. Campbell's company was ordered Christmas morning to drive out a party of paratroopers that had infiltrated the battalion's front line, and the major led the attack himself. When one platoon was pinned down by machine-gun fire, he should have deployed some of his men to outflank it. Instead, inexplicably, he seized a Tommy gun and, with "an inarticulate bellow," charged it alone. Riddled with bullets, Alex Campbell died in the cold mud of an anonymous field near Ortona.[121]

For the 48th Highlanders, Christmas and Boxing days were tense. The Germans had belatedly discovered the intrusion, and spent 25 December tightening a noose around the Torontonians, shelling, sniping, and aggressively patrolling. The 48th was in dire straits, because its food and ammunition supplies were running perilously low. However, a supply party led by the former Argonaut quarterback, Captain George Beal, arrived just before midnight, and the battalion braced for the counter-attacks that were sure to come.

They did not have long to wait. The first one was delivered at 1000 hours, the paratroopers slashing into the Canadian position behind a heavy deluge of shells. One shell demolished the farmhouse where Major Clarke had his headquarters; Clarke injured his back, but refused to be evacuated. As the Germans closed in on him, Company Sergeant-Major Gordon Keefler came to the rescue. Keefler had always insisted that a rifle and bayonet were better than a Tommy gun at close quarters, and he proved it now by killing eight Germans. The tough sergeant-major won the Military Medal for his efforts.[122]

Once, twice, three times, the paratroopers attacked, and each time they were driven back. But by noon, the 48th was in desperate straits. Even before the first assault, Colonel Johnston had dispatched his intelligence officer, Lieutenant John Clarkson, to round up some tanks. They were nowhere in sight, and Johnston knew that if they did not show up soon, he would not be able to hold this hill.

A Hollywood movie could not have been scripted better. Around 1400 hours, Johnston heard cheers; then, amid the steady shell-fire that was going on all around him, he detected the dull roar of approaching engines. There, churning through the sea of mud, were three Ontario Regiment Shermans, guided by the resolute Lieutenant Clarkson, who was later awarded the Military Cross. Their arrival was, according to Johnston, "almost miraculous. The fourth Sherman in line had bogged down in the mud – and the route was closed. If it had been the lead tank they would all have been blocked."[123]

Half an hour later, the 48th attacked. Led by a British barrage, supported by Ontario tanks, the Glamour Boys went after the paratroopers with a vengeance. They sent the Germans scurrying for shelter in the nearby villages of San Nicola and San Tommaso, leaving behind a hundred dead or prisoners. Padre Stewart East surveyed the carnage and dubbed the position "Cemetery Hill." But most of the graves dug here contained Germans; amazingly, the Highlanders suffered only eight casualties in this day-long battle.[124]

That tanks could operate in these conditions speaks volumes for the work of the "tank doctors." That was the nickname given to the men of the Royal Canadian Electrical and Mechanical Engineers, which provided a variety of units to recover and repair tanks knocked out during battle. Every armoured unit had its own light-aid detachment, and the armoured brigade had a heavy-recovery section; their job was to get the Shermans back into action as fast as possible. This involved everything from towing bogged-down tanks out of the mud to effecting minor repairs, sometimes in the midst of a minefield. More seriously damaged tanks had to be hauled away for repairs at workshops well to the rear. It was risky work. "I'm right-handed, but when I feel around inside a disabled tank in no man's land, I do it with my left hand," one tank doctor later stated. "Jerry has a habit of booby-trapping our tanks which are disabled and if I'm going to lose a hand I'd rather it be my left one."[125]

But there was still heavy fighting in Ortona, and the divisional commander, Chris Vokes, ordered more attacks west and north of the town: the 48th Highlanders were to carry out the original plan and capture San Nicola and San Tommaso, on high ground in the fork of a little stream called the Riccio, while two battalions of the Third Brigade pressed northwards. The Royal 22nd Regiment was to push the Germans back to the River Arielli, as the Carleton and York Regiment headed for the coastal village of Torre Mucchia, high atop a headland known as Point 59.

The 48th took its objectives, but neither the Van Doos nor the Carletons had much success. The Van Doos, under their new commanding officer, Major Jean Allard, ran into difficulties on the Riccio. The rock-jawed Allard, who wore "an American steel helmet which enveloped his head like a latrine-bucket" (Strome Galloway's description),[126] had taken command of the regiment during the fighting at Casa Berardi, and he would win the Distinguished Service Order for directing the battalion in this action. But the paratroopers proved once again that they could be formidable opponents, and not until the third try, on 30 December, did the Royal 22nd finally capture the high ground immediately north of San Nicola–San Tommaso. Meanwhile, the Carletons were pinned down by heavy and accurate fire from Torre Mucchia, defended by a fresh battalion of paratroopers. The brigadier, Graeme Gibson, ordered the New Brunswickers to take up defensive positions on the coast road, at the foot of Point 59.

But their troubles did not end there. On New Year's Eve, a thunderstorm descended upon the boggy, blood-soaked Ortona battlefields, and the resourceful enemy paratroopers used the storm as a cover for a surprise attack on the Carletons. Before they fully realized what was happening, two companies had been driven back, suffering fifty casualties in the process. As a result of this setback, Point 59 would remain in enemy hands for a few more days.[127]

By then, however, the battle in Ortona would be long over.

At 0800 hours on Tuesday, 28 December, the CBC's Matt Halton drove into Ortona. An unearthly quiet had fallen over the ruined town, punctuated by the occasional shell or machine-gun burst. Entering the Eddies' command post, the reporter met Colonel Jefferson. "Don't tell me?" he said to the colonel.

"Yes," Jefferson grinned, "I think we've got Ortona. There's a patrol going through the fort now. If they find no Germans there, the thing is over. We'll know any minute."

Ten minutes later, the radio operator took off his headset and turned to the colonel. "Sir, the Jerries have gone, or else they're all dead."[128]

The battle was over. Bloodied but unbowed, the paratroopers had pulled out of Ortona during the night.

"It was a feeling of relief," says the Edmonton major, Jim Stone, who was rewarded with the Military Cross for his efforts in Ortona. "Somebody had a big jug of Marsala, and I took a slug – went down to my boots. The world looked much better that morning."[129]

Ortona lay in ruins. Artist Charles Comfort, who went into the town later that day, was astonished by "the worst havoc we had yet seen. . . . The familiar world had disappeared, and in its place a grotesque and malignant forest of ruins crowded all about us, leaing, tottering crazily, reeking with the malodorous stench of death." Nothing saddened him more than the sight of the great cathedral, San Tommaso, which the retreating Germans had blown up, leaving it "half buried in its own masonry, looking as if a mighty cleaver had struck down through the dome and split it in half like a butchered deer." He was so upset that he was unable to do any sketching, although he returned to paint the wreckage of the once-great church.[130]

The Germans were gone, but Ortona was still a very dangerous place, as Halton discovered when he was taken on a tour. "As I stepped forward once I was pulled back by the officer with me. He bent down and picked up a piece of paper, set with cunning artlessness over a buried mine."[131] In fact, there would be casualties – particularly among returning civilians – for days and weeks, from the countless mines and booby traps in Ortona.

The price paid for this small corner of Italy was dear. The two infantry battalions had borne the brunt of the losses, the Eddies losing 172 and the Seaforths 103, either killed or wounded. Germans losses are unknown, but the Canadians recovered the bodies of 100 paratroopers scattered among the shattered streets and houses.[132]

It was with justifiable pride that the Edmontons and Seaforths painted a sign, which was posted at the entrance to the town:

THIS IS ORTONA,
A WEST CANADIAN TOWN.[133]

CHAPTER NINE

"A Haywire Outfit"

1

"We smashed 90 Panzer Grenadier Division," General Vokes later wrote of Ortona, "and we gave 1 German Para Division a mauling which it will long remember."[1]

One irony is that Germans had no desire to get too deeply involved in the defence of Ortona. But the battle attracted an unusual amount of media attention, which exerted an unfortunate influence on events. On 22 December, the American news agency, the Associated Press, referred (with some exaggeration) to the "miniature Stalingrad in hapless Ortona," and the Germans could not ignore the publicity being given to this minor action on Italy's Adriatic coast. On Christmas Day, Generalfeldmarschall Albert Kesselring complained that "we do not want to defend Ortona decisively, but the English have made it as important as Rome . . . you can do nothing when things develop in this manner; it is only too bad that- . . . the world press makes so much of it."[2]

Canadians would long remember Ortona, too – both the veterans who survived it, and the grieving families of the many who did not. December had been a grim month. In the slow, painful progress from the Moro past Ortona, Canadian casualties totalled 695 dead and 1,738 wounded, in addition to 1,773 sick, for a staggering total of 4,206.[3]

It would take months to rebuild the First Canadian Infantry Division. Even after the arrival of reinforcements during Christmas week, the division remained 1,050 below strength on the last day of December. General Vokes had to admit that it had lost its "sharp fighting edge," for most of the casualties had, as usual, fallen among the infantry, where rifle companies had been reduced by half or more.[4]

The condition of The Royal Canadian Regiment was typical of the appalling state of the division's nine infantry battalions. The RCR, recalls Strome Galloway, had undergone a dramatic transformation in the past few months:

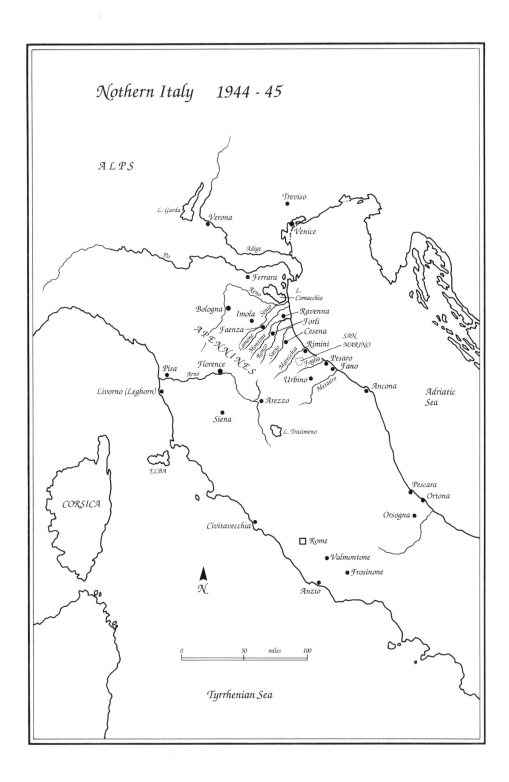

Nothern Italy   1944 - 45

ALPS

L. Garda

Treviso

Verona

Venice

Adige

Po

Ferrara

Reno

L. Comacchio

Bologna

Imola

Ravenna

Senio

Faenza

Forli

APENNINES

Lamone

Cesena

Montone

Rimini

Ronco

SAN MARINO

Savio

Pisa

Marecchia

Pesaro

Florence

Foglia

Fano

Arno

Urbino

Livorno (Leghorn)

Metauro

Ancona

Arezzo

Adriatic Sea

Siena

L. Trasimeno

ELBA

Pescara

Ortona

CORSICA

Orsogna

Civitavecchia

Rome

Valmontone

Frosinone

N

Anzio

0   50   miles   100

Tyrrhenian Sea

Of the 41 officers who had landed at Pachino less than six months before only nine remained with the battalion, and six of us had been wounded. We landed 756 strong. Now, more than 550 of these originals were among the killed, wounded, missing or prisoners of war. Or, they had gone out with jaundice, malaria or other ailments. Some had been wounded, returned and wounded again. New faces had appeared as reinforcements and had been evacuated or buried before we even learned their names.[5]

The infantry had borne the majority of the casualties, but they did not have a monopoly on misery. Gunners and tankers, engineers and signallers, truck drivers and tank doctors, stretcher-bearers and surgeons, quartermasters and cooks, had put in long, hard hours to make victory possible. "It was," observes the Second Brigade's Bert Hoffmeister, "a tremendous team effort."[6]

Ortona scarred men, both physically and mentally. One-quarter (484) of the Canadian sick were cases of exhaustion. "These, though classified as sick, in need of psychiatric rather than surgical treatment, were really battle casualties inflicted by intense strain instead of enemy weapons."[7] During the Great War of 1914–18, these unfortunates had been lumped together into the category of "shell shock," an umbrella term used dismissively by many experts to describe everything from cowardice to insanity. Major Arthur Doyle, the psychiatrist attached to First Division headquarters, was fascinated by what he found in Italy. "Every sort of clinical picture was seen," he reported as he travelled about the Canadian sector on a motorcycle, "gross hysterias with mutism, paralysis . . . the range went from these to the poor inadequate personality who showed little outward evidence of anxiety but said simply – 'I can't take it.'"[8]

One such casualty was Jack Anderson, a private in the RCR. Today, residing in a Halifax high-rise, he reflects on his wartime experiences, raging at the stupidity and waste and futility, chuckling at the characters he encountered, marvelling at the bravery he witnessed. A veteran of Sicily, Anderson reached his breaking point during the battle at Sterlin Castle. Afterwards, "I was useless," he confesses. "I did not have the nerve to face it any more." Already suffering from a painfully infected wisdom tooth, which caused the side of his face to swell, he developed a tic on his forehead when he was sent back to the battalion. The medical officer refused to have anything to do with him until Anderson's company commander, Captain Slim Liddell, intervened on his behalf. When Anderson was finally sent to the rear, his war was over. "I'm not ashamed of it, you know. It was battle fatigue. There was a time I was so shaky, you know – it happened all of a sudden. It took me months and months to get over it."[9]

There is no lack of criticism about the battle in and around Ortona in December 1943. Most of the critics focus on Chris Vokes, the rookie divisional commander. Geoff Walsh, the divisional engineer, comments: "Chris Vokes was very good with [i.e., under] Guy Simonds. . . . Guy knew what to do and how to handle Chris. But Chris on his own was very impulsive."[10]

The criticism started during the battle. During a Third Brigade conference on 20 December, Captain R.D. Prince noted that the consensus among senior officers was that The Gully should "have been turned earlier from the left flank. . . . It was impossible for a frontal attack to be successful. . . . The elementary manoeuvres of feeling out and attempting to turn the flank were not used here."[11] That belief is shared by Jim Stone, the heroic Loyal Eddy who came out of the battle with two minor wounds and the Military Criss. "Ortona was a frightfully-fought battle," he contends. It "should never have been fought."[12]

Historians, the Monday-morning quarterbacks whose hindsight is blessed with perfection, are even more critical. Brereton Greenhous writes that "Vokes, for all his bluster, was never a man for daring or momentum. Or for small leaps of logic." Greenhous argues "there seems no obvious explanation for Vokes' decision to attack the town itself instead of just leaving a brigade to mask it (or even a battalion . . .). His efforts should surely have been directed to deepening that [Morning Glory] salient. But, in a very humdrum way, taking Ortona itself was the next logical step: Ortona, after all, was the immediate, direct objective, and to push on north required a small leap of logic."[13]

Greenhous overlooks the fact that Vokes did attempt to outflank Ortona, as soon as it became apparent that the enemy was defending the town in strength. He also overlooks the difficulties encountered by the First and Third brigades and the Ontario tanks in the valiant attempts to fight their way through the quagmire west and north of Ortona. A pivotal figure in the battle was Bert Hoffmeister, the Vancouver businessman who emerged from the war as one of Canada's most successful soldiers. And Hoffmeister points out that Vokes did offer to call off the battle. "I think it was about day four or five," he says, "I felt that we were making progress . . . I could see light at the end of the tunnel. Chris Vokes asked me if I would like to quit, and I said, 'Absolutely not, to quit at this time would be letting the brigade down and the effect on the morale of the brigade would be such that it would be just shocking.'"[14]

Vokes's handling of the battle can be questioned in some respects – there were too many frontal assaults against The Gully, and he committed all of his reserves – but it is unfair to blame him. The real culprit resided at

Eighth Army headquarters. It was Bernard Montgomery who insisted on prolonging offensive operations in impossible ground and weather conditions, the same Monty who had built his reputation on sparing the lives of his troops. And whatever is said about Vokes's tactics, it should be noted that of the four divisions leading Monty's "colossal crack," only the First Canadian could claim a significant, if costly, success. The others, the British 5th, the 2nd New Zealand, and the 8th Indian, had encountered prolonged, and no less costly, failure.

But these facts were lost on the Canadian veterans who nicknamed Vokes "The Butcher." Perhaps, if they had known him better, they would not have been so unkind. One of his staff officers later told war correspondent Doug How: "I came in at Christmastime, and the soldiers were fighting at Ortona. Chris Vokes was having dinner all by himself in his own headquarters, and he was crying. There was only one reason he was weeping – he realized what these men were going through."[15]

In Canada, Christmas 1943 was subdued. It was not just the inconvenience of food rationing, and the limited quantity and quality of other commodities. Death had visited too many families, especially in the last six months, with the air force's escalating involvement in the bomber offensive against Germany and with the army's long-awaited commitment to action in Italy. There were many like W. D. Fereday, a Great War veteran living on Scarborough Road in Toronto. Fate dealt him and his wife a cruel blow in 1943. Their twenty-five-year-old son, Terry, a private in the 48th Highlanders, had been killed in action on 18 December at The Gully. The next day, Terry's younger brother, Eric, an RCAF pilot officer, died in a training mishap in Prince Rupert, British Columbia. Christmas in the Fereday household was not a happy one.[16]

Throughout December, all Canadians were riveted to their radios. The CBC was setting the standard for battlefront broadcasts, catapulting Matthew Halton into national prominence. Unlike some correspondents, Halton really did venture into the front lines to make his reports, but his self-centred nature did not endear him to his colleagues, who tired of his long-winded stories of hair-raising escapes from death. Ralph Allen once interrupted Halton in the middle of a story and advised him not to tell it any more. "Why not?" the radio reporter asked, indignantly. "Well," replied Allen, "every time you tell it it gets more and more hectic and one of these times you're going to get killed."[17]

Broadcasting was still in its infancy, and the equipment was extremely primitive, not to mention bulky. There were no tape recorders. To capture the sounds of battle, the technicians accompanying Halton had to cut a phonograph record inside the van which carried all of the necessary equipment. And Italy's weather did not make things easier for them, according to Arthur Holmes. "During the summer," he complained in late 1943, "heat made the discs almost too hot to handle. Now we find that we can hardly cut the discs as the cold makes them so hard, and low temperature produces high surface noises, too."[18] But so impressive was the quality of the CBC recordings that they were regularly broadcast by the BBC and the American radio networks.

Halton's words captivated the nation:

> Soaking wet, in a morass of mud, against an enemy fighting harder than he's fought before, the Canadians attack, attack and attack. The enemy now is fighting like the devil to hold us. He brings in more and more guns, more and more troops. The hillsides and farmlands and orchards are a ghastly brew of fire, and our roads for four miles behind the forward infantry are under heavy shelling. Not as bad as our own shelling, but bad enough. . . .
>
> Listen to the echo of those shells! Those are our guns far behind, in such a position that there is this wild echoing. . . .

When Ortona finally fell, Canada cheered. CANADA BAYONETS WIN ORTONA, proclaimed the banner headline of the *Toronto Star* on 28 December, with a smaller headline underneath: "Little Stalingrad." Ortona, said the Montreal *Gazette*, "will always rank and be remembered definitely as a Canadian show."[19] On a more sobering note, foreshadowing the conscription crisis of late 1944, Ottawa's *Evening Citizen* perceptively pointed out that fighting in Ortona had been "the hardest of any wherein Canadian troops have taken part in this war. Substantial reinforcements will evidently be needed to restore the 1st Division to full bayonet strength. The effectiveness of Canada's military organization is about to be put to the test."[20]

2

One of the best Canadian combat units in Italy did not fight as part of the Canadian army. Originally designated the 2nd Canadian Parachute Battalion, it was renamed the 1st Canadian Special Service Battalion. But this was for book-keeping purposes only. The members of this battalion served in a bi-national unit known as the First Special Service Force.

It had been a hot day in July 1942 when thirty-two-year-old Tom Gilday arrived at Fort William Henry Harrison, near Helena, Montana. As Major Gilday strode into the administration building to present his Canadian army papers, he noticed parachutes descending from the sky. "I remember standing in the orderly room," he recalls, "and the typist was typing out my form, asking me questions – name, number, et cetera – and while he was doing that, a parachutist landed on the roof of the building, rolled off the roof onto the ground, right outside our window. An ambulance came along and picked him up, and away he went. And all this time, the man who was doing the typing simply glanced out the window, came right back to his typewriter, and continued to ask me questions as though this was just an event that happened every five minutes. And I wondered what kind of a haywire outfit I had arrived into!"[21]

This "haywire outfit" was one of the élite units of World War II. The First Special Service Force traced its origins to early 1942 and a fantastic scheme to mount widespread wintertime raids on enemy installations in occupied Europe, ranging from Norway to northern Italy to Romania. The specially trained raiders were to be equipped with a tracked vehicle to carry them cross-country. This scheme, code-named "Plough," was enthusiastically embraced by Prime Minister Churchill, who subsequently offered it to the American army's chief of staff, George Marshall. Marshall, in turn, was sufficiently intrigued by the idea that he agreed to take it over. Plough was eventually cancelled, but not before a special unit had been created for this specific purpose.

A thirty-five-year-old U.S. Army colonel, Robert Frederick, was given *carte blanche* to raise and train the innocuously named First Special Service Force. For a base, Frederick selected an idle National Guard camp in Montana which offered the variety of terrain required for the specialized training he envisaged. He specified that only the best candidates were to be accepted: "Single men between ages 21 and 35 who had completed three years or more grammar school within the occupational range of Lumberjacks, Forest Rangers, Hunters, Northwoodsmen, Game Wardens, Prospectors, and Explorers." With no precedents, he organized this force as he saw fit. It would be composed of a combat and a service echelon, the latter responsible for work details, supply, and administration, and the former concerned solely with fighting. The combat echelon consisted of three regiments, each containing two battalions, with three companies of three platoons per battalion. It would be a compact force; the original plan authorized 32 officers and 385 other ranks per regiment, although this was later increased by 50 per cent.[22]

Frederick would also command a contingent of Canadians. The British had approached Canada with a proposal to participate in Plough, and these discussions led to Prime Minister King's personal approval on 26 June 1942. Within three weeks, Defence Minister Ralston authorized 47 officers and 650 other ranks to be seconded to the U.S. Army for this purpose. These men were given the administrative title 2nd Canadian

Parachute Battalion; this was changed to the 1st Canadian Special Service Battalion in May 1943. Thus, about half of the Force's initial combat element was to be Canadian. However, this fell to one-third when the enlisted strength was increased and, taking into account the service echelon, the Canadian component finally amounted to about a quarter of the Force's strength.[23]

The senior Canadian officer in the Force was John McQueen of the Calgary Highlanders. He was succeeded by a pair of Ontarians, D. D. Williamson and, later, Jack Akehurst. Canadians were well represented in the command structure; by the time the Force went into battle in Italy, Williamson, a full colonel, was one of the three regimental commanders in the Force, while five of the six battalion commanders (lieutenant-colonels) were Canadians.

One of the battalion commanders was Tom Gilday, whose initial involvement was to round up volunteers for the project. "I wasn't asked to volunteer," he points out, "I was told to go." A member of Montreal's Canadian Grenadier Guards since 1932, he had served as the army's only ski instructor since 1940, training men to travel and survive in the snow. This seemed to fit perfectly into Plough's intentions, and Gilday was sent out to sign up candidates. "I picked trappers and hunters, bushmen, farmers' sons, all good individual outdoor types who would know their way around in the woods and in the country and in all kinds of weather conditions."[24]

The results were intriguing. During the summer of 1942, men converged on Fort Harrison from every corner of North America. Among the first to arrive was a second lieutenant named Stan Waters, who would one day command the Canadian armed forces and, later, serve as Canada's first elected senator. "There were some Americans there and some Canadians there," he recalls. "We had a hodgepodge, a mixture of every possible uniform. I'd never seen so many different uniforms, both American and Canadian."[25]

The training was varied and rigorous. They were taught parachuting, skiing, and mountain climbing. Everything was done "at the double," and their physical conditioning was aided by calisthenics, obstacle courses, and long marches with hundred-pound packs. Each man learned how to handle explosives and to use every weapon in the Force's impressive arsenal. These included the M-1 (Garand) semi-automatic rifle, the Browning automatic rifle (the American equivalent of the Bren), a new rocket launcher better known by its nickname of "bazooka," the 60-millimetre mortar, the portable flamethrower, grenades, the Johnson light machine-gun, and the V-42 dagger. Hand-to-hand combat, night fighting, and use of captured weapons (German and Japanese) rounded out the training program.

For the Canadians, accustomed to the thriftiness of their own army, it was a new and wondrous experience. "We seemed to have unlimited resources for training – ammunition and equipment," says Waters. "Lots of special equipment, vehicles. The first oversnow vehicle, the Weasel, was prepared for the Force. They were designed and produced by Studebaker, and I believe the time-frame was something like sixteen months. Absolutely incredible."[26]

The days were long and busy, and there were many injuries. "I guess we lost almost as many people in training as we did in operations," recounts a bemused Waters. Many of these occurred during parachuting, he says, "because we had inadequate preparation. You were in an airplane and you got out."[27] Serious injury meant immediate reassignment elsewhere, as the senior Canadian officer, Lieutenant-Colonel McQueen, discovered when he broke his leg during a parachute exercise.

The Canadians had to learn the American way of doing things. For most of them this was not difficult, since the majority of the officers and NCOs were relative newcomers. But for long-time soldiers like Tom Gilday, there were substantial differences. "For one thing," he notes, "there was no special training for NCOs. They simply hung stripes on people and expected them to be natural leaders." Gilday was disappointed when the Americans rejected a proposal to adopt a British training innovation, battle drill, which emphasized section and platoon movements. However, he recognizes that this was just another difference in the way Americans operated. "Americans really don't fight sections, and they really don't fight platoons or companies. They are a huge, huge army; you just feel lost in it. Where we would throw in a company, they would throw in a battalion."[28]

Gilday, and a fellow Montrealer and battalion commander, John Bourne, a Black Watch veteran, set up a private school for NCOs, giving section and platoon leaders a crash course in battle drill. "It was one of our little secret ventures," Gilday recalls fondly, "and it worked. We are satisfied that, in the long run, it saved lives. And it gave us a chance to train our section leaders the way we felt a section leader should be trained. And our platoon sergeants and our platoon commanders, it gave them the ability to give orders and know exactly what they were talking about."[29]

One problem that was more annoying than real was that of pay. American army pay rates were higher than the Canadian army's, but Colonel Frederick's suggestion that Ottawa pay its troops at American rates was rejected. Even allowing for the fact that the Americans paid income tax and Canadians did not, a Canadian staff sergeant earned $99 a month, compared to the $93 earned by an American private, while an unmarried Canadian private earned a mere $63.[30] However, Sergeant Ken Cashman notes that the resourceful Canadians managed to get around this problem.

They were paid twice a month, while the Americans were paid but once, "and we took it upon ourselves to loan large amounts of our pay to the Americans at usurious rates. And, of course, the usual gambling games, you could increase your pay allotment that way."[31]

There was little to distinguish the Canadians from their American colleagues. Everyone wore American uniforms and rank badges, although provision was made for officers and enlisted men to wear brass CANADA insignia on their collars, and the Force's shoulder badge was a red spearhead with USA-CANADA in white letters. But these distinctions did not seem to matter, for there were no national sub-units within the Force: Canadians and Americans were mixed together, eating, sleeping, training, fighting, and, eventually, dying side by side. "After we had been working together for a few months," recalls Colonel Gilday, "actually it was hard to tell an American from a Canadian. We all had the same uniforms and it wasn't long before we forgot that we were anything except well-trained soldiers."[32]

Plough was cancelled during the winter of 1942–43, but it was clear that the Force had other uses. Not only was it superbly trained, but its skills and variety of automatic weapons made this an inordinately powerful formation. Although numerically smaller than a Canadian brigade or an American regiment, the Force boasted the firepower of a full division. A new task was found for the Force: it would be a shock formation. As such, it would go into action as an infantry unit, but in places too difficult for ordinary infantry formations, tackling objectives considered impregnable. "We continued to train very vigorously," says Stan Waters, "but perhaps spending more time on conventional infantry training, fire and movement, and command."[33]

Its first taste of action came in the summer of 1943, when the Force participated in the expedition to drive the Japanese from the Aleutian Islands, their only toehold in North America. The Force led the assault on an island named Attu, only to discover that the Japanese garrison had withdrawn earlier.

By the beginning of September, the Force had returned to the United States to resume its training and preparation for its next challenge – Italy.

The Force arrived in Italy on 19 November 1943. Two weeks later, as part of the U.S. Fifth Army, it underwent its baptism of fire.

With Rome the tantalizing but far-off objective, Mark Clark's Fifth Army was poised to launch its assault on the mountains below Monte Cassino. The army's advance in November had been halted before Monte la Difensa, the left shoulder of the Mignano Gap, which led to Cassino. "A veritable fortress," Difensa (also known as Hill 960, from its height in metres) was a looming grey hulk criss-crossed by perilous trails leading to perpendicular cliffs at its snow-capped peak. The Force was ordered to take it and Monte la Remetanea, just beyond.[34] "There was no doubt in anybody's mind about taking Difensa," recalls Colonel Gilday, whose battalion was in reserve for this action. "Everybody felt that if it was there, we could do it."[35]

The task of taking the mountain was given to Colonel D. D. Williamson's 2nd Regiment. The assault battalion was also commanded by a Canadian, Lieutenant-Colonel Tommy MacWilliam, who in more peaceful times was a history professor from New Brunswick. Because of the sheer difficulty of the ground, the operation was divided into two parts: the first night, the Force would make the seven-hour climb part-way up the mountain, hide during the day, then make the final ascent the next night.

That climb was both gruelling and unforgettable. "We were carrying our normal combat supplies, rations, ammunition, and we were carrying extra ammunition, which we knew we would need when we got up there," recalls Ken Cashman. "On top of this there was no water up there, we had to carry extra water," which is what Cashman carried up Difensa. "I honestly don't know how some of us did it. One of the mules broke down, and one of the Forcemen took the load off the mule and carried it the rest of the way himself." Sergeant Cashman found it inspiring to see the Force commander, Colonel Frederick, accompanying them. "He was always with us," Cashman says fondly of Frederick. "If he was not with us on the immediate assault, he was very close to it. He made it a point of being seen in the front lines. His idea was leadership, not drive."[36]

They took the Germans by surprise on Difensa. At dawn on Friday, 3 December, Tommy MacWilliam's assault battalion, climbing ropes and masked by fog, scaled the final cliffs and swarmed across the mountaintop.

It was all over in less than an hour. "Being new to combat, new to coming under shell fire, I think we were naïve about what was happening," says Cashman. "It was still more like a training exercise, until we got to the top and discovered that it wasn't a training exercise. It came as a bit of a shock. It scared the hell out of me." His terror was soon supplanted by anger. For two nights, he had sweated and strained under the weight of a five-gallon jerrycan of water; within ten minutes of getting to the top, he was hit by fragments from a mortar bomb or artillery shell. Slightly wounded, Cashman was more concerned about his jerrycan, which had been punctured. "And there went five gallons of water that I'd lugged up the mountain which didn't do anybody a damn bit of good."[37]

The Difensa triumph marked the start of a bloody, six-day battle, concluding with the capture of Monte la Remetanea. Its introduction to the Italian campaign had cost the Force 511 casualties, including seventy-three dead and 116 exhaustion cases.[38] Stan Waters, now a captain, went into action as a junior company commander; by the time it ended, he was commanding a battalion, for the losses included his colonel, Tommy MacWilliam (killed by a mortar blast), and both senior company commanders.[39]

When British troops of the 56th Division took neighbouring Monte Camino, and the U.S. 36th Division seized Monte Sammucro to the north, the Mignano Gap had been forced open. The next task was to punch through, but this could not be done until rocky Hill 720, west of Sammucro, had been taken, along with towering Monte Majo overlooking the Rapido valley northeast of Cassino. After a pause to rest and reorganize, the Force was sent to take these key positions.

Following a bloody battle on Christmas Day to capture Hill 720, the Force went about seizing Monte Majo's four-thousand-foot peak. While the weakened 1st and 2nd regiments (both down to half of their authorized strength) cleared the high ground leading to Majo from the south, Colonel Frederick's remaining regiment, the 3rd, was sent into the wilderness, to outflank the mountain from the north. By now, the beginning of January 1944, the Force was battling the elements as much as the enemy. "Winter was now full upon central Italy," says the unit history. "Strong winds whipped up the flat valleys and snow covered the lowlands. Above 500 meters there was zero [Fahrenheit] weather and three inches of snow; at 600 meters it was five inches and drifting. The elements and the mountainous route ahead promised no comfort to men on the trail."[40]

After the 3rd Regiment set out on its arduous journey, the 1st and 2nd attacked. (The latter was now commanded by an American, Bob Moore, when Colonel Williamson, suffering from ulcers, was invalided back to Canada.) In quick succession, they cleared the surprised Germans from Hills 670, 724, and 775 on 4 January. One German prisoner remembered his late-evening encounter with the Force. "We were standing alertly at our machine guns," he told his captors, "when a voice said 'Hands up!' The attack was very excellently accomplished."[41]

Now it was the 3rd Regiment's turn. Majo was assigned to the 1st Battalion, commanded by Lieutenant-Colonel Tom Gilday, who had been instrumental in organizing the Force's Canadian contingent. Gilday, a rugged outdoorsman (who still cross-country skis in his eightieth year), responded by staging what historian Robert Burhans called "a masterful piece of military work."[42] Gilday sent one company to slip around the enemy positions, while he led the main body in a frontal advance up Majo's steep, snowswept slopes.

It worked beautifully. On the night of 6–7 January, Gilday's battalion scaled the heights and swiftly routed the surprised Germans from their rocky fortress. Majo rivalled Difensa as a feat of physical endurance; and, like Difensa, the capture of the peak marked the beginning of a prolonged fight. "We used up all our ammunition in the main assault," Gilday recalls, "and Jerry left his machine-guns with lots of ammunition behind, when we pushed him out, and we had to use his weapons for the next day, or even two days, before we could get resupplied from our base." He estimates that the Germans launched forty-two counter-attacks in the next few days, and the captured weapons proved to be invaluable, as was the American artillery, which responded to countless calls for assistance. At one point, Gilday spotted Germans – he stopped counting at seventy – slipping through the snow into a little cluster of trees to form up for an attack. Gilday personally brought down shell fire on the wood. "I'm quite certain that there wasn't a single person in that company that could walk away from it. When I saw the stretcher-bearers coming up through the snow, I called off the fire." He admits that he took grim satisfaction in smashing the threatened attack. "I felt that it sort of balanced the books a little bit," he explains, "because I'd lost some awfully good men."[43]

Gilday's battalion held on for more than week, in adverse conditions. It was bitterly cold on Majo, as a young sergeant named Tony Planinshek can attest. A Montrealer, Planinshek survived the attack to celebrate his twenty-first birthday on 9 January, only to freeze his feet in the aftermath of the battle. "They carried me off the mountain," he says with a rueful smile, and he spent nearly two weeks in hospital in Caserta.[44] But Planinshek had been lucky. Sixty-seven Canadian members of the Force were either killed or wounded on Monte Majo.[45]

By the time the First Special Service Force was pulled out of the line in the middle of January, it had established an impressive record. After securing Majo, it drove the enemy from Hills 1109 and 1270, and other Fifth Army formations cleared the Germans from their few remaining positions east of Cassino. Thanks largely to the efforts of this élite Canadian–American unit, the Fifth Army was finally ready to launch its long-awaited offensive on Rome.

Success was directly due to its training. According to Ken Cashman, who had been wounded on Difensa, "We were taught to think for ourselves, but a lot of stuff that we did when we first came under fire was reaction to the training that we'd had. It was done more by instinct than by stopping to think a situation out. You instinctively did certain things. That reaction comes from being well trained."[46] As Colonel Gilday points out, "we had a tremendous advantage when it came to fighting in the mountains of Italy. We not only had the advantage of having trained in mountains, and trained with ropes, and pitons, et cetera, but we also had the clothing and the equipment that went with it, and no other soldiers had that."[47]

But the cost of the Force's first month in Italy had been dear. Out of a combat strength of 1,800, 1,400 were either dead or hospitalized for fatigue or ailments such as frostbite and trench foot.[48] The Canadian contingent had been cut in half.[49]

There was no time for regrets, and not much more for recovery. The Force was headed for a place called Anzio.

3

By late 1943, the Allied campaign in Italy was in serious trouble. While Montgomery's colossal crack was mired in the mud on Italy's Adriatic coast, Mark Clark's drive on Rome had run into the roadblock in the mountains before Cassino. Worse, the Allies were still uncertain about just how this increasingly difficult campaign fit into their overall strategy.

The campaign had fallen victim to its own confused guidelines. Its objectives were being continually altered in order to justify its existence. There were half a million Allied soldiers in Italy now, but their efforts were being hamstrung by serious administrative troubles. "Two campaigns were being fought at the same time," explained British military analyst J. F. C. Fuller, "one on the ground and one in the air." This was a product of the fuzzy premise for the invasion of Italy, for one of the main objectives, after the capture of the Foggia plain, was to utilize it as a base for long-range bombers striking into the heart of Germany and other targets, notably the oilfields in Romania. The air forces tied up vast amounts of shipping, which slowed the army's build-up during the last three months of 1943.[50]

Winston Churchill's mission was to salvage the campaign. "We had an army there which, if not supported, might be entirely cast away, giving Hitler the greatest triumph he had had since the fall of France," he later wrote. Although things had not gone as well as he had hoped, the Italian front had made a tangible contribution to the Allied cause. "It had attracted to itself twenty good German divisions. If the garrisons kept in the Balkans for fear of attack there were added, nearly forty divisions were retained facing the Allies in the Mediterranean."[51]

The British prime minister redoubled his efforts to keep alive the Italian campaign. With several months before the cross-Channel invasion could take place, he saw no sense in the planned withdrawal of troops and landing craft, because "in the Mediterranean alone are we in contact with the enemy and able to bring superior numbers to bear upon him now. It is certainly an odd way of helping the Russians, to slow down the fight in the only theatre where anything can be done for some months."[52]

It was a familiar theme, and he would once again have to overcome increasing American suspicions. In July 1943, Roosevelt's secretary of war,

Henry Stimson, had warned the president that the British were still haunted by their costly battles on the Western Front in the last war and by their defeat in 1940, which contributed to their "terribly dangerous" theories about winning the war.[53] Senior American planners had begun to suspect that the the British viewed the Allied build-up in Britain not as an invasion force but as "a gigantic deception plan and an occupying force" after Germany's inevitable collapse.[54]

Churchill was able to argue his case in late 1943. His concerns were addressed at Teheran where, between 28 November and 1 December, the first meeting of the so-called "Big Three" – Churchill, Roosevelt, and Stalin – took place. The historic conference concluded with a number of far-reaching decisions; they included, so far as the Mediterranean was concerned, limiting the advance in Italy to Pisa–Rimini, the retention of a certain number of landing craft in this theatre until mid-January, and "an operation" (code-named "Anvil") of unspecified size against southern France to coincide with Overlord.[55]

Afterwards, the Americans and British convened in Cairo in early December to work out a compromise. They must, said Roosevelt, balance "the integrity of Overlord" against the British desire "to keep the Mediterranean ablaze."[56] A compromise was reached, thanks to Dwight Eisenhower and his staff at Allied Force Headquarters. Eisenhower presented a paper which concluded that the Italian campaign had accomplished its goals, but that a further advance to the Po valley, in northern Italy, would greatly enhance Overlord's chances of success. The catch was that the Po could be reached only if the forces in Italy were built up "to maximum strength," which was clearly not practicable. Eisenhower's answer was "to follow a plan that would avoid reverses, costly attacks, and great expenditure of supplies. . . . Carefully planned minor offensives, with success assured in each, comprised the campaign I expected to use during the winter; it was dictated by the objective and by the need to sustain morale amidst the inescapably miserable conditions of the Italian mountains."[57]

Eisenhower's proposals were accepted at the Cairo conference. However, he would not conduct the campaign which he outlined, because on 6 December he was chosen to serve as the Allied supreme commander in Northwest Europe. He would be Overlord's overlord.

The chief of the Imperial General Staff, Sir Alan Brooke, was satisfied with the compromise, but his mood changed when, in the middle of December, he travelled to Italy. Although in possession of full reports and correspondence, he was unprepared for what he discovered on 14 December, after arriving at Montgomery's Eighth Army headquarters. "Monty strikes me as looking tired and definitely wants a rest and a change," the CIGS commented that night in his diary. "I can see that he does not feel that

Clark is running the Fifth Army right nor that Alex is gripping the show sufficiently. He ... asked me how much importance we attached to an early capture of Rome, as he saw little hope of capturing it before March. ... Frankly I am rather depressed from what I have heard and seen to-day."[58]

Nor was he reassured by a tour the next day of front-line divisions, including the First Canadian, locked in the bloody battle for The Gully, outside Ortona. "My impression of the day is that we are stuck in our offensive here and shall make no real progress till the ground dries, unless we make greater use of our amphibious power. ... The offensive is stagnating badly, and something must be done about it."[59]

That something was a major amphibious operation. Of course, such a landing had figured in the planning of Alexander's December offensive. Code-named "Shingle," the plan had called for a single division and supporting troops to land near Anzio, southwest of Rome, on 20 December, the earliest date by which the necessary shipping could be assembled. When the Fifth Army's offensive had stalled in the mountains south of Monte Cassino, Shingle had had to be shelved. But Churchill, bed-ridden by pneumonia, refused to let it die:

> I felt we were at one of the climaxes of the war. The mounting of "Overlord" was the greatest event and duty in the world. But must we sabotage everything we could have in Italy, where the main strength overseas of our country was involved? Were we to leave it a stagnant pool from which we had drawn every fish we wanted? As I saw the problem, the campaign in Italy, in which a million or more of our British, British-controlled and Allied armies were engaged, was the faithful and indispensable comrade and counterpart to the main cross-Channel operation. ... I was sure that a vigorous campaign in Italy during the first half of 1944 would be the greatest help to the supreme operation of crossing the Channel on which all minds were set and all engagements made.[60]

With bulldog determination, Churchill strove to save the Italian campaign. To do it, he had to ensure that enough landing craft, particularly that invaluable vessel, the LST (landing ship, tank), remained in the Mediterranean long enough to mount a major landing. Although perplexed by the perpetual shortage of LSTs, he sought and won Roosevelt's permission to retain sufficient shipping "to bring off 'Shingle' on a two division basis around January 20th."[61]

At last, there seemed to be reason for optimism about the campaign. Plans were hurriedly drawn up: Mark Clark's Fifth Army would carry out the main effort, smashing through the enemy's Gustav Line at Cassino, then, after linking up with the divisions landing at Anzio, driving for Rome. The Eighth Army's role was limited. Exhausted by its month-long struggle through the mud on the Adriatic coast, it would content itself with minor operations.

This was perhaps just as well, because it had a new commander. Sir Bernard Montgomery was departing the Mediterranean for England, where he would take command of the Twenty-first Army Group, which would spearhead the invasion of France the following summer. Monty had mixed emotions. "Though sad of course to leave the Eighth Army," he viewed the promotion as "a relief, because I was not happy about the overall situation in Italy.... No grand design for the opening of a new theatre of operations; no master plan; no grip on the operations; a first class administrative muddle.... For these reasons I was not sorry to leave the Italian theatre."[62]

Monty's departure was a blow, for he embodied the very heart and soul of the Eighth Army. There can be no question that the army in Italy lost some of its spirit when he flew to England on the morning of 31 December.

His successor was Sir Oliver Leese, described by Monty as "a very valuable officer . . . easily the best I have."[63] But he was no Montgomery, in ability or personality. A capable corps commander, he was out his depth commanding an army. The Canadians who served under him would learn first-hand his shortcomings.

CHAPTER TEN

"Just Like Passchendaele"

1

Tuesday, 1 February 1944, should have been a red-letter day. On that date, the headquarters of I Canadian Corps became operational, taking responsibility for a sector on the Adriatic north of Ortona. It marked the first time since the end of the Great War that a Canadian corps was active on a field of battle.

It should have been a red-letter day, but it was not, thanks largely to the corps commander, Harry Crerar. The fifty-five-year-old Hamilton native had been in the Mediterranean theatre since late October 1943, and he had wasted little time stepping on toes. A dour, dedicated professional, he expected the Canadians serving in Italy to meet his spit-and-polish standards.

Crerar's arrival in late 1943 had been a shock to the veteran First Division. As Chris Vokes later complained, "life became a sort of administrative hell on earth." The corps commmander, Vokes contended, had surrounded himself with staff officers who "didn't know what they were doing. They produced more useless paperwork containing more absolute bullshit than one could cover with an exploding No. 36 grenade." Crerar had not endeared himself to the First Division's veterans by insisting that names painted on tanks and trucks by their devoted drivers be removed, and demanding that dress standards improve markedly. "I love spit and polish – it is marvelous in its place – but spit and polish . . . has no place in the field," said Vokes. "Its place is the parade ground. . . . As far as I was concerned, my soldiers could go into battle in their BVDs or bare-assed if they wanted to. . . . But our new corps people wanted us to march into battle with gaiters and tie, every soldier impeccably dressed."[1]

Crerar had also run afoul of Montgomery. Their dispute centred on Crerar's lack of combat experience, something for which the Canadian had long lobbied. "I believe that I could run a good show in modern battle," he had written Monty in September, "but I would like to test out these beliefs by practical experience. In fairness to those whom I might command in battle, it seems to me an essential personal preparation."[2] When Simonds had come down with jaundice in late September, Andy McNaughton proposed that Crerar be sent to take temporary command of the First Division. "No question of seniority arises," he assured Montgomery, "as Crerar is quite content to serve under any of your Corps Commanders." But this cable to Eighth Army headquarters went unanswered.[3]

In October, with Crerar present in the Mediterranean and anxious to activate his corps headquarters, Montgomery had resurrected McNaughton's earlier proposal. Chris Vokes, he said, should take a holiday and let Crerar command the First Division for a while, "to get the feel of things before tackling a corps responsibility with his entirely green staff." According to Monty's Canadian liaison officer, Dick Malone, Crerar "simply refused to play," declaring that he had no intention of stepping down, even for a short time, to take command of a division. He moved his headquarters into the luxurious San Domenico Palace Hotel in Taormina, Sicily, where he intended to wait until I Canadian Corps was activated in the field. Montgomery, in a fit of pique, refused Crerar permission to visit army headquarters.[4]

Crerar's relations with Guy Simonds were even worse. An initial meeting at Campobasso on 30 October, on the eve of Simonds's takeover of command of the Fifth Armoured Division, had proved to be most unpleasant. Simonds, just out of hospital after his bout with jaundice, secretly harboured the belief that Crerar had not wanted him as his chief staff officer in England in 1942, and they had exchanged strong words at Campobasso. This was followed by what is surely one of the most bizarre episodes of the whole war, a trivial incident which Crerar magnified out of all proportion. While Canadian troops were sacrificing their lives in the bloody battles for The Gully and Ortona, the two senior Canadian officers in the Mediterranean theatre were engaged in a bitter and unseemly personal row.

It began soon after Crerar saw Simonds's headquarters caravan, or trailer. Most impressed, the corps commander decided that he had to have one just like it, and arranged in early December to send an engineer to take measurements and incorporate certain ideas in the construction of his own caravan. Captain G. T. Kirk was the unfortunate officer who was sent out to inspect Simonds's trailer. The youthful divisional commander must have been in a bad mood that day, for he took exception to the engineer's presence, claiming that he did not have permission to be there. After giving Kirk a tongue-lashing, Simonds had thrown him out. This brought, on 10 December, an irate letter from Crerar, who chose to make an issue of this incident. In addition to being a "personal discourtesy to me," Crerar told Simonds that "it tends to indicate that your nerves are over-stretched and that impulse, rather than considered judgment, may begin to affect your decisions. Should this, indeed, be the situation, I would be extremely worried, for you are now reaching a position in the Army when balance is becoming even more important to your future than brilliance."[5]

Crerar had even complained about Simonds to Montgomery. But that was a bad move, for Simonds had no more enthusiastic or influential supporter than the legendary Eighth Army commander, who approvingly saw in Simonds the mirror-image of himself. Monty sent a frosty, hand-written reply to Crerar:

> My views are that Simonds is a first class soldier. After a period with an armoured Division he will be suitable for a Corps. He will be a very valuable officer in the Canadian Forces as you have no one else with his experience; he must therefore be handled carefully, and be trained on. VOKES is not even in the same parish; I am trying hard to teach him, but he will never be anything more than "a plain good cook."
>
> I do not, of course, know what has taken place between you and Simonds. He is directly under my command for training and so on. . . . If you have been sending him any instructions or directions on training he might possibly ignore them!! He gets that from me – verbally.[6]

Still, Crerar would not let the matter rest. Indeed, early in 1944 he had redoubled his efforts, sending to Ken Stuart, the acting First Army commander in England, details of "the present and potential problem of Simonds" and his "egocentric mind." Crerar informed Stuart that he had shown his Simonds correspondence to Dr. Fred Van Nostrand, a Toronto specialist who was now the Canadian army's chief psychiatric adviser, summoned from London by Crerar for the purpose of determining Simonds's mental stability. He also called the corps medical director, Brigadier Emmet McCusker, for an opinion. "Van Nostrand," wrote Crerar, "after perusing the attached communications, stated that in spite of marked egocentricity, Simonds, in his opinion, could be relied upon to function effectively as a Senior Commander though very preferably *not* as an independent Cdn force Cmd. McCusker generally agreed, though a bit more worried about Simonds than Van Nostrand." Crerar, while not doubting that Simonds could be a successful corps commander, added: "I cannot see him going on and up the way and distance I had anticipated," suggesting to Stuart that this file be set aside until "some possible future time when the further employment of this brilliant, and comparatively young, man comes up for consideration."[7]

This incident had long-term ramifications. Simonds later served under Crerar in Northwest Europe, even temporarily taking his place when the army commander fell ill. But Crerar never forgot this little episode in Italy.

When the war ended, he saw to it that the man chosen to head the peace-time Canadian army as CGS was not brilliant Guy Simonds but bureaucratic Charles Foulkes. Although Simonds was later appointed CGS, he was, according to historian C. P. Stacey, "undoubtedly deeply hurt" when he was overlooked initially. Afterwards, Stacey stated, "Guy Simonds hated Harry Crerar with a most consuming hatred."[8]

In the meantime, Simonds's Fifth Division was to suffer for the rivalry with Crerar.

The Fifth Canadian Armoured Division had had a memorable journey from the United Kingdom. The convoy carrying the divisional and corps troops had sailed down the Clyde on the evening of 27 October 1943. Most of the twenty-four ships were American, which meant that they were provided with rations of unbelievable quality and quantity. Canadians who had spent up to three years surviving on a steady diet of canned "mystery meat" or mutton, boiled cabbage, overcooked carrots, and grey bread were amazed at the fabulous food. Unfortunately, many of these men soon lost their appetites to seasickness when the convoy encountered a violent storm in the North Atlantic.

Surviving the storm, the convoy had sailed through the Strait of Gibraltar into the sunny Mediterranean on Thursday, 4 November. Two days later, their pleasant cruise was rudely interrupted when, twenty miles off the North African coast, a dozen German torpedo-bombers swooped down on the convoy during the early evening. Anti-aircraft fire claimed three of the attackers, but not before three ships were sunk. These included an American destroyer, the Dutch transport *Marnix van Sint Aldegonde* (which had transported Canadian troops to Sicily in July), and the American transport *Santa Elena*.

Among the more than 1,800 Canadian personnel aboard *Santa Elena* were 121 nursing sisters, who were the first into the lifeboats when "Abandon ship" was sounded. "The crew of the *Santa Elena* did not know how to release the boats, so, directed by Matron Blanche Herman of Lunenburg, the nurses knocked the boats free of the falls, and, singing their hearts out took over the oars and pulled away." From the bridge, someone ordered the nurses to be quiet, which struck Lieutenant Duncan Fraser as rather odd. "It seemed unlikely that a bunch of Canadian nurses would add much to the clamour when our gun crew was trying to shoot down a German aircraft with the aft four inch gun, and all the ships in the convoy were tearing the night apart with anti-aircraft fire." There was, happily, no loss of life among the Canadians.[9]

The rest of the journey was uneventful, and the convoy split up, the ships heading for Palermo and Augusta in Sicily and Naples on the mainland. Another unpleasant surprise awaited the Fifth Division when it pitched its tents in olive groves and vineyards on the outskirts of Naples. Venereal disease had become a major problem, complicated by a typhus epidemic in the last two months of 1943. General Simonds soon expressed his desire "to get the troops away from this sort of suburban 'built up' area as quickly as I can. It is a very poor training area, the squalid slums are depressing and constitute a very bad atmosphere in which to condition troops."[10] A better camp was found on the Adriatic coast, at Altamura; but before the division could move, it had to pick up vehicles (everything except tanks, which were being supplied under a separate arrangement) from the British 7th Armoured Division, the famed "Desert Rats."

They were in for a shock. As the First Division had discovered earlier, British vehicles that had come through the desert campaign were on their last legs, or wheels, by the time they were handed over to the Canadians. The 7th Division's history candidly admits that many of these vehicles had been second-hand acquisitions in early 1943. Moreover, the 7th had swapped some of its better vehicles for the wrecks of other Eighth Army formations. The situation was exacerbated by a shortage of tools and spare parts.[11]

With vehicles such as these, it was a hair-raising trip across the Apennines. One wag dubbed it the "Pitiful Pilgrimage."[12] Canadian mechanical engineers spent three weeks recovering broken-down vehicles in the mountains. At Fifth Division headquarters, Lieutenant-Colonel J. L. Sparling ruefully noted that "the non-runners almost exceeded the runners."[13]

Canadian protests fell on deaf ears. Staff officers who appealed to their British counterparts at AFHQ encountered a complete lack of sympathy, or even interest, in the plight of I Canadian Corps. "Their reaction was one of surprise that we should be coming at all," remarked one Canadian officer, "and incredulity that we should be coming almost completely unequipped."[14]

There was an apparently simple solution to the problem. Crerar's headquarters units were to receive a shipment of 3,350 brand-new Canadian-built vehicles in December. Should these not be allotted instead to the combat troops? Crerar rejected the idea. He did not believe that it was "impossible" to find the necessary vehicles somewhere in this theatre, and he also feared that such a transfer might give the British "reason . . . to delay the formation of 1 Cdn Corps owing to the non-equipment of one or more Corps Troops units which Army or Army Group may then say are essential for the purpose."[15]

To one of Simonds's brigadiers, this was unbelievable. George Kitching contends that the reason can be found in Crerar's relationship with Simonds. He says Crerar "was becoming increasingly jealous of Guy

Simonds' success as a commander and also of his close contacts with Montgomery and other senior officers of the U.S. and British Armies." Kitching suspects that Crerar deliberately delayed the re-equipping of the Fifth, so that Simonds could not command it in combat.[16]

Eventually, sufficient vehicles were rounded up to mobilize the division, thanks to Guy Simonds's "pull" at Eighth Army headquarters. But tanks were another matter. Given the choice of accepting the Desert Rats' desert-worn, diesel-powered Shermans or waiting for new tanks with Chrysler engines, Simonds wisely chose to wait. The arrangement was that his division would receive fifty per week from the beginning of December; each shipment would enable him to equip one armoured regiment. However, because of shipping delays, it was not until the end of January that the division was fully equipped.[17]

Because of the vehicle problems, the division's infantry brigade was ready for action before its armoured formation. As early as 4 December, Simonds had notified Crerar that Kitching's brigade would soon be ready for "its first experience of contact with the enemy." Exactly one month later, Kitching was informed that his formation would relieve the First Division's Third Brigade north of Ortona; its mission was to be strictly defensive, with offensive operations limited to aggressive patrolling. "The intention is to 'break us in easily,'" remarked the brigade's war diarist. "We shall soon see whether it is 'easy' or not."[18]

The Canadian army's first action of 1944 on the Adriatic front was fought on 4 January. It was a Tuesday, and the Carleton and York Regiment exacted sweet revenge for its New Year's Eve setback at the hands of those tough paratroopers. At Point 59, overlooking Torre Mucchia on the coast, the Germans had established two strongpoints, defended by a half-dozen machine-guns and linked by trenches, protected by barbed wire and minefields. After a day-long bombardment, a single company of Carletons attacked from two directions. "The Germans were just like rats coming out of holes," declared Sergeant Edward Parker of Woodstock, New Brunswick, "and we had a field day."[19] By 2100 hours, the high ground had been secured at a cost of three dead and four wounded. Forty paratroopers were later buried here.[20]

Point 59 was the last significant success for the Canadians in what proved to be a long, miserable winter. It secured the Canadian line along the Riccio, a small stream meandering through a steep gully. Beyond lay a high ridge which blocked any advance to the next river, the Arielli, and to Pescara, further up the coast. Back in Ortona, an officers' lounge was decorated with a brave sign: "Watch for the opening of our Pescara premises."[21] But it would be months before Pescara's liberation, and Canadian troops would not participate in it.

There were two more attacks in January. The first was staged on the seventeenth by George Kitching's rookie Eleventh Brigade, while the veteran First Brigade mounted the other at month's end. Both actions were disappointing.

Brigadier Kitching's high-strung troops had moved up on 12 January to relieve the weary Third Brigade. "Morale was high," reads the war diary of Toronto's Irish Regiment of Canada, "as the Unit had long waited the chance to have a 'crack' at the enemy."[22] They taunted the troops of the First Division: "We'll show you Red Patch bastards how it's done."[23]

By the evening of the thirteenth, the relief was complete. Kitching's front, which stretched three thousand yards inland from the Adriatic, was held by two battalions, the Irish Regiment and the Cape Breton Highlanders, with the Perth Regiment in reserve. The spirited Irish wasted no time getting acquainted with the Germans. The battalion commander, Lieutenant-Colonel Bobby Clark, arranged for the pipe major to take his bagpipes and serenade the enemy from a forward slit trench. The tune chosen, "Lili Marlene," was a favourite of all armies in the Mediterranean theatre, despite its German origins; Clark knew that they would be enraged by the bagpipe version. He was right. Within five minutes, enemy mortars stonked the pipe major's position. He stubbornly refused to take cover ("You can't play the pipes standing still," he later explained from his hospital bed, "you have to march up and down"), and a shell fragment ended the concert.[24]

Brigadier Kitching's patrol program was barely under way when a dramatic change of plan took place. A major offensive was being prepared (scheduled for 24 January but later cancelled) by XIII Corps to distract the Germans from the impending amphibious operation at Anzio, on Italy's west coast. In a preliminary operation, on orders from the Eighth Army's General Leese, v Corps was to employ two battalions of Kitching's newly arrived brigade "to make every effort to gain the high ground east of R. Arielli. This operation to be supported by all artillery available. Heavy casualties are *not* to be incurred."[25]

Kitching came to regret this operation. "I must accept the blame for agreeing to that plan," he says. "I agreed because I felt that the overwhelming fire support of sixteen artillery regiments would neutralize the enemy during that critical period when our leading companies would close with him. I was wrong."[26]

His brigade went about its preparations with enthusiasm. Company and platoon commanders of the Perths went forward to reconnoitre the lay of the land, while the battalion practised in a secluded spot its attack over ground similar to that beyond the Riccio. In successive attacks on 17 January the Perths and Cape Breton Highlanders, supported by tanks of the Three Rivers Regiment, would cross the Riccio and drive the Germans back to the Arielli. They were unfazed by the fact that they were facing two battalions of the same paratroopers who fought so savagely in and around Ortona in December. "We were young, highly trained, full of the fires of youth and just spoiling for a fight," according to one rifleman, Stanley Scislowski. "There might even be some medals in it for us, who knows? We looked at the prospects of battle as being a game where honour and glory would be ours if we played it right."[27]

The Perths went in first, at 0545 hours. They soon learned that there is little honour and even less glory in this game of war. With the exception of a single platoon, the two Perth assault companies were stopped cold. The Germans had spent weeks surveying the valley and registering targets for their artillery, mortars, and machine-guns, and most of the Perths were trapped in the valley bottom. Major R. A. MacDougall led seven men in an attack on a nearby house, from which the enemy fire seemed to be heaviest. It was brave but futile. MacDougall and three of his men died, and the others were wounded. The major's C Company remained pinned down, except for a party under Lieutenant Robert Chamberlain of St. Thomas, Ontario. After fording the Riccio, Chamberlain's platoon had wiped out a three-man machine-gun post and moved up the ridge. His platoon split up, but the lieutenant and nine other ranks made it to the objective by 0730. For the rest of the day, Chamberlain and his heroic little band waited in vain for reinforcements to arrive.[28]

Brigadier Kitching, unaware that some of the Perths had reached the objective, slightly revised his plans. The Cape Breton Highlanders would still attack, but further right than originally planned. Two companies of Highlanders, known as "The Boys from the Bay," started forward at 1345 hours. They filed down into the valley, and the paratroopers waited patiently behind their cleverly concealed automatic weapons. "I think they waited until the last man got in the river – there were two companies of us – then they opened fire," remembers George Hall, then a twenty-two-year-old sergeant from Lunenburg, Nova Scotia. "Talk about the Fourth of July – it was the fourth, fifth, and sixth, too."[29]

Pinned down in water up to his chest, Hall says that movement was almost impossible. "You just couldn't move. You'd part the bunch of bramble bushes along the edge [and] just like a scythe, the machine-guns would turn right on you." Hall was huddled with his next-door neighbour from Lunenburg, Corporal Aubrey Smith, and two other men when the sergeant-major summoned him. Moments after Hall splashed away, a mortar bomb landed among his comrades, killing all three of them.[30]

With darkness falling, the surviving Highlanders and Perths made their way back to the safety of their own lines. Among the last to return was the brave Lieutenant Chamberlain, who had held the Perth Regiment's objective for the whole day. He was later awarded the Military Cross. Another latecomer was Lance-Sergeant Norman Bell, a small but muscular thirty-year-old Torontonian. He had found shelter in an enemy slit trench, but waited for the right moment to get out of there. "Come last light," he recalls, "and this German officer came over, and he looked right down into this slit trench. I just had to pull the trigger, because he looked right down the barrel of my rifle. That was the signal for us to get out."[31]

The battle had ended for the troops, but it had just begun for the stretcher-bearers and doctors behind the lines. At the advanced dressing station of the 24th Field Ambulance was Private Dave Gordon, a twenty-one-year-old stretcher-bearer from Hagersville, Ontario. The memories of that night remain etched in his memory. Among his patients was a man with a stomach wound, which Gordon attempted to dress by wrapping a bandage around the man's body. As he reached round his back, Gordon was horrified when "my hand almost disappeared" – the poor fellow had a gaping wound in his back as well. Gordon had enlisted with the field ambulance with an eye on a future medical career, but "I saw enough to make me decide that I didn't want to be a doctor."[32]

The casualty count on 17 January was grim. The Perth Regiment suffered the most: forty-seven dead, sixty-two wounded, and twenty-eight taken prisoner. The Cape Breton Highlanders lost forty-six men. The Germans reported sixty-three paratroopers killed and wounded. The enemy's lack of concern is illustrated by Albert Kesselring's curt comment in the wake of the battle: "The trial runs of green troops are nothing famous."[33]

Many reasons have been cited for the failure of the Riccio attack: the breakdown in communications, inadequate maps, a disjointed plan of attack, the inexperience of the troops. The brigadier, George Kitching, believes "we should have had more time to get to know the enemy."[34] And while he accepts full responsibility for the outcome, Kitching says his "biggest disappointment was the lack of vital support from the tanks of the Three Rivers Regiment in the early stages of the Perth attack."[35] For this, he blames Bob Wyman, the commander of the First Armoured Brigade. Kitching has since learned that his fellow brigadier "had told his units not to hazard his tanks by getting into too much of a dog fight. Certainly none of us had any knowledge of this restriction at the time. Had I known that tanks were not expendable but infantry were, I would never have agreed to put in the attack."[36]

It was a sobering experience for all concerned. According to the Cape

Breton Highlanders' Sergeant George Hall, "we were wet and defeated and disgusted," their earlier confidence a bitter memory. "We were going to lick the Jerries. Well, in one hour they let us know who was the boss, I can tell you that much."[37]

Two weeks later, it was the turn of the Hastings and Prince Edward Regiment. This attack was another dubious undertaking and, as at the Arielli, it was Charles Allfrey, the British v Corps commander, who arranged the Canadian attack. The purpose of the operation was simple: a "holding attack," to prevent the transfer of German forces from the Adriatic to the Anzio front.

The attack was to be carried out on 30 January, the day before Allfrey was due to hand over responsibility for this sector to Harry Crerar's I Canadian Corps headquarters. And Allfrey ordered it without the knowledge of the divisional commander, Chris Vokes, who had gone on leave. Vokes's temporary replacement, Bert Hoffmeister, handed the task to the First Brigade's Dan Spry. The youthful brigadier in turn assigned it to the Hasty Ps, who had proven so reliable so many times before. The objective was to clear the Germans from the high ground between the Riccio and Arielli rivers, west of Villa Grande. It meant a mile-long advance, in daylight, over "generally flat, exposed ground." Like the attack on the seventeenth, this one would be backed by tanks (the Calgary Regiment) and a heavy concentration of artillery (seven Canadian, Indian, and British regiments), as well as an aerial bombardment by two dozen Kittyhawks of the Desert Air Force.[38]

The Hasty Ps attacked at 1600 hours. Two companies led the assault, and things went well – for a while. They came very close to their objective, but an unbelievable volume of enemy fire forced them to fall back several hundred yards to the protection of a shallow gully, where they dug in for the night. In three hours, the Hasty Ps lost forty-eight men, but their ordeal was not over: they were ordered by Brigadier Spry to try again the next afternoon.

A fresh company was added to the assault, but the results were no different. The hour-long battle on 31 January swelled the Hasty Ps' casualty toll by another forty-three, killed or wounded. It was, noted the First Brigade's war diary, "A very heavy price to pay for the knowledge that the enemy is holding the approach to Tollo in strength."[39]

Much anger ensued as a result of this action. The commander of the Calgary Regiment, Cy Neroutsos, had opposed the operation as an inappropriate use of armour, and today he is still "damn mad" about the four tanks and fifteen crewmen he lost that day.[40] When Chris Vokes returned from his ten days' leave, he was enraged at the corps commander, Charles

Allfrey. "I had made it quite clear to him before I left I did not want any attacks carried out by my division except offensive patrolling, until the ground got better. He had agreed."[41]

But the Canadians had fought their last major action of the winter.

2

"It's just like Passchendaele." On a cold January day, looking out from the battered stone farmhouse which served as the headquarters of The Royal Canadian Regiment, Harry Crerar was reminded of the infamous Great War battle in which men and artillery pieces simply disappeared in the foul-smelling sea of Flanders mud.[42] The Ortona salient in early 1944 would bear for the men under his command the same evil connotations that the Ypres salient had borne for their fathers during 1917.

The Canadian sector north of shattered Ortona was truly forbidding. The countryside was filled with the "desolation of shattered farmhouses and villas, burnt haystacks, and shell-pocked fields, sodden with the winter rains and befouled with unburied German dead and a litter of equipment, shattered cannon, burnt-out tanks and vehicles."[43] And the weather made a bad situation that much worse. "For weeks," says the history of the 48th Highlanders, "the rain saturated everything; a battle dress was a cold clammy shroud that was often board-stiff from the frost, until the heat of a man's body converted it back to a stinking mush of sodden wool. Feet were numb stumps. They slept, ate and lived in the cold slime."[44]

After the failed attacks on the Riccio and Arielli rivers, the Adriatic front settled into static warfare. The two sides warily and wearily faced each other, peering over their barbed-wire entanglements and minefields and trip wires. "This war is so much like the last one," General Crerar concluded, "it's not even funny."[45]

Was it a valid comparison? In some ways it was, but not so in others. While the RCR's Strome Galloway admits that there were similarities with trench warfare on the Western Front, he points out that the situation in Italy was not as "sophisticated" as the 1914–1918 era. The earlier war featured two sharply-defined lines facing each other across a desolate no man's land. But the Italian front in early 1944 was considerably different. "Two ramshackle barricades of unconnected slit trenches and fortified farmhouses, the gaps between them sometimes filled with primitive barbed-wire entanglements, stretched across the torn vineyards and sodden meadows north of Ortona. One barrier was German, the other Canadian. A broad gully lay in between. This gully was no-man's land."[46]

During the Great War, the Canadians had won renown for their work in no man's land. They were famous for their trench raids, and aggressive patrolling staked the Canadian claim to that desolate strip between the opposing trenches. Crerar, convinced that his soldiers could live up to their fathers' reputation, instituted a policy of intensive patrol work on the Canadian front. It was one of the most controversial decisions of his brief tenure in command of I Canadian Corps.

There were several types of patrols. The smallest was the reconnaissance, or recce, patrol. In a recce patrol, an officer and three or four other ranks were sent out to study enemy positions. While recce patrols sought to avoid contact with the Germans, others were supposed to look for trouble. A standing patrol could be anything up to a platoon in size; it slipped out with the intention of ambushing enemy patrols. A fighting patrol, which could also be platoon-sized, attempted to draw the enemy into a fire fight, with the purpose of capturing or killing a German, in order to identify opposing formations.

Risks were considerable, and chances of success were slim. "The lucky ones came back to an enamel cup with an inch of rum in the bottom," says the RCR's Strome Galloway. "The unlucky ones stayed out and their skeletons were recovered in the spring."[47]

Worse, the results were unimpressive. Galloway's own unit, the RCR, at one point sent out forty fighting patrols in forty days, without once encountering the Germans. This was typical of other battalions in the tired First Division, and George Stevens, one of Canada's most eminent military historians, was scathing in his assessment of the Canadian soldiers. Their "sorry record," he argued, may be attributed to the fact that they lacked the frontier skills of their fathers. Stevens charged that "men whose tommy-guns squirted sixty shots a minute never would be the snipers, the hunters or the stalkers that their fathers had been." Moreover, said Stevens, they relied too heavily on the artillery. "Fighting patrols seldom felt it to be their duty to fight. Instead, on encountering an enemy a map reference would be flashed back to artillery and mortar supports and the patrol would make itself scarce in case it was caught in the 'shorts' of the shoot."[48]

The real culprit was not the Canadian soldier, but rather the patrol policy itself. One of the most vocal critics of that policy was a man who acquired an enviable reputation during the Italian campaign, Jim Stone of the Loyal Edmonton Regiment. "How many good men, especially platoon commanders, were wasted in fruitless patrolling in that dark close country, I would not hazard a guess. I do know that most of the patrolling was worthless, morale destroying and wasteful of manpower."[49] It was "stupidity," says Stone, and something the enemy seldom attempted. "I think all the time we were there, the Germans put two patrols out, and we must've been putting out about four a night. And they knew just as much, or more, about us as we knew about them."[50]

Long stretches passed in which no prisoners were taken, and corps headquarters became so concerned that General Crerar finally posted a reward – a bottle of whisky – for anyone bringing in one or more Germans. This went unclaimed until 20 February, when the Carleton and Yorks sent out a late-night fighting patrol which returned with "the coveted prize of two (2) Jerries." Whisky was unavailable, so Crerar sent £5 to Chris Vokes, "the most welcome payment I have ever made." Vokes relayed the money to the brigadier, Graeme Gibson, with the comment: "I'm very glad the spell of bad luck is now broken." Gibson was so pleased that he matched Crerar's reward.[51]

But there were many Canadians who functioned fairly well in this environment. One of the best was Corporal Charles Jeremy, a Micmac Indian of the West Nova Scotia Regiment. He never claimed a kill, but before this sniper was severely wounded in March 1944, admirers put his total as "something like sixty."[52] Another noted sniper was the Van Doos' Stan Chiasson, an Acadian from Bathurst, New Brunswick, whose stealth and marksmanship were renowned. Unshaven, camouflaged in netting and a German parachutist's groundsheet, Chiasson accounted for more than sixty enemy soldiers and won rave reviews from his regimental commander, Jean Allard. "He amazes me!" declared the CO. "He has brought back from his long, patient vigils more information than you would expect of a dozen patrols."[53]

It was people like Jeremy and Chiasson who made possible some notable successes. The Van Doos staged an impressive raid on Crecchio, a stone-walled village nicknamed "Little Stalingrad" by the Canadians. When patrols pinpointed a weak spot in the enemy defences, the VC-winner, Paul Triquet, led his company into Crecchio and, after blocking the only two exits, went door-to-door shooting and grenading the panic-stricken and surprised enemy. The raiders returned with only light losses.[54] Leslie Moore, a West Nova lieutenant, took out a patrol which surprised an enemy outpost; Moore and his men brought back two prisoners and a heavy machine-gun.[55] The Cape Breton Highlanders resorted to kidnapping, staging a daylight raid across the Arielli near the end of February, snatching a German from his slit trench, and dragging him screaming back to Canadian lines.[56]

The savagery of static warfare made rare moments of humanity that much more precious. One night, the Cape Breton Highlanders drubbed a forty-man enemy patrol that blundered into their positions. Dawn brought a grim sight: seventeen dead or wounded Germans scattered in front of the Canadian slit trenches. Under a white flag, a German lieutenant approached, calling out for a Canadian officer to step forward. The senior man was a sergeant, Fred Cederberg; the German was reluctant to parley with him, but when he realized that he had no choice, he introduced himself as Ernst Bröhm and said, "I wish to arrange for a short truce – some hour or so – to enable us to recover our dead and wounded." Cederberg hesitated, but reluctantly agreed. He watched as a dozen enemy stretcher-bearers hurried towards him and started their life-saving work.

Minutes later, Leutnant Bröhm returned. "I must ask a favour," he told the young Canadian sergeant. "We are short of stretchers. And morphine. Can you help?" Again, Cederberg hesitated, but after mulling it over he agreed to assist the enemy. As the last of the German casualties was carried away, one of Cederberg's Boys from the Bay muttered, "An' there goes our goddamned stretchers, 'cause you're never gonna hear from those bastards again."

He was wrong. Just before noon, Leutnant Bröhm returned under a white flag, accompanied by two soldiers carrying the Canadian stretchers and morphine to replace the medicine borrowed earlier – and a bottle of schnapps as a token of his appreciation.[57]

No one had to go looking for trouble to experience heartbreak. This was, after all, war, and terrible things were the norm. Even random shelling sometimes produced grim results, as the Perth Regiment discovered during a meal parade on 5 February 1944. B Company's kitchen had been set up inside a cave in the side of a ravine. The only approach to it was via a narrow ledge overlooking a thirty-foot drop. The angle was such that it was considered impervious to enemy fire, but the Germans proved otherwise. They deposited a single mortar bomb right in the midst of the company's lunch-time line-up. "It was a lucky shot of the Jerries," said the Perths' padre, Crawford Smith, "for two feet either way, and it would have landed on the crest of the hill, or dropped into the valley below."[58] In a split-second of horror, the Perths lost thirty-seven men, including nineteen dead.[59]

Reinforcements arrived, but they seemed to fill the field ambulances faster than the slit trenches. The newcomers were always warned about picking up souvenirs, because discarded enemy equipment was often booby-trapped. But the warnings were not always heeded. Victor Hall, the West Nova stretcher-bearer, recalls that within minutes of receiving this lecture, a reinforcement reached for a souvenir; the resulting blast blew off his hand "as if it was chopped off with a knife."[60] The ones who made it into the front lines often did not last very long. On 12 March, the Perth Regiment sent out a fighting patrol on "a dark, moonless night." After a brief firefight, the patrol returned, having lost one man killed. He was Private John McDonald; a newcomer, he had arrived only an hour before the patrol set out. No one knew him; no member of the patrol had even seen his face in the dark. "He came in anonymity, and he died in anonymity, with only his name being recorded in the Regiment's Roll of Honour."[61]

Casualty statistics are revealing. Between 1 February and 7 March, 120 Canadians were killed and 585 wounded in Italy. In approximately the same period, 3,466 were treated for illness.[62]

The losses would have been worse had it not been for the introduction of penicillin. The miracle drug made its first appearance in Canadian dressing stations in January 1944, although it was in short supply due to its high price. In early March 1944, a pair of PPCLI men, hideously injured by an enemy shell, were brought to an advanced surgical centre, where both underwent double amputations. But infection brought them to the brink of death. They were saved by the intervention of the corps medical chief, Brigadier McCusker, who ordered two million units of penicillin from Naples. The instructions accompanying the new drug were vague, and all of it was administered to these two patients. "Recovery was not only prompt but truly remarkable," Lieutenant-Colonel C. E. Corrigan later reported. "When the package had been emptied, the manufacturer's bill was found lying at the bottom. The price tag? – just under $500,000 Canadian."[63]

Pleasures were few and far between. Virtually every town and village in the vicinity was out of bounds to the Canadians, but troops could get passes for quick trips into Ortona and San Vito for a bath and a shave, a movie or concert, or a pub crawl. In the front lines, *vino* was the chief relief from the misery. The troops called it "liquid sunshine," and it seemed that every farm had a stock of red wine. A potent alternative was "steam," which the troops distilled from wine, but some officers and NCOs did not countenance the consumption of wine on or near the battlefield. One was the Loyal Eddies' Major Jim Stone, who had a ready answer, in the form of his Tommy gun. "When I could see barrels of wine," he says, "I shot holes in them."[64]

Another important pleasure was mail. A letter or parcel from home was one of the few ways the soldiers could keep in touch with reality, but the mail service available to the Canadians in Italy was relatively poor during the first few months of 1944. A measure of compensation was provided by the creation of a daily newspaper for the Canadian army. The first edition of *The Maple Leaf* rolled off the press on 14 January 1944. The editor-in-chief was Dick Malone, the tough-talking, cigar-smoking newspaperman, who had unwittingly requisitioned for a head office "one of the largest whorehouses in Naples." Finding a building, he recalled, was the least of his problems in launching *The Maple Leaf*. "The first was to locate a press and overcome the difficulties of operating Italian machinery. Paper had to be borrowed or stolen. There was none for sale. There were power failures, bridges washed out on the supply route, and even a threatened libel suit. . . . It wasn't all beer and skittles!"[65]

The Maple Leaf gave birth to Herbie. This sad-faced cartoon character was the creation of Bing Coughlin, a talented sergeant of the Princess Louise Dragoon Guards. Herbie was always in trouble, it seemed, and the troops adored him because they could relate to that. "There was one in every regiment," says the RCHA gunner, Henry Worrell.[66]

Herbie was not the only source of humour to be found in the front lines for these young Canadians. Some humour occurred right in their midst. The Germans used dogs in some of their outposts; the barking would alert them to the approach of Canadian patrols. The Canadians tried hunting the dogs but with indifferent results, and poisoned meat left at strategic locations did not have much effect either. The solution was a female dog in heat, according to war correspondent Wallace Reyburn, "and the German dogs came rushing across no-man's-land to our line by the dozens."[67]

A Canadian medal provided humour of a different sort. The Canadian Volunteer Service Medal was instituted in late 1943, and the first ribbons were pinned on Italian veterans in early 1944. Thousands of Canadian soldiers in the theatre qualified, for it was awarded to volunteers with eighteen months' service, with a silver maple-leaf clasp for those who had served overseas for six months. (Naturally, there were many newcomers who qualified for the clasp, but not the ribbon!) "What a farce!" was Strome Galloway's reaction when he first heard of it. "Somebody has already dubbed it the V.M.K., which letters stand for 'Vote Mackenzie King.' If they'd hand around a few more DCMs and MMs to the fighting troops instead of making a quartermaster's issue out of this new thing it would be a lot more to the point."[68]

The Canadians were able to make minor improvements in their lifestyle by taking advantage of the Italian peasants who stubbornly refused to leave their homes, even in the middle of the battlefield. "Whatever the Canadians could get to eat off these suffering people," declared the Perth Regiment's Stan Scislowski, "was often far more palatable than what our cooks tried to palm off on us."[69]

In so doing, however, they sometimes found themselves balancing precariously along the fine line that separates looting and liberating. The First Division's Chris Vokes attempted to explain the difference: "Liberating is putting something, not too valuable a something, to one's immediate use. If one liberated a goose for the purpose of eating it, all right. If one liberated a carpet for one's caravan, all right. Liberating can become stealing. Stealing is the taking of very valuable things for personal gain. Art treasures sent home, for example, is looting."[70]

This line was overstepped sufficiently often, however, that the reputation of neither Canada nor Canadians was enhanced. Major Jim Stone of the Loyal Eddies later discussed with an Italian nobleman the comparative merits of German and Canadian soldiers. "Well, I'd rather have Germans," the Italian replied when asked which nationality he preferred to have in his neighbourhood. "When the Germans were here, the commandant would come to me and he'd say, 'I want forty cows delivered tomorrow at a certain place.' And I knew who had the most cattle and who could best afford to lose them, so I sent word to each family to deliver a cow, two cows. And that was it. The Canadians, every man kills his own cow."[71]

Leave always ended too soon. The marginal comforts of stolen or bartered goods were quickly forgotten. Food parcels were devoured, and letters tucked away in packs. Then the deadly cycle of patrols resumed. "And war," comments Strome Galloway, "said to be long periods of boredom, punctuated with short periods of fright, proved to be just that. The weather was foul. Freezing rain, high chill winds and occasional snow flurries made life miserable in the extreme. The patrol program went on, too. The size of regimental cemeteries grew."[72]

Wholesale changes occurred among Canadian commanders during the first months of 1944. One reason for sending Canadians to the Mediterrean theatre was, of course, battle experience, and now senior officers and NCOs were being returned to England, assigned to formations of the First Canadian Army in order to share their experience in the preparation for the impending cross-Channel invasion. If Canadians were successful in northwestern Europe, much of the credit belongs to the lessons learned in the Spaghetti League.

The changes started right at the top. Harry Crerar departed in March to take command of the army in England. Crerar, with thirty-six days of operational experience in command of a corps, would lead into battle Andy McNaughton's beloved "dagger," and he would prove to be a capable if colourless commander. In England, Crerar would be reunited with Guy Simonds and Bernard Montgomery. Simonds, given command of II Canadian Corps, handed over the Fifth Armoured Division to the man with whom he had conducted a spirited pre-war debate in the pages of the *Canadian Defence Quarterly* about concepts of modern warfare. E. L. M. Burns, known to friends as "Tommy," took over from Simonds at the end of January; seven weeks later, he was appointed as Crerar's successor.[73]

The forty-six-year-old Burns admitted that the news came as "a great surprise to me." As Burns recounted in his memoirs, Crerar explained that "he had selected me, rather than the other divisional commanders because he judged that I had greater capacity for foresight and planning ahead than other possible candidates – though others might possess more dominating personalities and perhaps be better at fighting a division in a tight situation."[74]

Literate and literary (he had been encouraged by H. L. Mencken), trilingual (English-French-German), Tommy Burns was an engineer by training, a veteran of the Great War. He had a "sharp and penetrating mind," according to the future *Globe and Mail* publisher, Dick Malone, but was handicapped by "a very cold and austere personality." Burns "was almost devoid of humour. He seldom wasted a word and had little time for small talk in his few personal relationships."[75] He was known to his troops as "Smilin' Sunray" (Sunray was the code name for any commander).

Unhappily for Burns, his appointment resulted in considerable resentment. He chalked it up to professional jealousy, particularly by the veterans of Sicily who, he wrote, "assume[d] that the history of modern warfare had begun on July 10, 1943."[76] However, many knew him from training days in England, and remembered him as the brigadier who equipped his tanks with governors, devices which limited their maximum speed to six miles per hour![77]

There were numerous other changes. Burns's place at the head of the Fifth Division was taken by Vancouver's Bert Hoffmeister, whose rise had been meteoric: a battalion commander in Sicily, a brigadier at Ortona, now a divisional commander. Hoffmeister was succeeded in command of the Second Brigade by Graeme Gibson, whose Third Brigade was taken over by Paul Bernatchez, formerly of the Van Doos. The Eleventh Brigade's George Kitching continued his rapid rise, being promoted to major-general and taking over the Fourth Armoured Division in England. Kitching handed over command of his brigade to Eric Snow. Brigadier Bob Wyman went to England to take command of the Second Armoured Brigade, leaving the First Armoured Brigade in the hands of likeable Bill Murphy. Two battalion commanders, Jim Jefferson of the Loyal Eddies and the Three Rivers Regiment's Leslie Booth, departed for brigade commands in England. (Booth would be killed in Normandy, leading the Fourth Armoured Brigade into battle.) Many of these promotions bore Guy Simonds's stamp of approval, for he obviously wished to take with him men in whom he had complete confidence. His influence was unmistakeable in the transfer of other senior officers, including Bruce Matthews, the First Division's artillery commander, and the divisional engineer, Geoff Walsh.

At lower levels, the changes were even more pronounced. Majors, captains, lieutenants, and senior NCOs were soon making their way to England, to lend their experience to the formations that would soon be invading northwestern Europe. They included majors Snuffy Smith and Ned Amy, of the Ontario and Calgary tanks, respectively, and Doug Harkness, the anti-tank gunner. Most were glad to leave, but one man who did not want to go was the feisty regimental sergeant-major of the Hasty Ps,

Angus Duffy, who was posted to England as an instructor. Duffy protested – "I'll stay here as a corporal" – but to no avail.[78]

There can be no question of the impact made on the First Canadian Army by the arrival of the Italian veterans. The transfer, dubbed Operation "Pooch," was invaluable, says the former Calgary tanker, Ned Amy, "because when we went in at Normandy, at least we'd been shot at. The plan was a good one, to take some people who had been out there and put them into the units that were going into Northwest Europe."[79]

All agree that their Italian experience was beneficial. There was a limit to its value, of course, because the war in northwestern Europe was different in many ways from that being fought in the Spaghetti League. The scale was much larger, and the resources being made available were almost unbelievable, compared to the scrimping and scrounging that the Italian veterans often had to do. "I always felt that they had too much equipment in Northwest Europe," says the engineer chief, Geoff Walsh. "They were handicapped. I know damn well that some of the vehicles were never even unpacked."[80]

Despite the differences, the Spaghetti Leaguers were able to implement useful changes in training before the invasion was launched. "I stepped up the training," says Walsh, who ended the war commanding the First Canadian Army's engineers. "Battle discipline. I pointed out to them that no matter how perfect you are in training, once you got into battle you only got a certain percentage of that training."[81]

But what was the effect of all this on the veteran Canadian formations which remained in Italy? They had already lost many of their best and most experienced people to death, injury, or illness; now they were waving farewell to talented comrades and dear friends. Perhaps some of them were troubled by the nagging suspicion that the Italian campaign was of secondary importance. For now, this doubt would remain unspoken.

3

All hopes rested with Anzio. The only possibility of breaking the deadlock in the mountains and mud of Italy lay with Operation Shingle, the landing of two divisions on the west coast, just below Rome. It proved to be a bitter disappointment.

In a bid to draw German reserves away from the landing area, the Fifth Army renewed its offensive in the mountains around Cassino, guarding the vital Liri valley. To do it, Mark Clark had to breach the enemy defences along the Rapido and Garigliano rivers. Sir Richard McCreery's British X Corps, which had been part of the Fifth Army since Salerno, fought its way across the Garigliano on 17 and 18 January. But a direct assault on Monte

Cassino resulted in complete disaster on 21–22 January. The U.S. 36th Division suffered grievous losses in a matter of hours, but Clark was unapologetic. Although the divisional commander blamed the setback on Clark's "stupidity," Clark defended the operation: "Some blood had to be spilled on either the land or the SHINGLE front, and I greatly preferred that it be on the Rapido, where we were secure, rather than at Anzio with the sea at our back."[82]

For a while, it did indeed appear that the bloodshed on the Rapido was justified. During the pre-dawn hours of Saturday, 22 January, one American and one British division, supported by Ranger and Commando units, made an unopposed landing at Anzio. "We achieved what is certainly one of the most complete surprises in history," wrote the American commander, Major-General John Lucas. By nightfall, Lucas had 36,000 men ashore, with 3,200 vehicles. Aside from nuisance bombing by the Luftwaffe, there were no Germans in sight. "Thus far," says the American official history, "the amphibious operation was a resounding success."[83]

But Lucas, a fifty-two-year-old career soldier, was the wrong man for this job. Instead of taking advantage of the enemy's weakness, he preferred to consolidate his beachhead before venturing inland, despite Clark's exhortations to use "bold and aggressive action."[84] Clark poured in additional forces, including the élite Canadian–American First Special Service Force, but Lucas continued to plod along. It took him eight days to mount an attack towards the Alban Hills, twenty miles inland, which overlooked the landing site. By then, it was far too late.

While Lucas tiptoed around Anzio's sandy beaches, the Germans reacted with characteristic speed and skill. The enemy commander-in-chief, Generalfeldmarschall Kesselring, scrounged together "a jumble of multifarious troops" and put them under the command of the Fourteenth Army's Eberhard von Mackensen. Within days, they had not only sealed off the beachhead, but were mounting furious counter-attacks in a bid to crush it. The reinforcements sent in by Clark, instead of leading a triumphant advance on Rome, found themselves fighting a desperate defensive battle.[85]

Clark finally relieved Lucas on 22 February, a month after the landing. But Anzio's prospects had long since dimmed. "Anzio," says the British historian A. J. P. Taylor, "was like Gallipoli all over again: inspired by the same man [Churchill] and with the same result."[86]

Canadians had a small but splendid part to play at Anzio, both in the air and on the ground.

The First Special Service Force arrived in the embattled beachhead on 1 February. Although refreshed by a two-week rest, the Force was still numerically weak. A trickle of reinforcements, combined with the return from hospital of the lightly wounded and the ill, left it with a combat strength of 1,233, all ranks. Only one regiment, the 3rd, was intact; the other two were at half-strength. But numbers do not tell the story, because the Force promptly took over one-quarter of Anzio's thirty-mile-long front. The beachhead's right, or eastern, flank rested on a canal named after Mussolini, and it was this sector that was allotted to the Force. While the commander, Robert Frederick – now wearing the single star of a brigadier-general – held his 2nd Regiment in reserve, the other two regiments moved into the line on the evening of Wednesday, 2 February. It marked the beginning of ninety-eight days of continuous action.[87]

The Force was spread dangerously thin. Its front line was held by an average of only one man per twelve yards. There were, however, compensating factors. The Canale Mussolini was a natural tank trap, and it cut across the Pontine Marshes, "the flattest piece of ground in Italy," which would give defenders the advantage.[88]

They would need every advantage, because they were opposed by one of the best formations in the German army, the Hermann Göring Panzer Division (which the First Canadian Division had encountered in Sicily). The Germans were very aggressive, and wasted little time putting the Force to the test. Tom Gilday, the Montreal native who commanded a battalion of the 3rd Regiment, recalls that the enemy attacked the second night after the Force took over the line. Gilday had established his headquarters in a farmhouse within twenty-five yards of the front line, and the battle was soon raging at his very doorstep. Fearing the worst, he put out a call for reinforcements. "They told me that I was on my own, there was no such thing as reinforcements. We had to stand or go into the sea, so we stood. That was our introduction to Anzio."[89]

While movement during the day was dangerous, because the German artillery completely dominated the small beachhead, the Force's Americans and Canadians made the enemy's life miserable by a nightly program of patrols. "This was basically the way we had been trained," says Ken Cashman, a former sergeant. "We were trained as a force to do night fighting."[90] As Colonel Gilday points out: "Combined with being able to work and be comfortable at night, you have a very strong force, and a very capable force, and this was one of the things the Germans learned to dread about our boys – their quick movement at night and their ability to attack at an opportune time, and keep the element of surprise."[91]

The nightly forays produced almost immediate results. By 7 February, the Germans had withdrawn their outposts more than a mile from the canal, but that merely encouraged the Force to increase its efforts. With blackened faces, patrols went in search of trouble. One patrol brought back a blood-stained diary belonging to a German lieutenant who had been killed by the people he had been writing about: "The Black Devils are all around us every time we come into the line. We never hear them come." The Forcemen now had a nickname, "Black Devils," and the Force itself was commonly referred to as "The Devil's Brigade," a title that spawned both a book and a movie (starring William Holden and Cliff Robertson).[92] General Frederick was quick to exploit the enemy's anxiety. Resorting to psychological warfare, he ordered a batch of calling cards adorned with the Force's USA–CANADA shoulder patch and the words, *Das Dicke Ende Kommt Noch!* ("The Worst is Yet to Come!"). One prisoner reported being told by his superiors that he was "fighting an élite Canadian–American Force. They are treacherous, unmerciful and clever. You cannot afford to relax." A ten-day furlough, he said, would be granted to any German soldier who could capture a member of the Force.[93] Another prisoner, a lieutenant, admitted that the Germans had been having "great trouble finding definite information of the First Special Service Force. The prisoners we have taken do not talk. The best view in the Hermann Goering Division is that you are a division, by the frontage you hold and by having three regiments."[94]

One of the most successful raiders was a quiet sergeant from Manitoba. A great-great-grandson of the legendary chief, Peguis, twenty-eight-year-old Tommy Prince became Canada's most-decorated Native soldier, with the Military Medal and the Silver Star. The former lumberjack survived the war, and served in the Korean War; today, Prince's memory is honoured by a barracks at Camp Petawawa and by a statue unveiled in November 1989 in a Winnipeg park. According to his battalion commander, Tom Gilday, he was "a wonderful scout,"[95] whose daring exploits were renowned. The most famous occurred on 8 February, when he went tank-hunting with a field telephone.

Creeping across the canal after dark, paying out telephone line as went, Prince slipped into a deserted farmhouse two hundred yards from the enemy lines. Here, he patiently waited for daylight. From this vantage point he could clearly pinpoint German tanks as they rumbled back and forth, constantly changing position in order to avoid American shells. That morning, Prince spotted a pair of tanks and called down accurate artillery fire that destroyed both. The enemy did not realize that he was in the ruined house, but about noon some mortar bombs fell behind it, cutting Prince's telephone line. The quick-witted sergeant donned a black hat and jacket which he found lying in the house and, imitating an excitable Italian, rushed outside. He darted about, waving his arms, all the time searching for the break in the cable. He found it, made the necessary repairs, then went out front and performed "another little dervish dance" for the benefit of any Germans who happened to be watching. He went back in the house, and called down shell fire that destroyed two more tanks before nightfall.[96]

Prince won the Military Medal for his work here, but he "often complained that, had he not been an Indian, he would have won the VC."[97]

Despite outstanding performances like this, the Force's casualties at Anzio, while not heavy, mounted steadily. By the time it came out of the line on 9 May, it had lost 384 men, killed, wounded, or missing;[98] 117 were Canadians.[99]

One of the highlights of the long siege at Anzio was the air war. Like his men, Colonel Gilday witnessed "some wonderful dogfights," and some of these almost certainly involved Canadian Spitfires.[100]

The RCAF's 417 (City of Windsor) Squadron spent three months patrolling the Anzio beachhead, where "the Windsors enjoyed the best hunting of their career." By the time it was over, the squadron had chalked up nineteen kills, together with five probably destroyed and thirteen damaged.[101]

In sharp contrast, the past several months had been rather frustrating. Aside from a handful of dogfights, the Canadian fighter pilots had rarely seen enemy aircraft since moving from Sicily to mainland Italy in late September 1943. One of the few Canadians to enjoy a measure of success was an Ontario native, Bert Houle, who ended the year in command of 417 Squadron.

Houle was one of Canada's top aces in this war. Small but athletic and very competitive, Houle had spent much of his young life unwittingly honing the skills which would make him a terror of the sky. Growing up on a farm in northern Ontario, Houle was an experienced hunter before he was ten years old, learning "to shoot straight and to navigate in the bush without a compass." He dreamt about flying, and "read every book I could find" about Canada's Great War aces, like Billy Bishop and Roy Brown.[102]

He had enlisted in the air force as soon as the war broke out, and by the time he took command of 417 Squadron he was a veteran of long months of aerial combat in North Africa, where the primary British fighter aircraft was the Hurricane, which was outclassed by the enemy's Messerschmitt 109 and Focke-Wulf 190. "We were mainly sitting ducks while in Hurricanes," he recalls, but that situation changed dramatically when the squadron re-equipped with the faster, more manoeuvrable Spitfire. "We had the advantage then," he says. "If you used the Spitfire VIII or IX properly you should not have too much trouble shooting down Me 109s and FW 190s. You could climb with them and out-turn them. You could not dive with them, but the trick was not to dive at the same angle, but to stay above them until they had to level out, then use your height to catch them."[103]

Houle had claimed the squadron's first kill within two days of 417 becoming operational in Italy, but bad weather during most of the last three months of 1943 had made it difficult to hunt Germans. However, Houle made the most of his limited opportunities; on 3 December, he shot down two enemy fighters, the first of two occasions in which he recorded "double kills, and that was always exhilarating to me and to my squadron."[104]

However, the hunting was much better over Anzio. The scoring started with the very first mission over the beachhead on 22 January. Squadron Leader Houle was leading an eight-plane patrol at twelve thousand feet when he spotted four "bandits" dive-bombing the beaches. The Canadians jettisoned their long-range fuel tanks and swooped down on the FW 190s. Houle drew a bead on one of the enemy aircraft and fired two short bursts. "The bullets smashed into the fuselage and wing roots and around the engine, producing clouds of black smoke." It was the first of four aircraft Houle would personally destroy at Anzio.[105]

"A merry dogfight" occurred on 25 January, when seven Spitfires tangled with two enemy formations, eighteen FW 190s and ten Me 109s. The Canadians probably destroyed one and damaged two others, for the loss of one of their own aircraft. This was the first of four straight days in which the Canadian Spitfires broke up enemy air attacks on the Anzio beaches. In this period, the squadron shot down three German fighters (including one by Houle), probably destroyed two more, and damaged at least four others.[106]

The squadron was given a brief break at the end of January, when it was re-equipped with new Spitfires, the Mark VIII. The tired pilots welcomed the time off, sight-seeing in Naples, chasing nurses, and luxuriating in hot showers. The break was timely, for poor weather during the first of half of February limited 417's flying time. "The first person who says anything to any member of this squadron after the war about sunny Italy," fumed the squadron's war diary, "is a cinch to get slugged."[107]

When the Windsors returned to Anzio, Bert Houle wasted little time chalking up another kill. It occurred on 7 February, and it was unusual. Houle, leading a patrol of ten Spitfires, had spotted and chased a gaggle of enemy aircraft. The Germans scattered, and after a futile chase, the Canadians prepared to head for home. That was when somebody noticed that their patrol was larger than before: an Me 109 had mistakenly joined the Canadian formation! The newcomer noticed his error and tried to flee, with Houle hot on his tail. The German plane was soon billowing black and white smoke, and then the squadron leader got in "a really telling burst" which blew off the Messerschmitt's tail. The pilot took to his parachute and the fighter crashed.[108]

Meanwhile, a perplexing mechanical gremlin was plaguing the new Spitfires. The Mark VIII could fly faster, farther, and higher than its predecessors, but pilots were soon complaining that the engine would cut out at a certain speed. While mechanics were quick to pinpoint the carburettor as the problem, this meant removing the entire unit and sending it to a special repair shop, grounding the aircraft for a week or more. Richard Shunn, a member of the maintenance crew, studied coloured schematics of the carb and discovered a simple solution involving the tightening of a screw. It worked like a charm, he recalls, adding, "I never got thanks and could have been in trouble for what I did."[109]

The new Spits proved themselves on Valentine's Day. For 417 Squadron, 14 February would provide "the most successful action in its history" – three destroyed and three damaged.[110] Houle personally accounted for one of each, despite a close call in which a "20mm shell punched out a piece of the [cockpit's] armour plating, which lodged against my carotid artery."[111]

It was his last action as squadron leader. "An excellent leader and skilful pilot,"[112] a two-time winner of the Distinguished Flying Cross, Houle departed for Canada, having completed his second operational tour (a tour was two hundred hours in the air, or roughly the same number of missions). He had destroyed seven enemy aircraft in Italy (to go along with three earlier kills), making him the top Canadian ace in this theatre. "It was always a great satisfaction to shoot down an enemy aircraft, especially an enemy fighter," he says, but there was nothing personal about it, so far as he was concerned. "I did not hate Germans. . . . It was him or me, and I preferred it to be him."[113]

For a while after Bert Houle's departure, 417 Squadron continued to enjoy good hunting over Anzio. March saw the Windsors make 604 sorties, totalling 876 flying hours, which resulted in seven kills, a probable, and three damaged German fighters. The climax came on 29 March, when the Windsors shot down three Germans, along with a probable and a damaged.[114]

By then, the Luftwaffe had had enough. Three weeks passed before the Germans ventured into the sky over Anzio during the day, and 417 had to content itself with routine patrols, flying escort for medium bombers, and dropping "nickels," packages of propaganda pamphlets, along with the occasional air-sea rescue mission.

There were few kills now. An Me 109 and an FW 190, both of which fell victim to the Windsors on 23 April, marked the end of hunting season over Anzio, so far as 417 Squadron was concerned. The Canadian Spitfires still patrolled over the beachhead, but they had other duties, strafing ground transport and escorting bombers in the vicinity of Monte Cassino. By the beginning of May, it was apparent that something big was about to happen in Italy.

4

Prime Minister Churchill could scarcely conceal his disappointment over Anzio. "We hoped to land a wild cat that would tear out the bowels of the *Boche*," he fumed to his military advisers. "Instead we have stranded a vast whale with its tail flopping about in the water!"[115]

Allied strategy had been turned upside down. "Operation *Shingle*," notes American historian Robert Wallace, "had been launched to facilitate a breakthrough at Cassino. The breakthrough had failed, and now the situation was reversed. The troops at Cassino would have to keep pressing forward in order to take the pressure off the Anzio beachhead."[116]

The Liri valley appeared to Alexander to be "the gateway to Rome." Although it contained only one major road, Route 6, the valley, twenty miles long and ranging from four to seven miles in width, seemed to offer tantalizing possibilities of employing armour. The Germans, realizing that the rugged mountain ranges on either side of the valley would severely restrict if not preclude passage by Allied forces, had concentrated their strongest defences in this region. The main defensive belt was the Gustav Line, which ran from the mountains north of Monte Cassino to the coast and followed the Rapido, Gari, and Garigliano rivers. The Gustav Line blocked the entrance to the Liri valley; even if could be breached, no further advance would be possible until the mountain masses on either side were captured. To the north towered 5,500-foot Monte Cairo, and a spur, Cassino, with the town of the same name nestled at its foot. A secondary defensive line had been prepared several miles to the rear, but the Germans did not intend to utilize it. In January, Hitler had decreed that "the Gustav Line must be held at all costs."[117]

The battle to break into and through the Liri valley lasted more than five months. Americans, British, Indians, New Zealanders, French, Poles, and Canadians all had their turn, as the fight escalated in size and intensity.

The focus of attention was Cassino, and particularly the monastery perched on the mountaintop at the mouth of the Liri valley. It had been founded in 529, only to be destroyed by the Lombards in 581, by the Saracens in 883, and by an earthquake in 1349, and each time was rebuilt on a more majestic scale in order to withstand assault by man and nature. On 15 February 1944, it was destroyed for the fourth time in its history by

Allied bombers, but the tough 1st Parachute Division (so familiar to Canadians) promptly occupied the ruins and staged a stupendous defensive struggle. In the face of prolonged aerial and artillery bombardment, and spirited attacks, the paratroopers stood firm, causing a befuddled Alexander to comment, "I doubt if there are any other troops in the world who could have stood up to it and then gone on fighting with the ferocity they have."[118]

By the beginning of May, the campaign in Italy had been stalemated. The only vindication of Allied strategy thus far had been Hitler's decision to commit unusually large forces to this front. As one of his advisers later complained, "Hitler's Mediterranean strategy threw a far greater strain upon the German war potential than the military situation justified."[119]

Alexander's answer to the deadlock was a battering ram. Amid great secrecy, he had begun the task of transferring the bulk of the Eighth Army from the east coast. On 26 March, a change of boundaries took effect. Mark Clark's Fifth Army held the sixteen miles from the sea, while Sir Oliver Leese's Eighth Army headquarters took responsibility for the balance of the fifty-five-mile Allied front. But at the mouth of the Liri valley, Alexander concentrated four divisions of the British XIII Corps, with newly-arrived II Polish Corps on its right. These forces would be the sledgehammer which would smash the Gustav Line and capture Cassino, enabling Leese to commit his reserve formations to race through the Liri valley and lead the rush to Rome. Alexander's offensive, accompanied by what was hoped would be an overwhelming bombardment, was tentatively scheduled for 10 May, carefully timed to ensure the best support for the impending cross-Channel invasion, set for 5 June.

The code name for this great attack was "Diadem." And the key was I Canadian Corps, which would form Leese's reserve and exploit the breakthrough. But the corps had spent the winter on the Adriatic front, and this posed a problem. As in the Great War, the Germans had come to associate the presence of the Canadians with impending offensive operations. To transfer them across Italy's mountainous spine, in complete secrecy, posed one of the greatest challenges to Allied, and Canadian, ingenuity.

CHAPTER ELEVEN

"I Was a Nervous Wreck"

1

Spring had at last come to Italy's Adriatic coast. The ever-present fog and seemingly endless rain had given way to sunshine and warmer temperatures, drying the ground and bringing the sleeping vineyards, farmlands, and orchards back to life.

But the winter-weary Canadians had gone. When the headquarters of I Canadian Corps was moved into reserve on 7 March, with it went the Fifth Armoured Division. The First Armoured Brigade was withdrawn in late March, and in early April it became the first Canadian formation to cross the mountains to the west coast. The First Division remained in the Adriatic sector until the third week in April, when it was relieved by the 10th Indian Division.

The First Division welcomed the break. Continuous action breeds a certain sloppiness, in conduct and bearing, and in appearance; static warfare tends to cancel out the lessons and value of mobile warfare. This was true of all services, particularly the artillery. The division's new (since February) chief gunner, Brigadier Bill Ziegler, had been distressed to see the condition of his command. Ziegler's prescription was a period of "highly-specialized training," which did not please the divisional commander, Chris Vokes, who interpreted Ziegler's comments as criticism of his predecessor, Bruce Matthews. It took him some time to get out of Vokes's doghouse, says Ziegler, "but I knew they needed training. They had got slack in the mud. And I knew that, in the battles we had before us, they were going to have to be trained right up to the nth degree. For a month I worked the hell out of them – and out of myself, too – night and day." Ziegler was pleased with the results. "By the end of the month, which wasn't very long, they were pretty damn good," he recalls. "And by the time we got through with the Liri valley, they were the best."[1]

The Fifth Division, which was nicknamed "the Mighty Maroon Machine" because of its shoulder patches, also underwent a rigorous training program. "The division's preparation for active operations," notes

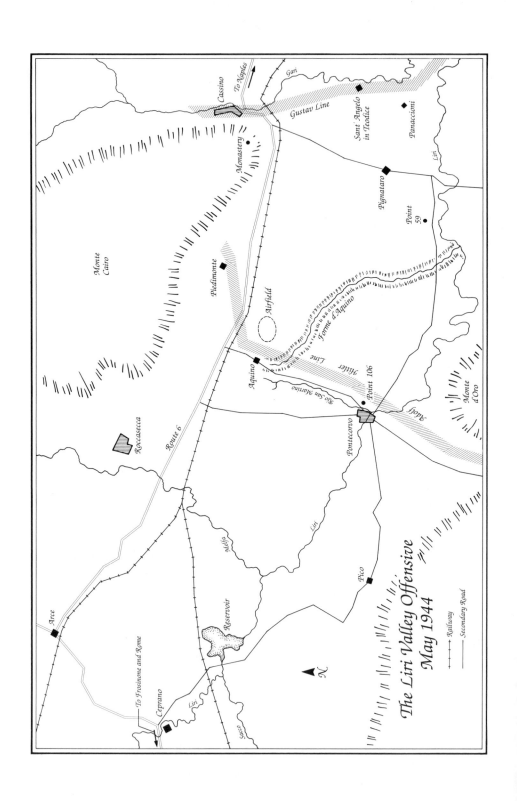

The Liri Valley Offensive
May 1944

⊢─⊣ Railway
──── Secondary Road

historian Bill McAndrew, "had been somewhat less than complete. It had had no opportunity to function as a formation since its arrival in Italy, and equipment shortages severely limited unit training." Nor did it help that the division had had four commanders in the space of less than six months.[2]

The newest divisional commander, Bert Hoffmeister, worked hard to correct the deficiencies of his untried formation. Conscious of the criticism that the infantry of the Eleventh Brigade had failed to follow the artillery barrage closely in their January operation on the Riccio, the divisional staff organized a series of exercises, using live ammunition; General Hoffmeister himself, an old hand at infantry tactics and training, "insisted on accompanying the lead platoons to demonstrate how close troops can safely follow their supporting gunfire."[3]

So far as his armour was concerned, Hoffmeister had to improvise, because tanks did not seem to have a place in this campaign. (Before coming out from England, Tommy Burns had solicited Montgomery's views on the role of armour in Italy, only to be told: "There is no role for an armoured division in Italy!")[4] The prevailing tank doctrine, laid down in the 1943 manual, *The Tactical Handling of the Armoured Division*, advocated speed and power to slash through enemy defences; as Bill McAndrew points out, this manual "had not been written with Italy in mind," for the terrain rarely lent itself to such dynamic employment. Until now, tanks had been utilized to supplement artillery fire in support of infantry.[5]

With one brigade of armour and one of infantry, Hoffmeister chose to strike a balance between "doctrinal theory and the realities of the ground over which he had to operate," and to perfect the cooperation between tanks and infantry. But this was easier to state than to achieve, because each arm believed that the other had let it down in previous operations. According to McAndrew:

> In the attack, infantry wanted tanks right with them and were extremely reluctant to move forward when the tanks became separated or were stopped; tankers complained that the infantry failed to appreciate the impossibility of their maintaining intimate contact while moving over broken ground and, moreover, that they could provide gun fire support just as effectively from long range. The infantry also wanted tanks with them in the defence, especially in the period before their own anti-tank weapons got forward; tankers objected that the infantry were reluctant to give them close protection in forward positions at night when they were blind and most vulnerable.[6]

To iron out these difficulties, the division's armoured and infantry elements trained together, learned each other's weapons and tactics, even bivouacked together. As incredible as it may sound, this was something new for the units of the Fifth Armoured Division. Unfortunately, this training was interrupted during the second week in April. Only one divisional exercise had been staged when the Eleventh Brigade was detached and sent to the Cassino front for a month-long tour under New Zealand command. By the time the brigade returned in early May, the division was preoccupied with planning and preparations for its first great battle, in the Liri valley.

The Eleventh Infantry Brigade spent a memorable month in the line near Cassino. The brigadier, Eric Snow, commanded about 7,500 troops during this period; besides his own three infantry battalions (Perth Regiment, Irish Regiment of Canada, and Cape Breton Highlanders), Snow had under him the motorized Westminster Regiment, a variety of artillery and engineer units, and a battalion of Italian sailors who had volunteered to serve as soldiers after surrendering their ship at Malta.

Snow's brigade group came under the command of the 2nd New Zealand Division on 15 April, and remained there until 5 May, occupying a mountainous nine-thousand-yard sector five miles northeast of Cassino. "In truth," writes Cape Breton subaltern Duncan Fraser, "our tour in the line was not very onerous. But it was different." All thoughts of working with tanks were forgotten, he notes. Instead, the infantry learned to work with "man-packs, jeep trains and mules. Above all mules."[7]

It was a monumental struggle just to get into the isolated, rocky positions allocated to the Canadians. There was only one way in or out, a treacherous trail known as the "Inferno Track," a "steep and rough" road, recalls Lieutenant Fraser. "It was passable only in the dark – and then only by mule, jeeps and trailers – and foot soldiers."[8]

It was just as difficult to get out. Canadian losses here were relatively light (125), which was fortunate. "Casualties had to be taken out at night," says Perth Regiment stretcher-bearer Dave Gordon. "And while the casualty rate wasn't that high, it was really difficult to take them a couple of miles over those mountain trails."[9] The Westminster Regiment found that three relays of bearers required four to six hours to carry a wounded man on a stretcher to the nearest medical station.[10]

From their positions, Monte Cassino could be seen in the distance; through binoculars, the Canadians could pinpoint the ruins of the famous monastery. "My platoon was lucky," records Fraser; "we occupied two well-built Italian houses; and our slit trenches and sangars provided good shelter and protection. We were dry for a change," although the rations left a lot to be desired. Fraser recalls that he and his men existed on a steady diet of compo packs containing tinned steak-and-kidney pudding. Since fires were not allowed, and there was no other way to warm up the meals, "we lived off cold steak and kidney pud for the nearly three weeks we were in the position."[11]

Very quickly, the Canadians learned to hide during the day. The Germans, occupying the neighbouring peaks, had a good view of the Canadian positions, and the slightest movement was certain to bring a mortar stonk. And the enemy's accuracy with these weapons was frightening. Sergeant Norman Bell, of the Perth Regiment, describes the fire as "deadly accurate. I was a nervous wreck when I came out of there. You couldn't sleep in the daytime, and you couldn't move."[12]

Days were thus reduced to "sheer boredom," while nights were a sharp contrast. "There was plenty of activity by night," recalls Duncan Fraser, "when we patrolled the defensive wire in front of us to make sure that German patrols were not infiltrating our lines; or that German vehicles were not making a 'sneak and peak' before assaulting us. . . . We were resupplied with food and ammunition at night by soldiers of our Headquarters Company who picked up man-packs from the mule trains and humped them over the mountain track to us."[13]

There were few regrets when South African troops arrived to relieve the Canadians near Cassino on 5 May. "It's a god-awful piece of real estate," commented one Cape Breton Highlander, and no one would have disagreed with him.[14]

The remainder of the Canadian corps, scattered across the central Apennines, was part of an elaborate deception scheme. To pull it off, the "playwrights" at General Alexander's headquarters decided to take advantage of the enemy's respect for the Canadians, and of their fear of another Allied landing somewhere on Italy's west coast.

As the main body of the corps took up its positions for the Liri valley offensive, dummy signal traffic was prepared, simulating a massive amphibious training scheme in the Salerno area, south of Naples. It would involve I Canadian Corps, with the First and Fifth divisions, plus an American division under command, which purportedly was preparing to land at Civitavecchia, forty miles north of Rome. On 18 April, the headquarters of these formations went off the air – a clear and entirely normal indication to German wireless interceptors that a move was under way. Four days later, Canadian signal detachments began operating near Salerno; for the next three weeks, they broadcast phony messages, both clear and in cipher, carefully regulated to approximate the signal traffic of a corps and its subordinate units. It was hoped that two factors would convince the Germans that the simulation was real: the First Canadian Division's extensive amphibious experience, and the close similarity of the coastline south of Salerno to that of Civitavecchia.[15]

The deception was reminiscent of that which accompanied the famed move of the Canadian Corps in 1918, prior to the offensive that ended the Great War – and it was equally successful. In early May, German Tenth Army intelligence reported "the concentration of enemy troops in the Salerno-Naples area. Amongst others, 1 Cdn Inf Div," while they mistakenly placed the entire Fifth Armoured Division at Acquafondata, northeast of Cassino (thanks to the identification of a prisoner of the Eleventh Brigade). Despite the radio traffic, the Germans were unable to pinpoint even the false location of I Canadian Corps headquarters, which was recorded as "unlocated." The German commander-in-chief, Albert Kesselring, accordingly kept the Gustav Line, his main defensive position at the mouth of the Liri valley, thinly manned, while spreading his sparse reserves along the coastline to meet an emergency that would never come.[16]

Kesselring was not especially concerned, but he would have been much more uncomfortable had he been aware of the vast array of forces assembling at the mouth of the Liri valley for Alexander's Diadem offensive. On the Eighth Army's front alone were the Canadian corps (43,487 strong), XIII Corps (98,431), and II Polish Corps (45,626), backed by 1,193 guns.[17] Vast stockpiles of supplies had been brought up on successive nights before the attack, all carefully camouflaged to avoid detection during daylight hours. "In the daytime," recalled Colonel M. V. McQueen, a corps staff officer, "the valley looked as quiet as could be, but at night it was a beehive of industry – everybody going someplace."[18]

Moving the nightly convoys of trucks was an imposing challenge for the drivers. They moved under the cover of an artillery smokescreen, thickened by smoke generators. Headlights were forbidden; instead, a Jeep would lead the line of trucks along the appropriate one-way road to the correct location. Each truck had a small white light mounted on its differential; the vehicle behind would follow this beacon. "If you didn't pull out in time," recalls Lloyd Oliver, then a twenty-one-year-old Manitoba farm lad who drove a truck for the Fifth Armoured Division, "you didn't know what would happen." Once under way, he says, the tiny beacon on the lorry ahead had a hypnotizing effect after a while, and there were many accidents.[19]

A lot of toil and sweat went into the artillery's preparations for the coming battle. So many Canadian guns were packed into a small area that it was dubbed "Gun Alley."[20] Dick Fuller, a twenty-three-year-old Niagara Falls native, says the work started three or more weeks ahead of time. "We dug gun positions, camouflaged them, and brought our guns up, put them in our positions – and we did all this at night, and slept under the camouflage nets by day." Fuller's unit, the 10th Battery, discovered after getting its 25-pounders put in place, that an olive grove on a nearby hill blocked the line of fire. So a party went out with saws and "cut every tree about three-quarters of the way through, and braced it so that it still stood up. Then, about an hour or so before the big barrage started, there were parties of people rushing up the hill and pushing those trees over!"[21]

At I Canadian Corps headquarters, General Burns and his staff were busy, too. Uncertainties dogged the Canadian preparations at this level. As the Eighth Army's reserve formation, the Canadian corps was to pursue the defeated enemy after the breaching of the Gustav Line. But Burns and his planners were conscious of a secondary defensive position in front of Aquino and Pontecorvo, eight miles further up the Liri valley. How strong was it, and would the Germans make a serious attempt to defend it? No one could answer those questions. Indeed, little was known about it, other than its name. When construction began in December 1943, it had been dubbed the Führer Riegel; soon afterwards, Hitler forbade the use of his title, and it was renamed Senger Riegel, after Generalleutnant Fridolin von Senger und Etterlin, whose XIV Panzer Corps was responsible for this sector. But the Allies continued to refer to the mystery position as the Adolf Hitler Line.[22]

Burns, mindful that senior Allied commanders had not wanted another corps headquarters in this theatre, knew only too well that his every effort would be scrupulously studied by the Eighth Army staff. It was already painfully clear that he and his army commander, Sir Oliver Leese, had little in common. During a planning session at Eighth Army headquarters, Burns was baffled by Leese's lecture. Turning to Chris Vokes, the corps commander asked, "What the hell is he talking about?"

"Our attack on the Hitler Line, sir."

"Then why in hell doesn't he say so instead of prancing about waving his hands like a whore in heat?"[23]

Another consideration overshadowed Burns's planning. On 5 May, he attended a conference in Naples with Brigadier Ted Weeks, who informed him that there was a shortage of reinforcements in the Mediterranean theatre. On 11 May, Burns delivered the bad news to his divisional commanders and brigadiers. Only 325 reinforcements per battalion were available, said Burns. If casualties exceeded that rate in the coming operation, he warned, "we shall be completely out of [reinforcements] by the middle of July – save those that return from hospital, etc – and no further [reinforcements] to speak of can be expected before that date, due to priorities in the other theatre."[24]

It was a gloomy forecast. The cross-Channel invasion had not even begun, and already the Canadian forces in Italy had been relegated to second-class status.

2

Expectations for Diadem were high. "Everything is now ready, all plans and preparations are complete," Sir Harold Alexander cabled Prime Minister Churchill on 11 May. "Our object is the destruction of the enemy south of Rome and we have every hope and every intention of doing that."[25]

Half a million Allied soldiers were taking part in the great offensive. While the Eighth Army bludgeoned its way past Cassino and into the Liri valley, the Fifth Army would be making a two-pronged thrust. One would be made by the newly arrived Corps Expéditionnaire Français, striking through the mountains south of the Liri, while the other would come a few days later from the Anzio beachhead. The latter operation, soon to be shrouded in controversy, was designed "to cut Highway 6 in the Valmontone area, and thereby prevent the supply and withdrawal of the troops of the German Tenth Army opposing the advance of Eighth and Fifth Armies." If all went according to plan, the deadlocked Italian front would become, at long last, a war of movement, in which the Allies would be able to utilize their superior armoured strength to full advantage.[26]

Thursday evening, 11 May, was auspiciously pleasant. It was warm and the sky clear, with small pockets of mist forming the valleys of the Gari and the Liri. Fireflies soon twinkled in the darkness and nightingales chirped "enchantingly" amid the usual warlike sounds that could be heard on any battlefront: the occasional harassing shots by isolated batteries which the Germans had come to expect, along with the odd burst of machine-gun and mortar fire.

That all changed at 2300 hours. Night turned into day as 1700 guns of the Fifth and Eighth armies simultaneously belched fire and destruction. A military policeman from Calgary, Dick Whittington, interrupted his traffic-control duties to stare in awe. "I didn't have a newspaper," he recalls, "but I had a bunch of papers and I could read them in the flashes that were going back and forth across the front."[27]

Canadian tanks played a critical role in the attack across the Gari. Although the Canadian corps was relegated to reserve status, the First Canadian Armoured Brigade was part of the spearhead, supporting the 8th Indian Division, with which it had served following a personality clash between Chris Vokes and the former brigadier, Bob Wyman. During the fighting in and around Ortona, Vokes had complained about Wyman, calling him "a bull-headed guy, a little lord unto himself." Vokes subsequently let it be known that he would be happy not to work with Wyman's brigade, and he got his wish. However, in February 1944, Wyman had been replaced by Bill Murphy, a "first class" officer, according to Vokes, who by then regretted his words.[28] But the damage had been done; except for a brief reunion in the Liri valley, the armoured brigade would seldom serve alongside major Canadian formations in Italy.

As with any river crossing, the key to the Gari operation was to get tanks into action as quickly as possible. No one doubted that the 8th Indian Division could establish a foothold on the west bank, but they would need armour in order to break out beyond the river. During the early hours of 12 May, the Indians did manage to claim a precarious toehold on the other side of the Gari, and the engineers went to work to get tanks across. Three bridging sites had been selected, one (code-named "Plymouth") for the Calgary Tanks and two ("Cardiff" and "Oxford") for the Ontario Regiment. By the morning of 12 May, Oxford and Plymouth had been completed, and Shermans were pouring across the river.

While the Oxford crossing was a standard Bailey bridge, Plymouth's was an experiment derived from a "hare-brained idea," according to Lieutenant-Colonel Cy Neroutsos of the Calgaries. The tank commander had been discussing with Major-General Dudley Russell, commanding the 8th Indian Division, the difficulties of getting over the sixty-foot-wide Gari, when a staff officer joked about building a Bailey bridge and simply pushing it across the river. Colonel Neroutsos was intrigued by the suggestion and talked it over with his tank doctor, Captain Tony Kingsmill. Kingsmill's solution was both simple and effective. A hundred-foot Bailey bridge was built on and carried by two Sherman tanks, the front one with its turret removed and replaced by rollers. This tank would drive halfway across the river and stop, while the second tank continued to push the bridge until it was secured on the far bank.[29]

Two training runs with Kingsmill's bridge went poorly, and Neroutsos decided to hedge his bets by sending one squadron across Plymouth and one across Oxford, in the Ontario sector. In fact, there were problems at Plymouth. Confusion caused by smoke, darkness, and enemy fire delayed the placement of the unusual bridge until 0930 hours on Friday, 12 May. Kingsmill, who survived a mortar blast to win the Military Cross, was surprised to see that "the first persons to take advantage of the bridge were a group of about six Germans who in the smoke and general confusion ran to relative safety across the river from where they had been hiding in the waist-deep rushes."[30]

Unfortunately, this marvellous bridge was soon knocked out. Only four Shermans managed to get over it before enemy shelling put it out of commission.

Oxford saved the day. Completed at 0840, it enabled both Calgary and Ontario tanks to cross the Gari. But even this turned into a "considerable shambles," according to the Ontario commander, Bob Purves. The ground on both banks was boggy and mined; many Shermans of both regiments were either trapped in the mud or knocked out. The Ontarios were able to get only half a dozen tanks into action, while four more Calgary Shermans joined the battle on the far bank.[31]

There were not many of them, but the Canadian tanks did deadly work on the Gari that day. The Calgary and Ontario Shermans spent the afternoon and early evening of 12 May roaming about the countryside, shooting up enemy transport and guns and pinpointing targets for the artillery. The Calgary objective was the village of Panaccioni, and Shermans commanded by Lieutenant Al Cawsey and Corporal Bill McWithey headed for it. *En route*, they knocked out at least four anti-tank or self-propelled guns.

Things went even better on Saturday, 13 May. More Bailey bridges were built overnight, and infantry and armoured reinforcements crossed the Gari. Two of the heroes were tank doctors, Captain G. L. Patton and Sergeant F. L. Carson, who recovered no fewer than twenty-three Ontario tanks and put them back into action. Many of these tanks were mired in the marshy flats, directly in front of enemy positions, and Patton and Carson carried out their work under heavy fire. Patton was later awarded the Military Cross, Carson the Military Medal.

While the Ontarios supported the Indians in clearing the town of Sant' Angelo in Teodice, the Calgaries captured Panaccioni, bagging a battalion headquarters and 125 prisoners in the process.[32] The bridgehead was secured by 14 May, enabling the Three Rivers Regiment to cross the Gari. But the situation remained confused and dangerous; the terrain precluded any rapid movements, and there seemed to be Germans everywhere in the valley. Repeatedly, the Three Rivers tanks would reach their objectives, only to be called back to help the embattled infantry clear a stubborn machine-gun post. That evening, the sluggish advance reached Marchisella, a village a mile north of Pignataro, where the tanks awaited the arrival of fresh troops the next day.[33]

A sharp counter-attack at dawn on Tuesday, 16 May nearly took the Three Rivers Regiment by surprise, but it was driven back. "Increasing numbers of [prisoners] were taken, most of them being 'dead beat' from what they had been through," recounted a regimental report. "When you got close to them they would usually throw up their hands."[34]

The Canadian tanks won high praise for their efforts on the Gari. The Eighth Army's Sir Oliver Leese called the First Armoured Brigade "the best armoured formation in the MEDITERRANEAN Theatre."[35]

The Gustav Line had been breached. The German commander-in-chief, Kesselring, tried desperately to minimize the damage; during the evening of 15 May, he ordered that a new line of defence be established across the

Liri valley, through Pignataro, to enable "the continued defence of the Cassino massif" by the 1st Parachute Division. But this position had already been occupied by the 8th Indian Division and its Canadian tanks, and the following afternoon, Kesselring was finally forced to face defeat. In a telephone conversation with the Tenth Army's Generaloberst Heinrich von Vietinghoff, Kesselring stated, "I consider withdrawal to the Senger position as necessary." Within an hour, Vietinghoff's staff had issued orders for a general withdrawal to the Adolf Hitler Line.[36]

Kesselring's command was facing a crisis. Although his paratroopers at Cassino continued to hold out, the right wing of Vietinghoff's Tenth Army had been shattered. The most alarming incursion had occurred not in the Liri valley, but in the mountains immediately south, where the Corps Expéditionnaire Français had achieved an amazing success against surprisingly weak German forces. Unless something could be done to check the rapid advance by the French, and that of the U.S. II Corps along the coast, the German Tenth Army would be faced with utter destruction.

While Kesselring was trying to salvage his battered army group, Sir Harold Alexander was exultant. That same evening, 16 May, he signalled the CIGS, Sir Alan Brooke: "We can now claim that we have definitely broken the Gustav Line."[37]

Eighth Army headquarters had already taken steps to prepare the next phase of the battle. On the evening of the fifteenth, Sir Oliver Leese ordered I Canadian Corps to take over the southern half of the Liri valley front; together with XIII Corps, the Canadians would advance to the Hitler Line. Given the extent of the enemy's disorganization, Leese hoped that his army might be able to "bounce" this position before it could be properly manned. Failing this, a full frontal assault would have to be mounted.

Dan Spry's First Canadian Infantry Brigade went into action on Tuesday morning, 16 May. The youthful brigadier passed two battalions through the left flank of the 8th Indian Division, The Royal Canadian Regiment near the River Liri, and the Hastings and Prince Edward Regiment near Pignataro.

The Canadians whistled and sang as they marched forward, and the pleasant countryside might have had something to do with their happy mood. They were in the heart of the Liri valley, "a green paradise," according to Thomas Raddall, "one of the show places of Italy, walled in by high mountains and rolling its length north-westward in farmland thickly dotted with bushes and trees and watered by clear mountain streams. There were orchards and fields of tall grass or young wheat thigh-deep, and the dusty roadsides were speckled with wild flowers, notably the poppy, whose scarlet bloom reminded everyone of 'Flanders Fields.'"[38] But the valley's beauty masked countless dangers, as these Canadians soon discovered.

It was slow going for both units. The Hasty Ps, under their new commanding officer, Don Cameron, ran into heavy fire. The Germans "appeared to have unlimited supplies of shells and mortar bombs,"[39] as the RCR discovered on Point 59, a knoll overlooking the Liri on the road to Pignataro. The Royal Canadians captured it, along with fifty prisoners, but the enemy saturated the hilltop with artillery and mortar fire, which cost the battalion twenty killed and thirty-six wounded.[40] In complete disregard for his own safety, Private R. E. Deadman answered the enemy fire with his 2-inch mortar, for which he was later awarded the Military Medal.

The modest advance that day had far-reaching consequences. Even as the divisional commander, Chris Vokes, planned the next day's advance towards the Hitler Line, he received a disturbing message from the corps commander, Tommy Burns. General Leese, Burns reported, "is disappointed that no greater progress was made in the face of quite light opposition and is very urgent that a determined advance should be made tomorrow."[41] This brief message speaks volumes about Burns's leadership qualities, or lack thereof. Rather than meekly passing along Leese's comments, he should have gone forward to find out if the army commander's judgement was correct. If so, he should have reprimanded Vokes personally; if not (as was the case), he should have notified Leese that his criticism was unfounded. Without even fighting a major action, Burns seemed to have shown the veterans at First Division headquarters that their doubts about him were justified.

Vokes widened his front that evening, bringing Paul Bernatchez's Third Brigade into line on the right of the First. The advance resumed on the morning of the seventeenth, and things went much better when the Royal 22nd Regiment went into action, supported by tanks of the Three Rivers Regiment. Fourteen tanks fell by the wayside (seven lost to mines, seven bogged down), but these losses were offset by the capture of 120 prisoners.[42]

Brigadier Bernatchez, the former Van Doos' CO, was a familiar sight all day long, ranging the battlefield in his Jeep, keeping tabs on his troops. The West Nova Scotia Regiment passed through the Van Doos later that morning, and the Carleton and Yorks continued in the advance during the late afternoon and evening. While scattered resistance was encountered, the biggest difficulty was presented not by the enemy but by poor maps, according to the West Novas' history. "More than once what the map showed as a road turned out to be merely a grassy cattle track through the fields."[43] Despite the many difficulties, the Carletons brought the brigade's advance to the gully of the Forme d'Aquino, and pushed across after dark to establish a solid bridgehead beyond.[44]

As on the previous day, the First Brigade encountered more formidable opposition, in the form of a fresh foe, the 190th Panzer Reconnaissance Battalion, which took full advantage of the lush terrain to slow the Canadians. Despite strong resistance, Toronto's 48th Highlanders, advancing along the road to Pontecorvo, also reached the Forme d'Aquino, to the left of the Third Brigade. The Canadians were now within three to four miles of the Hitler Line.

Darkness brought a last-gasp counter-attack, and it fell on the Toronto Highlanders. Three self-propelled guns and thirty infantry moved down the road from Pontecorvo, but a quick-witted sergeant gave the Germans all they could handle. Bob Shaw was a member of the battalion's anti-tank platoon, which was derisively known as "The Popcorn Shooters," because its 6-pounder anti-tank guns rarely made themselves useful. Sergeant Shaw, who would win the Military Medal for this night's work, more than made up for missed opportunities. A mortar flare revealed the alarming situation: one self-propelled gun was on the bridge, with one on either side of the little stream. As the flare fizzled, Shaw fired his 6-pounder at the gun on the bridge. He evidently hit the fuel tank, for there was a spectacular explosion and fire, which gave the Toronto Bren gunners lots of light to pick out their targets. While they mowed down the German infantry, Shaw calmly knocked out the vehicle trapped on the near side of the gully. The scrap cost the 48th nineteen casualties, but it was the enemy's last attempt to prevent the Canadians from closing on the Hitler Line.[45]

Thursday, 18 May, brought them to the edge of the German fortifications. The First and Third brigades continued their cautious advance, still uncertain about the enemy's intentions. Scattered fire was encountered, and the Van Doos took a dozen prisoners.[46] But the 48th Highlanders lost two men as prisoners, when a patrol walked into the midst of forty Germans hidden in a field of grain.[47]

That night, the Third Brigade was ordered to assault the Hitler Line. Divisional headquarters had notified Brigadier Bernatchez "that, based on intelligence lately received, it was felt that the enemy had not had time to man the Adolf Hitler Line."[48] Bernatchez elected to send in the Van Doos and Carletons; however, when he learned that only limited artillery support was available (most Canadian guns were to engage targets around Aquino, which was to be attacked by the British 78th Division), Bernatchez sent in the French-Canadians alone, backed by British tanks. The Van Doos' commander, Jean Allard, was not happy about this operation. "The front was too calm for my taste," he later wrote, "and I could not believe that the fortified points had in fact been abandoned."[49]

His fears were justified. The Van Doos attacked at 0630 hours on 19 May, under cover of a thick mist. They made steady progress, opposed only by snipers and scattered riflemen. Around 0800, the fog lifted, and with the French-Canadians in plain view, the enemy "opened up with all he had." With the two assault companies pinned down, the support companies passed through and made a brave attempt to press home the attack. But by late morning it was clear the Van Doos could go no further in the storm of steel that enveloped them.[50]

Allard was livid. The operation had cost him fifty-seven casualties which he viewed as needless. "I felt that my regiment had been the victim of recklessness of the High Command, which had sent it on a dubious mission on the basis of relatively limited information and without artillery support to surprise the defenders. . . . I was left with a bad taste in my mouth about the whole affair . . . after this event I retained serious doubts about the competence of commanders who had blindly made the decision to hurl us, without preparation, against lines supposed to be abandoned shortly anyway."[51]

Allard blames First Division headquarters for this unfortunate operation, but the blame goes much higher. General Alexander had ordered General Leese to maintain the pressure on the Germans, and Leese, in possession of intelligence reports that seemed to indicate that the Hitler Line might be bounced, ordered I Canadian and British XIII corps to make the attempt. The latter operation was mounted by the 36th Infantry Brigade of the neighbouring 78th Division, and it was no more successful than the Canadian attack.

But 19 May had not been a wasted day. "It was now apparent," wrote Brigadier Bernatchez, "that the enemy intended to fight for the Hitler Line, and that a properly teed-up attack with strong artillery support would be necessary."[52]

The British high command had reached the same conclusion. On the morning of 20 May, Sir Oliver Leese issued verbal orders for a two-phase operation "to pierce the Adolf Hitler Line and exploit towards Arce-Ceprano." I Canadian Corps, attacking on a one-division front, would break through between the Forme d'Aquino and Pontecorvo. The British XIII and II Polish corps would assist the Canadians by mounting diversionary attacks at other points along the line between Aquino and Piedimonte. The Canadians, said Leese, must destroy the garrison of the fortifications and then strike towards the River Melfa five miles to the northwest. I Canadian and British XIII corps would then exploit the breakthrough.[53]

The attack on the Hitler Line would be mounted on Tuesday, 23 May. That would give the Canadians two full days and part of a third in which to prepare for their most difficult battle of the entire Italian campaign.

3

Even as General Leese was outlining his plans, the Adolf Hitler Line was being attacked – by two Canadians and a water truck. Gunners Ernie Buss and "Stan" Stanyer were prairie boys; their job was to keep the 3rd Field Regiment supplied with fresh water, pumped from the nearest river or stream. By the early morning of 20 May, when they drove out in the pre-dawn darkness in search of water for the field guns, they had been on the move for nearly forty-eight hours without rest. In unfamiliar territory, eyes heavy from lack of sleep, they did not find the road they thought they were looking for until well after daylight, and they followed it – in the wrong direction! Instead of going east, towards the rear, they were headed west, towards the front lines.[54]

They were on the Pignataro–Pontecorvo road; without realizing it, they almost drove right through the Hitler Line. There was "no traffic about," says Buss, "but we were in a hurry so didn't notice anything wrong." They might have driven all the way into Pontecorvo had their truck not hit a mine. The explosion sheared off the front of the big vehicle, and after the dust had cleared, they crawled out of the truck to survey the situation. The twenty-five-year-old Buss told Stanyer to stay by the truck while he went in search of help. As he walked along the road in the direction they had come, Buss spotted blood on his trousers and, belatedly realizing that he was injured, shouted for Stanyer to come and have a look. Buss recalls what happened next:

> Just as he stepped away from the truck, I heard a sharp crack from a rifle and saw Stan grasp his shoulder and fall onto the road. I was stunned for a second, not knowing what was happening here. It was only then that it dawned on me that we were in enemy territory. Should I run for help or what? Then another sharp crack, and a bullet hit the ground a few inches from my feet. I then ran towards the ditch by the road when another hit. I then ran ducking back and forth along the line of trees that were growing along the roadside.

Buss reached a Canadian outpost, where he was given first aid. While he was taken to the rear for further treatment, an infantry patrol went out that night and rescued the wounded Stanyer.[55]

Massive artillery support was arrayed for the Canadian assault on the Hitler Line, code-named "Chesterfield." When the First Division attacked on the morning of 23 May, it would be backed by 810 Canadian, British, Polish, Indian, American, and French guns – twice the total that backed the famous barrage at El Alamein in November 1942. Because it was a divisional operation, most of these batteries were placed under the command of the division's chief gunner, Bill Ziegler. Tall, bespectacled, studious, Ziegler was a Calgary native and a former militia officer who went about his preparations with professional skill. Ziegler huddled with his staff in a captured dugout thirty feet underground to draw up the fire plan that would, it was hoped, deliver victory. "We worked there with no break whatsover, just steadily, hour after hour after hour, for seventy-two hours," he recalls. The time element was, he insists, "not excessive at all. You couldn't have done it in any less time, because you don't want to make any mistakes, and every single map reference had to be double-checked."[56]

It was the most complex fire plan Ziegler ever produced. With so many guns, and so many targets, it could scarcely be otherwise. The gunners prepared a series of powerful concentrations on selected targets with a creeping barrage, a curtain of high explosive that moved a hundred yards every three minutes. There were also counter-battery (aimed at the enemy's guns and mortars) and counter-preparation (aimed at supply routes, suspected ammunition depots, and headquarters) programs, along with steady harassing fire, at the rate of a thousand shells per hour.[57]*

In another dugout nearby, Ziegler's boss was busy with his own plans for Chesterfield. Chris Vokes had elected to make his breakthrough on a two-thousand-yard front between the Forme d'Aquino and Pontecorvo, believing that it offered the best possibilities for his assault formation – two battalions of the reserve Second Brigade, supported by two regiments of British tanks and by the vast artillery barrage described above. "There was about enough room," Vokes later explained, "for the two forward battalions of the brigade to do their various manoeuvrings."[59] Two roads running roughly perpendicular to the line of advance provided convenient objective lines: the nearer, linking Pontecorvo and Aquino, lay immediately behind the Hitler Line; one to two thousand yards further west was the road from Pontecorvo to Route 6.

The corps commander, General Burns, endorsed Vokes's plan at a conference on 20 May, but it was soon changed. As Burns later wrote, "it was quickly pointed out to me by General Leese that the front of attack was too narrow and should be extended by at least one more battalion frontage." Burns notified Vokes, who broadened the front of attack by another thousand yards, to accommodate a battalion of the Third Brigade. Burns noted that Vokes "was not too pleased at having to alter his preparations."[60]

---

* The barrage planned by Ziegler was his "first and last." Afterwards he reassessed the fire plan and concluded that barrages were "one hell of a waste and what I could almost call 'a lazy man's way of doing the job.'" Ziegler takes great satisfaction in noting that present-day gunners to do not employ barrages, "so I maintain that I was the author of the death of the barrage."[58]

Before this battle ended, relations between the volatile Vokes and the stolid Burns would get much worse.

In the meantime, preparations continued for the big attack. "While infantry and engineer patrols probed cautiously into the fringe of the German defences, lifting mines and reconnoitring tank routes, the narrow valley roads between the Gari and the Forme d'Aquino were clogged with the unaccustomed weight of military traffic moving up for the offensive."[61]

Slowly but surely, a picture of the Hitler Line was emerging. Aerial photographs revealed much, but not all, about it. The fortifications, about eight hundred yards deep, were fairly standard, consisting mainly of weapon-pits for machine-guns and rifles, concrete shelters, portable steel pillboxes, and observation posts for all weapons.[62]

On the ground, from a distance, the defences were almost invisible, hidden behind "orchards, olive groves, copses of small trees with thick undergrowth, and standing crops." But the patrols which boldly scouted the position found that the enemy had cleverly cleared their fields of fire. An anti-tank ditch (in reality a string of craters fifteen to thirty feet wide) covered most of the front, along with barbed-wire entanglements of varied depth, interspersed with trip wires and mines.[63]

But there was a lot that was not known about the Hitler Line, and some unpleasant surprises awaited the Canadian infantry and British tanks who were getting ready to attack it. Adjoining each of the subterranean bunkers, 150 or more yards apart, "was a 'Tobruk' weapon-pit. This was an underground concrete chamber with a circular neck-like opening projecting a few inches above the ground. A metal track inside the neck provided for the rotation of an anti-tank turret or machine-gun mount." More ominous was something new in Italy (although used previously in the desert fighting), *Panzerturm*. The Germans had removed turrets from older-model Mark III and IV tanks, and installed them atop a base of bricks and reinforced concrete. Each turret mounted a long-barrelled 75-millimetre anti-tank gun, a machine-gun, and a rocket projector, manned by a specially-trained three-man crew; and each position was protected by a brace of self-propelled guns. There were eighteen of these miniature fortresses, including eight in the Canadian sector. They remained concealed until the Canadians attacked; their low profile made them very hard to hit, and they proved impervious to all but direct hits by certain calibres of shells.[64]

Despite the awesome power of the enemy defences, and despite the experience of the Third Brigade in closing up to them, General Vokes continued to hope that the Germans would not make a determined bid to hold the Hitler Line. His belief was influenced by events in the mountains on either side of the Liri. After capturing Cassino on 18 May, the Poles were threatening Piedimonte, at the north end of the Hitler Line, while to the south the Corps Expéditionnaire Français had already breached it. The Hitler position was lightly fortified in front of the French, who had driven the Germans from the high ground overlooking Pontecorvo on 20 May. The next night, patrols entered that part of the town on the French side of the Liri, much to the discomfiture of the Canadians, immersed in the preparations for their frontal assault. "The French are making our faces more than a little red," reads the First Division's war diary, "although we realize the reason for this waiting."[65]

Vokes was quick to see the possibilities presented by the French success. The Hitler Line had already been outflanked: perhaps he could take advantage of the situation. He sent the First Brigade's Dan Spry to visit the French on 21 May, in the hope of arranging an assault-boat crossing of the River Liri that would enable the Canadians to take Pontecorvo from the rear. Spry's report was disappointing. In his opinion, the Liri's steep, twelve-foot bank, defended by machine-guns, would make a crossing extremely hazardous; and, to get into Pontecorvo, the Canadians would have to cross the river not once but twice.

However, Vokes was toying with another alternative to Chesterfield. That morning, his reconnaissance regiment, the Princess Louise Dragoon Guards, had taken twenty-two prisoners, members of the low-quality 44th Field Replacement Battalion. When he learned of this incident, the divisional commander concluded that the Pontecorvo end of the Hitler Line was but lightly held.[66]

Vokes went to General Burns and proposed to attack the area to the left of his divisional front with Spry's brigade on the morning of the twenty-second. If it went well, as he expected, there would be no need to mount Chesterfield. Instead of making that frontal assault, the Second Brigade could instead be summoned from reserve and exploit the First Brigade's breach. To Vokes's hard-working chief gunner, Bill Ziegler, it was a logical undertaking. "In battle, opportunities arise; the good officer takes advantage of the opportunities."[67]

Not everyone saw it that way. "I agreed to this operation," Burns later wrote, "although I was not very happy about it," fearing that it might distract attention from Chesterfield's preparations.[68] Most unhappy of all was the man who was ordered to make the attack. Ian Johnston, the officer commanding the 48th Highlanders of Canada, was aghast when told of this operation. It was midnight when Brigadier Spry informed him of the plan: the 48th Highlanders were to attack at 0400 hours on 22 May, supported by tanks of the 142nd Regiment and the artillery program already arranged for this sector under Chesterfield. If the attack succeeded, Spry would send in The Royal Canadian and Hastings and Prince

Edward regiments to widen the breach, and the Second Brigade would soon follow.

Colonel Johnston asked to be relieved of his command. With only four hours to prepare, with no preliminary bombardment or time to lift mines, and unconvinced that either the tanks or the artillery could properly support his troops, Johnston viewed the operation as suicidal. Spry tried to talk him out of it; Johnston was adamant. Finally, the brigadier telephoned Vokes, who assented to a four-hour delay. That seemed to satisfy the battalion commander, who hurried forward to organize the assault.[69]

While the 48th Highlanders were preparing to storm the Hitler Line, Vokes launched a preliminary attack by the Princess Louise Dragoon Guards and the 142nd Royal Tank Regiment near the Pignataro–Pontecorvo road. Attacking at 0700, the armoured cars and tanks punched four hundred yards into the enemy fortified zone, before being stopped by a minefield. Three British tanks were destroyed, but the Plugs captured sixty more demoralized prisoners.[70] If nothing else, the probing attack allowed the reconnaissance regiment to claim "the distinction of being the first unit in the Eighth Army to penetrate the Hitler Line."[71]

After two more postponements, the 48th attacked at 1030. The Highlanders came under fire while they were still working their way through the barbed wire. The lucky ones found gaps blown by the artillery's harassing fire of the past couple of days. The unlucky ones were tangled in the wire, in plain sight of the enemy. "That was a fearful thing," one survivor recalled. "If you fight with barbwire it only gets worse. You must ignore the machine-gun bullets plucking at your sleeves, and quietly take out the barbs . . . one . . . by . . . bloody . . . one."[72]

But the 48th got through the barbed wire and across the anti-tank ditch. With Colonel Johnston at their head, all four companies were now in the midst of the Hitler Line. His casualties had been surprisingly light, but the British tanks, attempting to manoeuvre past the wreckage of Ernie Buss's water truck, were having a terrible time: mines and anti-tank fire took a grim toll. A single *Panzerturm* brewed up three British Shermans, but a Canadian 17-pounder of the 1st Anti-Tank Regiment knocked out the enemy position, scoring two direct hits at sixteen hundred yards – nearly a mile.[73]

Johnston rearranged his line, and dug in to await the counter-attacks which must come. The 48th's position by late afternoon was seemingly hopeless. Without armoured support, the battalion occupied a bridgehead six hundred yards wide and four hundred yards deep, surrounded on three sides by the enemy. Indeed, there appeared to no help of any kind available. A coded message arrived from brigade headquarters, and Johnston anxiously waited for the intelligence officer to decipher it. He grabbed the potentially life-saving message, and read it in disbelief: "A supply of red paint is now available for divisional patches on vehicles."[74]

Tommy Burns had watched the 48th make the attack. At 0830 he drove up to a mountaintop observation post belonging to the neighbouring French. The corps commander lost interest quickly; after watching for less than an hour, he returned to his headquarters. "I concluded that it was not going to succeed," he later explained.[75] He telephoned Chris Vokes, "who informed me that the attack was making better progress than had appeared from my own observations." Then Oliver Leese phoned to caution Burns "against getting too involved in this subsidiary operation in prejudice of the main CHESTERFIELD operation."[76]

By late afternoon on 22 May, Vokes had to admit that his gambit had failed. Chesterfield would have to be launched after all, he informed Burns, who only now learned that Vokes had held the Second Brigade in limbo for most of the day. "He had been intending to ask permission to do this," Burns later wrote, "but I was not aware at the time that this alternate plan of his was delaying the deployment for the main planned attack." By the time the brigade's two assault formations, Princess Patricia's Canadian Light Infantry and the Seaforth Highlanders of Canada, moved into the front line, they were left with "insufficient time for reconnoitring approaches to the Hitler Line fortified zone, and especially little opportunity to lift mines to allow clear passage for the tanks."[77]

"We should've patrolled more," says Cam Ware, who commanded the Patricias. "But we couldn't patrol more, because we just moved into the line that night." For two days, Ware had been uncertain about his role; orders were being issued and plans prepared, only to be revised. If the First Brigade succeeded at Pontecorvo, the PPCLI, along with the Seaforths and Loyal Edmontons, would move to that flank. If not, they would relieve the West Novas of the Third Brigade and mount the main attack. There is, he points out, a time-honoured military adage which deals with this sort of uncertainty: "Order, counter-order, disorder."[78]

Chesterfield was scheduled for 0600 hours on the twenty-third. Three minutes before H-Hour (a term recently introduced to replace zero hour), the artillery would lay down the creeping barrage, paving the way, it was hoped, for the three leading assault battalions, the PPCLI, the Seaforths, and the Carleton and York Regiment. The Loyal Edmonton Regiment was arrayed behind the Patricias, to lend weight and impetus to the main drive through the Hitler Line, while the West Nova Scotia Regiment backed up the Carletons. Two British armoured units would support the infantry: the North Irish Horse (which included a captain named Randolph Churchill, the prime minister's son) would back up the PPCLI and Seaforths, while the 51st Royal Tank Regiment would go into action with the Eddies and Carletons. The battle plan called for a one-hour pause on the initial objective, the Pontecorvo–Aquino road, before the advance to the Pontecorvo–Route 6 road. Chesterfield would be completed by the Fifth Armoured Division pouring through the breach.*

Tommy Burns spent an anxious night, as he awaited the start of his first major action as a corps commander. For any commander, the waiting is always the worst part of an operation. Burns, at least, was satisfied that he and his senior subordinates had done everything possible to ensure success in the morning. On his desk was a note from Sir Oliver Leese. "My dear Tommy," the army commander had written, "I am confident that you will add the ADOLF HITLER LINE to those epics of Canadian battle history – SANCTUARY WOOD; VIMY; ORTONA."[81] Burns hoped that Leese was right.

---

* The assault on the Hitler Line is a striking illustration of the small numbers of combatants on a modern battlefield. It is estimated that, excluding reserve units, there were 1,085 German soldiers manning the fortifications between Piedimonte and Pontecorvo;[79] of these, "probably not more than 800" were facing the Canadians.[80] The three Canadian assault battalions each attacked with two companies forward and two in support; each company went into action with two platoons up and one behind. If those twelve front-line platoons were each at full strength (35), which they almost certainly were not, there would have been, at most, 420 Canadian soldiers leading the assault.

CHAPTER TWELVE

The Valley of Death

1

Tuesday, 23 May, dawned in a shroud of mist. By the middle of the morning, however, "a muggy heat lay on the rolling farmland as stifling as a blanket, and above the battle haze the clouds were gathering with a threat of rain."[1] By H-Hour, the sun had been up for twenty minutes, but the attackers had been awake for a couple of hours. After a cold breakfast, the Canadians "trudged through the meadows to their Forming-Up Points. There they spread out, sat down, and waited for the barrage to begin."[2]

They did not have long to wait. A ten-minute bombardment of enemy positions had been carried out at 0505, followed by a half-hour counter-battery program. Since this was combined with the creeping barrage that opened at 0557, the infantry could take some solace in the fact that this "spectacular fire plan . . . was the heaviest ever to be utilized by the Western Allies up to this stage of the war."[3] Would it be enough?

The western Canadians of the Second Brigade walked into disaster. For Princess Patricia's Canadian Light Infantry on the right, supported by the Loyal Edmonton Regiment, with the Seaforth Highlanders of Canada on their left, 23 May 1944 would be forever associated with misfortune and grief.

Three minutes after the barrage opened, the infantry started forward. Bucko Watson, the popular major who commanded A Company of the Patricias, cheerfully called out, "See you on the objective," to no one in particular.[4]

At first, the going was relatively easy. The barrage was "satisfactory," according to the Patricias' colonel, Cam Ware, who notes that his men dealt swiftly and decisively with the enemy they discovered in the woods that lay in the path of their advance.[5] Twenty minutes after the attack started, the two leading companies had reached the initial objective line (there were five for the PPCLI, each about three hundred yards apart), and at 0710 the second line had been passed. Major Watson's company reported that it was past the barbed-wire entanglements that marked the leading edge of the Hitler Line. It was the last thing that went right for the Patricias.[6]

Actually, difficulties had begun earlier. As Colonel Ware had feared, the oak forest in front of the battalion proved to be a hindrance to the attackers. "It was difficult to follow the barrage through dense woods," Major Watson later commented, "and we soon began to find the wounded of 'C' Company in our path, whereas they should have been on our right. . . . We had not seen our supporting tanks but we knew we had reached the Hitler Line for we could see rows of barbed wire ahead."[7]

As soon as the infantrymen cleared the woods, they were engulfed in a storm of enemy fire, from the front and from the right, where paratroopers were holding Aquino. But it was at this point that the Patricias paid the price for their inability to properly reconnoitre the area before the attack. Their tank support, Churchills and Shermans of the North Irish Horse, forced into a bottleneck by the lay of the land, had blundered into an undetected minefield at this critical moment. Unable to move forward, the tanks presented wonderful targets to the *Panzerturm* mounting 75-millimetre guns. As tank after tank brewed, the survivors were forced to fall back to the dubious protection of the woods. The infantry pushed on alone, trying to keep up to the barrage. At every step, men fell: some were victims of *Nebelwerfer* fire, many were dropped by machine-gun bullets, and others trod on mines scattered about the barbed-wire entanglements.

It was a brutal baptism of fire for Private Allan "Curly" Gurevitch, a former soft-drink salesman from Calgary who had just joined the PPCLI in April. Four days shy of his twenty-eighth birthday, Gurevitch was lugging a 2-inch mortar into his first battle. Even today, he marvels that he survived. "There was heavy artillery coming down, medium artillery, there was machine-gun fire that we were going into. You could see the tracer bullets passing by. I was waiting to get hit – nothing happened. I just don't know how I lived." Eventually, Gurevitch sought refuge in a shell hole, where he and a handful of other Patricias were pinned down for the rest of the day.[8]

Only one Patricia made it to the objective. The intrepid Major Watson worked his way through the barbed wire, accompanied by a few of his men. Within minutes, all the others had been killed or wounded, but Watson went on alone. Ahead was the Pontecorvo–Aquino road, the battalion's objective, "so I went on to it," the major later wrote. "I could find no trace of my men but the enemy was there. By that time I had been wounded twice and realized that the attack had failed." Like Curly Gurevitch, Watson took refuge in a "large and quite comfortable shell hole," and prayed for help to arrive.[9]

To make matters worse, radio communications had broken down. The last message to reach Colonel Ware, shortly after 0700, was that two companies of attackers were through the wire. Runners were sent forward to contact the company commanders, but none returned. Ware went up to take personal charge, but he soon regretted it. "I was in a stupid position," he says, "I was too far forward. There was nothing I could do. I kept calling for smoke, but we got no smoke, as far as I could see. And we were trapped."[10]

By now, the reserve Loyal Eddies were mixed up in the fighting. The Alberta battalion was supposed to keep pace with the Patricias, moving forward at certain times before passing through and leading the final advance. As soon as the Pats had moved into action, Lieutenant-Colonel Rowan Coleman led his battalion into its assigned positions, but before the Edmontons and tanks of the 51st Regiment had gone a hundred yards, trouble had become evident. The area was under heavy mortar and shell fire; there were casualties, and the Eddies were nowhere near the designated start line. Colonel Coleman radioed brigade headquarters and requested a half-hour delay in his scheduled advance. He received permission, but events rendered this arrangement meaningless. The Eddies passed through the Patricias' reserve company, working their way into the shell- and bullet-riddled oak wood and emerging into the wheatfield beyond, where they were greeted by what one report described as "without doubt . . . the worst enemy fire the battalion has ever experienced."[11]

The battle swiftly turned into a shambles for the Eddies. The high-water mark of the advance was achieved by two sections of one company who managed to cut their way into the wire, only to be trapped among the mines by the relentless machine-gun fire. Colonel Coleman was wounded in the hand and leg. Radio communications were knocked out. The only immediate support was provided by three disabled British tanks, but even this was snuffed out late in the morning, when a German self-propelled gun rumbled up to within five hundred yards and blasted the British tanks into submission. The Eddies, intermingled with the surviving Patricias, were deadlocked along the wire and in the woods.

Things were only slightly better to the immediate left of the Patricias and Eddies, where Vancouver's Seaforth Highlanders were in action. Minutes after starting the attack, the Seaforths had encountered the same heavy fire that the Second Brigade's other two battalions were facing. Nevertheless, the Highlanders made steady and promising progress, backed by two squadrons of the North Irish Horse. Visibility was extremely poor, due to the smoke, dust, and fog that enveloped them.

This was the first combat in Italy for the tanks of the North Irish Horse, and the British veterans of the North African desert were finding that this warfare was very much different. In one field alone, on the Seaforths' right flank, fifteen tanks had been brewed up by the deadly *Panzerturm*.[12]

Major James Allan took charge at this critical juncture. Within two hours of the beginning of the battle, Allan was the only Seaforth company commander who was still in action. Allan did not have much with which to work. His company had suffered 20 per cent casualties by the time it reached the wire, which, fortunately, was not much of an obstacle. Although it was sown with anti-tank mines, there were no anti-personnel mines, and the shelling had chopped big gaps in the entanglement. Every tank of the North Irish Horse had been knocked out, but the major led his company to the Pontecorvo–Aquino road. As he deployed them, he spotted one of the concrete-emplaced tank turrets that had done so much damage to the British tanks. Set low in what appeared to be a pile of rubble, the turret was protected by a sunken track, filled with felled trees and laced with slit trenches and machine-gun posts. But Allan spotted the Achilles heel, a shallow gully to the south. A party of Seaforths slipped around the enemy position and knocked out the turret by killing the crew at close range with small-arms fire.[13]

By mid morning, Allan had rounded up about a hundred survivors of the four rifle companies in a line of dugouts and slit trenches just east of the Pontecorvo–Aquino road. He reported this situation to battalion headquarters; shortly afterwards, his radio was knocked out.

Allan's brave little band was soon counter-attacked. Isolated on the objective, with no tanks to help them, the Seaforths fought like tigers. When German self-propelled guns approached from the right, Company Sergeant-Major J. M. Duddle took a two-man PIAT team out to greet them. They had only two bombs for their anti-tank weapon, but these were sufficient. Knocking out one gun, Duddle and his PIAT men escaped in a hail of bullets. The sergeant-major reported to Allan, whose radio had been repaired long enough to get through a call to battalion headquarters for anti-tank guns, PIAT bombs, and reinforcements.[14]

But no help could get through. The 90th Anti-Tank Battery tried to get guns up to both the Seaforths and the Patricias, to no avail. So great was the volume of fire that ammunition parties were unable to get through. Major Allan and his men were cut off, in the heart of the Adolf Hitler Line.

At Second Brigade headquarters, Graeme Gibson was helpless. He was another victim of the flawed plan of attack. Although the PPCLI had been stopped, the Seaforths had attained a partial breakthrough – but Brigadier Gibson had no reserves to commit, because the Loyal Eddies were already involved in the fighting. "With all the benefits of hindsight," says one divisional staff officer, "I think that the . . . Edmontons should have been kept back, as far as possible clear of counter-bombardment until actually committed. It is a well-tried military maxim that a commander should reinforce success. The Edmontons should have been prepared to attack in the second phase either on the right through the PPCLI or on the left through the Seaforths."

The survivors of the Patricias, Eddies, and Seaforths, blinded by clouds of smoke, huddled in shell holes and behind shattered tree trunks and burning tanks, could only hold on and hope for the best. "But," notes the British official historian, "unknown to all these steadfast men, their Division was winning the battle."[15]

If 23 May was a black day for Western Canada, it was a grand day for the Maritimes.

It was no coincidence that the Carleton and York Regiment was the only battalion which broke through the Hitler Line, and the only one to have had a chance to properly reconnoitre the fortifications. Indeed, the Carletons had been in the forefront since bumping into the German line on 18 May. They had patrolled aggressively and effectively in the meantime, but the most valuable work came on the morning of 22 May, when the Carletons made a diversionary attack to aid the 48th Highlanders. Although suffering twenty-five casualties, the assault company brought back "priceless information" about the enemy's defences.[16]

The New Brunswickers put the information to good use in their attack. Unlike the westerners of the Second Brigade, they knew what to expect; the Hitler Line had few surprises for them. Many of their British tanks came to grief in front of the *Panzerturm*, which proved as deadly here as elsewhere, but the Carletons forged ahead, "following closely on the heels of the barrage. . . . The greatest obstacle to our advance was the relentless pounding of the hostile mortars, *Nebelwerfers* and artillery which the Germans had in great numbers behind the lines."[17]

Within seventy-five minutes of H-Hour, the Carleton and York Regiment had breached the powerful defences. Digging in along the Aquino–Pontecorvo road, they rounded up dozens of prisoners – all together, two hundred by the end of the day – and sent them to the rear in a steady stream. Victory cost the Carletons sixty-two casualties.[18]

Behind them, the men of the West Nova Scotia Regiment were in high spirits. The previous night, they had taken bets "as to how long it will take to smash the Adolf Hitler line," and the battalion had prepared to go into action that morning "with amazing precision. An air of confidence about everywhere, orders being quietly given and quickly obeyed. . . . Everyone knows exactly what is expected of them and what they are to do."[19] The battalion commander, Lieutenant-Colonel Ron Waterman, notified Third Brigade headquarters at 1040 that he was ready to continue the attack.

The Nova Scotians were anxious to move. Not only were men being lost to the intense shell fire, they were seemingly surrounded by brewed-up

British tanks. There were few things more horrifying that watching human beings incinerated in their steel coffins. Stretcher-bearer Victor Hall recalls that the regimental aid post was equipped to handle minor burns, but the medical people were virtually helpless to deal with the massive burns suffered by many of the tankers who were literally ablaze. "Nothing you can do. Just get him on a stretcher and get him to the RAP. All they could do was put a wet blanket over him and get him the hell out. And morphine."[20]

But, instead of attacking in support of the Carletons, the West Novas were ordered to dig in. This was not good news, according to a mystified Colonel Waterman. "More tanks on fire, casualties being taken out as quickly as possible, shell and mortar fire intense, everyone is getting a bit worried, no news, what can be holding up the attack?"[21]

Not until late Tuesday morning did an accurate picture of the battle begin to take shape at First Division headquarters. "For the first few hours," says the divisional gunner, Bill Ziegler, "the fog of battle prevailed. And that is absolutely according to form."[22]

The belated realization of the failure on the Second Brigade's front, the division's main thrust, forced General Vokes and his staff to re-evaluate their plans. One fact was clear: Aquino was a trouble spot. The Canadians were paying a high price for the Eighth Army's informality, and Sir Oliver Leese's preference for verbal orders. The British 78th Division, on the right of the Canadians, had been instructed to distract the defenders of Aquino, but there was a wide divergence between what the Canadians expected the British to do and what the British actually did, which seems to have been very little.

The Canadians were finally forced to take matters into their own hands. After consulting with Second Brigade headquarters, Brigadier Ziegler decided upon a radical course: a William target, in which every available gun in the Eighth Army would fire simultaneously on the stubborn para-troopers at Aquino. This raised a few eyebrows; no artillery commander had ever called for one before. Ziegler submitted his request to the corps artillery chief, E. C. "Johnny" Plow, at 1227. Approval came, says Ziegler, "in very short order," and he and his staff went to work. "I gave the fire orders, and those fire orders had to pass from my headquarters down to all these fire units." All was ready within thirty-three minutes, an "amazingly short" time, according to Ziegler.[23]

At 1300 hours, 668 guns opened fire. It was all over in less than a minute. In that brief span, 3,509 shells, totalling ninety-two tons of high explosive, fell on Aquino and its airfield.[24]

The William target achieved the desired effect, and the enemy fire was noticeably reduced. A few days later, Bill Ziegler, the man responsible for this devastation, was flying over the Liri valley when his light plane ran out of fuel. The pilot told him not to worry, that they could land at Aquino. "The hell we will," exclaimed Ziegler. "I've blown it all to hell!" The aircraft had to make an emergency landing on the highway, Route 6.[25]

While the artillery pulverized Aquino, Chris Vokes had come to some conclusions of his own. By noon, with the main attack by the Second Brigade getting nowhere, he gave serious consideration to the possibilities of exploiting the break achieved by the Carleton and Yorks on the Third Brigade front. Vokes called the corps commander, Tommy Burns, who later wrote that "with my advice and agreement he took the bold course of exploiting the success on the left."[26] Vokes decided to commit his divisional reserve units, the Van Doos and the Three Rivers tanks, to the Carletons' front; together with the West Nova Scotia Regiment, they would pry open the Hitler Line.

Even as he made this decision, Vokes might well have recalled Sir Oliver Leese's intervention a few days earlier. Vokes's original plan, approved by Burns, had called for an attack by the Second Brigade alone; at Leese's insistence, the assault frontage had been widened to include the Carleton and Yorks. Vokes was most annoyed at the time, but he should have been grateful for Leese's fortuitous meddling.

The only problem was that it would take time to organize the attack, issue the necessary orders, and get troops and tanks into position. H-Hour for the renewed attack was set for 1530, but this was later delayed until 1650; the final H-Hour was not confirmed until twenty minutes before the attack.

Meanwhile, the 48th Highlanders had continued to wage their forgotten fight trapped inside the Hitler Line near Pontecorvo. It seemed to one veteran that the Germans had "more Spandaus [machine-guns] than we'd ever seen congregated. More mortars, too. And we had no tanks."[27]

But British tanks were on the way. The divisional reconnaissance unit, the Princess Louise Dragoon Guards, had discovered a route between the Pontecorvo road and the River Liri that was not mined, enabling a squadron of Churchills to reach the 48th shortly after dawn. The Highlanders and their tanks attacked at 0800, in an effort to take Point 106, the high ground to the right that they had failed to capture the previous day. Within moments, the Canadians discovered that the Germans had reinforced the position during the night, and even with armoured support they were unable to make much progress in the face of heavy small-arms fire. The Highlanders tried repeatedly to break through the enemy defences. One by one, their tanks were knocked out. Instead of taking Point 106, the Glamour Boys from Toronto were trapped on the bullet-swept slopes.

The Hastings and Prince Edward Regiment came to their rescue. At noon, when it became clear that the 48th could not take Point 106, Brigadier Spry ordered the Hastings and Prince Edward Regiment into action. Lieutenant-Colonel Don Cameron hastily drew up a plan of attack. One company, D, would swing through the Hitler Line where the 48th had broken in, while B attacked further to the right, where gaps had been cut in the wire the previous night. A Company would be held in reserve to exploit success.[28]

D Company moved out at 1400 hours. No artillery support could be provided, for fear of hitting the 48th Highlanders, but the Hasty Ps did not need the gunners' assistance. Once inside the Hitler Line's barbed wire, the company deployed and attacked as if it were on a training exercise in England. Firing from the hip, they overran the enemy, taking thirty-two prisoners. Nineteen were captured single-handedly by Sergeant Jack Loshaw, who was later awarded the Military Medal. Then, at 1500, B Company and tanks of the 142nd Royal Tank Regiment attacked from the other direction. Plough Jockeys from Ontario and British Churchills and Shermans overran the defenders, enabling A Company to follow through and capture Point 106.[29]

By 1900, it was all over. At the cost of thirty casualties, the Hasty Ps had saved the 48th Highlanders and seized the last obstacle before Ponte-corvo, capturing three hundred Germans and killing or wounding another hundred. "It was," says Farley Mowat, "probably the most brilliant single action fought by the Regiment in the entire course of the war."[30]

The West Novas and Van Doos attacked north of Pontecorvo behind a powerful barrage.

It had been a long, hard day for the gunners. After firing the barrage for the morning's big attack, they had, as scheduled, laid down a curtain of shells just beyond the Pontecorvo–Aquino road. The protective barrage had been planned to last an hour; they had to maintain it for more than nine hours, in addition to answering periodic requests for concentrations of fire on certain targets. Now, they continued to labour over their red-hot gun barrels, ramming home one round after another, the piles of brass shell casings growing bigger by the minute.

The Nova Scotians had been waiting all day for this moment. Expecting to have carried out this operation before noon, they had not brought rations. Everyone was hungry, but the worst part was having to dig in among the burning tanks. When the Three Rivers Shermans finally appeared, it was not even necessary for them to stop. "As they rolled into our position through the wrecks of the Churchills we just waved them on, got up, and started forward," recounted one West Nova officer. "Our aim was clear enough – to get forward out of that hell hole."[31]

"Good luck, West Novas!" the Carletons called out, as their exuberant fellow Maritimers passed through them, heading for the narrow gravel road that connected Pontecorvo with Route 6. They lost a few men to their own shell fire, but they stayed close behind the barrage. The gully of a small river, the San Martino, proved to be a natural tank obstacle, and the Three Rivers Shermans halted on its eastern lip. A heavy thunderstorm swept across the battlefield during the advance, but it would take more than slippery ground to slow the West Novas. As the enemy's counter-barrage fell on the open ground behind them, the Canadian infantry pressed forward; by sunset they were on the objective, after meeting "spotty resistance" along the way. Upon reaching the road, they pushed ahead to a low ridge just beyond it, where they dug in.[32]

The Germans counter-attacked almost immediately. With Pontecorvo cut off by the Canadian advance, every available enemy soldier and tank was dispatched to drive the West Novas away. The Germans lost heavily in the face of Canadian shell fire, but still managed to overrun part of A Company, taking thirty prisoners. The West Novas did not remain prisoners for long. Their captors, apparently unaware that a full battalion of Canadians was there, marched up the road towards Route 6 – right under the noses of B Company, which was watching in disbelief.

Privates Walter Peach and R. L. Hall sized up the situation immediately; they fired their Bren gun over the heads of the Canadians in the middle of the column. Then, as their buddies hit the ground, they cut down the Germans. Peach and Hall died in the exchange that followed, but the enemy, caught in the road with no cover, stood little chance in the face of B Company's rifles and Bren guns. "Not a German escaped."[33]

In sharp contrast, the Van Doos on the right of the West Novas had a relatively uneventful evening. The Royal 22nd Regiment also crossed the San Martino gully, and moved northwards; by 2115, and with thankfully light losses, the French-Canadians were consolidating their gains, twelve hundred yards north of the West Novas. While digging in, the Van Doos discovered dugouts that had served as an enemy headquarters. Inside, they found detailed maps and documents, office equipment, and twenty Iron Crosses, "which were probably to be issued to the men for their successful defence of the Hitler Line," the battalion report speculated. "I wonder how Hitler himself feels in knowing that the line bearing his wretched name has been broken and that a lot of his Iron Crosses are now in the hands of many of our Canadians, and that they are nothing more than souvenirs."[34]

Between them, the West Novas and Van Doos had widened the breach in the Hitler Line to more than a mile. After the day's hard fighting, the Third Brigade's relatively easy success seemed to be almost too good to be true. A very relieved General Vokes later called it "the 1st Division's most out-standing tactical success in any single day of fighting in the war."[35] With this attack, he later commented, "the Hitler Line folded like a militia tent in a high wind."[36]

Vokes summoned to his dugout the division's chief gunner, Bill Ziegler, whose artillery preparations had kept him on his feet for three days. The Calgary native, aware that they had not hit it off since his arrival in February, was hesitant about attending a private meeting with the abrasive Vokes.

The divisional commander surprised him. Handing Ziegler a bottle of rye and nodding to a tumbler on the desk, Vokes told him to have a drink. Ziegler poured a bit of liquor into the glass, but Vokes was dissatisfied with the miniscule amount. "Goddammit," he roared, "I said, 'Pour yourself a drink'!"

Ziegler added a little more.

"Goddammit, Ziegler, don't you understand English? *Pour yourself a drink!*"

This time, the gunner filled the tumbler to the top.

Satisfied, Vokes sat on his desk and said, "Now drink it."

Ziegler obeyed; in minutes, he recalls, "I was out like a light. I slept like a baby," and when he awoke several hours later, "I was a new man." This was precisely what Vokes had intended, says Ziegler. "He knew that I would keep on going until I dropped, so he decided to put me to sleep." Ziegler had seen a hitherto hidden side of Vokes. From that moment, they were fast friends.[37]

Cam Ware could have used a good, stiff drink and a long sleep, too. The PPCLI colonel was in a state of near-shock as he returned to his battalion headquarters that night. War correspondent Doug How remembers meeting Ware, whose "eyes were glazed,"[38] and understandably so. The colonel had survived a nightmare in which he had seen his beloved regiment killed all around him. "They were fine boys," he said to Captain Howard Mitchell of the Saskatoon Light Infantry. "They are gone. I haven't anybody left. They are all gone."[39] So it must have seemed; by nightfall, he had been able to find only seventy-seven able-bodied men with whom to hold the division's right flank.

There were survivors and stragglers, of course. Among them was Curly Gurevitch, who helped a wounded man to the rear, then returned to aid a second soldier in the shell hole where he had taken refuge during the day. Only later did he discover that he had made a total of four trips through a minefield, emerging unscathed. However, a mortar blast had partially deafened him; it was an injury that would end his combat career.[40]

Bucko Watson was found the next morning in his shell hole near the

Pontecorvo–Aquino road. According to the unit war diary, the major was "suffering from a wound in one arm, a piece of his helmet and a schmeisser bullet in his forehead (and a tremendous appetite)."[41]

The Second Brigade, the victor at Ortona, had been cut to pieces at the Hitler Line. Its casualties numbered 543, a total "unequalled in a single day's fighting by any Canadian brigade during the entire Italian campaign." This was well over half the division's losses (879) in its hardest day's fighting of the entire Italian campaign.[42]

The death toll was heartbreaking. "We had so many casualties," recalls an SLI officer, Rupe Leblond, "they were using bulldozers to scoop our troops into trenches, and then later our people would come up, identify them, and give them a proper burial. That was how bad our casualties were."[43] The padre of the Seaforths, Roy Durnford, was a busy man for the next few days, for he had to oversee the burial of fifty-two Seaforths in the regimental cemetery. "Bodies keep coming in," the weary padre wrote in his diary, "mute testimony to awful victory. The cemetery is filling up fast. Work goes on at a fast and furious pace. . . . I go to bed but not to sleep."[44]

The British tanks who had so valiantly supported the Canadians suffered huge losses, too. The three units, the North Irish Horse, the 51st Royal Tank Regiment, and the 142nd Regiment lost a total of forty-four tanks destroyed; a great many more were knocked out, but a substantial number were salvaged and returned to action after repairs.[45] All three armoured units were later authorized to add the maple leaf to their regimental badges, as a reward for their sacrifices at the Hitler Line.

Chris Vokes later called the Hitler Line "the best battle I ever fought, or organized, even though we suffered so heavily."[46]

Frontal attacks are almost always costly, and the Hitler Line was no exception. Yet failure is even costlier, as the German defenders discovered when their fortifications were breached by both the First and Third brigades. The number of prisoners alone (more than seven hundred) nearly matched the total Canadian casualties, while the German dead numbered "several hundred." Almost every unit holding the Hitler Line was afterwards written off by the enemy high command.[47]

And it was failure that cost the Canadians the majority of their losses. The Second Brigade's disaster on the right flank can be attributed to any number of factors. The corps commander, Tommy Burns, blamed the inability of the attacking battalions to properly reconnoitre the approaches to the Hitler Line, which he traced to the First Brigade's attack on 22 May. "Looking back," he later wrote, "it seems I should not have agreed to Vokes' idea to get round the Hitler defences by the Pontecorvo flank."[48]

Vokes sharply disagreed. He contended that the Second Brigade had met with disaster because of the failure of the British on the right to mask Aquino. "That division," Vokes insisted of the 78th, "was supposed to exert strong frontal pressure on the Aquino defences during our own attack. If it did so, it had no noticeable effect. The real blame may be attributed to the employment of two corps in the narrow valley instead of one. If one corps commander had planned and co-ordinated the assault, Aquino would have been dealt with properly, and the 2nd Brigade debacle might not have occurred."[49]

There was no shortage of analysis in the wake of the Hitler Line. Almost everyone, it seems, had a suggestion for improving future operations of this nature. But perhaps the most valid commentary comes from the former gunner, Bill Ziegler, whose hard work won him the Distinguished Service Order and Chris Vokes's lifelong friendship. "You cannot take twenty thousand men, put them into a complex operation like this, however good they might be – and we were good, let me tell you, we were bloody good, but you can't expect that we were perfect. We made some mistakes. We didn't make as many mistakes as the Germans made. The acid test is, 'Who won?' You can't argue with success."[50]

There had been mistakes, and there would be more. But the road to Rome lay open at long last.

2

The Canadian breach in the Hitler Line created a new crisis for the Germans. Half an hour after the Canadian attack began on the morning of 23 May, American forces launched their long-awaited breakout from the embattled Anzio beachhead. The U.S. VI Corps struck northwards for Valmontone. If the Americans could reach it, they would cut off the line of retreat for the bulk of the two German armies in Italy.

The Eighth Army had not endeared itself to senior officers in the Fifth Army. Both Mark Clark and the French commander, Alphonse Juin, were bitterly critical of the slow advance along the Liri valley and the ponderous preparations for the attack on the Hitler Line. Juin complained that the British XIII Corps had wasted a whole day, 17 May, waiting for the fall of Cassino before launching a serious drive down the valley. This delay, said Juin, enabled the Germans to shift forces to meet the French threat in the south, and "we were forced to mark time and wait for the attack, they having hardly begun to make contact with the Hitler Line." Clark was even more outspoken in his condemnation of British efforts. On 21 May, after visiting Sir Oliver Leese's headquarters to discuss the Eighth Army's assault on the Hitler Line, he told his diary: "All their actions are always dictated by their desire to save manpower and let someone else do it."[51]

However, Allied problems seem rather petty by comparison to those the Germans were facing. From the onset of Diadem, the enemy had met one crisis after another. They had been totally surprised by the Allied offensive. Two key commanders, the Tenth Army's Heinrich von Vietinghoff and Fridolin von Senger und Etterlin, the Rhodes scholar and former Benedictine monk who commanded XIV Panzer Corps, had been in Germany, receiving medals from Hitler, when the attack began. They hurriedly returned to the front, where they were forced to utilize their considerable skills to avert disaster.

Privately, Vietinghoff was optimistic that the Hitler Line could be held. "The defence works," he wrote, "were excellent; effective concentrations of artillery and anti-aircraft artillery under the direct command of the Army's senior artillery commander . . . ; the two divisional commanders [Ernst Gunther Baade of the 90th Panzer Grenadier and the 1st Parachute's Richard Heidrich] were in a class all by themselves."[52]

By the evening of the twenty-third, reality had rudely intruded upon the German commanders. With the Anzio beachhead suddenly coming to life and posing a threat to the Tenth Army's line of communications, Kesselring telephoned Vietinghoff. "Contrary to all expectations," the field-marshal said, "things do not look good."[53]

As the German defences crumbled, there was only one possibility of stabilizing the situation in the Liri valley. Six miles northwest of the ruptured Hitler Line, a little river meandered across the the floor of the valley. Its name was the Melfa, and if the Germans could hold it, the Tenth Army might yet be saved.

The pursuit started slowly. The original Canadian plan called for the Fifth Armoured Division to pass through the First Division as soon as the breakthrough had been made, and General Hoffmeister intended to do precisely that. Brigadier Desmond Smith's Fifth Armoured Brigade would lead the way, establishing a bridgehead on the Melfa, enabling Brigadier Eric Snow's Eleventh Infantry Brigade to pass through and lead the way to Ceprano, where Route 6 crossed the River Liri. Smith's tanks would once again take over the advance, "which with luck would turn into a pursuit before the Germans were able to recover."[54]

But the pursuit was delayed. After receiving approval from Tommy Burns to commence the advance early Tuesday evening, Hoffmeister soon found that there were insurmountable difficulties. The division had planned to pass through the Second Brigade's front; the switch to the Third Brigade sector, a mile south, meant having to select new assembly areas and a new start line in unfamiliar territory. This was compounded by the heavy rain, which reduced every road and track to muddy trails, and by traffic congestion caused by British tanks coming back from the Hitler Line to refuel and reorganize. As a result, Hoffmeister reported to Burns that he could not get going until morning.[55]

The Mighty Maroon Machine was champing at the bit to get into action. With the exception of the three infantry battalions of the Eleventh Brigade, most of the division had not been in battle before. None were more anxious than the Governor-General's Horse Guards, better known as the "GeeGees,"* the divisional reconnaissance regiment. "At last the day has arrived," says the unit's war diary. "Four long years lie behind us. . . . Years of waiting. Four long years with a single purpose – to hit the Hun where it hurts."[57]

To lead the dash to the Melfa, two strike forces had been organized. Vokes Force, commanded by Lieutenant-Colonel Fred Vokes (Chris Vokes's younger, hot-tempered brother), consisted of his British Columbia Dragoons and the Irish Regiment. Vokes Force would go about halfway to the Melfa, and allow Griffin Force to pass through. Lieutenant-Colonel P. G. "Paddy" Griffin commanded his own Lord Strathcona's Horse and the motorized infantry of the Westminster Regiment. The enthusiastic GeeGees would cover the flanks during the advance.

Vokes Force plunged into action at 0757 hours on Wednesday, 24 May. Shermans of the B.C. Dragoons roared past the gully of the San Martino, emerging from the vineyards and copses in a tangle of wires, vines, and branches. The noise drowned out the incongruous sound of church bells ringing out over the battlefield. That morning, The Royal Canadian Regiment had occupied Pontecorvo, which had been reduced by prolonged aerial and artillery bombardment to "a heap of stone and mortar, with the mangled corpses of its defenders lying everywhere in the streets." After Private J. J. Griggs knocked out an anti-tank gun on the outskirts, for which he was awarded the Military Medal, Lieutenant Bill Rich led the RCR scout platoon into Pontecorvo. While dozens of dazed Germans stumbled from the rubble to surrender, Rich boldly climbed into the church tower and rang the bell to announce the capture of the hotly-contested town. Rich won the Military Cross for his exploit.[58]

It was 1030 when Vokes Force encountered a formidable adversary. The B.C. Dragoons became the first Allied force to engage Mark V Panther tanks. These fifty-ton monsters belonged to the 1st Panzer Regiment, the first German unit in Italy to be equipped with the new Panthers and kept in reserve until an emergency such as this one. Lieutenant Nigel Taylor never forgot his shock at seeing a Panther, "the most enormous tank I had ever

---

* They were also known, from their initials (GGHG), as "God's Gift to Hungry Girls" and "Good God, How Gorgeous!"[56]

seen." Fortunately for Taylor, he spotted the Mark v before the Germans saw him. His gunner, Trooper Cecil Shears, was "a crack shot," and he drilled two rounds into the Panther at a thousand yards. "I got him, sir," said Shears, and the Sherman crew cheered. It was the first Panther to be killed in Italy. The partying was short-lived; Shears died moments later when Taylor's tank was brewed up by a self-propelled gun.[59]

By the time the smoke cleared, Vokes Force had routed the Germans. Three Panthers had been destroyed and a self-propelled gun captured, along with ninety paratroopers. Victory had cost four Shermans and thirty-three Dragoon and Irish casualties.[60]

Griffin Force passed through Vokes Force in the early afternoon. In the lead was the Strathcona's "recce" troop, equipped with American-made Honey tanks (the Honey was merely a light Stuart tank with the turret removed), commanded by a young lieutenant named Edward Perkins. With only three Honeys, Perkins's job was to get to the Melfa as quickly as possible and seize and hold a crossing for the rest of Griffin Force. It would prove to be a tall assignment.

Perkins reached the Melfa at 1500 hours, after exchanging shots along the way with an enemy half-track and a Panther. Like so many rivers in Italy, the Melfa was insignificant, a small stream flowing through a bed fifty yards wide. Perkins quickly got his three Honeys across the Melfa, posted them, then set out to secure the bridgehead, surprising and capturing eight German paratroopers in a farmhouse. After sending two men to take the prisoners away and guide the Strathconas and Westminsters to the proper crossing, Perkins had only twelve men to hold his ground. But they were heavily armed, because each Honey carried a pair of Browning machine-guns, and the five-man crew had a Bren gun, a PIAT, and Tommy guns, in addition to a stock of prepared charges and grenades.[61]

On the other side of the Melfa, a major tank battle was developing. This was one of the rare times in Italy that a substantial number of Canadian tanks clashed with German armour. Panthers, Marks IVs, and self-propelled guns, determined to snuff out the Canadian threat to the Melfa line, attacked repeatedly. Thanks to the trees and hedges which abounded along the banks of the Melfa, it was impossible to exert high-level control over the fighting, which deteriorated into a multitude of bitter duels between Shermans and Panthers that lasted from late afternoon until dusk.

It had turned into "a beautiful day, soft and warm, and overhead the sun shone down from a sky of cloudless blue." Captain John Windsor, a twenty-three-year-old Calgarian, admitted to a feeling of exhilaration as his tank rolled into action, rumbling through an orchard in search of the enemy. "Others had been hit, but I was indestructible," he later wrote. But his sense of invincibility was rudely shattered seconds later. "One moment the world around me was full of vivid colour, green and blue, red and brown, yellow and golden, there were trees and grasses, mountains and people, then suddenly, in the fraction of an instant, everything turned to inky blackness. It was rather like being in a brightly lighted room when suddenly the electicity fails and everything is plunged into darkness." Windsor knew instantly what had happened to him. "This was not the blackness of unconsciousness, nor the blackness of death. I was alive, that was certain, but I was blind." His face had been riddled with fragments from the enemy shell that had hit his Sherman. As the tank brewed up, Windsor's crew guided him to the shelter of a German slit trench.[62]

It was a costly battle, on both sides. That evening, the normally placid banks of the Melfa presented a scene of utter destruction. "As far as one could see . . . the eerie light from burning tanks blended grotesquely with the glow of the setting sun; smoke from burning oil and petrol mingled with the dust that hung over the valley to give the effect of a partial eclipse."[63] Losses were heavy on both sides. The Strathconas destroyed seven Panthers, four Mark IVs, and nine self-propelled guns, and took twenty-two prisoners. Thirty-six dead Germans were found in the area. The Strathconas lost seventeen Shermans and fifty-five men, including Herman Buss, the younger brother of Ernie, whose water truck had come to grief in the Hitler Line just four days earlier.[64]

Reinforcements reached Lieutenant Perkins at 1700 hours, in the form of Major John Mahony's company of the Westminster Regiment. Five weeks shy of his thirty-third birthday, Mahony was an athletic former newspaper reporter from New Westminster. He would later be described by journalist Doug How as "a quiet, mild fellow,"[65] but he was anything but quiet and mild this day. Rolling up to the Melfa in their White scout cars (this was one of the few occasions in Italy that this motorized infantry unit was able to take these American-built armoured vehicles into action), the Westies dismounted and smartly crossed the river, taking up positions in Perkins's little bridgehead.

Quickly taking charge of the bridgehead, Mahony organized an attack on a house where enemy machine-gunners were making life unbearable for the Canadians. That foray netted twenty prisoners.[66] When some of his men were trapped in the open by a German tank which was systematically picking them off with machine-gun fire, Mahony rescued them by throwing some well-aimed smoke grenades.[67]

Trooper Jacob Funk of the Strathconas typified the heroism. Funk, armed with a PIAT, hunted a self-propelled gun that was firing on the Shermans across the river. He crept along the bank until he was within 150 yards; his first round exploded prematurely in the overhanging foliage. He crawled still closer, and his next two shots went high and wide. However, his fourth bomb hit the mark, and the crew bailed out of the burning wreck; one was killed by the Bren gunners and the rest were captured. This performance brought Funk the Military Medal.[68]

Shortly before dusk, the Germans launched a strong counter-attack. A half-mile away, four tanks escorted by several dozen infantrymen rumbled slowly across the stubble fields, and headed directly for the centre of the bridgehead. At five hundred yards, Mahony ordered his two PIATs at a high angle, "in the hope that we might get a lucky hit." As the tanks came closer, Mahony gave the order for every available weapon to open fire. "I even fired with my Tommy gun, which I afterwards thought was pretty stupid at that range, but a man does funny things in a situation like that," Mahony said later.[69]

The small-arms fire had the desired effect. The German infantry went to ground, while the tanks came to within two hundred yards before turning around and rumbling off. "Why, I shall never know," Mahony later remarked. "I can only guess, and my guess is that they thought they were walking into a trap and that we had anti-tank weapons concealed behind the bank and were going to open up on them, like sitting ducks, when they got a little closer." Whatever the reason, Mahony was glad to see them go.[70]

However, they turned up again a short time later. The four tanks followed the river bank, evidently hunting for the Canadians, and one tank stopped a few feet from a slit trench occupied by a private of the Westies. John Culling, a farm lad from Swift Current, Saskatchewan, watched as the enemy commander opened the turret and started to climb out, intent on having a closer look around. Private Culling pulled the pin out of a 36 grenade and tossed it. The blast, said Mahony, "killed the officer who slumped out of the turret and fell forward onto the hull of the tank." Alerted, the tank crew began to swivel the turret towards Culling, searching for their tormentor with powerful machine-guns. Culling tossed another grenade. It hit the edge of the hatch and, like a basketball rolling round the hoop before scoring, dropped into the tank. The explosion killed the driver and disabled the tank. The three surviving crew members tried to flee, but Culling killed two and captured the third .[71] His bravery brought Culling a well-merited Military Medal.

But the other tanks found prey in the form of a four-man section in one of the foremost positions. "After an uneven struggle in which one man was severely wounded and later died, the remaining three were taken prisoner by the Jerries." Later, the three tanks could be seen moving about in plain sight, and Mahony lamented the lack of heavier anti-tank weapons. "At times they made beautiful targets and we would have given our shirts for a couple of 6-pounder anti-tank guns. They were beyond the range of our PIATs."[72]

With nightfall, Mahony and Perkins regrouped, moving their men closer together and making the bridgehead a bit smaller. The tireless major with the quick smile was amazed by his men's high spirits as he made the rounds during the night. "They were still joking and laughing about some of the humorous and exciting incidents of the day. When a Canadian infantryman can't crack a joke . . . then things are pretty bad."[73]

Reinforcements arrived during the night, in the form of another company of Westies. A weary Mahony greeted them with a smile and a joke: "What a way to spend the 24th of May!"[74]

The Germans continued to threaten a counter-attack, but the bridgehead was secure; the Canadians were over the Melfa to stay. John Mahony was rewarded with the Victoria Cross, the second to be awarded to a Canadian in Italy, while Ed Perkins received the Distinguished Service Order.

3

The Canadian push to the Melfa had completely disrupted German plans.

Orders were outdated even before they were issued. Early on the twenty-fifth, as the Fifth Canadian Division was reinforcing its bridgehead on the Melfa, the German high command was issuing orders calling for the "fanatical defence of the designated main defence lines," and Generalfeldmarschall Kesselring forbade "the withdrawal of any division and the giving up of any strongpoint without my prior explicit consent." At midday, the Tenth Army's commander, Vietinghoff, telephoned Valentin Feurstein, commanding LI Mountain Corps, "to emphasize that according to the Führer's orders the Melfa line must be held for several days. An early withdrawal is out of the question."[75]

The Germans were in a perilous position. While the Eighth Army was advancing through the Liri valley, American forces breaking out of the Anzio beachhead were endangering the line of retreat for the Tenth and Fourteenth armies. While the Canadians were crossing the Melfa, the U.S. VI Corps had captured Cisterna, halfway to Valmontone. The crisis was reaching a climax. Vietinghoff's chief of staff, Fritz Wentzell, declared: "We have to get out of here as fast as we can or we shall lose the whole 14th Panzer Corps!"[76]

Canadian veterans who return to Italy today never fail to be surprised at the tremendous changes that have taken place since the war. Aside from the military cemeteries (many in disappointingly obscure locations), there are few reminders of the terrible struggle that took place across the length and breadth of Italy in 1944. One of the most impressive changes in present-day Italy is the *autostrada* network of superhighways. Unfortunately, many of these have been built across Canadian battlefields. One of these is the Melfa, and veterans of the Westminster Regiment are saddened to find that a great highway, the A2, passes over the place where they fought their magnificent battle. "Four lanes each way cross this widened expanse of the Melfa, and Ferraris, Bugattis, Alfa Romeos, Porsches, etc. pour by in both directions with the speed of 88s," recalls Ron Hurley, who was a sergeant in the Westies. "One could get the feeling that the chances of becoming a casualty at this Melfa crossing were almost as great as 1944."[77]

Today's traffic moves much faster and more efficiently than it did during May 1944, when traffic jams of nightmarish proportions threatened to disrupt the Eighth Army's push along the Liri valley. In 1944, there was only one highway, Route 6; the few secondary roads were merely "insubstantial dirt tracks."[78] To make matters worse, the terrain proved to be far more rugged than aerial photographs had indicated. "Our biggest headache was keeping our vehicles out of ditches," the VC winner, John Mahony, attested. "Italian roads at their best were none too good and several times we had to leave the roads and strike out across country. At those times it became a nightmare of pulling our cumbersome White scout cars out of one drainage ditch after another."[79]

These difficulties were compounded by General Leese's decision to exploit the Hitler Line breakthrough on a two-corps front, I Canadian on the left and British XIII on the right. This arrangement had already hurt the Canadians in their assault on the Hitler Line, and they were going to suffer for it during the pursuit phase of the operation. Leese's plan allocated Route 6 to the British corps, and relegated the Canadians to sideroads. "This plan," notes the British official historian, "contained seeds for trouble. . . . Even if the going was as good as it was expected to be, traffic congestion was bound to occur." To make matters worse, Leese had "introduced the principle that one Corps might use, at need, roads and tracks in another Corps' area. On paper this arrangement seems sensible; in practice it depends on the communication of complicated and changing movement tables to large numbers of drivers and military policemen, and on sweet reasonableness of commanders at every level."[80]

The results were as unpleasant as they were predictable. "In an area of not more than twenty-five square miles," noted Canadian historian George Stevens, "four infantry and three armoured divisions were operating. That meant that more than 20,000 vehicles were moving about in this restricted space. They crossed and recrossed the battlefield in every direction; they tangled in hour-long traffic jams at bottlenecks; they created a maze of misleading tracks; they often coagulated in such great clots as to hinder the movement of troops on foot."[81]

In these circumstances, there were few opportunities for spectacular armoured thrusts. One was made in an unexpected quarter by the Fifth Canadian Armoured Division's reconnaissance regiment. With the British XIII Corps getting off to a slow start because of a bottleneck at Aquino, where stubborn German paratroopers held out long after the Hitler Line had been smashed, the Canadian division's flank was wide open for the first couple of days of the pursuit. The job of guarding it went to the Governor-General's Horse Guards, who had been so excited about seeing action for the first time in the war.

The GeeGees did their job better than anyone had a right to expect. "Our last intelligence before crossing the start line," writes Major Allan Burton of Toronto, who led a squadron of GeeGees into battle, "was that there were 48 heavy German tanks facing my twelve Shermans and light recce vehicles, so we weren't at all concerned about Rome or the Pope!" Luckily, he says, the enemy armour "retreated steadily in front of our small group without firing a shot. They thought we were part of a much larger group and didn't realize that we were alone out in left field!" During 24 and 25 May, Burton's squadron captured a hundred prisoners, including an officer who was carrying enemy codes. This performance brought Burton the Distinguished Service Order.[82]

Unfortunately, successes like this were few and far between for most of the Canadian units plodding along the valley.

On Friday, 26 May, "a hot, dusty day,"[83] the Eleventh Infantry Brigade took over the lead of the Fifth Division's advance. By nightfall, the Cape Breton Highlanders and Perths, supported by tanks of the 8th Hussars, had come to within a mile of Ceprano, on the River Liri.

But they had a terrible time getting there. At one point, patrols of the two infantry units clashed; the mistake was realized, according to Perth padre Crawford Smith, "before they took each other apart."[84] Working their way along rough and narrow tracks, blinded by thick brush, tormented by mines and booby traps, by snipers, and by long-range artillery and mortar fire, they made slow progress. While there was no organized resistance, there was plenty of isolated opposition. A sniper high in a tree calmly picked off six Boys from the Bay, whose comrades pinpointed their antagonist for a Sherman. The tank fired a round into the top of the evergreen, then raked it with machine-gun fire. There was no more sniper fire. "When we got up to him," one Canadian recalled, "he was sitting against a tree with a cigarette going. He had one leg off and he'd taken off his belt and made a tourniquet. His sniper's rifle had six notches in it."[85]

It did not help when the tanks ran out of gasoline. Thanks to the traffic tie-ups to the rear, petrol supplies had failed to arrive during the night. Running low on fuel, the 8th Hussars had no choice but to pull over and wait for gas to be brought up. The infantry went on without the tanks, which were finally refuelled in the late afternoon. But the Hussars could testify to the presence of enemy soldiers all round them. While they were waiting, Lieutenant Sted Henderson opened the hatch to let in some fresh air; what he got was a German stick grenade which clattered on the floor. Henderson's driver picked up the grenade and handed it to him, and the lieutenant lobbed it out, where it exploded harmlessly.[86]

That night, the Irish Regiment from Toronto came up and patrolled to the Liri. All bridges had been destroyed, but parties of the Irish swam the river to find Ceprano had been abandoned.

The Liri was crossed in force on Saturday, 27 May. Although Ceprano was unoccupied, enemy artillery on the high ground beyond dominated most of the crossing sites. It appeared that the Canadians would have to undertake that most difficult of military operations, an opposed river crossing, until a Perth patrol discovered a blind spot in a sharp bend in the river, a thousand yards below the town. There was a break in the steep banks, screened by trees, and the Perths brought up an assault boat and crossed the Liri. Only one boat could be used because of the limited cover, and it took all morning to get the whole battalion over the Liri and into Ceprano. The Cape Breton Highlanders followed, and by dark they had established a firm bridgehead, enabling the engineers to go to work on a bridge.

Canadian engineers worked all night to construct the 120-foot Bailey, but "efficiency was apparently sacrificed to speed." At 0730 on 28 May, just as the bridge was being pushed to the far bank, it broke apart and the whole span collapsed into the river. Another bridge was built during the day, under the personal supervision of the division's chief engineer, Lieutenant-Colonel Jack Christian. This Bailey was ready for traffic by 1730 hours, but Christian had to admit that the episode "has given us a bit of a black eye."[87]

Canadians built the bridge, but the British were the first to use it. The Eighth Army continued to insist that I Canadian Corps stay to the left of Route 6, which jogged from Arce to Ceprano. To allow XIII Corps to continue its pursuit along the highway, General Leese's staff ordered the Fifth Canadian Armoured Division to give priority of passage to the 78th Division.

This decision not only severely restricted the frontage allotted to the Canadians, it threatened to hamstring the Fifth Division's advance. Until receipt of the army's orders, Desmond Smith's Fifth Armoured Brigade had been poised to cross at Ceprano. A day had already been lost because of the collapsed bridge, and Smith had to find some way of getting over the Liri. He found it, in the First Division's sector, where Baileys were already in use; a long detour was clearly preferable to a long wait, and Smith's tanks rumbled through the night. By dawn on Monday, 29 May, his brigade was ready to resume the advance towards Frosinone, further along Route 6.

The previous day, the three battalions of Eric Snow's Eleventh Brigade had cautiously expanded their bridgehead on the Liri. The brigade pushed forward with the Cape Breton Highlanders on the left, the Perth Regiment on the right, and the Irish Regiment in the centre. It was during this move that John Lovelace of the Irish was severely wounded. The twenty-two-year-old Bren gunner was in an olive grove that came under enemy shell fire, and Lovelace was among three men hit by a blast of high explosive. The world went black for the young private, and forty-four years elapsed before he found out exactly what happened to him.

A stretcher-bearer named Nelson Maddeau was the first to reach the scene. "Although German shells were still falling, I could only think to get to the men." Finding the others dead, he turned his attention to Lovelace. "I did not even know if John was alive," Maddeau writes, "until he moved. I cleared his nostrils and mouth so he could breathe. How he had survived, I don't know. He had been blown about ten feet from his gun." Maddeau and his driver loaded the wounded man onto a stretcher, then carried him to an ambulance. They parted ways at the hospital.[88]

Lovelace, unconscious for weeks, spent the best part of three months in hospital, in Caserta and Avellino. He eventually recovered, although he was not allowed to return to his unit. That was almost as much a blow to him as his battle wounds, for he "felt that I had failed" the Irish in their hour of need. Long-term psychiatric treatment followed, as Lovelace grappled with that blank spot in his memory in the summer of 1944.[89] The veil was finally lifted in the spring of 1988, when he attended a veterans' reunion in Orillia, Ontario. Also present was Nelson Maddeau, who had driven up from his home in Scarborough. The former stretcher-bearer describes his meeting with the man whose life he saved on that faraway battlefield:

> I was sitting in a chair at the far end of the hall. I noticed a small chap with an Irish cap come in. . . . he started to go around to tables and I got a good look at him. Even though older, I still remembered the face. Names elude me but faces – never. When he came to my table, I told him I knew him from Italy and told him what had happened to him. He put his arm around me and I could see the tears in his eyes. For he had finally found the person who could fill in part of his life.[90]

While battered, bleeding John Lovelace was on his way to hospital, Canadian armour plunged into the wild terrain leading to Pofi, on the way to Frosinone. The ground was worse than anyone could have imagined, and limited the forces Brigadier Desmond Smith could commit to action. On the morning of 29 May, the British Columbia Dragoons led the push, supported by the motorized Westminster Regiment. They occupied Pofi that night, after a day no veteran could ever forget.

They had had to negotiate steep, thickly wooded ridges separated by gullies and "troublesome streams with their bridges blown." Only two narrow, twisting trails were available to the Canadians, and these had been heavily mined by the retreating Germans. The Dragoons reached Pofi with only nine tanks. "Of the remainder," the regiment reported, "five had been destroyed by enemy action and the rest were bogged down, stuck on banks, rocks, tree stumps." The Westies' cumbersome White scout cars fared no better. By dusk, the unit diarist recorded, "bits and pieces of the Regiment were all over the countryside, numerous vehicles being suspended over cliffs or jammed in sunken roads."[91]

The next morning, the Perths entered undefended Arnara, two miles northwest of Pofi. "It was a bloodless victory," Perth veteran Stan Scislowski later observed, "but no one was heard to complain. We were getting to appreciate such unstirring victories."[92] Beyond lay three hills, code-named "Tom," "Dick," and "Harry." The first two were taken with little difficulty by the Cape Breton Highlanders and Irish Regiment, respectively, and the 8th New Brunswick Hussars reached Ceccano. But Lord Strathcona's Horse fought a major battle on this "glorious summer day."

German forces were reportedly retreating along Route 6, and the Strathconas were ordered to cut them off. They were greeted at the crossroads near the village of Torrice by tanks and self-propelled guns of the 26th Panzer Division, desperately trying to keep open this vital link. The enemy got the upper hand early, swiftly knocking out three Shermans. But the Strathconas more than made up for the early setback. In one remarkable piece of shooting, a Sherman knocked out a Panther with a single round at eighteen hundred yards – a full mile. Another Sherman, commanded by Corporal J. B. Matthews, accounted for a Panther, a Mark IV, and a self-propelled 75, for which Matthews won the Distinguished Conduct Medal. Darkness brought the fighting to an end, with the Canadians in control of the crossroads. It had been won at the cost of five Shermans; four German tanks were destroyed. The Strathconas also captured an undamaged Panther, its lights on and its wireless tuned to the Canadian frequency.[93]

Tuesday, 30 May, marked the end of the line for the Fifth Armoured Division in the Liri valley. Two days earlier, General Burns decided that the terrain was simply unsuitable for armour, that infantry could move just as quickly as tanks, and he ordered Chris Vokes's First Division to pass through Hoffmeister's formation.

The Canadians captured Frosinone on the last day in May. At dawn all three battalions of the Second Brigade closed in on the provincial capital, perched on a rocky hill three hundred feet above Route 6. Just before daylight, the Loyal Edmonton Regiment had slipped a four-man patrol into the town to determine whether the place was being held in force. It was, and they were quickly taken prisoner. They attempted to bluff the Germans into surrendering, but the enemy fled instead, taking the four captive Eddies with them. The journey ended in Tivoli, east of Rome, where they had a memorable meeting with a German intelligence officer. "He was very interested in the Loyal Edmonton Regiment, and amazingly enough, told us practically the whole history of our Regiment. About the only thing he didn't know was the meaning of our colors, and, of course, we didn't tell him, because we didn't know either." The prisoners were treated well enough (except for an alarming outburst from an excited major who raged at their guard, "Didn't you have orders that all prisoners were to be shot?"), although there was little food to be had. Twice they were given champagne because the Germans had no water. All four later escaped.[94]

The captured scouts were not missed. Frosinone fell after a brief skirmish with the rearguard, which retreated after losing a number of men, including five taken prisoner. "One of the prisoners taken volunteered his services to direct artillery fire on his own positions," the Edmonton war diary noted. "It proved to be effective but nothing but the utmost contempt could be felt for such a traitor."[95]

Frosinone's fall left the Canadians with a clear and tantalizing view of "the rolling plain that stretched towards Rome."[96] Also clearly seen from Frosinone was the next Canadian objective, Ferentino, a hilltop town seven miles to the northwest. The task of taking it was given to The Royal Canadian Regiment, under its new commanding officer, Lieutenant-Colonel Jim Ritchie. The RCR, following a screen provided by the Princess Louise Dragoon Guards, reached Ferentino on the evening of 1 June. Entering the virtually undefended town shortly after midnight, they received "a terrific welcome from the inhabitants."[97]

However, there was no time to enjoy the party. The Royal Canadians immediately set out for Anagni, ten miles down the road, which they entered early on Saturday, 3 June, without losing a man. The Canadians were treated as liberators, as the second-in-commmand, Major Strome Galloway, noted: "The town is *en fête*. Last night the populace laid on a big celebration, handing out food and kisses, with everyone in a carnival mood."[98]

Before the third of June was very old, there were signs that the Canadians were not going to be on the road very much longer. An American technical sergeant took a wrong turn and drove his Jeep from Valmontone down Route 6 into the Canadian lines. The First Brigade's commander, Dan Spry, invited him to lunch, to commemorate the first contact between the Fifth and Eighth armies in the Sacco valley. During the afternoon, the Princess Louise Dragoon Guards sent a patrol to Colleferro, ten miles up the road from Anagni, where French troops were met.[99]

Rome was ever so close, but I Canadian Corps and the rest of the Eighth Army would have no part in its capture. Two days earlier, General Leese had notified Tommy Burns that Anagni would mark the end of the Canadian advance. The Canadians were to halt here, so that the Corps Expéditionnaire Français could move onto the highway and cover the Fifth Army's right flank.

There were mixed feelings about being pulled off the road so close to the Italian capital. Some, like Sergeant Bill Ross of the Loyal Eddies, were irate. "We didn't think very much of it," he says of the order to halt, "because we could've been in Rome in two days if they'd have left us alone."[100] On the other hand, Private Victor Hall of the West Novas shrugs when asked if he was disappointed. "I don't know if anybody was. I couldn't say if they even gave it much thought."[101]

Rome fell the next day, 4 June. "We are all a little bit disappointed and envious of the Americans," notes the First Division's war diary. "Surely Rome depended on Pontecorvo. Or are we the only soldiers to think so?"[102] The same day, the Canadian corps headquarters passed into reserve. The Liri valley campaign was over.

CHAPTER THIRTEEN

"Distinctly Troublesome"

1

The eyes of the world watched as the Allies entered Rome in early June 1944. For one day, world attention was focussed on Italy. For one day, the Allied armies battling in that thankless campaign basked in the limelight. President Roosevelt attempted to keep the achievement in perspective, pointing out that "it would be unwise to inflate in our minds the military importance of the capture of Rome."[1]

One day of glory. Then came a day called "D," when the eyes of the world looked elsewhere, and afterwards seldom spared a sideways glance at Italy.

"Mr. King, the invasion has started." The prime minister awakened from his slumbers as the RCMP officer knocked at his bedroom door. "Mr. King, the invasion has started." King switched on the light and looked at his bedside clock. It was 4:30 A.M. on Tuesday, 6 June 1944.[2]

The Mountie was referring to Overlord, which had begun a few hours earlier. In Normandy, on the coast of France, the Allies had stormed ashore in the greatest amphibious operation in history. There were 5,000 vessels in the invasion fleet, with thousands of aircraft in the sky. Some protected the fleet, others attacked enemy troops and installations, and still others dropped the first invaders – 23,400 American, British, and Canadian paratroopers – shortly after midnight. At 0630, American troops hit their beaches (code-named "Omaha" and "Utah"), followed an hour or so later by the British (at "Gold" and "Sword" beaches) and the Canadians ("Juno"). Its ranks leavened by veterans from the Spaghetti League, units of the Third Canadian Infantry Division (headquartered aboard an old friend from Sicily, HMS *Hilary*) stormed ashore and pushed further inland than any of the D-Day invasion forces. By nightfall, the Allies had 130,000 men, 6,000 vehicles, and 600 guns ashore. They were there to stay.

Mackenzie King had returned from Britain just two weeks earlier. During his second wartime visit to Britain, King had addressed both houses of the British Parliament and met with fellow Commonwealth prime ministers, discussing the progress of the war, the prospects for peace, and foreign policy. He had dined with the Royal Family and with Overlord's commander, General Eisenhower, who, recalling the hassle over acknowledgement of Canadian forces in the invasion of Sicily, sought the prime minister's cooperation to ensure that there would be no premature publicity of their presence in Normandy.

King returned to Canada in triumph. The nation was filled with optimism and expectation about the impending invasion, for everyone knew that it was coming soon, if not the exact date. On 22 May, the day after his return, the prime minister stood in the House of Commons and told MPs that he was "never more proud to be a Canadian than I am at this hour and I was never more proud to be a citizen of the British Empire." During his three-week stay in Britain, King claimed, he had been able to "gain exceptional information from the inside" about the Allied preparations for the forthcoming invasion of northwestern Europe. Naturally, he said, for the sake of security he could divulge nothing.[3]

The Opposition cheered his words, and King revelled in the attention. Before his British junket, he had unveiled plans to introduce legislation for a modest family allowance, the so-called "baby bonus," which had been greeted by considerable opposition not only from his political opponents but from within his own Liberal party as well. Having had his fill of criticism, King could see no reason to spoil the mood of the moment by admitting that he knew no more about Overlord than anyone else in that hallowed hall.

Italy had not yet been altogether forgotten. Regardless of the distractions posed by domestic affairs and the coming invasion of Europe, CBC correspondents covering the Italian campaign continued to provide Canadians with their most up-to-date, colourful, and dramatic war news. Even Mackenzie King's morale was boosted by recent events. On 23 May, when the Canadians attacked the Hitler Line, King stayed in bed late, reading newspapers and listening to radio news reports. "I felt most what our army is now accomplishing in Italy," he confided in his diary, "and of the tremendous crushing blows that are being brought against the Germans. They will be literally crushed. I cannot see how they can hope to hold out beyond this year."[4] He had been so moved by word of the Hitler Line breakthrough that he sent a cable to the corps commander, General Burns. The battle, King said, was "another memorable chapter of the military record of our country. . . . Our pride in your accomplishments is beyond all words."[5]

Rome had special meaning for King. In 1900, as a twenty-five-year-old, he had toured European capitals on a travelling scholarship from Harvard University, from which he had received a doctorate in economics. It was in

Rome that he received a cable offering him the civil service appointment (deputy minister of labour) that launched his long Ottawa career. Yet, for all the personal significance which Rome held for him and the importance he attached to the fighting in Italy, where he had sent nearly half of Canada's overseas army, King never did visit the Italian battlefields. It was a puzzling oversight by this man of unusual complexity.

2

While the Canadian army was denied the opportunity of liberating Rome, there was a definite Canadian presence in the Eternal City. Canadian soldiers were among the first to enter Rome, and other Canadians were already there, living a life of subterfuge and danger.

The Black Devils of the First Special Service Force were the first liberators to enter the city.

When it came out of the line at Anzio, the Force had spent nearly a hundred days in continuous action. Now, it was given a twelve-day respite, to rest, reorganize, and plan for the breakout battle. Reinforcements strengthened the Force to "the highest point in its history."[6] They included, for the first time, Canadian reinforcements (15 officers and 240 other ranks); hitherto, it had been the Canadian government's policy not to reinforce the 1st Canadian Special Service Battalion.[7] Sergeant Ken Cashman was sent to oversee the Canadian reinforcements assembled at Avellino. "Some of them had been in combat before with various Canadian units. They came to us, in most cases, as trained people familiar with combat. Some of them who had come out as reinforcements and never got to their units, came to us. They were well trained, but they took a conversion period of about ten days, and we converted them to American equipment, to our American table of organization."[8]

This inadvertently resulted in one of the most embarrassing moments in the Force's history. Among the Canadian newcomers were four blacks, and their arrival caused shock waves. The American army at that time was not racially integrated; blacks served in separate units, usually under white officers. According to one of the Force's Canadian majors, Stan Waters, "the senior Canadian, Jack Akehurst, had to sit these guys down and say, 'I'm sorry, but you can't stay with us.' I remember him talking about it afterwards; it was one of the hardest things he had to do. That was very embarrassing to everyone. Shows you how little our own people understood about what was going on."[9]

The embarrassment was quickly forgotten in the midst of the breakout from the Anzio beachhead, on 23 May, four months and a day after the original landing. At 0630, half an hour after the start of the Canadian assault on the Hitler Line, the U.S. VI Corps burst out of its trap and launched a drive towards Valmontone. That morning, the Force, with its right flank resting on the Canale Mussolini, punched towards Route 7 (the fabled Via Appia, or Appian Way), one of the two highways to Rome from the south. The Force reached the road, but a counter-attack by a dozen tanks checked any further advance that day. The tanks included a new and unbelievable monstrosity, the Tiger. Armed with the superb 88, the fifty-six-ton Tiger was so heavily armoured that it was virtually impervious to a frontal shot, and the Force found out that a bazooka made little impression on the cumbersome tank. One patrol scored a direct hit at point-blank range on a Tiger, but the rocket merely "burned a patch of paint off the hull; nothing else."[10] The Black Devils had the dubious distinction of being the first Allied troops in Italy to tangle with Tigers.

The breakout at Anzio was one of the toughest battles the Force faced. And it was costly, too. By the time the Black Devils secured Rome, Canadian casualties alone totalled 185, or about one-third of the Force's Canadian contingent.[11] But this élite unit was able to absorb heavy losses with minimal effect on performance or morale.

Once the breakout was well under way, the Force found itself in the mountainous terrain in which it was so formidable. Monte Arrestino fell on 25 May, commanding the entrance to the valley leading northwards to Valmontone. After the bitter initial battle, the breakout quickly turned into a pursuit, and the Force seized Artena, near Valmontone, on the twenty-seventh. But the Germans were not to be taken lightly; they launched unsuccessful armoured counter-attacks against the Black Devils at dusk on 28 May and early on 30 May.

On 2 June, Jack Akehurst's 2nd Regiment took Colleferro, together with four hundred prisoners, and linked up with Algerians of the Corps Expéditionnaire Français. The next day, patrols of the First Canadian Infantry Division would reach Colleferro; this would be the closest the First Special Service Force and Canadian formations ever got to each other.

The approach to the Eternal City was made on 3 June. By now, the push to Rome had become a race involving every division of the two American corps; everyone wanted to be able to say, "We were the first into Rome." It had been declared an open city by the Germans, and while there was no organized resistance, the liberators had to deal with isolated snipers, tanks, and self-propelled guns. By midnight on the third, the Force had reached Rome's suburbs. An hour later, the Force commander, Brigadier-General Robert Frederick, was ordered to seize the Tiber bridges in the capital.

The Force entered Rome at 0620 hours on Sunday, 4 June. "We knew we were the first ones into Rome," says Calgary's Jack Parfett, a twenty-three-year-old sergeant.[12] But there was no time to dwell on it. Fanning out across the capital, the Force seized key locations in the heart of Rome, including eight bridges. By 2300 hours, the city had been secured. But, contrary to popular belief, there was fighting in Rome, and men died before the Germans finally pulled out. Among the Force's casualties was one of the American regimental commanders.

The reaction of Romans was cautious at first. Lieutenant-Colonel Tom Gilday remembers driving into the city before dawn on 5 June, in search of his battalion.

> I had never been in Rome before, and much to my amazement, there was the Colosseum on my left, and I continued on and somehow or other I found myself at the top of the Spanish Steps, so went bump, bump, bump down the steps. Eventually, I found the Victor Emmanuel Monument, and went bump, bump, bump up the steps and around the pillars at the top and I found my boys there.
>
> Absolutely nothing was happening. The city was dead. Nobody dared stick their noses out. They didn't know if the Germans had gone. They didn't know which flag to put out or whether to cheer or cry.

After daylight, a man stopped Gilday and asked who he was. Using sign language and pidgin Italian, Gilday tried to explain that he was a Canadian officer. "Then I somehow or other conveyed to him that the Germans had gone. He threw up his hands in the air and let out a yell, and within two minutes the streets were full and everybody was out celebrating."[13]

The Force literally disappeared at this point. However, Colonel Gilday says this is understandable. "They had been sitting in Anzio. They hadn't seen a girl or a nightclub or any other place worth while in over a hundred days and nights. And they were pretty well scattered around the city for maybe three days, four days, maybe five days, some of them. But eventually they came crawling back into camp like old hound dogs that had been out looking for a bitch, with their tails hanging down. And things eventually got back to normal."[14]

Although Rome was full of Canadians, the city was, for the time being, off-limits to Canadian servicemen. This was nothing new to most members of I Canadian Corps, who had been pulled off the road south of the city. Most Canadians shrugged it off, since it seemed as if practically every town and village in Italy had been posted with an OUT OF BOUNDS sign.

But Rupe Leblond took it personally. When the fun-loving captain in the Saskatoon Light Infantry heard over his radio that the Americans had entered Rome, and that the city was out of bounds to everyone else, it was like waving a red flag at a bull. Leblond strolled over and spoke to a fellow captain, Les Clough, a plump, red-haired, six-footer from Moose Jaw. Leblond went right to the point: "Why don't we go into Rome?"

"How the hell are you going to get in?" asked an incredulous Clough. "They're going to have guards posted all the way into Rome."

The irrepressible Leblond waved off Clough's arguments and the two captains hopped into a Jeep and hit the road. They had travelled but a short distance when they fell in behind a convoy of Jeeps. The convoy was American, and the lead Jeep was flying a flag, probably that of a general. As Clough predicted, there were guardhouses along the way, but the guards were slow to notice the different uniforms of the men in the last Jeep. Each time the guards attempted to flag down the Canadians, Leblond would just wave to them, as if to say, "We're with those guys!"

A huge party was under way by the time they got into Rome. The streets were jammed with people, singing, dancing, drinking, kissing. "I couldn't see where to drive my Jeep, for people hanging over it and trying to pour booze into it."

Leblond eventually made his way to the Excelsior Hotel, in the centre of Rome, where he had been told to expect a superb party. The merry-making lived up to expectations, fuelled by extraordinary quantities of alcohol and food, but the SLI captain was surprised to meet other Canadians. Dressed in rags, they were escaped prisoners of war, and their presence was due to a remarkable organization.[15]

It was a hot, sunny Saturday in Sicily when Henry Byrnes had been captured by the Germans. A captain in the Royal Canadian Army Service Corps, "Barney" (as he was known to his friends) Byrnes had been sent out to establish an ammunition supply point for the advancing First Canadian Division. Whether he took a wrong turn or was given incorrect map references, he never knew. Whatever the reason, he was ambushed by German soldiers; his driver was killed and he was captured. The date was 24 July 1943.

Byrnes was treated quite well. With other prisoners, including a group of Hasty Ps, he was ferried across the Strait of Messina and put on a train for CCPG 66 at Capua, just north of Naples. After the Allied invasion of mainland Italy, the Capua camp was evacuated, and Byrnes ended up at CCPG 122, on the northern outskirts of Rome. Again, most of the prisoners were removed from here and shipped to Germany, but Byrnes was left behind, with a pair of British officers. On 24 September, they were marched by disinterested Italian guards to a nearby railway station to begin their journey to Germany. The trio had little difficulty ditching the guards and hitch-hiking to the Vatican.

They pulled up to the Santa Maria Gate, and when the ceremonial

Swiss Guards were looking the other way, the three escapers hurried into the Vatican's neutral territory. Their luck held; when guards attempted to throw them out, two men from the British embassy intervened on their behalf. Allowed to remain in the Vatican, the Canadian captain and his British companions were free in the very loosest sense of the word. "They locked us up for about a month in the [Papal] Gendarmerie barracks," Byrnes recalls. "We had good food, wine, and the British embassy sent us down reading material, so it wasn't such a bad set-up at all."

As time passed, they were gradually given more freedom. First, there were escorted trips to the British embassy for occasional meals, "and they finally gave us the run of the whole Vatican area. Except for the afternoons, when we had to clear the garden because His Holiness was out meditating and he wasn't supposed to see any of us rough characters."

Byrnes was soon involved with the Rome Escape Line. In the wake of Italy's surrender, this had been launched by Father Hugh O'Flaherty, an Irish monsignor who was deeply offended by the actions of the Germans – particularly their treatment of Roman Jews. O'Flaherty, who resided in the Collegium Teutonicum (German College), used his Irish neutrality and his clerical garb to cloak his activities, assisted by the British minister to the Holy See, Sir D'Arcy Osborne, and "his most amazing butler," John May, along with a British artillery officer, Sam Derry. These hard-working men provided support and assistance for the many hundreds of escaped prisoners who had flooded the countryside in the wake of the Italian surrender. Byrnes's typing ability was put to use when the Rome Escape Line started compiling lists of escapees in and around Rome. "The thing gradually grew and grew," says Byrnes, who estimates that the organization eventually supported three hundred prisoners in Rome, and another three thousand in the immediate vicinity. As the numbers grew, so did the tasks involved:

> First of all, we had contact with the Swiss who were running the Red Cross. We made arrangements for the Red Cross parcels to be broken apart, the labels pulled off the tin cans, so they could not be identified as Red Cross, and sent out with runners to these various people. We collected clothing and sent that out. Then we were able to raise money. Some of us wrote cheques on pieces of paper, and the Italians took them because they knew who was going to win the war, and gave us a very good rate of exchange. And we were able to raise loans from private Roman citizens, and with that, of course, could buy supplies. Once we got the thing going, we were able to get money from the British Foreign Office.

A multitude of details required attention. During the winter of 1943–44, footwear became an urgent problem; the boots of the escaped prisoners fell apart, and Byrnes says high-quality replacements were provided. "The factory that repaired German boots was very, very close to the Vatican, and we worked out a set-up whereby we would take in our old beat-up boots and trade them for brand-new Jerry ones, all done on the basis of a 'midnight requisition.'"

Health problems were handled by a medical officer and a dentist. The latter was outfitted with Italian equipment, and he could deal with virtually any dental crisis. The doctor, however, was unable to perform major surgery. Byrnes points out that other arrangements had to be made in certain emergencies: "We had one case of a ruptured appendix, out in the country, and we were able to sedate him, bring him in, deliver him to a hospital that had a sympathetic operating staff. So they operated on him, and we immediately got him out of the OR into a car, and got him under cover again."

Despite the elaborate support system, says Byrnes, the key to success was the generosity of Italian civilians. Nearly all of the escapees were billeted in private homes in and around Rome. Surprisingly, the supply of billets exceeded the demand. "You weren't anybody in Roman society," Byrnes explains, "unless you could say, 'Psst, I've got a PW living up in the attic!'" Among the Romans who hid escapees was the film star, Gina Lollobrigida.

It was a dangerous game. The Gestapo, the dreaded German secret police, were aware of the existence of the Rome Escape Line, and relentlessly pursued both the organizers and the Italians who aided them. Arrest could – and for several, did – mean imprisonment and execution.

The Allied entry into Rome was a great occasion for Barney Byrnes and his co-workers in the Rome Escape Line, and for the escaped prisoners and the Italians who had so selflessly supported them. The Anzio landing in January had raised expectations of an early liberation, but these hopes had been shattered when the invaders were bottled up in the beachhead. "Once Rome fell, strictly speaking," says Byrnes, "we should have been kept in the Vatican until the end of the war. But they just opened the gates and out we went. It's quite a sensation, sticking your foot out for the first time."

Free once more, Barney Byrnes remained in Rome. He helped to establish the Allied Screening Commission, which sought to compensate the Italians who had assisted the escaped prisoners. This "clean-up job," as Byrnes describes it, lasted eighteen months. Sam Derry was the first head of the commission, but Byrnes succeeded him; by the time its work was complete, it had investigated ninety thousand cases in which Italians had assisted Allied soldiers, sailors, and airmen.[16]

3

Rome's fall obscured the most serious split of the war between the British and Americans. The Americans, never happy about the ever-growing commitment of manpower and material resources to Italy, still viewed with suspicion British efforts to nourish a secondary theatre. The British, on the other hand, were infuriated by American reluctance to support a campaign which was, in their opinion, making a major contribution to the war effort.

The continued viability of the Italian campaign faced a new threat in early 1944. At the Quebec Conference in August 1943, the Allies had agreed to undertake an amphibious landing, code-named "Anvil," in southern France. Its timing had always been in doubt. Ideally, it would precede Overlord, the cross-Channel invasion, and so draw German forces away from the main landing sites; failing that, it would take place either coincidentally with or soon after Overlord, in order to provide the maximum benefits. Anvil was one Mediterranean operation that appealed to the Americans. Among other considerations, they liked the idea because the deep-water ports in southern France would enable them to dramatically step up the movement of reinforcements and supplies which were essential to the success of the invasion of northwestern Europe.

The problem with Anvil, so far as the British were concerned, was that the invasion forces would come from Italy. To undertake this operation, the Americans planned to pull out three of their own divisions and the four divisions of the Corps Expéditionnaire Français. The CIGS, Field-Marshal Sir Alan Brooke, fumed that his American counterpart, General George Marshall, "does not begin to understand the Italian campaign. He cannot realise that to maintain an offensive a proportion of reserve divisions is required. He considers that this reserve can be withdrawn for a new offensive in the South of France and that the momentum in Italy can still be maintained."[17]

But, for a time, it seemed that Brooke would have little to worry about. Thanks to the persistent shortage of assault shipping, most of which had been allocated to Overlord, Anvil was placed on the back burner. Anvil was apparently doomed. After prolonged discussions, the American chiefs of staff agreed to postpone Anvil until after Diadem, General Alexander's grand offensive.

Rome had fallen, but Diadem had been a hollow victory. Although the Fifth and Eighth armies captured Rome and mauled the German defenders, they had failed in their bid for a decisive victory. Statistics told a disappointing story, so far as the Allies were concerned. Alexander's great offensive had reached Rome at the cost of 43,746 casualties in the Fifth and

Eighth armies. German losses have been estimated at slightly more than 50,000, which includes 24,334 prisoners.[18] "True, the battle ended in a decisive victory for us," Alexander admitted in his memoirs, "but it was not as complete as it might have been."[19]

One reason was Mark Clark, the ambitious Fifth Army commander whose primary objective was to get into Rome ahead of the British; trapping the Germans between the Anzio breakout forces and the main armies was, to him, a secondary consideration. "The capture of Rome," he told his generals, "is the only important objective."[20] On 3 June, the Germans declared Rome an open, or undefended, city; two days later Clark entered the city in triumph, while the Germans escaped. The escape routes in the mountain passes, combined with the slow advance of the Eighth Army, made it most unlikely that the Germans could have been destroyed – but Clark's failure even to attempt to destroy them left him open to criticism.

Even as the Allies struggled to pursue the Germans north of Rome, Overlord had eclipsed the campaign in Italy. "British strategy in the Mediterranean lost all significance," commented historian A. J. P. Taylor.[21] Although this was precisely what had been planned since Casablanca, Sir William Jackson says that it must have been "galling for the men who had fought so long and so hard to find their victory overshadowed by armies which, to them, had been sitting comfortably in England while they had been struggling through muddy rivers and over brutally jagged mountains in the foul weather of the Italian winter."[22]

Alexander sensed that his theatre was in danger of being forgotten. In a situation report to Prime Minister Churchill on 30 May, even before the fall of Rome, he had voiced his private concern: "I hope our tap will not be turned off too soon . . . and prevent us from winning the full fruits of our present advantageous position." Although Diadem had been disappointing, he had no intention of relaxing his efforts.[23]

Most of the month of June was taken up in debate over the future of the Italian campaign. While the Americans pressed for an invasion of southern France, and the British argued the benefits of crushing the Germans in northern Italy, President Roosevelt intervened decisively on 28 June. In a cable to Churchill, Roosevelt declared that the British proposal to commit "practically all the Mediterranean resources to advance into Northern Italy and from there to the north-east is not acceptable to me." The important matter now was to defeat the Germans in northwestern Europe and invade Germany, he said. "I am convinced that we will have sufficient forces in Italy with 'Anvil' forces withdrawn to chase Kesselring north of Pisa-Rimini, and maintain heavy pressure against his Army at the very least to the extent necessary to contain his present force . . . history will never forgive us if we lost precious time and lives in indecision and debate."[24]

The British chiefs of staff reluctantly bowed to the Americans. In the interests of Allied solidarity, they consented to the invasion of southern France, enabling the Combined Chiefs of Staff to issue their directive on 2 July, authorizing Anvil, which was later given a new code name, "Dragoon," for security reasons. It would be mounted on the basis of a three-division landing, which would be reinforced by ten divisions, plus an airborne landing of undetermined size. The target date was 15 August.[25]

Churchill was most upset. He drew up a telegram to the president expressing his "very grave dissatisfaction" with "the way in which the control of events is now being assumed one-sidedly, by the United States Chiefs of Staff." Churchill went so far as to threaten to separate the British command from the American in the Mediterranean. Cooler heads prevailed, and the prime minister's telegram was not sent. But Churchill was still unhappy, as he notified his chiefs of staff: "Let us at least have a chance to launch a decisive strategic stroke with what is entirely British and under British Command. I am not going to give way about this for anybody. Alexander is to have his campaign."[26]

By early July, four divisions had already been withdrawn from the Fifth Army, and three more departed shortly. This reduced Mark Clark's army by 40 per cent, but the loss of the four-division French corps, the most experienced mountain troops in Italy, was a cruel blow to Allied hopes. Alexander was deeply disappointed. "Whatever value the invasion of Southern France may have had as a contribution to operations in Northwestern Europe," he later wrote, "its effect on the Italian campaign was disastrous. The Allied Armies in full pursuit of a beaten army were called off from the chase, Kesselring was given a breathing space to reorganize his scattered forces and I was left with insufficient strength to break through the barrier of the Apennines."[27]

4

Introspection and recrimination followed the Canadian campaign in the Liri valley.

The campaign had, as always, been costly. Between 15 May and 4 June, I Canadian Corps lost 789 men killed, 2,463 wounded, and 116 taken prisoner. On the other side of the ledger, the corps had captured more than 1,400 Germans and killed and wounded a great many others, while smashing one of the enemy's strongest defensive positions and advancing forty-one miles.[28]

"On the whole, I think we can be well satisfied with our performance," the corps commander, Tommy Burns, informed Harry Crerar on 7 June. "We did what was asked of us from the start, and the troops fought exceptionally well. But after the first few days, when it was a question of pursuit, really, overcoming the resistance of rearguards and obstacles, we were too slow, and several opportunities were missed."[29]

However, the Eighth Army's General Leese was entirely dissatisfied. Oblivious to his own glaring faults, he had made it clear very early in the campaign that he was unhappy with the Canadian performance, from that of Burns on down. On 26 May, Burns had learned via Leese's Canadian liaison officer (the former Hasty P, Lord Tweedsmuir) that the army commander felt that the Fifth Division's staff work "was not entirely satisfactory." Burns immediately telephoned Leese and assured him "that I thought in the main the faults were due to inexperience, and that they would be corrected with further practice and advice."[30]

Then had come the foul-up at the Liri, where the Fifth Division's Bailey bridge had collapsed. "I should have come down to see for myself how things were," Burns later admitted, "when the slowdown became apparent." Burns received a "rocket" from Leese about the delay. Still, the Canadian commander was not too worried, believing that it had more to do with Leese's hope of getting to Rome ahead of the Fifth Army than with concerns about any real Canadian shortcomings.[31]

The day after the Allies entered Rome, Burns had a private meeting with Leese, to clear the air. They discussed Burns's capabilities, openly and frankly, and the Canadian left the interview satisfied that everything had been straightened out. "My impression, perhaps naive, was that General Leese was prepared to have me carry on."[32]

He could not have been more mistaken. In fact, Leese wanted Burns's head on a platter. Seeking a change in the corps command, Sir Oliver offered to provide the "best British officer that could be made available," if no suitable Canadian could be found. Failing that, Leese and Alexander recommended "that the Corps be broken up and the divisions placed under the command of a British Corps." Alexander, in a telegram to Sir Alan Brooke, noted that the Canadian corps, with one division of infantry and one of armour, was "sadly unbalanced" and "very extravagant in overheads."[33] At the same time, Alexander informed Brooke, Leese lacked confidence in Burns and "will not place British or Indian divisions under his command. The choice is either giving the Corps tasks beyond the capability of the Corps HQ, or tasks below the fighting capacity of their troops."[34]

This caused a flap at Canadian Military Headquarters in England. Still waiting for First Canadian Army headquarters to be activated in France, General Crerar recalled British unhappiness at his own arrival in the Mediterranean in late 1943. In a long rebuttal, Crerar pointed out that this attitude was quite typical of the British. "No Canadian, or American, or other 'national' Commander, unless possessing quite phenomenal qualities is ever rated as high as an equivalent Britisher. It also means that to a British Army Commander, such as Leese, the Canadian cohesiveness created by the existence of a Canadian higher formation, such as a corps, is a distinctly troublesome factor."[35]

Of course, Crerar had a personal investment in this discussion, since he had selected Burns as his successor in command of I Canadian Corps. Nevertheless, at Crerar's insistence, Lieutenant-General Ken Stuart, the chief of staff at CMHQ, flew to Italy to investigate. Soon after arriving, Stuart interviewed the two Canadian divisional commanders, Chris Vokes and Bert Hoffmeister. Stuart ordered Vokes to frankly assess Burns's qualities as a commander, and Vokes did so.

"He hasn't got the experience and flair for command," Vokes explained. "He's dour. He is called Laughing Boy by the troops. You know how they always go the opposite way in nick-naming, or he is called Smiling Sunray, because he never smiles. He hasn't any 'presence.'. . . He is in a league of generals who are extroverts. Every British general out here is an extrovert. Burns is an introvert. He's not 'in the club.' He hasn't had any experience commanding a brigade or a division in action. He doesn't know the form."[36]

However, when Vokes pledged to loyally support his corps commander, Stuart subsequently informed Leese that he was quite satisfied with the colourless Burns, declaring his preference for "a Canadian Commander with the mental equipment to make sound decisions even though short on personality to one with plenty of personality but without the 'grey matter' to make sound decisions." Leese did not take it well. "The decision to retain Burns makes my task as Army Commander more difficult," he fumed. "It makes my Army inflexible, since at any rate I shall not be able to employ Burns on any task which I consider beyond him. There is a further serious handicap, as through my lack of faith in their Commander, I may be prevented from employing my best troops on the most critical task."[37]

Burns was far from secure, but he retained his post, for the time being – "in effect on probation," as C. P. Stacey later wrote, "a devilish situation for any commander" – but several senior Canadian officers were denied even probation. Burns was given the unhappy task of replacing a number of career officers at corps headquarters, all of whom he knew personally. The chief victims included his senior staff officer, Nick McCarter, and the corps engineer, A. B. Connelly. McCarter later confided in his colleague, historian Stacey, "that part of the trouble was that the veteran 1st Canadian Division resented being placed under a corps headquarters that had never fought. [McCarter] thought that he himself had been made a scapegoat for the Corps Commander."[38]

McCarter's replacement was the youthful Desmond Smith, whose Fifth Armoured Brigade had done well enough in the Liri valley to win the brigadier the Distinguished Service Order. Smith, who admits that he was no fan of Burns's ("certainly Fifth Armoured Division could have led the way into Rome had there been more responsible individuals at the top of Canadian Corps") and that he accepted the appointment at the request of Sir Oliver Leese, soon found himself caught in the crossfire of animosity between the corps and divisional headquarters. Until this assignment, he felt that he had been on good terms with his colleagues in the First and Fifth divisions. Now, these officers seemed to regard him as "a traitor."[39]

Divisional and brigade staffs emerged virtually unchanged. Vokes "did very well," Burns informed Crerar, "with a little direction and an occasional prod," while Hoffmeister had done "an excellent job," leading "his green division with all the drive we expected of him." But some brigadiers did not fare so well. Graeme Gibson, whose Second Brigade had been wrecked at the Hitler Line, had been "disappointing," according to Burns, who had already begun to rule him out for promotion to divisional command. Brigadier Eric Snow, whose Eleventh Brigade had encountered difficulties during the pursuit phase of operations, "did not produce the goods," said Burns, ignoring the fact that most of the difficulties were not the brigadier's fault.[40] Snow was replaced by the 48th Highlanders' Ian Johnston. That left Bert Hoffmeister with two new brigadiers, for Desmond Smith's replacement at the head of the Fifth Armoured Brigade was Ian Cumberland, whose Governor-General's Horse Guards had done such impressive work in the Liri valley.

The introverted Tommy Burns consoled himself by writing at length, analysing and assessing the just-completed campaign. Burns produced two detailed papers, one entitled, "The 'Set-Piece' Attack: Lessons from the Breakthrough of the Hitler Line," the other, "The Pursuit from the Melfa to Anagni: Lessons."

It may well be that these papers were the reason General Leese wished to get rid of him. Burns accepted full responsibility for any Canadian failings, but he also pointed out problems that were not of his making. For example, he noted two occasions in which British units passed into the Canadian operational area, and "excessive confusion developed through inability to get the change of orders and plans down to units and individual drivers and traffic control pointsmen."[41] Burns could not have endeared himself to Leese by criticizing Eighth Army headquarters.

Most of the lessons and changes are extremely technical. They range from the tactics employed by the combat arms (infantry, armour, and artillery), to improved communications, to redefined job descriptions for certain staff officers. Nevertheless, some interesting innovations resulted. One vital lesson of the Liri campaign was the need for improved traffic control. To their credit, the Canadians decided to do something about it, even though many of the problems emanated from mistakes at army head-quarters; other problems were due to the rough terrain and to the absence of real roads in the valley. Burns handed the matter to his senior adminis-trative staff officer, Brigadier J. F. Lister, who came up with a simple but effective solution. According to Burns, "it resembled the 'block' system used by railways. The forward and return routes were divided into blocks of several miles in length. At the junctions between blocks, strong traffic control posts were established, each in radio communication with the posts forward and rear and with the corps traffic control centre. At each control post there was a parking area, or 'siding,' into which convoys could be 'shunted' if the route ahead was blocked or congested, or if it was necessary to give precedence to a convoy coming up from the rear."[42]

Perhaps the most significant change involved the organization of the Fifth Division. If the Liri valley operations had proved one thing, it was that the armoured division, with one armoured and one infantry brigade, was unbalanced. To become more effective in the Italian countryside, a second infantry brigade was necessary. The Eighth Army had already recognized this shortcoming in British armoured divisions, and Leese strongly recommended that the Canadians do likewise. Burns, who was receptive to the idea, was informed by CMHQ in London that he could proceed with the alteration. The only catch was that no new formations would be made available to him; all units for the new infantry brigade would have to be found within existing Canadian resources in Italy.[43]

There were two possibilities: he could simply shuffle the Canadian brigades already in Italy, or he could create an entirely new brigade. In the first scenario, which Burns claimed that he "very strongly" favoured,[44] the First Canadian Armoured Brigade could have been integrated with the First Division, which could have transferred one of its three veteran infan-try brigades to the Fifth Division. This would have created, in effect, two very powerful, and experienced, armoured divisions.

But this obvious solution was not practicable. Not only was the First Armoured Brigade jealous of its independent status (since the beginning of the year, it had seldom served with the Canadian corps), but it was now highly valued by the British corps to which it was attached. Indeed, Burns had appealed repeatedly to have the armoured brigade returned from the British XIII Corps, but his requests had been refused, for General Leese considered it to be "the most experienced armoured brigade in Italy and therefore in great demand."[45] This was, said Burns, a "sincere tribute to the Canadian Armoured Brigade's effectiveness (though one that I failed to appreciate)."[46]

Faced with this reality, Burns opted for the other alternative, to form a new brigade. It was "a serious commitment . . . in the face of a shortage of infantry reinforcements," he admitted, but he insisted that the benefits far exceeded the risks. By adding a second brigade of infantry, he estimated that the Fifth Division's "fighting value . . . was increased by a third. . . . The establishment of an armoured division was 750 officers and 14,219 other ranks; so by adding the [new brigade's] 79 officers and 1,269 other ranks, or less than a tenth, we got a third increase in fighting value."[47]

This formation was created on 13 July. The Twelfth Infantry Brigade was commanded by highly regarded Brigadier Dan Spry, transferred from the First Brigade (his place was taken by the Saskatoon Light Infantry's Allan Calder). Spry's new command consisted of the Westminster Regiment, the Princess Louise Dragoon Guards, and a battalion eventually known as the Lanark and Renfrew Scottish Regiment. Of the three, the Westies were affected the least; a motorized battalion, they had had much experience in infantry tactics and training.

On the other hand, the Plugs were enraged. Rightly proud of the reputation they had achieved as the First Division's reconnaissance regiment – Leese had called it "the best reconnaissance unit in the Eighth Army"[48] – they did not want to lose their armoured cars. The Plugs dubbed 13 July "Black Thursday." That night, the officers held a wake, while the other ranks fired flares and smoke bombs to express their unhappiness. The next day, the divisional commander, General Vokes, dropped by to say farewell, but the bitterness remained. In front of the mess, a grave was dug and a cross erected, bearing the words: "R.I.P., 4 Cdn Recce Regt. (4 P.L.D.G.) 13 Jul 44 – STABBED IN THE BACK."[49]

The other battalion was created from scratch. The majority of the men came from two light anti-aircraft batteries, the 89th and 109th, which had been rendered unnecessary because of the absence of enemy aircraft at which to shoot. Just finding a name for this unit became a major undertaking. It was temporarily dubbed the 89th/109th Battalion, then redesignated (at the suggestion of Tommy Burns) the 1st Canadian Light Anti-Aircraft Battalion. When this was judged unsatisfactory, in view of the "majority wish among officers and ORs to make this a Highland Regiment," there was a proposal to rename it the 2nd Battalion, 48th Highlanders of Canada.[50] Other possibilities included the Gordon Highlanders of Canada and the Royal Scots of Canada; the minister of defence, Layton Ralston, suggested Laircroft Scots of Canada.[51]

The battalion commander, an experienced infantryman named

Lieutenant-Colonel W. Clement Dick, had a better idea. Aware that Ontario's Lanark and Renfrew Scottish had not been mobilized, Dick suggested seeking the militia unit's approval and support. "Within weeks," he recalls, "we had balmorals, shoulder patches, etc., and [had been] renamed Lanark and Renfrew Scottish."[52]

Although Dick was able to procure a large number of experienced junior officers and NCOs, some veterans were not optimistic about this unit's chances in battle. The Lanarks were nicknamed the "Slaughterhouse Battalion," because their first time in action was sure "to be a slaughter," said one veteran. "Four years on the guns and now they're infantry."[53]

5

Following the loss of Rome, the German objective in Italy was greatly simplified: to buy time for a stand further north.

The withdrawal of enemy forces was notable in two respects. First, it was successful. The German commander-in-chief, Albert Kesselring, managed to extricate his two battered armies and retreat more than a hundred miles northwards, virtually unhindered. The field-marshal later credited this to "the remarkable slowness of the enemy's advance. . . . The Allies utterly failed to seize their chances."[54] But the retreat was even more noteworthy because it had been permitted by Adolf Hitler. This was a startling departure for the Führer, who normally insisted on fighting to the last man and for every square inch of territory. However, Hitler quickly made it clear to Kesselring that further retreats would be unacceptable. He pointed to a line drawn across the map of northern Italy, from Pisa to Rimini, and insisted that this would be "the final blocking line, since the enemy's entry into the Po plain would have incalculable military and political consequences."[55]

But the situation in Italy was far from promising for the Germans in the summer of 1944. Construction of the new defensive line on which Hitler was pinning his hopes had begun in the fall of 1943, but had been interrupted in favour of work elsewhere, when the nature of the campaign changed. Originally known as the "Apennine position," it had been given a more sinister name in April 1944, when it was designated the "Gothic Line." While the Germans renamed it the "Green Line" in June, the Allies continued to refer to it as the Gothic Line.[56]

Aside from a brief outburst of activity in the wake of Anzio, work on the Gothic Line defences proceeded in a "fairly leisurely fashion" until the beginning of June. With Rome's fall imminent, the Germans drew up elaborate plans for the Gothic Line. Areas considered vulnerable to tank attacks were to be protected by *Panzerturm*, the concrete-emplaced tank turrets that had proven so effective at the Hitler Line; fortifications were to be built at all key points, "even on those mountain fronts which are considered almost inaccessible." Extensive minefields would shield the entire line, along with a four-mile-wide dead zone, or *Vorfeld*, created "by lasting demolition of all traffic routes, installations and shelters." Civilians living in the area were to be evicted from their homes, and Italian males were to be conscripted to provide much of the labour force, under the supervision of engineering experts from the paramilitary construction agency, Organization Todt.[57]

However, the Germans needed time to complete the construction of the Gothic Line, and they hoped to buy that time by manning a series of incomplete defensive positions. Furthest south was the Albert–Frieda Line, which centred on Trasimeno, a large lake about midway between Rome and Florence, where the legendary Carthaginian general, Hannibal, had won a great victory over the Romans in 217 B.C. Kesselring was not very happy about having to defend partial defences such as these, but he obeyed Hitler's orders. The commander-in-chief issued instructions that Army Group C would "stand and defend the Albert–Frieda Line. . . . Every officer and man must know that upon reaching this line the delaying tactics will come to an end and the enemy advance and break-through must be stopped."[58]

Canadian tanks helped to upset German hopes and plans.

Slowed by extensive demolitions and bad weather, the Eighth Army did not reach the Albert–Frieda Line until the end of the third week in June. The First Canadian Armoured Brigade had been held in reserve north of Rome until 18 June, when it underwent training with the British 4th Division. After XIII Corps encountered the enemy defences about Lago Trasimeno, the 4th Division was moved up to support the assault, with the 78th and 6th South African Armoured divisions. Shermans of the Ontario Regiment went into action on 21 June with the 78th in sight of the lake, "a beautiful body of water set like a gem in the heart of the highlands."[59] In four days of fighting, the Ontarios destroyed a total of five German tanks, a sufficiently impressive total to warrant a message of congratulations from the army commander, Sir Oliver Leese, to Lieutenant-Colonel Bob Purves.[60]

The Three Rivers Regiment, in action nearby, encountered problems. They went into battle with the 4th Division's 28th Brigade, a formation whose training and experience with tanks left much to be desired. They also ran into an old foe, the remnants of the 1st Parachute Division, who fought with customary ferocity despite their depleted numbers. Attack and counter-attack raged back and forth among the steep, terraced hillsides and lush orchards and vineyards. It was poor tank country, and the Three

Rivers' casualties mounted steadily. "Co-operation with the infantry," fumed an unidentified tank officer, "was conspicuous by its absence." On one occasion, the tanks arrived late for an attack; another time, the attack was postponed an hour, but the tanks were not notified.[61]

By the time the Three Rivers Regiment was pulled out of the line on 1 July, it had endured "its heaviest fighting since landing in Sicily." Its losses totalled ninety-four men and twenty-six tanks, more than it had lost during the battles in the Gustav and Hitler lines in May.[62]

The Germans were now falling back to their next improvised position, the so-called Arezzo Line, which blocked the final approach to Florence. While the Ontario and Three Rivers tanks rested, Shermans of the Calgary Regiment supported the British advance northwards. Enemy rear-guards disputed river crossings and other awkward sites, and progress was slowed by demolitions and mines along the few roads. "The weather was beautiful – glorious," recalls Sergeant Bob Sharp of the Calgaries, but the rugged hill country made for "rough going." He says that he did not really appreciate how bad it was until he returned to Italy in 1975. "It's just amazing. When you come down from Florence to Rome, looking at the mountains, it just shocked me that we tried putting tanks in there."[63]

The laboured advance abruptly halted at the Arezzo Line. On 6 and 7 July, the Calgary Tanks supported two British battalions in their assault on the olive-terraced slopes overlooking the village of San Pancrazio. But the Shermans could do little to help, and the attack failed in the face of "rocks, gorges, precipitous hills, sniping, mortaring and the exhaustion of their accompanying infantry."[64] The Calgaries' report concluded "that we were up against a stone wall. Our infantry had suffered heavily, were dead-beat and fed-up."[65]

A week-long deadlock ensued. It was finally broken by a joint attack by the 6th South African Armoured and 2nd New Zealand divisions on 15 and 16 July. Combined with a steady advance to the west by the Fifth Army, the Germans reluctantly relinquished their hold on the Arezzo Line, and slowly withdrew towards Florence.

The First Canadian Armoured Brigade soon found itself with new duties. As part of a realignment of the Fifth and Eighth armies – namely, the removal of the four divisions of the Corps Expéditionnaire Français for the invasion of southern France – the Canadian tanks were attached to the 8th Indian Division, an old acquaintance from the Adriatic and from the Liri valley. The Calgaries were the first into line, accompanying the Indians in a slow but steady advance southwest of Florence. "We were scarcely playing an inspired role," complained the Calgary war diarist. "The engineers and assault personnel were worked to the limit, while the enemy retired leisurely laying still more mines."[66]

The Three Rivers Regiment took over the escort duties on 27 July. They were in Chianti country, and were able to make good time on decent roads winding between steep hills covered with vineyards and olive groves. Halting at the Pesa, a tributary of the Arno, the river that flows through Florence, the 8th Indian Division paused to await a major attack on the enemy's last delaying position in front of Florence. The defences were not broken until 3 August, and the Indian infantry and Canadian tanks contributed by forcing their way across the Pesa two nights earlier and clearing the Germans from the south bank of the Arno. The New Zealanders and South Africans entered the southern outskirts of Florence at dawn on the fourth.

Kesselring commented in 1944 that waging war in Italy was like fighting in a museum. Virtually every city, town, and village contained treasures of historical or religious significance: "frescoes, statues, churches, medieval monasteries, Roman bridges and aqueducts, Baroque fountains and Renaissance paintings." Both sides were guilty of abusing these valuables. The Allies deliberately destroyed the centuries-old monastery atop Monte Cassino in February 1944; but inadvertent acts, such as the incendiary-bombing of the Chiesa di Santa Maria in Naples, were no less anguishing to art-lovers. The Germans indulged in some high-level looting on behalf of Adolf Hitler. His Kunstschutz, or art-protection commission, requisitioned priceless works of art in July 1944 and transported them to secluded spots in northern Italy and Austria.[67]

Yet both sides also made efforts to preserve these priceless artifacts. And classical Florence, with its magnificent museums and monuments, was one place where the antagonists were able to cooperate. The Germans provided trucks for the Italian authorities who evacuated masterpieces for safe-keeping in neighbouring castles. To protect the city, the Germans had conferred "open city" status on Florence the previous winter, but its fate became more doubtful as the battlefront inched closer and closer. Kesselring believed that the British attached "much more than average significance" to Florence, that its capture would be seen as a "prestige success," somewhat offsetting the American capture of Rome. The paratroop officer who commanded the city warned Swiss officials that the Germans rated "the beauties of Florence" well below military considerations.[68]

Before abandoning the south side of the Arno, the Germans blew up all but one of Florence's six ancient bridges. The only one to be spared was the Ponte Vecchio, built in 1345 and considered too weak and narrow to be of military value. Just in case the Allies were tempted to use it, the Germans dynamited the medieval buildings at the south end of Florence's first bridge. But the bridges were the only major victims; as the British official history points out, "it is ironical that the treasures of Florence suffered more from the floods of 1966 than from either the Germans or the Allies in 1944."[69]

The First Canadian Division arrived in Florence a few days later.

After being pulled out of the drive towards Rome in early June, I Canadian Corps had been transported to the upper Volturno valley, a barren, isolated region of central Italy, to rest, reinforce, and reorganize. On the way, they heard the news of the invasion of France, which caused a sensation. A typical reaction was that of Bert Hoskin, a major in the Westminster Regiment, who remembers saying, "It's about goddam time those lazy buggers in England got something to do!"[70]

The First Division's Chris Vokes had advised his troops to "work hard and play hard," and all ranks had taken his words to heart.[71] There was plenty of training to be done, but there was also lots of free time for visits to rest camps in Bari and Salerno. But the most popular resort of all was, predictably, Rome. Leave to the Eternal City was provided for 180 officers and 1,000 other ranks at a time. A British NCO who watched the Canadians in action marvelled at them: "They give candy to every child in sight, shove all Italian males off the pavement, and make an instant sexual advance to every woman of child-bearing age they encounter."[72]

Rome's sights were exciting and varied. Charles Comfort, seeing Rome from an artist's perspective, never forgot "the overwhelming beauty of a well-groomed city. Since I left Montreal I had not seen a modern city which had escaped being crushed and burned. . . . It was wonderful to behold."[73]

Parties were the most popular pastime. "The quantity of *vino* and other Italian mixtures consumed," the war diary of The Royal Canadian Regiment noted in the middle of July, "was a marvel of human endurance."[74] Declared one weary nursing sister: "When the Army sets out to amuse itself, it does not fool."[75]

However, right on cue had come a plethora of silly orders from corps headquarters. These rules and regulations merely served to widen the gulf "between the minority who had fought and the majority who served behind the lines," according to historian George Stevens. Under one regulation, "a maximum number of cigarettes was prescribed for every soldier even though they came as gifts. The cigarette had become the principal medium of exchange in bartering with the civilian population, and this restriction was regarded as an arbitrary interference with a soldier's perquisites." An even sillier order, "apparently aimed at restricting the consumption of local wines, warned all ranks that Italian red wine possessed the same alcoholic content as Canadian rye whiskey – an intimation which was received sardonically but enthusiastically and which accomplished exactly the reverse of its intention."[76]

One worth-while undertaking was a solution for the vexing problem of neuropsychiatric, or NP, cases. Of the 1,231 casualties incurred by the First Division's nine infantry battalions in the Liri valley, nearly one-quarter were classified as NP, a figure that Harry Crerar, comfortably ensconced in his headquarters in far-off England, considered to be unacceptably high. Although the campaign in Normandy would provide comparable statistics, the Canadian army commander believed that there was something seriously wrong in Italy, due to what he called the "reprehensible objection of a small proportion of other ranks of I Cdn Corps to risk death or serious injury for their country. . . . The 'angles' include such things as desertion, self-inflicted wounds, attempts to be diagnosed as 'exhaustion cases,' VD re-infection and so on."[77]

Fortunately, Crerar's nonsensical views were not shared by the officers who had to deal with these shattered men. Major Arthur Doyle, a psychiatrist at I Corps headquarters, assembled statistics showing that the NP problem was virtually the same as it had been during the previous winter, despite tougher disciplinary measures advocated by Crerar and other generals. Doyle's compassionate efforts resulted in the creation of special employment companies, which enabled NP cases to perform light engineering duties. As historian Bill McAndrew points out, this answer "proved to be a reasonable institutional compromise which acknowledged, however uneasily, the gulf between attitudinal preconceptions about soldierly behaviour and stark ugly reality."[78]

The end of July had brought a sure sign that the Canadian corps would soon be back in action. On the thirty-first, the Canadians were visited by King George VI, travelling incognito for security reasons as "General Collingwood." The King presented the Victoria Cross to Major Mahony of the Westminster Regiment, and inspected the Royal 22nd, of which he was the colonel-in-chief.

When the King had departed, a veil of secrecy descended across the Volturno valley. Jim McAvity, the new commanding officer of Lord Strathcona's Horse, recalls that "it was an offense to throw away a cigarette package, a chocolate bar wrapper or anything bearing the name 'Canada,' it was an offense to speak to an Italian or even allow a native to overhear a conversation; all unit and divisional patches and markings were removed from our uniforms and vehicles – nothing was left to indicate that we might be Canadians."[79] The next day, the First Division boarded trucks and disappeared from the valley, followed on successive days by the rest of the Canadian corps.

Their route took them past Rome and northwards. The First Division moved into Florence on the nights of 5 and 6 August, relieving the 2nd New Zealand and 6th South African divisions on a ten-mile front along the Arno. Accompanying the Canadians was Charles Comfort, the war artist whose anticipation at witnessing the wonders of Florence was displaced by anger and indignation over the destruction of the city's beautiful bridges. Comfort, who was soon to leave Italy, was especially saddened by the "depressing discovery" of the ruins of the Ponte Santa Trinita.[80]

Florence may have been an open city, but this did not mean the war was forgotten. While the Allied troops had been forbidden to shell the nine-tenths of Florence held by German paratroopers north of the Arno, the enemy was not so shy about using mortars and snipers against the newly arrived Canadians. In one afternoon alone, The Royal Canadian Regiment lost fourteen men wounded by mortar fire.[81] When a member of the Hastings and Prince Edward Regiment was killed by a sniper, the battalion sharpshooters went to work with a vengeance, picking off seven enemy soldiers in a single day.[82] Both sides sent fighting patrols across the river, and the Loyal Edmonton Regiment lost half a dozen men in one clash with the paratroopers; six more Eddies were lost to a mine.[83]

Still, Florence was a generally pleasant if brief interlude, particularly for the three battalions of the First Brigade that were billeted inside the city. The Royal Canadians were headquartered in a sixty-four-room mansion, and Major Strome Galloway found himself enoying unexpected luxury, with amenities that included a comfortable bedroom, a marble bathroom, a library with thousands of books (including many in English), and meals served in a splendid dining room. "We left our temporary home unviolated," Galloway says, "though God knows what happened to its contents when the next occupants arrived."[84]

The division's tour of Florence ended on 8 August. Its brief stay had served its purpose, and that evening, the Canadians slipped out of the city to rejoin I Canadian Corps in the Perugia–Foligno area, thirty miles south. Fresh commitments, including another secret move, awaited the corps.

PART THREE

Backwater

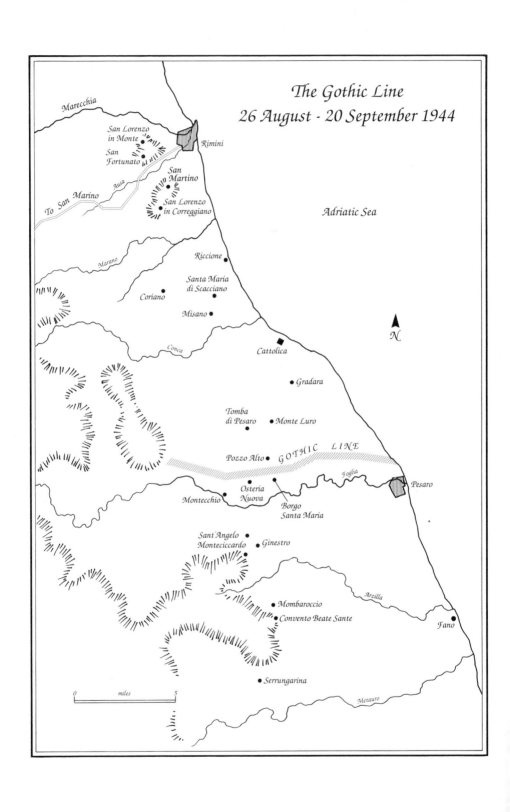

The Gothic Line
26 August - 20 September 1944

Marecchia

San Lorenzo in Monte

Rimini

San Fortunato

Ausa

San Martino

To San Marino

San Lorenzo in Correggiano

Adriatic Sea

Marano

Riccione

Santa Maria di Scacciano

Coriano

Misano

Conca

Cattolica

N

Gradara

Tomba di Pesaro

Monte Luro

Pozzo Alto

GOTHIC LINE

Foglia

Pesaro

Montecchio

Osteria Nuova

Borgo Santa Maria

Sant'Angelo Monteciccardo

Ginestro

Arzilla

Mombaroccio

Convento Beate Sante

Fano

Serrungarina

Metauro

0   miles   5

CHAPTER FOURTEEN

"It's Awful to Die"

1

The Canadians were crucial to both Allied and German plans in August 1944.

General Alexander's plan was to employ his two weakened armies in a joint blow in early August against the Gothic Line opposite Florence and drive towards Bologna. It meant punching through thirty miles of mountains, but this appeared to be the most promising location for what seemed certain to be the decisive offensive. Alexander had already set in motion the massive administrative preparations required for an operation of this size, including the concentration of the necessary forces and the stockpiling of supplies of ammunition, food, and medicine. An elaborate deception, code-named "Ottrington," was an integral feature of the August offensive. Ottrington was designed to distract the Germans from the Florence front by simulating threats in two other sectors: an amphibious landing near Genoa, in northwestern Italy, and a major attack on the Adriatic coast. The latter was aided by a vigorous offensive during July by II Polish Corps, which captured the port of Ancona.

This was the reason for the secrecy-shrouded move of the Canadian divisions from the Volturno valley in early August. However, the plan changed even before I Canadian Corps completed its northward movement. Instead of trying to keep the Canadian presence a secret, the Allies now wished to advertise their presence, and so moved the First Canadian Division into the front lines in and around Florence.

Sir Oliver Leese had changed his mind about the Eighth Army's role in Alexander's offensive plans. Leese met Alexander privately on 4 August and proposed that while Mark Clark's Fifth Army should proceed with its attack on the Florence–Bologna axis, the Eighth Army should shift its weight to the Adriatic, where its superiority of guns and armour could be more easily brought to bear. Leese's proposal directly countered his own staff's recommendations. As recently as 27 July, Eighth Army planners, asked to reassess the potential of the Adriatic front for offensive operations, concluded that such "an attack ... would be difficult to mount, would not allow us to bring the necessary concentration of forces to bear, and would not offer any good opportunities for exploitation. To get involved in a series of river crossing operations is playing into the hands of a withdrawing enemy."[1]

Leese was conscious of the risks. "We realise that it is not an easy operation," he explained in a 7 August letter to the War Office in London. "It goes against the grain of the country. ... But in order to defeat the enemy we have got to fight another big battle somewhere; and we would far sooner fight this battle in the low ground than in the mountains."[2]

Surprisingly, no one objected. Alexander felt that he had no choice but to accept Leese's proposal, and when Mark Clark agreed, Alexander's summer offensive was completely recast. The price of Clark's agreement was the British XIII Corps being sent to serve in the Fifth Army, to compensate for the forces lost to Dragoon, the invasion of southern France. Preliminary orders were issued on 6 August, just two days after Leese requested the alternative operation. The Eighth Army would shift its main forces across the mountains to the Adriatic coast and attack when Leese decided he was ready; the Fifth Army would conduct preliminary operations in mid-August and be prepared to exploit any success gained by the Eighth Army. The offensive was code-named "Olive."

It was all done hastily, at the eleventh hour. "The decision was taken without adequate staff examination of all the repercussions, or sufficient time for the senior commanders themselves to probe the consequences of such a major change in operational policy," the British official history points out. "Changing plans at so late a stage took great moral courage. Had the change led to a brilliant military coup Alexander would have been applauded for a stroke of military genius."[3] That it fell short of the intended mark was due to the bungling of the man who was most responsible for the last-minute change: Sir Oliver Leese.

Leese's detailed plans boggle the imagination. He decided to employ three corps along the Adriatic: the British V, I Canadian, and II Polish. In so doing, he left out his best and most experienced subordinate, Richard McCreery of X Corps. In contrast, V Corps had not conducted a major operation since the previous December, and its commander, Charles Keightley, had just taken over on 3 August. The untested Keightley would be commanding one armoured and five infantry divisions, "a small army," according to historian Bill McAndrew.[4] The inclusion of the Canadians was not surprising; although he had no use for Tommy Burns, Leese wanted and needed the hard-hitting Canadian divisions. The Poles were very good but, experiencing dire manpower shortages, were capable of no more than limited operations.

The army commander presided over a planning conference on 9 August. His staff had produced a memorandum, envisaging V Corps as the pursuit formation, and giving Leese two options: to employ all three corps side-by-side, with the Poles on the coast, V Corps in the centre, and the Canadians on the hilly inland flank; or to keep V Corps in reserve until the Canadians and Poles had broken the Gothic Line. Leese's preference was to use the three corps in the initial attack; as Canadian historian Brereton Greenhous observes, Leese "apparently [had not] learnt much from the congestion which had marked his attack in the LIRI Valley."[5] It was Leese's idea that the Poles would take Pesaro on the right, while the Canadian corps "was to break the Gothic Line, secure the dominating ground on the left of the sector and protect the left flank of the break-through." In the centre, the oversized V Corps, after punching through the enemy fortifications, would pour its armoured divisions through the hole and drive along the coastal highway, Route 16.[6]

Although Burns endorsed this plan, Leese threw it aside when the Polish representative pointed out, according to his experience, "that progress along the coast road axis was generally slower than inland. The Germans did extensive demolition and mining on the coast road but did not pay so much attention to the inland routes."[7] Leese casually reversed the positions, but not the roles or composition, of the British and Canadian corps. The consequences of this decision were enormous. Observes historian Bill McAndrew:

> The Canadian Corps was now placed in the sector best suited for launching the pursuit, as it directly controlled access to the coastal highway leading on past Rimini to Bologna; but Burns was not given the additional forces he would need to take advantage of his situation. V Corps, with the divisions to exploit initial success, was now to operate over ground ill-suited for vehicle movement of any kind.... One can only surmise that Leese let his optimistic enthusiasm outrun his map sense, and assumed he could break out wherever he chose.[8]

Four days later, written instructions from Eighth Army headquarters confirmed Leese's verbal orders, setting in motion the assembly of ten divisions, 1,276 tanks, and 1,122 guns on the Adriatic. These forces would deliver what Leese was certain would be a decisive blow against the enemy.

"If only I knew where the Canadians are!" exclaimed the Tenth Army's chief of staff, Generalmajor Fritz Wentzell, at the beginning of July.[9]

The Germans, knowing that the presence of the Canadians would reveal enemy intentions, were desperate to locate them. "One of these days," predicted Oberst Henning Werner Runkel, chief of staff of LXXVI

Panzer Corps, "the Canadian Corps is going to attack and then our centre will explode." The capture of the crew of a Three Rivers tank near Lago Trasimeno had led the enemy to conclude, mistakenly, that the entire Fifth Canadian Armoured Division was present. Tenth Army intelligence officers declared, "Only Canadians attack like that." Not until the end of June did they determine that only one Canadian armoured brigade was involved; the whereabouts of I Canadian Corps remained a mystery.[10]

It is little wonder that the enemy was having trouble tracking down Canadian formations, because German intelligence was abysmal. With the Allies in complete command of the sky, the Germans were deprived of aerial surveillance, but that scarcely excuses their laxity in August 1944. Amid the multitude of erroneous, nonsensical, and misleading reports, enemy commanders were unable to discern the few gems of accuracy. Among those dismissed as being unfounded was this Fourteenth Army intelligence assessment: "Unusually large supply movements are being carried out at the present time in the Adriatic sector . . . it seems that the enemy is making preparation for large-scale operations."[11]

Great things were happening everywhere in August 1944. On all fronts, the Germans were being defeated. They were reeling in the face of overwhelming and relentless attacks by the Soviets, whose summer offensive had reclaimed nearly all of the territory lost in 1941 and 1942; the end of July saw the Soviet army standing at the gates of Warsaw. In France, the American, British, and Canadian invasion forces were at last breaking out of the Normandy beachhead; Paris would be liberated before the end of the month. On 15 August, the Allies invaded southern France, the attack spearheaded by the First Special Service Force, rested and reorganized after its capture of Rome.

The Canadians in Italy were ready to do their part. Refreshed by their two months in the Volturno valley, they were honed to a peak. Infantry battalions depleted by the blood-letting at the Hitler Line had been rebuilt, each at full strength, 845 officers and other ranks. And the camaraderie of leave, partying, and training proved to be an effective combination. "It was good to see the newcomers and the oldtimers melded together," recalls Jim Stone of the Loyal Eddies.[12]

The move across the mountains was a triumph of administrative and engineering skill, for the Eighth Army as a whole and for the Canadian corps in particular. Undertaken at short notice and amid strict security, the week-long transfer to the Adriatic was nothing short of remarkable. "The Canadian Corps alone moved some 280 carriers, about 650 tanks and some 10,700 wheeled vehicles."[13] From Foligno, the Canadians moved to the vicinity of Iesi, fifteen miles from the coast. Travelling overnight, without headlights, the convoys required about eight hours to reach their destinations. The tireless Canadian engineers built a 120-mile-long route for their own and British tanks, so that they would not chew up the roads required by the infantry formations.[14]

By 20 August, the Canadians had taken up their positions, behind the Polish corps. When they went into action, I Canadian Corps would take over a four-mile front on the left of the Poles, along the River Metauro, the fabled site of Hasdrubal's defeat in 207 B.C., which sealed Hannibal's fate in Carthage's war with ancient Rome. The Metauro was a delaying position in front of the *Vorfeld*, the zone of desolation before the main Gothic Line positions, which were arrayed behind another river, the Foglia, ten miles to the northwest. On 21 August, General Burns outlined a four-phase plan for his Canadians. With the First Division leading, a bridgehead would be established across the Metauro. The second phase would involve a rapid advance past Pesaro to the Foglia. The third, the actual breaching of the Gothic Line, involved two possibilities: if the Germans were taken by surprise and seemed disorganized, the Canadians would try to "gate-crash" the defences with an immediate attack; otherwise, both divisions would mount a full-scale assault. In the final phase, they would take Rimini.

The last few days and hours before the attack were busy. Infantry commanders studied their maps, pinpointed the objectives, and explained the plans to their subordinates; gunners picked out their targets, prepared fire plans, and supervised the stockpiling of ammunition. There would be no preliminary bombardment, in the interests of secrecy, but the Desert Air Force had carried out a wide-ranging program of bombing and strafing.

Tommy Burns, characteristically, did not allow himself to be carried away by the wave of optimism which swept through the Eighth Army on the eve of Olive. "Let every one of us go into this battle with the determination to press forward until the enemy is destroyed; to strike and pursue until he can fight no longer," Burns implored his troops. "Then, and only then, shall we have won what we, as Canadians, have been fighting for – security, peace and honour for our country."[15]

2

Friday, 25 August, was hot and sunny. It was also very quiet on the Tenth Army's front; so quiet, in fact, that Generaloberst Vietinghoff was away on leave. That morning, the commander-in-chief, Generalfeldmarschall Kesselring, telephoned Vietinghoff's chief of staff, Fritz Wentzell. Wentzell, oblivious to the onslaught that would be unleashed on his army that night, assured Kesselring that all appeared to be normal. Three nights earlier, Vietinghoff had authorized a withdrawal of the weak forces defending the Metauro; they were being pulled back several miles, to another delaying position (the Red Line) behind a small stream, the Arzilla. Wentzell reported that this move was going smoothly.

"Otherwise nothing of importance?" Kesselring queried.

"Otherwise," Wentzell assured the field-marshal, "nothing."[16]

The four Canadian assault battalions crossed the Metauro during the last ninety minutes of 25 August. It was a silent attack; no shell fire was scheduled until one minute before midnight. The Metauro was a gentle stream, nowhere more than three feet deep, and the battalions had been able to select their crossing points the night before. There were no Germans on the riverbank, and the Canadian infantrymen, their waterlogged boots making obscene noises, crept through the vineyards and olive groves and fanned out along their first objective, Route 3, which ran parallel to and just beyond the Metauro.[17]

At 2359 hours, the bombardment exploded over their heads, 350 guns firing in concert. The artillery program was considerably different than that utilized at the Hitler Line. The First Division's chief gunner, Bill Ziegler, had scrapped the creeping barrage in favour of a series of concentrations on the series of ridges where the Germans were likely to have defensive positions. Moving from target to target at the rate of a hundred yards every six minutes, the gunners laid down a curtain of shell fire along the far edge of the perimeter of the bridgehead. This feature would not only protect the troops but guide them to their objectives in the darkness.[18]

The operation went like clockwork. Princess Patricia's Canadian Light Infantry, losing three men to mines, captured the village of Serrungarina, while The Royal Canadian Regiment took nearby Saltara; the 48th Highlanders of Canada and the Loyal Edmonton Regiment secured either flank. By dawn, the British 21st Tank Brigade was preparing to move across the Metauro to reinforce the three-thousand-yard-deep bridgehead. "The ease of the operation astonished everyone," noted the PPCLI historian, George Stevens.[19]

The advance resumed Saturday morning. Unlike the previous day, battalions of the First and Second brigades fought a series of spirited battles for the high ground in front of them, notably Monte della Mattera, a sixteen-hundred-foot rise flanked on the left by Monte San Giovanni and on the right by Point 393, crowned by the Convento Beate Sante.

They carried out their attacks on 26 August under the watchful eyes of a pair of distinguished visitors. Major Rusty Wilkes, the padre of The Royal Canadian Regiment, was amazed when, during the afternoon, a staff car pulled up to the farm being used as the unit's tactical headquarters

After Ortona, the Adriatic front settled into a period of static warfare. In order to keep the enemy off balance, the Canadians mounted an intensive program of patrolling, which proved costly both in terms of casualties and of morale. Above, a daring daylight patrol by the Perth Regiment, January 1944. (National Archives of Canada / PA 130601)

Sergeant Tommy Prince became Canada's most decorated Native soldier as a member of the élite Canadian–American First Special Service Force. (National Archives of Canada / PA 142287)

Lieutenant-General Harry Crerar (right), and his successor in command of I Canadian Corps, Lieutenant-General E. L. M. Burns. Neither was very imaginative, but while Crerar enjoyed considerable success, the unsmiling Burns proved to be a disappointing failure. (National Archives of Canada / PA 132784)

Tough, profane, and a much better commander than generally recognized, the First Division's Major-General Chris Vokes (left) studies a map with a close personal friend, Lieutenant-Colonel Cam Ware of Princess Patricia's Canadian Light Infantry. (National Archives of Canada / PA 162145)

A battalion commander in Sicily, a brigadier at Ortona, Major-General Bert Hoffmeister forged the Fifth Canadian Armoured Division into a potent weapon in 1944. (National Archives of Canada / PA 115880)

The peaceful Liri valley today provides a striking contrast to the heavy fighting that occurred here in May and June 1944. (Cindy Delisle)

Major John Mahoney of the Westminster Regiment won the Victoria Cross on 25 May 1944 for his part in establishing and holding a vital bridgehead on the Melfa River in the Liri valley. (National Archives of Canada / PA 167002)

Among the sinister defences in the Adolf Hitler Line was the *Panzerturm*, a tank turret emplaced in concrete, which played havoc with Canadian and British tanks on 23 May 1944. (National Archives of Canada / PA 114917)

Snipers such as this camouflaged veteran of the 48th Highlanders of Canada were able to thrive in the rough country during the approach to the River Foglia. Beyond the Foglia stood the imposing Gothic Line, which both divisions of I Canadian Corps smashed in three days of hard fighting, 30 August to 1 September 1944. (National Archives of Canada / PA 116842)

The capture of Rimini, here being entered by a Canadian patrol on 21 September 1944, was the culmination of a series of furious and costly battles that began at the Gothic Line. (National Archives of Canada / PA 136213)

Major Strome Galloway, photographed in early 1944. A company commander in Sicily, he later served as second-in-command and occasionally as acting commander of The Royal Canadian Regiment. (Strome Galloway)

Engineers played an important part in the ground war in Italy. Bulldozer drivers, who often worked under heavy fire, were known as free spirits, as indicated by this top-hatted fellow working near Rimini in September 1944. (National Archives of Canada / PA 142070)

Private Ernest "Smoky" Smith of the Seaforth Highlanders of Canada won the Victoria Cross for single-handedly defeating a German counter-attack on the vulnerable Savio bridgehead on 21 October 1944. (National Archives of Canada / PA 140011)

The present day Savio. In October 1944, the river was in spate, its floodbanks nearly brimful of water. (Cindy Delisle)

The River Lamone as it appears today. In December 1944, when the Canadians attempted to cross it, the Lamone's steep banks were bereft of vegetation and filled with icy-cold fast-flowing water. (Cindy Delisle)

Gino Farnetti, the five-year-old Italian boy who was befriended by truck drivers of the Fifth Canadian Armoured Division. Although the drivers failed in their bid to take Gino with them when they were transferred to northwestern Europe in early 1945, they were able to track him down long after the war and bring him to Canada for reunions in 1980 and again in 1990. (Vic Worley)

(Tac HQ). Out stepped the impeccably attired commander of the Fifteenth Army Group, General Sir Harold Alexander, and the portly prime minister, Winston Churchill, outfitted in sun helmet and tropicals. Wilkes fetched the nearest combat officer, Lieutenant Ted Shuter, who later wrote:

> As Mr. Churchill peered at the enemy positions through binoculars our supporting twenty-five pounders opened up in the rear. The Prime Minister lowered his glasses, looked around for an instant and in a voice that bespoke a warrior's satisfaction on being on a battlefield, exclaimed, "Ah! Cannon!" He was indeed too far foward for a person of his importance; General Alexander showed considerable concern over his safety. The couple left and within a half-hour a concentration of enemy mortar bombs fell where the eminent visitors had stood.[20]

Churchill was very pleased with the view from this vantage point. "The Germans," he later wrote, "were firing with rifles and machine-guns from thick scrub on the far side of the valley, about five hundred yards away. Our front line was beneath us. The firing was desultory and intermittent. But this was the nearest I got to the enemy and the time I heard most bullets in the Second World War."[21]

The Canadian infantry division continued the chase on Sunday, 27 August. But it was not easy, for the Germans retired behind a screen of demolitions carried out with customary skill and thoroughness. "Blown bridges, cratered roads, buildings toppled into every defile by his demolition parties, delayed the armour; skilfully posted rearguards and well placed shelling held up the infantry." The few roads meandered aimlessly among jungles of vines and olives. The forested, cultivated hills and valleys hindered radio communications and made map-reading a nightmare; the RCR's Lieutenant-Colonel Jim Ritchie and his intelligence officer got lost for several hours in a maze of gullies, and a company of the PPCLI disappeared for a whole day.[22]

By Sunday evening, the leading units found themselves overlooking the valley of the Arzilla, a "muddy trickle"[23] dominated by a long, hilly ridge on the far side. Although the ridge was shrouded in a haze, subalterns checking their maps could identify the key villages of Montecicardo, Sant' Angelo, and Ginestreto. It was an ideal position for a delaying action, and the Germans took full advantage of it. They were able to do this, because there was no way to get around the ramparts of this natural fortress. It stood directly in the path of the advancing Canadians, who had no choice but to force their way through. Once again, they were hindered by General Leese's decision to put three corps into action, each on a narrow front. The British and Poles on either side of the Canadians were of little help at this point; both neighbouring formations were lagging behind.

In a day of sharp fighting on 28 August, the Canadians cleared the Germans from the ridge overlooking the Arzilla and advanced towards the Foglia. During the morning of the twenty-ninth, Canadian patrols combed the broad valley; all reported no sign of the enemy on this side of the river.

Now, at close range, the Canadians studied the fortifications of the Gothic Line. Only later would the statistics be available. Although the defences were incomplete on the Tenth Army's front, they were nevertheless considerable: "2,375 machine-gun posts, 479 anti-tank gun, mortar and assault-gun positions, 3,604 dug-outs and shelters of various kinds (including 27 caves), 16,006 riflemen's positions (of trees and branches), 72,127 'T' (Teller, anti-tank) mines and 23,172 'S' mines laid, 117,370 metres of wire obstacles, and 8,944 metres of anti-tank ditch." The position in the sector opposite the Canadians was naturally strong. Beyond the Foglia stood another long, steep ridge, frowning over the remains of the villages of Montecchio, Osteria Nuova, and Borgo Santa Maria, linked by the lateral road from the coastal community of Pesaro. Behind stood the imposing hill mass of Tomba di Pesaro and Monte Luro, a "series of irregular spurs reaching like crooked fingers down to the Foglia," and featuring a number of nameless but important hills, Points 111 and 120 guarding Montecchio, Points 115 and 147 overlooking Osteria Nuova, and Points 131 and 133, the keys to Borgo Santa Maria. Other important positions in the area included the village of Pozzo Alto and the heights of Monte Marrone, Monte Peloso, and Points 119 and 204.[24]

The Germans had turned the valley of the Foglia into a killing ground. The Canadian army historian, Gerry Nicholson, has described it in chilling detail:

It was true that the Foglia in this season of drought had more gravel in its bed than water . . . but the low-lying meadows were treacherous, and the valley itself, from one to two miles broad, with every house and tree razed to the ground to clear the field of fire, would be costly to cross in daylight against a well manned defence. The minefields in the river flats were sown in wide overlapping panels and were backed by the anti-tank ditch, some fourteen feet across, which zig-zagged in front of the road through most of the Canadian sector. The slopes beyond were planted with numerous machine-gun posts, many of them encased in concrete and the majority connected by covered passages to deep dug-outs. Wire obstacles, more formidable than any that the Canadians had yet encountered in Italy, surrounded these positions, and behind them more wire ran in a broad belt along the whole front. This in turn was covered by fire from another zone of mutually supporting pillboxes and emplacements. Killing-ground had been proportioned off with geometric skill. All comers were provided for: anti-tank guns awaited the armour, dug-in flamethrowers the infantry. A mile or two back, the few Panther turrets whose installation had been completed commanded a wide sky-line that must leave the attacking tanks (if any got through) exposed in silhouette as they sailed into view over the rising ground.[25]

Major Howard Mitchell, who commanded a company of machine-gunners with the Saskatoon Light Infantry, was appalled by what he saw as he studied the enemy positions. "This," he feared, "could only be a stupid slaughter."[26]

General Burns had already decided on a set-piece attack. His original plan had envisaged a somewhat speedier advance to the Foglia, and when it became apparent that it would take longer than expected to reach the river, Burns had put his staff to work on a full-scale assault, utilizing both of his divisions to breach the Gothic Line. The Canadian attack on the Gothic Line, tentatively scheduled for 2 September, was closely patterned on these lines. To carry it out, of course, meant launching an armoured division against prepared positions. This was hardly the classic method of employing armour, but Burns had no choice, because the Canadian corps in its present composition was unbalanced, and his army commander refused to give him the infantry division he required for this operation.

Infantry and engineer patrols probing the enemy positions made some interesting discoveries on 29 August. The elaborate minefields in the valley had been badly damaged by Allied aerial attacks during the past three days. But the engineers encountered a new kind of mine. This was the *Schutzenmine*, or Schu-mine. A small wooden box, which made it almost impossible to detect with the available equipment, the Schu-mine contained a seven-ounce explosive. It was designed not to kill but to maim: the blast would blow off a man's foot. The advantage to the Germans was obvious: a dead man could be left where he fell, but an injured man had to be physically removed for treatment, which temporarily took two or more others out of action.

The patrols also discovered that the defences were strangely quiet. Many slipped through gaps in the wire and minefields to the road beyond the Foglia. The impression of enemy unpreparedness was confirmed by the personal observations of the Fifth Division's Bert Hoffmeister, who went out with a patrol to study the enemy lines. "There was no life around the place at all. I did not expect German officers to be swanking up and down but the whole thing looked terribly quiet."[27]

Either the Germans were simply lying low, or they really were not ready to face an attack. Whatever the case, a new possibility was presenting itself to the Canadians. Perhaps a full-scale assault would not be required; if, as it appeared, the Germans had not been able to man the Gothic Line, the defences might be breached by bold action by the leading battalions.

The Germans were uncharacteristically slow to react to the threat materializing on the Tenth Army's Adriatic front. The commander-in-chief, Albert Kesselring, fearing an amphibious landing somewhere along the coast, refused to commit his reserves until he had proof that this was the real thing. "This whole affair," he declared, "gives me the impression of a large-scale diversion."[28]

Part of the problem, from Kesselring's point of view, was that the attack neatly dovetailed with his own planned withdrawal from the Metauro. He perceived the British advance on the heels of his own retiring troops as a natural follow-up, despite urgent claims by the Tenth Army's chief of staff that the danger was real. Fritz Wentzell was particularly disturbed by the reported presence of the Canadians opposite Generalleutnant Wilhelm Raapke's 71st Infantry Division and the 1st Parachute Division of Generalleutnant Richard Heidrich, "for if they really are Canadians we will have to adopt quite other measures. For then it will be a true major operation."[29]

Proof of Allied intentions arrived on 28 August. A copy of General Leese's eve-of-battle message to the troops fell into German hands. General der Panzertruppen Traugott Herr, commanding LXXVI Panzer Corps, was convinced of its authenticity. "On the basis of the captured document," he informed the Tenth Army's Heinrich von Vietinghoff, just returned from leave, "it is now certain that the enemy intends to carry out a big push to the plains of the Po." Herr's corps was authorized to fall back to the Gothic Line, with instructions to defend it "under all circumstances."[30]

Even Kesselring was finally convinced. "I now agree with you," he told Fritz Wentzell, "that the matter on the coast is dangerous."[31] He authorized the transfer of two divisions, 26th Panzer and 29th Panzer Grenadier, to the danger point.

It would take time (at least two days) to move these forces, but the field-marshal was not unduly concerned. While the Eighth Army had closed up to the Gothic Line, Kesselring was familiar with their "customarily deliberate battle procedure." If the British followed their usual ponderous practice, they would pause, redeploy their guns, and marshal their other resources, before attacking. Kesselring was confident that the Tenth Army had plenty of time to spare.[32]

The field-marshal was wrong again.

3

The Canadians attacked on Wednesday afternoon, 30 August. It marked the start of a terrific, three-day battle to smash the Gothic Line.

The first to test the defences were the hardy Maritimers of the West Nova Scotia Regiment. The West Novas set out across the Foglia at 1600 hours. An eerie silence greeted them, for there was no accompanying artillery bombardment, and enemy defenders, huddled in their dugouts and shelters, held their fire.

The West Novas walked into a nightmare. Arrayed along the north bank, between Osteria Nuova and Borgo Santa Maria, stood a vast minefield, and the West Novas strode right into it. Schu-mines blew off unsuspecting feet, and other men were victimized by S-mines, *Schrapnellminen*, known to the troops as "Bouncing Betsys" or "daisy-cutters" because they sprang several feet into the air before scattering ball-bearings or scraps of steel for up to two hundred yards in every direction. The explosions and screams had barely begun when the patient, invisible Germans opened fire. Stretcher-bearer Victor Hall of Lunenburg watched helplessly as friends died in the maelstrom. "The verges, the gutters, were mined along the road," he recalls, and when the enemy started shooting, the West Novas naturally dived for cover along the roadside. "A lot of them jumped onto the mines."[33]

Mines have no respect for rank: two company commanders, Major Allan Nicholson and Captain Stanley Smith, each lost a leg in that minefield. Radios were knocked out within minutes. The West Novas were trapped.[34]

Ninety minutes later, two battalions of the Eleventh Brigade tried their luck. The Cape Breton Highlanders and the Perth Regiment attacked the high ground behind Montecchio, the Perths heading for Point 111 and the Highlanders for Point 120. The brigadier, Ian Johnston, had received word that a company of the First Division had reached the road to the right, and he was mindful of the Cape Breton patrol, which had crossed the river and walked along the road that very morning, in broad daylight, without drawing fire. The key to the attack was Point 120, "a sharp and rocky crag 300 feet high."[35]

The Boys from the Bay had their hands full. As soon as they started across the valley, "all hell broke loose," according to Bill Matheson, a twenty-three-year-old lieutenant from Westville, Nova Scotia. "Caught in the open, the only way we could advance was by crawling on our bellies." Three times they reached their objective, Point 120, and three times they were driven back. Their last attempt was made after midnight, when two companies attacked, following a twenty-minute bombardment. As young Lieutenant Matheson found, night attacks can be tricky operations:

> We started off in the dark with my platoon leading, and me leading the platoon. We got across the valley and on the hill encountered all sorts of wire obstacles. Suddenly we were out of the wire, which we had been hopscotching through for at least 30 minutes, when we heard voices off to our left. Three Germans had left their bunkers and were standing not more than 50 yards from me. I turned to my leading section leader and told him to cover with his section while I moved the remaining sections to attack the enemy position.
>
> He whispered urgently to me, "Do you know how many of us are here?"
>
> I said, "No, but I should think the whole company is behind us."
>
> He said, "You and I are the only ones here."

It was true! Matheson later discovered that his company commander had had a change of heart about the approach route, and had hurried up to halt the advance. Unfortunately, he grabbed the second man back of Matheson, and the lieutenant and his NCO continued along their way in the darkness, thinking that the company was right behind them. Finding that they were alone, they threw some grenades at the Germans, then scurried back down the hill "in some haste" in search of their comrades.[36]

While the Cape Bretons were being frustrated at Point 120, the Perths were storming Point 111. Losing a half-dozen men to mines, the Ontario battalion found a bridge across the anti-tank ditch (which was fifteen feet wide and ten feet deep) and deployed at the foot of the steep hill. One company was pinned down here, but Lieutenant-Colonel Bill Reid went forward and organized a second attack, which went in at 2030 hours. Captain Sammy Ridge led D Company up the slope. In the gathering darkness, the Germans inexplicably held their fire until the Canadians were almost at the crest. The hail of machine-gun bullets failed to daunt the Perths, according to one veteran, Stan Scislowski. "Every single mother's son of them on that slope broke into a maniacal howling charge in the final twenty yards."[37]

The Perths took the hill at bayonet-point, and became the first Canadians to break into the Gothic Line. Later that night, one company took advantage of the darkness to slip around Point 147, capturing it from the rear.[38]

The Fifth Division had prised open the door; the next step was to smash it open.

Thursday, 31 August, proved to be another hot, sunny day. Visibility would have been perfect, had it not been for the haze of smoke and dust that shrouded the valley of the Foglia and the ridges and hills beyond.[39]

The day began with an attempt by the West Nova Scotia Regiment to recover from their disaster in the minefield between Osteria Nuova and Borgo Santa Maria. Under the personal direction of the colonel, Ron Waterman, the West Novas launched a new attack towards their objective, Point 133, only to blunder into yet another minefield. Within twenty minutes, Waterman called for a smoke screen which enabled his battered battalion to withdraw across the Foglia. The attack had cost the West Novas seventy-eight casualties.[40]

While the Red Patches struggled, the key battles were being fought and won by the Mighty Maroon Machine, as Bert Hoffmeister's Fifth Armoured Division was known. The First Division was hampered by its inability to get a firm bridgehead in the enemy defences; until it was firmly lodged, the supporting British tanks could not be committed. On the other hand, the Fifth Division had plenty of its own armour, and Hoffmeister used it. His willingness to use tanks to break through the Gothic Line might not have impressed the authors of the tanker's bible, *The Tactical Handling of the Armoured Division*, but the situation demanded something beyond the ordinary. New Brunswick's dashing 8th Hussars, the British Columbia Dragoons, and Lord Strathcona's Horse were destined to play crucial roles in the day's fighting.

The 8th Hussars helped the Irish Regiment of Canada to capture Point 120 and Montecchio. The Eleventh Brigade's Ian Johnston had hoped to launch the attack under the cover of darkness, but the Irish had difficulty getting through the traffic jam that was developing on the Foglia, where engineers were constructing a bridge. The southern Ontario regiment spent most of the morning getting into position, losing fifty men to fire from Point 120 while doing so.[41]

The Irish more than made up for the delay. Their noon attack, accompanied by an artillery stonk, proved to be "a dashing example of tank-infantry co-operation," according to historian Doug How.[42] The Canadians were in Montecchio before the defenders realized what was happening; the Irish lost one man taking the town. They captured 130 Germans in the ruins of the village, and 117 more on the hill which frowned over it. The haul of prisoners netted this day, and the intensity of the fighting, would make it clear that the enemy had had time to man the Gothic Line in ample strength.[43]

Other Hussars, meanwhile, had plunged deeper into the German defences, towards Monte Marrone. The eleven Shermans of A Squadron were commanded by Major P. M. "Frenchy" Blanchet, who was so ill with jaundice that "his face looked like a duck's foot." Without infantry support, however, the tanks were soon in trouble, and a savage battle developed. When Sergeant Bill McIntee's tank was knocked out and the crew members forced to bail out, they were mowed down by a nearby machine-gun post. One died in the hail of bullets, and the other four were wounded; as they lay on the ground, German soldiers rushed forward and bayoneted two of the helpless crewmen. Captain Doug Lewis, watching from his Sherman, reacted first in horror and then in mute rage. He turned the tank's machine-gun on the Germans, then jumped out and used his pistol to kill two more. One of Lewis's crewmen shared his anger, tackling one German and strangling him with his bare hands. In the face of this onslaught, six Germans tried to surrender, but it was too late for that. The Sherman's machine-gun riddled them.[44]

Blanchet's squadron was forced back, but the 8th Hussars were not to be denied. The regiment's remaining squadron moved up with the Cape Breton Highlanders during the late afternoon, and this time Monte Marrone fell to the Canadians. Losses were surprisingly light, considering the defences atop the hill. "Concrete emplaced 88 and 75mm high-velocity guns mounted in steel tank turrets were all over the place," a Hussar major, Bob Ross, recounted. "They covered every avenue of advance. A great many of them had been captured still intact by Canadian units. They were sighted with perfect fields of fire and it certainly looked as though they should have been able to wipe us out in detail as we crossed the completely open ground."[45]

After being overrun by the Canadian Shermans, one bewildered English-speaking prisoner muttered to the Highlanders' Sergeant George Hall, "You fellows have got too many tanks."[46]

The *coup de main* was staged by the B.C. Dragoons. The CO, Lieutenant-Colonel Fred Vokes, was ordered to take the Perths under his command and push towards Point 204. The Dragoons had trouble getting across the Foglia, and when Vokes failed to find the Perths' headquarters, he impetuously ordered the tanks to go ahead without the infantry. Fifty Shermans roared between Point 147, held by the Perths, and Point 115, still in German hands. "Looking at the map now, we find that the total distance was not much more than 3 miles," recalled Major Jack Letcher, "and yet it seemed like it must be 30 miles."[47]

The survivors, for good reason, would call the regiment's route "Death Valley," because it had been designed as a killing ground for tanks. In the rolling, treeless countryside, they had to run a gauntlet of anti-tank fire designed to prevent precisely the kind of attack that the Dragoons were making. Only eighteen tanks survived, and the unit's fifty-one casualties included Colonel Vokes, who was fatally wounded by a mortar blast after leaving his disabled Sherman. By 1430 hours, however, they had taken Point 204 and sounded the death knell of the Gothic Line.[48]

They had paid a hefty price, but the Dragoons had made an invaluable contribution. "Had Pt 204 not been taken that day, and the enemy been given a few more hours to organize his defences," notes historian Brereton Greenhous, "it is unlikely that it could have been taken subsequently without a significant pause to organize the traditional 'set-piece' assault."[49] The victory was sealed by the Perths, who arrived soon afterwards, escorted by Shermans of Lord Strathcona's Horse, who took over from the Dragoons.

Point 204 was a key position, and the Germans were not about to let the Canadians keep it without a fight. Elements of the 26th Panzer Division were now entering the battle, being fed piecemeal into the tumult as they arrived. During the evening, and all night long, paratroopers, tanks, and self-propelled guns attempted to reclaim vital Point 204.

The Germans were good, but the Canadians were better. The Perths and Strathconas proved to be a deadly combination. The infantrymen's CO, Colonel Reid, seemed to be everywhere, hurrying from danger point to danger point, exhorting his men to hold their ground, and leading counterattacks whenever the infiltrating paratroopers gained a toehold. Though twice wounded, Reid gathered up his PIAT teams and went on a tank-hunting expedition, scoring several direct hits on self-propelled guns, for which he was later awarded the Distinguished Service Order. When daylight came, the Canadians still held Point 204. Forty dead Germans on the hillside attested to the night's savage battle.[50]

Slowly, but surely, the breach in the Gothic Line was being widened. During the afternoon of the thirty-first, Princess Patricia's Canadian Light Infantry took advantage of the favourable situation on the left and broke out of Osteria Nuova. The paratroopers defending Points 115 and 133, preoccupied by the tank battle raging beside and behind them, were overrun before they could recover. The Patricias, backed by a squadron of tanks from the 48th Royal Tank Regiment, took both hills and rounded up 210 prisoners, many of them paratroopers. Encouraged by PPCLI's success, the Second Brigade's Graeme Gibson committed the Seaforth Highlanders of Canada, supported by tanks of the 145th Regiment, through the PPCLI's bridgehead. By dusk, this force had reached the outskirts of the hilltop village of Pozzo Alto, midway between Borgo Santa Maria and Point 204.[51]

With the arrival of darkness on 31 August, the situation on the Canadian corps front was rather promising. Thanks to the Fifth Division's successes, the Canadians had ripped open a hole more than a mile wide and two miles deep in the Gothic Line. Secure on Monte Marrone on the left and Point 204 on the right, the Canadians were within a mile of Monte Peloso and Monte Luro, twin peaks which marked the last high ground in the area. Beyond, the country sloped gradually down to the broad coastal plain where the River Conca and Rimini lay.

So far, the Fifth Division's exploits had overshadowed the veteran First Division, and Chris Vokes was determined to make amends on the first day of September. In fact, that fateful Friday was to be a day of sparkling successes by both divisions and marked the climax of the battle.

Before the fighting, frenzied activity was taking place, both in and behind the battle zone. Between the Metauro and the Foglia, a steady stream of trucks rolled back and forth, bringing up the necessary supplies and equipment to sustain the combat units. "In places the dust lies like powdered snow to a depth of three or four inches," wrote a Canadian officer. "It is impossible to see a moving tank. You are only aware of its presence by the turbulent cloud of dust which accompanies it." A traffic sign attested to the prevailing mood of optimism: DRIVE CAREFULLY IF YOU WANT TO SEE VIENNA.[52]

The Royal 22nd Regiment moved into action before dawn in a bid to secure the right shoulder of the breach. Engineers worked through the night to clear three narrow paths in the minefield where the West Novas had earlier come to grief, then Lieutenant-Colonel Jean Allard hurried two companies forward. Beyond the mines, the two companies parted ways. Captain Yvon Dubé led B Company towards Borgo Santa Maria, which the Van Doos attacked from the rear. "The defenders put up very little resistance," and shortly after 0636, the wrecked village was in Canadian hands.[53]

Major Tony Poulin's company had a much more difficult fight for Point 131. Despite several fierce bayonet charges, the French-Canadians were stopped by heavy fire from the main defences along the crest of the hill, four concrete bunkers linked by tunnels and guarded by machine-gunners. Even artillery fire failed to dislodge the determined defenders, so Poulin sent his sergeant-major to notify Colonel Allard at battalion headquarters. Allard responded by sending up four armoured carriers mounting Vickers medium machine-guns. When the tracked vehicles arrived, Poulin organized his final assault, arranging the carriers in a semi-circle, with his fifty surviving men (he started the day with eighty-five) following close behind. While the carriers used their machine-guns to pin down the defenders at close range, the infantry rushed up and dispatched them with hand grenades. "The plan worked to perfection," Poulin reported. "In ten minutes we took the four German hilltop positions."[54] By 1425 hours, Point 131 was secured by the Van Doos.[55]

The situation on the right was further improved that afternoon when the Seaforths and their British tanks took Pozzo Alto and its five-hundred-foot hill. The Seaforths then drove northwards and took Point 119, nearly a mile away.

In the centre, the Fifth Division had not been idle. Monte Peloso and Tomba di Pesaro were its primary objectives, but it took most of the day to complete their capture. The original plan called for the Perths and Strathconas to attack Peloso, but this had to be revised when it became apparent that fresh infantry would be needed. The Perths had come through thirty-six hours of fighting, losing ninety men, including their CO, Bill Reid (wounded after only eighteen days in command of the regiment). General Hoffmeister looked at the three battalions of the recently organized Twelfth Brigade, and selected the Princess Louise Dragoon Guards, the former First Division reconnaissance regiment. It took time for the Plugs to work their way forward, braving heavy shelling that caused a number of casualties near Point 204.

It was 1310 hours when the attack on Monte Peloso was finally launched, but it could hardly have been timed better. As the Plugs and Strathcona Shermans crossed the cultivated fields, they overran large numbers of panzer grenadiers. "Row after row of them were found, crouching or lying in the open with no slit trenches or fire positions," Strathcona Colonel Jim McAvity later wrote, "and it was obvious that we had caught a battalion in the act of attacking us. In all, over 120 German dead were counted and about the same number of wounded passed through our R[egimental] A[id] P[ost] to the prisoner of war cage or to our hospitals."[56] So many Germans were killed here that bulldozers were later used to bury them in a mass grave.

The Plugs were not only new to infantry tactics, they had a new commanding officer. Lieutenant-Colonel Bill Darling won the Distinguished Service Order this day, leading his green troops into a fierce cross-fire. As casualties mounted alarmingly, Darling ignored sniper and machine-gun bullets to rally the men and keep them moving forward. By the time the Plugs reached the foot of Monte Peloso, there were only forty survivors in the two assault companies. With two hundred yards still to go to reach the crest of the hill, Darling paused to consult with the Strathconas. Darling's plan was to send the tanks halfway up the slope on their own; if the opposition was not too bad, he would lead the handful of infantrymen to the top.[57]

The Shermans roared up the hillside, knocking down the few houses still standing, firing their 75s and machine-guns at every likely defensive position. When Darling saw the tanks making steady progress, he led the Plugs to the crest. Only fifteen men made it to the top with him; even at that, they covered "the last 50 yards literally on hands and knees."[58]

Monte Peloso now belonged to the Plugs and Strathconas. The tanks had performed to their usual high standards, but for the Plugs, whose armoured cars were still a recent and cherished memory, it had been a truly remarkable achievement. Their heavy casualties (129, including 35 dead) were at least partly attributable to inexperience. But stragglers wandered into the position during the next few hours; by dark, Darling had 100 men with whom to hold the hill. The Plugs were also reinforced by a handy bottle of whisky that was passed around to celebrate the victory.[59]

The Irish Regiment and the 8th Hussars completed the victory that evening. The Irish and ten Shermans moved up to Monte Peloso, capturing seventy prisoners along the way, and shortly after 1800 hours they passed through the ragged ranks of the heroic Plugs. The objective was Tomba di Pesaro, less than half a mile to the west. The hilltop village proved to be undefended, and the wild Irish celebrated. A sign told the story: "BOBBY CLARKEVILLE – IN BOUNDS TO ALL CDN TROOPS."[60] It was both a tribute to the likeable colonel who commanded the regiment (although his name was misspelled), and a commentary on the infuriating practice by which most towns and villages were placed out of bounds to Canadians. (Indeed, two overzealous military policemen were captured just before the Gothic Line, when they inadvertently crossed the Foglia to post OUT OF BOUNDS signs. This incident was later the subject of a famous, and very popular, *Herbie* cartoon.)[61]

While the Irish were taking Tomba di Pesaro, the Loyal Edmonton Regiment was having an equally easy time on Monte Luro, the most northwesterly feature. The 940-foot hill should have been the site of a hard fight; according to historian George Stevens, it was "deeply entrenched and studded with machine guns and anti-tank cupolas." What it did not have was a garrison. The defenders, after being subjected to heavy artillery and aerial bombardment for several hours, "proved more anxious to escape than to stand and fight."[62] According to Captain John Dougan, who commanded C Company, "We walked on to the objective, took 4 PW and reorganized."[63]

It was a deceptively easy ending to a hard-fought battle. The Gothic Line had been shattered, and even as night descended over the smoking, bloody battlefield, the Canadians started their pursuit of the defeated enemy.

For many, an important struggle was still taking place: the fight to live. The three-day battle exacted its inevitable toll: 235 Canadian soldiers died and another 591 were wounded.[64] The medical services were inundated. Dave Gordon, the slender, twenty-year-old orderly from Hagersville, Ontario, remembers the Gothic Line as his busiest experience of the war. He went without sleep for forty-eight hours during one stretch; only an occasional tea break could be allowed.[65] It was just as busy at 16 Field Dressing Station, where the former Three Rivers padre, Waldo Smith, helped tend to the battered and broken bodies which were being brought in.

"I came to know by the amount of blood on the floor under the stretcher," Smith later wrote, "whether the soldier was going to die."[66]

For days afterwards, burial parties carried out their heartrending work under Italy's brilliant sun and blue sky. Death at any time is tragic, but Martha Gellhorn, the journalist wife of Ernest Hemingway, who had watched the Canadians make their assault on the Gothic Line, believed that there was a special sadness about this battle. "It is awful to die at the end of summer or in the gentle days of the new autumn when you are young and have fought a long time . . . and when you know that the war is won anyhow. It is awful and one would have to be a liar or a fool not to see this and not to feel it like a misery, so that these days every man dead is a greater sorrow because the end of all this tragic dying is so near."[67]

Unfortunately, the end was not so near as it appeared.

CHAPTER FIFTEEN

"...And Be Goddamned If We'll Surrender!"

1

The speed and power of the Eighth Army's attack on the Gothic Line had taken Kesselring and other senior Germans by surprise. A synopsis of the Tenth Army's telephone conversations on 31 August reveals the extent of the crisis. "Time and again the situation is being described as very grave, as immediate commitment of reserves which have just arrived makes it barely possible to seal off the enemy penetrations. All reserves (elements of 98 Inf and 26 Pz Div) are brought forward, and the artillery is sharply concentrated."[1]

Although both the British and Poles on either flank had broken into the Gothic Line, it was in the Canadian sector that the enemy fortifications had been decisively breached. The capture of Monte Peloso and Monte Luro, which dominated the land for miles around, had sealed the enemy's fate. Worse, from the enemy's point of view, was the fact that the Canadian corps was threatening to drive a wedge between the Tenth Army's two best divisions, the 26th Panzer and 1st Parachute.

During the night of 1–2 September, the Germans began a two-stage withdrawal to avoid complete disaster. By morning, the 26th Panzer and 1st Parachute divisions were to be on the Misano ridge, behind the next river, the Conca. Over the next two nights, they would fall back to a line of improvised ridges. This was the Green Line II, a back-up to the Gothic Line. Although not a prepared position, it was naturally strong, and it would be manned not only by the defeated Gothic Line forces, but by fresh formations being rushed to the scene by Kesselring.[2] The Tenth Army issued orders that the Green Line II must be held at all costs, "in order to gain time for the reinforcements to arrive."[3]

The Germans fled with the Canadians hot on their heels. Speed being the primary concern, there was little time even to grieve, as the First Division's Chris Vokes discovered. After his younger brother, Fred, had been killed on 31 August, leading the B.C. Dragoons against Point 204, he had attended the brief funeral ceremony the next day. "And it *was* a very sad thing, to see this only brother of mine, whom I loved very much ... baled up in a blanket and put into a hole in the ground. In fact, I broke down. I cried."[4]

It was still dark when the chase began on Saturday morning, 2 September. It proved to be a rather uneventful day. "Jerry had pulled out so suddenly," a First Division gunner, Bombardier Charlie Phelan, related in his diary, "that many of the '*Minen*' signs still marked the minefields."[5] Aside from isolated pockets of resistance, both divisions rarely spotted the enemy *en route* to the Conca.

Tommy Burns was understandably elated by the work of his corps. In triumph, he had notified Eighth Army headquarters earlier in the day that the Gothic Line had been "completely broken." He was summoned to Leese's advanced headquarters, where the army commander and Sir Harold Alexander greeted him. "They were highly pleased," Burns later wrote, "and, I thought, a little surprised at the speed of the Canadians' advance." But it was Burns who was surprised, when Alexander informed him that he was recommending the Canadian commander for the Distinguished Service Order. "I considered the decoration as an honour for the corps whose bravery and sacrifice had won the victory," said Burns. "But I also took it as a sign that the generals had decided that I could handle my command and that confidence had replaced the doubts which had formerly existed."[6]

Leese must have been grinding his teeth as he watched Alexander congratulate Burns. While he was pleased that the Canadians had "gate-crashed" the Gothic Line, the battle had developed almost exactly opposite to what he had anticipated. His secondary formation, the Canadian Corps, had breached the Gothic Line and was pursuing the enemy; his pursuit corps, Charles Keightley's V, was having all sorts of problems and lagging far behind the Canadians. Their roles had been reversed by the fortunes of battle: the oversized V Corps was now guarding the flank of the undersized Canadian corps. Burns had tried to warn him that the British forces would have difficulty advancing on the inland flank, and this was happening. Leese's sole hope lay with the fresh 1st Armoured Division, a veteran formation of the North African campaign, now moving up to take over the lead. The army commander was certain that this tank thrust on V Corps' front would unhinge the German delaying positions and carry the Eighth Army past Rimini.

2

With the Canadian corps across the Conca on the morning of 3 September, Burns and his colleagues were having difficulty keeping their optimism under control. Burns knew that it was unwise to underestimate the Germans, who had shown a remarkable, at times unbelievable, capacity to recover from defeat. But, surely, this time it would be different. From the Conca, it was just nine miles to Rimini and the River Marecchia. Beyond that stream stood the Romagna plain, the east end of the Po valley.

The Po valley exerted a hypnotic influence. This was legendary tank country; once there, the Allies could turn the Italian slugging-match into a foot-race across the northern Italian plain. What senior commanders had forgotten as they gazed longingly at their maps of the Po was the intervening ground, the foothills and coastal plain between the Conca and Marecchia rivers. It would take the Canadians eighteen agonizing days to fight their way to the Marecchia.

The First Division, staying close to the coast along Route 16, put two battalions of Allan Calder's First Brigade across the Conca on 3 September. The Royal Canadian Regiment established the bridgehead during the night; it was an easy crossing, because the river bed was virtually dry. "For miles around burning homesteads and haystacks, glowing like hundreds of cigarette butts in a darkened room, illuminated the otherwise pitch-dark landscape," recalls Major Strome Galloway, who points out that the fires had been set deliberately, "so as to deprive our advancing army of cover from the view of his artillery [observation posts]."[7]

The Royal Canadians had their first skirmish shortly after dawn. Shooting broke out as the RCR rifle companies advanced towards the resort of Riccione, a pre-war summer retreat of the late Galeazzo Ciano, Mussolini's son-in-law, who had been executed by the Italians for his part in Il Duce's forced resignation in the summer of 1943. The Royal Canadians were forced to clear some beach-front cottages on the outskirts of Riccione, where five paratroopers were captured. That signalled the start of a bitter battle on the eastern end of the Misano ridge. The presence of the enemy "in great strength" was an unpleasant surprise, in view of reports that the Germans had withdrawn all the way to Rimini.[8]

To assist the RCR in Riccione, Brigadier Calder committed the Hastings and Prince Edward Regiment. The Hasty Ps were sent to take the village of Santa Maria di Scacciano, a mile off the coast road. Two companies approached the village in the dark, under cover of "vineyards, olive groves, orchards and brush hedges." Scouts sent into Santa Maria reported it to be "lightly held," speculating that it was an outpost protecting a nearby mortar and self-propelled gun position. But the morning of 4 September brought a much different tale, when a furious door-to-door battle ensued. Santa Maria, in fact, was garrisoned by a substantial number of Germans;

B Company alone captured twenty-five, without making an appreciable dent in the enemy's defences.[9]

At one point, there was a lull in the shooting and a paratroop officer approached the Hasty Ps under the cover of white flag. He called out: "Surrender you English gentlemen – you are surrounded and will only die."

"We *ain't* English," Private "Slim" Sanford shouted back. "We *ain't* gentlemen – and be Goddamned if we'll surrender."[10]

The deadlock on the First Brigade's front was finally broken, if only briefly, the next day. Brigadier Calder, an experienced soldier, came forward and after studying the situation decided to commit his remaining battalion, Toronto's 48th Highlanders. Calder's solution was a three-pronged attack, with all the tanks and artillery available, at 0600 hours on 5 September. The Hasty Ps, in the centre, withdrew its two companies from Santa Maria under the cover of darkness; at H-Hour, after the village had been pulverized by the artillery, the Hasty Ps took over the ruins without a fight. Afterwards the 48th Highlanders pursued the defeated enemy to the bluff-lined banks of the dry River Melo, more than a mile beyond Santa Maria. The Royal Canadians pushed into and past Riccione, only to face some of their heaviest fighting since Cider crossroads near Ortona. The German paratroopers chose to make a stand in the hamlet of San Lorenzo in Strada, where a savage battle ensued, in and around the church. At one point, an RCR platoon broke into the building and waged a hand-to-hand struggle in the nave. Although they could not hold it, Corporal Rodesse Duhaime won the Military Medal for wiping out a German anti-tank crew in the sanctuary.

Casualties mounted alarmingly. Calder's First Brigade had lost more than three hundred men, more than half of them in the RCR alone.

On the left, the Fifth Division also had its hands full. Early on the sultry morning of 4 September, New Brunswick's 8th Hussars rumbled past Monte Gallera, intent on following the road which ran along the crest of Besanigo ridge. This road offered the most direct approach to Besanigo, but it was swept by fire from a parallel ridge a half-mile to the west, crowned by Coriano, described by former war correspondent Doug How as "one of those stone villages with a central square and the inevitable dominant church and the inevitable back alleys of poverty and stench." Coriano was in the British sector, but its name would soon take a proud place in Canadian military history.[11]

The Hussars came to grief long before reaching Besanigo. Three Shermans fell into the dry bed of a steep-sided stream being used as an anti-tank ditch. One tank brewed up soon afterwards, while the other two frantically sought an escape route. But there was no way out; the banks were too steep. Major Howard Keirstead and Sergeant Keith Fraser, the crew commanders, knew that they were in desperate straits. Soon enough, the Germans were stalking them, trying to get close enough for a point-blank shot with a *Faustpatrone*, a portable anti-tank weapon similar to the PIAT. As long as there was daylight, they were able to use their machine-guns to keep the enemy at bay – but nighttime would almost certainly bring doom.[12]

Attempts to rescue them proved costly. After losing five Shermans (including one commanded by Sergeant Billy Bell, who lost seven tanks during the war – and survived), Lieutenant-Colonel George Robinson forbade any more rescue missions. They would have to hope the infantry could get to Keirstead and Fraser before the Germans did. Four crewmen from the latter's tank later staggered into Canadian lines and gave exact details of the position of the two Shermans. After dark, a patrol of the Irish Regiment of Canada crept up to the anti-tank ditch. Within seventy-five yards of the last reported position of the trapped tanks, the infantrymen heard German voices: the remaining crewmen were assumed to be either dead or captured.[13]

Besanigo ridge, including the village of that name, was occupied the next day by the Irish Regiment and the Cape Breton Highlanders, who dubbed it "Graveyard Hill." This advance brought the Fifth Division's line into conformity with the First Division on the right, along the Melo. But the Canadians could move no farther until Coriano was taken. This position offered perfect observation and fields of fire over the four miles of vineyards and grainfields leading down to the blue Adriatic. "The town," writes Canadian historian Brereton Greenhous, "anchored the enfilade position and there were sufficient farm houses and haystacks along the eastern slope of the ridge to provide a network of mutually supporting forward outposts. Tanks, and [self-propelled] guns could move relatively freely on the reverse slope, while the valley bottom behind the ridge provided good cover for guns and mortars."[14]

Even worse, light showers fell Tuesday night. These turned to steady rain on Wednesday, 6 September, and meteorologists predicted several days of unsettled weather.

"Though not strong in numbers," Heinrich von Vietinghoff patiently explained to Albert Kesselring, "the Canadians are very good soldiers. I am told that the 5th Canadian Armoured Division was excellent."[15]

In the face of the Canadian performance, the German delaying positions, first near Misano, now at Coriano, were proving invaluable. Frantic efforts were under way to construct another line of defence in the bottleneck between Rimini and the ostensibly neutral little republic of San

Marino. Designated the Rimini Line, it followed a line of hills and ridges, generally north of another meandering little river, the Ausa. An estimated ten thousand Italians had been conscripted to construct defences, and they were joined by all available German labour battalions. "Each day's delay in the enemy offensive," an enemy staff report later stated, "represented a gain of several times that period for the defence."[16]

The rain that started falling on 6 September bought even more time for the desperate Germans. While the precipitation proved to be a blessing for them, it was a nightmare for Kesselring's Allied counterpart, Oliver Leese. The Eighth Army commander was painfully aware that the last-minute change of plan that he had foisted on General Alexander had cost more than two weeks of perfect weather. At first the showers merely settled the dust and offered a measure of relief from the oppressive early-September heat, but as the rainfall persisted, the Eighth Army bogged down.

"The mud was soon many inches deep," writes Brereton Greenhous. "Breakdown detachments hauled out vehicles only to see them slide off the road again and again, and as soon as rain began to fall in the hills to the west the shallow streams that trickled over wide gravel beds became angry torrents. A watercourse which in the morning could be crossed on a 20-foot Bailey span would need piers and several spans by nightfall."[17]

The weather-induced lull in the battle gave Leese time to reflect on events of the past few days. Although he approved of the rookie corps commander, Charles Keightley, Leese was deeply disappointed in the performance of v Corps as a whole. "It is extraordinary how difficult it is," he complained on 8 September in a letter to the War Office, "to make new troops realise the inter-dependence of tanks and infantry until they have gained the knowledge by bitter experience in battle." The British 1st Armoured Division, which had not fought since Tunisia in early 1943, was ample proof that experience in the desert meant nothing in Italy. On 4 and 5 September, the British tanks were hurled at Coriano ridge in a costly failure.[18]

As the rain fell, Leese finally admitted that changes were in order. Designating the Canadian Corps his pursuit corps, he swallowed his earlier reservations about General Burns's capabilities and, on 6 September, placed additional formations under his command. These included the British 4th and 2nd New Zealand divisions, the British 25th Army Tank Brigade, and the 3rd Greek Mountain Brigade. Leese intended to renew his offensive as soon as it stopped raining. First, v Corps would take crucial Coriano, enabling the Canadians to punch across the River Marano. Both corps would jointly break through the Rimini Line and cross the Marecchia. There he would unleash his Canadian, British, and New Zealand tanks across the plain.[19]

The rain also played havoc with Allied aerial operations, including those of the Canadian 417 Squadron. During the summer, the squadron's Spitfires had been converted to fighter-bombers, each aircraft being fitted with a rack which carried a 500-pound bomb. Since enemy aircraft were rarely seen, 417's main role now was to bomb and machine-gun ground targets. It was to prove to be far more dangerous than air combat had been: between September 1942, when the squadron had become operational in Egypt, and the end of May 1944, 417 had lost nine pilots; in the last year of the war, these low-level bombing missions would claim nineteen flyers.[20]

There was no shortage of targets for the Spitfires' bombs and machine-guns. Their quarry included railway bridges, crossroads, and gun positions over a wide area, "a rough triangle extending from the Po River near Ferrara south through Bologna to Piato and thence eastward to the Adriatic coast about Fano." 417 Squadron also participated in a recent innovation in the increasingly complex area of aerial support for ground operations. Aircraft were sent out on "Rover" missions; they had no specific target until they reported to a forward control post which radioed them an assignment. The fighter-bombers assembled in so-called "cab-ranks," just like London taxis, which could be "whistled up" at short notice for intervention in ground battles.[21]

The soldiers raved about this innovation by 417 Squadron and the rest of the Desert Air Force. The Canadian commander, General Burns, later wrote that the air force "contributed much to the success of the attacks" mounted by the Canadians along the Adriatic.[22] Toronto's Norman Bell, then a sergeant in the Perth Regiment, can attest to the air force's work. "You know," he says, "all you needed was one lone Spitfire just floating around up there, and you could pretty well relax a little."[23]

Allied aircraft had played a small but important part in the Gothic Line battle. Fighter-bombers had ravaged Borgo Santa Maria, Osteria Nuova, and Montecchio in the course of the fighting, and every plane that flew over or near Tomba di Pesaro was instructed to swoop down and strafe it when returning from any mission, in order to harass the enemy observers atop this key hill.[24]

Throughout the battles that lay ahead, the army would turn to the air force for help, weather permitting. In September, 417 Squadron averaged thirty cab-rank missions a day. While these were great for the soldiers' morale, ground-support operations were not the most satisfying undertakings for the airmen. The veteran flyers of 417 gazed longingly into the sky, but "not an enemy aircraft was seen."[25]

Tommy Burns energetically plunged into the preparations for battle. He was, naturally, very pleased that Sir Oliver Leese had placed additional formations under him, taking it as a show of confidence in his capabilities. Canadian units would benefit, because Burns could now afford to rest them occasionally.[26]

Burns issued his plan of battle on 10 September. It would be an eight-phase operation, beginning with the capture of Coriano ridge by Bert Hoffmeister's Fifth Canadian Armoured Division, with assistance from the British 1st Armoured Division. Then Major-General Dudley Ward's British 4th Division would relieve the Fifth and join Chris Vokes's First Canadian Division in a northward drive, crossing the Marano, breaching the Rimini Line, and establishing bridgeheads on the Marecchia. The Greek brigade would protect the First Division's right flank.[27]

The intervening days were were far from quiet. According to historian Gerry Nicholson, "the Canadian divisions were experiencing their heaviest shelling so far in the Italian campaign." The enemy took full advantage of their superior positions and excellent observation posts to pound the Canadian lines along the Besanigo ridge to the coast.[28]

The rain added to the misery. For the men in the front lines, this meant long hours in water-logged slit trenches. Behind the lines, it meant more work for everyone. The efficiency of the Canadian engineers can only be admired. At the peak of the storm on 7 September, both of the Fifth Division's traffic routes were closed when the Foglia flooded; the engineers re-opened the roads after working all night. Despite the mud and untold difficulties, the armoured division's traffic-control experts still managed to move an average of fifty vehicles per hour, sometimes getting up to three hundred.[29]

Rain or shine, the Canadians patrolled steadily, aggressively, pinpointing the strongest defences, selecting the best lines of approach over ridges, across the hills, through valleys. There were clashes with enemy patrols, and more than a few surprises. During one nighttime foray into enemy territory, on 9 September, a patrol of the Perth Regiment made a singular discovery. Crawling up to a deep ditch, they observed two large, immobile shadows in the moonlight. "Christ," declared one of the soldiers, so surprised that he said it out loud, "those are Shermans."

A weak, pain-racked voice called out in reply, "What unit are you from?"

When the lieutenant said they were Perths, he heard weeping. Cautiously moving up to the Shermans, the patrol realized that these were the tanks that had been lost five days earlier. The three surviving crewmen had a remarkable tale to relate.

On 4 September, with dusk falling, Sergeant Keith Fraser had ordered the other four members of his crew to get out of the Sherman to try to reach safety; they did, and reported the precise position of the tanks. Fraser had made one last attempt to contact regimental headquarters over the dying radio, but he lingered too long. German infantry approached under the cover of darkness and opened fire with *Faustpatronen* at close range: Fraser's Sherman was hit once, while two rockets hit Major Howard Keirstead's tank. Keirstead ordered his men to bail out of the brewing-up Sherman: they were greeted by a hail of machine-gun bullets. Trooper E. R. Hilckey fell dead, while Trooper Charlie Stevens was paralysed from the waist down. The major took seven bullets in the thigh and two more in his arm. Lance-Corporal John Wentworth safely emerged from the tank, but when he rushed to Keirstead's side, he was riddled in both legs. Only one member of the crew, Sergeant C. M. Stevenson, escaped the fusillade unhurt. Huddled around their tank, the survivors waited in the darkness to be captured.

A short distance away, Keith Fraser realized that he had delayed his escape too long. Slipping out of the escape hatch in the floor of the burning Sherman, he froze. "I could hear the Germans talking a yard or so away," he recounted. "They were right alongside the tank. All I could do was keep still. All I had with me was a .38 pistol and 23 rounds of ammunition."

(It was at this point that the patrol of the Irish Regiment arrived nearby, and the sound of German voices seemed to indicate that they were too late to save the tankers.)

While Fraser hid under his tank, Keirstead's crew was in dire straits. They lay there silently, the badly injured Stevens and Wentworth fighting the urge to cry out in pain, hoping against hope that the Germans would somehow miss them. When the enemy patrol departed, the unwounded Sergeant Stevenson agreed to go for help, but he did not even get close. Moments later, there was a burst of machine-gun fire, then silence. Their worst fears were confirmed in the morning, when they found Stevenson's body slumped over the tank turret; evidently he had tried to make one last attempt to use the Sherman's radio to call for help.

Major Keirstead decided that he would have to go himself. Leaving his rations with Wentworth and Stevens, he started crawling in the general direction of Besanigo ridge. Within several hundreds yards, however, he was bracketed by mortar bombs. The major, already weakened by the loss of blood from nine bullet wounds, was hit by mortar fragments in the head, shoulder, and leg. Keirstead lay there for a while to recover some of his strength, then continued crawling. He could hear the distinctive sound of Canadian 25-pounders in the distance, but he was uncertain of the direction the noise was coming from. Keirstead finally reached a farm, where the family fed him and tended to his wounds. The last thing he remembered before passing out was the sound of footsteps at the front door and the sight of three German soldiers entering the house.

When Keirstead recovered consciousness the next day, the three Germans were still there. Before passing out again, he realized that they were deserters, who were just as anxious as he to reach the Canadian lines. Then one of the Italians ventured out, returning some time later with an Irish Jeep. The unconscious Keirstead was rescued without even knowing it.

Back at the ditch, John Wentworth and Charlie Stevens were having a rough time. Both of Wentworth's legs were broken, and Stevens had four bullets in the back. Propped up against their Sherman, they lay there in silent agony for two days before they were joined by Keith Fraser, who had waited that long before scrambling out from underneath his tank. When Fraser spotted his fellow Hussars, he hurried to their aid, treating them with sulfa powder and morphine. After burying Trooper Hilckey, he dug a hole in the side of the embankment where they could hide. The ditch was shelled occasionally, usually by Canadian guns; this was the one opportunity for the severely injured Stevens to scream his lungs out.

Fraser tried a number of times to go for help, but he was driven back by machine-gun fire. "I'll never know why the Germans didn't come and take us," he shrugged afterwards. "God knows, they knew we were there."

By the fifth day of their ordeal, Stevens was usually unconscious. Fraser was knocked out by a shell burst. When he awoke, he administered the last of the morphine to Wentworth, then they both fell asleep. They were awakened by the Perth patrol that stumbled onto them.

They were soon on their way to medical treatment. Unfortunately, Charlie Stevens did not survive; he died a few days later. But both John Wentworth and Howard Keirstead recovered, although the major spent several months in hospital. And Keith Fraser went to Buckingham Palace, where he was presented with the Military Medal by King George for displaying "the highest devotion to duty" for staying with his wounded comrades.[30]

3

The Canadians stormed Coriano ridge when Wednesday, 13 September, was an hour old.

The attack was backed by seven hundred guns, every piece of artillery the Eighth Army could muster. It was a two-pronged operation, beginning at 2300 hours on 12 September, when the British 1st Armoured Division, bolstered by British and Indian infantry, struck the south end of the ridge. Then, with the defenders distracted by that blow, the Fifth Canadian

Armoured Division attacked the north end. The work of the gunners was invaluable. During the days leading up to the attack, the artillery had fired a complex and confusing program of harassing and destructive fire along and around the ridge. Some of the shells contained propaganda leaflets, and several Germans deserted with these scraps of paper in their pockets. Aerial bombardment also took its toll on the enemy's nerves.

Night operations always contain an element of risk, and this one proved to be no exception. The Cape Breton Highlanders and Perth Regiment led the initial assault, behind a creeping barrage. But the battle swiftly degenerated into confusion. The young Cape Breton lieutenant, Bill Matheson, who was among the first to reach the crest of the Coriano ridge, says the confused situation actually worked to his advantage:

> I thought at the beginning of the battle that I was very fortunate to be the reserve platoon of one of the two reserve companies. We weren't too far beyond the start line, however, when it became obvious that something had gone awry. Our wireless radio sets never were worth a great deal in battle, and our set went "out" earlier than usual. We found out afterwards that somone had called for a "repeat" of the artillery support, so we walked right into the barrage and walked up to the objective in it.
>
> How it happened is absolutely inexplicable, but both our forward companies and the two forward platoons of my own company got completely astray, so that my platoon became the leading element of the battalion and the only one that reached the objective. When our barrage lifted we found the Germans completely disorganized and retreating into Coriano village and their reverse-slope positions.[31]

Matheson was in an uncomfortable position, holding the entire battalion front with just his own twenty-two-man platoon. Yet he lost only one man here (the stretcher-bearer, ironically enough, wounded in the foot by shell fragments). He sent a runner across the valley to the Highlanders' headquarters, which replied with word that help was on the way and that it was Matheson's job to sort out the platoons and companies as they straggled in and to put them in their proper places. This he did, and by dawn the Highlanders, and the Perths on their left, were secure on the ridge.[32]

The Irish Regiment of Canada, passing through them to take the village of Coriano, was soon involved in a street battle as vicious and deadly as Ortona. Shermans of the 8th Hussars made one foray into Coriano, losing one tank, but when it became evident that the narrow streets precluded effective use of their firepower, they pulled back to the outskirts and let the infantry go to it. The Germans, said one Hussar, "had some damnably clever positions dug into the cellars of houses, places we couldn't get at with our tank guns. It was tough to have to sit there and watch them nail one infantryman after another and not be able to do anything about it. We could fire but it didn't do much good. Then you'd see a Canadian making a break from one place to another. There'd be a burst of fire and, like as not, he'd go down."[33]

The fighting in Coriano lasted all day long and through the night. Thursday morning, 14 September, found the rubble-choked village strangely quiet: the Germans had pulled out, leaving the Canadians in complete control of Coriano ridge. The enemy had left behind a Mark IV tank, in perfect condition; the explosive charge that was supposed to destroy it failed to detonate, and the Hussars later presented the tank to General Hoffmeister. The Irish had captured sixty prisoners in the course of the fighting in the village, but the total should have been far higher. "A big bunch of Gerries [sic] who should have been our prisoners surrendered instead to the British off to our left. Their surrender was part of the battle of Coriano. They'd been in the town."[34]

Coriano ridge cost the Eleventh Brigade 210 casualties. The heaviest toll was incurred by the Cape Breton Highlanders, who lost eighty-five men, including twenty-two dead. "It was a hard fight," Sir Oliver Leese later said of Coriano, "and a decisive action in the battle."[35]

With its left flank secured, the First Canadian Division was free to launch its attack across the Marano.

After a cool, clear night, Thursday, 14 September, turned into another exceedingly hot day. The Third Brigade (temporarily commanded by the First Division's chief staff officer, Lieutenant-Colonel Pat Bogert, in place of Paul Bernatchez, who had been injured in a flying accident a few days earlier) put two battalions into action during the morning, the West Nova Scotia and Royal 22nd regiments.

Both battalions had difficulty getting across the Marano in the face of heavy fire. However, the West Novas managed to capture a bridge, wired for demolition but intact, and when the Van Doos forced a crossing to the right, they pushed towards the brigade objective, an oblique ridge topped by the villages of San Lorenzo in Correggiano and San Martino in Monte l'Abate.

Disaster awaited both units. The Nova Scotians, moving against San Lorenzo, had to cross a slope which "was utterly bare except for a scatter of young olive trees from which the leaves had been blasted by shell-fire." The British tanks accompanying them were knocked out one by one, but the infantry used the cover of smoke and dust to reach the outskirts of the village, perched on the crest of the ridge. But without tank support, they were unable to break into the fortress, and they fell back to regroup.[36]

Further right, the Van Doos endured their "blackest day of the war." To reach the objective, San Martino, at the north end of the ridge, they had to pass San Lorenzo, and the Germans had plenty of firepower to deal with both the West Novas and the French-Canadians. Three times the Royal 22nd tried to cross the naked, sun-baked fields east of the ridge, only to be driven back each time. Finally, they withdrew under the cover of darkness. That day, 14 September, had cost the battalion ninety-three casualties.[37]

A measure of the intensity of the enemy fire is revealed by the sixty casualties suffered by the Carleton and York Regiment, which was not actively engaged during the fourteenth. These losses, which included the commanding officer, Lieutenant-Colonel E. D. "Dick" Danby, who was wounded, were almost the same as the battalion's toll in its brilliant break-through at the Hitler Line.[38]

The West Novas, however, persisted in their efforts to get into San Lorenzo. The battalion commander, Ron Waterman, drove up in his carrier to direct operations personally. Although he had no more tanks, he ordered another assault at 2000 hours. It failed.

He ordered yet another attempt, at 0230 the next morning. It failed, too.

Waterman ordered them to do it again, after daylight on the fifteenth. The fourth assault on San Lorenzo was launched at 0830, this time with tank support. The Nova Scotians were not to be denied, but it took them most of the day to take the battered village. Within an hour, C Company had lost every one of its officers; within two hours, the attack had seemingly failed, despite the excellent smoke screen laid down by the Canadian gunners. The tanks were unable to get past the deadly fire of the enemy's self-propelled guns, and the infantrymen were pinned down by the machine-guns in the houses lining the crest of the ridge. But the West Novas brought forward their own 6-pounder anti-tank guns, hauled them up the bullet-swept slope, and blasted the Germans out of their positions. Having gained a toehold, they fought their way into San Lorenzo; by 1830, it was reported secure.

It had been a notable achievement. To take the heavily defended village, the West Novas had fought for forty hours. But it was their last battle under Colonel Waterman. The next day, Major Frank Hiltz took over the battalion and Waterman was summoned to a meeting with the divisional commander, Chris Vokes. Vokes knew only too well that, under Waterman, the West Novas had clinched victory at the Hitler Line in May. But their performance at the Gothic Line had fallen far below expectations; here, too, they had failed to measure up to their own high standards. After investigating, Vokes came to the painful conclusion that "proper leadership of the West Novas had broken down." He hated to do it, but he relieved Waterman of his command.[39]

A career soldier, Ron Waterman was a victim of the system. Nine months in command of an infantry battalion had burned him out. If anything, it was remarkable that he lasted as long as he did, because it was the most demanding position on the battlefield. Senior officers and their staffs were mainly concerned with planning and preparing battles, and lower-ranking officers led their men into the fight. Battalion commanders did all that, and more, in a seemingly never-ending cycle. "The Allies learned something from the war in Italy," says Tom Gilday, who commanded a battalion in the First Special Service Force. "After that, in northwest Europe, they wouldn't let a battalion commander command for more than six months, because they knew he would be pretty well fagged out by then."[40]

While the West Novas were slugging it out in San Lorenzo, the Van Doos were having success further north. Midway between the villages at either end of the ridge stood Palazzo des Vergers, a "balustraded mansion of 700 rooms, with its deep cellarage providing ample protection for head-quarters staffs, and its flat roof giving long perspectives over the surrounding country."[41] Lieutenant-Colonel Jean Allard selected this as his first objective, after which the battalion would drive along the ridge to take San Martino. The attack was launched at 1450 hours, and once again, the British tanks gave German anti-tank gunners valuable target practice, and burning hulks soon dotted the bare, flat fields.

But the fast-moving Van Doos "were extraordinary," according to Allard; "nothing could stop them." They captured the mansion in less than an hour, and headed for San Martino. Despite fierce machine-gun fire, the French-Canadians prevailed, thanks largely to the bravery of one man, Sergeant Yvon Piuze. When C Company was pinned down by heavy fire halfway up the slope, a trio of Van Doos raced ahead by themselves. Two were quickly shot, but the third, Piuze, picked up a Bren gun and raced through the enemy bullets to wipe out a machine-gun post, then a second. He was killed while attacking another nest, but his rampage gave the French-Canadians the opening they needed, and they charged into San Martino, capturing it shortly after 1700 hours. Piuze was recommended for the Victoria Cross; he did not get it, Allard maintains, "only because the authorities failed to recognize the importance and valour of his action."[42]

Unfortunately, a careless error robbed the Canadians of their just rewards. General Vokes ordered Graeme Gibson's Second Brigade up to San Lorenzo–San Martino to embark on the next stage of the multi-phase Rimini operation. The Second Brigade was to debouch from San Martino and push nine hundred yards north to the railway embankment overlooking the Ausa; this would serve as the start line for the subsequent assault on the Rimini Line. Things were looking rosy for the Canadian corps during the night of 15–16 September, until the Seaforth Highlanders of Canada relieved the Van Doos at San Martino. Either the French-Canadians moved out too quickly, or the Seaforths took over the wrong positions (no one seems to know for sure what went wrong), but San Martino was left vacant for a short time – long enough for fifty paratroopers to slip back into the village. It would take three days of heavy fighting to recapture San Martino.

The Seaforths soon found that the paratroopers planned to fight to the bitter end. There were perhaps a dozen houses in San Martino, but each "had been transformed into a pillbox and in the cellars concrete shelters had been built which were impervious to all but the heaviest plunging fire."[43] The Seaforths attacked the next afternoon, behind a powerful artillery bombardment, but to no avail; only a handful of Seaforths broke into the village, after most of the tanks were knocked out. By 1600 hours, after a battle which "almost rivalled Ortona for bitterness," the Seaforths had been driven back.[44]

In the hope that darkness might give them the upper hand, they tried twice more after midnight. These efforts merely added to the casualty toll. The battalion's ninety casualties were the most in a single day since the Hitler Line. Parties collected the dead and wounded by the light of burning haystacks and buildings.[45]

A company of Van Doos had better going on the left of the Seaforths, capturing the hamlet of Belvedere, on an outcropping from the main ridge, southwest of San Martino. But San Martino was the key; unless and until it could be captured, the First Division could not close up to the Rimini Line. The 48th Highlanders of Canada learned to their regret just how dangerous it was to try to get past the north end of the ridge. The Toronto battalion tried twice, on 16 September and again the following day. These efforts resulted in eighty-five casualties, with precious little in the way of results.[46]

San Martino was not the only trouble spot. On the left of the Canadians, v Corps was lagging far behind in mountainous terrain. The British 4th Division, under Canadian command, was having difficulty with the high ground near the border of the Republic of San Marino; these heights commanded the Canadian approaches to the Rimini Line. Until they were taken, there could be no assault on the enemy fortifications. But there was also a problem on the right, where a major battle was raging across and around the airfield south of Rimini.

The airfield was the objective of the 3rd Greek Mountain Brigade. The

Greeks, strengthened by New Zealand tanks and Canadian anti-tank guns and mortars, had been assigned to the coastal flats, rather than to the mountains for which they were trained, because it was mistakenly assumed that the fighting would be easier here. The Rimini airfield proved to be anything but easy. The ground was perfectly flat, of course, giving the Germans vast fields of fire for their automatic weapons. Artillery fire directed by observation posts at San Martino and San Fortunato added to the attackers' troubles.

When the Greeks were stopped at the edge of the airfield, The Royal Canadian Regiment entered the fray during the morning of 16 September. It was an auspicious debut, thanks to Corporal N. J. McMahon. As D Company worked its way forward, McMahon's section was pinned by machine-gun fire from a nearby house. The corporal jumped up and led his men in a wild charge; breaking into the house, they killed twelve Germans and captured two others. McMahon personally accounted for half the enemy dead, and was awarded the Distinguished Conduct Medal for his heroism. For the rest of that day, and the next, the Royal Canadians "inched forward."[47]

The Greeks caused almost as many problems as the Germans. The difficulties of working with them were almost insurmountable, according to the acting RCR commander, Strome Galloway. "We couldn't speak Greek and they couldn't speak English – at least not well enough to know what was really meant." As a result, the Greek brigade stopped at the southern edge of the airfield, instead of advancing along the north side and covering the Canadians. "They left our right flank open," insists Galloway, "and that was one reason we lost so many men." The RCR suffered ninety casualties before conquering the airfield.[48]

By the afternoon of 17 September, General Burns was growing concerned about the slow progress across the Canadian corps' front. He summoned two of his divisional commanders, Chris Vokes and the Britisher, Dudley Ward, to discuss their plans. Burns reminded them that he was still hoping to get across the Ausa by the next day. Ward, having received word that a key ridge on his left had finally fallen, assured the Canadian commander that he was prepared to attempt a crossing that night.

The situation on the First Canadian Division's front was not so happy. Unlike Ward, Vokes was unable to offer any assurances about getting over the Ausa on the eighteenth. He knew that nothing could be done until San Martino had been captured and his brigades had moved up to the Rimini railway line. Burns took him aside for a private chat. Was he sure that the First Division could keep going? If not, Burns was prepared to commit the

2nd New Zealand Division, "which was so strong in armour that it could practically rate as an armoured division." Vokes would not hear of it.[49]

Events on Monday, 18 September, did little to enhance Vokes's position. Finesse had not worked thus far; the divisional commander decided to try brute force. While the First Brigade, with the 48th Highlanders and the RCR, fought towards Rimini, Vokes moved up fresh troops for the main thrust west of San Martino. The weary Seaforths were relieved by the Loyal Edmonton Regiment, which would clear troublesome San Martino, enabling Princess Patricia's Canadian Light Infantry to reach the railway embankment. Brigadier Gibson was given the First Brigade's Hasty Ps as a reserve formation. Attacking on the left, the Third Brigade would lead with the Carleton and Yorks, with the Van Doos and West Novas passing through to the Ausa.

The Eddies fared poorly in their attack on San Martino. Two companies supported by five British tanks attacked at 0600 hours. "The enemy allowed us to get down into the bottom of the gully . . . and then opened up with a terrific fire," Captain John Dougan recounted. "He had the gully absolutely covered – snipers, MGs, a tank on the right, one on the left. . . . We stayed there from 0600 to 0930 hours, and all that time his fire never let up."[50] The Eddies, fifty-eight fewer in number, withdrew under a smoke screen.[51]

But their sacrifice was not in vain. By distracting the paratroopers in San Martino, the Edmontons gave the Patricias a fighting chance to advance to the railway. It was a cloudy morning, but the infantry and their tanks provided fine targets for enemy gunners as they crossed the fields and vineyards on the river flats. Each step of the way, they were under fire from almost every direction. Half the tanks were knocked out. Out of two companies (127 strong), only sixty men under Major Colin McDougall got close to the objective, digging in within two hundred yards of the embankment. "How anyone survived the enemy fire directed from San Martino behind us and San Fortunato ahead is a miracle," says PPCLI Lieutenant Syd Frost.[52]

The Patricias' success, limited though it was, endangered the line of retreat for San Martino's defenders. Patrols of the 48th Highlanders entered the battered little village that night to find that it had been abandoned. They discovered an underground strongpoint that defied belief: its five-foot-thick concrete walls could protect a hundred men; three long tunnels led to observation points equipped with high-powered telescopes, which offered a perfect view of the entire Canadian sector.[53]

Only the Carleton and Yorks reached the Ausa on 18 September. The New Brunswick battalion, a thousand yards to the left of the PPCLI, moved slowly and steadily. As if the enemy fire were not heavy enough, the Carletons were bombed and strafed by their own aircraft.

By 0910 hours, the leading elements of the battalion had crossed the railway embankment and reached the river. Here the Carletons were pinned down by machine-gun and artillery fire. Despite surprisingly light losses (twenty-six by day's end), Major Jack Ensor, the acting commander, reported that the Ausa "was a tank obstacle, and held in strength and could not be cleared without 75% casualties." Ensor had his men dig in along the rail embankment.[54]

Although only one battalion had made it to the Ausa, the situation held some promise. Heartened by the report from the Carletons, General Vokes decided to exploit their success. Finally displaying some of his characteristic drive, which had been noticeably absent since his brother's death, Vokes ordered Graeme Gibson's Second Brigade "to take a short breather"[55] and transferred the Hasty Ps to Pat Bogert's Third Brigade, which would cross the river that very night.

The Ausa's steep banks posed an obstacle to tanks but, according to historian George Stevens, "a broad jumper could cross it dry-shod,"[56] and that is what the sturdy New Brunswickers of the Carleton and York Regiment did after dark on 18 September. Despite heavy shelling, there were no casualties as two companies worked their way over the Ausa and established a bridgehead.[57] Behind them, the engineers matched the Carletons' efficiency by constructing a tank crossing: bulldozers carved out the banks, while an Ark bridge, the first used by Canadians, was installed nearby. The Ark, designed to bridge narrow streams, was a turretless Churchill tank which carried treadway tracks. When the tank was parked in midstream, the tracks were spread fore and aft to either bank.

Two more battalions passed through the bridgehead at dawn on 19 September. The West Novas and the Hasty Ps, both supported by the 48th Royal Tanks, hoped to surprise the enemy on the ridge beyond. The attackers had little trouble reaching their initial objective, Route 22, the Rimini–San Marino highway, which became the start line for the attack on the heights that loomed beyond. At 0630 hours, a powerful bombardment signalled the second phase of the advance. Neither unit got much farther than the lower slopes. The West Novas ran into paratroopers; after a struggle that lasted for several hours, they were forced back to the road, having lost sixty-three men.[58] The Hasty Ps almost reached the top of the ridge before being driven back by heavy fire. Lieutenant-Colonel Don Cameron believed that the operation could have succeeded with a little more preparation. "There was no time for a recce," he later wrote, "and none of the Company officers had seen the ground in day-light."[59]

Vokes was undaunted. That afternoon he conferred with his brigadiers and prepared a full-scale night assault on the ridge. The main thrust would be made by the Second Brigade's Loyal Eddies and Seaforth Highlanders, supported on the left by the Van Doos of Pat Bogert's Third Brigade. An elaborate artillery program was prepared at short notice by the divisional gunner, Bill Ziegler, who had at his disposal the artillery of both Canadian divisions, as well as of the British 4th and 2nd New Zealand. Ziegler and his staff devised a brilliant fire plan which "consisted of a series of linear targets in three diverging lanes – a lane a thousand yards wide for each attacking company. These targets lifted in groups, as in a barrage, with the infantry able to control each lift as required." Each assault company would maintain a wall of shell fire six hundred yards ahead.[60]

The Canadians would also use artificial moonlight, their first experience with it in Italy. Artificial moonlight utilized anti-aircraft searchlights and had been introduced that summer in Normandy. British formations had employed it during various phases of the Gothic Line operation. Normally, night operations required a full moon, so that there was some light; artificial moonlight, General Burns noted, made night attacks possible at any time. "In addition to helping the attackers find their way," he later wrote, "it showed up the defenders' movements, and often dazzled them, making it all the more difficult to bring the attackers under fire."[61]

The failed assault by the Third Brigade had one beneficial effect, since it provided a detailed look at the defences that anchored the Rimini Line. From the north end, where the hamlet of La Grazie was nestled, a mile from Rimini, the 470-foot ridge ran in a southeasterly direction for more than two miles. Midway along the crest stood the villages of Covignano and San Fortunato, which lent its name to the ridge, and a pair of mansions, Palazzo Paradiso and Villa Belvedere. Behind, three spurs protruded northwestward like fingers, overlooking the Marecchia. The front slopes were "honeycombed with dugouts, and a number of emplacements contained Panther turrets," according to historian Gerry Nicholson. "The defenders had the further protection afforded by a winding sunken road which meandered along the length of the ridge, years of travel having worn it down in places to a depth of 20 feet between banks of earth and shale."[62]

The Van Doos went in first. The two assault companies, moving in single file, worked their way up the slope. They left their supporting British tanks of the 145th Regiment at the foot of the ridge, to ensure surprise and to preserve them for the vital consolidation phase, when the Van Doos would be vulnerable to a counter-attack. In a series of short, sharp clashes, they fought their way towards the crest, by-passing the strongest opposition in order to conserve their strength for the main objective, Villa Belvedere, six hundred yards from San Fortunato.

The mansion fell, together with ninety-five prisoners. "At that time it seemed evident that the enemy was taken by surprise," reads the battalion's report, "because they themselves had blown up one of their tanks and an infantry gun." Colonel Allard committed his remaining two companies, and the Van Doos spent the rest of the night mopping up the area, filling the villa's spacious basement with more than two hundred prisoners. In addition, over fifty German corpses were later counted in the vicinity.[63] The cost to the Van Doos: one dead and "two or three wounded," according to a proud Allard, who was rewarded with a bar to the Distinguished Service Order he had won at the end of December.[64]

This stunning success was equalled by the western Canadians of the Second Brigade. Brigadier Gibson's plan called for the Loyal Edmontons to silently infiltrate the enemy positions atop the ridge and take a road junction on the spur beyond it. That done, Vancouver's Seaforths were to follow, swing right, and clear the north end of the ridge from San Fortunato to La Grazie.

The Eddies, after reconnoitring the ground during the evening, started forward at 2100 hours. Engineers accompanying them cleared mines along the way, and the operation appeared to be going smoothly until D Company clashed with some surprised Germans. In the ensuing confusion, the company dispersed, and Major J. H. McDougall arrived at the top of the ridge with only sixteen men. The area was alive with Germans, and the major deployed his little force along the sunken road to await reinforcements.[65]

The enemy arrived first. The clanking roar warned McDougall's party that a tank was coming, followed by infantry. The Eddies held their fire until the tank passed, then wiped out the Germans behind it. The tank rumbled off, but returned soon afterwards, in search of its infantry protection. Sergeant H. O. W. Powell laid a string of Hawkins anti-tank grenades across the road, then readied his PIAT. He might have been a little intimidated had he realized that this was no ordinary tank. It was a Tiger, a fifty-six-ton monstrosity that was virtually impervious to pea-shooters like Powell's PIAT. The Tiger was immobilized when it ran over a grenade, which blew off a track. Powell casually looked for weak points, then fired two bombs at close range. The shaken crew surrendered.[66]

With the Eddies off to a good start, the Seaforths received the word to move out at 0430. Both assault companies made steady progress, although one captured so many prisoners "that its mobility was embarrassed." By dawn, the Seaforths were on their objectives, and the support company, C, hurried up to reinforce the ridge. Major Haworth Glendinning, the company commander, was later awarded the Distinguished Service Order for his skilful leadership. At the cost of only two casualties, C Company took 115 prisoners, boosting the battalion's capture count for the day to 214.[67]

With fighting raging on either side of them, the Edmontons forged ahead as dawn approached on Wednesday, 20 September. It was a cloudy, cool morning with a promise of rain, but most were too busy to notice. B Company had secured an important crossroads, code-named "Bovey," and Captain John Dougan led his C Company through to the village at the end of the spur, San Lorenzo in Monte. This vital position, which commanded the entire reverse slope of the ridge, was undefended, but Dougan's men occupied the village "just in time, for as we got in we saw that Jerry was coming up to do likewise. Our Bren gunners had a grand time against them, mowing them down right and left," the captain reported. Another large counter-attack developed twenty minutes later, with the Germans approaching under the cover of vegetation. Dougan called for artillery support, and the Canadian gunners broke up the attack.[68]

Help was on the way. While British tanks were having trouble getting past the sunken road atop the ridge, the Edmontons' second-in-command, Major Jim Stone, whose front-line leadership would be rewarded with the Distinguished Service Order, had begun bringing up the battalion's 6-pounder anti-tank guns. Commanded by Captain George Brown, these guns inflicted a considerable amount of damage on the enemy tanks and self-propelled guns that were roaming about the ridge. One of Brown's gunners, a Scottish sergeant named Bill Ross, won the Military Medal for his cool work.

By now, Captain Dougan, who would add a bar to the Military Cross he had won in Sicily, faced another problem: his company was running short of ammunition. A surprising solution materialized in the form of a pair of Germans who surrendered and reported that one of their half-tracks was in the valley below. Dougan sent a sergeant to fetch it; despite its Red Cross markings, this vehicle was stocked with a thousand rounds of .303-calibre ammunition, which Dougan distributed to his men.[69]

This half-track was put to good use. The anti-tank captain, George Brown, used his rudimentary German to convince the senior enemy officer that it should evacuate the wounded, both Canadian and German. The catch was that the vehicle needed a German driver, who seemed rather reluctant to get involved. Brown swung a deal with the officer. "If he'll drive that vehicle," said the captain, "we'll send out all the wounded prisoners, and our own wounded. Starting with our own in the first one, then yours next, then ours, until we get them all out." This was agreeable, and the carrier had made three trips and was returning for another load of wounded when it was hit by a shell; the German driver was killed.[70]

The view from the ridge was remarkable. "We could see for miles," recalls the MM-winning sergeant, Bill Ross.[71] All morning long, the Edmontons used their vantage points to pick out unbelievable targets for the artillery. Before noon, Captain Dougan reported, "I counted 24 [self-propelled] guns or tanks which rolled by our position at a distance of 400 to 1,000 yards. I also saw a couple of companies of German infantry moving off to the flanks, and one isolated company marching towards the church where we were." Sixty Germans attempted to run the gauntlet under the cover of a white flag; the ruse did not work.[72]

The Eddies could be pleased with themselves. Combined with the fine feats on either flank by the Van Doos and Seaforths, their attack had been decisive. The regimental history ranks San Fortunato with Ortona as "the proudest emblazure on the Loyal Edmonton colours."[73] Their 55 casualties were offset by the estimated 200 Germans killed or wounded in this sector, with an additional 110 prisoners.

Even the weary West Novas helped out, attacking between the Eddies and Van Doos. Under the cover of darkness, Major Frank Hiltz, the acting commander, deployed his companies below Palazzo Paradiso, just down the road from Villa Belvedere. While two companies attacked the mansion frontally, the other two outflanked it. By 1100 hours, the Nova Scotians had prevailed. More than two hundred prisoners attested to the strength of the garrison.[74]

The corps commander, General Burns, was particularly pleased with the First Division's hard-fought victory. He marvelled at the durability of the assault troops, pointing out that the battle had been won by battalions which "had suffered repulse and heavy casualties in the actions against San Martino and in the plain they now looked back upon."[75]

It now remained for the Canadians to clinch their victory by getting across the Marecchia and breaking onto the flat, broad plain that lay so tantalizingly on the other side.

Early Wednesday afternoon, with the disheartened and disorganized Germans still falling back from the ruined Rimini Line, the Second Brigade attempted to pursue the defeated enemy. Rain was falling as the PPCLI crossed the ridge and descended into the valley of the Marecchia, only to be checked by powerful Tiger tanks at the crossroads north of San Lorenzo. This stubborn rearguard checked the Canadian advance, and it was dawn on 21 September before the Patricias reached the Marecchia. By afternoon, the battalion had established a firm bridgehead, in preparation for the First Division's relief by the 2nd New Zealand Division.

Rimini's fall was now a foregone conclusion. While the rest of the division punched through the San Fortunato defences and across the Marecchia, the 48th Highlanders and the Royal Canadian Regiment had fought an almost forgotten battle to capture the coastal town. Between Allied air raids and German demolitions, Rimini was in ruins. It was estimated that 75 per cent of its buildings had been destroyed or damaged beyond repair, including many historical sites. But two major landmarks somehow survived: the Arco d'Augusto, the Roman triumphal arch dating back to 27 B.C., and a bridge, the Ponte di Tiberio, constructed in A.D. 27.

During the night of 20–21 September, the sound of explosions signalled the enemy's withdrawal, and patrols of the RCR and 48th cautiously entered ruined Rimini. But they were ordered to halt: the honour of liberating Rimini was to go to the Greek brigade, which entered the town in triumph during the morning of the twenty-first. Unable to find a Union Jack or Canadian ensign to fly beside their own flag, the Greeks hoisted the banner of an auxiliary service organization. This was meagre consolation to the RCR, which felt cheated. "The Greeks paraded ceremonially, the Canadians licking their wounds in the background," Strome Galloway recalls. "Later we read in the newspapers from home the annoying headline, HEROIC GREEK BRIGADE TAKES RIMINI. What price glory?"[76]

Friday, 22 September, marked the last day of action for the First Division. Casualties had mounted steadily as the Patricias awaited the arrival of the New Zealanders who would take their place. By now, young Lieutenant Syd Frost had begun to doubt that he or any of his seventeen-man platoon would be alive to greet the Kiwis. Deployed around a sturdy *casa*, the Patricias had been pounded by a terrifying bombardment from dawn on the twenty-second. The five-room house was systematically destroyed, but Frost decided that it was the safest place around, so he gathered his platoon inside. The shelling continued, and soon the house was reduced to just two intact rooms, presenting Frost with a dilemma. Should he split the platoon in two, in an effort to minimize his losses, or keep everyone together in the room they were in? Relying on his "phenomenal luck at poker," he kept his platoon together. Shortly afterwards, a shell smashed the other room to pieces.[77]

Frost was lucky, indeed. At one point, he bent over to speak to one of his wounded men, and an armour-piercing shell punched through the wall where he had been standing just moments before. By noon, the situation was desperate. Then, faintly, over the explosions rocking the house, Frost detected the clanking of approaching tanks. They were Churchills of the New Zealand division, much to Frost's delight.[78]

In 1985, Syd Frost returned to the *casa*. He was pleased to find that it had been rebuilt by the owners, who treated him to a meal of "the best spaghetti I had tasted in years," washed down with *vino* of "considerable authority." It was served in the same room where he and his platoon had come so close to death that September day in 1944.[79]

The battles from the Gothic Line to the Marecchia had seen the heaviest sustained fighting by the Canadians in Italy. This unfortunate fact is reflected in the casualty toll. From 25 August until 22 September, the First Division had sustained 2,511 battle casualties, including 626 killed. In addition, 1,005 were evacuated because of illness. The Fifth Division's losses for the same period totalled 1,385; of that number, 390 were fatalities. "Canadian losses," states the official history, "were heavier than for any period of equal length before or after, during the Italian campaign."[80]

"The cutting edge has been blunted," a saddened Chris Vokes reported of the First Division's state. The bulk of the casualties had, typically, been borne by the combat units, the artillery, armour, and especially the infantry. Worse, according to Tommy Burns, was the fact that "the losses had been heaviest among the leaders of sections, platoons and companies, trained and experienced on the battlefield. Reinforcements could replace these leaders physically, but could not replace their battle-craft, their knowledge of what could be done in the conditions of close combat."[81]

Still, Burns had reason to be happy in the last week of September. His eight-stage plan for the capture of Rimini, he wrote, "had been carried out substantially as foreseen," albeit a few days later than planned. The Canadian corps, with the Fifth Armoured and 2nd New Zealand divisions leading, was poised for what Burns hopefully described as "a rapid pursuit of the defeated enemy over ground favourable to the action of armoured forces."[82]

4

"Something unpleasant has happened." That was how Generaloberst Vietinghoff attempted to inform Generalfeldmarschall Kesselring about the loss of the Rimini Line.[83]

Crisis management had reached new heights for the enemy commanders since the beginning of September. First, the Gothic Line was broken, followed by the furious battles beyond the Marano. The fighting at Coriano was worrisome, not so much for the loss of the ridge (which was, after all, merely a delaying position), but for the notable improvements in British and Canadian tactics. A Tenth Army report pointed out that "during the first few days of the attack," the enemy had shown "no hesitancy, but smart follow-through after initial success." And, most important, "enemy armoured formations, particularly Canadian tanks, [are] no longer sensitive to artillery fire, but carry on under heaviest fire concentrations."[84]

The breaking of the Rimini Line seemed to be the end so far as the Germans were concerned. "I have the terrible feelng," Kesselring commented, "that the thing is beginning to slide." The field-marshal, looking at his maps, saw what British and Canadian commanders were seeing – the broad, flat plain to the north, ideal tank country. Not even the weather would cooperate with him. He had been hoping and praying for rain since early September, but he sadly told Vietinghoff on the eighteenth that "there is no promise of a change in weather. The rainy season this year is late by two weeks: this is two weeks past the European mean."[85]

Kesselring's thought was to retreat. A plan had already been drawn up. Code-named *Herbstnebel*, "Autumn Fog," it called for a withdrawal behind the River Po, combined with stubborn delaying actions south of that line. On 23 September, the field-marshal sent his chief of staff to Germany to seek Adolf Hitler's permission to carry out this plan. However, Kesselring was informed that "the Führer, for political, military and administrative reasons, had decided to defend the Apennine front and to hold upper Italy not only until late Autumn, but indefinitely." Hitler considered that "a withdrawal of the front behind the Po might be too much of a shock for the German people." Northern Italy's industrial and agricultural production, he felt, was too valuable to endanger.[86]

As a sign of good faith, Hitler agreed to meet Kesselring's demands for reinforcements. The field-marshal had requested 23,800 men to make good his losses during September; the Führer promised to send 20,000 by the beginning of October.[87]

The fighting in Italy would continue. The Tenth Army's Heinrich von Vietinghoff issued his instructions accordingly. His forces were "not to relinquish one foot of soil to the enemy without inflicting heavy casualties. . . . The enemy's reserves are not inexhaustible. Heavy casualties in particular would press very heavily on him. The battles of Ortona and Cassino have demonstrated this."[88]

On the other side of the world, Winston Churchill was making another bid to keep alive his cherished Italian campaign.

After several efforts, the prime minister had managed to talk the Americans into another conference to discuss strategy. On 12 September, Churchill and President Roosevelt, together with their key advisers, met for the second time in Quebec. The four-day conference, code-named "Octagon," was their first meeting since Cairo in December 1943. Octagon turned out to be the last Anglo-American strategic conference of the war.

Things were going exceedingly well for the Allies in early September 1944. In the east, the Soviet juggernaut had rolled through Romania and was crushing the German forces in Bulgaria. In northwestern Europe, the British Second Army had liberated Brussels and Antwerp, while the First Canadian Army had begun the thankless task of clearing the Channel ports. The Americans were approaching the German frontier. In Italy, Operation Olive offered impressive possibilities. By now, the attempted assassination of Hitler on 20 July was public knowledge, and there seemed to be good reason to believe that the war was almost over – Christmas, at the latest.

Churchill sailed to Canada aboard the fast ocean liner, *Queen Mary*, determined to ensure that General Alexander was provided with the means to deliver a decisive victory in Italy. The prime minister had just returned to England from the Mediterranean, where he had viewed Dragoon, the invasion of southern France, on 15 August, and then had toured the battlefront in Italy. His trip convinced him that he had been right all along. Dragoon, a virtually unopposed landing, had proven to be superfluous; Overlord had contributed to its success, rather than the other way around. On the other hand, Italy offered access to eastern Europe and the possibility of thwarting Soviet designs in that area. Additionally, as C. P. Stacey has written, "Italy was a British sphere of command, and British prestige would hardly have allowed people like Churchill and Alexander to see it become a mere static backwater while Eisenhower's forces marched across North-West Europe to victory."[89]

If Churchill went to the second Quebec Conference expecting another dog-fight with the Americans, he was pleasantly surprised. "In the first flush of victory," notes British historian Arthur Bryant, "allies find it easy to be cordial,"[90] and Quebec proved it. With the European war now certain to end in victory, the lion's share of the discussions concerned the war in the Pacific. The Mediterranean, so long a sore point between the western allies, hardly raised a ripple. The Americans had earlier expressed a desire to close down the Italian campaign as soon as possible, but they readily agreed "that no major units should be withdrawn from Italy until the outcome of General Alexander's present offensive is known."[91]

Churchill also reached a behind-the-scenes decision that affected Italy. At the urging of Sir Alan Brooke, the CIGS, he agreed to transfer the Eighth Army's commander, Sir Oliver Leese, to the Pacific theatre. Brooke considered Leese to be "a serious disappointment. . . . I may be wrong but he gives me the impression of stickiness and lack of thrust." Even the British official history concludes that Leese's overall record was mediocre: "8th Army never lost a battle under his command, nor could it claim a resounding victory."[92]

Leese's departure came too late to save Alexander's offensive. The fine weather lost by the last-minute change of plans that Leese had forced on Alexander could never be recovered. The Fifth Army's campaign, launched north of Florence in the second week of September, had caught the Germans by surprise and had made slow but steady progress, despite Leese's misgivings about mountain fighting. The Fifth Army eventually fell short of its goal, Bologna, simply because it lacked the strength to break the Gothic Line in the centre. Recalling that Alexander's original plan had called for a joint offensive by the two armies in this sector, the British official history contends it almost certainly would have resulted in the decisive victory Churchill sought. Leese's objections led to the Fifth and Eighth armies fighting separate battles and achieving indifferent results, instead of working together.[93]

The celebration over the Canadian-led breakthrough to Rimini was premature and short-lived. Alexander confidently predicted that the Germans would likely retire to the Po, and he warned that, without substantial reinforcements, "we shall have to continue the battle of Italy with about twenty divisions, almost all of which have had long periods of heavy fighting this year, and some for several years, against the twenty German divisions committed to the battle front, with the prospect of four more German divisions, and probably two Italian divisions, joining in the battle at a later stage." Alexander declared that he required a three-to-one superiority in order to achieve "a really decisive success."[94] However, his request was rejected.

Victory carried a substantial price in blood. The Eighth Army's battle casualties, exclusive of sick cases, totalled 14,000. The British were running short of men in every theatre, but the Mediterranean accounted for half of the 42,000-man deficiency, and drastic measures were required. Even before Rimini fell, Alexander's headquarters had been pondering alternatives. Finally, on 22 September, he accepted his staff's proposals. The 1st Armoured Division was to be broken up to provide reinforcements for other formations, and all British infantry battalions would be reduced from four to three companies, with a corresponding reduction in the overall strength of each battalion, from 845, all ranks, to 730.[95]

It was a crisis shared by the Canadians.

Prime Minister William Lyon Mackenzie King was rather pleased with the situation in September 1944. He was basking in the glow of the second Quebec Conference, where he had again rubbed elbows with Churchill and Roosevelt. His controversial family-allowance legislation was on its way to parliamentary approval, and the country at large seemed to be thriving. Although Ottawa had suffered through a sweltering summer, Western Canada had enjoyed ideal weather, reflected in bumper crops of wheat in the Prairie provinces and fruit in British Columbia.

Yet all of this took a back seat to the euphoric war news. There were widespread predictions that the conflict would soon be over. "LOOK FOR COLLAPSE OF REICH BY OCT. 31, trumpeted a headline in the Ottawa *Citizen* on 13 September. Indeed, Ottawa had become the first city in Canada to establish a committee to oversee its victory celebrations.[96] Canadians were taking quiet pride in the part being played by their fighting men. Harry Crerar's First Canadian Army headquarters became operational in Normandy at the end of July; for the first time ever, Canada was represented by a field army (although only half of the forces within it were Canadian). With the three divisions of Guy Simonds's II Corps seeing action during August, the *Citizen* noted on 26 August, "Canada's entire overseas military establishment, the 1st Canadian Army headquarters organization, two corps headquarters, five divisions and two army tank brigades now are in action against the enemy in Italy and France." It was one of the few mentions of the Italian campaign, which had been virtually forgotten by the Canadian news media. Until 6 June and the invasion of Normandy, Italy had been front-page news; after that date, it had been relegated to small items buried on the inside pages of papers from coast to coast.

That was of little concern to Mackenzie King, who exulted in the certainty that the war would end without the need to implement conscription for overseas service. He had taken much abuse over his odd policy of conscripting men for home defence (the conscripts were derisively known as "zombies"), while maintaining an exclusively volunteer overseas army. His own defence minister, Layton Ralston, had declared in the House of Commons as recently as 10 July that Canada had "sufficient reserve general service men to complete our quotas right up to the calendar year end."[97] King could also refer to a 2 August report from Ken Stuart, the chief of staff at CMHQ in London, who stated: "I am satisfied . . . with the general reinforcement situation."[98]

Stuart, so eager to please his political masters that he was nicknamed the "Great Appeaser,"[99] clung to this position in the face of contradictory information. On 4 August, General Crerar signalled CMHQ that he was nineteen hundred infantrymen short of his requirements in Normandy. "I consider this the most serious problem of Cdn Army at the moment," Crerar stated, but Stuart did not share his concern. "The present situation," he explained in a 26 August cable to the chief of the General Staff, J. C. Murchie, "is not a manpower problem in the true sense. We have the men. It is not a problem of general supply. It is a problem of detailed distribution."[100]

And then Conn Smythe blew the whistle. The forty-nine-year-old sports entrepreneur from Toronto had won the Military Cross during the Great War; commanding an anti-aircraft battery in this war, he had been wounded in Normandy in late July. While in hospital, Smythe was able to compare notes with officers of other units, particularly infantry. They all told the same story: casualties were being replaced by half-trained young men who had little chance of survival on the battlefield. Smythe arrived back in Canada and promptly informed George McCullagh, the publisher of Toronto's *Globe and Mail*, that some of the reinforcements being sent into action had "never thrown a grenade."[101] McCullagh printed the charges on 19 September, and every newspaper in the country soon carried them. It was "disgraceful," said the *Ottawa Journal* on 20 September: "No official brush-off can dispose of these charges by Major Smythe. They are true or they are not true."

True or untrue, they were timely. Ralston was scheduled to depart on 24 September for a tour of the overseas forces in Italy and France. A proponent of conscription, Ralston was determined to find out for himself just how bad the situation really was. The minister arrived in Naples on 26 September, flying via New York and Casablanca. Before returning to England on 4 October, Ralston would have had no doubt about his course of action.

Having battled its way through the Gothic and Rimini lines and past the bloody Coriano and San Lorenzo–San Martino ridges, I Canadian Corps was in desperate need of men, especially infantrymen. A report for the week ending 23 September showed that the two Canadian divisions were short a thousand men.[102]

The state of the Canadian combat units was alarming. For example, the West Nova Scotia Regiment, which had suffered 252 casualties after crossing the Marano, received only 119 reinforcements, many of them men recovered from previous wounds.[103] According to Bill Matheson, a platoon commander in the Cape Breton Highlanders, the shortage was most obvious among the riflemen. "A soldier deficit at the section level," he writes, "made a lot more work for the remaining private soldiers, and one missing was very noticeable; more than one missing was catastrophic."[104]

Unfortunately, there was a job to be done, a war to be won. Full-strength or half-strength, says the RCR's Strome Galloway, there was no change in tactical assignments. "Companies of 50 were given the same tasks, related to the terrain, as though they went into action with 100-plus men; in the same way platoons of 15 were expected to do the job as though they consisted of 30 or more men. 'Realism' was seldom a factor at higher headquarters!"[105]

Not only were battalions under strength, but the newcomers were little more than cannon fodder. The Cape Breton Highlanders went into action on Coriano ridge the day after receiving a batch of reinforcements. Bill Matheson remembers digging in with his platoon on the ridge, and one of the new men came up to him with a Bren gun in hand. "The fellow beside me dropped this," said the rookie, "and I thought it might be useful, so I picked it up and here it is." When Matheson pointed out where to set it up, the young man gaped at him and replied, "I don't know how to fire one of these." Later, fearing a German counter-attack, Matheson called for the

PIAT. Another recent arrival ran up with it and flopped beside him: "Is this what you're looking for?"[106]

To send an untrained man into battle was to give him a virtual death sentence. "I can remember one poor little bugger who came up to us," says Bert Hoskin, then a company commander in British Columbia's Westminster Regiment. "He was dead in an hour. He didn't know how to take advantage of cover."[107]

The difficulty was that there just was not enough time to train people properly. Reinforcements were needed immediately, and they had to be processed faster than the system allowed. An emergency training centre was established at Avellino, nestled in the mountains thirty miles from Naples. The adjutant here was Lieutenant Duncan Fraser, a Cape Breton Highlander who had been wounded in late May in the Liri valley. Fraser recalls his despair when faced with giving fuzzy-cheeked youngsters what amounted to a ten- or fourteen-day survival course:

> Some of them were totally unacquainted with the rifle, grenades were a total and terrifying mystery, the light machine-gun was a mechanical monster, they had no knowledge of map reading or of the techniques of fieldcraft or of section and platoon movement in battle formation. We had scarcely time to do more than demonstrate the weapons and techniques they needed to function as infantry soldiers before the reinforcement depot was ordered to send them forward.[108]

And now James Layton Ralston was going to learn all of this first-hand. Ralston was greeted by Brigadier Eric Haldenby, who commanded the reinforcement depot in Italy. The brigadier's message was short but not sweet. "One month or less will finish the reinforcements even if we use specialists," he informed the minister.[109] When Ralston challenged the veracity of the figures, Haldenby hotly replied: "Do you want some figures to simply back up the government's stand, or do you want the truth?"[110]

Ralston toured the combat units, at rest and at the front. He went out of his way to visit the Cape Breton Highlanders, the successor to the Great War's 85th Battalion, which Ralston had commanded. One of Ralston's encounters was the stuff of legend. Inspecting Toronto's 48th Highlanders, he was introduced to William Crossley, the regimental sergeant-major. Crossley, who was nicknamed "Bulldog Bill," bluntly told the minister that he had no business sending out poorly trained recruits. "In fact, sir," he added, "they know little more than a man straight out of a Yonge St. tavern."[111]

By the time Defence Minister Ralston reached London and heard similar stories from the commanders in northwestern Europe, his course was even more clear. "I regret to say that conditions and prospects of which I have learned," he cabled Mackenzie King on 13 October, "will, I feel, necessitate reassessment in light of the future, particularly regarding infantry involving, I fear, grave responsibilities."[112]

King knew what that meant. The cable caused the prime minister "great concern," he told his diary. It was clear that Ralston "was coming back with the intention of making proposals which may involve the whole question of conscription." King braced himself for what Stacey called "the most serious Cabinet crisis of the war."[113]

CHAPTER SIXTEEN

"A Nice Christmas Present"

1

Intent on debouching into the broad valley of the Po, I Canadian Corps poured troops and tanks through the Marecchia bridgehead. General Burns had designated three successive rivers as the main objectives of the coming operations, the Fiumicino, the Savio, and the Ronco, twenty-five miles beyond the Marecchia. Relieving the First Canadian Division during 22 September, the 2nd New Zealand Division set out immediately, pushing along the coastal highway, Route 16.

The next day, Bert Hoffmeister's Fifth Division joined the pursuit. The Canadian armoured formation found itself without a major road; the only other main highway, Route 9 to Bologna, had been allotted to the British V Corps. To reach the Fiumicino, the Fifth had to negotiate two smaller watercourses, the Uso and, two miles further along, the Salto. The division would have to fight almost every step of the way.

Its advance was checked in front of the Uso. The footsloggers of the Princess Louise Dragoon Guards had had to wait for the arrival of their supporting Strathcona Shermans before setting out on the secondary road to San Vito. Leading the Twelfth Brigade, barely a half-mile from their start line, they ran into outposts of the 29th Panzer Grenadier Division in the hamlets of Casale and Variano, hidden among vineyards five hundred yards apart. Heavy artillery and mortar fire raked the Plugs, who were forced to deploy and clear the enemy positions. They were able to use the cover of vine rows, but these also provided refuge for German snipers and interfered with the Shermans by forcing the Strathcona tank commanders to fight with their hatches closed.

By noon, the Plugs were hopelessly pinned down. Their casualties were surprisingly high – six officers and seventy-one other ranks – for such a short fight.[1] The Strathconas' Lieutenant-Colonel Jim McAvity was appalled to find his tanks fighting their way through a "veritable jungle," where every advantage lay with the Germans, who fought with their usual tenacity and skill, "expending lavishly and accurately the ammunition from the dumps built up on [the] line of withdrawal, and employing small groups of infantry and tanks so sited as to bring murderous cross-fire on our advancing infantry."[2]

It marked the beginning of a four-day battle for the Twelfth Brigade and its new commander, Brigadier J. S. Lind, who had succeeded Dan Spry in August, when the latter was made Canada's youngest major-general and transferred to command the Third Canadian Infantry Division in northwestern Europe. It was a rough initiation for the rookie brigadier, as Lind was forced to commit all three of his infantry battalions, along with the Strathconas and Governor-General's Horse Guards to secure a crossing on the Uso. It proved to be costly both in terms of time and of blood: the recently-formed brigade lost 275 killed, wounded, and missing.[3]

There was a sense of betrayal among the black-bereted tank men. The "high-priced help," senior commanders and their staff officers, had blown it again, according to the Strathconas' Colonel McAvity. "All of us . . . had confidently expected to find open, flat country – and conservative estimates beforehand as to the number of days it would take us to reach the Po River did not exceed 12. And now, at the end of the fourth day, we had crossed only the first of the score of rivers and ditches between us and the legendary Po."[4]

Just as the Liri valley had proven to be far rougher than aerial photographs had indicated, so this area was much different than anticipated. According to the corps commander, General Burns:

> A great part of this area was reclaimed marsh, with a network of drainage canals banked high on the sides – and ditches, most of which became tank obstacles when it rained. And it did rain – earlier and more heavily than could have been forecast from the meteorological records. . . .
>
> The soil was a light clay, made slippery by even a light shower. When there was much rain it became so soft that wheeled vehicles and even tanks sank deeply into it and could not move. The only practicable routes for movement of vehicles were the few and indifferently paved roads – and of course, the enemy could readily build a strong defence against armour which was confined to the roads.[5]

After the delay on the Uso, Bert Hoffmeister pulled the Twelfth Brigade out of the line and sent in the Eleventh. The brigadier, Ian Johnston, put two battalions across the Salto during Wednesday, 27 September, the Irish Regiment on the left and the Cape Breton Highlanders on the right. The Salto was no obstacle for the foot soldiers, but tanks and self-propelled guns had to await the construction of Bailey bridges, and the infantry forged ahead on their own. The Irish were the first to reach the Fiumicino,

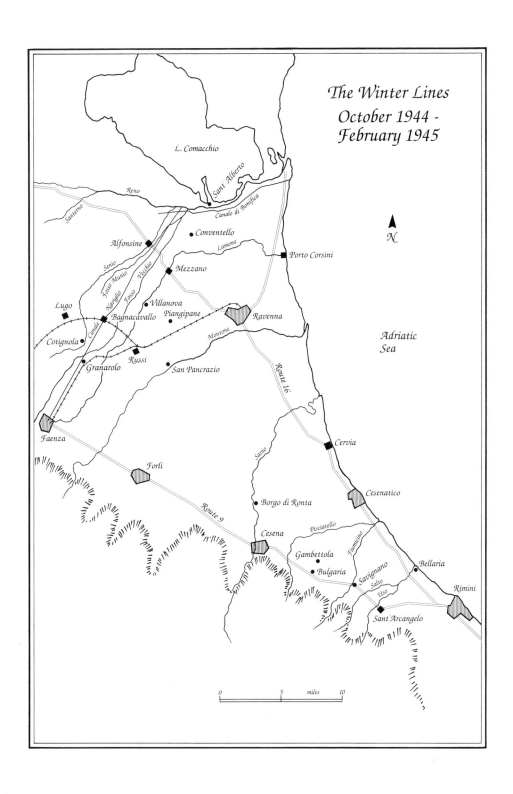

The Winter Lines
October 1944 -
February 1945

one of several rivers in the region reputed to be the legendary Rubicon, which Julius Caesar had crossed twenty centuries earlier.

Unfortunately, the Irish allowed their exuberance to carry them away. During the night, A Company waded the Fiumicino and occupied a road junction three hundred yards beyond. Dawn found them cut off and under attack by German tanks and infantry of the 26th Panzer Division. Reinforcements rushed to the rescue, including B Company of the Irish and a squadron of New Brunswick's 8th Hussars. The Shermans were able to get across the river on the ruins of a blown bridge, and it was here that they met a Tiger tank for the first time. Major Cliff McEwen would never forget it. "The shells just bounced off, like peas off a wall," he later remarked. McEwen lost four tanks before admitting defeat and ordering a withdrawal.[6]

The Hussars watched helplessly as disaster befell the Irish. "We had a grandstand seat," one of them recalled. "Some of us could see the infantry across the river, getting up and then going down when the shells came. And then we could see them in a helpless position with the Germans around them and the Irish with their hands up, surrendering."[7] Fifty-three were taken prisoner. At the crossroads the bodies of one German and nine Canadians were later found; except for a single section left behind to cover the crossing site, A Company had been wiped out.

The Cape Breton Highlanders, on the right, were having troubles of their own. Slowed by machine-gun and sniper fire, they needed two days to fight their way into the village of Fiumicino, which lent its name to the river and where it was reported that the bridge was still intact. By the time Fiumicino fell, on 28 September, the bridge had been long since destroyed.[8]

Further efforts to cross the Fiumicino were washed out – literally. It started raining during the afternoon of the twenty-eighth. The rainfall continued throughout the night; by the next morning, the Fiumicino had been transformed from a meandering stream into a raging torrent thirty feet wide. The bed of the Rubicone had been dry for the past two or three years; practically overnight, it filled with fast-flowing, icy water sixteen feet deep.[9] The Uso and Marecchia rivers underwent similar transformations, with fords being flooded and Bailey bridges swept away. Indeed, the only bridge to survive was the venerable Ponte di Tiberio in Rimini.

In a matter of hours, the Fifth Division's advance had been stopped in its tracks. Remarked the war diary of the 17th Canadian Field Regiment: "Not exactly the romp over the Lombardy Plains that was expected."[10]

2

The rain continued for the first ten days of October. During this period, the Fifth Division could do no more than consolidate its positions on the Fiumicino. The situation facing the Cape Breton Highlanders was typical:

We occupied the houses on the east side of the river and the enemy occupied those on the west side. In many cases we were no more than 100 yards apart. Enemy snipers were very active but we had the greatest success in combatting them with our Piats. It is by no means easy to be certain of the exact point from which a sniper is operating, but we found that a Piat bomb, striking somewhere near, had the desired effect of silencing him one way or another. The bad weather continued and the mud did not improve. The only vehicles that could move at all were jeeps with chains and carriers, and these only with the greatest difficulty.[11]

Behind the lines, there was much activity. It was during this rainy interlude that Defence Minister Ralston made his fateful visit to Italy. Besides entertaining the minister, General Burns met the Eighth Army's new commander, Sir Richard McCreery. At forty-six, the tall, slender McCreery was a highly regarded officer who had commanded the British X Corps since Salerno. Historian John Strawson describes him as a man "who combined great love of and skill with horses, a fine intellect and an almost eccentric personality."[12] While Burns has not recorded his thoughts on Oliver Leese's departure, he must have been glad to see him go. Moreover, he knew McCreery well and would have hoped to get along with him better than with Leese. The only problem, from Burns's point of view, was that McCreery was another member of the exclusive "Eighth Army club," that "crowd of breezy, huntin'-n-shootin' extroverts," as historian Bill McAndrew puts it. This in particular did not bode well for Burns.[13]

They were soon working at cross purposes. McCreery intended to renew the offensive as soon as possible, but the rain forced a series of cancellations. Burns did not relish attacking at this time. On 9 October, after discussing the situation with his divisional commanders, he noted in his diary that they "pointed out the very bad going, and expressed the opinion that we might be drifting into the carrying on of an offensive in similar conditions to those of last autumn and winter, where hard fighting and numerous casualties resulted in no great gain." Burns passed these views along to McCreery, making it clear that he concurred with them.[14]

McCreery ignored Burns's recommendation to halt offensive operations. His staff at Eighth Army headquarters had already drawn up an elaborate battle plan, and he had no intention of changing it. Under this plan, the Canadian corps would take over the full eight-mile front on the Fiumicino, up to and including Route 9. Accordingly, McCreery instructed Burns to maintain steady pressure on the Germans, while the rest of the Eighth Army shifted the weight of its attack into the mountains, where better progress might be expected because the rainfall had had less effect there. The new army commander could not have been pleased with Burns's forthright views.

To prepare for the resumption of offensive operations, Burns juggled his front-line formations. Extending the corps sector to the left, he inserted the First Canadian Division in the British 56th Division's bridgehead west of Savignano. The Fifth Armoured Division, in the centre, was replaced by the New Zealanders who sidestepped from the right, which was taken over by an improvised formation. "Cumberland Force" took its name from Brigadier Ian Cumberland, the officer commanding the Fifth Armoured Brigade. "Cumberland Force was one of those set-ups so peculiar to the Eighth Army," the brigadier later wrote. "A mixed force holding a wide front which . . . was not very vital to the Army plan."[15]

Cumberland Force began its eighteen-day life on Tuesday, 10 October. Its Canadian content included the Perth Regiment, the British Columbia Dragoons, the Royal Canadian Dragoons, the Governor-General's Horse Guards, with the 3rd Greek Mountain Brigade, assorted units of Canadian artillery, and British and New Zealand armoured units. Aside from patrolling and the occasional raid, there was little action on its three-and-a-half-mile front until 16 October, when the Germans fell back a short distance, conforming to a forced withdrawal further inland, where the First Canadian Division was mounting the main attack on the corps front. As the Germans withdrew, Cumberland Force followed. It was slow going at times, according to the brigadier, since "the country was ideally suited for demolitions."[16]

The first large town liberated by this mixed-bag formation was the seaside resort of Cesenatico, which fell on 20 October to the GeeGees. The Germans abandoned it without a fight, but the Horse Guards found that the coastal highway, Route 16, was impassable to vehicles, thanks to the enemy's demolition work. When his tanks were unable to move forward, Lieutenant-Colonel A. K. Jordan rode a bicycle ("Canada's Mechanized Army!" joked Ian Cumberland) into Cesenatico and liberated the jubilant population. Late on 24 October, assisted by Italian partisans, the leading elements reached the River Savio. Next morning, a company of Perths crossed the Savio and established a bridgehead. The engineers installed a bridge and the GeeGees roared across to consolidate the position.[17]

Cumberland Force had forged ahead to the next river, the Bevano, when a torrential downpour swept the entire corps front on 26 October. The effect was immediate, according to Brigadier Cumberland: "Operations came to a standstill; roads became a series of ruts and mud holes; communications were disrupted; the Savio became a raging torrent and washed out all its bridges." By the time the rain let up, Cumberland Force had outlived its usefulness. At noon on 28 October, its brief history ended.[18]

The First Division's return to action had been highlighted by the third and final Victoria Cross won by a Canadian in Italy.

The division was allotted a narrow front, restricted by the Rimini–Bologna railway to the right of Route 9 and by the mountains on the left, and Chris Vokes led with a single brigade, Allan Calder's First. When the advance reached a canalized stream known as the Pisciatello, Vokes planned to commit the other two brigades for the crossing of the Savio, north of Cesena.

The Hastings and Prince Edward Regiment was the first to cross the Fiumicino. During the morning of Wednesday, 11 October, the battalion began leap-frogging its companies out of the British bridgehead near Savignano. The Hasty Ps found themselves in a gloomy landscape, according to Farley Mowat. "The raised banks of ditches covered the low land like worm-casts, and water stood or flowed almost everywhere, turning the rich soil into heavy muck."[19] After a brief skirmish which cost a German rearguard force, the Hasty Ps had reached the Scolo Rigossa. Although there was no sign of the New Zealanders and British who were supposed to be on either side, Lieutenant-Colonel Don Cameron decided to keep pushing along the highway the next morning. One company waded the *scolo*, or drainage canal, and the rest of the battalion followed. By the afternoon of 12 October, Cameron had established a bridgehead five hundred yards deep.

The Hasty Ps found themselves in a worrisome position. The New Zealanders had been held up and were two and a half miles behind them, and to help fill the yawning gap, Brigadier Calder moved The Royal Canadian Regiment along the railway, as the Hasty Ps plunged deeper into enemy-held territory. Ahead stood the village of Gambettola and a hamlet, Bulgaria, with the rail line running between them. On 13 October, Calder sent up Strathcona Shermans and ordered the Hasty Ps to break out of their bridgehead and capture Bulgaria.

After a day-long aerial and artillery bombardment, the Hasty Ps attacked at dawn on a sunny Saturday, 14 October. For a while, it looked as if they would have to leave their tank support behind, for the Ark bridge installed during the night in the *scolo* sank in the ooze. The only other possible crossing was a partially-demolished bridge, which engineering officers had already ruled out, declaring that it would not support Shermans. Colonel McAvity decided to take "a gamble on the old bridge," and the risk was justified.[20] The tanks got across in time to accompany the Hasty Ps, who were glad to have the help in their day-long fight for

Bulgaria. After the Shermans blasted the buildings with high-explosive shells and machine-gun bullets, the riflemen moved from door to door, completing the job with their Lee-Enfields, Tommy guns, and grenades. "The whole operation," recalls Brigadier Calder, "was a perfect example of infantry-tank cooperation."[21]

By 1630 hours, the ruins were clear of the enemy, except for the dead. Besides killing an unknown number of Germans, the Hasty Ps had captured fifty-five prisoners. Victory cost thirty casualties, including Huron Brant, the Ontario Native who had won the Military Medal in Sicily. Brant had been among half a dozen men killed when they were trapped in a drainage ditch by an enemy machine-gun.[22]

Bulgaria's fall had a magical effect. Gambettola was now untenable, and the Germans were forced to withdraw along almost the entire Canadian corps front between the mountains and the sea. On 15 October, the 5th New Zealand Infantry Brigade found Gambettola undefended, as the enemy took up new positions behind the Pisciatello. By the evening of the sixteenth, the Canadians had closed on this line. Because of the widening front, General Vokes inserted the Second Brigade between the First Brigade on the left and the New Zealanders on the right.

The Second Brigade had undergone a number of command changes in the last few days. Graeme Gibson had been evacuated on medical grounds, and with the return of Paul Bernatchez to the Third Brigade, his temporary replacement, Pat Bogert, now took over command of the Second. A personality conflict between Gibson and Syd Thomson, the colonel of the Seaforth Highlanders, had finally come to a head, costing Thomson his job. Thomson's replacement was Henry "Budge" Bell-Irving, who now returned to the Seaforths after a brief stint as commanding officer of the Loyal Edmonton Regiment, while Jim Stone was, at long last, given the Eddies.

For the next several days, the weather would be unsettled, but Pat Bogert wasted no time getting the Second Brigade across the canalized stream. His plan was to make a silent crossing the next night, near the wrecked railway bridge, and establish a bridgehead around the village of Ponte della Pietra. A ford three hundred yards north of the rail line would, it was hoped, enable British tanks to reinforce the bridgehead and allow the engineers to install a bridge. Bogert handed the assignment to Jim Stone's Loyal Eddies and the 12th Royal Tank Regiment.

A steady drizzle fell as the leading company splashed across the Pisciatello shortly after 2200 hours. Stone sent a second company across when fighting broke out with panzer grenadiers, who made a determined effort to smash the bridgehead. The Eddies held on during the night, and at daybreak they looked for the British tanks that were supposed to be fording the Pisciatello. However, they had been delayed when engineers pronounced the river's sandy bottom too soft to permit the passage of Churchills or any other heavy equipment; a bridge at this point was out of the question, in their opinion. Luckily for the Eddies, a British tank officer gambled that the engineers were mistaken and sent a squadron of Churchills across the river at mid-afternoon. A third company of infantry crossed now, and the Eddies and their British tanks widened the bridgehead during the late afternoon of 18 October, clearing Ponte della Pietra by 1830 hours.[23]

Jim Stone's luck continued to hold. At midnight, having lost radio contact with his three companies beyond the river, he decided to go across himself. As his Bren carrier approached the bank, it hit a mine. Everyone was killed, except for Stone. "So much in war depends on luck," he reflects. "I was in the first battle the Edmonton Regiment was in; I missed the Hitler Line battle, but I was in every other. I got shot once through the finger, I had four or five little nicks, but nothing else. Now, I should have been killed fifty times on the law of averages. But it was just luck. Or maybe I just knew how to hide!"[24]

During the night, the engineers installed an eighty-foot Bailey bridge. The Eddies had won. At the cost of thirty-five casualties, they had established a key bridgehead, capturing fifty-three Germans in the process.[25] Stone considers the Pisciatello to have been "my best show." At the time, the stream was thirty yards wide; "nowadays," he says, "it's an irrigation ditch. And that's Italian rivers, that's exactly what happened in Italy – they're a river one day and an irrigation ditch the next. And that country was thick, black soil – the valley of the Po – no stones, just black soil. It was miserable country to fight through."[26]

The sun peeked through the clouds on Thursday, 19 October, as the First Division advanced towards the next river, the Savio. Princess Patricia's Canadian Light Infantry passed through the Edmonton bridgehead, while the Third Brigade moved up on the left, led by the Carleton and York and Royal 22nd regiments. Carleton patrols entered Cesena to find that the Germans had abandoned the city, and the next morning Lieutenant-Colonel Jack Ensor was "royally welcomed as the 'liberator' of Cesena."[27] The Carletons then moved up to the Savio, where they were joined by the Van Doos and, further upstream, by the Patricias.

It soon became apparent that any attempt to get over the Savio would be a major undertaking. The volume of fire drawn by patrols indicated that the Germans were holding the river in force. The Savio was the biggest obstacle the Canadians had so far encountered in northern Italy. "It lay in a muddy trough about fifteen feet below ground level; at this time of the year the river was swollen with storm water from the mountains and at many places it was too deep to ford. The near bank had been cleared of clumps and canes and trees; the western bank, which was slightly higher, afforded the enemy an excellent field of fire."[28]

The Pats were the first to test the Savio defences. The Eighth Army was demanding that I Canadian Corps continue to press the enemy; Tommy Burns instructed Chris Vokes to "get a bridgehead over the Savio," and Vokes handed it to the Second Brigade's Pat Bogert. The plan called for the PPCLI to put two companies across the Savio, and the Seaforth Highlanders would pass through and cut the Cesena–Ravenna highway.[29]

The attack took place at 1700 hours on 20 October, and both companies of Patricias were decimated by the heavy fire that greeted them. In D Company, one platoon and part of another worked their way past the mines that were liberally sown on the steep bank, splashed across the waist-deep Savio, and huddled below the far bank, where enemy fire prevented any further movements. Meanwhile, A Company's Major Ted Cutbill counted heads on the far bank and found that he had only sixteen men. Cutbill's radio refused to work, so he was out of touch with battalion headquarters. After dark, having waited in vain for stragglers, and seeing no sign of D Company (the platoon-and-a-half pulled back under the cover of darkness), Cutbill led his men on a daring foray deep into enemy territory. However, Cutbill concluded that his best bet would be to dig in along the riverbank and send a sergeant to fetch reinforcements. The Germans were aware of the presence of these pesky Patricias, and Saturday, 21 October, proved to be a long and difficult day. The Canadians endured a terrific pounding by the enemy artillery, and repulsed repeated localized counter-attacks. "Several times," the major later wrote, "the situation [became] quite critical."[30]

Since they were running low on food, water, and ammunition, Sergeant F. H. Sparrow had volunteered to make another trip across the Savio. He had gone over before dawn, returning with a radio and a handful of reinforcements. Now he did it again, to fetch supplies and to provide as many details as possible about the German positions. Sparrow survived the daylight venture (and was later awarded the Military Medal), bringing back word that an attack was to be made that night by the Seaforth Highlanders and Loyal Eddies.

It rained all day as Pat Bogert's battalions prepared for their attack. Unlike the Pats, the Seaforths and Eddies had time to reconnoitre the river, and they knew what to expect when they launched their attack. There was plenty of artillery, in the form of two medium and six field regiments, plus every mortar and machine-gun in the Saskatoon Light Infantry (the Savio marked the first time in its history that the SLI fought together as a complete unit). The bombardment began at 1955 hours, and half an hour later two companies of Seaforths and, a thousand yards to their left, one of Eddies started across the Savio.[31]

The Seaforths attacked on either side of Cutbill's little force. Captain Don Duncan's D Company, on the left, crossed the Savio in single file, and scrambled up the slippery far bank, where they contacted the Patricias. Some of the Seaforths, finding their weapons filled with mud, traded with Cutbill's men. At the same time, Captain Anthony Staples and B Company crossed six hundred yards to the north. Both companies, taking advantage of the darkness and steady rain, used speed and maneouvre to clear the Germans from numerous farmhouses and machine-gun posts in the area. By dawn, B Company alone had rounded up fifty-one prisoners.[32]

On the other hand, the Edmontons suffered a setback within minutes. As he scaled the slimy bank on the far side of the Savio, Major Bill Longhurst, the officer who had devised the mouse-holing technique that had been invaluable at Ortona, was killed in the first burst of enemy fire. Longhurst was adored by his battalion. "You know," says Sergeant Bill Ross, "he came up to get his majority confirmed, and he should never have been in the line. He was a sick man, really, he wasn't in good health."[33] Riddled with bullets, Longhurst died on the muddy bank of the Savio, and the attack seemed to die with him.

Some of Longhurst's men were captured, others scattered, but Company Sergeant-Major W. G. Davies rounded up ten survivors and dug in along the embankment. As soon as Colonel Stone realized what had happened, he rushed a second company across the river. That was the turning point; the Eddies quickly established a firm bridgehead, and during the night both battalions sent across their reserve companies.[34]

Counter-attacks were not long in coming. As the Seaforth commander, Budge Bell-Irving, later observed, "Getting there and staying there were two acutely different problems."[35] According to George Brown, then a twenty-two-year-old captain, this was true of any operation, but particularly so when water obstacles were involved. The rivers made it "hard to get anything across. So they'd get over to the other side without their heavy guns; all they had was their small arms. They wouldn't have their supporting guns, mortars, and they wouldn't have any vehicles to help them, and tanks couldn't get across" until a bridge had been built. "It'd be frustrating as hell."[36]

As German tanks and soldiers converged on the Seaforth position near the Cesena–Ravenna highway, Colonel Bell-Irving played his trump card, a newly created tank-hunting platoon, comprised of sixteen soldiers, equipped with four PIATs. All battalions had an anti-tank platoon, but its role was primarily defensive; Bell-Irving's tank hunters, on the other hand, went looking for trouble. Their tactics were simple: Hawkins anti-tank grenades would be used to immobilize the tank, which would then be knocked out by a PIAT, and the crew dispatched with Tommy guns.[37]

At 0230 hours, four Panther tanks, accompanied by two self-propelled guns and about thirty infantry, rumbled out of the gloom. The Seaforth tank hunters were waiting for them. Sergeant K. P. Thompson carefully laid a string of Hawkins grenades across the road and deployed his two-man PIAT teams nearby. Their first victim was a German staff car, which miraculously missed the grenades but was riddled with small-arms fire, and both occupants were killed. A self-propelled gun followed; it hit a grenade, and PIATs finished it off. Private James Tennant fired his PIAT "at such close range that either a piece of shrapnel from the bomb or the ring from the bomb's tail-piece flew back into his eye." Next came a Panther, and Private Ernest Alvia Smith hurried to out to meet it. A former track star from New Westminster, B.C., the stocky, thirty-year-old Smith, was nicknamed "Smoky" by his friends. And this night's fighting would bring him the Victoria Cross.[38]

Smith hurried into a field with a PIAT team. He left a single man and a PIAT there, then crossed the road with his injured friend, Private Tennant, and fetched another PIAT. The two Seaforths just got into position when the Panther approached, its machine-guns raking the roadside ditches. Tennant was hit, and Smith jumped onto the road in clear view of the fifty-ton tank. At a range of only thirty feet, he fired his PIAT, knocking out the Panther. Ten Germans riding on the back of the tank leaped off and charged Smith, who picked up his Tommy gun and cut down four of his enemy; the rest fled.

A second Panther came at him. Smith steadfastly stood over his wounded friend, and when more German infantry attacked, he calmly reloaded his Tommy gun with magazines collected from the ditch. Time and again the enemy swarmed around the stubborn Seaforth, only to be driven back in a hail of bullets. The Germans retreated, but another Panther came into action. Unable to ignore the shell fire, Smith helped Tennant to cover and medical aid. Then he returned to his post to await further counter-attacks.[39]

This spectacular performance brought Smoky Smith the second Victoria Cross to be awarded to a New Westminster native in the Italian campaign. He was characteristically modest. "It was a job to do, and you did it," he shrugged, "and I was scared the whole time. Who wouldn't be?"[40] Later, when asked what the VC meant to him, he answered quietly: "A nice Christmas present to take home to Mom."[41]

The grey, wet dawn brought a host of surprises for the Seaforths. It began with the discovery and capture of a Panther hopelessly bogged down in a nearby ditch. Colonel Bell-Irving recounted some of the other morning activities of his battalion:

About first light the German machine-gunners on the river bank behind us became hungry. They got out their mess-tins and came up to their former kitchen, now D Coy HQ, for their food. This surprised and surprising breakfast line-up netted us 56 PWs. Another innocent group were taken by a simple ruse. Our chaps cut a telephone line down to the river. A line party came up to repair it and were taken PWs. The remaining enemy on the river bank were cleaned out without any fighting. The result of the night and morning efforts was some 150 PWs.[42]

However, the picture was far from pleasant. The Second Brigade had established a bridgehead more than a mile wide and up to 1,400 yards deep in the Seaforth sector. But everyone – two full battalions – on the far side of the Savio was cut off, because it was proving impossible to build a bridge in the face of near-flood conditions. Bill Ross, the Edmonton sergeant, says the transformation of the Savio was almost unbelievable. "That river rose three feet in two hours," he remembers. "We waded across it at night, and by morning you couldn't swim across it."[43]

The situation was causing concern at both divisional and corps headquarters. "I remember a midnight telephone conversation with Vokes," Tommy Burns later wrote. "He was worried, and wanted my decision whether he should try to hang on, or withdraw the unsupported infantry. I told him to hang on, as it seemed to me that the Germans really would not have the power to throw us back, and the engineers might have better luck the next day."[44]

Engineers ruled out a bridge in this area for at least twenty-four hours. Rafts were able to get supplies across, including 6-pounder anti-tank guns, and to bring out some of the wounded. But this was only a half-measure. Something more had to be done, and a British tank officer offered a possibility. He pointed out a potential crossing site a mile downstream from the bridgehead, near Borgo di Ronta, and Canadian engineers confirmed that it seemed suitable for a bridge. Chris Vokes promptly placed the West Nova Scotia Regiment under the command of the Second Brigade's Pat Bogert and ordered him to establish a bridgehead there. Since the West Novas were still in Cesena, Bogert ordered a company of the Patricias to hurry to Borgo di Ronta to guard the site.

Time was of the essence, and the hurried operation went poorly. Not until 2200 hours did Captain A. G. Robinson, the officer commanding the PPCLI's D Company at Borgo di Ronta, learn that he had been placed under command of the West Novas for a midnight attack. The Nova Scotia unit was still *en route* from Cesena, so Robinson led his company across the raging Savio. The captain later reported that "the water [was] up to the men's chests, and the current so swift that when a man crossed he was 25 yards downstream from the place he started at." Robinson believed that at least two of his men drowned, but more died when the first platoon blundered into an enemy patrol on the far bank. The ensuing fire fight raised the alarm, and the Germans were ready when the West Novas started to cross the swollen Savio.[45]

Braving heavy fire, two companies of the Maritime battalion made it across the river in assault boats by daylight. But they were in desperate straits. As they fought their way along the muddy riverbank, there seemed to be no end to bad news. Lieutenant A. C. Mackenzie reported that there were three German tanks, supported by infantry, two hundred yards to the left. A platoon of the Patricias, holding a house some distance from the river, was practically wiped out by a counter-attack. But the biggest blow of all was delivered by a Canadian engineer officer, who informed them that because of the soft banks and rising waters, it was impossible to build a bridge here after all.[46]

The West Nova bridgehead was soon under a violent counter-attack, and, with no possibility of reinforcing it, Lieutenant-Colonel A. L. Saunders ordered his companies to withdraw. After fighting a magnificent rearguard battle, the West Novas were back on the near side of the Savio by 1130 hours.

By midday on 23 October, the Second Brigade was still across the Savio, but without a bridge to show for the 191 casualties incurred during the past four days. That morning, after discussing the situation with Chris Vokes, Tommy Burns decided to make another effort. But the army commander, Dick McCreery, told him not to bother, because things were going well elsewhere. The British had developed a solid crossing in Cesena, where a Bailey bridge had been installed on the solid arches of the city's centuries-old Ponte Vecchio. And in the mountains to the south and west, McCreery's strategy was working well. The Poles and V Corps were making steady progress, as was the Anglo-American Fifth Army, approaching Bologna. The Savio was no longer safe for the Germans to defend in strength; they had to pull back or be outflanked.[47]

The West Novas returned to the far side of the Savio that night. Colonel Saunders ordered a patrol to probe the enemy defences, and at 2045 hours, Lieutenant C. H. Smith set out with ten other ranks. Smith's patrol found an assault boat and paddled across, and for several hours they explored the west bank of the Savio. They found the house where the PPCLI platoon had been wiped out; the place was littered with dead Canadians, and the ground around was marked by the deep tracks of Tiger tanks and scattered with German equipment, but there were signs that the enemy was present. Smith led his men inland, to Route 9. Eventually, he arrived at a farm, where he was greeted by a happy Italian family who told him that the Germans were gone. Smith hurried back to report this valuable information.[48]

A slow-motion pursuit started the next day, 24 October. The lack of bridges in the Canadian sector meant that there were no vehicles heavier than Jeeps on the far side of the Savio. The Carleton and Yorks started to wade the river (to assist the men against the swift current, a rope was later put across and secured to a church tower) during the morning, but it was late afternoon before the whole battalion was across the Savio and advancing along the railway.[49]

The Patricias led the Second Brigade's "break-out" from the bridgehead. The battalion crossed on a footbridge installed by the engineers, but the advance was painfully slow. Lieutenants like Syd Frost cursed his maps, which "were so bad," he writes, "that we were convinced the cost of production had been secretly subsidized by the Germans." And, of course, there was the mud, which, says Frost, "reminded me of father's stories of the mud and filth of the battlefields of France in the First War. There was no escaping the sticky stuff."[50]

By late evening on the twenty-fourth, the First Division's leading battalions had moved only two miles. The next day they reached the Bevano, and pushed on towards the Ronco, six miles beyond. Syd Frost reflected on a book he had tucked in his pack. It was John Galsworthy's novel, *One More River to Cross*, "a particularly apt choice, I thought."[51]

On the right, the Fifth Armoured Division had also joined the chase. Bert Hoffmeister's formation had relieved the 2nd New Zealand Division during the night of 22–23 October, marking the end of the New Zealanders' service in I Canadian Corps. Although his division was committed to a holding role on the Savio, Hoffmeister felt that the situation "seemed to justify a crossing." The Irish and Perth regiments clambered aboard assault boats and established bridgeheads two miles apart on 24 October. When the engineers constructed bridges at both points, the Cape Breton Highlanders and the Irish were at the Bevano the next day.[52]

The engineers were also busy in the First Division's sector. A suitable crossing was finally located just north of the demolished railway bridge. Work started at noon on 24 October, and a seventy-foot Bailey bridge was opened the next morning, enabling tanks to cross; by the end of the twenty-fifth, the Second and Third brigades were over the Savio.

It was a short-lived success. Rain started to fall that evening, and grew heavier during the night. By daylight on 26 October, the Savio was rising at an alarming rate. The First Division's engineers watched helplessly as nature destroyed not only their Bailey bridge, but every bridge in the Canadian corps sector. The only bridge that survived the flood was Cesena's Ponte Vecchio, spanned by a Bailey. For the next three days this single passage carried the heavy traffic of both the Canadians and their British neighbours in V Corps.

Only now was the futility of their efforts apparent. Had it been done deliberately, the Canadian corps could hardly have selected a more unsuitable front than along the raging Savio north of Cesena. "During the last 2,000 years, the natives of Italy have built good and numerous bridges," Lieutenant-Colonel Ted Webb, the First Division's chief engineer, ruefully noted in his report, "but never had they bridged the River Savio in the 7-mile stretch from Cesena north to Mensa. This the Canadians attempted to do, and failed."[53]

The Ronco was also in spate. While the bridges on the Savio were being washed away, the Carletons and Patricias reached the Ronco, to find that "it was now about 200 yards wide and six feet deep with a very strong current," as the PPCLI's Lieutenant Syd Frost reported. "Boats could not be launched on the steep riverbanks. . . . It looked as though the battalion had another river to cross by wading or even swimming."[54]

The Canadians were spared that agonizing prospect. The entire Eighth Army needed rest by now, but the two Canadian divisions were in urgent need of it. They had been in action almost continuously, with only brief breaks, since late August. The army commander, General McCreery, had decided before the Savio to take the Canadian corps out of the line, so that it would be refreshed and ready to go for the resumption of action in late November or early December. After a one-day delay caused by the flooding on the Savio, the Canadian formations were relieved on 28 October by the British 4th Division and by an improvised formation known as "Porterforce," after the British lieutenant-colonel who commanded it. Porterforce, with various Canadian and British armoured, artillery, and engineering units, took over a sector extending ten miles inland from the coast.

So ended a month of operations which can only be termed disappointing. Instead of a dazzling dash across the plains to the Po, the Canadians had had to battle both enemy rearguards and "the worst October weather in Italy in living memory."[55] They had reached their objective, the Ronco, but had advanced only twenty-three miles in the previous thirty-three days. The single saving grace was that there had been few big battles, a fact which was reflected in the relatively low casualty count: 355 killed, 1,471 wounded, 92 taken prisoner.[56]

As they travelled south to the Rimini rest area, no one relished the thought of further fighting in this forbidding area. Captain Dave Rowland, the padre of Toronto's Irish Regiment, spoke for many when he wrote in his diary: "The authorities over here have us pretty well convinced that we will be another winter in Italy. The weather has been so bad I'm sure it has set us back a few months. I'm still hopeful that we won't have to stay here. I would welcome a change to another front in preference to another Italian winter."[57]

3

The Italian campaign had been Dragooned.

It was a bitter realization, but no surprise to the British, who had tried so hard to prevent that very thing from happening. The Anglo-American offensive petered out at the end of October 1944, short of its twin objectives, Bologna and Ravenna. Mark Clark's Fifth Army suspended its attacks on 27 October; the Eighth Army continued limited operations into November. The Allies enjoyed a material superiority over the Germans, including complete command of the air, but Dragoon, the August invasion of southern France, had removed their numerical advantage. Now, ever so close to victory, both armies had run out of fresh forces.

Winston Churchill, Italy's champion, never forgave his American allies for mounting Dragoon. "It seems certain that but for the deprivations and demands of [Dragoon] the campaign in Italy could have been over by Christmas." Dragoon's benefits were limited, he charged, while it had deprived Alexander's army group of "its opportunity to stike a most formidable blow at the Germans, and very possibly to reach Vienna before the Russians, with all that might have followed therefrom."[58]

General Alexander weighed his alternatives. Like the campaign in northern Italy, the fighting in northwestern Europe had bogged down on Germany's western doorstep. General Eisenhower had already decided to embark upon a winter campaign, in order to wear down the enemy for the decisive spring battles. At Eisenhower's urging, Alexander determined "to continue the offensive on the Italian front at full stretch to the limits set by exhaustion and material shortage."[59]

After meeting his army commanders, McCreery and Clark, on 29 October, Alexander notified the Mediterranean supreme commander, Sir Henry Wilson, that the Fifth and Eighth armies would launch a combined effort during the first half of December to reach Bologna and Ravenna. All offensive operations would cease by 15 December, in order to allow proper time for the preparation of the spring offensive, tentatively scheduled for 1 Feburary 1945.[60]

If nothing else, American and British views on Italy had been belatedly reconciled. As the official American history notes:

Thus bringing to battle the maximum number of German divisions and denying their use on other, more critical fronts, would from that point constitute the sole mission of the Allied armies in Italy. Actually, as far as the Americans were concerned, that had always been the mission, certainly since the QUADRANT [Quebec] Conference of 1943. In American eyes the British had finally been brought around to recognition of a long-standing reality.[61]

The only trouble was that the Allied forces in Italy, while considerably superior to the enemy in both manpower and equipment, were too weak to accomplish anything decisive. Moreover, their psychological state was also unsettled. "Allied morale suffered a decline after the euphoria of August and September," observes British historian Sir William Jackson. "The end of the war had seemed so near that it engendered an enthusiasm in men to be in at the kill. In October the end seemed just as inevitable but much further off."[62]

Defeat in Italy was a foregone conclusion for the Germans. The Allies' slow but relentless advance up the Italian boot was made possible by their quantitative superiority in men and equipment, which would have been even greater had this not been a secondary theatre, and which, as the attacker, they could bring to bear on battlefields of their choice. Yet, as it did on both the Russian and Western fronts in 1944, the German army in Italy confounded the Allies with its fighting prowess in the face of adversity, its ability to rebound from near-catastrophic defeats.

German military men had to cope with many disadvantages. Not the least of these was the Führer, Adolf Hitler, whose constant interference proved to be more of a hindrance than a help to his beleaguered armies. One American general later remarked that "one's imagination boggled at what the German army might have done to us without Hitler working so effectively for our side."[63] Another detriment was Allied control of the air, which made a nightmare out of large-scale troop and supply movements. The German armed forces were also plagued by perpetual shortages of virtually everything, from food to gasoline, but the most serious shortage was manpower. The manpower problems faced by the Allies in the fall of 1944 were nothing compared to those faced by the Germans, who were putting old men and young boys into uniform and sending them off to war. By the fall of 1944, the German army was a pale shadow of its former self.

Albert Kesselring's Army Group C in Italy contained a typical cross-section of German divisions: several superb formations, such as the formidable 1st Parachute Division, which had confronted the Canadians so many times; a majority of average units; and a handful of unreliable and even bizarre outfits, such as the 162nd Turcoman Division, which was comprised of men conscripted from countries occupied by the Germans and which the Canadians virtually destroyed during the battle for Rimini. (In the fighting at Riccione, Lieutenant Jimmy Quayle and two scouts of the Royal Canadian Regiment encountered eleven Turcomen, armed to the teeth, who wished not to surrender but to join the Canadians and help them kill Germans!)[64] The best units were kept in reserve and used as fire brigades, rushing from crisis to crisis – but there were never enough of them to decisively defeat the Allies.

Unlike Allied soldiers, who went into battle after battle confident of ultimate victory, their enemies were under no illusion about the eventual outcome of the war. By now, German fighting men "were sustained by a compound of fatalism and blind faith," in the words of British historian Max Hastings. "We no longer expected total victory, but we still felt an absolute sense of loyalty," recalled one German veteran, while another maintained that his motivation was provided by "two words – 'unconditional surrender.' If for the rest of my life I was to chop wood in Canada or Siberia, then I would sooner die."[65]

The dogged determination of so many German soldiers was enhanced by the superior efficiency of the army as an organizational entity. A senior German headquarters contained only half as many officers as its Allied counterpart. German divisions might have been very small numerically, but they contained a far higher percentage of combat personnel than Allied divisions. For example, fighting soldiers accounted for as much as 90 per cent of a 1944 *panzer grenadier* division, compared to 65.56 per cent in an American division.[66]

The efficiency of the German army was characterized by its admirable flexibility and remarkable durability, which allowed it to adapt to adverse conditions. Observes historian Hastings: "It is striking to contrast the manner in which Allied units which suffered 40 or 50 per cent losses expected to be pulled out of the line, even disbanded, with their German counterparts, who were merely reassembled into improvised battlegroups – the *kampfengruppen* – which were an essential ingredient of so many of the German army's victories. . . . Cooks, signallers, isolated tank platoons, stray Luftwaffe flak units were all grist to the mill of the *kampfengruppen*, which proved astonishingly cohesive and effective in action."[67]

Superior weaponry aided the Germans immensely. It is a sad fact that, while in the air and at sea Allied technology and ingenuity matched or exceeded that of the enemy, this was rarely the case in the ground war. American, British, and Canadian soldiers utilized weapons that were almost always outclassed by those brought to bear by their opponents. The British 25-pounder artillery piece was good enough, but paled beside the German 88-millimetre gun. A German soldier could throw his potato-masher hand grenade farther than the pineapple-shaped grenades used by

Allied soldiers. The MG 42 could fire twelve hundred rounds per minute, compared to five hundred for the British Bren gun. The Germans were masters of the use of their 81-millimetre and 120-millimetre mortars, which accounted for a very high proportion of Allied casualties. Hand-held anti-tank weapons fielded by the Germans were invariably better than the PIAT used by the British and Canadians or the American bazooka. It was the same story with German-built Tiger and Panther tanks, compared to the American-designed Sherman used by the Allies in Italy. Fortunately for the Allied cause, Tigers and Panthers were available in very limited numbers, but Max Hastings has asked a very valid question: "How could American and British industries produce a host of superb aircraft, an astonishing variety of radar equipment, the proximity fuse, the DUKW, the jeep, yet still ask their armies to join battle against the Wehrmacht equipped with a range of tanks utterly inferior in armour and killing power?"[68]

The Germans also enjoyed the advantage of being on the defensive, in territory which favoured the defence: Italian battlegrounds were either mountainous or flat and criss-crossed by treacherous watercourses. The weather also seemed to favour them; heavy rainfall had severely hampered the Allies in the last months of 1944, and it would continue to do so. But much of the German success in delaying the inevitable in northern Italy was directly attributable to Generalfeldmarschall Kesselring, who repeatedly juggled his slender resources to parry each Allied thrust.

However, a traffic accident cost the Germans his invaluable services. On 23 October, while touring the battlefront, his staff car collided with a gun being towed onto Route 9 between Bologna and Imola. The field-marshal suffered a severe concussion which incapacitated him for nearly three months. (It did not affect his sense of humour. "Soon after the accident," he later wrote, "the story got about that the Field-Marshal was doing well, but that the gun had had to be scrapped.")[69]

Kesselring's temporary replacement was the Tenth Army's Heinrich von Vietinghoff. The artistocratic Vietinghoff believed, like Kesselring, that there was only one practicable course – immediate withdrawal to the Alps, where the mountainous terrain could be easily defended. But it did not take Vietinghoff long to realize that "Hitler made all the decisions." And, as before, the Führer bluntly forbade any "voluntary withdrawal"; Army Group C must hold, he decreed, "at every point."[70]

However, Vietinghoff did take advantage of the limited authority vested in his position, authorizing LXXVI Panzer Corps to "disengage a little" on 23 October. His hope was to make a fighting withdrawal to the Genghis Khan Line, running from south of Bologna to Lago Comacchio. Construction of these defences started the same day that Vietinghoff took charge of Army Group C.[71]

The Germans would attempt to defend the water-logged Po plain to the bitter end.

4

While Canadian soldiers were battling the bullets, shells, and rivers of mud in northern Italy, the biggest political battle of the war had broken out at home. The lid had been blown off the conscription crisis.

Prime Minister Mackenzie King dreaded the return of Defence Minister Ralston from his overseas trip, for he knew that Ralston was coming home to recommend that conscription be implemented to provide reinforcements for Canada's combat units in Italy and northwestern Europe. Ralston arrived at Ottawa's Rockcliffe Airport on Wednesday, 18 October. Accompanied by Ken Stuart, the chief of staff at CMHQ in London, Ralston met King at the prime minister's East Block office on Parliament Hill that very afternoon. The defence minister described his trip and meetings with prominent people, including Eisenhower and Montgomery, who had warned that there was still much fighting to be done before the war could be brought to a successful conclusion. The minister made it clear that, in his opinion, there was only one answer: some of the soldiers conscripted for home defence under the 1940 National Resources Mobilization Act (NRMA) must be sent overseas.

The conscription crisis King faced was "an artificial one," as historians W. A. B. Douglas and Brereton Greenhous have pointed out.[72] The army had a projected shortfall of fifteen thousand infantry, which the NRMA men would be expected to make up – yet the Canadian army contained nearly half a million men.

The Canadian army that evolved during World War II was a bureaucrat's dream. It was, to be blunt, an army of pencil-pushers and paper-shufflers, grotesquely top-heavy in staff officers, with bloated and duplicated support services of sometimes dubious value. Tommy Burns, in his brilliant post-war analysis, *Manpower in the Canadian Army*, described the statistical story. At the time of the 1944 conscription crisis, there were 465,750 men and women in the Canadian army. This figure included 59,699 NRMA men and 16,178 nurses and members of the Canadian Women's Army Corps. Subtracting these numbers from the total, one is left with 389,873 soldiers available for "general service." Of these, 257,203 were in the United Kingdom, northwestern Europe, and Italy, with approximately 158,000 in the field formations (First Canadian Army, I and II Canadian Corps) and 99,000 in base and line-of-communication units. The five Canadian divisions had a total estimated strength of 85,000; 37,817 were infantrymen.[73]

How was it possible that sufficient reinforcements could not be found among 390,000 volunteer soldiers for the army's 38,000-man infantry corps? Burns's study showed that the organization of the Canadian army was, as he delicately put it, "uneconomical." Much of the inefficiency was a direct result of the decision to create a field army, which in turn can be traced to the years following the Great War. According to historian Steve Harris, who has explored this area in some depth, "senior officers had a fixation with a six-division army from 1919 on, and believed that a force of this size was the appropriate contribution for Canada to make in any major war. Yet the general staff between the wars never once undertook demographic studies to ascertain whether an army of this size could be sustained through voluntary enlistment."[74]

The First Canadian Army had been established, Burns argued, for reasons "more political than military. The idea of a unitary Canadian Army was more gratifying to national patriotic sentiment than the idea of an equivalent number of troops operating in divisions or even corps, scattered throughout the British or Allied Armies." But a modern army headquarters is a complex organization, offering administrative and support services for the formations under its direction. This resulted in a duplication of many of the functions of CMHQ in London, which were further duplicated by the decision to send a corps to Italy, leaving Canada's overseas forces with "too many high formations and administrative headquarters for the number of fighting troops."[75]

The army made no end of problems for itself. A temporary surplus of junior officers led to a scheme to lend two thousand of them to the British army. This was arranged in February 1944, when I Canadian Corps was recovering from the costly and traumatic battles in and around Ortona. National Defence Headquarters belatedly realized (three months later) that the "Canloan" officers were needed in our army, but not before 673 were seconded to the British forces, where they served with distinction (forty-three won the Military Cross). It was one of a number of dubious moves, according to war correspondent and historian Doug How. "They kept setting up these [outfits] like the Special Service Force. You took these very aggressive guys into it, just to impress the Americans. The parachute battalion – was it necessary? You have all sorts of corporals there who might well have been damn good platoon lieutenants."[76]*

---

* The First Special Service Force was one victim of the conscription crisis. General Stuart had already recommended its disbandment, pointing out that, since the Force's departure from Italy for southern France in August, "effective Canadian administrative control is quite impossible." Stuart contended "that this unit appears now to be submerged to such an extent with the U.S. Forces that the value to Canada of its retention is no longer apparent."[77] When the Americans concluded that it had, in any case, outlived its usefulness, the Force was disbanded on 5 December.

To make matters worse, the Canadian military hierarchy consistently underestimated infantry casualties, despite repeated warnings that it was doing so, and CMHQ blindly adhered to British forecasts, which were originally based on the fighting in the North African desert, where infantry losses had been deceptively small. The British grudgingly revised their forecasts as the war progressed. In 1942, they had estimated that 20 per cent of all reinforcements would be required for the infantry; this figure was hiked to 40–45 per cent in 1943, and to 50 per cent in January 1944. It was finally increased to 75 per cent in September of that year, but even that figure was a bit low. The infantry's share of Canadian casualties ran as high as 78 per cent.[78]

Warnings about possible infantry shortages were bluntly rejected, and the other services eventually ended up with more men than they required. By December 1944, when the Canadian army was crying for more infantry, there were 46,567 men in the reinforcement pool in Europe, but most of them had been trained to be almost anything besides infantry. As Burns noted, "while there was a shortage of infantry reinforcements, there were more reinforcements for other arms than were needed. The maladjustment derived primarily from using erroneous wastage rates, i.e., the rates at which officers and men of the various corps, fighting and administrative, became non-effective through battle casualties or sickness."[79]

However, CMHQ seems to have had second thoughts in March 1944, when it instituted a program of remustering, converting officers and other ranks from various services to infantry. This started with 2,000 general-duty gunners, tankers, and engineers; as well, 250 artillery officers and an equal number of service-corps officers were transferred to the infantry. When the fighting in Normandy threatened to dry up the reinforcement pool, CMHQ stepped up the remustering, switching 3,500 more artillery and service-corps men to the infantry.[80]

In Italy, remustering had, by the beginning of May, become virtually the sole manner of reinforcing Canadian combat units. Burns started with eight hundred general-duty men from the armoured and other corps, and this policy remained in effect for the rest of 1944. "Only the reinforcements so remustered and retrained made it possible, up to the end of September, to replace casualties in the infantry as they occurred, or at any rate to ensure that there were no units seriously under strength for any length of time," Burns wrote. "The situation grew more difficult thereafter, as few infantry reinforcements had been sent out from the United Kingdom since the spring, and the reservoir of men in other corps who could be remustered had been exhausted."[81]

In April and May 1944, 5,656 infantrymen were sent from Canada, while another 1,875 were remustered in the same period, just in time for the

Liri valley fighting in May and June. Despite the influx of soldiers, CMHQ reported a deficit of 3,337 infantry on 31 May. Lieutenant-General J. C. Murchie, Ken Stuart's successor as chief of Canada's general staff, proposed that some infantry formations be broken up to meet the shortfall, but Stuart objected. "It would not be understood here or in the U.S. or in Canada," he cabled on 2 June, "and would be detrimental to the morale of whole Canadian Army." Stuart urged a "wait and see" policy. "I am confident that we can meet demands during next four months giving priority of course to [Overlord] over [Italy]." When the Canadians invaded France, the drain on infantry reinforcements was twice the forecast rate.[82]

Defence Minister Ralston was kept in the dark about all this. Soon after assuming his duties in London in late December 1943, Stuart had informed Ralston that he would select the information that the minister would see, in order to control what he called "alarmist cables." Thereafter, Stuart, with Ralston's acquiescence, "enforced a policy of soft-pedalling on this question and saw to it that communications which he considered 'alarmist' were not sent to Ottawa."[83]

It was unusually effective. Ralston later admitted to Prime Minister King that "until he was in Italy he was not fully apprised of the reinforcement situation."[84]

Despite his knowledge of the situation, Stuart had advised the King government, at the beginning of August 1944, that he was satisfied that there was no cause for concern about manpower. Clearly, he was hoping for an early end to the war, as many believed possible that summer. But now, in October, he had to retract his optimistic forecast. "I am forced to the conclusion ... that the time has come," he informed Prime Minister King, "when the future effective maintenance of our Canadian forces in two theatres requires that NRMA personnel be made available for service overseas."[85]

The result was a full-fledged political crisis.

When Prime Minister King was presented with the manpower figures, he was astounded, and so were members of his cabinet. "My God, if that is the case," cried Air Minister Chubby Power, "what are you talking about getting more men under conscription?"[86]

Day after day, in meeting after meeting, Ralston remained intractable. "As I see it at the moment," he told his cabinet colleagues, "I feel that there is no alternative but to recommend the extension of NRMA personnel to overseas."[87] True, fifteen thousand men could certainly be found elsewhere in the army, "but they would not have been trained infantrymen and training them would have taken a great deal of time," as historian C. P. Stacey has observed. "The only place where *a large body of trained infantrymen* was actually available was among the N.R.M.A. soldiers."[88]

Other possible solutions were proposed, and each was rejected in turn: smaller battalions; financial incentives to convince zombies to volunteer; an approach to the French government-in-exile with a request "to let one or two of their units fight with one of our French units." King felt that these were worthy of consideration, but his military advisers disagreed. "What annoys me about the Defence Dept.," he fumed in his diary, "is that any proposal made, short of conscription of N.R.M.A. men, meets with instant rejection."[89]

As the crisis mounted, one solution became apparent to King: he could get rid of Ralston. Indeed, King had a replacement waiting in the wings. He had already met privately with the old warrior, Andy McNaughton, vetting him as a possible governor-general. But now it appeared McNaughton would be more valuable as a member of cabinet, holding the defence portfolio – poetic justice, in King's view. "The whole business really goes back to the struggle between Ralston and McNaughton: the separation of the Army for Italy at Ralston's insistence as against McNaughton and Churchill's wishes at the time. It is now clear that had the army been kept intact in England, there would be no need for reinforcements at this stage."[90]

On the last day in October, King summoned McNaughton to Laurier House. After satisfying himself that they both agreed "that it was questionable whether it was necessary to resort to conscription at this stage," the prime minister made up his mind. The next day, he invited McNaughton to become his minister of national defence; when the general accepted, King tendered Ralston's resignation. During the 1942 conscription crisis, Ralston had angrily resigned from King's cabinet. He had been talked out of quitting but had neglected to withdraw his letter of resignation. King now presented it to the afternoon cabinet meeting. "I said that in regard to a resignation from Ralston, that he had tendered his resignation to me two years ago; that that had been a very trying thing for me to go on day in and day out for this period with this resignation not withdrawn, but simply held."[91]

Andy McNaughton was sworn in on Tuesday, 2 November. In replacing Ralston, he had gained a measure of revenge against one of the two men he held responsible for his own fall from grace a year earlier. The other culprit was Ken Stuart, who, according to Stacey (serving at CMHQ at that time), "vanished instantly from the scene. . . . We never saw him again; other people had to sort out the disorganized mass of important papers in his office."[92]

His revenge complete, McNaughton now set about to find the volunteers to fill the openings in the overseas infantry battalions. But his appointment was one of Mackenzie King's rare misreadings of public sentiment. Instead of rallying the country to the cause, McNaughton's appeals for more volunteers produced the opposite effect. His speeches were greeted with outright hostility, and he was heckled mercilessly. Toronto's pro-conscriptionist *Globe and Mail* denounced him for promoting "the Government's cowardly and shameful policy of keeping the zombie army in futile idleness in Canada, and refusing to provide adequate reinforcements for the army he once commanded."[93]

Everything King had sought to avoid was now happening. The country was divided in the worst way since the 1917 conscription crisis. C. P. Stacey, who visited Canada briefly in December 1944, was shocked by what he described as "the febrile and, indeed, psychopathic tone in which the conscription issue was being discussed in the newspapers, and particularly the unmeasured abuse which was being hurled at General McNaughton ... by the opposition press. Politically the state of the country was tragic."[94]

McNaughton, shaken by the outcome of his first two, and only, public appearances, complained that he was now "the most hated man of Canada today."[95] The results of his appeals fell far short of expectations. In the first three weeks of November, only 649 zombies volunteered to go overseas. McNaughton finally conceded defeat on 22 November, telephoning the prime minister to say "that the voluntary system would not get the men."[96]

King, who had visions of "civil war," made his decision at that moment. "It is apparent to me that to whatever bad management this may have been due, we are faced with a real situation which has to be met and now there is no longer thought as to the nature of the military advice tendered, particularly by Gen. McNaughton. And if so tendered by Gen. McNaughton who has come into the government to try to save the situation, it will be my clear duty to agree to the passing of the Order in Council and go to Parliament and ask for a vote of confidence."[97]

Whether it was prescience or just pure luck, King had averted a full-scale revolt in his cabinet. Even as he decided to implement limited overseas conscription, six of his ministers, including C. D. Howe, were meeting privately to prepare their simultaneous resignation to protest the government's conscription policy. The order-in-council, introduced the next day in the House of Commons, authorized the minister of defence to send overseas "such personnel, in such numbers as may be approved by the Governor in Council (the number hereby approved being sixteen thousand), who are serving by reason of their having been called out for training, service or duty pursuant to the provisions of the National Resources Mobilization Act, 1940."[98]

The storm that King had feared proved to be a tempest in a teapot. There were minor disturbances in Quebec involving civilians, but the most serious protests occurred in British Columbia, where there was at least one instance of "mutiny," as King called it, and lesser disorders involving zombies stationed in that province. He survived a vote of confidence in the Commons, and only one cabinet minister, Chubby Power, resigned from his cabinet.[99]

The first NRMA men to go overseas sailed from Halifax on 3 January 1945. Altogether, 12,908 were sent, and they served their country well. Only 2,463 actually joined combat units; 331 became casualties, including 69 who were killed.[100]

However, Prime Minister King's half-measure came too late to benefit I Canadian Corps, languishing in the backwater of a nearly-forgotten campaign. Not a single zombie went to Italy.

CHAPTER SEVENTEEN

Rivers of Blood

1

War-weariness hit them like a sledgehammer. Many of the dwindling number of the Canadian veterans in Italy had been in action for a year and a half; some were approaching their fifth year in uniform.

The infantry had borne the brunt of the battles, and now they were tired of it all. "There were men with children four and five years old, whom they had never seen," writes Farley Mowat.[1] The corps commander, Tommy Burns, sensed the growing disillusionment among his men. "I felt that some of the discouragement came from the realization that the promises of victory in 1944 and a speedy return home could not be fulfilled."[2]

Their regimental families were changing, too. The local or regional identities borne by most infantry battalions had become hazy since early 1944, when "the process of funnelling recruits towards their own provincial regiments was discontinued; the thinning trickle of men from Canada was pooled in the reinforcement depots and 'rationed' impersonally to all units in the field."[3] Cross-posting further diluted regimental identities. Because it was almost impossible to forecast casualties in a given unit, there were times when it was necessary to divert reinforcements to formations "in worse circumstances . . . than the unit to which such reinforcments rightfully belonged," says Strome Galloway of The Royal Canadian Regiment. "Cross-posting was by no means popular, and when the battle was over efforts were made to send these men back to their own parent battalion as soon as possible" – if they had survived.[4]

To make matters worse, wounded men who would normally have been shipped back to Canada were instead returning to the battlefront. One of these was Arnold McCourt of the Three Rivers Regiment. Suffering from a damaged ear-drum and multiple shell-fragment wounds, McCourt was hospitalized at Caserta, where he was classified as Medical Category E, under which he would be evacuated to Canada. During the summer of 1944, he was reclassified as a category A and sent back to battle. "At least the pill was sweetened a bit," he later commented, "in that we did return to our own units and not to some other regiment."[5]

Home leave might have helped, but it was available for only a select few. The reason: there were not enough men to take the place of those who went home. The measures adopted were inadequate, to say the least. The first was the "Tri-wound Scheme," for veterans who had been wounded three times; eighty-eight Canadians left Italy in September under this program. After Defence Minister Ralston's visit to the front, it was modified to give a six-month tour of duty in Canada for three-year veterans who had been twice wounded. Veterans of five years' continuous overseas service qualified for thirty-day leaves in Canada.[6] But this was another half-measure; only three men per battalion were allowed to go. For example, there were forty-one veterans of the RCR who qualified, and the lucky trio had their names drawn from a hat.[7]

The conscription crisis in Canada did nothing to improve morale. It would be impossible to say who was more unpopular at this moment, Prime Minister Mackenzie King or the zombies. Even now, nearly a half-century after the war, the depth of feeling aroused by the mere mention of King's name can be surprising. RCHA gunner Henry Worrell maintains that "Mackenzie King was the greatest traitor Canada ever had. If I'd seen Mackenzie King over there, and I'd had a rifle in my hand, I'd have shot him dead."[8] The zombies were viewed with equal derision. Charlie Phelan, also of the RCHA, noted in his diary that his fellow gunners had agreed upon a motto for the reluctant conscripts: "Ladies before gentlemen: CWACs overseas first."[9]

Andy McNaughton came in for his share of abuse, too. Word of his appointment as defence minister was greeted with unbounded enthusiasm, but this mood turned to anger within days, when it was realized that McNaughton would not willingly bring in conscription. "They felt that they had been betrayed," wrote noted poet Douglas LePan, who served as a gunner in Italy, "and betrayed by someone they had trusted, trusted supremely. They believed it was impossible to raise sufficient reinforcements by voluntary means and they believed the General knew that, too. . . . It is impossible to exaggerate the bitterness."[10]

The infantry shortage in Italy peaked in early November. On the fourth, the Canadian corps was 1,209 other ranks below its requirements.[11] The fighting troops might not have been aware of the precise numbers, but the weakness of front-line companies, platoons, and sections was painfully obvious to every soldier. Morale suffered accordingly, writes the RCR's Strome Galloway. "Our rifle companies were always under strength, the reinforcements poorly trained. The eyes of the world were now on the great destructive battles of the [Western] Front. By October, 1944, we were floundering in a backwater of the war. Only some of us could remember the road to Ortona and our distant walk in Sicily's sunshine."[12]

Underlying all else were feelings of irrelevancy. The war was being won elsewhere, these men knew, and anything that happened in Italy made little difference to the eventual outcome. "The thing that always hung over there, even before the Second Front," recalls war correspondent Doug How, "was that there was always a nagging feeling that it really wasn't relevant, that it wasn't going to matter a helluva lot. It was a secondary front."[13]

Their sensitivity on this point gave rise to one of the most famous songs of the war. When the Normandy invasion was plastered all over the front pages of newspapers (including *The Maple Leaf*) as D-Day, Mediterranean veterans were far from impressed. Hitherto, D-Day had been the reference point for any tentatively scheduled military operation, and Canadians had been involved in two D-Days in the Mediterranean, the landings at Pachino and Reggio di Calabria. Other D-Days in this theatre included North Africa, Salerno, and Anzio, but all were overshadowed by the most famous D-Day of all, Normandy.

Veterans of Italy, of all nationalities, call themselves "D-Day Dodgers," a term they use with justifiable pride. Its origins are doubtful, but the name is commonly attributed to Nancy Astor. Wealthy and beautiful, charming and outspoken, the American-born Lady Astor had a fond connection with Canadians, dating back to the Great War, when she allowed the Canadian Red Cross to establish a hospital on her estate. Britain's first female member of Parliament, she flirted with a number of unpopular causes, including fascism and prohibition, and during the war vicious rumours about her circulated in the armed forces. The most notorious rumour blamed her for demeaning the Italian campaign by referring to the troops there as "D-Day Dodgers." Her biographer, John Grigg, insists it was all very innocent: that she received a letter from a British soldier, who signed it "D-Day Dodgers." Writes Grigg: "She, assuming this was a humorous nickname like 'Desert Rats,' began her reply 'Dear D-Day Dodgers,' only to find that it was soon being put around she had cast an odious slur on the army in Italy."[14]

The soldiers, including Canadians, reacted with anger, which was vented in the derisive lyrics of a song that became their theme. Sung to the tune of their favourite, "Lili Marlene," it was entitled, "We Are the D-Day Dodgers":

We are the D-Day Dodgers, out in Italy,
Always on the vino, always on the spree.
Eighth Army skivers and their tanks,
We go to war, in ties and slacks,
We are the D-Day Dodgers, in sunny Italy.

We fought into Agira, a holiday with pay;
Jerry brought his bands out to cheer us on our way,
Showed us the sights and gave us tea,
We all sang songs, the beer was free,
We are the D-Day Dodgers, in sunny Italy.

The Moro and Ortona were taken in our stride,
We didn't really fight there, we went there for the ride.
Sleeping 'til noon and playing games,
We live in Rome with lots of dames.
We are the D-Day Dodgers, in sunny Italy.

On our way to Florence, we had a lovely time,
We drove a bus from Rimini, right through the Gothic Line.
Then to Bologna we did go,
We all went swimming in the Po,
We are the D-Day Dodgers, in sunny Italy.

We hear the boys in France are going home on leave
After six months' service, such a shame they're not relieved.
We were told to carry on a few more years,
Because our wives don't shed no tears,
We are the D-Day Dodgers, in sunny Italy.

We are the D-Day Dodgers, way out in Italy.
We're always tight, we cannot fight.
What bloody use are we?

When the Canadians came out of the line at the end of October, the relentless rain was depressing. The *bora*, the winter gale that blows across the Adriatic from the mountains of Yugoslavia, left them cold and miserable. "It looks as if they're trying to drown us here," fumed a Hasty P in a letter home, while another commented: "So help me, it's so Goddamned wet out here that even our hair is rusting. Somebody seems to have it in for us."[15]

Discontent with rations hit new heights. "Interminable bully beef and Australian dehydrated mutton with dehydrated vegetables and inedible margarine – these were the staples," Farley Mowat remembers. "Scrounging was no longer a hobby, but a virtual necessity." They traded anything and everything, with anyone and everyone, in the hope of improving their lot.[16]

There were the usual recreational activities: sports, concerts, card games, parties, trips to Rome and Florence, which were accompanied by an alarming rise in venereal disease.[17]

There was also a return to spit and polish, which infuriated these veterans. It seemed like an unnecessary aggravation, according to the RCHA's Charlie Phelan, whose diary reveals his fury: "Everyone is getting fed up with our alleged 'rest.' The bull is getting pretty thick. For example, we in our room are so crowded that we have difficulty moving around once the beds are made down – especially as there are no lights – yet each morning we have to lay out our kit according to a mimeographed diagram. What a war!"[18]

The resumption of training was made more interesting by a menagerie of new weapons and equipment: "Firefly," "Crocodile," "Wasp," "Weasel." The Firefly was a Sherman mounting a 17-pounder gun instead of the 75-millimetre, an improvement which enabled the Canadians to meet enemy tanks on nearly equal terms. The Crocodile was a Churchill tank equipped with a flamethrower capable of squirting a stream of burning fuel up to two hundred yards; the Wasp was a carrier-mounted flamethrower, which was allotted four per battalion. (A portable flamethrower, named the "Lifebuoy," was also introduced.) The Weasel was an American amphibious vehicle originally developed for the First Special Service Force.[19]

The engineers also had some new toys. Their training emphasized, for obvious reasons, bridging and rafting, and Canadians were responsible for two innovative bridges. Captain B. S. Brown developed an eighty-foot assault bridge braced by a pair of tanks, with the advantage that no tank was lost, unlike the previous versions, in which a turretless tank carried the bridge into the water and remained there as the foundation.[20] The infantry's need for a portable foot-bridge was filled by Captain E. A. Olafson, on the staff at Third Brigade headquarters. He designed a bridge in fifteen-foot segments of half-inch steel; up to five segments, each weighing two hundred pounds, could be connected with relative ease under fire.[21]

They would soon have a chance to test these innovations in the mud of northern Italy.

2

November's rains brought the winds of change to I Canadian Corps.

The main victim was Tommy Burns. The forty-seven-year-old career soldier had few admirers, fewer friends. A theorist, he was more suited temperamentally and professionally to the role of a senior staff officer. He was, in many ways, a pathetic figure, aware of his own shortcomings and uncomfortable with the realization that he was in over his head.

By now, Burns had become all but isolated at corps headquarters. His divisional commanders, Chris Vokes and Bert Hoffmeister, had no use for him; Vokes, in particular, recalls one senior officer, "made no secret of his dislike for Tommy Burns. . . . He was clever, but his austere, almost unfriendly manner contrasted so strongly with the rough and extroverted manner of Vokes that it seemed that co-operation between them was impossible."

Few knew Burns better than his chief staff officer, Brigadier Desmond Smith. In Smith's opinion, Burns had been "extremely fortunate" to reach his high rank, which merely focussed attention on his shortcomings. "The man as a leader lacked the personality that has that basic human touch." Burns, says Smith, "seemed to find it very difficult to ever enjoy a pleasant comment or a joke with any of his colleagues. He spent more time stopping his Jeep on the highway or on the roads and telling off a private soldier who was not wearing his beret or who had his battledress in a state of dishevelment." According to Smith, Burns's personality traits translated into trouble whenever the corps was in action. "When the battle was engaged, any plans which he might have worked out in considerable detail and with great integrity, once they started to fall apart, as a commander, he lost complete control. He lost control of his divisional commanders."[22]

Burns's days had been numbered. He had retained his command only by the narrowest of margins in the wake of the Liri valley campaign, but Defence Minister Ralston had heard enough complaints about him that, during his visit to Italy in early October, he had cornered Brigadier Smith, whose views on Burns's capabilities he sought. Smith, naturally, refused to offer his opinion of a superior officer, but "it became quite clear to me at this point in time that the powers that be had decided that Burns should be removed from command of the corps."[23]

On 24 October, when the Canadians were still battling on the Savio, Burns was summoned to the Eighth Army's headquarters. There, General McCreery "informed me that he was not satisfied with me as corps Commander, and had recommended that I be replaced." Burns "was surprised; I had thought that after the victories of the corps in the Adriatic offensive the higher command had revised its previously unfavourable opinion of my ability."[24]

Tommy Burns's fate was sealed. He went on leave to Rome on 2 November, but this was interrupted when Harry Crerar ordered him to fly to England, where he would be assigned to other duties. At the time, Burns recalled, "I was very resentful of the way in which my service in the Italian Theatre had been terminated." Years later, however, he was able to "look at it in a more philosophical way." While he proudly pointed out that under "my command the corps had taken all objectives assigned to it, inflicting heavy losses on the enemy," he did not find it "surprising that General McCreery would want to replace any of his subordinate commanders whom he considered would not be fully effective in the hard, forbidding operations which apparently lay ahead."[25] Burns ended up as the senior Canadian officer at Twenty-first Army Group headquarters – the kind of staff job for which he was eminently suited.

It seemed that Vokes would be the beneficiary of this upheaval at corps headquarters. When Burns left Italy on the evening of 6 November, Vokes was named as his temporary replacement, and it was widely assumed that he would be confirmed in this appointment shortly. Desmond Smith, the senior corps staff officer, was named as acting commander of the First Division, and George Kitching, an old hand in Italy, who had briefly commanded the Fourth Canadian Armoured Division in Normandy, was brought in to replace Smith.

But Harry Crerar had other ideas about the corps command. Crerar had recently been ill, and while Guy Simonds had temporarily taken his place at First Canadian Army headquarters, Simonds's II Corps had been run by Charles Foulkes, a forty-one-year-old professional soldier. Foulkes had filled the position for five weeks, and Crerar evidently liked what he saw. On 9 November, he commended Foulkes on the job he had done; three days later, over lunch, he informed Foulkes that he was going to Italy to take over I Corps.[26]

Crerar had ulterior motives for appointing Foulkes. Besides their professional careers, Crerar and Foulkes had one thing in common: they did not get along with Guy Simonds. Crerar, his Italian contretemps with Simonds still very much in his thoughts, had one eye on the post-war period, and he had no intention of giving Simonds a free run to the top of Canada's peacetime army. The way things stood now, Simonds had no competition; but the smooth-talking Foulkes might provide it, if he were promoted soon enough.

A comedy of errors ensued. Word of Foulkes's promotion was relayed to General Alexander's Fifteenth Army Group headquarters. Somehow, there was an error in transmission. It may be that some anonymous operator did not recognize Foulkes's name and substituted the better-known Vokes. In any case, Alexander sent a telegram to Vokes on 14 November, congratulating him on his appointment. Vokes's staff, assuming that this meant that his position was permanent, staged a celebratory dinner that evening.

The mistake was not realized until the next day, when a top-secret cable arrived for Vokes. The corps commander was away from headquarters, inspecting units, so Brigadier Kitching opened and read it, as he was empowered to do under these circumstances. Kitching was "horrified" when he saw the contents: Charles Foulkes had been named as corps commander, and Vokes was being transferred to northwestern Europe to take over the Fourth Armoured Division; that division's commander,

Harry Foster, would get the First Division. This was, according to Kitching, "Army politics of the worst kind. Chris Vokes was senior to him, had four times as much operational experience, was well known to the troops who had confidence in him, and he was well known at 8th Army Headquarters. I could not help but feel that this was General Crerar at his worst."[27]

Now it was Chris Vokes's turn to be philosophical. "I have often wondered," he later wrote, "whether someone got the names Vokes and Foulkes mixed up. . . . I have lost no sleep over that command shuffle, but I have sometimes speculated about what later might have been." It has been speculated that Vokes switched places with Foster as a face-saving measure after the embarrassing confusion over names, but Vokes had other ideas: "No doubt the top brass knew I'd be able to stomach Foulkes even less well than I had Burns, as my Corps Commander." Vokes's acquaintance with Foulkes dated back to before the war, and he "had always disliked the man. I thought he was nothing but a military nincompoop, a complete horse's ass, a military politician."[28]

Foulkes's arrival was less than auspicious. Vokes, hiding his disappointment, arranged a warm welcome at the Rimini airport, complete with a guard of honour from Foulkes's peacetime unit, The Royal Canadian Regiment, a band, and all senior officers. The welcoming party waited in vain; when the corps commander's aircraft failed to show up, the parade was dismissed.

It turned out that Foulkes had been taken to the wrong airfield. To add insult to humiliation, the American flight crew dropped him at the far end of the runway, with all his luggage. "In a towering rage," he staggered with his bags to a nearby hangar, where he introduced himself as the Canadian corps commander, and demanded a ride. A Canadian corporal working on a vehicle refused to believe him; as far as he was concerned, Chris Vokes was the corps commander, and this officer was clearly not Vokes. The corporal ignored him and Foulkes hitch-hiked to Eighth Army headquarters, where he was able to find transportation to Rimini.[29]

Unfortunately, his formal introduction to the corps was not much better. Foulkes assumed an attitude of superiority; this was, after all, just the Spaghetti League, and he was a veteran of the "real war," in northwestern Europe. Gathering 125 senior officers in Teatro Dante, an opera house in Riccione, he lectured them on his expectations. "He started off by telling us that he expected some 'spirited leadership' in the next operation, thus giving us the impression that he did not believe we had been giving that type of leadership in the past," recounts the RCR's Strome Galloway, who resented the implication, especially in view of the latter's lack of experience. "Those of us who had experienced sixteen months of fighting in

Sicily and Italy did not need this high-ranking tyro to tell us how to lead men. His contempt for the fighting troops was apparent."[30]

It was not an auspicious beginning for Foulkes.

Within days, planning was under way for the next offensive. The object was the capture of Bologna by a pincer movement of the two armies. General Alexander reserved for himself the right to set the date, some time after 7 December. In the meantime, the Eighth Army would conduct preliminary operations to the River Santerno, its designated start line for the drive on Bologna. To get there, the Eighth would have to get across two other major rivers, the Lamone and the Senio. General McCreery's instructions called for I Canadian Corps to go into action on the army's right flank, where it would drive straight northwards through Russi to Route 16, cutting off Ravenna, then swing west through Lugo and establish a bridgehead on the Santerno.

Corps planners filled in the details. The Canadian phase of operations was code-named "Chuckle," an unfortunate name, in retrospect, but it was really an innocent choice, according to Brigadier Kitching. "Code names were allotted by Army in blocks," he explains, "so we at Corps would be given a number of them, probably all starting with 'C.' 'Chuckle' just happened to come out at the top."[31]

Foulkes intended to commit both Canadian divisions to the battle. They would start out together from the vicinity of Casa Bertini, on the Montone. The Fifth Division, on the right, would swing through San Pancrazio and Godo to cut Route 16 and capture Ravenna, while the First Division made the main drive on Russi, followed by the multiple river crossings to the Santerno. The starting date depended on the 10th Indian Division's ability to capture Casa Bertini, but the ground ahead of the Canadian corps was hardly promising, interspersed by rain-swollen streams, irrigation ditches, and canals, while each of the major rivers flowed between high flood-banks, "which gave the enemy excellent observation of the intervening flats and provided him with sites for burrowed-out shelters and machine-gun positions. . . . To move forward between the rivers was an arduous task; to cross them a formidable one indeed."[32]

3

The 10th Indian Division cleared Casa Bertini during the early morning of Friday, 1 December. In the next few hours, three Canadian infantry battalions moved into the bridgehead. On the right was the Twelfth Brigade's Princess Louise Dragoon Guards, with the Royal 22nd and West Nova Scotia regiments of the Third Brigade on the left. At 2100 hours, General

Foulkes assumed command of the sector stretching from this bridgehead to the Adriatic, as final plans were distributed to the assault units.[33]

Operation Chuckle started the next morning. At 0900 on that sunny Saturday, a punishing artillery and aerial bombardment cleared the way for the initial infantry advance a half-hour later. Leading the First Division's advance, the two battalions of the Third Brigade had little trouble at first, although the West Novas were mistakenly strafed by British fighters. In the face of growing opposition in the approach to Russi, however, both battalions laid low until after dark, not a long wait, because the sun started to go down at 1630. The Germans facing the Van Doos withdrew under the cover of darkness, and the French-Canadians chased them all the way to the rail line west of Russi. The West Novas, assisted by engineers of the 4th Field Company, were in Russi by 0700 on 3 December.[34]

While the Third Brigade manoeuvred into position to seize a bridgehead on the Lamone, the Twelfth Brigade was doing equally well. The Princess Louise Dragoon Guards, like the West Novas and Van Doos, got off to a smooth start on Saturday morning, pushing northeastwards along the Montone. And, like the other two battalions, they were also stopped by fierce resistance, in a bottleneck formed by opposing bends in the parallel waterways, the Montone and the Scolo Via Cupa. The Westminster Regiment saved the day.

It had been Brigadier J. S. Lind's intention that the Westminsters remain on the east side of the Montone until San Pancrazio had been cleared, but a thick fog in the river flats appeared to offer the Westies a chance to cross earlier. The battalion commander, Lieutenant-Colonel Gordon Corbould, called in one of his company commanders, Bert Hoskin, and the thirty-two-year-old major agreed to attempt it.[35]

The Westies wasted little time. A platoon under Sergeant J. D. Jones slipped across the Montone and cleared mines from the far bank, while assault boats were brought up and tied side-by-side to form a fifty-foot bridge. As Hoskin deployed his men to rush the river, "we got the goddamnedest stonking you ever saw in your life. And we were just lying there, and when the stonking stopped for a minute, I jumped up and said, 'Let's go!'" At a dead run, the Westies raced across the Montone and fanned out on the far side. The Germans opened fire on them, but it was too late: six surprised defenders were killed and seventeen taken prisoner in the next few minutes. "It worked like a charm, thank God," says Hoskin, who was awarded the Distinguished Service Order for this action. By nightfall the whole battalion was over the Montone.[36]

It was a fine coup, but the Westies were just getting warmed up. After capturing San Pancrazio on 3 December, they were ordered to take Piangipane, a crossroads village five miles north, midway between Russi and

Route 16. They set off in single file in the late afternoon, with darkness descending. It was a risky venture, in the dark, in unfamiliar territory alive with enemy tanks, and with unreliable maps their only guide, but it went surprisingly well. Using a demolished bridge to cross the *scolo*, they were across the Godo–Ravenna road by midnight. Here they ambushed an enemy convoy. At the cost of seven casualties, the Westies killed ten Germans and captured twenty-three more, knocking out two tanks and three half-tracks.[37]

They pushed on towards Piangipane, which they captured during the afternoon of 4 December. At the same time, the Plugs, supported by Shermans of the British Columbia Dragoons, roared up the road from Godo towards Ravenna, a walled city of thirty thousand, famed as Dante's burial place. It was an easy conquest, for the Germans had evacuated Ravenna to avoid being trapped.[38]

Things were going exceedingly well for Bert Hoffmeister's Mighty Maroon Machine. Ravenna had been captured, and the fall of Piangipane enabled the Eleventh Brigade to join the advance towards the Lamone. By the morning of 6 December, the armoured division held a five-mile front along the river.

The First Division, however, was having problems. Despite committing his reserve unit, the Carleton and York Regiment, the Third Brigade's Paul Bernatchez was unable to get his battalions beyond the Lamone. By the morning of 4 December, forty-eight hours after launching its first attacks, the brigade had finally closed up to the river, to find that the Germans had retired behind the blown railway and road bridges.

Now came a fateful decision. The previous afternoon, Brigadier Bernatchez had requested that the First Brigade take over from his Third Brigade, "due to casualties suffered." The divisional commander, Brigadier Smith, waited until shortly after midnight, and when it became apparent that the Third Brigade was not going to be able to establish a bridgehead on the Lamone, he instructed the First Brigade to complete the Third's phase of the operation.[39]

Historians, and survivors of the First Brigade, have been critical of the last-minute change of plan. George Stevens later pointed out that the Third Brigade's casualties, "slightly over a hundred," did not justify the concern shown by Bernatchez.[40] But this was Desmond Smith's maiden battle in command of a division, and Paul Bernatchez was a highly regarded brigadier: if Bernatchez felt that his brigade could not continue, Smith was hardly in a position to argue.

Neither was the First Brigade's commander, Montreal's Allan Calder, who would pay the price for this hastily-conducted operation. "If I had known then what I know now," says Calder, "I would have refused the order. Of course, refusing an order is a 'no-win' proposition, because it can never be proved what would have happened if the order had been carried out." At the time, however, there was the ever-present "sense of urgency and haste after we had dislodged the enemy from a defensive position – urgency to press on and deny him the opportunity to comfortably settle into his next defensive position. Within reason, this made sense, because allowing him to man his next position would cause more casualties to our troops than if he was kept in retreat."[41]

In the haste lay the seeds of disaster. Calder says that he received no fewer than four different sets of orders in a matter of hours.[42] Eventually, a set-piece attack was planned, with two battalions backed by the entire divisonal artillery and four regiments of medium guns. The Royal Canadian and Hastings and Prince Edward regiments were scheduled to make their assault at 0100 hours on Tuesday, 5 December.

But it was not going to be easy. The first troops to reach the Lamone, patrols of the RCR, were dismayed to discover that the river was a far more serious obstacle than had been indicated by initial intelligence reports. Instead of being "3–5 feet deep, and the banks fairly good and not very high," reported Major Jim Houghton, "the river was 10–15 feet deep, the current very swift, and the water very cold, and the water gap approximately 35 feet wide." An RCR scout officer drowned in the icy torrent.[43]

The operation started poorly for the Hasty Ps. The assault companies of both battalions were instructed to keep away from the river bank during the ten-minute preliminary bombardment by the medium guns. This precaution was necessary because the mediums fired their shells in a flat trajectory, and it was almost certain that there would be some hits on the Canadian side. However, the two companies of Hasty Ps moved right up to the embankment, thanks to the darkness and fog and their unreliable Italian maps. At 0050 hours, when the bombardment began, one Canadian shell after another smashed into them; by the time the mediums ceased firing after ten minutes, the Hasty Ps were a battered, bloody mess. Forty-eight of them had been either killed or wounded; the survivors were in a state of shock.[44]

The Royal Canadians went ahead alone. Major Jim Houghton, whose A Company was to be the first to cross the Lamone, led his men to the water as soon as the bombardment ended, only to find that the collapsible canvas boats that were supposed to be there had not yet arrived. "I spread the men out below the dyke wall and waited." Half an hour later, the boats were hauled up, and Houghton hurriedly put two platoons across; when the boats returned, he boarded his remaining platoon and his headquarters. "A shell burst near my boat," the English-born professional later wrote, "and killed or wounded all in it except myself."[45]

Despite this mishap, Houghton established his company on its objectives by 0215 hours, with Major Eric Thorne's B Company on the left, towards the rail line. The only concern was that one of Thorne's platoons was missing. (Only later would it become clear that the platoon was not merely missing, but practically wiped out. It had crossed the Lamone on the ruins of the railway bridge, only to be stonked by enemy mortars at the far end; eighteen out of twenty-three men were killed or wounded.) With the bridgehead seemingly secure, Captain Jimmy Wilkinson brought C Company across on a pair of Olafson foot-bridges and led his troops inland. Aside from scattered shelling and small-arms fire, the foggy night was quiet.[46]

By dawn, things seemed to be going smoothly, not only with the RCR but with the Hasty Ps. After they had been shelled by their own medium guns, Major Cliff Broad had led the forty-odd survivors of B Company over the Lamone and linked up with the RCR, digging in on the right flank. The acting battalion commander, Major Stan Ketcheson, ordered up his two reserve companies, and sent them across the Olafson bridges.[47]

Then the Germans counter-attacked. Under the cover of a "thick grey mist," and hidden by the twenty-foot embankment that carried the Ravenna–Lugo railway line, elements of the 114th Jäger and 356th Infantry divisions, supported by self-propelled guns, struck the RCR at daybreak. As luck would have it, the enemy hit the bridgehead where it was weakest. The platoon that had been wiped out crossing the ruined railway bridge was supposed to guard the battalion's left flank, which was instead left wide open to the German counter-attack.[48]

The results were disastrous. C Company was all but wiped out. Captain Wilkinson was captured; only twelve of his men escaped. B Company was also overrun, losing forty-one officers and other ranks, out of seventy-two who went into action; Major Thorne was fatally wounded.[49]

Huddled over his radio set in a house near the riverbank was Private Ray Eaton. "I was talking to a forward platoon that was being slashed to pieces," he remembers. "I could hear them on my radio, but I wasn't able to get through to them." His company commander had ordered him to "tell them to drop everything and get out. And I kept at this and kept at this. My company sergeant-major told me to move, and my company commander stuck his head in the door and shouted to move. I didn't move quick enough, and by the time I got out it was too late – the Germans were on top of us." Eaton ended up at Stalag VIIA in Moosburg, but not before enduring numerous privations, as well as an Allied air raid and a derailment.[50]

Without heavy weapons to help them repel the enemy assault, the Royal Canadians and Hasty Ps fought a stubborn rearguard action during the morning. The survivors gradually withdrew, and by 0900 hours, the only Canadians on the far side of the Lamone were either dead or prisoners.

It had been a stunning reversal of fortunes. "The apparent success of 0630 hrs," commented the RCR war diary, "had turned into a ghastly failure before 1200 hrs." In less than twelve hours, the two assault battalions had suffered 164 casualties. The RCR lost 106 men, including 31 taken prisoner; almost all of the losses suffered by the Hasty Ps came at the hands of their own artillery before the attack started.[51]

At corps headquarters, Charles Foulkes was enraged by the failure that had blighted his first major operation. Desmond Smith was absolved of any blame, but the First Brigade's Allan Calder provided a convenient scapegoat, as Foulkes explained in a letter to Harry Crerar:

> I thoroughly investigated this party and I have come to the conclusion it failed mainly because of the lack of inspired leadership and ability to command on the part of Calder. The consolidation was not properly buttoned up, and Calder was unable to read the battle properly and take the necessary action with his reserve when things were going badly. . . . I'm afraid that Calder will not do as a brigade commander.[52]

It was hardly a fair assessment, which Calder believes was based more on personal animosity than on professional ability. The First Brigade had performed effectively under Calder's command through every engagement during the past four months, and at the Lamone it had been rushed in to fight a battle that rightfully belonged to the Third Brigade. The real reason for the reversal at the Lamone was the latter's commander, Brigadier Bernatchez.

"The fact that the Lamone battle was not the success that it might have been," says Desmond Smith, "is no reason to suggest that Calder was not an effective brigade commander." Nevertheless, Calder's misfortune was a stroke of luck for Smith, who now assumed command of the First Brigade. His command of the First Division had been temporary, pending the arrival of Major-General Harry Foster, and Smith had expected to return to corps headquarters as the chief staff officer at I Corps. However, that posting had gone to George Kitching, much to Smith's surprise. Had the First Brigade not become available to him, Smith would have been left without a job.[53]

Allan Calder quietly returned to the so-called "Cease-Fire League" in England, where he was given command of a training unit, but he was not the only scapegoat for the Lamone misadventure. More heads rolled when the new divisional commander, Harry Foster, arrived from northwestern Europe the day after the Lamone. Foster, a forty-two-year-old Nova Scotia native, who was not very happy about being "exiled to Italy" in Chris

Vokes's place, promptly fired the two battalion commanders at the Lamone, Lieutenant-Colonel Jim Ritchie of the RCR and Major Stan Ketcheson of the Hasty Ps.[54]

The first few days of Chuckle had not greatly inconvenienced the Germans. The opening blow had fallen on a newly organized formation, LXXIII Corps, commanded by General der Infanterie Anton Dostler. This corps, comprising only two divisions, the 114th Jäger and 356th Infantry, was assigned the coastal sector, which coincided almost exactly with that held by the opposing I Canadian Corps.

The subsequent loss of Ravenna had not been unexpected, and the Germans had fallen back in an orderly fashion behind the Lamone. The assault by the First Canadian Infantry Brigade barely rated a mention in the day's summary of operations prepared by Vietinghoff, who was far more concerned with the situation south of Route 9, where a joint Polish and British attack on 3 December had crossed the Lamone. By the seventh, the Allied thrust was threatening Faenza and Imola. Vietinghoff hesitated to commit his reserves, fearing a Fifth Army attack on Bologna if he overreacted to the Eighth Army drive. But when there appeared to be no activity on the Bologna front and the lengthy Canadian sector along the Lamone fell quiet, he gambled on a counter-attack on 9 December, sending his 90th Panzer Grenadier Division to smash the British south of Faenza. The British 46th Division skilfully parried the attack, leaving the situation of Vietinghoff's Tenth Army unimproved.

Just as Kesselring had been doing for so many months, Vietinghoff found that his main role as commander-in-chief was to juggle his few reserves, particularly of armour, to meet the multiple threats across the front. For the time being, at least, it seemed that he had things under control. Then the Lamone front "burst into flames" once more, as the Canadians stormed across the bloody, muddy river.[55]

Defeat did not sit well with Charles Foulkes. The new corps commander ordered his staff to draw up plans for another assault on the Lamone, this time by both Canadian divisions, on the night of 6 December.

It was in the midst of this adversity that Foulkes won over some of the doubters at both corps and divisional headquarters. The Lamone fiasco notwithstanding, George Kitching, the top corps staff officer, came to admire the general. "The more I worked with Charles Foulkes in Italy the more I respected his judgment in tactical matters."[56]

The plan approved by Foulkes called for the First Division to establish a bridgehead in the same area where the RCR and Hasty Ps had come to grief, while the Fifth Division crossed several miles north, at Villanova and

Borgo di Villanova. Both divisions, after breaching the Lamone defences, were to strike for the next river, the Senio, four miles west. Between the rivers lay terrain which was anything but encouraging. In the space of less than two miles stood four dyked watercourses, Fosso Vetro, Fosso Vecchio, Canale Naviglio, and Fosso Munio, each one a naturally strong defensive position.

But the operation had to be postponed. Weather forecasts were not promising; possible storms in the mountains would not only jeopardize any bridgeheads which might be established on the Lamone but would also wash away the Canadian bridges on the Montone, thus cutting off the entire Canadian corps.

The intervening days were not wasted. The river crossing sites were carefully reconnoitred, in sharp contrast to the previous attempt, and each assault unit "had time to get down to really detailed planning," according to the commander of the Carleton and York Regiment, Jack Ensor. "The whole plan was put down to every man, and every man knew exactly what he was going into, where he was going, and how he was to do his job."[57]

It was "a dark moonless"[58] Sunday night, 10 December, when the Canadian corps crashed across the Lamone. The Fifth Division, mounting a silent attack by two battalions of the Eleventh Brigade, moved first. At 1930 hours, two companies each from the Perth Regiment and the Cape Breton Highlanders scrambled across the embankment, leapt into assault boats, and paddled over the swift Lamone. The Highlanders "got across practically unopposed," capturing the village of Villanova and forty-three prisoners,[59] while the Perths, in "an attack delivered with speed, precision, and complete success,"[60] stormed into Borgo di Villanova, a mile south of Villanova. The Westminster and Irish regiments were rushed across to secure and widen the bridgehead, and they moved so rapidly that they captured intact a bridge on the Fosso Vetro, an irrigation ditch. Driving off two small counter-attacks, they pushed on to the next ditch, the Fosso Vecchio, where they were forced to stop, for the enemy had had time to destroy the bridge. By midday on the eleventh, the Irish had "advanced 3,000 yards, taken 50 prisoners and killed and wounded probably as many more."[61]

At the same time, the First Division was making amends for its earlier setback on the Lamone. In sharp contrast to the silent attack employed by the Fifth Division, the First employed a massive and imaginative thirty-minute bombardment, which ceased for twenty minutes, then resumed in the hope of catching the defenders in the open. This program was orchestrated by the division's chief gunner, Bill Ziegler, who had introduced another innovation. With the enemy taking refuge behind the floodbanks of the rivers and canals, there was a need for more plunging fire, like that of mortars. Since 25-pounders could fire at no more than a 45-degree angle, Ziegler had the trails of the guns dug into the ground, which increased the angle of fire. There were no range tables for this type of shooting, but "we had a lot of mathematical brains," says Ziegler (himself a civil engineer in peacetime), "and we corrected them by actual fire."[62]

The assault, under eerie artificial moonlight, started at 2130 hours. This was, as originally planned, a Third Brigade operation, and Brigadier Bernatchez was given an extra battalion, the 48th Highlanders, to ensure success. Bernatchez put three battalions in the cross-river assault: the Carleton and Yorks on the right, with the West Novas in the centre, and the 48th on the left.[63]

Two companies led the Carletons across the Lamone. They travelled in a dozen assault boats, each capable of carrying up to fifteen men. Everyone who crossed the Lamone that night was surprised at the swift current. "I luckily managed to grab some overhanging willow branches," recalled Captain Pete Newell, "or else we would have been on our way to the Adriatic."[64]

Once across, the Carletons charged up the embankment, firing their Bren and Tommy guns and throwing grenades. Still reeling from the punishing bombardment, the Germans were taken completely by surprise. "Those who did not come out of their weapon pits quickly," Major Rowland Horsey wrote, "were treated to a 36 grenade." Within twenty minutes, his men were on their objectives. "The mopping up was not a great task," Horsey recounted. "I have never seen so many wounded, maimed and dead Germans in another area of similar size. Most of these casualties [were] caused by our small-arms fire and grenades." Later, when the bridgehead expanded, Horsey saw the "excellent" but grim results of the artillery's work, "a good many" dead Germans, who had been lured into the open during the pause in the shelling.[65]

The painstaking preparations had paid off. Toronto's 48th Highlanders matched the Carletons' success and, while the West Novas had minor difficulties, by dawn the Third Brigade had firmly established a bridgehead on the Lamone. Unlike the previous week's débâcle involving the First Brigade, the successful crossing was achieved at relatively small cost. The Carletons had one man killed and twelve others wounded in this operation.[66]

During the night of 11–12 December, the Germans withdrew behind the Canale Naviglio, seven hundred yards west of the Fosso Vecchio. The Naviglio's twenty-foot earthen embankment stood out clearly, ominously, above the misty, flat, treeless fields. According to intelligence reports, the bed of the canal was dry here; the Germans had dammed it further south. It was known, too, that the enemy had rushed up reinforcements to block the Canadian advance. The two-division LXXIII Corps had been bolstered by the relatively fresh 98th Infantry Division and by an élite unit, the Kesselring Machine-Gun Battalion, one of only two such heavily armed units in Italy, employed for emergencies like the one developing on the Canadian front.[67]

General Foulkes prepared another set-piece attack. Once again, both divisions would take part, supported by tanks now pouring across the Lamone bridges built by the engineers. The stage was set for the last full-scale battle by Canadians in Italy.

The battle for the Naviglio began after dark on Tuesday, 12 December. Four battalions spearheaded the operation. On the right, the Fifth Division sent into action the only two infantry units that had not yet been involved in the fighting, the Princess Louise Dragoon Guards and the Lanark and Renfrew Scottish, while the First Division committed the Carleton and Yorks and Hasty Ps, the latter still shaken by their dire experience on the Lamone a week earlier.

It was an overcast evening, with a thick mist giving way to drizzle as the troops slogged forward. The Plugs and Lanarks crossed the Fosso Vecchio without much difficulty, and patrols slipped across the fields towards the canal. Not until they approached the shadow-shrouded embankment did they realize what they were up against. The grass-covered floodbank loomed over them, its twenty-foot slope seemingly perpendicular.[68]

Sergeant Fred Cederberg of the Lanarks grabbed one of his men and crawled up to explore the bank. As he pulled himself to the top, Cederberg found himself looking at Schmeissers held by a pair of grim-faced Germans. Luckily for the sergeant, his partner was fast on the draw, and the bullet-riddled Germans tumbled into the dry bed of the canal. That set off a battle royal, according to Cederberg. "Long strings of tracers slit the darkness, followed by a series of detonating Jerry potato-masher grenades, the eye blinking pinpoints of flame searing the ground mists. Hoarse, maddened shouts were flung at the forbidding sky. The slow, rhythmic thump-thump-thump of a Bren gun, spouting incendiaries, sprayed the faint outline of the dyke, followed by the intermittent harsh crack of our own 36 grenades."[69]

The Lanarks were pinned right there, unable to cross the canal, unwilling to go back to the Fosso Vecchio. And so they dug in and doggedly held on. Their 111 casualties[70] included 16 cases of trench foot, a malady usually associated with the trenches of the Great War and caused by prolonged exposure to cold and wet.[71]

The Plugs, a mile to the right, had fared even worse. Two squadrons (the former reconnaissance regiment stubbornly refused to call its sub-units companies) fought their way across the canal, only to be trapped there by German shell-fire. At 0140, after only four hours of fighting, the acting battalion commander, Major A. E. Langston, ordered a withdrawal, but it was too late for Private Cecil Cook and many of his buddies holed up in a battered house. Cook's party fought until they ran out of ammunition, he recalls. "One of our officers just about had his stomach blown out, so he said to the sergeant, 'Holler "surrender."' The sergeant wouldn't give up. He said, 'You're still in command, you do the hollering.' So the officer – his stomach was hanging out – he hollered. Then we went out with our hands over our heads and lined up outside." Those were Cook's first steps into captivity that would end in a prison camp in southern Germany.[72]

The Naviglio cost the Princess Louise Dragoon Guards eighty-eight casualties, including forty-six men captured – more than half of all the Plugs lost as prisoners during the whole war.[73]

Things went better on the First Division's front, but the fighting was no less severe. Desmond Smith's First Brigade, reinforced by the Carleton and Yorks, drew this assignment. Smith wisely decided to send in the Carletons first, to establish a bridgehead on the Naviglio, then support with the Hastings and Prince Edward Regiment. Time was short: the plan was outlined to company commanders at 1900 hours, and H-Hour was at 2200. But the New Brunswick battalion, still flushed with its easy and impressive success on the Lamone two nights earlier, carried out its part quickly and confidently. The two leading companies cleared the far side of the canal, just north of the village of Bagnacavallo, in the face of "little opposition," rounding up forty-five prisoners. Three companies of the Hasty Ps then entered the bridgehead and extended it to the right, while the remaining two companies of the Carletons did likewise to the left.[74] By 0415 on 13 December, the bridgehead was more than a thousand yards wide and seven hundred yards deep.

In the grey, misty light of dawn, the Germans counter-attacked in force. Tanks and infantry swarmed across the flat fields from what seemed to be every direction. With help from the artillery, the Carletons held their own at first, but as the morning wore on, and the enemy pressure mounted steadily, the Carletons fell back to the canal bank, where they made their stand. "By noon the situation was critical," Major Rowland Horsey reported. Their only hope was that the tanks that had been promised them would arrive in time.[75]

The Hasty Ps were in even worse shape. One by one, the companies on the right were crushed by Mark IVs: first B Company, then A Company. C Company fell back, its toehold beyond the Naviglio reduced to a single house. Desperate radio messages to battalion headquarters told the alarming tale, but there was little that Lieutenant-Colonel Don Cameron could do for them, except assure them: "Help is on the way, hold on."[76]

The British Columbia Dragoons were indeed on the way. Unfortunately, the first tanks to reach the beleaguered Carletons mounted the old 75-millimetre guns, which were ineffective against the Panthers and Tigers roaming this battlefield. But the presence of the Shermans, and the knowledge that Fireflies, armed with the superior 17-pounders, were on the way, inspired the Carletons to fight even harder. The Fireflies arrived in the nick of time. A pair of them appeared shortly after 1500 hours, "and from that time on the day was ours," said Major Horsey, whose steadfast leadership was rewarded with the Distinguished Service Order.[77]

For the second time in three nights, the Carleton and Yorks had excelled in a major operation, and escaped with light losses: six killed and twenty-seven wounded. But for the Hasty Ps, their second major operation in just over a week had been costly. The battalion had suffered sixty-nine casualties, most of them captured when A and B companies were overrun.[78]

The bridgehead, or what was left of it, had been saved, but the battle was not yet over. It remained for the Canadians to recover the ground lost earlier in the day, and then using this solid base to exploit as rapidly as possible to the Senio. The task of restoring the bridgehead went to Jim Stone's Loyal Edmonton Regiment, supported by the B.C. Dragoons. The Eddies had been warned late in the morning, giving Colonel Stone several hours to reconnoitre and draw up his plans. "Time spent in *proper preparations*," he later wrote, "is not wasted." Stone's battalion advanced at 1600, with daylight just beginning to fade. The situation was fluid, with German tanks and self-propelled guns still roaming the area, but the Eddies took up their assigned positions during the evening, aided by artificial moonlight and supported by the Seaforth Highlanders. By midnight, the bridgehead had been restored.[79]

During the night, the sound of enemy armour could be heard around the perimeter of the bridgehead, and soon after daybreak on 14 December, the tanks and self-propelled guns counter-attacked, only to be crushed by Canadian artillery fire. By the end of the day, the smoking hulks of two Tigers and four Panthers in front of the Seaforths testified to the enemy's determination to smash the bridgehead.[80]

The artillery also came to the assistance of the neighbouring Edmontons, who organized a company attack on a group of houses held by the Germans. The enemy attacked first, but their timing – just two minutes before the Eddies' artillery support opened up – was terrible. The mixed force of German armour and infantry advanced right into the Canadian shell fire. The counter-attack was destroyed before it ever got going, without costing the Edmontons a single casualty.[81]

The Eddies captured ninety-one Germans, and killed or wounded another forty. Fifty of their own had fallen, including a dozen dead. One of those killed was Sergeant Joseph St. Germain, a Native from northern Alberta, who had fought at Ortona. When Stone had congratulated him after that battle, St. Germain had stated matter-of-factly, "That's fine, sir, but I hope I'm killed in this war. Here, I lead a platoon and the boys call me 'Saint,' but back in Canada, I'm just a poor goddam Indian," with no right to vote, unable even to go into a bar. Sergeant St. Germain got his wish, on the muddy banks of the Naviglio.[82]

Although it was still under attack, the bridgehead was already proving its worth. With his efforts to cross the canal having come to naught, the Fifth Division's Bert Hoffmeister arranged to use the First Division's crossing. At midday on 14 December, a company of the Westminster Regiment swung through the Loyal Eddies and, backed by Shermans of Lord Strathcona's Horse, pushed straight northwards. With help from fighter-bombers of the Desert Air Force, the Westies peeled the Germans away from the canal, capturing 106, suffering only twenty casualties themselves. That night, the Lanarks crossed the Naviglio and cleared the Germans from the village of Osteria; by daylight on the fifteenth, the Fifth Division had a foothold five hundred yards deep.[83]

While the Fifth Division pushed across the Naviglio and closed up to the Fosso Munio, the First Division staged a series of local attacks to widen its bridgehead for a break-out. During the night of 14–15 December, Princess Patricia's Canadian Light Infantry moved over the canal, with the task of driving the Germans out of ancient, walled Bagnacavallo, where many of the enemy counter-attacks had originated.

The bridgehead battles raged unabated on Friday, 15 December. If the Germans lacked the strength to drive the Second Brigade from the bridgehead, the Canadians were equally unable to break the resistance provided by enemy tanks and the élite Kesselring machine-gunners. Gains were modest as all three battalions, the Seaforths in the centre, flanked by the PPCLI on the left and the Eddies on the right, attempted to improve their holdings. When the Patricias were stopped short of Bagnacavallo, the Canadian gunners focussed their fury on the tall, stone church towers which gave the enemy excellent vantage points overlooking the entire battlefield. The towers were pounded to rubble by the 7th Canadian Anti-Tank Regiment, using 17-pounders and M10 self-propelled guns firing armour-piercing shells.[84]

It was apparent at corps headquarters that the battlefront would have to be widened. As General Foulkes assessed the situation, the key was Bagnacavallo; its fall would surely force the Germans back to the Senio. But this would not be easy, for the enemy still held the Fosso Vecchio as well as the

Canale Naviglio south of the Ravenna–Lugo railway line. Indeed, the railways that intersected the watercourses east of the Senio segmented the entire area into odd-shaped but easily-defended little fortresses.

At daybreak on 16 December, the 48th Highlanders of Canada attempted to close up to the Fosso Vecchio, the drainage ditch a mile east of its positions. The Toronto battalion employed a "patrol-and-crump tactic," in which patrols would creep forward and locate defensive positions, then call in an artillery "crump" to destroy them. The Highlanders actually managed to capture intact a bridge over the Fosso Vecchio, but were ordered to withdraw on 17 December to make way for a more powerful assault on the eighteenth.

The new divisional commander, Harry Foster, had grown impatient with the slow, time-consuming approach. To carry out the full-scale assault, the First Brigade's Desmond Smith had to count on the same battalions, the Royal Canadians and Hasty Ps, which had been crushed on the Lamone, and it should have been no surprise that the result was remarkably similar. The RCR was a mere shadow of its former self; it had suffered five hundred casualties in the past five months, and only nine officers and twenty-four other ranks remained of the men who had landed in Sicily in July 1943.[85] The Hasty Ps were simply burned out. The Lamone and Naviglio operations had cost the Hasty Ps all four of their company commanders, and every company was weak, "one being made up of drivers, batmen and cooks. Some platoons were led by corporals."[86]

Things went wrong from the start. The Hasty Ps seem not to have made it to the Fosso Vecchio (the official history notes, rather delicately, that they "appear to have become disorganized east of the canal"),[87] while one of the two RCR assault companies was hit by German shell-fire even before the attack began. The only sizeable force to cross the Vecchio was A Company, led by Major Jim Houghton, who was able to establish a small bridgehead.

But it only lasted until the Germans counter-attacked at 0615 hours. Canadian artillery fire slowed the enemy drive, but without heavy weapons the infantrymen were soon facing a familiar choice: retreat or die. Most of the Royal Canadians managed to escape, thanks in large part to a one-man wrecking crew named H. G. Otis. While his comrades were withdrawing, Private Otis crawled forward with a PIAT and ambushed the advancing German tanks. He scored a hit on the lead tank, causing it to brew up. He also hit the following tank, but the bomb failed to detonate; another round missed the tank but exploded among the infantry behind it. With the enemy swarming around him, Otis made his way back, picking up a wounded man and carrying him to safety. Otis won the Distinguished Conduct Medal.[88]

It had been another costly operation. The RCR lost seventy-one men on the Fosso Vecchio, many of them newcomers who had been remustered from other services or previously wounded with other units. First the Lamone and now the Fosso Vecchio had left the battalion understandably disillusioned, as the second-in-command, Major Strome Galloway, has described:

> During December changes in personnel had been so frequent that it would be an impossible task to list them here. Reinforcements arrived in a continuous flow and streamed back from whence they came – only on stretchers, or were consigned to the sodden soil of the province of Emilia. In many cases the same day's return showed name after name of those who had been "Taken on Strength" and "Struck off Strength" within a matter of hours. Switches in the command of companies occurred frequently and to list them . . . would be but a dreary recital of names. Men became section commanders and platoon sergeants without ever sewing stripes on their sleeves and were wounded or dead before they could be officially promoted.[89]

There was no let-up. A determined Charles Foulkes met Harry Foster and Bert Hoffmeister at the latter's headquarters within hours of the First Brigade's failure on the Fosso Vecchio. They drew up plans for yet another joint assault by the two divisions that very night. The object was to force the Germans to abandon the S-shaped Fosso Munio and retire behind the Senio, and the task was given to two infantry brigades, the Second and Eleventh, both using two assault battalions. It would be a silent operation, beginning at 2000 hours on 19 December, with artillery support being made available after the element of surprise had been lost.[90]

It was a cool evening, but no rain was falling when the Loyal Edmonton Regiment and Princess Patricia's Canadian Light Infantry went into action on the Second Brigade's front. For the first few hours, the infantry had to do their fighting without the benefit of armoured support; "the many small tree-bordered fields and vinerows restricted tank movement to the roads – and these were all heavily mined."[91] The Germans had, typically, turned every farmhouse in the area into a miniature fortress, but the Loyal Eddies proved equal to the task, repeatedly outflanking enemy strongpoints and leaving them with the unpalatable choice of surrendering or being wiped out. Despite savage counter-attacks, all objectives were taken by 1650 hours on 20 December, at the cost of 66 casualties, while 99 prisoners were captured.[92] The Patricias had also prevailed, capturing 108 Germans for the loss of 87 of their own, killed and wounded.[93]

The key to the fighting on 19–20 December was on the right, where the

Eleventh Brigade won a hard-fought battle to establish a bridgehead on the Fosso Munio. Brigadier Ian Johnston chose the Irish and Perth regiments for this job, and the Perths were not very pleased about it. After enduring a week of constant sniping and shelling, the battalion had just withdrawn for a rest, and more than a few men were hoping that they would remain in reserve for Christmas, now less than a week away.

The Perths were even less impressed when they were given a quick look at the terrain over which they would have to attack. According to Private Stan Scislowski, the Munio itself was not much of an obstacle, a thirty-foot-wide ditch with eight-foot banks; the water was only four feet wide. But the "billiard-table flats" beyond it were much more worrisome. "For more than a mile in front of the attacking battalions the area was so open that not a tree or single dwelling broke the monotony of open space."[94]

Both the Perths and the Irish were in trouble within a short time. On the right, the Irish almost made it to their objective, a cluster of houses a few hundred yards from the Munio. But the two assault companies ran into such a hail of machine-gun bullets that they were forced back. They tried repeatedly to renew the attack, only to be greeted by deadly fire in the flat fields. And the Perths had even worse problems. The lead platoon crossed the Munio unopposed and entered a roadside ditch. Splashing through the icy ankle-deep water, they approached a stone culvert, unaware that a two-man machine-gun crew was hiding behind it, waiting for the Canadians to get closer. At twenty-five yards, the Germans opened fire with terrible effect, as Scislowski described:

> The first twelve men were knocked over backwards and died instantly. The survivors of that first burst flung themselves against the slick sides of the ditch in a vain effort to scramble out of the line of fire. Their efforts delayed only for seconds their own deaths as the bullets stitched a murderous path along the full length of the ditch. The wounded, the dying, and the dead lay piled in heaps in a bloody mess of torn bodies. The cold water beneath them ran red from the blood that poured into it.[95]

The two assault companies were pinned along the Munio, and it appeared that the Perth operation was doomed to failure. "It was beyond belief," Scislowski observed, "that the Germans had so many shells to expend against this comparatively minor attack." But Major Bob Cole and A Company slipped to the right and found a blind spot in the enemy defences. "Like ghosts in the dead of night," they crossed the Munio and worked their way past several outposts. Others, which could not be avoided, were silently eliminated as the Perths pushed towards their objective, Casa della Congregatione, a thousand yards away. The farmhouse fell to them around 0330, and Cole's company dug in for the inevitable counter-attacks.[96]

The enemy did not disappoint them. While German troops and tanks repeatedly stormed Cole's isolated company, Canadian engineers worked feverishly to provide a crossing of the Munio for tanks of Lord Strathcona's Horse. It was after 1300 hours when a bulldozer finally carved out a route for the Shermans, which rumbled to the rescue of the Perths who were still fighting at Casa della Congregatione. At 1535, the first Sherman rolled into the farmyard, moments after the Perths had defeated a final counter-attack. For his outstanding leadership, Major Cole was later awarded the Distinguished Service Order.[97]

The Perths paid dearly for their bridgehead. Their casualties totalled eighty-one, nearly half of whom had been killed, an unusually large proportion. Eight of the Irish Regiment's forty-two casualties were dead.[98]

The Perths' regimental sergeant-major, George Curtis, was very nearly one of these statistics. That morning, he was captured while leading a carrying party with ammunition for Major Cole's "lost" company, and he spent nine hours as a prisoner of war. Curtis managed a hair-raising escape when his captors were caught in Canadian shell-fire. "It was a screaming hell," he remarked after rejoining the Perths.[99]

Casa della Congregatione pulled the plug on the German defences in this area. Under the cover of darkness, the enemy withdrew behind the Senio, leaving behind isolated snipers and machine-gunners to slow the Canadian pursuit. Even Bagnacavallo was evacuated; the Carleton and Yorks entered it unopposed the next morning. During the twenty-first, the Canadians closed up to the Senio. Among the Cape Breton Highlanders was a dashing sergeant named Dan MacDonald. His former lieutenant, Bill Matheson, calls MacDonald "the bravest soldier I ever met." Sergeant MacDonald paid for his bravery on 21 December, when he was wounded during intense shelling.[100] He lost an arm and a leg, but recovered to forge a fine career as a politician, eventually serving as a federal cabinet minister.

The Canadians dug in along the Senio and prepared to celebrate Christmas. Operation Chuckle, while not quite as successful as hoped, had resulted in a 9-mile advance during the first three weeks in December, in which I Canadian Corps had breached three major and heavily defended water lines, had captured 1,670 Germans, and had forced the enemy to rush in a fresh division and an élite machine-gun battalion from a shrinking reserve. But, as always, there was a cost in blood. In twenty days, the Canadians had lost 548 officers and other ranks killed, 1,796 wounded, and 212 prisoners. The daily average was almost the same as the Gothic Line losses.[101]

Many of the dead were buried in an improvised cemetery near Villanova. After supervising the funerals for the Irish Regiment's fatalities, padre Dave Rowland wrote in his diary on 22 December: "I'm afraid many of the families [at home] will just be sitting down to their Christmas dinner when the sad news will arrive."[102]

4

Christmas 1944 was not a happy one in Canada. It was the sixth wartime Christmas, and the wounds of the recent conscription debate were still tender. C. P. Stacey, the Canadian army historian, returned to Canada from Britain during December, and found that while life in Canada was incomparably better than in Britain, spirits were sagging at home: "Men and women were tired of the war and were anxious to see the end of it. . . . The long casualty lists of the past couple of years had had their due effect, bereaving thousands of households and touching others with constant fear. And the bitter political controversy then in progress over conscription certainly added to the general sense of strain."[103]

It was a typically quiet Christmas for Prime Minister Mackenzie King. King spent the holidays at Laurier House in Ottawa, where he was awakened Christmas morning by church bells. The greatest joy in his life at that time was provided by his pet dog, as recounted in his diary: "Went over to little Pat's crib and had a little talk with him. Talked of the members of the family and of others and of men fighting at the front." Christmas Day was uneventful, but he made this touching entry in his diary:

> I wonder if the day will come when that loveliest of hymns "Silent Night" will come into the minds of the people throughout the world to express the German heart. When that day comes Christendom will have won its complete triumph. I believe it is an expression of the heart of many Germans as it is of the real heart of most people throughout the world. That is the appalling tragedy of all that we are witnessing today.[104]

Lieutenant-Colonel Jim Stone was determined that this would be a better Christmas for his Loyal Edmonton Regiment than the last. A year before, he had been a company commander engaged in the bloody battle for Ortona, where "my Christmas dinner was a cold pork chop at ten o'clock at night on the street – came up in a carrier. And I said, 'By God, if I'm still alive next Christmas, it'll be different.'"[105]

Soon after taking command of the battalion, in September, Stone had started a farm. One of his veterans was given the job of collecting and caring for any live turkeys "liberated" by the Eddies during their coming operations. The brigadier, Pat Bogert, gave Stone permission to pull the battalion out of the front lines on Christmas Eve, and the Eddies boarded trucks for Cervia, a coastal resort midway between Ravenna and Rimini. More than five hundred men took over a local hotel where, Stone recalls, "we had the most wonderful turkey dinner. I think we sat there in three relays." Despite copious quantities of wine, there were no lingering after-effects. "I must say that the next morning we got out on the trucks to go back at eight o'clock, there wasn't a single man missing – all there, and all of them sober. Quite a thing for morale. It had been a very wonderful Christmas, I think the best I ever had in my life."[106]

Surprising as it may sound, there were many Canadians who, like Jim Stone, enjoyed Christmas 1944. Scrounging parties fanned out across the countryside, trading for and liberating the goods and supplies needed for countless dinner parties. This region of Italy was a hot-bed of fascism (Mussolini had been born here), which was all the encouragement the Canadians needed for double-dealing with the civilians. A sergeant of New Brunswick's 8th Hussars went around procuring poultry with chits entitling the bearer to compensation by the Allied Military Government; he signed the receipts "Mickey Mouse."[107]

Of course, somebody had to remain in the front lines at Christmas, but even that experience could be memorable. Christmas Day was sunny, cold, and quiet, but Captain George Fraser of the 48th Highlanders spent it with, as he put it, "a flame-thrower in one hand and a Christmas cracker in the other."[108] It was sobering to listen to their enemies, on the other side of the Senio floodbanks, singing "Stille Nacht, heilige Nacht." "The Germans, indeed, did sing 'Holy Night' on Christmas Day," remembers the Cape Breton Highlander subaltern, Bill Matheson. "They also rode a white horse along the top of the dyke on their side of the river without any hostile reaction on our part. . . . I do not believe there was any exchange of fire during Christmas Day and, contrary to other reports, there was no fraternization with the enemy."[109]

Then, all too soon, the killing and suffering resumed.

CHAPTER EIGHTEEN

"We'll Show 'Em"

1

Mired in half-frozen mud and cloaked in obscurity, the Italian campaign had staggered to a standstill. On 30 December, Sir Harold Alexander called off further offensive operations. It was not an earth-shaking decision; it merely recognized reality. The Allied armies in Italy were simply too weak to overcome both the Germans and the weather, thanks largely to the forces diverted for the sake of Dragoon, the invasion of southern France, Winston Churchill bitterly pointed out in early December. "Consequently we cleared the Apennines only to find the valley of the Po a bog. Thus both in the mountains and on the plains our immense armour superiority has been unable to make itself felt." And Churchill had little hope of resuscitating the Italian offensive. Lamenting his diminishing stature beside Roosevelt and Stalin, Churchill noted that "it is not so easy as it used to be for me to get things done."[1]

Not even a change in senior commands could alter its fortunes. In the middle of December, Alexander had been promoted to field-marshal and named supreme commander; his place as commander of the Fifteenth Army Group was taken by the American, Mark Clark. Although Alexander's original plan called for the December offensive to end around the middle of the month, Clark announced on 20 December that "the time is rapidly approaching when I shall give the signal for a combined all-out attack of Fifth and Eighth Armies."[2]

It was clearly impossible. The Fifth Army had been relatively inactive during December, while the Eighth Army had worn itself out clawing its way to the flooded Senio. To make matters worse, there was a shortage of artillery ammunition. In fifteen days, the Eighth Army had consumed a half-million rounds of 25-pounder ammunition; even with stringent rationing, its stockpile of 612,000 rounds for the envisaged five-week offensive was obviously inadequate. The Eighth Army's Dick McCreery informed Clark of this situation on Christmas Day and requested that he reconsider his offensive plans. The Fifth Army, meanwhile, was hit by a minor counter-attack on 26 December; it was a small setback, but since it came just ten days after the last-gasp offensive mounted by the Germans in the Ardennes on the Western Front, it was impossible to ignore the possibility of a similar desperation attack in Italy.

It did not help that Clark and McCreery could hardly stand each other. Clark considered McCreery to be "a washout . . . a feather duster type."[3] McCreery's view of Clark was no more flattering. "I had only two problems," he later observed of the campaign in Italy. "One was Mark Clark."[4]

"Tomorrow," the First Division's Harry Foster wrote on the night of 25 December, "we return to the cold reality of war and all its ugliness but we won't forget Christmas 1944, because for 24 hrs men became human again and war seemed very far away."[5]

Small-scale operations predominated in the week following Christmas, as the Canadians mounted aggressive patrols and periodic hit-and-run raids. As a river, the Senio was not much of an obstacle. But its enormous floodbanks were another story, looming "like a wall running through the flat farmland."[6] In several spots, the Germans were on the near side of the Senio, sheltered by the towering bank, scant yards separating their slit trenches from the Canadians. These small parties of enemy soldiers were linked to the far side of the river by a number of foot-bridges, which were replaced as quickly as the Canadians destroyed them.

The year drew to a deceptively peaceful close on the Senio front. "No gains anywhere," a PPCLI officer wrote. "The front is so quiet that a staff officer went all the way in daylight forward to an observation pit 50 yards from the Senio and there watched our planes attack the reverse slope of the near bank. Yet he did not draw enemy fire."[7]

The First Canadian Armoured Brigade was *en route* to the Senio sector. Since August, its three tank regiments had served with British and Indian troops in XIII Corps in the Fifth Army near Bologna. In mountains and in mud, these Canadians had further enhanced their reputation as one of the best armoured formations in the Mediterranean theatre. "Tanks of this formation," the brigadier, Bill Murphy of Vancouver, pointed out in his Christmas message, "have been in action for all but 14 of the last 365 days."[8]

"I hope you haven't got so that you feel like orphans," Defence Minister Ralston had told the brigade during his visit in October.[9] Far from feeling like orphans, the men of the Calgary, Ontario, and Three Rivers regiments rather enjoyed being separated from the main Canadian forces in Italy. "I think we *preferred* fighting with the Brits and Indians and Ghurkas," comments Dick Maltby, a Calgary subaltern, "because we escaped the chickenshit with which the Canadian troops were afflicted."[10]

Now, their enforced separation was about to end. On New Year's Eve, the Calgary Tanks started out on a memorable passage through the Apennines to rejoin the Eighth Army. The all-night trek took place in a raging snowstorm. Trooper Keirn Wallace, a twenty-five-year-old from Saskatchewan, remembers watching as several of the big Shermans came dangerously close to falling off the steep, winding road. "They were going right over the edge. I'll never know why they didn't."[11] Brigadier Murphy later congratulated the Calgaries, calling the hair-raising trek "the most outstanding work [the regiment] has performed in the face of the enemy from Sicily to the Western Apennines."[12]

The quiet along the Senio was about to be shattered. At either end of the Canadian sector were pockets of enemy troops, and I Corps headquarters had decided to get rid of them before settling down for the winter. On the right, north of Ravenna, the Germans were huddled behind a web of canals and rivers, below Lago Comacchio, along a line extending from the coast to Alfonsine, where it linked up with the Senio defences. On the left, there was the salient protruding south from Cotignola to the village of Granarolo. General Foulkes assigned the Comacchio pinching-out operation to the Fifth Division, while Harry Foster's First Division would cooperate with the neighbouring British 56th Division to destroy the Granarolo salient.

The Granarolo operation, carried out by all three battalions of the Second Brigade, went like clockwork. Following a diversionary attack by the Royal 22nd Regiment near Bagnacavallo during the afternoon of 3 January, the PPCLI attacked a half-mile south of Granarolo and took the Germans by surprise. By 2130, the Patricias had captured fifty-five prisoners, subsequently adding a self-propelled gun and an Opel staff car to their trophies. At midnight, the Seaforth Highlanders crossed the Naviglio behind the PPCLI, swinging north to the Fosso Vecchio to threaten the Granarolo garrison from the rear. (The Vecchio lies west of the Naviglio here, crossing underneath it just north of Granarolo.) The next day, the Loyal Edmonton Regiment entered Granarolo to find that the Germans had pulled out. The Second Brigade had captured seventy-five of the enemy, and killed or wounded another sixty, for a loss of twenty-nine men in the three participating battalions. The brigadier, Pat Bogert, later described it as "one of the neatest battles this Brigade has ever had."[13]

Bert Hoffmeister's Mighty Maroon Machine matched this performance in the face of considerably stiffer resistance. General Hoffmeister planned a two-stage operation: in the first, the Eleventh Brigade would mount a set-piece attack to capture the defences in the thousand-yard gap between the village of Conventello and a drainage canal, the Fosso Basilica; the Fifth Armoured Brigade would then pass through and take advantage of the frozen ground to seize a bridgehead on the Canale di Bonifica and take Sant' Alberto, on the south shore of Comacchio. The line of advance offered the advantage of having only one water crossing; the disadvantage was that it left the division vulnerable to a counter-attack from Alfonsine.

H-Hour was 0500 on Tuesday, 2 January. Accompanied by a massive barrage, the Irish and Perth regiments, supported by the 8th New Brunswick Hussars, moved forward under artificial moonlight. Opposition was spotty, and the infantry had little difficulty in reaching their objectives by early afternoon, with seventy-three prisoners to show for their efforts. During the afternoon, the Hussars and the British Columbia Dragoons, with infantry support provided by the Cape Breton Highlanders, launched the second stage of the operation. The armoured spearheads rolled northwards, slowed by small rearguard defences and occasional counter-attacks from the west, which warned that something larger was astir in that direction.

A major counter-attack was delivered by a battle group drawn from the 16th SS Panzer Division – rated by the enemy high command as "the strongest combat division" available – at 0500 hours on Thursday, 4 January, and a desperate fight ensued on the Fosso Basilica near Conventello. This was the first, and only, time that Canadians in Italy fought SS troops, whose fanaticism was matched only by that of the paratroopers with whom they were so familiar. The Germans planned to recapture Conventello and cut off the Canadian armour, forcing it into the marshlands north of Ravenna. The blow fell on the Westminster Regiment, borrowed from the Twelfth Brigade to take the place of the Perths.[14]

At first, the Westies were slow to grasp the danger developing on their front. But once they realized that they were under attack, the British Columbians took a terrible toll of the SS men. Sergeant Harry Herman later described the carnage:

> I gave the order to fire and all hell broke loose. Our Vickers and Bren guns and rifles were going all at once for about 30 minutes. Then we saw the white flag going up and I gave orders to cease fire. At first 3 Germans came in with their faces covered with blood, yelling "Kameraden nicht schiessen." I told the first German to call out to the others to come in with their hands up. He called as loud as he could and they all came in with their hands up. It was getting light by then, and we counted 17 dead and 30 prisoners.[15]

This grim scene was repeated elsewhere. By 0900, the reserve Irish Regiment and a squadron of the 8th Hussars had counter-attacked and crushed the Germans who had actually got across the drainage canal to within five hundred yards of Conventello. The Canadians, who suffered remarkably light casualties (the Westies lost only seven men wounded), captured 180 prisoners. Captured officers complained that the Germans had been unable to get their supporting arms over the multiple water hazards east of Alfonsine, which the official history observes was "a problem only too familiar to the Canadians."[16]

Enemy resistance collapsed at this point. The Cape Breton Highlanders, learning from deserters that the defenders on the Canale di Basilica were very demoralized, crossed on the remains of a bridge that had been blown up by the Germans. Late in the day, the B.C. Dragoons put their Shermans across at a nearby bridge that had been rigged for demolition (the Canadian engineers removed a ton of explosives from it), and at daylight on the fifth, the two units entered Sant' Alberto, which was undefended. The Highlanders rounded up fifty dispirited prisoners before moving north to the River Reno.[17] The Dragoons and Perths pushed eastwards to the coast, linking up with the British 12th Lancers coming up from Porto Corsini.

It had been an impressive five days for the Mighty Maroon Machine. Hoffmeister's division had taken six hundred prisoners, and three hundred enemy dead were counted in the area, while Canadian losses were less than two hundred. Eight Panther tanks and twenty anti-tank guns had been destroyed or captured.[18]

Charles Foulkes was delighted. "This was really the first time I had a chance to see Hoffmeister handling his division as an armoured division," he wrote Harry Crerar, "and I was quite satisfied with the results."[19]

None knew it, but the Canadians had had their last hurrah in Italy.

2

It was a dreary, depressing scene. "Winter was full upon the plains," Farley Mowat writes of the Senio in January 1945. "Snow mingled with the freezing rains. Heavy frosts coated the muddy sloughs and the contorted skeletons of shell-torn olive trees."[20]

For most Canadian infantry units, winter meant a return to the dreadful, and deadly, routine of patrolling. Patrols went out every night, to probe the enemy defences, to ambush the enemy, or to seek a battle. "It was last year's Arielli war all over again," historian Thomas Raddall later commented, "with all its mud and cold and bloodshed."[21]

At least one battalion, however, did not participate. As a company commander in early 1944, Jim Stone of the Loyal Eddies had watched in helpless rage as the battalion's moral and physical strength was decimated by meaningless patrols, and now, commanding the unit in the shadow of the Senio's towering banks, he kept the patrolwork to a minimum. "We didn't bother trying to patrol over the Senio," Stone recalls. "We disputed the banks where the Germans were – nothing like the nonsense we had on the Arielli, of trying to patrol all the time."[22]

The Canadians held a front twenty-seven miles long. That meant that they were spread very thin – "as thinly as the jam in an English war-time sandwich," according to one writer.[23] The answer was defence in depth; the Lamone and Montone rivers were designated as "stop lines," in the event of a German breakthrough, and all bridges were wired for demolition.[24]

These defensive arrangements were handicapped by the strict rationing of artillery ammunition. When his company of the 48th Highlanders got into a scrap, Captain Mike George asked for a barrage of 25-pounders. The forward observation officer agreed, and after a brief pause, four shells screamed overhead. George, assuming that these were ranging shots, waited for some time before asking, "When is our barrage coming?"

The gunner replied over the radio: "That's your ration."[25]

To shore up the overstretched Canadian corps, the Eighth Army entrusted General Foulkes with an Italian unit. This was the Gruppo di Combattimento Cremona, the size of a reinforced Canadian brigade, one of five such combat groups serving with the Allies. The Italians moved into the front lines in January, relieving part of the Fifth Armoured Division, but the Canadians were unimpressed with their new allies. As the RCR's Strome Galloway relates, Lieutenant Des Egan was sent out with a patrol to contact the neighbouring Italians one frosty February night. Approaching an outpost, Egan called the password and, getting no response, crawled up to have a look inside. He found two soundly sleeping Italians, one of them clutching a white flag. "We were always a bit uncertain after that, when the *Gruppo Cremona* held the line on our flank," says Galloway.[26]

The Canadians resorted to a variety of improvised weapons. Some of these morale-builders worked rather well, as Budge Bell-Irving, the commanding officer of the Seaforth Highlanders, recounted:

> One night our men filled a metal garbage can with a centre core of mines surrounded by winter deposits from a latrine. Fused and lidded this was rolled up and over the dyke. The enormous explosion, the silence, then a rather splashy rain, was followed by hoots of mirth and loud laughter. I suspect that there was considerable damage to enemy morale, though possibly no damage. On another occasion a makeshift vehicle constructed by the pioneers was bedecked with mines and pushed up and over.[27]

The bizarre arsenal included the "Dagwood," a creation of the Lanark and Renfrew Scottish, featuring a 36 grenade sandwiched between a pair of Hawkins anti-tank grenades, placed in a sandbag, and tossed over the bank. Giant slingshots were popular. The Seaforths dubbed theirs the "V-2," after the German missile; the smaller Canadian version, an inner tube slung from the forks of a tree, tossed a grenade up to a hundred yards.[28] PIATs used as mortars also proved to be surprisingly effective.

Both sides used booby traps, particulary in and around houses in contested areas, but the Germans were acknowledged masters of the art of booby-trapping. On 3 February, the Patricias attacked a group of enemy-held houses on the Fosso Vecchio. The garrison fled when the Canadians approached, and they soon discovered why. Moments after a platoon occupied one of the houses, a charge demolished the place, burying several men in the rubble. When another platoon hurried to their aid, the rescuers were bracketed by "a perfectly ranged salvo of mortar shells." Six Pats died, twenty-eight others were wounded, and one was listed as missing.[29]

The Germans were aggressive, and the Canadians had to be constantly alert. On 8 January, a white-hooded enemy patrol attacked an outpost of the West Nova Scotia Regiment, and captured seven men and a Lifebuoy flamethrower.[30] Later that month, it was the turn of the Loyal Edmonton Regiment to be victimized, when two Eddies were snatched from their outpost and trundled off before anyone realized that they were gone.[31]

The Royal Canadian Regiment fell victim to what the official history calls "the most neatly executed raid of the whole period."[32] The Germans cleverly isolated a company position with artillery and mortar fire; during the forty-minute bombardment, a twenty-five-man patrol slipped up to a three-storey house manned by a platoon. When the shelling ceased, the Germans rushed the building and seized seventeen occupants of the main floor, without firing a shot. The prisoners were carried off into the night, their buddies in the upper floors watching helplessly, unable to fire for fear of hitting their own people. Strome Galloway remembers the episode ruefully, for he was in acting command of the battalion at the time. The First Brigade's Desmond Smith was "furious," says Galloway, who investigated and "determined that we could not be faulted for the way we were holding our sector. It was just one of those things."[33]

The biggest raid staged by the Germans was a spoiling attack on 24 February against the Seaforths and Eddies. An estimated 150 Germans, equipped with flamethrowers, crossed the Senio during the evening, after an all-day bombardment by mortars and artillery. The attackers were stopped cold in the Edmonton sector, but the Seaforths were overrun in several places, and Colonel Bell-Irving called for an artillery stonk right on top of his own positions. "Because we were in slit trenches and the enemy was running around in the open, we got away with it," he later commented. By daylight on 25 February, no Germans remained east of the Senio in this sector, save the dead and the prisoners.[34]

It was a period not without humour. In late January, a German patrol stole a stretcher from the Carleton and Yorks, but later returned it, together with a bottle of cognac.[35] Psychological warfare was still a hit-and-miss proposition, as the RCR found when a loudspeaker was set up in their sector and "broadcast the sound of a fairly noisy patrol. Unfortunately the recording had been made during a soft period and the sound of slushing through mud and water was broadcast to the enemy on a night when the ground was frozen hard."[36] On 15 February, a German sniper put a bullet through a periscope being used by the Seaforth Highlanders, who were so impressed that they rewarded him with a tin of meat-and-vegetable stew. Some time later, the enemy tossed back a hammer with a note attached: "I tried to give your can of M and V to my dog but he wouldn't eat it."[37]

The winter took its toll on everyone's nerves, from the highest to the lowest ranks. Charles Foulkes, accustomed to the lavish array of equipment in northwestern Europe, was disgusted by the prevailing shortages of specialized vehicles of every type in Italy. Amphibious vehicles were in great demand in this water-logged area, but the supply fell far short of requirements, and Foulkes complained about "operating across Caesar's rivers using almost the same equipment."[38]

The other senior exile to the Spaghetti League was also unhappy. Harry Foster, commanding the First Division, was not particularly impressed with what he was seeing in Italy, where it appeared that "each side [was] prepared to do a lot of shooting but without the devotion necessary for serious battle," as he later remarked. There was something else about Italy that Foster did not like – Charles Foulkes. They had never really got along, but it reached the point during these dreary days of early 1945 that Foster would excuse himself from his headquarters whenever he learned that the corps commander was on the way to visit him. "I thought Foulkes suffered from a sense of inferiority," Foster commented. "He was not liked by any senior British or Canadian officer that I ever saw. . . . He reminded me of someone who, knowing he has overstepped his abilities, tried to bluff his way through."[39]

It was a trying time for everyone, and some simply could not handle it any more. Mentally and physically exhausted in a war zone that seemed to have been forgotten, they were incapable of functioning effectively. After the middle of December, Colonel Ken Hunter, the Fifth Division's chief medical officer, noted an alarming increase in neuropsychiatric cases attributable to exhaustion.

By now, NP cases had fallen into a predictable pattern. Depending on the circumstances, they could account for up to one-third of a unit's casualties, a figure common to other Allied armies, according to historian Bill McAndrew. Colonel Hunter noted that "these casualties appear among the most susceptible individuals very early in action. Following this initial influx the incidence becomes gradually greater according to the length of time a unit or formation is in action, the weight of enemy shelling, the state of physical exhaustion of the personnel, the magnitude of the [battle] casualties suffered by a unit, and the discomfort resultant from bad weather conditions."[40]

Stress casualties in Italy were little different from those suffered on other battlefronts, in the Canadian or other armies. However, Canadian medical authorities did identify in the Mediterranean theatre "a small group of cases that suffered acute psychoses, apparently different from any met elsewhere. The onset was sudden, and recovery frequently occurred as soon as the patient was evacuated by ship to the United Kingdom."[41]

While the treatment of NP casualties remained a contentious issue until the war's end, some commanders found that a little kindness and understanding went a long way. Jim Stone, the Eddies' commander, recounts how, during the late-February attack on his battalion and the Seaforths, one of his officers went to pieces. As soon as the battle began, Stone hopped in his carrier and rounded up three Shermans. Arriving at the scene of the action, he found the anxious company commander preparing to withdraw. Stone calmed him down with a few quiet words of reassurance: "You've got nothing to worry about. There are three tanks back there lacing the hell out of everything in front of us, your platoon's holding in front. You're fine. Just sit tight." Afterwards, Stone sent the officer for a long rest.[42]

Whole units were susceptible. Even after active operations had ceased in early January, the corps medical director, Brigadier H. M. Elder, advised Foulkes that certain battalions "if put into action without more rest would not give a good account of themselves." Foulkes ordered three-to-five-day rests at regular intervals for all front-line units.[43]

Some, such as the Hastings and Prince Edward Regiment, needed more than rest. This battalion, whose thirty-one battle honours were the most won by any Canadian unit in the Second World War, had fallen on hard times recently, first at the Lamone and then at the Naviglio. When the Hasty Ps staggered out of the front lines for Christmas, Lieutenant-Colonel Don Cameron prescribed bitter medicine. He put his battered battalion back on the parade square, and imposed a gruelling spit-and-polish regimen reminiscent of Aldershot in 1940. After restoring its pride, Cameron rebuilt the unit; on 6 January, the Hasty Ps received their first large batch of reinforcements. When they returned to the front lines, Cameron broke them in gently, sticking to small-scale actions with a high probability of success to rebuild confidence. With firm but compassionate handling, the Hasty Ps gradually recovered.[44]

It was no shame that men broke down under the strain. The remarkable part is not that some men fell victim to the stress of battle, but that so few did. Strome Galloway, the RCR veteran, has nothing but admiration for the Canadians who endured the seemingly endless misery of that Italian winter. "Looking back," he writes, "it is hard to believe that ordinary, peaceable men from the cities and farms of Canada could face the terrors and brutalities of that particular battlefield day after day and night after night. The calibre of the men was quite magnificent. Most were between 20 and 25, quite a few were younger. A man over thirty was a rarity."[45]

Their suffering, thankfully, was nearly over.

3

For months, Canada had been lobbying to reunite its army. Even before I Canadian Corps had fought its first battle, at the Hitler Line, the Canadian government had sought to reverse its policy of splitting up its overseas formations. In June 1944, Ken Stuart, then chief of staff at CMHQ in London, had presented the government's position to the CIGS, Sir Alan Brooke, stressing that the unification of Canada's forces was desirable "as soon as military considerations permit." Brooke's reply promised that the Canadian request would be met when "military *and shipping* considerations allowed."[46] Even after Stuart's departure, CMHQ wasted no opportunity to remind British authorities of the desire to reunite the Canadian army.

By late October, at the height of the conscription crisis in Canada, the reunion of Canadian combat forces was becoming a political concern. Prime Minister King noted in his diary that the First Army's General Crerar "had told me there was nothing he was more anxious for than for [the army] to be all together at the end of the war." One of his cabinet ministers, Ian Mackenzie, urged King to "communicate with Churchill and that we should demand that our men return from Italy and have one Canadian army."[47]

Andy McNaughton's arrival in the King cabinet ensured that the matter would be pursued. McNaughton told the prime minister that he had "always felt it was a mistake to divide the army and to have some of our men fighting in Italy as well as in northern Europe. That it was nonsense to talk about sending battalions there for training. . . . That a great many men were used up in maintaining lengthy communications." With

McNaughton orchestrating the political pressure, the Canadian government soon took a formal position. In November 1944, Ottawa notified the British of the wish to have Canada's overseas army reunited "even before the defeat of Germany."[48]

The Canadian reunion was, understandably, low on the list of Allied priorities. It had come up briefly at the second Quebec conference in September, and in response to the formal request, the British government pointed out that such a move might not be possible, citing transportation difficulties. They did not mention that Sir Harold Alexander, who was still in command of the Fifteenth Army Group at the time, was opposed to the move. In October, while planning for his 1945 offensive, he sought assurances that the Canadians would not be sent "to join their comrades in France"; he was told that there was "no present intention to withdraw any of the forces now at your disposal."[49]

As 1944 gave way to 1945, there was little reason for Canadian authorities to hope for the reunion of their army. Too much was happening, not only in embattled Europe but in the Pacific war, where the Japanese were being systematically crushed by American naval and air power. With the Allies trying to bring the conflict to a conclusion, the Canadian wish to bring their overseas forces together, for reasons of national sentiment, seemed trivial.

The decision, when it was made, came with surprising suddenness. At the end of January, the Combined Chiefs of Staff met in Malta. Their discussions reached a consensus on two points: that the war in northwestern Europe was the decisive theatre of operations and that the Allied forces should be reinforced to ensure victory. When the chiefs further agreed that the British needed reinforcements more urgently than did the Americans, Field-Marshal Brooke noted the "great advantages in moving the Canadian divisions to enable them to join up with the remainder of the Canadian forces in France."[50]

The Combined Chiefs of Staff concurred, and the Canadians were soon packing their bags.

The transfer operation was code-named "Goldflake," after a brand of cigarettes.[51] Plans for the move were speedily drawn up. Authorization was contained in a directive issued to Alexander on 2 February, and corps headquarters received notification two days later. The first Canadians sailed from Leghorn (Livorno) for the southern French port of Marseilles on 15 February.

It was a remarkable undertaking. Canadian combat units and administrative centres were spread all over Italy. With corps headquarters in Ravenna, the First Division was in the line along the Senio, while the Fifth was in reserve and scattered along the Adriatic coast from Cervia to Cattolica. The First Armoured Brigade was in transit across the mountains. There were the reinforcement depot at Avellino, hospitals, punishment camps, leave centres, convalescent depots, medical and dental stores, graves-registration units, and a host of other miscellaneous units, from one end of Italy to the other. Nearly sixty thousand men and women, and thousands of vehicles, "had to be funnelled through the two ports [Leghorn and Naples] on the west coast, and the task of directing the bulk of them across the 15th Army Group's lines of communications without interrupting the normal maintenance of the Eighth and Fifth Armies required careful planning and skilful timing of the necessary trains and road convoys."[52]

And, of course, it had to be done secretly. "Penknife" was the code name for the deception plan devised to hoodwink the Germans. Although the absence of the Canadians could not be disguised, the Allied high command hoped that the Germans could be convinced that it was merely the result of a regrouping prior to the impending offensive in northern Italy. For this purpose, a special 230-man unit was set up at Macerata, south of Ancona; its job was to send people "hither and thither putting up formation and unit signs and pulling them down again. Widely scattered detachments of the Royal Canadian Signals maintained the normal flow of wireless traffic by filling the air with dummy messages: the measure of their success was the enemy's frequent attempts to 'jam the air.'" An added touch was the continued publication of *The Maple Leaf* until the middle of March, and "all Canadian clubs, hostels, leave centres and hospitals were kept open as long as possible."[53]

(The Germans were completely fooled by Penknife. Maps issued by the enemy high command on 17 March, when Goldflake had been all but completed, showed I Canadian Corps in reserve at Ancona; another month passed before the Germans realized that there were no Canadian formations in Italy.)

A series of daily conferences at corps headquarters laid the groundwork for Goldflake, and General Foulkes flew to First Canadian Army headquarters in Holland to plan the role of I Corps in the coming offensive on the Rhine. By road and rail, Canadian troops and equipment were shipped across Italy for their departure. Corps headquarters and units immediately under its jurisdiction moved first, followed by the Fifth Armoured Division and the First Armoured Brigade. The First Infantry Division remained in the front lines on the Senio until the end of February, when it was relieved by the 8th Indian Division. By then, the Fifth Division had reached the Netherlands, and on 15 March, I Corps headquarters became operational.

A shakedown accompanied the departure from Italy. During the campaign, every Canadian unit had acquired non-essential and unauthorized equipment, and even personnel. The most obvious surplus was in transport. In addition to their own Canadian-built trucks, there was a bewildering collection of cannibalized British vehicles, which had lasted far longer than anyone could reasonably have expected them to, as well as liberated Italian and German makes and still others stolen or traded from the Americans. Before leaving Italy, a determined effort was made to weed out the surplus baggage. Corps orders were explicit: only those vehicles on a unit's establishment would be taken to northwestern Europe. All others would be turned over to British and Indian formations.

One armoured regiment submitted a request to take four extra "command" tanks. This aroused suspicion at corps headquarters, and General Foulkes had his senior staff officer, George Kitching, arrange to pay the unit a surprise visit to inspect these tanks. He and Kitching were taken to "four rather scruffy tanks" separated from the rest of the regiment. Foulkes was greeted by the faint sound of clucking from within; he struck the tank with his walking stick, and a great commotion of squawking and feathers resulted. It turned out that the tanks were mobile chicken coops, which produced two hundred fresh eggs every day. "Charles had a good sense of humour on these occasions," writes Kitching, "but he wouldn't allow the regiment to retain their egg-laying tanks."[54]

Despite the strict rules, it was remarkable what the Canadians managed to take with them. The PPCLI took the Opel staff car captured at Granarolo in January, along with an assortment of small dogs stashed in individual kit bags.[55] New Brunswick's 8th Hussars constructed a hidden compartment in the back of a truck and smuggled out Princess Louise, a horse rescued at Coriano ridge and now serving as the regimental mascot.[56] The Calgary Regiment somehow brought out its prized possession, a battered piano (which was later exchanged for a brand-new model in a posh piano shop in Arnhem).[57]

A group of Fifth Division truckers tried to take Gino Farnetti with them. They had picked up the five-year-old orphan the previous May, near Frosinone, close to the end of the Liri valley campaign. When Lloyd Oliver, a twenty-one-year-old farmer from western Manitoba, found the youngster, he and his fellow truck drivers adopted Gino. "I made him a pair of pants and found an Italian seamstress to make a jacket," Oliver recalls, "and we made him a corporal." Gino had some unusual habits for a five-year-old; among other things, says Oliver, he "smoked like a trooper when he first came to us." Oliver and his buddies wanted to take Gino with them; the lad had no close family, and they looked on him as their own by now.

But a sharp-eyed officer spotted him, and the jig was up. Arrangements were made to leave Gino with a foster family in Ravenna, and Oliver was given the unhappy job of delivering him.[58]

(Although Oliver soon lost track of Gino and his foster family, he started searching for him in 1977, and his efforts culminated in a 1980 reunion with Gino at Oliver's farm at Miniota, Manitoba, with fifteen of the men who had looked after the waif in war-torn Italy. Gino, who had grown up to be an engineer, was overjoyed to meet his benefactors once again. "I wanted all these years to find the men who saved me," he told reporters. "I was very surprised and very excited that Lloyd found me."[59] The reunion was so successful that it was repeated in 1990.)

The majority of the 58,172 Canadians who were shipped out of Italy passed through Harrod's Camp at Leghorn. For weeks, rumours had been flying about their destination. When it was made official, the news caused quite a sensation. The Strathconas' colonel, Jim McAvity, remarked "that everyone was excited and everyone was happy in the extreme . . . the idea of joining our own Army was rather like going home."[60] The PPCLI, Syd Frost recalls, reacted boisterously: "We'll show 'em that the D-Day Dodgers know how to fight." This brought a gentle admonition from Brigadier Pat Bogert, who "warned us against bragging about our actions in Sicily and Italy – 1st Division would prove itself by deeds rather than words."[61]

The vast majority of Canadians were only too happy to leave Italy. The Perths' padre, Crawford Smith, called it "a relief" to "leave behind the land that had few, if any, pleasant associations."[62] But by the time they had boarded the LSTs and troopships that would take them to France, other emotions had come into play. It occurred to some, like Dick Maltby of the Calgary Regiment, that they were leaving behind a family, "the 8th Army, where we figured we lived a more relaxed life style than we would under Canadian command and, under which, we had developed successful battle tactics."[63]

Good or bad, there was no shortage of memories. Reginald Roy, the fine historian of the Seaforth Highlanders of Canada, has eloquently pointed out some of them:

> Behind them they left many of their comrades who would rest forever beneath the soil of Italy. . . . There were Italian place names, too, which they would always remember, many of which would appear ultimately on [regimental] colours as battle honours. Memories flooded back with each mile the ships drew away from the harbour – the vino, the spaghetti dinners, the fighting at Agira, the warmth of Sicily, the charge through the hell-fire at the Hitler Line, the unexpected beauty of the countryside after turning a bend in the road, the wretched poverty of

the villages, the mud of the Senio dykes and the almost unreal Christmas dinner at the front line in Ortona.[64]

Some of these thoughts occurred to Syd Frost, on board LST 692, which sailed at 0600 hours on 13 March. Standing on the deck, the twice-wounded Frost watched as the Italian coastline "slowly dipped below the horizon. Suddenly I felt overcome by a wave of sadness and regret that surprised me. . . . Despite all the dirt, blistering heat, bitter cold, rain, mud, rugged mountains and treacherous torrents I knew I loved this land and its people."[65]

"The Best in the World"

1

The D-Day Dodgers were received with open arms. "We are all very proud of what you have accomplished. . . . And, now that we are all together, let us add speed to the victory in no uncertain manner," declared the First Army commander, Harry Crerar.[1]

Crerar had borne well the responsibilities of high command. A full general since November, and the highest-ranking Canadian wartime commander, he had survived several spats with Montgomery and other senior British officers. While no one, Canadian or British, thought much of him as a military man, Crerar had shown one admirable attribute: he was a general who made few mistakes. With the arrival of I Canadian Corps from Italy, Crerar now commanded the biggest armed force ever fielded by Canada.

The Fifth Armoured Division arrived in Belgium in late February, followed by the First Armoured Brigade in early March, and the First Infantry Division later that month. They had had pleasant journeys. The weather was generally bright and sunny, a sharp contrast to the storm which had greeted the First Division's arrival off Sicily in July 1943. Although the Germans were still a threat, there were no attacks at sea like those endured by both the First and Fifth divisions on their way to Italy. Even better, the American ships that carried the Canadians to southern France were lavishly supplied with food – white bread, butter, canned wieners, frozen chicken, ice cream – that most of these Canadians had merely dreamed about. "They accepted the lavish generosity of their hosts," says Farley Mowat, "with the pleasure of children at a birthday party."[2]

However, there were worrisome indications that it was not going to be an entirely happy reunion. The First Division was the army's senior formation, but it had little in common with the army it was joining, as Mowat points out: "The names of Carpiquet, Falaise and the Scheldt meant as little to [them] as the names of Cassino, Ortona and Ravenna mean to those Canadians who had fought their war in Northern Europe." They were ordered to wear the Canadian Volunteer Service Medal, which they dubbed EBGO, "Every Bastard's Got One."[3]

Their uniforms were given a major overhaul. "I like to dress, and I had the most garish outfits you could think of, all made by Italian women," recalls Rupe Leblond of the Saskatoon Light Infantry, "and I'd go into battle with these fancy outfits, never wearing a helmet, wearing shorts, and carrying this cane. You could go into battle with any uniform you wanted." That had been in Italy; now, in northwestern Europe, "we were regimented. You wore your helmet, you wore whatever they said you had to wear."[4]

Nor were they happy when they were ordered to take down signs announcing the arrival of the D-Day Dodgers, although the order was given not out of rancour or condescension, but for the sake of security. The official announcement of the move from Italy was made on 23 April, but Prime Minister King had been badgering Winston Churchill for a month, pointing out that it was common knowledge in Canada "through the interruption of the mails from Italy and other causes." A Canadian Press dispatch dated 3 April broke security, but the report was not confirmed until the twenty-third.[5]

The newcomers' first order of business was to reorganize. Changes that had been instituted in Italy were deemed unnecessary for the fighting in northwestern Europe, and I Canadian Corps was expected to conform to the First Canadian Army. For example, armoured divisions here did not require two infantry brigades, which resulted in the disbanding of the Twelfth Infantry Brigade. Effective 15 March, the brigade's three infantry battalions reverted to their former roles: the Westminster Regiment resumed its duties as the Fifth Division's motorized infantry unit; the Princess Louise Dragoon Guards returned to the First Division as the reconnaissance regiment; and the men of the Lanark and Renfrew Scottish went back to being anti-aircraft gunners. Of the three, the Westies were affected the least, and the Plugs were delighted to get back to their armoured cars. But it came as "a bitter shock and disappointment" to the Lanarks, whose war diary called it "a severe blow to everyone in the regiment who has fought and worked so hard to make this in a very short time a first class fighting unit ready to fight against the most severe opposition.[6]

There were other changes; most, but not all, involved the dissolution of units that had been created to meet specific needs during the Italian campaign. These included Tommy Burns's special traffic-control section (eleven officers, 235 other ranks), formed in the wake of the Liri valley traffic jams, and the counter-mortar staff, consisting of seven officers and fifty-eight other ranks, which had been organized when Burns realized "that the Germans relied on mortars as their principal element of support-ing firepower." The medical establishment, also overhauled in Italy, reverted to its original format. In September 1944, Brigadier Emmet McCusker reduced the number of personnel in his field ambulances and found other work for the surplus people. "Economizing in manpower in no way lowered efficiency," maintained Burns, who later called McCusker "the only officer that I can remember who, of his own accord, concluded that he had too many men on his establishment for the job to be done, and reduced their numbers."[7]

But there were undeniable advantages. "The one thing we found on our arrival in the northwest Europe theatre was the plethora of support: avia-tion support, artillery support, a plethora of equipment, no shortage of troops," the First Infantry Brigade's Desmond Smith recalls. "The north-west theatre seemed to be a haven as compared to how we were slugging it out in Italy with the minimum of reserves, the minimum of ammunition, and the minimum of all sorts of military support."[8] Some men were allowed to go on leave to England, and reinforcements arrived, including the controversial conscripts. A zombie would be the last member of the Loyal Edmonton Regiment to be killed in action.[9]

The fresh faces and bountiful equipment would come in handy, for there was one more river to cross.

When the D-Day Dodgers reached Belgium in March 1945, they found themselves in the midst of the series of mighty blows that shattered the Third Reich. The First Canadian Army, on the extreme left of the Allied forces, played an impressive and important part in the bloody battles of February and March. General Crerar's army, containing half a million Canadian, American, and British soldiers, had breached the Siegfried Line and cleared the west bank of the River Rhine, trapping thousands of German troops. On 23 March, the Canadians launched Operation "Plun-der," the push across the Rhine itself and into the heart of Germany.

The veterans of Italy found themselves facing an old adversary. Albert Kesselring had been brought north by Hitler to take over supreme com-mand of the embattled Western Front, the Führer hoping that the field-marshal's brilliance at defensive warfare could somehow stabilize the situation.

When they were finally sent into action in early April, the D-Day Dodgers were given a tough assignment. While the main Allied forces pushed eastwards, it fell to Charles Foulkes's I Canadian Corps to deal with the German pocket in the western Netherlands, which was held by 120,000 heavily armed and desperate enemy troops. The Canadians were in a race against time, for the civilian population was on the verge of starvation.

They pulled it off brilliantly. The first step was made in the middle of April, when Harry Foster's First Division punched across the River Ijssel and captured the key city of Apeldoorn. George Kitching, the senior staff officer at I Corps headquarters, recalls being told by British officers "that our troops were far superior to those of the 2nd Canadian and 3rd Canadian Divisions. They commented that our 1st Div regiments were really anxious to get to grips with the enemy and that their morale was far superior to that of II Canadian Corps." Bert Hoffmeister and the Fifth Division then struck north from Antwerp, catching the Germans in a classic pincer movement and reaching the Ijsselmeer, or Zuider Zee, in a spectacular thirty-mile dash. Then, while a ceasefire was arranged in order to deliver life-saving supplies to the starving Dutch, the Eleventh Brigade shifted northwards for a final battle in and around the port of Delfzijl, which fell on 2 May. General Foulkes's "plan was sound," says Kitching, "but I am quite sure that its success was due to the excellence of the Canadian troops taking part."[10]

The D-Day Dodgers took it all in stride. "There was not too much difference between some of our Italian battles, e.g., clearance of the Comacchio region, and the polder country of Holland," says Bill Matheson of the Cape Breton Highlanders. "There was a much greater variety of terrain in Italy, with the mountainous interior and the flat coastal areas. A water obstacle is a water obstacle, be it in Italy or [northwestern] Europe."[11] No one was prouder of them than General Foster. Based on what he had seen here and in Italy, Foster flatly declared that his troops "were the best in the world. More imaginative than the Germans; more flexible than the British; more sensible than the Russians; better trained and led than the Americans and worth any six of their soldiers when it came to close combat."[12]

Casualties were thankfully light, but some long-time veterans of Italy were among them. Don Mackenzie, the young commanding officer of the 48th Highlanders, was killed by an enemy shell; the Seaforths lost Major Haworth Glendinning, who had won the Distinguished Service Order at San Fortunato and who had just arrived from leave in England, where he had been married a week earlier. The Royal Canadian Regiment grieved for Captain Freddie Sims. As a subaltern, Sims had been the first Royal Canadian to land in Sicily on 10 July 1943, and he had survived the subsequent twenty months of fighting in Italy, only to become the very last RCR to be killed in action in northwestern Europe.

Surrender was the by-word in the first few days of May 1945. On 4 May, the Germans opposite the Twenty-first Army Group surrendered to Field-Marshal Montgomery, and the next day, in a battered hotel in Wageningen, Charles Foulkes accepted the surrender of Generaloberst Johannes Blaskowitz, commander of the German forces in the Netherlands. Early on 7

May, formal surrender documents were signed at Eisenhower's headquarters, taking effect at midnight.

It was hard to believe that it was really over. "I think we were all a bit numb," recounted the First Division's Harry Foster. "Six and a half years is a long time for any man to be thinking about just trying to stay alive and hoping to see that day when it's all over. Of course we were pleased. . . . But I think everyone was just too bloody tired to get excited."[13]

2

The war in Italy, to which Canadians had made such an important contribution, ended on 2 May.

The final Allied offensive followed familiar lines. The army-group commander, Mark Clark, borrowed from Sir Harold Alexander the "strategy of the two-handed punch." The first punch was delivered on 9 April, when the Eighth Army stormed across the Senio, supported by 150 Wasp and Crocodile flamethrowers and 825 heavy bombers. As anticipated, this drew enemy reserves to the Adriatic sector, and when the Fifth Army attacked on the fourteenth, the Germans were doomed. On 20 April, Hitler's birthday, the German commander, Heinrich von Vietinghoff, authorized a general withdrawal.

Polish forces entered Bologna on 21 April, and the next day the Americans reached the Po. Allied fighter-bombers ravaged the retreating enemy, turning their attention to the Po's ferries and pontoon bridges. Those Germans who escaped had to swim for their lives, including the tough paratroop general, Richard Heidrich. But little heavy equipment went with them. "Every approach was choked with vehicles, guns and tanks which had been destroyed by air attacks or artillery shelling or abandoned by the enemy in his headlong flight." By 25 April, the Allies had captured fifty thousand Germans.[14]

The Po barely slowed the Allied advance. The Americans captured Verona on 27 April; two days later, Venice was occupied by the British.

Surrender was already in the works by then. Serious and secret negotiations had begun in February through Swiss intermediaries, leading to discussions between the American agent, Allen Dulles, and an SS general, Karl Wolff, in March. Wolff was able to convince Vietinghoff that capitulation was the only way to prevent unnecessary bloodshed, and in late April, representatives of Wolff and Vietinghoff secretly signed surrender documents in Caserta.

Complications briefly threatened the arrangement. Kesselring, who on 28 April had been appointed supreme commander of both the western and southern fronts, refused to sanction the surrender. On the thirtieth, he replaced Vietinghoff and his chief of staff, Hans Röttiger, with General der Infanterie Friedrich Schulz and Generalmajor Fritz Wentzell, respectively. Wolff had Schulz and Wentzell arrested to prevent them from interfering with the impending ceasefire, but it all became academic late in the evening of 1 May, with the announcement of Hitler's death the previous day. Released from his oath of allegiance to the Führer, Kesselring consented to the Italian armistice early the next morning.

At midday on 2 May, 207,425 Germans laid down their arms. It was the enemy's first mass capitulation, the culmination of a bitter and bloody twenty-two-month campaign that had started with the invasion of Sicily on a hot July day in 1943. No Canadian veteran would have been surprised to learn that the 1st Parachute Division was the last German formation to surrender. "We have done our duty to the end," declared Generalleutnant Heidrich in his final orders, "and we do not feel we have been defeated. . . . Each of you must know that the darkest hour of our people demands manly dignity."[15]

With the departure of I Canadian Corps, the only Canadian combatants left in Italy were airmen. Many belonged to RAF squadrons; there was just one Canadian unit here now, 417 (City of Windsor) Squadron. "As the only RCAF squadron in the Desert Air Force," recalls the squadron leader, Dave Goldberg, "we already felt somewhat orphaned from the RCAF before the removal of the Canadian corps from Italy to France." The army's move, he admits, "tended to compound our existing perceptions for a while."[16]

Goldberg had commanded the squadron since November 1944. Later a prominent Hamilton lawyer, Goldberg was a veteran of northwestern Europe; shot down over France in March, he had evaded capture. Transferred to Italy, Goldberg was to be 417's last wartime commander.

The squadron had spent an indifferent winter. Poor weather had restricted the Windsors to just eighteen flying days in November, and in early December they had moved to a new base, at Bellaria, just north of Rimini, in time for a paralysing winter storm which precluded operations until 9 December. The weather did not improve; on average, every second day was a wash-out, and January 1945 was little better, with 226 sorties – the smallest number recorded by the Windsors in any month since Sicily. But the squadron made the most of its limited opportunities, dropping forty-six tons of bombs and bagging 116 railway cars.

More notable was the alarming fatality rate. The squadron lost six pilots during December and January, beginning on 10 December when two Spitfires collided while manoeuvring into position to attack ground targets, claiming the lives of Pilot Officer Al Shannon and Warrant Officer R. W. "Tex" Rideout, one of the squadron's small contingent of Americans. On the last day of 1944, Warrant Officer Ken Hanson experienced engine trouble on take-off, and radioed that he was heading out to sea, presumably to jettison his bomb before returning to the airfield. Hanson was never heard from again; his body washed ashore several months later.[17]

Bad luck had continued to plague the squadron early in the new year. On 15 January, Warrant Officer Bob Ashley was escorting Kittyhawks to bomb a bridge. Along the way, his engine failed, and he radioed that he was bailing out; he was never seen again. Five days later, two more men disappeared. Flight Lieutenant Jimmy Waslyk and Flying Officer Raymond Edge took off from Bellaria to bomb a gun position west of Imola. They never returned.[18]

Christmas had been one pleasant distraction. Cards were printed, bearing the Italian Christmas and New Year's greeting, *Auguri di Buon Natale e Capodanno*, and Christmas dinner "was a sit-down meal with dishes and cutlery," a pleasant change from the usual cafeteria-style service and mess tins. "It was a rowdy drunk," Leading Aircraftsman Stu Egglestone of Calgary recalls. "The CO stood to say a few words and could not be heard; he gave up."[19]

January 1945 had witnessed 417's last dogfight of the war. Everyone knew that German aircraft were around; Messerschmitts had been seen, but not engaged, in December. On 23 January, the New Zealander who commanded 244 Wing, W. E. Bary, was leading five Canadian rookies when he spotted eleven Me109s north of Padua. "Jettison bombs!" cried Bary. "This is it!" The Germans scattered, with pairs of Spitfires in hot pursuit. "A grand dogfight" ensued, with fighters darting in and out, weaving, circling, firing the occasional burst. The Germans fled without losing a plane, but the Canadians went home happy.[20]

February, when the Windsors had learned that they were being orphaned by the Canadian army, was another dismal month. Thirteen fogbound days restricted operations, but there were no casualties, and life at Bellaria was bearable, thanks to the Windsor Club and its legendary bar.[21] To survive the frigid nights, the ingenious Windsors installed makeshift gas stoves (according to Stu Egglestone, "We were using about 120 gallons of 100-octane aircraft gasoline a month per tent" – while gas was being rationed in wartime Canada). However, the stoves were outlawed when a half-dozen tents burned down.[22]

The weather had improved in March. The "clear, sunny days" resulted in some impressive statistics. The squadron flew 529 sorties, 140 more than any other squadron in 244 Wing (a tribute to the maintenance crews who worked so long and hard to keep the Spitfires airworthy), delivering 106 tons of bombs, which destroyed a locomotive, eighty freight cars, seven passenger coaches, forty-seven vehicles, and sixteen barges.[23]

Another claim enshrined Dave Goldberg in squadron mythology. On 9 March, northwest of Padua, the squadron leader and three Spitfires spotted a trio of horse-drawn vehicles, which the Canadians strafed. "But one of the vehicles behaved in a very curious manner; although hit repeatedly it refused to stop. The horse 'just ambled on' and negotiated a corner of the road in a strange unequine fashion. The pilots were convinced it was a camouflaged vehicle of some sort with a dummy horse attached."[24] When Goldberg filed his report, it resulted in a host of mirthful comments about this "horse-drawn tank." Goldberg contends that it "has been embellished over the years beyond the reality of the incident at the time . . . and upon reflection I would have preferred to have never made any observations in that regard."[25]

April 1945 had proved to be a fitting climax for the Windsors. It was the squadron's busiest month of the entire campaign, with 938 hours' worth of missions, the pilots flying an average of two dozen sorties per day. The Canadian Spitfires chalked up "an impressive tally of cratered rail lines, broken bridges, and battered locomotives, rolling stock, tanks, vehicles, carts, barges and guns," but a good portion of their work came in close support of the army against "occupied buildings, slit trenches, dugouts, gun posts, tanks and similar targets."[26]

This superlative effort coincided with the launching of the final offensive by the Fifth and Eighth armies. The part played by 417 Squadron began at 1500 hours on 9 April, with a pair of bombing and strafing missions. As the temperatures increased, so did the squadron's workload. Between dawn and dusk on 12 April, the Windsors flew forty-nine missions; bad weather interrupted operations for the next two days, but the Canadians returned to the sky with a vengeance between 15 and 21 April, flying an average of thirty-three sorties a day. On 16 April, the squadron had recorded its final fatality of the war: Flying Officer Jack Rose crashed while strafing slit trenches.[27]

The Windsors enjoyed superb hunting during the last week in April. Splendid weather, combined with the enemy's chaotic retreat, presented the squadron with unprecedented targets: trucks, tanks, wagons, staff cars, motorcycles. In the space of four days, the Canadian Spitfire pilots flew 129 sorties "to bomb and strafe the retreating Germans. Road targets were numerous as the pilots hunted from the Po to the Piave, strafing anything that moved, and the holocaust resembled that in the Falaise Gap in August 1944."[28]

On 29 April, 417 Squadron flew its last mission of the war. During the evening, Dave Goldberg led six Spitfires to shoot up enemy traffic. They found a convoy of about a hundred vehicles; the Canadians destroyed or damaged at least one-quarter of them before zooming into the darkening sky.[29] Today, the squadron leader is philosophical about the carnage inflicted during these sorties. Theirs was "a somewhat impersonal" sort of war, unlike the close-quarters fighting that the army experienced. "The scenes presented to us on the roads in Italy were viewed as the natural outcome of the war," he explains, "but at the same time underlined a personal involvement, suffering, and death of an enemy whom we were trained to fight."[30]

At the beginning of May, the Windsors waved farewell to Bellaria and moved to Treviso, north of Venice. As they journeyed to the new base, the war in Italy ended.

Like most of his men, Squadron Leader Goldberg felt "great relief." There was little celebrating, he recalls: "Oddly enough, quiet reflection coupled with the awareness of having survived war dominated. . . . All were very tired and weary."[31]

The Windsors participated in the Desert Air Force's victory fly-past at Udine on 28 May, and for the next month prepared to return to Canada. Flying training was cut back, while generous leave was provided for the weary warriors. On 28 June, the squadron's 260 men boarded a convoy of twenty-two trucks for Forli to catch a train. At midnight on 30 June, 417 Squadron officially ceased to exist as an operational unit, ending a journey that started in November 1941 with its formation in England.

Just as the Canadian soldiers who served in Italy took great pride in having served with the Eighth Army, the flyers went home with fond memories of their association with the Desert Air Force. Although its name was inappropriate to Italy's fall and winter rains, the DAF had won an admirable reputation in the course of the campaign. Comments Goldberg: "The unique combination of military professionalism and teamwork without the undue application or presence of unduly stringent and impractical rules, regulations, and formalities always proved to be refreshing and added to the great esprit de corps."[32]

3

The Italian campaign was the longest sustained offensive undertaken by the Allies during the war. It was characterized by suspicion and animosity between the British and Americans; in all other respects they were the ideal allies, yet they nearly came to a parting of the ways over their Mediterranean strategy. The symbolism of the campaign is inescapable, for Italy was the one theatre of operations in which the British had predominance in manpower and material resources; this secondary front can be seen as the last grasp for glory by a fading empire that was being overshadowed in every way by two superpowers, the United States and the Soviet Union.

Nearly a half-century after the war, historians are unable to agree on the merits of the Italian campaign. Whatever one's views, it must be admitted that there is something inherently unsatisfying about the war in Italy, caught in the middle of the protracted dispute between the British, who exaggerated its importance, and the Americans, who tried to minimize it. Field-Marshal Alexander tried to place it in perspective when he wrote at the end of the war: "The Allied Armies in Italy were not engaged with the enemy's main armies and their attacks were not directed, as were those of the Allies in the West or the Russians in the East, against the heart of the German Fatherland and the nerve-centres of Germany's national existence. Our role was subordinate and preparatory." Despite their subordinate status, Alexander's forces still managed to come close to conclusive victory, particularly in the battle for Rome in May and June 1944, which led to heightened and unreasonable expectations. "It was only when Allied leaders began to look for decisive results in Italy itself," argues British veteran and historian John Strawson, "that they reaped such disappointment and frustration."[33]

The campaign has generated exaggerated claims and criticisms over the years. Not surprisingly, the keenest supporter and apologist for the Italian campaign was its chief architect, Winston Churchill. "The principal task of our armies had been to draw off and contain the greatest possible number of Germans. This had been admirably fulfilled," he later wrote. "Except for a short period in the summer of 1944, the enemy had always outnumbered us. At the time of their crisis in August of that year no fewer than fifty-five German divisions were deployed along the Mediterranean fronts. Nor was this all. Our forces rounded off their task by devouring the larger army they had been ordered to 'contain.' There have been few campaigns with a finer culmination."[34]

Critics, both British and American, were unimpressed with such claims. George Marshall, the American army's chief of staff, never did buy Churchill's arguments in favour of the protracted campaign in Italy. As late as March 1945, he dismissed it as "a grave strategical mistake."[35] Some British writers have denounced the campaign, such as J. F. C. Fuller, who caustically commented that Italy was "tactically the most absurd and strategically the most senseless campaign of the whole war."[36]

The campaign's problems were rooted in the lack of direction. It was launched, after all, for the sake of employing the half-million British and American troops who were in the Mediterranean at the conclusion of the North African campaign, and who were basically stranded there for lack of shipping. Historians Dominick Graham and Shelford Bidwell point out also that its goals were repeatedly changed to suit the circumstances, "from a cheap victory over Italy, to prove to the Russians that the Western Allies were really fighting in Europe, to support the strategic bombing policy, and finally to contain Army Group 'C.'"[37]

This put the soldiers in an impossible position. Sir Richard McCreery, the last of the Eighth Army's commanders, called it "a ridiculous situation. Not only we were battle-weary, depleted, depressed, out-numbered and generally mucked about but we who could least afford to find manpower were being asked to send whole formations to France and to Greece, and at a time, I may add, when we were being ordered simultaneously to nail down sufficient divisions of the enemy to make a worthwhile contribution to the whole war effort. It was like being asked to pull a rabbit out of the hat when one has found that the rabbit has disappeared and then to one's horror one found that one had been deprived of the hat as well."[38]

Whatever the merits of the campaign, whatever success was achieved, can be attributed to the German decision to contest the peninsula. Churchill recognized this fact, writing in December 1944 to President Roosevelt. Describing with alarm the "marked degree of frustration in Italy," the prime minister pointed out that "the Germans are still keeping 26 divisions, equivalent to perhaps 16 full strength or more, on our front. They could however at any time retreat through the Brenner and Ljubljana and greatly shorten their line by holding from Lake Garda to the mouth of the Adige. By this they might save half their Italian forces for home defence. ... This would be a powerful reinforcement to the German homeland, according to events, either in the east or in the west."[39]

Italy was as much a conundrum to the enemy as it was to the Allies. The Germans lost far more than they gained by contesting the peninsula, but Albert Kesselring, the mastermind of the Germans' defensive strategy, remained unrepentant, writing in his memoirs:

> To have evacuated the whole of Italy and defended the Reich from positions in the Alps would not have been to economize our effectives; it would have given the enemy untrammelled freedom of movement in the direction of France and the Balkans, and have meant sacrificing an indispensable deep battle-zone and unleashing the air war on the whole of southern Germany and Austria.
>
> Similarly to have evacuated southern and central Italy and held the Apennines and Alps only would not have resulted in any saving of men and materials, nor have appreciably lessened the danger of sea- and airborne landings or the extension of the air war as above.

Kesselring contended "that the battle for Italy was not only justified but even imperative and the problem one of simply doing whatever seemed best for one's own theatre irrespective of the general strategic plan."[40]

Whatever the reasons for fighting the campaign in Italy, whatever doubts and criticisms have been raised, there is a bottom line – casualties. As the Canadian official history observes, "there is no question as to which side had its strength drained more by the campaign." Allied losses from D-Day in Sicily on 10 July 1943 to 2 May 1945 totalled 320,955, while the Germans and Italians lost 658,339, exclusive of the quarter-million troops who were involved in the final capitulation.[41] The historian wishing to justify the campaign need look no further.

The Canadians were among twenty-six nationalities represented in the Allied forces in Italy. A total of 92,757 Canadians of all ranks served in this theatre, and more than a quarter of them became casualties. The final toll includes 5,764 dead, 19,486 wounded, 1,004 captured.

There are few memorials to their efforts. Unlike Normandy, where every city, town, and village has a picturesque plaque or monument recalling its liberation, with a park or street named for the unit or units responsible, Italy (perhaps understandably) has virtually turned a blind eye to its recent past. Churches rebuilt since the war (Passionisti, outside Pontecorvo, and Ortona's San Tomasso) are decorated with paintings depicting their destruction, and there is a plaque at Casa Berardi, commemorating "Cap. Paul Triquet, Royal 22e Reggiment [sic] Canadian – Ortona 1943." But these are the exceptions. Superhighways have been built over the battle-fields, and most of the concrete fortifications constructed by the Germans have been removed.

Only the cemeteries tell the tale of what happened here in 1943, 1944, and 1945. Canada's dead can be found in seventeen war cemeteries, between Agira, Sicily, and Argenta in northern Italy. Some (notably Cassino, at the foot of the rebuilt monastery, and Gradara, overlooked by a fairy-tale castle) are strikingly beautiful; others less so. But all are immaculately maintained. And all bear striking, if mute, testimony to the sacrifices of Canadian soldiers, flyers, and sailors.

The veterans of Italy, living and dead, are Canada's forgotten heroes. They fought a campaign that, for eleven months, was front-page news; after the invasion of Normandy on 6 June 1944, they toiled in virtual anonymity. Although many fine correspondents remained at work in Italy, the most famous of all, Ross Munro, had long since left to cover the cross-Channel operation. The effect was dramatic: in compiling his official history, *The Canadians in Italy*, Gerald Nicholson recounted that "we had the greatest difficulty in finding suitable photographs for the last ten months of the campaign" – most of the photographers had left for France![42]

This inferior status is reinforced annually. The anniversary of D-Day in

Normandy is celebrated on 6 June, with even more impressive ceremonials every five or ten years – and deservedly so. But who marks the anniversary of the landings in Sicily, the capture of Ortona, the assaults on the Hitler or Gothic lines? Notes Duncan Fraser, the veteran of the Cape Breton Highlanders, who returned to Nova Scotia to become a professor of political science, "some of the bloodiest battles of the Second World War have been dismissed from the national memory."[43]

They are still the D-Day Dodgers. It is a name of which they are fiercely, and rightly, proud, and the comments of Victor Hall of the West Nova Scotia Regiment typify their views. "I'm glad I was a D-Day Dodger," he states emphatically. "Anybody that was in Italy at the time had to laugh at this D-Day business. Because they [the Normandy invasion forces] were in action from June the sixth until the war was over, May the eighth – eleven months. We were in action eleven months *before* they went into action, from July tenth to June sixth. So we did twice as much time [in action], and yet we're never mentioned. Ignored. Italy was just a forgotten part of the war."[44]

Official indifference has not helped their cause. They have been forced to endure other indignities that denied recognition of their unique contributions to the war effort. During the summer of 1944, the Canadian veterans of Sicily and Italy were awarded the 1939–43 Star; this was later revised to the 1939–45 Star, "to cover both fronts. We all thought this was a degrading affair towards the Italian and Sicilian participants who received it," says Ray Cross, a tank doctor with the First Canadian Armoured Brigade. Another proposal, to put the number 8, reflecting their affiliation with the Eighth Army, on the Italian Star ribbon, was not sanctioned by the Canadian government. "Here again," Cross writes, "another black eye for the Italian campaign veterans."[45]

Some have tried to do something about it. In Orillia, Ontario, Cliff Evans, a veteran of the Saskatoon Light Infantry, organized an annual D-Day Dodgers' reunion, which has grown by leaps and bounds in a dozen years. Fifty attended the first reunion; now it attracts several hundred army, navy, and air force veterans each May.[46]

None of this should be necessary. "The gallant record of the Canadians in Italy speaks for itself," writes the PPCLI's Syd Frost. "It is enshrined in a host of Battle Honours of the Regiments who fought there. This is a good thing, for otherwise their deeds would soon be forgotten – unremembered by all except the D-Day Dodgers. They will never forget."[47]

This is especially sad for veterans from Canada's Maritime provinces. According to Duncan Fraser, the former Cape Breton Highlander, Italy embodied the main military effort of the Maritimes. "In northwest Europe, two Maritime infantry battalions saw battle. But in Italy, the

Maritime Provinces' component of the Canadian army comprised three . . . infantry battalions, one infantry close-support machine-gun and mortar company, one armoured regiment, an anti-tank battery, an anti-aircraft battery, in addition to many Maritimers in other service and support units, as well as the large contingent of . . . Maritime nursing sisters and doctors."[48]

The Canadian D-Day Dodgers have good reason to be proud of their achievements. In a 1956 speech, official historian Gerry Nicholson pointed out that the Canadians always faced the cream of the German forces in Italy:

> Looking over the list of the 20 German divisions which at one time or another opposed the Canadians, it is difficult to pick out more than two or three that were manned by low-grade troops. On the other hand the list includes a number of divisions that constituted the elite of the German armies in Italy . . . for, as we have learned from enemy records, it is a fact that the reported appearance of the Canadians in a given sector was generally the signal for the Germans to commit their best formations in the theatre.[49]

It is no coincidence that the Canadians hold their adversaries in high regard. "We overcame them with equipment, and the number of shells – firepower – and the numbers of troops," says Jim Stone, the former commanding officer of the Loyal Edmonton Regiment. "The Germans fought a magnificent delaying battle the whole way up Italy."[50]

Ironically, so far as their prime minister was concerned, the Canadians sent to Italy *really were* dodging D-Day. Although they had other motives (notably, getting rid of Andy McNaughton as the army commander overseas), Mackenzie King's advisers won his support by playing on his fears of the heavy casualties that could, and did, accompany the cross-Channel invasion. King hoped to spare the country these forecast losses by sending a substantial part of the First Canadian Army to Italy. Yet, when the conscription crisis that he sought to avoid finally exploded, the prime minister attributed it to the decision to split the army.

Was it the right decision? The answer to that question is subjective, and every participant, every historian, has his own views. A senior King adviser, Major-General Maurice Pope, later argued: "It was better . . . to fight divided than not to fight until victory had been practically assured." Pope, conveniently ignoring the casualty lists, believed "that if some of our formations and units had not taken part in the operations in Sicily and Italy, the Canadian people would have been denied a sense of having played their due part in the defeat of Germany."[51]

Certainly McNaughton considered it an unnecessary waste of

resources. At the end of March 1945, the defence minister chatted privately with Prime Minister King, who recorded their conversation in his diary:

> He made clearer to me today than I have seen before just what is the cause of his strong feeling about Ralston. It began with what he feels Ralston–Stuart worked in with Sir Alan Brooke and Montgomery to change altogether the plans on which the Army had been built up with a view to its part in the invasion of Northern Europe. He has a statement from Ralston in which Ralston says that unless there were casualties to a certain amount, we would have no voice in the peace. That, I can vouch for, is something very familiar to what he said in Council and to which I took exception – that it was necessary for us to be fighting in Italy. . . . The General also says he has a telegram from Eisenhower to him with words something to the effect not to break up the army in Britain but to keep it intact for invasion purposes. [McNaughton] was quite favoured to allowing officers to go to Italy for battle training but saw no need for moving the troops . . . there was no justification for our men going on in to Italy [after Sicily]. . . . McNaughton feels that having the two divisions go to Italy meant extra lines of supply with a demand for very large numbers of additional men, reduced the effectiveness in the long run of the invasion and really was accountable for the [manpower] shortage that came later on the continent. I think events show that he is right.[52]

Consider, too, the stinging indictment of Canada's pre-eminent historian, the late C. P. Stacey. Accepting the validity of using the Italian operations to acquire experience for key officers and senior NCOs taking part in Overlord, Stacey pointed out that I Canadian Corps was effectively orphaned. "Although the lives of so many Canadian soldiers were involved in the strategic decision to continue the offensive in Italy after we reached the Gothic Line," he wrote, "no Canadian authority was consulted upon it or even informed of it." According to Stacey this was directly attributable to the "fundamental" error in splitting Canada's field army. As a consequence, the Canadian government "reduced its own control of it and exposed the fragments to the sort of situation which the corps in Italy became involved in the autumn of 1944. And it merely made itself ridiculous when, having realized the error it had made, it began asking to have the Mediterranean force brought back at a time when it had not yet fought a major battle."[53]

The campaign revealed the strengths and weaknesses of the Canadian army. Its tradition of militia enthusiasm and professional competence was admirably reflected in the consistent successes in platoon and company actions, and often at the battalion level. At the brigade, division, and corps levels, inconsistency was a problem. According to the historians W. A. B. Douglas and Brereton Greenhous, "the paucity of talent at the higher levels of command" can be attributed to the neglect of the military before the war. "Success at those levels normally requires both long and careful training and natural talent, but the small budget and low profile of the Canadian forces in the pre-war days meant that young officers had little opportunity to get the necessary training." They identify Guy Simonds, Chris Vokes, and Bert Hoffmeister as Canada's only "first-rate" generals; all three served in Italy. (And it was no coincidence that Hoffmeister, a militia officer before the war, was later appointed to command the division organized for but not sent to the Pacific theatre.)[54]

Orphaned by their government, neglected by the news media after 6 June, the Canadians fought their lonely war in distant Italy. Half a century later, it remains, to the public at large, an unknown aspect of Canada's war effort, much to the disgust of D-Day Dodgers like Duncan Fraser:

> The war in Italy was cruel and dirty. Under-equipped with everything but spirit, guts, and determination, the Canadians in Italy made a reputation as tough and courageous fighters. They slugged victoriously northwards against an implacable, efficient, and seasoned enemy army, through the most difficult and heartbreaking terrain encountered by any army in the Second World War. . . .
>
> Living amongst us are many Canadian widows of infantrymen killed on the Italian battlefields nearly half a century ago. If for no other reason than this we should as a nation honour the Canadians who fought, bled, and died in that far-off land.
>
> To do otherwise is totally unconscionable.[55]

Canadian Army Formations in Italy, 19 August 1944

I Canadian Corps

I Corps Headquarters Signals
I Corps Defence Company (Lorne Scots)
I Corps Transport Company, Royal Canadian Army Service Corps
I Corps Troops Workshop, Royal Canadian Electrical and Mechanical
    Engineers

7th Anti-Tank Regiment
1st Survey Regiment

4 Casualty Clearing Station, Royal Canadian Army Medical Corps
5 Casualty Clearing Station

First Canadian Infantry Division

First Infantry Divisional Signals

Royal Canadian Dragoons (1st Armoured Car Regiment)
Saskatoon Light Infantry (Machine-Gun)

First Canadian Infantry Brigade
    The Royal Canadian Regiment
    Hastings and Prince Edward Regiment
    48th Highlanders of Canada

Second Canadian Infantry Brigade
    Princess Patricia's Canadian Light Infantry
    Seaforth Highlanders of Canada
    Loyal Edmonton Regiment

Third Canadian Infantry Brigade
  Royal 22nd Regiment
  Carleton and York Regiment
  West Nova Scotia Regiment

1st Field Regiment (Royal Canadian Horse Artillery), Royal Canadian
  Artillery
2nd Field Regiment
3rd Field Regiment
1st Anti-Tank Regiment
2nd Light Anti-Aircraft Regiment

2nd Field Park Company, Corps of Royal Canadian Engineers
1st Field Company
3rd Field Company
4th Field Company

4 Field Ambulance, Royal Canadian Army Medical Corps
5 Field Ambulance
9 Field Ambulance

First Infantry Divisional Troops Company, Royal Canadian Army Service
  Corps
First Infantry Brigade Company
Second Infantry Brigade Company
Third Infantry Brigade Company

First Infantry Brigade Workshop, Royal Canadian Electrical and
  Mechanical Engineers
Second Infantry Brigade Workshop
Third Infantry Brigade Workshop

Fifth Canadian Armoured Division

Fifth Armoured Divisional Signals

Governor-General's Horse Guards

Fifth Canadian Armoured Brigade
  Lord Strathcona's Horse (2nd Armoured Regiment)
  8th Princess Louise's Hussars (5th Armoured Regiment)
  British Columbia Dragoons (9th Armoured Regiment)

Eleventh Canadian Infantry Brigade
  Perth Regiment

Cape Breton Highlanders
Irish Regiment of Canada

Twelfth Canadian Infantry Brigade
    4th Princess Louise Dragoon Guards
    Lanark and Renfrew Scottish Regiment
    Westminster Regiment (Motor)

17th Field Regiment, Royal Canadian Artillery
8th Field Regiment (Self-Propelled)
4th Anti-Tank Regiment
5th Light Anti-Aircraft Regiment

4th Field Park Squadron, Corps of Royal Canadian Engineers
1st Field Squadron
10th Field Squadron

7 Field Ambulance, Royal Canadian Army Medical Corps
8 Field Ambulance
24 Field Ambulance

Fifth Armoured Divisional Troops Company, Royal Canadian Army
    Service Corps
Fifth Armoured Brigade Company
Eleventh Infantry Brigade Company
Twelfth Infantry Brigade Company

Fifth Armoured Brigade Workshop, Royal Canadian Electrical and
    Mechanical Engineers
Eleventh Infantry Brigade Workshop
Twelfth Infantry Brigade Workshop

First Canadian Armoured Brigade

First Armoured Brigade Signals

Ontario (11th Armoured) Regiment
Three Rivers (12th Armoured) Regiment
Calgary (14th Armoured) Regiment

2 Light Field Ambulance, Royal Canadian Army Medical Corps

First Armoured Brigade Company, Royal Canadian Army Service Corps

First Armoured Brigade Workshop, Royal Canadian Electrical and
    Mechanical Engineers

Other Units

First Canadian Army Troops:
  Elgin (25th Armoured Delivery) Regiment
  1 Army Group, Royal Canadian Artillery
      1st Medium Regiment
      2nd Medium Regiment
      5th Medium Regiment

Royal Canadian Army Service Corps:
  31 Corps Troops Company
  32 Corps Troops Company
  1 Motor Ambulance Company
  1 Headquarters Corps Car Company
  41 Army Transport Company

Royal Canadian Army Medical Corps:
  1 General Hospital
  3 General Hospital
  5 General Hospital
  14 General Hospital
  15 General Hospital
  28 General Hospital
  1 Convalescent Depot

Canadian Dental Corps:
  1 Dental Company
  3 Dental Company
  8 Dental Company
  11 Base Dental Company

Royal Canadian Ordnance Corps:
  201 Infantry Ordnance Sub-Park
  205 Armoured Ordnance Sub-Park
  1 Corps and Army Troops Sub-Park

Royal Canadian Electrical and Mechanical Engineers:
  1 Army Tank Troops Workshop
  1 Infantry Troops Workshop
  5 Armoured Troops Workshop
  1 Recovery Company

Canadian Provost Corps:
    1 Provost Company (RCMP)
    3 Provost Company
    5 Provost Company
    1 Line of Communication Provost Company
    35 Traffic Control Company

Reference Notes

Throughout the notes, NAC refers to the National Archives of Canada and DHist to the Directorate of History, National Defence Headquarters, Ottawa.

Prologue: "Things Are Getting Very Monotonous"

1. Churchill, *The Grand Alliance*, 5.
2. Gilbert, *Road to Victory*, 181.
3. Ibid., 253.
4. Ready, *Forgotten Allies*, 192.
5. Churchill, *The Grand Alliance*, 652.
6. Gilbert, 263.
7. Ellis, *Cassino*, 10.
8. Bruce, *Second Front Now!* 96-7.
9. Liddell Hart, *History of the Second World War*, 451.
10. D'Este, *Bitter Victory*, 50.
11. Ibid., 72.
12. Ibid., 71-2.
13. Bradley, *A General's Life*, 160.
14. Molony, *The Mediterranean and Middle East*, V/12-13.
15. D'Este, 113.
16. Blumenson, *The Patton Papers*, 229.
17. D'Este, 93.
18. Thompson, *The Montgomery Legend*, 227.
19. Blumenson, *The Patton Papers*, 283.
20. D'Este, 107.
21. Hamilton, *Master of the Battlefield*, 268.
22. D'Este, 108.
23. Molony, V/31.
24. Stevens, *The Royal Canadian Regiment*, 67.
25. Molony, V/46.
26. Ibid., 4fn, 28fn.
27. Nicholson, *The Canadians in Italy*, 86.
28. Nicolson, 211.
29. Hamilton, 472-3.

30. Bradley, 162–3.
31. Molony, v/24.
32. Trevor-Roper, *Hitler's Table Talk*, 10–11, 660.
33. Irving, *The Trail of the Fox*, 346.
34. Molony, v/37.
35. Nicholson, *The Canadians in Italy*, 55.
36. Howard, *Grand Strategy*, 467.
37. D'Este, 193.
38. Ibid., 195.
39. Nicholson, *The Canadians in Italy*, 56–7.
40. Nolan, *King's War*, 1.
41. Ibid., 87–8.
42. How, *The Canadians at War*, 210.
43. Douglas, *Out of the Shadows*, 103.
44. Nolan, 116.
45. Ready, 19.
46. Moir, *History of the Royal Canadian Corps of Signals*, 82.
47. Interview with author, 7/8/89.
48. Mitchell, RCHA, 89.
49. Malone, *A Portrait of War*, 123.
50. Stursberg, *Journey into Victory*, 79.
51. Shapiro, *They Left the Back Door Open*, 3–4.
52. Nicholson, *The Canadians in Italy*, 21.
53. Swettenham, II/246–7, 267.
54. Bryant, *The Turn of the Tide*, 488–9.
55. Pickersgill, *The Mackenzie King Record*, I/500.
56. Ibid., 495–7.
57. Nicholson, *The Canadians in Italy*, 24.
58. Ibid., 3, 26.
59. Swettenham, *McNaughton*, II/291–2.
60. Kitching, *Mud and Green Fields*, 140.
61. Nicholson, *The Canadians in Italy*, 26.
62. Interview with author, 25/7/89.
63. Hamilton, 507.
64. Nicholson, *The Canadians in Italy*, 31–2.
65. Ibid., 32.
66. Maltby, "Hi-Ho! Hi-Ho!" in *Informal History of the Calgary Regiment*, 2.
67. Nicholson, *The Canadians in Italy*, 36–7, 39fn.
68. Stacey, *Arms, Men and Government*, 210–11, 218.
69. Kitching, 157.
70. Graham, *Citizen and Soldier*, 140, 143–4.
71. Kitching, 158–9.
72. Nicholson, *The Canadians in Italy*, 40–1.
73. Stevens, *Princess Patricia's Canadian Light Infantry*, 60.
74. Nicholson, *The Canadians in Italy*, 42.
75. Mowat, *And No Birds Sang*, 55–6.
76. Mitchell, *My War*, 70.
77. B. Sharp, interview with author, 15/6/89.
78. Interview with author, 7/8/89.

79. Interview with author, 25/7/89.
80. NAC, RG 24 C3, volume 13,726, war diary, 6/7/43.
81. Interview with author, 9/6/89.
82. Nicholson, *The Gunners of Canada*, 138.
83. NAC, RG 24 C3, volume 13,726, war diary, 5/7/43.
84. Kitching, 160.
85. Mowat, *And No Birds Sang*, 63–4.
86. NAC, RG 24, volume 15,156, July 1943 war diary, Appendix 12.
87. Ibid., volume 15,113, July 1943 war diary.

PART ONE
Chapter 1: "Fun and Games"

1. Nicholson, *The Canadians in Italy*, 65–6.
2. Ibid., 66.
3. Stursberg, *Journey into Victory*, 316.
4. Molony, *The Mediterranean and Middle East*, V/57.
5. Schull, *Far Distant Ships*, 204.
6. Air Historian, *No. 417 Squadron*, 27.
7. Mitchell, *My War*, 71.
8. Munro, *Gauntlet to Overlord*, 363.
9. NAC, RG 24, volume 15,156, July 1943 war diary, Appendix 12.
10. Ibid.
11. Malone, *A Portrait of War*, 147–8.
12. Nicholson, *The Canadians in Italy*, 68.
13. Graham, *Citizen and Soldier*, 150.
14. Nicholson, *The Canadians in Italy*, 69–70.
15. Smith, *Duffy's Regiment*, 83.
16. Letter to author, 27/3/90.
17. Ibid.
18. Mowat, *And No Birds Sang*, 76; *The Regiment*, 58.
19. Mowat, *And No Birds Sang*, 79–80, 85.
20. Nicholson, *The Canadians in Italy*, 70.
21. Stursberg, 106–7.
22. Graham, *Citizen and Soldier*, 154.
23. Stevens, *A City Goes to War*, 233.
24. Beattie, *Dileas*, 222–3.
25. Stursberg, 107.
26. Raddall, *West Novas*, 84.
27. Nicholson, *The Canadians in Italy*, 72.
28. Mitchell, *My War*, 72.
29. Galloway, *Some Died at Ortona*, 33–4.
30. NAC, RG 24 C3, volume 13,726, war diary, 10/7/43.
31. Mowat, *The Regiment*, 63.
32. NAC, MG 26 J13, diary, 10/7/43.
33. Ibid., 9/7/43.
34. Ibid.
35. Pearson, *Mike*, I/242.
36. Nicholson, *The Canadians in Italy*, 74.

37. Ottawa, *Evening Citizen*, 10/7/43.
38. NAC, MG 26 J13, diary, 9–10/7/43.
39. *Toronto Star*, 9/7/43.
40. Ottawa, *Evening Citizen*, 9/7/43.
41. Pickersgill, *The Mackenzie King Record*, 1/517.
42. How, *The Canadians at War*, 329.
43. Interview with author, 17/7/89.
44. Munro, 377.
45. Interview with author, 17/7/89.
46. How, *The Canadians in Italy*, 329.
47. Interview with author, 17/7/89.
48. NAC, MG 26 J13, diary, 10/7/43.
49. Shapiro, *They Left the Back Door Open*, 49.
50. Molony, V/52.
51. Macmillan, *War Diaries*, 153.
52. Nicholson, *The Canadians in Italy*, 90.
53. D'Este, *Bitter Victory*, 312.
54. Kesselring, *Kesselring: A Soldier's Record*, 196–7.
55. Molony, V/87.
56. Molony, V/87.
57. Graham and Bidwell, *Tug of War*, 21–2.
58. Molony, V/88–9.
59. Blumenson, *The Patton Papers*, 290, 293–4.
60. Hamilton, *Master of the Battlefield*, 319–20.
61. D'Este, 527.
62. Hamilton, 321.
63. D'Este, 404.

Chapter 2: "Too Fat"

1. Beattie, *Dileas*, 229.
2. Historical Section, General Staff, *From Pachino to Ortona*, 42.
3. Munro, *Gauntlet to Overload*, 379.
4. NAC, RG 24 C3, volume 13,726, war diary, 12/7/43.
5. Nicholson, *The Canadians in Italy*, 82.
6. Malone, *A Portrait of War*, 158.
7. Stursberg, *Journey into Victory*, 114.
8. Malone, *A Portrait of War*, 159.
9. Galloway, *Some Died at Ortona*, 37.
10. Stevens, *The Royal Canadian Regiment*, 72.
11. Interview with author, 17/7/89.
12. Mowat, *And No Birds Sang*, 86.
13. Beattie, 233.
14. Mowat, *And No Birds Sang*, 87.
15. Hamilton, *Master of the Battlefield*, 305.
16. Mowat, *And No Birds Sang*, 89.
17. H. Graham, *Citizen and Soldier*, 156.
18. Hamilton, 309.

19. Butcher, *My Three Years with Eisenhower*, 361.
20. Swettenham, *McNaughton*, ii/297.
21. Ibid., 298.
22. Stacey, *Arms, Men and Government*, 225.
23. Montgomery, *Memoirs*, 184.
24. Hamilton, 332.
25. De Guingand, *Generals at War*, 153.
26. NAC, MG 27 III B11, volume 51, "Report on Visit to North Africa and Sicily, 6–20 July 1943," Appendix v.
27. Ibid.
28. NAC, MG 30 E133, volume 324, memo, 21/9/46.
29. Stacey, *Arms, Men and Government*, 226.
30. Swettenham, ii/304.
31. Hamilton, 333.
32. Stacey, *Arms, Men and Government*, 227.
33. Stevens, *A City Goes to War*, 238.
34. Vokes, *Vokes: My Story*, 97.
35. Nicholson, *The Canadians in Italy*, 90.
36. Ibid., 53.
37. Mowat, *And No Birds Sang*, 103.
38. Munro, 380.
39. Gaffen, *Forgotten Soldiers*, 41.
40. Mowat, *And No Birds Sang*, 103.
41. Beattie, 241.
42. Interview with author, 25/7/89.
43. Ibid.
44. Nicholson, *The Canadians in Italy*, 92.
45. Beattie, 242–3.
46. Nicholson, *The Canadians in Italy*, 93–4.
47. H. Graham, 158–9.
48. Smith, *Duffy's Regiment*, 87.
49. H. Graham, 161–2.
50. Hamilton, 341.
51. H. Graham, 162–3.
52. Ibid., 163.
53. Kitching, *Mud and Green Fileds*, 169.
54. H. Graham, 163.
55. Interview with author, 17/7/89.
56. Ibid.
57. Munro, 392–3.
58. Raddall, *West Novas*, 90.
59. Mowat, *And No Birds Sang*, 106–7.
60. Ibid., 42, 111.
61. Nicholson, *The Canadians in Italy*, 99.
62. Galloway, *Some Died at Ortona*, 54–5.
63. Beattie, 251.
64. Nicholson, *The Canadians in Italy*, 99–100.

Chapter 3: The Red Patch Devils

1. Beattie, *Dileas*, 255.
2. Mansikka, *Pack Up Your Troubles*, 9.
3. Vokes, *Vokes: My Story*, 107.
4. Beattie, 261.
5. Nicholson, *The Canadians in Italy*, 101–2.
6. H. Graham, *Citizen and Soldier*, 166–7.
7. Mowat, *And No Birds Sang*, 124.
8. Mowat, *The Regiment*, 84.
9. Mowat, *And No Birds Sang*, 127.
10. Tweedsmuir, *Assoro, July 21–23, 1943*, 10–11.
11. Mowat, *And No Birds Sang*, 128.
12. Smith, *Duffy's Regiment*, 94.
13. Mowat, *And No Birds Sang*, 129.
14. Tweedsmuir, 13–14.
15. Letter to author, 31/8/89.
16. Mowat, *And No Birds Sang*, 131.
17. Ibid., 133–4.
18. Tweedsmuir, 23–4.
19. Ibid., 18.
20. Letter to author, 31/8/89.
21. Ibid.
22. Ibid.
23. Ibid.
24. Ibid.
25. H. Graham, 171.
26. Beattie, 266.
27. Ibid., 268.
28. Mowat, *The Regiment*, 91.
29. Smith, *Duffy's Regiment*, 101.
30. Nicholson, *The Canadians in Italy*, 106.
31. Stevens, *Princess Patricia's Canadian Light Infantry*, 81.
32. Mitchell, *My War*, 74.
33. NAC, RG24, volume 15,156, July 1943 war diary, Appendix 16.
34. Vokes, 111.
35. Letter to author, 26/10/89.
36. Interview with author, 17/7/89.
37. Vokes, 100.
38. Interview with author, 25/7/89.
39. Nicholson, *The Canadians in Italy*, 108–9.
40. Interview with author, 25/7/89.
41. Nicholson, *The Canadians in Italy*, 108.
42. Stevens, *A City Goes to War*, 238.
43. Nicholson, *The Canadians in Italy,* 108.
44. Vokes, 111.
45. NAC, RG24, volume 15,156, July 1943 war diary, Appendix 16.
46. Stevens, *A City Goes to War*, 239.
47. NAC, RG24, volume 15,156, July 1943 war diary, Appendix 16.

48. Ibid.
49. Ibid.
50. Letter to author, 20/1/90.
51. NAC, RG24, volume 13,796, November 1944 war diary, Appendix 11.
52. Nicholson, *The Canadians in Italy*, 110.
53. Ibid., 118.
54. Mowat, *The Regiment*, 94.
55. McAndrew, "Fire or Movement?" 142.
56. Interview with author, 23/8/90.
57. Letter to author, 31/1/90.
58. McAndrew, "Fire or Movement?" 142.
59. Letter to author, 18/2/90.
60. Galloway, *Some Died at Ortona*, 69.
61. Nicholson, *The Canadians in Italy*, 124.
62. Galloway, *Some Died at Ortona*, 70.
63. Ibid., 70-1.
64. Stevens, *The Royal Canadian Regiment*, 80.
65. Letter to author, 18/2/90.
66. Ibid.
67. Kitching, letter to author, 20/1/90.
68. Mowat, *The Regiment*, 94.
69. Nicholson, *The Canadians in Italy*, 124-5.
70. Letter to author, 20/1/90.
71. Mowat, *And No Birds Sang*, 145.
72. Smith, *Duffy's Regiment*, 100.
73. Tweedsmuir, 2-3.
74. Nicholson, *The Canadians in Italy*, 125-6.
75. Mowat, *The Regiment*, 96.
76. *The Plough Jockey* (newspaper of Hastings and Prince Edward Regiment), July 1988, 18.
77. Letter to author, 18/2/90.
78. Ibid.
79. McAndrew, "Fire or Movement?" 144.
80. Galloway, *Some Died at Ortona*, 72-3.
81. Letter to author, 20/1/90.
82. H. Graham, 177.
83. Letter to author, 31/1/90.
84. Ibid., 27/3/90.
85. Interview with author, 8/8/89.
86. Raddall, *West Novas*, 92.
87. Nicholson, *The Canadians in Italy*, 126-7.
88. Ibid., 126.
89. Ibid., 122.
90. H. Graham, 175.
91. Letter to author, 31/1/90.
92. McAndrew, "Fire or Movement?" 144.
93. Letter to author, 24/10/89.
94. Ibid., 31/1/90.
95. Nicholson, *The Canadians in Italy*, 128-9.

96. Ibid., 129.
97. NAC, RG24, volume 15,156, July 1943 war diary, Appendix 19.
98. Nicholson, *The Canadians in Italy*, 129.
99. Vokes, 114.
100. Nicholson, *The Canadians in Italy*, 130.
101. Roy, *The Seaforth Highlanders of Canada*, 181–2.
102. Shapiro, *They Left the Back Door Open*, 68.
103. Historical Section, 60.
104. Roy, *The Seaforth Highlanders of Canada*, 188.
105. Nicholson, *The Canadians in Italy*, 132.
106. Shapiro, 62.
107. NAC, RG24, volume 15,156, July 1943 war diary, Appendix 20.
108. Nicholson, *The Canadians in Italy*, 134.
109. Galloway, *Some Died at Ortona*, 73.

Chapter 4: "A Proper Schemozzle"

1. Nicholson, *The Canadians in Italy*, 135.
2. Lochner, *The Goebbels Diaries, 1942–1943*, 418.
3. Ibid., 403; D'Este, *Bitter Victory*, 203.
4. Hamilton, *Master of the Battlefield*, 336–9.
5. Blumenson, *The Patton Papers*, 301, 306.
6. Hamilton, 328.
7. Nicholson, *The Canadians in Italy*, 137.
8. Tooley, *Invicta*, 132.
9. Raddall, *West Novas*, 93.
10. Ibid., 95.
11. Nicholson, *The Canadians in Italy*, 141.
12. Raddall, 98.
13. Nicholson, *The Canadians in Italy*, 143.
14. Ibid., 142–3.
15. Ibid., 144.
16. Interview with author, 7/8/89.
17. Nicholson, *The Canadians in Italy*, 147.
18. Ibid., 148–9.
19. Galloway, *Some Died at Ortona*, 83–4.
20. Ibid., 86.
21. Ibid., 87–9.
22. Letter to author, 24/10/89.
23. Letter to author, 31/8/89.
24. Stursberg, *Journey into Victory*, 137–8.
25. Nicholson, *The Canadians in Italy*, 153.
26. Ibid., 154.
27. Raddall, 86–7.
28. Roy, *The Seaforth Highlanders of Canada*, 172–3fn.
29. Warren, *Wait for the Waggon*, 240.
30. Stursberg, 141.
31. Nicholson, *The Canadians in Italy*, 162.
32. Munro, *Gauntlet to Overlord*, 424.

33. Nicholson, *The Canadians in Italy*, 158.
34. NAC, RG24, volume 14,074, August 1943 war diary, Appendix 11.
35. Nicholson, *The Canadians in Italy*, 160–1.
36. Roy, *The Seaforth Highlanders of Canada*, 196.
37. Vokes, *Vokes: My Story*, 114, 120.
38. Interview with author, 7/7/89.
39. Tooley, 142.
40. Nicholson, *The Canadians in Italy*, 163.
41. Ibid., 165.
42. Galloway, *Some Died at Ortona*, 95.
43. Interview with author, 25/7/89.
44. Gilbert, *Road to Victory*, 458.
45. Hamilton, 343.
46. Stacey, *Arms, Men and Government*, 228.
47. NAC, RG24, volume 14,074, August 1943 war diary, Appendix 15.
48. Feasby, *Official History of the Canadian Medical Services, 1939–1945*, I/129.
49. Munro, 384.
50. Stursberg, 133.
51. Powley, *Broadcast from the Front*, 48.
52. Reyburn, *Some of It Was Fun*, 75.
53. Interview with author, 17/7/89.
54. Reyburn, 128–9.
55. Stacey, *A Date with History*, 119, 142.
56. Ibid., 119.
57. McAndrew, "Recording the War," 44–5.
58. Stacey, *A Date with History*, 127–30.
59. Ibid., 119.
60. McAndrew, "Recording the War," 46.
61. Stacey, *A Date with History*, 119.
62. Churchill, *Closing the Ring*, 40.
63. Nicholson, *The Canadians in Italy*, 172–4.
64. D'Este, 522.
65. Nicholson, *The Canadians in Italy*, 173–4.
66. Fuller, *The Second World War, 1939–1945*, 266.
67. Kesselring, *Kesselring: A Soldier's Record*, 199.

Chapter 5: "Morale Is Excellent"

1. Nicholson, *The Canadians in Italy*, 181.
2. Loewenheim, *Roosevelt and Churchill*, 324.
3. Nicholson, *The Canadians in Italy*, 181–2.
4. Ellis, *Cassino*, 12.
5. Churchill, *The Grand Alliance*, 810.
6. Nicholson, *The Canadians in Italy*, 189.
7. Montgomery, *Memoirs*, 190–1.
8. Shepperd, *The Italian Campaign*, xi.
9. Jackson, *The Battle for Italy*, 78.
10. Stacey, *Arms, Men and Government*, 137.
11. Ibid., 180.

12. Pickersgill, *The Mackenzie King Record*, I/528.
13. Bruce, *Second Front Now!*, 133.
14. Ellis, 16.
15. Churchill, *Closing the Ring*, 83.
16. Ehrman, *Grand Strategy*, 8–9.
17. Churchill, *Closing the Ring*, 96, 151.
18. Bryant, *The Turn of the Tide*, 582.
19. Pickersgill, I/544–5.
20. Swettenham, *McNaughton*, II/293.
21. Nicholson, *The Canadians in Italy*, 188.
22. Galloway, *Some Died at Ortona*, 101.
23. Mitchell, RCHA, 97.
24. Feasby, *Official History of the Canadian Medical Services, 1939–1945*, I/125, 146.
25. Interview with author, 17/7/89.
26. Mowat, *And No Birds Sang*, 90.
27. Bob Sharp, interview with author, 15/6/89.
28. Galloway, *Some Died at Ortona*, 93.
29. NAC, RG24, volume 14,074, August 1943 war diary, Appendix 15.
30. Beattie, *Dileas*, 258.
31. Interview with author, 25/7/89.
32. Mowat, *The Regiment*, 103; *And No Birds Sang*, 161–2.
33. Vokes, *Vokes: My Story*, 123, 127; letter to author, n.d.
34. Nicholson, *The Canadians in Italy*, 119.
35. *The RCAF Overseas*, I/349.
36. Molony, *The Mediterranean and Middle East*, V/469fn.
37. Air Historian, *No. 417 Squadron*, 30–1.
38. Robbins, *417 Squadron History*, 15.
39. Olmsted, *Blue Skies*, 123.
40. Ibid., 124.
41. Ibid., 125–6.
42. Robbins, 15–16.
43. Galloway, *The General Who Never Was*, 180–1.
44. Ibid., 181–2.
45. Chalfont, *Montgomery of Alamein*, 210.
46. Nicholson, *The Canadians in Italy*, 179.
47. Ibid., 193.
48. Ibid., 190–1.
49. Galloway, *Some Died at Ortona*, 112.
50. Munro, *Gauntlet to Overlord*, 438.
51. Nicholson, *The Canadians in Italy*, 202.

PART TWO
Chapter 6: "A Most Curious War"

1. Munro, *Gauntlet to Overlord*, 440.
2. Interview with author, 17/7/89.
3. Munro, 439.
4. Schull, *Far Distant Ships*, 213.

5. Nicholson, *The Canadians in Italy*, 204.
6. Munro, 444.
7. Nicholson, *The Canadians in Italy*, 205.
8. Raddall, *West Novas*, 118–19.
9. Powley, *Broadcast from the Front*, 53.
10. Hamilton, *Master of the Battlefield*, 396.
11. NAC, RG24, volume 14,161, war diary, 3/9/43.
12. Mowat, *The Regiment*, 107–8.
13. Beattie, *Dileas*, 332.
14. Interview with author, 7/8/89.
15. Munro, 448.
16. Simonds, *Maple Leaf Up, Maple Leaf Down*, 157.
17. Beattie, 341.
18. Kerry, *The History of the Corps of Royal Canadian Engineers*, 153.
19. Interview with author, 9/6/89.
20. Beattie, 334.
21. Nicholson, *The Canadians in Italy*, 209.
22. Stevens, *A City Goes to War*, 251.
23. Unpublished memoir, loaned to author.
24. Letter to author, 10/3/90.
25. Raddall, 121.
26. Letter to author, 10/3/90.
27. Raddall, 121.
28. Mitchell, *RCHA*, 104.
29. Maltby, "'X' Force," in *Informal History of the Calgary Regiment*, 1–3.
30. Interview with author, 15/6/89.
31. Maltby, "'X' Force," 4.
32. Mowat, *The Regiment*, 109–10.
33. Frost, *Once a Patricia*, 157.
34. Kerry, 154.
35. Beattie, 341.
36. Kerry, 154.
37. Interview with author, 25/7/89.
38. Raddall, 126.
39. Ibid., 127.
40. Nicholson, *The Canadians in Italy*, 226–7.
41. Letter to author, 10/3/90.
42. Nicholson, *The Canadians in Italy*, 226–7.
43. Ibid., 233.
44. Feasby, *Official History of the Canadian Medical Services, 1939–1945*, I/157.
45. Vokes, *Vokes: My Story*, 140.
46. Interview with author, 6/8/89.
47. Irving, *Trail of the Fox*, 346.
48. Nicholson, *The Canadians in Italy*, 196.
49. Irving, *Hitler's War*, 578.
50. Strawson, *The Italian Campaign*, 209.
51. Irving, *Hitler's War*, 572.
52. Liddell Hart, *The Other Side of the Hill*, 365.
53. Greenfield, *Command Decisions*, 317.

54. Nicholson, *The Canadians in Italy*, 268.
55. Greenfield, 321.
56. Hart, *The Rommel Papers*, 447.
57. Montgomery, *Memoirs*, 190.
58. Ibid., 195.
59. Gilbert, *Road to Victory*, 497–8.
60. Ibid., 503.
61. Hamilton, 423.
62. Ibid., 419.
63. Ibid., 439–40.
64. Gilbert, 538.
65. Ibid., 540.
66. Hamilton, 420.
67. Ottawa, *Evening Citizen*, 2/9/43.
68. NAC, MG26 J13, memo attached to diary, 10/7/43.
69. Letter to author, 15/9/89.
70. Stacey, *Arms, Men and Government*, 237, 246–7.
71. Pickersgill, *The Mackenzie King Record*, I/605.
72. Swettenham, *McNaughton*, II/308.
73. Pickersgill, I/605–7.
74. Ibid., 520.
75. Letter to author, 7/10/89.
76. Pickersgill, I/558, 607.
77. NAC, MG30 E133, volume 139, McNaughton memo, 18/10/43.
78. Ibid., Stuart to McNaughton, 28/9/43.
79. Nicholson, *The Canadians in Italy*, 346–7.
80. Pickersgill, I/610.
81. NAC, MG30 E133, volume 139, Eisenhower to CCOS, 19/10/43.
82. Nicholson, *The Canadians in Italy*, 344.
83. Swettenham, II/327.
84. Pickersgill, I/621–2.
85. Shapiro, *They Left the Back Door Open*, 92.
86. Stacey, *The Victory Campaign*, 647.
87. Stacey, *Arms, Men and Government*, 229.

Chapter 7: "Monty's Mountain Goats"

1. Nicholson, *The Canadians in Italy*, 235.
2. Galloway, *Some Died at Ortona*, 137–9.
3. Galloway, *The General Who Never Was*, 157–8.
4. Interview with author, 15/6/89.
5. Nicholson, *The Canadians in Italy*, 237.
6. Letter to author, 9/10/89.
7. Nicholson, *The Canadians in Italy*, 247.
8. Ibid., 226fn.
9. Mitchell, *My War*, 77.
10. Beattie, *Dileas*, 357.
11. Nicholson, *The Canadians in Italy*, 241.
12. H. Graham, *Citizen and Soldier*, 188.

13. Nicholson, *The Canadians in Italy*, 248-9.
14. H. Graham, 188.
15. Nicholson, *The Canadians in Italy*, 248.
16. Stevens, *The Royal Canadian Regiment*, 102.
17. Mitchell, RCHA, 105.
18. Galloway, *A Regiment at War*, 100.
19. Ibid., 261.
20. Mowat, *And No Birds Sang*, 126.
21. Beattie, 392-4; Nicholson, *The Canadians in Italy*, 262.
22. Smith, *Duffy's Regiment*, 118; Nicholson, *The Canadians in Italy*, 262-3.
23. Stevens, *Princess Patricia's Canadian Light Infantry*, 117.
24. Nicholson, *The Canadians in Italy*, 264.
25. Feasby, *Official History of the Canadian Medical Services, 1939-1945*, 1/160.
26. Vokes, *Vokes: My Story*, 140.
27. Tooley, *Invicta*, 146.
28. Interview with author, 17/7/89.
29. Nicholson, *The Canadians in Italy*, 264.
30. Comfort, *Artist at War*, 45.
31. Stevens, *Princess Patricia's Canadian Light Infantry*, 118fn.
32. Mowat, *And No Birds Sang*, 204-5.
33. Mitchell, RCHA, 108.
34. G. Walsh, interview with author, 25/7/89.
35. Nicholson, *The Canadians in Italy*, 286.
36. Ibid., 280-1.
37. Interview with author, 7/8/89.
38. Nicholson, *The Canadians in Italy*, 283-4.
39. Interview with author, 7/8/89.
40. D. W. McLarty, interview with author, 4/3/82.
41. Interview with author, 7/3/82.
42. Ibid.
43. Interview with author, 4/3/82.
44. Ibid.
45. Moorehead, *Eclipse*, 55.
46. Smith, *Forty Nights to Freedom*, 84.
47. Interview with author, 7/3/82.
48. Interview with author, 4/3/82.
49. Ibid.
50. Ibid.
51. Ibid.
52. Ibid.
53. Ibid.
54. Krige, *The Way Out*, 128.
55. Interview with author, 4/3/82.
56. Dancocks, *In Enemy Hands*, 74.
57. Letter to author, 19/11/89.
58. Ibid.
59. Krige, 253fn.
60. Letter to author, 19/11/89.
61. Hamilton, *Master of the Battlefield*, 446.

62. Ibid., 441–2, 448.
63. Ehrman, *Grand Strategy*, 69–70.
64. Wallace, *The Italian Campaign*, 106.
65. Hamilton, 445.
66. Galloway, *Some Died at Ortona*, 165.
67. Hamilton, 449.
68. Ibid., 449–50.
69. Ibid., 450–1.
70. Nicholson, *The Canadians in Italy*, 291.

Chapter 8: Bloody December

1. Beattie, *Dileas*, 412.
2. Galloway, *The General Who Never Was*, 170.
3. Molony, *The Mediterranean and Middle East*, v/501.
4. Nicholson, *The Canadians in Italy*, 289.
5. Comfort, *Artist at War*, 76.
6. Nicholson, *The Canadians in Italy*, 290.
7. Interview with author, 7/7/89.
8. Ibid.
9. Nicholson, *The Canadians in Italy*, 295.
10. Mowat, *And No Birds Sang*, 226–7.
11. Mowat, *The Regiment*, 151.
12. Smith, *Duffy's Regiment*, 129.
13. Roy, *The Seaforth Highlanders of Canada*, 241.
14. NAC, RG24, volume 14,691, war diary, 6/12/43.
15. Nicholson, *The Canadians in Italy*, 297.
16. Roy, *The Seaforth Highlanders of Canada*, 244fn.
17. Dewar, *True Canadian War Stories*, 210.
18. Comfort, 77.
19. Beattie, 420–3.
20. Galloway, *A Regiment at War*, 108.
21. Galloway, *Some Died at Ortona*, 176–7.
22. Quayle, "Mitch," 38–9.
23. Nicholson, *The Canadians in Italy*, 300–1; Kerry, 169; How, *The Canadians at War*, 361; G. Walsh, interview with author, 25/7/89.
24. Nicholson, *The Canadians in Italy*, 300.
25. Interview with author, 7/8/89.
26. Ibid.; NAC, RG 24, volume 14,243, war diary, 9/12/43.
27. Roy, *The Seaforth Highlanders of Canada*, 246–7.
28. Interview with author, 7/7/89.
29. Nicholson, *The Canadians in Italy*, 301.
30. Interview with author, 8/8/89.
31. Quayle, 38–9.
32. Galloway, *Some Died at Ortona*, 184–5.
33. Ibid., 186; letter to author, 26/11/90.
34. Nicholson, *The Canadians in Italy*, 302–3.
35. DHist, 145.2H1013(D1), "Battle of the Moro River" (henceforth, HPER report).
36. Nicholson, *The Canadians in Italy*, 303.

37. Stevens, *The Royal Canadian Regiment*, 111.
38. Roy, *The Seaforth Highlanders of Canada*, 250.
39. Ibid.
40. Stevens, *A City Goes to War*, 267.
41. Interview with author, 7/7/89.
42. Ibid.
43. Nicholson, *The Canadians in Italy*, 306.
44. Letter to author, 9/10/89.
45. Raddall, 156-7.
46. Nicholson, *The Canadians in Italy*, 307-8.
47. Mitchell, RCHA, 111.
48. NAC, RG24, volume 15,050, war diary, 13/12/43.
49. Interview with author, 4/8/89.
50. Raddall, *West Novas*, 161-2.
51. Roy, *The Seaforth Highlanders of Canada*, 254; Nicholson, *The Canadians in Italy*, 309.
52. How, *The Canadians at War*, 362.
53. Allard, *Memoirs*, 59.
54. How, *The Canadians at War*, 362.
55. McNeil, *Voice of the Pioneer*, 216.
56. Nicholson, *The Canadians in Italy*, 311.
57. Ibid., 312.
58. Painton, "What It Takes To Win the V.C.," 47.
59. Nicholson, *The Canadians in Italy*, 312.
60. How, *The Canadians at War*, 364.
61. Raddall, 167.
62. Mitchell, RCHA, 113.
63. Good, *The Bridge at Dieppe*, 94.
64. Nicholson, *The Canadians in Italy*, 312.
65. McNeil, 217.
66. Ibid.
67. Interview with author, 25/7/89.
68. Vokes, *Vokes: My Story*, 141.
69. Malone, *A Portrait of War*, 214.
70. Nicholson, *The Canadians in Italy*, 317.
71. Mitchell, RCHA, 114-15.
72. Interview with author, 7/8/89.
73. Raddall, 168.
74. Beattie, 438-40.
75. Nicholson, *The Canadians in Italy*, 318.
76. Letter to author, 26/10/89.
77. Ibid.
78. Galloway, *A Regiment at War*, 113; letter to author, 26/11/90.
79. Galloway, *Some Died at Ortona*, 196.
80. Letter to author, 26/11/90.
81. Ibid.; Nicholson, *The Canadians in Italy*, 320.
82. Galloway, *Some Died at Ortona*, 195.
83. Letter to author, 26/11/90.
84. Nicholson, *The Canadians in Italy*, 322-3.

85. Ibid., 324–5; Historical Section, General Staff, *From Pachino to Ortona*, 144–5.
86. Nicholson, *The Canadians in Italy*, 325–6; Historical Section, General Staff, 145–7.
87. Historical Section, General Staff, 159.
88. DHist, 145.2E2011(D1), Account by Lt.-Col. J. C. Jefferson, 12/1/44 (henceforth, Jefferson account).
89. Interview with author, 6/7/89.
90. Stevens, *A City Goes to War*, 275.
91. Wallace, *The Italian Campaign*, 107.
92. NAC, RG24, volume 13,727, February war diary, "Ortona" (henceforth, Ortona report).
93. Ibid.
94. Ibid.
95. NAC, RG24, volume 15,114, December war diary, Matthew Halton report, 4/1/44 (henceforth, Halton report).
96. Interview with author, 6/7/89.
97. Ortona report.
98. Jefferson account.
99. O'Dell, *Bogie Wheels*, 44–5.
100. Ibid., 45.
101. Jefferson account.
102. *The Maple Leaf*, 28/1/44.
103. Interview with author, 7/6/89.
104. *The Maple Leaf*, 14/1/44.
105. Halton report.
106. Interview with author, 6/7/89.
107. Roy, *The Seaforth Highlanders of Canada*, 272.
108. Halton report.
109. Interview with author, 9/6/89.
110. Mitchell, *My War*, 89.
111. McAndrew, "Stress Casualties," 54–5.
112. How, *The Canadians at War*, 371–2.
113. Mowat, *And No Birds Sang*, 237.
114. Nicholson, *The Canadians in Italy*, 333–4.
115. Mowat, *And No Birds Sang*, 236.
116. Ibid., 239–40.
117. Mowat, *The Regiment*, 157; HPER report.
118. Beattie, 457.
119. Galloway, *The General Who Never Was*, 176.
120. Galloway, *Some Died at Ortona*, 208–9.
121. Mowat, *And No Birds Sang*, 250.
122. Beattie, 478.
123. Ibid., 479.
124. Ibid., 482; Nicholson, *The Canadians in Italy*, 336.
125. *The Maple Leaf*, 10/6/44.
126. Galloway, *Some Died at Ortona*, 213.
127. Nicholson, *The Canadians in Italy*, 337.
128. Halton report.
129. Interview with author, 6/7/89.

130. Comfort, 112–14.
131. Halton report.
132. Nicholson, *The Canadians in Italy*, 333.
133. Stacey, *A Date with History*, 131.

Chapter 9: "A Haywire Outfit"

1. Stacey, *Historical Documents of Canada*, 625.
2. Nicholson, *The Canadians in Italy*, 328.
3. Feasby, *The Canadian Medical Services, 1939–1945*, I/165.
4. Nicholson, *Official History of the Canadians in Italy*, 339.
5. Galloway, *The General Who Never Was*, 179–80.
6. Gaffen, *Ortona*, 46.
7. Feasby, I/165.
8. McAndrew, "Stress Casualties," 48.
9. Interview with author, 8/8/89.
10. Interview with author, 25/7/89.
11. Tooley, *Invicta*, 193.
12. Interview with author, 6/7/89.
13. Greenhous, "'Would It Not Have Been Better to Bypass Ortona Completely . . . ?'" 54.
14. Ibid., 54–5.
15. Interview with author, 6/8/89.
16. *Toronto Star*, 31/12/43.
17. Reyburn, *Some of It Was Fun*, 133–4.
18. Powley, *Broadcast from the Front*, 60
19. *Gazette* (Montreal), 28/12/43.
20. *Citizen* (Ottawa), 29/12/43.
21. Interview with author, n.d.
22. Burhans, *The First Special Service Force*, 14–15.
23. Stacey, *Six Years of War*, 105.
24. Interview with author, n.d.
25. Interview with author, 10/1/90.
26. Ibid.
27. Ibid.
28. Interview with author, n.d.
29. Ibid.
30. Stacey, *Six Years of War*, 107.
31. Interview with author, 27/9/89.
32. Interview with author, n.d.
33. Interview with author, 10/1/90.
34. Burhans, 95.
35. Interview with author, n.d.
36. Interview with author, 27/9/89.
37. Ibid.
38. Burhans, 124.
39. Interview with author, 10/1/90.
40. Burhans, 143.
41. Ibid., 145.

42. Ibid., 154.
43. Interview with author, n.d.
44. Interview with author, 5/10/89.
45. Nicholson, *The Canadians in Italy*, 455.
46. Interview with author, 27/9/89.
47. Interview with author, n.d.
48. Burhans, 162.
49. Nicholson, *The Canadians in Italy*, 455.
50. Fuller, *The Second World War, 1939–1945*, 270.
51. Churchill, *Closing the Ring*, 253.
52. Ibid., 332–3.
53. Eisenhower, *Eisenhower at War, 1943–1945*, 22.
54. Greenfield, *Command Decisions*, 262.
55. Ehrman, *Grand Strategy*, 182–3.
56. Jackson, *The Battle for Italy*, 161.
57. Eisenhower, *Crusade in Europe*, 199–202.
58. Bryant, *Triumph in the West*, 120.
59. Ibid., 122.
60. Churchill, *Closing the Ring*, 426.
61. Gilbert, *Road to Victory*, 622.
62. Montgomery, *Memoirs*, 203–4.
63. Hamilton, *Master of the Battlefield*, 461.

Chapter 10: "Just Like Passchendaele"

1. Vokes, *Vokes: My Story*, 152–4.
2. NAC, MG30 E157, volume 7, Crerar to Montgomery, 20/9/43.
3. Nicholson, *The Canadians in Italy*, 354–5.
4. Malone, *A Portrait of War*, 197–8.
5. NAC, MG30 E157, volume 7, Crerar to Simonds, 10/12/43.
6. Ibid., Montgomery to Crerar, 21/12/43.
7. Ibid., Crerar to Stuart, 13/1/44.
8. Stacey, *A Date with History*, 233.
9. D. Fraser, "When the Santa Elena Went Down," 16/9/89, loaned to author and used by permission of the Halifax *Herald* Limited.
10. Nicholson, *The Canadians in Italy*, 355.
11. Ibid., 356.
12. Moir, *The Royal Canadian Corps of Signals, 1903–1961*, 137–8.
13. Warren, *Wait for the Waggon*, 247.
14. Nicholson, *The Canadians in Italy*, 358.
15. Ibid.
16. Kitching, *Mud and Green Fields*, 178.
17. Nicholson, *The Canadians in Italy*, 358–9.
18. Ibid., 364.
19. *The Maple Leaf*, 14/1/44.
20. Nicholson, *The Canadians in Italy*, 337.
21. Stevens, *Princess Patricia's Canadian Light Infantry*, 140.
22. NAC, RG 24, volume 15,085, war diary, 12/1/44.
23. Galloway, *The General Who Never Was*, 187.

24. Kitching, 185–6.
25. Nicholson, *The Canadians in Italy*, 366.
26. Kitching, 186–7.
27. Scislowski, *Return to Italy, 1975*, 34.
28. Johnston, *The Fighting Perths*, 65–6.
29. Interview with author, 8/8/89.
30. Ibid.
31. Interview with author, 19/7/89.
32. Interview with author, 16/7/89.
33. Nicholson, *The Canadians in Italy*, 370–1.
34. Letter to author, 23/8/89.
35. Kitching, 189.
36. Letter to author, 23/8/89.
37. Interview with author, 8/8/89.
38. Nicholson, *The Canadians in Italy*, 376–7.
39. Ibid., 376fn, 378.
40. Quoted by G. Kitching, interview with author, 23/8/90.
41. Vokes, 151.
42. Galloway, *The General Who Never Was*, 184.
43. Raddall, *West Novas*, 169.
44. Beattie, *Dileas*, 493.
45. Burns, *General Mud*, ix.
46. Galloway, *The General Who Never Was*, 185–6.
47. Ibid., 193.
48. Stevens, *The Royal Canadian Regiment*, 129.
49. J. R. Stone memoir, loaned to author.
50. Interview with author, 6/7/89.
51. NAC, RG24, volume 15,050, war diary, 20/2/44; Appendix 1, Crerar to Vokes, 23/2/44, Vokes to Gibson, 21/2/44, Gibson to LCol F. L. Nicholls, n.d.
52. Raddall, 180.
53. *The Maple Leaf*, 28/1/44.
54. Allard, *Memoirs*, 69.
55. Raddall, 175–6.
56. Nicholson, *The Canadians in Italy*, 382.
57. Cederberg, *The Long Road Home*, 107–10.
58. Manuscript lent to author by Mrs J. K. Smith.
59. S. Johnston, 70–1.
60. Interview with author, 7/8/89.
61. Scislowski, *The Winter Front, 1944*, 13.
62. Feasby, *The Canadian Medical Services, 1939–1945*, I/172.
63. Nicholson, *Seventy Years of Service*, 186–7.
64. Interview with author, 6/7/89.
65. Malone, *A Portrait of War*, 221.
66. Interview with author, 17/7/89.
67. Reyburn, *Some of It Was Fun*, 52.
68. Galloway, *Some Died at Ortona*, 188.
69. Scislowski, *Return to Italy, 1975*, 32.
70. Vokes, 162.
71. Interview with author, 6/7/89.

72. Galloway, *The General Who Never Was*, 191.
73. Burns, *General Mud*, 123.
74. Ibid., 132–3.
75. Malone, *A Portrait of War*, 233.
76. Burns, *General Mud*, 133.
77. J. D. Smith, interview with author, n.d.
78. Smith, *Duffy's Regiment*, 141.
79. Interview with author, 7/8/89.
80. Interview with author, 25/7/89.
81. Ibid.
82. Blumenson, *Salerno to Cassino*, 347–8.
83. Ibid., 358–60.
84. Ibid., 389.
85. Wallace, *The Italian Campaign*, 132.
86. Strawson, *The Italian Campaign*, 27.
87. Burhans, *The First Special Service Force*, 165–6.
88. Ibid., 166.
89. Interview with author, n.d.
90. Interview with author, 27/9/89.
91. Interview with author, n.d.
92. Routhier, *The Black Devils*, 37.
93. Ibid., 38.
94. Burhans, 185.
95. Interview with author, n.d.
96. How, *The Canadians at War*, 375; Sealey, *Thomas George Prince*, 23–4.
97. Gaffen, *Forgotten Soldiers*, 55.
98. Burhans, 209.
99. Nicholson, *The Canadians in Italy*, 456.
100. Interview with author, n.d.
101. Air Historian, *No. 417 Squadron*, 49.
102. Letter to author, 1/9/89.
103. Ibid.
104. Ibid.
105. Air Historian, 49.
106. Ibid., 50–1.
107. Ibid., 53, 56.
108. Ibid., 53–4.
109. Letter to author, 27/8/89.
110. Air Historian, 54–5.
111. Letter to author, 1/9/89.
112. Air Historian, 55–6.
113. Letter to author, 1/9/89.
114. Air Historian, 57–8, 63.
115. Bryant, *Triumph in the West*, 153, 160.
116. Wallace, 138.
117. Ehrman, 227–8.
118. Molony, *The Mediterranean and Middle East*, v/799.
119. Strawson, 27.

Chapter 11: "I Was a Nervous Wreck"

1. Interview with author, 6/10/89.
2. McAndrew, "5th Canadian Armoured Division," 5.
3. Ibid., 8.
4. Burns, *General Mud*, 123.
5. McAndrew, "5th Canadian Armoured Division," 8-9.
6. Ibid., 10-11.
7. Fraser, "The Inferno Track" (henceforth, Fraser memoir), loaned to author and used by permission of the Halifax *Herald* Limited.
8. Ibid.
9. Interview with author, 16/7/89.
10. Oldfield, *The Westminsters' War Diary*, 63.
11. Fraser memoir.
12. Interview with author, 19/7/89.
13. Fraser memoir.
14. Cederberg, *The Long Road Home*, 113.
15. Nicholson, *The Canadians in Italy*, 392-3.
16. Ibid., 393.
17. Molony, *The Mediterranean and Middle East*, VI/61fn, 97.
18. Warren, *Wait for the Waggon*, 255.
19. Interview with author, 14/8/89.
20. Mitchell, RCHA, 123.
21. Interview with author, 18/7/89.
22. Nicholson, *The Canadians in Italy*, 395.
23. Foster, *Meeting of Generals*, 418.
24. NAC, RG24, volume 17,507, diary, 5/5/44, Appendix 1.
25. Molony, VI/9-10.
26. Ibid., 57-8.
27. Interview with author, 18/9/89.
28. Vokes, *Vokes: My Story*, 147.
29. Maltby, "Background to the Kingsmill Bridge," in *Informal History of the Calgary Regiment*, 1.
30. Ibid., "A Bridge Too Soon," in *Informal History of the Calgary Regiment*, 10.
31. DHist, 141.4A11013(D1), Account by Lt Col R. L. Purvis (sic), OC 11 CAR, 24/5/44.
32. DHist, 141.4A14013(D1), Report on Operations of 14 CAR (Calgary R) for the period 10 May to 28 May 44, 31/8/44 (henceforth, Calgary report).
33. DHist, 141.4A12013(D1), Report on Operations of 12 CAR (TRR) 11 May to 26 May 44, 31/7/44.
34. Ibid.
35. Maltby, "The Gari River and Beyond," in *Informal History of the Calgary Regiment*, 3-4.
36. Nicholson, *The Canadians in Italy*, 406-7.
37. Molony, VI/126.
38. Raddall, *West Novas*, 187.
39. Mowat, *The Regiment*, 183.
40. Nicholson, *The Canadians in Italy*, 408.
41. NAC, RG24, volume 17,507, May war diary, Appendix 2.
42. Three Rivers report.

43. Raddall, 190-1.
44. NAC, RG24, volume 15,050, May 1944 war diary, Appendix 16 (henceforth, CYR report).
45. Beattie, *Dileas*, 534-5.
46. NAC, RG24, volume 15,239, May 1944 war diary, Appendix 10 (henceforth, R22R report).
47. DHist, 145.2H3013(D1), The Liri Valley and the Adolph (*sic*) Hitler Line, n.d.
48. NAC, RG24, volume 14,084, May 1944 war diary, Appendix 17 (henceforth, Bernatchez report).
49. Allard, *Memoirs*, 74.
50. R22R report.
51. Allard, 76-7.
52. Bernatchez report.
53. Molony, VI/180-1.
54. E. Buss memoir, loaned to author.
55. Ibid.
56. Interview with author, 6/10/89.
57. Ibid.
58. Ibid.
59. Vokes, 159.
60. Burns, *General Mud*, 146.
61. Nicholson, *The Canadians in Italy*, 412-13.
62. Ibid., 396; Molony, VI/183.
63. Ibid.
64. Nicholson, *The Canadians in Italy*, 396, 414; Molony, VI/181.
65. NAC, RG24, volume 13,728, war diary, 21/5/44.
66. Nicholson, *The Canadians in Italy*, 413; Molony, VI/188.
67. Interview with author, 6/10/89.
68. Burns, *General Mud*, 147.
69. Beattie, 542-3.
70. Nicholson, *The Canadians in Italy*, 414.
71. Jackson, *The Princess Louise Dragoon Guards*, 190.
72. Beattie, 556.
73. Ibid., 561.
74. Ibid., 564.
75. Burns, *General Mud*, 148.
76. NAC, RG24, volume 17,507, diary, 22/5/44.
77. Burns, *General Mud*, 148.
78. Interview with author, 7/7/89.
79. Molony, VI/185.
80. Nicholson, *The Canadians in Italy*, 416.
81. NAC, RG24, volume 17,507, May 1944 diary, Appendix 6.

Chapter 12: The Valley of Death

1. Raddall, *West Novas*, 192.
2. McDougall, *Execution*, 108-9.
3. Nicholson, *The Canadians in Italy*, 417-18.
4. NAC, RG24, volume 15,157, war diary, 23/5/44 (henceforth, PPCLI war diary).

5. Interview with author, 7/7/89.

6. PPCLI war diary.

7. Stevens, *Princess Patricia's Canadian Light Infantry*, 161.

8. Interview with author, 6/6/90.

9. Stevens, *Princess Patricia's Canadian Light Infantry*, 161.

10. Interview with author, 7/7/89.

11. NAC, RG24, volume 14,078, May war diary, Appendix C (henceforth, LER report).

12. Roy, *The Seaforth Highlanders of Canada*, 303.

13. DHist, 145.2S5011(D3), J. C. Allan interview, 2/7/44.

14. Ibid., CSM Duddle interview, 1/7/44.

15. Molony, *The Mediterranean and Middle East*, VI/194.

16. NAC, RG 24, volume 15,050, May 1944 war diary, Appendix 16.

17. Ibid.

18. Tooley, *Invicta*, 234, 236.

19. NAC, RG24, volume 15,289, May 1944 war diary, Appendix 5 (henceforth, WNSR report).

20. Interview with author, 7/8/89.

21. WNSR report.

22. Interview with author, 6/10/89.

23. Ibid.

24. DHist, 142.21013(D1), CCRA, I Canadian Corps, Report on Operations, May–June 1944, n.d.

25. Interview with author, 6/10/89.

26. Burns, *General Mud*, 151.

27. Beattie, *Dileas*, 568.

28. NAC, RG24, volume 15,093, May 1944 war diary, Appendix 5.

29. Mowat, *The Regiment*, 188; Nicholson, *The Canadians in Italy*, 424.

30. Mowat, *The Regiment*, 189.

31. Raddall, 195.

32. Ibid., 195-7.

33. Ibid., 200.

34. NAC, RG 24, volume 15,239, May 1944 war diary, Appendix 10.

35. How, *The Canadians at War*, 418.

36. Vokes, *Vokes: My Story*, 160.

37. Interview with author, 6/10/89.

38. Interview with author, 6/8/89.

39. Mitchell, *My War*, 97.

40. Interview with author, 6/6/90.

41. Stevens, *Princess Patricia's Canadian Light Infantry*, 162-3.

42. Nicholson, *The Canadians in Italy*, 423, 425.

43. Interview with author, 12/7/89.

44. Roy, *The Seaforth Highlanders of Canada*, 312.

45. Molony, VI/194.

46. Vokes, 160.

47. Nicholson, *The Canadians in Italy*, 425.

48. Burns, *General Mud*, 149.

49. How, *The Canadians at War*, 418.

50. Interview with author, 6/10/89.

51. Ellis, *Cassino*, 408-10.

52. Jackson, *The Battle for Rome*, 150–1.
53. Nicholson, *The Canadians in Italy*, 426.
54. McAndrew, "5th Canadian Armoured Division," 14–15.
55. Nicholson, *The Canadians in Italy*, 428.
56. G. A. Burton, letter to author, 28/2/90.
57. NAC, RG24, volume 14,199, war diary, 24/5/44.
58. Galloway, *A Regiment at War*, 139–40; letter to author, 28/11/90.
59. Roy, *Sinews of Steel*, 250.
60. Nicholson, *The Canadians in Italy*, 429.
61. DHist, 141.4A2(D4), Account of Action, Lt E. J. Perkins, n.d. (henceforth, Perkins account).
62. Windsor, *Blind Date*, 46–8.
63. McAvity, *Lord Strathcona's Horse*, 77.
64. E. Buss, letter to author, n.d.
65. Interview with author, 6/8/89.
66. Perkins account.
67. DHist, 145.2W1011(D3), The Melfa Crossing (henceforth, Mahony account).
68. Perkins account.
69. Mahony account.
70. Ibid.
71. Ibid.
72. Ibid.
73. Ibid.
74. Oldfield, *The Westminsters' War Diary*, 94–5.
75. Nicholson, *The Canadians in Italy*, 436.
76. Graham and Bidwell, *Tug of War*, 337.
77. Hurley, *Ritorno in Italia*, 11, 14.
78. McAndrew, "5th Canadian Armoured Division," 16.
79. Mahony account.
80. Molony, VI/181.
81. Stevens, *Princess Patricia's Canadian Light Infantry*, 154.
82. Letter to author, 28/2/90.
83. Johnston, *The Fighting Perths*, 78.
84. Smith memoir, lent to author by Mrs. J. K. Smith.
85. How, *8th Hussars*, 219.
86. Ibid., 218.
87. Nicholson, *The Canadians in Italy*, 441.
88. Letter to author, n.d.
89. Interview with author, 17/7/89.
90. Letter to author, n.d.
91. Nicholson, *The Canadians in Italy*, 443.
92. Scislowski, *Pilgrimage*, 9.
93. McAvity, 94–6; Nicholson, *The Canadians in Italy*, 444–5.
94. NAC, RG24, volume 15,114, June 1944 war diary, Appendix 11.
95. Stevens, *A City Goes to War*, 298.
96. Nicholson, *The Canadians in Italy*, 445.
97. DHist, 145.2R13011(D1), Capture of Ferentino and Anagni by the RCR, 4/6/44.
98. Stevens, *The Royal Canadian Regiment*, 142.
99. Nicholson, *The Canadians in Italy*, 449.

100. Interview with author, 21/9/89.
101. Interview with author, 7/8/89.
102. NAC, RG24, volume 13,729, war diary, 5/6/44.

Chapter 13: "Distinctly Troublesome"

1. *The Maple Leaf*, 7/6/44.
2. NAC, MG26 J13, diary, 6/6/44.
3. Victoria *Daily Colonist*, 23/5/44.
4. NAC, MG26 J13, diary, 23/5/44.
5. NAC, RG24, volume 17,507, May diary, Appendix 13.
6. Burhans, *The First Special Service Force*, 211.
7. Nicholson, *The Canadians in Italy*, 455-6.
8. Interview with author, 27/9/89.
9. Interview with author, 10/1/90.
10. Burhans, 228.
11. Nicholson, *The Canadians in Italy*, 457.
12. Interview with author, 21/9/89.
13. Interview with author, n.d.
14. Ibid.
15. Interview with author, 12/7/89.
16. Interview with author, 1/2/82.
17. Bryant, *Triumph in the West*, 152.
18. Molony, *The Mediterranean and Middle East*, VI/284.
19. Alexander, *The Alexander Memoirs*, 127.
20. Kurzman, *The Race for Rome*, 17.
21. Strawson, *The Italian Campaign*, 26.
22. Jackson, *The Battle for Italy*, 230.
23. Molony, VI/312.
24. Ibid., 330-1.
25. Ehrman, *Grand Strategy*, 357-8.
26. Molony, VI/334-5.
27. Nicholson, *The Canadians in Italy*, 464-5.
28. Ibid., 452.
29. NAC, MG30 E157, volume 7, Burns to Crerar, 7/6/44.
30. NAC, RG24, volume 17,507, diary, 26/5/44.
31. Burns, *General Mud*, 159, 161.
32. Ibid., 162-3.
33. Nicholson, *The Canadians in Italy*, 451.
34. McAndrew, "Eighth Army at the Gothic Line: Commanders and Plans," 54.
35. Ibid., 53.
36. Vokes, *Vokes: My Story*, 183-4.
37. McAndrew, "Eighth Army at the Gothic Line: Commanders and Plans," 54.
38. Stacey, *A Date with History*, 144.
39. Interview with author, n.d.
40. NAC, MG30 E157, volume 7, Burns to Crerar, 7/6/44.
41. McAndrew, "5th Canadian Armoured Division," Appendix A.
42. Burns, *General Mud*, 168.
43. Ibid., 170.

44. NAC, RG24, volume 17,507, July diary, Appendix 1, Burns to Leese, 2/7/44.
45. Nicholson, *The Canadians in Italy*, 465.
46. Burns, *General Mud*, 171.
47. Burns, *Manpower in the Canadian Army*, 175–6.
48. Jackson, *The Princess Louise Dragoon Guards*, 193.
49. NAC, RG24, volume 14,205, war diary, 13-14/7/44.
50. NAC, RG24, volume 14,587, war diary, 24/7/44.
51. NAC, MG27 III B11, volume 62, P. J. Montague to J. C. Murchie, 16/10/44.
52. Letter to author, 22/8/89.
53. Broadfoot, *Six War Years, 1939–1945*, 156.
54. Kesselring, *Kesselring: A Soldier's Record*, 248–9.
55. Gilbert, *Road to Victory*, 822.
56. Nicholson, *The Canadians in Italy*, 198, 460fn.
57. Ibid., 494–5.
58. Ibid., 461.
59. Stevens, *A City Goes to War*, 302.
60. Nicholson, *The Canadians in Italy*, 467.
61. DHist, 141.4A12013(D1), Notes on the Battle of the Lake Trasimeno Line, 4/7/44.
62. Ibid., Report on Operations of 12 CAR (TRR) 2 June to 30 June 44, 1/8/44.
63. Interview with author, 15/6/89.
64. Nicholson, *The Canadians in Italy*, 472.
65. DHist, 141.4A14013(D1), Report on Operations 14 CAR (Calgary Regt) for period 12 June – 17 July 44, 28/7/44.
66. Nicholson, *The Canadians in Italy*, 476.
67. Wallace, 120, *The Italian Campaign*, 127–9.
68. Jackson, *The Mediterranean and the Middle East*, 73, 91, 94.
69. Ibid., 96.
70. Interview with author, 8/7/89.
71. NAC, RG24, volume 14,079, October 1944 war diary, 2 Cdn Inf Bde from the Metauro to the Marecchia, n.d.
72. Greenhous, *Dragoon*, 343.
73. Comfort, *Artist at War*, 155.
74. Stevens, *The Royal Canadian Regiment*, 144–5.
75. Nicholson, *Seventy Years of Service*, 188.
76. Stevens, *The Royal Canadian Regiment*, 144.
77. McAndrew, "Stress Casualties," 50.
78. Ibid., 50–1.
79. McAvity, *Lord Strathcona's Horse*, 110.
80. Comfort, 172.
81. Galloway, *The General Who Never Was*, 217.
82. Mowat, *The Regiment*, 198.
83. Stevens, *A City Goes to War*, 303.
84. Galloway, *The General Who Never Was*, 217.

PART THREE
Chapter 14: "It's Awful to Die"

1. Greenhous, "5 CAD in Operation *Olive*," 1.
2. Jackson, *The Mediterranean and the Middle East*, 122.

3. Ibid., 124–5.
4. McAndrew, "Eighth Army at the Gothic Line: Commanders and Plans," 57.
5. Greenhous, "5 CAD in Operation *Olive*," 3.
6. McAndrew, "Eighth Army at the Gothic Line: Commanders and Plans," 54–5.
7. Jackson, *The Mediterranean and the Middle East*, 128.
8. McAndrew, "Eighth Army at the Gothic Line: Commanders and Plans," 55.
9. Nicholson, *The Canadians in Italy*, 488.
10. Ibid., 470.
11. Ibid., 492–3.
12. Interview with author, 6/7/89.
13. Greenhous, "5 CAD in Operation *Olive*," 4.
14. Nicholson, *The Canadians in Italy*, 497.
15. Ibid., 503–4.
16. Ibid., 503.
17. Ibid., 504.
18. Ibid.
19. Stevens, *Princess Patricia's Canadian Light Infantry*, 181.
20. Stevens, *The Royal Canadian Regiment*, 151.
21. Churchill, *Closing the Ring*, 122.
22. Nicholson, *The Canadians in Italy*, 508.
23. Ibid., 507.
24. Ibid., 497, 512–13.
25. Ibid., 514.
26. Mitchell, *My War*, 101.
27. McAndrew, "Eighth Army at the Gothic Line: Commanders and Plans," 56.
28. McAndrew, "Eighth Army at the Gothic Line: The Dog-Fight," 55.
29. Greenhous, "5 CAD in Operation *Olive*," 14.
30. Nicholson, *The Canadians in Italy*, 511–12.
31. McAndrew, "Eighth Army at the Gothic Line: The Dog-Fight," 55.
32. Ibid.
33. Interview with author, 7/8/89.
34. Raddall, *West Novas*, 216.
35. How, *8th Hussars*, 233.
36. Letter to author, n.d.
37. Scislowski, *Return to Italy, 1975*, 44.
38. NAC, RG24, volume 14,159, September 1944 war diary, The Attack on the Gothic Line, n.d. (henceforth, Eleventh Brigade report).
39. NAC, RG24, volume 14,085, September 1944 war diary, The Battle for the Gothic Line, n.d.
40. Raddall, 219–20.
41. Eleventh Brigade report; Nicholson, *The Canadians in Italy*, 516.
42. How, *8th Hussars*, 235.
43. Eleventh Brigade report.
44. How, *8th Hussars*, 236–7; NAC, RG24, volume 14,056, October 1944 war diary, Report on Operations, n.d.
45. How, *8th Hussars*, 245.
46. Interview with author, 8/8/89.
47. DHist,141.4A9(D1), Major Jack Letcher account, n.d.
48. Roy, *Sinews of Steel*, 305.

49. Greenhous, "5 CAD in Operation *Olive*," 18–19.
50. NAC, RG24, volume 14,056, September 1944 war diary, Account of Operations, n.d.
51. NAC, RG24, volume 14,079, October 1944 war diary, 2 Cdn Inf Bde from the Metauro to the Marecchia, n.d.; Nicholson, *The Canadians in Italy*, 516–17.
52. Nicholson, *The Canadians in Italy*, 519.
53. NAC, RG24, volume 15,239, September 1944 war diary, Battle Report of Gothic Line Offensive, n.d. (henceforth, R22R report).
54. How, *The Canadians at War*, 531.
55. R22R report.
56. McAvity, *Lord Strathcona's Horse*, 125.
57. Jackson, *The Princess Louise Dragoon Guards*, 204.
58. Ibid.
59. Ibid., xii, 205; Nicholson, *The Canadians in Italy*, 521.
60. NAC, RG24, volume 15,086, war diary, 1/9/44.
61. Dick Whittington, interview with author, 18/9/89.
62. Stevens, *A City Goes to War*, 310.
63. DHist, 145.2E2011(D1), Statement by Capt J. A. Dougan, 11/10/44.
64. Feasby, *Official History of the Canadian Medical Services, 1939–1945*, I/194.
65. Interview with author, 16/7/89.
66. Smith, *What Time the Tempest?*, 267–9.
67. NAC, RG24, volume 14,079, September 1944 war diary, Appendix 39.

Chapter 15: " . . . And Be Goddamned If We'll Surrender!"

1. Greenhous, "5 CAD in Operation *Olive*," 18.
2. Jackson, *The Mediterranean and the Middle East*, 254.
3. Nicholson, *The Canadians in Italy*, 523.
4. Vokes, *Vokes: My Story*, 165, 169.
5. Mitchell, *RCHA*, 138.
6. Burns, *General Mud*, 188–9.
7. Galloway, *The General Who Never Was*, 220.
8. Galloway, *A Regiment at War*, 156–7.
9. NAC, RG24, volume 15,073, Appendix 8.
10. Mowat, *The Regiment*, 217.
11. How, *8th Hussars*, 249.
12. Ibid., 252.
13. Ibid.
14. Greenhous, "5 CAD in Operation *Olive*," 24.
15. Nicholson, *The Canadians in Italy*, 564.
16. Greenhous, "5 CAD in Operation *Olive*," 26.
17. Ibid., 25–6.
18. Jackson, *The Mediterranean and the Middle East*, 277, 305.
19. Nicholson, *The Canadians in Italy*, 532–3.
20. Air Historian, *No. 417 Squadron*, 73.
21. Ibid., 80–1.
22. Burns, *General Mud*, 196.
23. Interview with author, 19/7/89.
24. NAC, RG24, volume 16,193, Feb 1943 to Dec 1944, Report on Air Operations, 24

August to 22 September 44.

25. Air Historian, 85.
26. Burns, *General Mud*, 191–2.
27. Nicholson, *The Canadians in Italy*, 533.
28. Nicholson, *The Gunners of Canada*, 229.
29. Greenhous, "5 CAD in Operation *Olive*," 26.
30. How, *8th Hussars*, 255–62.
31. Letter to author, n.d.
32. Ibid.
33. How, *8th Hussars*, 268–9.
34. Ibid., 270.
35. Nicholson, *The Canadians in Italy*, 535, 537.
36. Raddall, *West Novas*, 225–6.
37. Nicholson, *The Canadians in Italy*, 539.
38. Tooley, *Invicta*, 273–4.
39. Vokes, 170.
40. Interview with author, n.d.
41. Nicholson, *The Canadians in Italy*, 541.
42. Allard, *Memoirs*, 90–2.
43. Stevens, *Princess Patricia's Canadian Light Infantry*, 189.
44. Roy, *The Seaforth Highlanders of Canada*, 334.
45. DHist, 145.2S5011(D3), Account of the action of the Seaforth of Canada, n.d.
46. Beattie, *Dileas*, 653, 656–9.
47. Stevens, *The Royal Canadian Regiment*, 157–8.
48. Galloway, *The General Who Never Was*, 223–5.
49. Burns, *General Mud*, 202.
50. DHist, 145.2E2011(D1), Account by Capt J. A. Dougan, 11/10/44 (henceforth, Dougan account).
51. Stevens, *A City Goes to War*, 312.
52. Frost, *Once a Patricia*, 278.
53. Beattie, 664.
54. NAC, RG24, volume 14,085, September 1944 war diary, Battle for the Gothic Line, n.d. (henceforth, CYR report).
55. NAC, RG24, volume 14,079, October 1944 war diary, 2 Cdn Inf Bde from the Metauro to the Marecchia, n.d.
56. Stevens, *Princess Patricia's Canadian Light Infantry*, 193.
57. CYR report.
58. Nicholson, *The Canadians in Italy*, 553.
59. NAC, RG24, volume 15,073, September 1944 war diary, Appendix 9.
60. Nicholson, *The Gunners of Canada*, 234.
61. Burns, *General Mud*, 203–4.
62. Nicholson, *The Gunners of Canada*, 232.
63. NAC, RG24, volume 15,239, September 1944 war diary, Battle Report of Gothic Line Offensive, n.d.
64. Allard, 97.
65. DHist, 145.2E2011(D1), The Loyal Edmonton Regiment, Campaign Narrative, n.d. (henceforth, LER report).
66. Ibid.; Stevens, *A City Goes to War*, 317.
67. Roy, *The Seaforth Highlanders of Canada*, 346–7; Nicholson, *The Canadians in*

Italy, 557.

68. Dougan account.
69. Ibid.
70. Interview with author, 7/6/89.
71. Interview with author, 21/9/89.
72. LER report.
73. Stevens, *A City Goes to War*, 318.
74. Raddall, 234.
75. Burns, *General Mud*, 202, 206.
76. Galloway, *The General Who Never Was*, 226.
77. Frost, 290.
78. Ibid.
79. Ibid., 506.
80. Nicholson, *The Canadians in Italy*, 562.
81. Burns, *General Mud*, 209.
82. Ibid., 207.
83. Nicholson, *The Canadians in Italy*, 557.
84. Greenhous, "5 CAD in Operation *Olive*," 29.
85. Nicholson, *The Canadians in Italy*, 558, 565.
86. Ibid., 570–1.
87. Jackson, *The Mediterranean and the Middle East*, 301.
88. Nicholson, *The Canadians in Italy*, 571.
89. Stacey, *Arms, Men and Government*, 199.
90. Bryant, *Triumph in the West*, 271.
91. Churchill, *Triumph and Tragedy*, 158.
92. Jackson, *The Mediterranean and the Middle East*, 361–3.
93. Ibid., 360.
94. Ehrman, *Grand Strategy*, 530.
95. Jackson, *The Mediterranean and the Middle East*, 304, 371–2.
96. *Citizen* (Ottawa), 14/9/44.
97. Dawson, *The Conscription Crisis of 1944*, 13.
98. NAC, MG27 III B11, volume 86, file Conscription, Aug–Oct 44.
99. Whitaker, *Tug of War*, 234.
100. Stacey, *Arms, Men and Government*, 437.
101. Granatstein, *Conscription in the Second World War*, 55.
102. NAC, MG27 III B11, volume 86, Report of Canadian section, GHQ, 2d Echelon, AAI, 23/9/44.
103. Raddall, 237.
104. Letter to author, n.d.
105. Letter to author, 24/10/89.
106. Letter to author, n.d.
107. Interview with author, 8/7/89.
108. D. Fraser, "Canada's Manpower Policy Folly," 11/11/88, loaned to author and used by permission of the Halifax *Herald* Limited.
109. NAC, MG27 III B11, volume 62, Col H. A. Dyde diary, 27/9/44.
110. Malone, *A World in Flames*, 146.
111. Beattie, 671.
112. Stacey, *Arms, Men and Government*, 442.
113. Ibid., 441–2.

Chapter 16: "A Nice Christmas Present"

1. NAC, RG24, volume 14,162, September 1944 war diary, Report on Operations of 12 Cdn Inf Bde, n.d. (henceforth, Twelfth Brigade report).
2. McAvity, *Lord Strathcona's Horse*, 150.
3. Twelfth Brigade report.
4. McAvity, 150.
5. Burns, *General Mud*, 208-9.
6. How, *8th Hussars*, 275.
7. Ibid., 276.
8. DHist, 145.5013 (D1), Report on Operations of the CB Highrs, 17/10/44 (henceforth, CBH report).
9. Tooley, *Invicta*, 286.
10. Nicholson, *The Gunners of Canada*, 237-8.
11. CBH report.
12. Strawson, *The Italian Campaign*, 17-18.
13. McAndrew, "Eighth Army at the Gothic Line: Commanders and Plans," 53.
14. Burns, *General Mud*, 213-14, 219.
15. NAC, RG24, volume 14,056, October 1944 war diary, History of Cumberland Force, n.d.
16. Ibid.
17. Ibid.
18. Ibid.
19. Mowat, *The Regiment*, 235.
20. McAvity, 156.
21. Letter to author, 7/5/90.
22. Mowat, *The Regiment*, 242.
23. Stevens, *A City Goes to War*, 322.
24. Interview with author, 6/7/89.
25. Stevens, *A City Goes to War*, 323.
26. Interview with author, 6/7/89.
27. NAC, RG24, volume 14,085, November 1944 war diary, Report on Ops, 12 - 28 Oct 44 incl, n.d. (henceforth, CYR report).
28. Stevens, *Princess Patricia's Canadian Light Infantry*, 201.
29. Nicholson, *The Canadians in Italy*, 585.
30. DHist, 142.4F3, Report on Operations, n.d., Appendix.
31. Nicholson, *The Canadians in Italy*, 586.
32. Roy, *The Seaforth Highlanders of Canada*, 357-9.
33. Interview with author, 21/9/89.
34. Stevens, *A City Goes to War*, 324.
35. DHist, 145.2S25011(D3), Account by Lt. Col. H. P. Bell-Irving, DSO, 12/11/44 (henceforth, Bell-Irving account).
36. Interview with author, 7/6/89.
37. Roy, *The Seaforth Highlanders of Canada*, 351.
38. Ibid., 362, 363fn.
39. Ibid., 363.
40. McNeil, *Voice of the Pioneer*, 219.
41. Good, *The Bridge at Dieppe*, 120.
42. Bell-Irving account.

43. Interview with author, 21/9/89.
44. Burns, *General Mud*, 217.
45. DHist, 145.2P7011(D3), Account by Capt A. G. Robinson, 2i/c "D" Company, PPCLI, 20/11/44.
46. Raddall, *West Novas*, 239–40.
47. Nicholson, *The Canadians in Italy*, 590.
48. Raddall, 244.
49. CYR report.
50. Frost, *Once a Patricia*, 317–18.
51. Ibid., 319.
52. Nicholson, *The Canadians in Italy*, 593–4.
53. DHist, 143.131013(D1), Account of Bridging Operations across R Savio, 21 Oct to 28 Oct 44, n.d.
54. Frost, 341.
55. Jackson, *The Mediterranean and the Middle East*, 445.
56. Nicholson, *The Canadians in Italy*, 596.
57. Rowland, *The Padre*, 90.
58. Churchill, *Triumph and Tragedy*, 85, 100.
59. Nicholson, *The Canadians in Italy*, 595.
60. Ibid., 596.
61. Fisher, *Cassino to the Alps*, 538.
62. Jackson, *The Mediterranean and the Middle East*, 433.
63. Hastings, *Overlord*, 179.
64. Galloway, *The General Who Never Was*, 223.
65. Hastings, 65, 185.
66. Ibid., 184.
67. Ibid.
68. Ibid., 190.
69. Kesselring, *Kesselring: A Soldier's Record*, 265.
70. Jackson, *The Mediterranean and the Middle East*, 422, 424, 429–30.
71. Ibid.
72. Douglas, *Out of the Shadows*, 246.
73. Burns, *Manpower in the Canadian Army*, 6.
74. Letter to author, 14/11/88.
75. Burns, *Manpower in the Canadian Army*, 32, 42.
76. Interview with author, 6/8/89.
77. NAC, MG27 III B11, volume 63, Stuart to Ralston, 7/10/44.
78. Burns, *Manpower in the Canadian Army*, 91, 100.
79. Ibid., 77.
80. Ibid., 92, 96.
81. Ibid.
82. Stacey, *Arms, Men and Government*, 428–35.
83. Ibid., 426–7.
84. Pickersgill, *The Mackenzie King Record*, II/264.
85. NAC, MG27 III B11, volume 63, file Fall 1944, Draft Memorandum, n.d.
86. Stacey, *Arms, Men and Government*, 451.
87. Granatstein, *Conscription in the Second World War*, 57.
88. Stacey, *Arms, Men and Government*, 451–2.
89. Ibid., 447.

90. Nolan, *King's War*, 137–8.
91. Dawson, *The Conscription Crisis of 1944*, 44.
92. Stacey, *A Date with History*, 151.
93. *Globe and Mail*, 3/11/44.
94. Stacey, *A Date with History*, 156.
95. Stacey, *Arms, Men and Government*, 465.
96. Dawson, 83–4.
97. Stacey, *Arms, Men and Government*, 471.
98. Ibid., 473–4.
99. Ibid., 475, 477–8.
100. Ibid., 479.

Chapter 17: Rivers of Blood

1. Mowat, *The Regiment*, 231–2.
2. Burns, *General Mud*, 220.
3. Raddall, *West Novas*, 237.
4. Letter to author, 24/10/89.
5. O'Dell, *Bogie Wheels*, 21.
6. Nicholson, *The Canadians in Italy*, 608.
7. Stevens, *The Royal Canadian Regiment*, 169.
8. Interview with author, 17/7/89.
9. Mitchell, RCHA, 143.
10. Quoted in Ibid., 148.
11. Stacey, *Arms, Men and Government*, 438fn.
12. Galloway, *The General Who Never Was*, 233.
13. Interview with author, 6/8/89.
14. Grigg, *Nancy Astor*, 167.
15. Mowat, *The Regiment*, 244.
16. Ibid., 222–3.
17. Feasby, *Official History of the Canadian Medical Services, 1939–1945*, I/203.
18. Mitchell, RCHA, 144.
19. Nicholson, *The Canadians in Italy*, 607.
20. Ibid.
21. Johnston, *Canada's Craftsmen*, 37.
22. Interview with author, n.d.
23. Ibid.
24. Burns, *General Mud*, 218.
25. Ibid., 220.
26. NAC, MG30 E157, volume 15, diary, 9-12/11/44.
27. Kitching, *Mud and Green Fields*, 232.
28. Vokes, *Vokes: My Story*, 186, 200.
29. Kitching, 233–6.
30. Galloway, *The General Who Never Was*, 236–7.
31. Letter to author, 23/8/89.
32. Nicholson, *The Canadians in Italy*, 612–13.
33. Ibid., 614.
34. Ibid., 615–16.
35. Oldfield, *The Westminsters' War Diary*, 148.

36. Interview with author, 8/7/89.
37. Oldfield, 154.
38. Nicholson, *The Canadians in Italy*, 620–1.
39. NAC, RG24, volume 14,077, war diary, 3-4/12/44.
40. Stevens, *The Royal Canadian Regiment*, 172.
41. Letter to author, 7/5/90.
42. Ibid.
43. DHist, 145.2R13011(D1), Account by Major J. M. Houghton, 30/1/45 (henceforth, Houghton account).
44. NAC, RG24, volume 15,073, war diary, 5/12/44.
45. Houghton account.
46. Ibid.
47. NAC, RG24, volume 15,073, war diary, 5/12/44.
48. Nicholson, *The Canadians in Italy*, 617–28.
49. Galloway, *The General Who Never Was*, 238.
50. Interview with author, 17/3/82.
51. Nicholson, *The Canadians in Italy*, 619.
52. NAC, MG30 E157, volume 7, Foulkes to Crerar, 7/12/44.
53. Interview with author, n.d.
54. Foster, *Meeting of Generals*, 419.
55. Nicholson, *The Canadians in Italy*, 623.
56. Kitching, *Mud and Green Fields*, 238.
57. DHist, 145.2C6011(D2), Account by Lt Col J. A. Ensor, 14/1/45.
58. Scislowski, *Return to Italy, 1975*, 57.
59. DHist, 145.2C5013(D10), Report on Operations of the CB Highrs for period 2 Dec to 27 Dec 44, 24/1/45.
60. Johnston, *The Fighting Perths*, 105.
61. Nicholson, *The Canadians in Italy*, 626.
62. Interview with author, 6/10/89.
63. Nicholson, *The Canadians in Italy*, 624–5.
64. Mitchell, *RCHA*, 146.
65. DHist, 145.2C6011(D2), Account by Major R. M. Horsey, OC "D" Coy, Carlt and York R, 13/1/45.
66. Tooley, *Invicta*, 317.
67. Nicholson, *The Canadians in Italy*, 628.
68. Cederberg, *The Long Road Home*, 200.
69. Ibid., 201.
70. Nicholson, *The Canadians in Italy*, 629.
71. Nicholson, *Seventy Years of Service*, 198.
72. Interview with author, 15/3/82.
73. Nicholson, *The Canadians in Italy*, 628–9.
74. DHist, 145.2C6011(D2), Account by Major R. M. Horsey, OC "D" Coy, Carlt and York R, n.d. (henceforth, Horsey account).
75. Ibid.
76. Mowat, *The Regiment*, 280.
77. Horsey account.
78. Tooley, 322; Nicholson, *The Canadians in Italy*, 630.
79. DHist, 145.2E2011(D1), Consolidation of 1 Cdn Inf Bde Bridgehead, n.d.
80. Roy, *The Seaforth Highlanders of Canada*, 380, 382.

81. Stevens, *A City Goes to War*, 332.
82. J. R. Stone memoir, loaned to author.
83. Nicholson, *The Canadians in Italy*, 631; Oldfield, 164.
84. Nicholson, *The Gunners of Canada*, 254.
85. Stevens, *The Royal Canadian Regiment*, 178.
86. Nicholson, *The Canadians in Italy*, 634–5.
87. Ibid., 635.
88. Stevens, *The Royal Canadian Regiment*, 177.
89. Galloway, *A Regiment at War*, 185–6.
90. Nicholson, *The Canadians in Italy*, 635–7.
91. Ibid., 638.
92. DHist, 145.2E2011(D1), Loyal Edmonton Regiment: Enlarging of Bridgehead over Canale Naviglio, n.d.
93. Stevens, *Princess Patricia's Canadian Light Infantry*, 219.
94. Scislowski, *Return to Italy, 1975*, 59.
95. Ibid., 60.
96. Ibid., 61–3.
97. Nicholson, *The Canadians in Italy*, 638.
98. Ibid.
99. *Toronto Star*, 23/12/44.
100. Letter to author, 31/3/90.
101. Nicholson, *The Canadians in Italy*, 640.
102. Rowland, *The Padre*, 100.
103. Stacey, *A Date with History*, 155.
104. NAC, MG30 J13, diary, 25/12/44.
105. Interview with author, 6/7/89.
106. Ibid.
107. How, *8th Hussars*, 296.
108. Beattie, *Dileas*, 722.
109. Letter to author, n.d.

Chapter 18: "We'll Show 'Em"

1. Gilbert, *Road to Victory*, 1081–2.
2. Nicholson, *The Canadians in Italy*, 641.
3. Blumenson, *Mark Clark*, 230.
4. Harpur, *The Impossible Victory*, 121–2.
5. Foster, *Meeting of Generals*, 423.
6. Roy, *The Seaforth Highlanders of Canada*, 388–9.
7. Stevens, *Princess Patricia's Canadian Light Infantry*, 279.
8. Moir, *The Royal Canadian Corps of Signals, 1903–1961*, 149.
9. *The Maple Leaf*, 7/10/44.
10. Letter to author, 8/11/89.
11. Interview with author, 16/10/89.
12. Maltby, "Slip and Slide o'er the Apennines," in *Informal History of the Calgary Regiment*, 1.
13. Nicholson, *The Canadians in Italy*, 646.
14. Ibid., 649.
15. Oldfield, *The Westminsters' War Diary*, 172–3.

16. Nicholson, *The Canadians in Italy*, 650.
17. DHist, 145.2C5013(D1), Report on Operations of CB Highrs for period 2 Jan to 13 Jan 45, 21/1/45.
18. Nicholson, *The Canadians in Italy*, 651.
19. NAC, MG30 E157, volume 7, Foulkes to Crerar, 14/1/45.
20. Mowat, *The Regiment*, 289.
21. Raddall, *West Novas*, 260-1.
22. Interview with author, 6/7/89.
23. McAvity, *Lord Strathcona's Horse*, 178.
24. Nicholson, *The Canadians in Italy*, 651-2.
25. Beattie, *Dileas*, 724.
26. Galloway, *The General Who Never Was*, 249.
27. Roy, *The Seaforth Highlanders of Canada*, 399.
28. Ibid., 398.
29. Stevens, *Princess Patricia's Canadian Light Infantry*, 226.
30. Raddall, 267-8.
31. Stevens, *A City Goes to War*, 337.
32. Nicholson, *The Canadians in Italy*, 653.
33. Galloway, *The General Who Never Was*, 250-1.
34. Roy, *The Seaforth Highlanders of Canada*, 405.
35. Tooley, *Invicta*, 336.
36. Galloway, *A Regiment at War*, 187.
37. Roy, *The Seaforth Highlanders of Canada*, 403.
38. Nicholson, *The Canadians in Italy*, 645.
39. Foster, 420, 424-5.
40. McAndrew, "Stress Casualties," 53.
41. Feasby, *Official History of the Canadian Medical Services, 1939-1945*, II/68.
42. Interview with author, 6/7/89.
43. Nicholson, *Seventy Years of Service*, 197.
44. Mowat, *The Regiment*, 286.
45. Galloway, *The General Who Never Was*, 243.
46. Nicholson, *The Canadians in Italy*, 657.
47. Pickersgill, *The Mackenzie King Record*, II/159, 175.
48. Ibid., 177; Nicholson, *The Canadians in Italy*, 658.
49. Nicholson, *The Canadians in Italy*, 658.
50. Ibid., 659.
51. Warren, *Wait for the Waggon*, 267.
52. Nicholson, *The Canadians in Italy*, 661.
53. Ibid., 664-5.
54. Kitching, *Mud and Green Fields*, 245.
55. Stevens, *Princess Patricia's Canadian Light Infantry*, 229fn.
56. How, *8th Hussars*, 312.
57. Maltby, "Operation Goldflake," in *Informal History of the Calgary Regiment*, 2.
58. Interview with author, 14/8/89.
59. *Toronto Star*, 24/8/80.
60. McAvity, 189.
61. Frost, *Once a Patricia*, 405.
62. Smith memoir, loaned to the author by Mrs. J. K. Smith.
63. Maltby, "Operation Goldflake," 1.

64. Roy, *The Seaforth Highlanders of Canada*, 409.
65. Frost, 408.

Epilogue: "The Best in the World"

1. NAC, RG24, volume 15,050, March war diary, Appendix 10.
2. Mowat, *The Regiment*, 294.
3. Ibid., 297–8.
4. Interview with author, 12/7/89.
5. Nicholson, *The Canadians in Italy*, 666.
6. NAC, RG24, volume 14,587, war diary, 10/3/45.
7. Burns, *Manpower in the Canadian Army*, 47, 64–9.
8. Interview with author, n.d.
9. Jim Stone, interview with author, 6/7/89.
10. Letter to author, n.d.
11. Letter to author, 31/3/90.
12. Foster, *Meeting of Generals*, 439.
13. Ibid., 443.
14. Nicholson, *The Canadians in Italy*, 676.
15. Kuhn, *German Paratroops in World War II*, 236.
16. Letter to author, 19/10/89.
17. Air Historian, *No. 417 Squadron*, 98.
18. Ibid., 101.
19. Interview with author, 5/9/89.
20. Air Historian, Appendix L.
21. Ibid., 96, 105.
22. Interview with author, 5/9/89.
23. Robbins, *417 Squadron History*, 31.
24. Air Historian, 115.
25. Letter to author, 19/10/89.
26. Air Historian, 117.
27. Ibid., 121.
28. Ibid., 123.
29. Ibid., 125.
30. Letter to author, 19/10/89.
31. Ibid.
32. Ibid.
33. Strawson, *The Italian Campaign*, 197–9.
34. Churchill, *Triumph and Tragedy*, 531.
35. Pope, *Soldiers and Politicians*, 189.
36. Fuller, *The Second World War, 1939–45*, 265.
37. Graham and Bidwell, *Tug of War*, 396, 403.
38. Harpur, *The Impossible Victory*, 124.
39. Loewenheim, *Roosevelt and Churchill*, 617.
40. Kesselring, *Kesselring: Soldier's Record*, 267.
41. Nicholson, *The Canadians in Italy*, 679.
42. NAC, MG31 G19, volume 6, speech, 28/11/56.
43. D. Fraser, "Italian Countryside Site of War That Never Was," 3/6/89, loaned to author and used by permission of the Halifax *Herald* Limited.

44. Interview with author, 7/8/89.
45. Letter to author, 24/8/89.
46. Letter to author, 24/2/89.
47. Frost, *Once a Patricia*, 412.
48. D. Fraser, "Nova Scotians in Italy," 2/9/89, loaned to author and used by permission of the Halifax *Herald* Limited.
49. NAC, MG31 G19, volume 6, speech, 22/10/56.
50. Interview with author, 6/7/89.
51. Pope, 153.
52. Pickersgill, II/347–8.
53. Stacey, *Arms, Men and Government*, 199–202.
54. Douglas, *Out of the Shadows*, 218.
55. D. Fraser, "Italian Countryside Site of War That Never Was," 3/6/89, loaned to author and used by permission of the Halifax *Herald* Limited.

Bibliography

Adleman, Robert H., and George Walton. *Rome Fell Today*. Boston: Little, Brown, 1968.

Air Historian. *No. 417 Squadron: A Narrative History*. n.p., 1954.

Alexander of Tunis. *The Alexander Memoirs*. London: Cassell, 1962.

Allard, Jean V. *The Memoirs of General Jean V. Allard*. Vancouver: University of British Columbia Press, 1988.

Allen, Ralph. *Ordeal by Fire*. New York: Popular Library, 1961.

Baldwin, Hanson W. *Battles Lost and Won*. New York: Harper & Row, 1966.

Beattie, Kim. *Dileas*. Toronto: 48th Highlanders of Canada, 1957.

Blumenson, Martin. *Salerno to Cassino*. Washington: United States Army, 1969.

_____. *The Patton Papers, 1940-1945*. Boston: Houghton Mifflin, 1974.

_____. *Mark Clark*. New York: Congdon & Weed, 1984.

Bothwell, Robert, Ian Drummond, and John English. *Canada, 1900-1945*. Toronto: University of Toronto Press, 1987.

Bradley, Omar N., and Clay Blair. *A General's Life*. New York: Simon & Schuster, 1983.

Braithwaite, Max. *The Hungry Thirties*. Toronto: Canada's Illustrated Heritage, 1977.

Broadfoot, Barry. *Six War Years, 1939-1945*. Toronto: Doubleday, 1974.

Bruce, George. *Second Front Now!* London: Macdonald & Jane's, 1979.

Bryant, Arthur. *The Turn of the Tide*. London: Collins, 1957.

_____. *Triumph in the West*. London: Collins, 1959.

Burhans, Robert. *The First Special Service Force*. (Reprint. Toronto: Methuen, 1981.)

Burns, E. L. M. *Manpower in the Canadian Army*. Toronto: Clarke, Irwin, 1956.

_____. *General Mud*. Toronto: Clarke, Irwin, 1970.

Burton, G. Allan. *A Store of Memories*. Toronto: McClelland & Stewart, 1986.

Butcher, Harry C. *My Three Years with Eisenhower*. New York: Simon & Schuster, 1946.

Canadian Encyclopedia. 3 volumes. Edmonton: Hurtig, 1985.

Carroll, Jock. *The Life and Times of Greg Clark*. Toronto: Doubleday, 1981.

Cederberg, Fred. *The Long Road Home*. Toronto: General, 1984.

Chalfont, Alun. *Montgomery of Alamein*. London: Weidenfeld & Nicolson, 1976.

Churchill, Winston S. *The Hinge of Fate*. Boston: Houghton Mifflin, 1950.

_____. *The Grand Alliance*. Boston: Houghton Mifflin, 1950.

_____. *Closing the Ring*. Boston: Houghton Mifflin, 1951.

_____. *Triumph and Tragedy*. Boston: Houghton Mifflin, 1953.

Comfort, Charles. *Artist at War*. Toronto: Ryerson, 1956.

Costello, John. *Love, Sex and War*. London: Collins, 1985.

Coughlin, Bing. *Herbie!* Toronto: Thomas Nelson, 1946.

Creighton, Donald. *Canada's First Century*. Toronto: Macmillan, 1970.

Curchin, Leonard A., and Brian D. Sim. *The Elgins*. St Thomas, Ont.: Sutherland Press, 1977.

Dancocks, Daniel G. *In Enemy Hands*. Edmonton: Hurtig, 1983.

Dawson, J. MacGregor. *The Conscription Crisis of 1944*. Toronto: University of Toronto Press, 1961.

De Guingand, Francis. *Generals at War*. London: Hodder & Stoughton, 1964.

D'Este, Carlo. *Bitter Victory*. London: Collins, 1988.

Dewar, Jane, ed. *True Canadian War Stories*. Toronto: Lester & Orpen Dennys, 1986.

Douglas, W. A. B., and Brereton Greenhous. *Out of the Shadows*. Toronto: Oxford University Press, 1977.

Dunn, Walter Scott. *Second Front Now – 1943*. University of Alabama Press, 1980.

Ehrman, John. *Grand Strategy*. Volume 5. London: Her Majesty's Stationery Office, 1956.

Eisenhower, David. *Eisenhower at War, 1943–1945*. New York: Random House, 1986.

Eisenhower, Dwight. *Crusade in Europe*. Garden City, N.Y.: Doubleday, 1948.

Ellis, John. *Cassino: The Hollow Victory*. London: Andre Deutsch, 1984.

Eubank, Keith. *Summit at Teheran*. New York: William Morrow, 1985.

Feasby, W. R., ed. *Official History of the Canadian Medical Services, 1939–1945*. 2 volumes. Ottawa: Queen's Printer, 1953, 1956.

Field of Honour. Montreal: Gazette Printing, 1950.

Fisher, Ernest F. *Cassino to the Alps*. Washington, D.C.: United States Army, 1977.

Foster, Tony. *Meeting of Generals*. Toronto: Methuen, 1986.

Franklin, Stephen. *A Time of Heroes*. Toronto: Canada's Illustrated Heritage, 1977.

Fraser, W. B. *Always a Strathcona*. Calgary: Comprint, 1976.

Frost, C. Sydney. *Once a Patricia*. St. Catharines, Ont.: Vanwell, 1988.

Fuller, J. F. C. *The Second World War, 1939–45*. London: Eyre & Spottiswoode, 1962.

Gaffen, Fred. *Forgotten Soldiers*. Penticton, B.C.: Theytus, 1985.

_____. *Ortona: Christmas 1943*. Ottawa: Canadian War Museum, 1988.

Galloway, Strome. *A Regiment at War*. Royal Canadian Regiment, 1946. (Reprint. 1979.)

_____. *Some Died at Ortona*. n.p., n.d.

_____. *The General Who Never Was*. Belleville, Ont.: Mika, 1981.

Garland, Albert N., and Howard McGaw Smith. *Sicily and the Surrender of Italy*. Washington, D.C.: United States Army, 1965.

Gilbert, Martin. *Road to Victory*. Toronto: Stoddart, 1986.

Gingrich, Earl, ed. *Short Stories, W.W. II*. Winterburn, Alta.: n.p., 1988.

Good, Mabel Tinkiss. *The Bridge at Dieppe*. Toronto: Griffin House, 1973.

Goodspeed, D. J. *The Armed Forces of Canada, 1867–1967*. Ottawa: Queen's Printer, 1967.

Graham, Dominick, and Shelford Bidwell. *Tug of War*. London: Hodder & Stoughton, 1986.

Graham, Howard. *Citizen and Soldier*. Toronto: McClelland & Stewart, 1987.

Granatstein, J. L. *Conscription in the Second World War, 1939–1945*. Toronto: McGraw-Hill Ryerson, 1969.

_____. *Mackenzie King: His Life and World.* Toronto: McGraw-Hill Ryerson, 1977.

_____, and Desmond Morton. *A Nation Forged in Fire.* Toronto: Lester & Orpen Dennys, 1989.

Greenfield, Kent R., ed. *Command Decisions.* Washington, D.C.: Department of the Army, 1960.

Greenhous, Brereton. *Dragoon.* Ottawa: Royal Canadian Dragoons, 1983.

_____. "Would It Not Have Been Better to Bypass Ortona Completely . . . ?" *Canadian Defence Quarterly,* April 1989, 51-5.

_____. "5 CAD in Operation *Olive,* 26 Aug – 14 Sep 1944," Directorate of History study paper, n.d.

Grigg, John. *Nancy Astor.* London: Sidgwick & Jackson, 1980.

Gunther, John. *D Day.* New York: Harper & Brothers, 1944.

Hamilton, Nigel. *Master of the Battlefield.* London: Hamish Hamilton, 1983.

Harpur, Brian. *The Impossible Victory.* New York: Hippocrene, 1981.

Harris, Stephen J. *Canadian Brass.* University of Toronto Press, 1988.

Hastings, Max. *Overlord.* New York: Simon and Schuster, 1984.

Hibbert, Joyce. *Fragments of War.* Toronto: Dundurn, 1985.

Higgins, Trumbull. *Soft Underbelly.* New York: Macmillan, 1968.

Historical Section, General Staff. *From Pachino to Ortona.* Ottawa: King's Printer, 1946.

Hoskin, Herbert. *Sometimes with Laughter.* n.p., 1982.

How, Douglas. *8th Hussars.* Sussex, N.B.: Maritime, 1964.

_____. *Night of the Caribou.* Hantsport: Lancelot Press, 1988.

_____, ed. *The Canadians at War.* 2 volumes. Montreal: Reader's Digest, 1969.

Howard, Michael. *Grand Strategy.* Volume 4. London: Her Majesty's Stationery Office, 1972.

Hurley, Ron, and Ian Douglas. *Ritorno in Italia.* New Westminster B.C.: Royal Westminster Regiment Association, 1976.

Hurst, Alan M. *The Canadian Y.M.C.A. in World War II.* National War Services Committee of the National Council of Young Men's Christian Associations of Canada, n.d.

Irving, David. *The Trail of the Fox.* New York: Avon, 1977.

_____. *Hitler's War.* New York: Viking, 1977.

Jackson, H. M. *The Princess Louise Dragoon Guards.* n.p., 1951.

Jackson, W. G. F. *The Battle for Italy.* London: B. T. Batsford, 1967.

_____. *The Battle for Rome.* London: B. T. Batsford, 1969.

_____. *Alexander of Tunis.* New York: Dodd, Mead, 1972.

_____. *The Mediterranean and Middle East.* Volume 6 (Part 2). London: Her Majesty's Stationery Office, 1987.

Johnston, Murray. *Canada's Craftsmen.* Land Ordnance Engineering Association, 1984.

Johnston, Stafford. *The Fighting Perths.* Stratford, Ont.: Perth Regiment Veterans' Association, 1964.

Kerry, A. J., and W. A. McDill. *The History of the Corps of Royal Canadian Engineers.* Volume 2. Ottawa: Military Engineers Association of Canada, 1966.

Kesselring, Albert. *Kesselring: A Soldier's Record.* Westport, Ct.: Greenwood, 1973.

Kitching, George. *Mud and Green Fields.* Langley, B.C.: Battleline Books, 1986.

Krige, Uys. *The Way Out.* Cape Town, South Africa: Maskew Miller, 1968.

Kuhn, Volkmar. *German Paratroops in World War II.* London: Ian Allan, 1978.

Kurzman, Dan. *The Race for Rome*. Garden City, N.Y.: Doubleday, 1975.

Lavigne, J. P. A. Michel, and J. F. (Stocky) Edwards. *Kittyhawk Pilot*. Battleford, Sask.: Turner-Warwick, 1983.

Lennon, Mary Jane, and Syd Charendoff. *On the Homefront*. Erin, Ont.: Boston Mills Press, 1981.

Lewin, Ronald. *Hitler's Mistakes*. London: Leo Cooper/Secker & Warburg, 1987.

Liddell Hart, B. H. *The Rommel Papers*. London: Collins, 1953.

———. *The Other Side of the Hill*. London: Cassell, 1953.

———. *History of the Second World War*. London: Pan, 1970.

Lochner, Louis, ed. *The Goebbels Diaries, 1942-1943*. Garden City, N.Y.: Doubleday, 1948.

Loewenheim, Francis L., and Harold D. Langley and Manfred Jonas. *Roosevelt and Churchill: Their Secret Wartime Correspondence*. New York: Saturday Review Press/E.P. Dutton, 1975.

Lower, Arthur R. M. *Colony to Nation*. Toronto: Longmans, Green, 1946. (Reprint, 1977)

Lynch, Charles. *The Lynch Mob*. Toronto: Key Porter, 1988.

Lynch, Mark, ed. *Salty Dips*. Volume 2. Ottawa: Naval Officers Associations of Canada, 1985.

McAndrew, William J. "Eighth Army at the Gothic Line: Commanders and Plans." *RUSI*, March 1986.

———. "Eighth Army at the Gothic Line: The Dog-Fight." *RUSI*, June 1986.

———. "Fire or Movement? Canadian Tactical Doctrine, Sicily – 1943." *Military Affairs*, July 1987.

———. "Stress Casualties: Canadians in Italy – 1943-45." *Canadian Defence Quarterly*, Winter 1987.

———. "Recording the War: Uncommon Canadian Perspectives of the Italian Campaign." *Canadian Defence Quarterly*, Winter 1988.

———. "5th Canadian Armoured Division: The Background." Directorate of History study paper, n.d.

McAvity, J. M. *Lord Strathcona's Horse*. Toronto: Bridgens, 1947.

McDougall, Colin. *Execution*. Reprint. Toronto: Macmillan/Laurentian Library, 1967.

Macmillan, Harold. *War Diaries*. London: Macmillan, 1984.

McNeil, Bill. *Voice of the Pioneer*. Volume 2. Toronto: Macmillan, 1984.

Malone, Richard S. *Missing from the Record*. Toronto: Collins, 1946.

———. *A Portrait of War, 1939-1943*. Toronto: Collins, 1983.

———. *A World in Flames, 1944-1945*. Toronto: Collins, 1984.

Maltby, Dick and Jessie, eds. *The Informal History of the Calgary Regiment – 14th Canadian Armoured Regiment*. Vancouver: n.p., 1989.

Mansikka, Eric. *Pack Up Your Troubles*. Toronto: Methuen, 1987.

Masters, Anthony. *Nancy Astor*. New York: McGraw-Hill, 1981.

Mitchell, G. D. *RCHA – Right of the Line*. Ottawa: RCHA History Committee, 1986.

Mitchell, Howard. *My War*. Rosetown Publishing, n.d.

Moir, John S., ed. *History of the Royal Canadian Corps of Signals, 1903-1961*. Ottawa: Corps Committee, RCCS, 1962.

Molony, C. J. C. *The Mediterranean and Middle East*. Volumes 5 and 6 (Part 1). London: Her Majesty's Stationery Office, 1973, 1984.

Montgomery of Alamein. *Memoirs*. London: Collins, 1958.

_____. *El Alamein to the Sangro/Normandy to the Baltic*. New York: St. Martin's Press, 1974.

Moorehead, Alan. *Eclipse*. London: Hamish Hamilton, 1945.

Morison, Samuel Eliot. *Strategy and Compromise*. Boston: Little, Brown, 1958.

_____. *Sicily – Salerno – Anzio*. Boston: Little, Brown, 1962.

Morton, Desmond. *Canada and War*. Toronto: Butterworths, 1981.

_____. *A Military History of Canada*. Edmonton: Hurtig, 1985.

Mowat, Farley. *The Regiment*. Toronto: McClelland & Stewart, 1955. (Reprint, 1974)

_____. *And No Birds Sang*. Toronto: McClelland & Stewart, 1979.

Munro, Ross. *Gauntlet to Overlord*. Toronto: Macmillan, 1946.

Murray, Joan. *Canadian Artists of the Second World War*. Oshawa: Robert McLaughlin, 1981.

Nicholson, G. W. L. *The Canadians in Italy*. Ottawa: Queen's Printer, 1956.

_____. *The Gunners of Canada*. Volume 2. Toronto: McClelland & Stewart, 1972.

_____. *Seventy Years of Service*. Ottawa: Borealis, 1977.

Nicolson, Nigel. *Alex*. London: Weidenfield & Nicolson, 1973.

Nofi, Albert, ed. *The War Against Hitler*. New York: Hippocrene, 1982.

Nolan, Brian. *King's War*. Toronto: Random House, 1988.

O'Dell, J. M., ed. *Bogie Wheels*. Volume 1. Three Rivers Regiment Veterans Association, 1989.

Oldfield, J. E. *The Westminsters' War Diary*. New Westminster, B.C.: Mitchell Press, 1964.

Olmsted, Bill. *Blue Skies*. Toronto: Stoddart, 1987.

Origo, Iris. *The War in Val D'Orcia*. Boston: David R. Godine, 1984.

Pack, S. W. C. *Operation "Husky."* Vancouver: Douglas David & Charles, 1977.

Painton, Frederick C. "What It Takes to Win the V.C." *Liberty*, 21 April 1945.

Parkinson, Roger. *A Day's March Nearer Home*. London: Hart-Davis, MacGibbon, 1974.

Parrish, Thomas, ed. *The Simon and Schuster Encyclopedia of World War II*. New York: Simon & Schuster, 1978.

Pearson, Lester B. *Mike*. Volume 1. University of Toronto Press, 1972.

Peniakoff, Vladimir. *Private Army*. London: Jonathon Cape, 1950.

Pickersgill, J. W. *The Mackenzie King Record*. Volume 1. University of Toronto Press, 1960.

_____, and D. F. Forster. *The Mackenzie King Record*. Volume 2. University of Toronto Press, 1968.

Pope, Maurice. *Soldiers and Politicians*. Toronto: University of Toronto Press, 1962.

Pawley, A. E. *Broadcast from the Front*. Toronto: Hakkert, 1975.

Prasad, Bisheshwar, ed. *The Campaign in Italy, 1943–45*. Calcutta: Orient Longmans, 1960.

Quayle, J. T. B. "Mitch." *The Connecting File*, 1988, 38–40.

Raddall, Thomas. *West Novas*. Liverpool: n.p., 1947. (Reprint, 1986)

Rannie, William F. *To the Thunderer His Arms*. Lincoln, Ont.: W. F. Rannie, 1984.

RCAF Overseas, The. 3 volumes. University of Toronto Press, 1944, 1945, 1949.

Ready, J. Lee. *Forgotten Allies*. Jefferson, N.C.: McFarland, 1985.

Reyburn, Wallace. *Some of It Was Fun*. Toronto: Thomas Nelson, 1949.

Robbins, Keith, ed. *417 Squadron History*. Stittsville, Ont.: Canada's Wings, 1983.

Routhier, Ray. *The Black Devils*. Great Falls: Advanced, 1982.

Rowland, Barry D. *The Padre*. Scarborough: Amethyst, 1982.

_____, and J. Douglas MacFarlane. *The Maple Leaf Forever*. Toronto: Natural Heritage, 1987.

Roy, R. H. *Sinews of Steel*. Brampton, Ont.: Charters, 1965.

_____. *The Seaforth Highlanders of Canada*. Vancouver: Seaforth Highlanders of Canada, 1969.

Schull, Joseph. *Far Distant Ships*. Reprint. Toronto: Stoddart, 1987.

Scislowski, Stanley. *Pilgrimage*, n.p., n.d.

_____. *Return to Italy, 1975*. n.p., 1975.

_____. *The Winter Front, 1944*. n.p., n.d.

Sealey, D. Bruce, and Peter Van De Vyvere. *Thomas George Prince*. Winnipeg: Peguis, 1981.

Shapiro, L. S. B. *They Left the Back Door Open*. Toronto: Ryerson, 1944.

Shepperd, G. A. *The Italian Campaign*. New York: Frederick A. Praeger, 1968.

Shirer, William. *The Rise and Fall of the Third Reich*. New York: Fawcett, 1965.

Simonds, Peter. *Maple Leaf Up, Maple Leaf Down*. New York: Island Press, 1946.

Sixsmith, E. K. G. *British Generalship in the Twentieth Century*. London: Arms & Armour Press, 1970.

Smith, D. Crawford. *Perth Regiment – Italian Campaign*. n.p., n.d.

Smith, Gladys E. *Forty Nights to Freedom*. Winnipeg: Queenston House, 1985.

Smith, Kenneth B. *Duffy's Regiment*. Toronto: Dundurn Press, 1987.

Smith, Waldo E. L. *What Time the Tempest*. Toronto: Ryerson, 1953.

Stacey, C.P. *The Canadian Army, 1939–1945*. Ottawa: King's Printer, 1948.

_____. *The Military Problems of Canada*. Toronto: Ryerson, 1940.

_____. *Six Years of War*. Ottawa: Queen's Printer, 1956.

_____. *The Victory Campaign*. Ottawa: Queen's Printer, 1960.

_____. *Arms, Men and Government*. Ottawa: Queen's Printer, 1970.

_____. *Historical Documents of Canada*. Volume 5. New York: St Martin's Press, 1972.

_____. *A Very Double Life*. Toronto: Macmillan, 1976.

_____. *A Date with History*. Ottawa: Deneau, 1982.

_____, and Barbara M. Wilson. *The Half-Million*. University of Toronto Press, 1987.

Stamp, Robert M. *The World of Tomorrow: A View of Canada in 1939*. Toronto: Fitzhenry & Whiteside, 1985.

Stead, Gordon W. *A Leaf Upon the Sea*. Vancouver: University of British Columbia Press, 1988.

Stevens, G. R. *Princess Patricia's Canadian Light Infantry, 1919–1957*. Volume 3. Montreal: Southam Printing, 1958.

_____. *A City Goes to War*. Brampton, Ont.: Charters, 1964.

_____. *The Royal Canadian Regiment, 1933–1966*. London: London Printing, 1967.

Stone, Norman. *Hitler*. Boston: Little, Brown, 1980.

Strawson, John. *The Italian Campaign*. London: Secker & Warburg, 1987.

Stursberg, Peter. *Journey into Victory*. London: George G. Harrap, 1944.

Swettenham, John. *McNaughton*. Volumes 2 and 3. Toronto: Ryerson, 1969.

Thompson, R. W. *The Price of Victory*. London: Constable, 1960.

_____. *The Montgomery Legend*. Volume 1. London: George Allen & Unwin, 1967.

Tooley, Robert. *Invicta*. Fredericton: New Ireland Press, 1989.

Trevelyan, Raleigh. *Rome '44*. London: Secker & Warburg, 1981.

Trevor-Roper, H. R., ed. *Hitler's Table Talk*. London: Weidenfeld & Nicolson, 1953.

Turner, Henry Ashby, ed. *Hitler – Memoirs of a Confidant*. Boston: Yale University

Press, 1985.

Tweedsmuir, Lord. *Assoro, July 21–23, 1943*. n.p., 1988.

Vokes, Chris. *Vokes: My Story*. Ottawa: Gallery, 1985.

Wallace, Robert. *The Italian Campaign*. Alexandria, Va.: Time-Life, 1981.

Warren, Arnold. *Wait for the Waggon*. Toronto: McClelland & Stewart, 1961.

Wedemeyer, Albert C. *Wedemeyer Reports!* New York: Henry Holt, 1958.

Whitaker, W. Denis, and Shelagh Whitaker. *Tug of War*. Toronto: Stoddart, 1984.

———. *Rhineland*. Toronto: Stoddart, 1989.

Whiting, Charles. *The Long March on Rome*. London: Century, 1987.

Windsor, John. *Blind Date*. Sidney, B.C.: Gray's Publishing, 1962.

Wood, Herbert Fairlie, and John Swettenham. *Silent Witnesses*. Toronto: Hakkert, 1974.

Worthington, Larry. *"Worthy."* Toronto: Macmillan, 1961.

Wyatt, Bernie. *Two Wings and a Prayer*. Erin, Ont.: Boston Mills Press, 1984.

Index

INDEX OF FORMATIONS, UNITS AND CORPS